Hemingway

Eight Decades
Hemingway
of Criticism

EDITED BY
Linda Wagner-Martin

Michigan State University Press · *East Lansing*

 Michigan State University Press
East Lansing, Michigan 48823-5245

Printed and bound in the United States of America.

16 15 14 13 12 11 10 09   1 2 3 4 5 6 7 8 9 10

LIBRARY OF CONGRESS CATALOGING-IN-PUBLICATION DATA
Hemingway : eight decades of criticism / edited by Linda Wagner-Martin.
p. cm.
Fourth collection of essays in a series providing contemporary criticism of the work and life
of Ernest Hemingway.
Includes bibliographical references and index.
ISBN 978-0-87013-839-3 (pbk. : alk. paper) 1. Hemingway, Ernest, 1899–1961—Criticism and
interpretation. I. Wagner-Martin, Linda.
PS3515.E37Z58673 2008
813'.52—dc22
2008017045

Cover design by Heather Truelove. Cover photo is used with permission of the Ernest
Hemingway Archive, The John F. Kennedy Library & Museum, Boston, Massachusetts.
Book design by Sharp Des!gns, Inc., Lansing, Michigan

**g green
press**
INITIATIVE Michigan State University Press is a member of the Green Press Initiative and is
committed to developing and encouraging ecologically responsible publishing
practices. For more information about the Green Press Initiative and the use of recycled paper
in book publishing, please visit *www.greenpressinitiative.org.*

Visit Michigan State University Press on the World Wide Web at *www.msupress.msu.edu*

For
Wiliam Duff and Tommy Wagner
   and
Paul, Carly, and Jessica Kate Wagner

Contents

PART 4. Places of Continuing Reassessment

PART 5. Endings

Introduction

Linda Wagner-Martin

Hemingway: *Eight Decades of Criticism* is the fourth collection of criticism in this series about Ernest Hemingway's writing. The first (*Five Decades*) appeared in 1974; the second (*Six Decades*) was published in 1987; the third (*Seven Decades*) appeared in 1998. All have been published by Michigan State University Press, and the existence of what has become a series of critical books owes its start to the generosity of former Press Director Lyle Blair and former Press Editor Jean Busfield.

In the 1970s, Michigan State University Press was already known as the publisher of two important collections of criticism on the other great American modernist: *William Faulkner: Two Decades of Criticism* (1951) and *William Faulkner: Three Decades of Criticism* (1960). Both books were edited jointly by Frederick J. Hoffman and Olga W. Vickery. By the early 1970s, unfortunately, both Professor Hoffman and his colleague and former doctoral student Vickery had died, so Blair asked me to prepare what would be *William Faulkner: Four Decades of Criticism*; it was published in 1973. I then asked to edit such a collection on Hemingway (who was not a favorite of Lyle Blair's). I argued that with Hemingway's strong ties to the Mid-Michigan area, and with so many faculty on campus teaching Hemingway (as well as a bevy of such good young writers as Jim Harrison, Tom McGuane, Dan Gerber, Jim Cash, Gary Gildner, and others), such a book was a natural for Michigan State University Press. So the following year, *Ernest Hemingway: Five Decades of Criticism* was published.

We chose the designation *Five Decades* in part to differentiate the Hemingway collection from the Faulkner *Four Decades* but also because (perhaps ironically) serious criticism on Hemingway's work began appearing earlier than criticism on Faulkner's writing—almost as soon as Hemingway found an American publisher. *In Our Time* appeared in the States in 1925, with *The Sun Also Rises* following in 1926 (1926 had earlier seen Scribner's publication of *The Torrents of Spring*, the satire Hemingway wrote to break his three-book contract with Boni & Liveright so that he could move on to Scribner's). From the Edmund Wilson 1924 *Dial* review of Hemingway's earliest work, *3 Stories & 10 Poems* and the lowercased *in our time,* through the immensely important assessments of the 1960s by such critics as Richard Bridgman (on Hemingway's "colloquial style"), Frederick I. Carpenter (on the "fifth dimension"), Joseph Waldmeir (on the author's religious beliefs), and Richard P. Adams (on possible literary sources), and through seminal critiques by Nathan Scott Jr., Robert Penn Warren, John Reardon, Carlos Baker, and others, the book provided provocative readings of Hemingway's work. The collection also included George Plimpton's *Paris Review* interview with Hemingway, an invaluable source of the writer's comments about the aesthetics that ruled his writing and his life.

More than ten years later, by the time of *Ernest Hemingway: Six Decades of Criticism,* the treasure trove of Hemingway's manuscripts, papers, and correspondence had opened in the John F. Kennedy Library, and scholars from around the world were making the pilgrimage to Boston, Massachusetts, to peruse the holdings. The Ernest Hemingway Society had been formed, and international biennial conferences were held in such locations as Madrid, Spain; Schruns, Austria; and Boston itself. Scholarship benefited accordingly from the wider perspective. No longer was Hemingway seen as the lucky Midwestern writer who had gone to Paris and become the quintessential American modernist—the recipient of the 1954 Nobel Prize for Literature— but rather he was regarded as the creator of the carefully crafted voice of an angst peculiar to the twentieth century. Though seen as male gendered and criticized for his masculinist perspective, Hemingway himself shattered this monolithic profile, as E. L. Doctorow and Nelson Algren note in this collection, by committing suicide in 1961.

Much of the criticism collected in the 1987 *Six Decades* benefited from access to Hemingway's manuscripts, a scholarly means of putting "writer" back into the author's own self-description. As he had said near the time of his death, "From my very first novel . . . I never for a moment doubted that I was the pioneer of a new era."[1] The essays by Bernard Oldsey (on Hemingway's beginnings and endings) and Nicholas Gerogiannis (on his poetry), and the biographical studies by Michael S. Reynolds, Scott Donaldson, and others, which were so much enhanced by the holdings in the Kennedy Library, led to new and refreshed readings of the work.

By the 1998 publication of *Hemingway: Seven Decades of Criticism*, the critical community had been reenergized both by the availability of new archival materials and by new currents in critical thought itself. New considerations of Hemingway's gender and sexual proclivities, as well as of the author's often ambivalent treatments of racial matters, were prompted in part by the posthumous publication of one of the last of his manuscripts to be brought to the reading public, *The Garden of Eden*. Unleashing a flurry of interest in a writer who had earlier been written off as unreservedly male, even macho, the 1986 novel led to a number of essays that were collected in *Seven Decades* as an important group for study. The work of Carl Eby, Debra A. Moddelmog, Mark Spilka, Robert Scholes, Nancy R. Comley, and other critics made the consideration of *The Garden of Eden* a kind of set piece for what was new in Hemingway studies. Just as Rose Marie Burwell's book *Hemingway: The Postwar Years and the Posthumous Novels* became the definitive word on the unpublished manuscripts that led to novels and memoirs printed after Hemingway's death, so this important critical work with *The Garden of Eden* became a critical norm for new evaluations of modernism itself.

In the introduction to *Seven Decades* I noted that within the three collections I had not included more than one work by any given critic: the writing of younger scholars, as well as of those new to Hemingway critique, provided ample material to choose from. I used this point to show how rich the criticism of Hemingway's work was becoming and, along with the caveat that I chose from essays rather than reprinting parts of books—thinking that libraries would more easily be able to supply books for interested scholars—to justify the processes of my selection.[2] The conditions that existed when I prepared the *Seven Decades* collection have only expanded: "the quality and range of criticism on Hemingway's writing has improved/increased dramatically. Part of this impetus comes from the activity of the 600-member Hemingway Society. . . . Part comes from the more critically sophisticated editorship of The *Hemingway Review,* the society's journal, which has recently attracted the best of current scholarship [fourteen of these essays are reprinted from that journal]. Another part is the continuing interest in the Hemingway works that have seen posthumous publication, *A Moveable Feast* in 1964, *Islands in the Stream* in 1970, and—most controversial—*The Garden of Eden.*"[3] I also pointed out that teachers and academics pay attention to criticism, and that it may therefore be that "Hemingway's work lives as much through the secondary criticism devoted to it as through its valid existence as text. The best criticism changes the lenses, and thereby gives readers new ways of reading, seeing, visualizing the art. It is in the interaction between the literature and its criticism that Hemingway's œuvre remains most vital."[4]

One notable difference between this collection and its predecessors is that there is no segment devoted to Hemingway's biography per se. With the current interest in cultural criticism, the author's biography suffuses much of the critique. But to separate out one essay as being more biographical than another has little merit. We have learned through Michael S. Reynolds's five-volume work, and through shorter biographies by various hands, that though accumulating salient detail is useful, it may not be the best means of determining why a text maintains its power. For instance, in this collection's first essay, Miriam Marty Clark's "Hemingway's Early Illness Narratives and the Lyric Dimensions of 'Now I Lay Me,'" the critic assumes that the reader understands the trauma of the young Hemingway's wound during the First World War and focuses on his *use* of the structural and linguistic patterns that injury and illness contribute to characterization in his stories. To emphasize the inclusive method of her writing, Clark draws from recent psychoanalytic, disability, and illness theories, using the work of such critics as Arthur Kleinman, David Morris, Rita Charon, Shoshana Felman, Arthur Frank, and others. In Clark's words, because Hemingway "begins within the wounded body" in many of his early stories, he draws on the condition of the character to "beget speech." She shows in her essay the way Hemingway is able in his work to find "a way 'out of narrative wreckage' produced by illness and into story."[5]

Clark's essay is indicative, I think, of the present critical moment: many strands of theoretical readings coalesce to provide an enriched view of the way critique can enhance both reading and textual work. It is the century of the blend—Derridean approaches exist beside, and sometimes within, psychoanalytic; Freudian-based readings coexist with French feminist; cultural critique with Marxist. I have arranged the essays included in *Eight Decades* to point to possible interrelationships among not only the author's works but also the critics' views of those works. For example, in part 1 of the collection, the Clark essay links with Diane Price Herndl's influential reading of Hemingway's 1929 novel, *A Farewell to Arms*. Price Herndl—as her title suggests—moves from injury and illness to considerations of masculinity, delving into gender roles within hospitals to further her argument about power among Hemingway characters.[6]

Conjoined with these essays in part 1 of the book are Dana Fore's very current assessment of the merging of guilt, disability (a different kind of reading for the wound trauma of not only Jake Barnes but also Brett Ashley in *The Sun Also Rises*), and the masculine; Greg Forter's Freudian reading of the same novel, with interesting emphasis on the added dimensions of mourning and melancholy; and Marc Seals's essay, which relates contemporary studies of trauma theory not to Hemingway's physical wounding but to his devastation following his wife's loss of his early manuscripts. The range of interpretation available from these five essays—all of them published within the last six years, making them truly representative of the twenty-first century of Hemingway critique—is not only surprising; it is doubly rewarding for the serious reader. Their separable bibliographies provide routes to new knowledge, yet because the essays are all based in the Hemingway texts we know so well there is also a congruence of vision.

Just as Hemingway's 1986 novel *The Garden of Eden* was the subject of much criticism in *Hemingway: Seven Decades of Criticism,* his *A Farewell to Arms* inspired much good work in the new century. War obsesses readers even more than usual today, and the essays by Alex Vernon, Matthew C. Stewart, and Jennifer A. Haytock—in their great variety—show several dimensions of reader concern. As in the essays in part 1, gender serves as a prompt for new readings in several of the essays in part 2, and Gary Harrington's linguistic analysis augments many of the readings within this group of essays.

The essays in the third group are unified in stemming from manuscript study with attention to issues of craft, or in the case of the Ron Berman and Lisa Narbeshuber pieces, with an interdisciplinary casting over to graphic art. Barbara Lounsberry's study of the manuscripts of Hemingway's *Green Hills of Africa* is a model of textual criticism, and the conclusions Robert W. Trogdon draws from his intense scrutiny of the pages of the *For Whom the Bell Tolls* manuscript show the practicality of such immersion.

My separation of materials in part 4 from those in part 3 hinges on what I wanted to emphasize as different kinds of perspective. For instance, in "The Taxation of Ernest Hemingway" Anthony E. Rebollo works to provide explanations for the author's supposed paranoia about the IRS and the federal government's taxation policies, and his seemingly unreasonable guilt. Rebello's description of the uses and abuses of the U.S. taxation of artists—writers, musicians, painters; people whose incomes varied widely year by year—makes Hemingway's apparent obsessive worry that he had an FBI file (and it turned out that he did) more than understandable. And

Laura Gruber Godfrey's process of explaining an important Hemingway short story through her "cultural geographic" approach is also a means of opening existing readings to the newest of critical approaches.[7]

The kind of superb alignment that exists among essays by very diverse critics, group by group in the collection, is perhaps best illustrated in the three essays of the last section. In returning to *The Old Man and the Sea,* the novella that won Ernest Hemingway his most consistent praise—and probably the Nobel Prize for Literature—three critics with varied perspectives supply a kind of prolegomena for the excellence of that work, particularly in relation to Hemingway's other writing. In Suzanne del Gizzo's "Going Home: Hemingway, Primitivism, and Identity," nonrestrictive anthropological reading links *The Old Man and the Sea* with Hemingway's later African writings of various kinds; in Susan Beegel's intertextual "Thor Heyerdahl's *Kon-Tiki* and Hemingway's Return to Primitivism in *The Old Man and the Sea*" we are reminded of Hemingway's need to place himself in the center of the popular imagination, often with good effect; and in William E. Cain's "Death Sentences, Rereading *The Old Man and the Sea*" we are privy to the accomplished senior scholar giving us, and himself, a new awareness of the dark significance of Hemingway's later work. The del Gizzo essay first appeared in *Modern Fiction Studies* and the Cain piece in *The Sewanee Review*; the Beegel essay has not been previously published.[8] Professor del Gizzo has just begun her career, only a few years after receiving her doctorate, whereas the other scholars are more established: the views, however, regardless of their place of publication and the status of the critic, coalesce helpfully for the reader.

In retrospect, the fact that these four collections of criticism—*Ernest Hemingway: Five Decades of Criticism, Ernest Hemingway: Six Decades of Criticism, Hemingway: Seven Decades of Criticism,* and the current book, *Hemingway: Eight Decades of Criticism*—have given a kind of permanence to the writing of nearly a hundred Hemingway scholars seems apt thanks for the work of selecting, producing, and indexing the volumes. The life of the scholar exists at a far remove from that of the writer Ernest Hemingway, who tormented himself with his need for celebrity, but it has ample satisfactions.

My thanks to Director Emeritus Fredric C. Bohm, Assistant Director and Editor in Chief Julie L. Loehr, Acquisitions Editor Martha A. Bates, Production Editor Annette Tanner, and Project Editor Kristine M. Blakeslee of the Michigan State University Press.

NOTES

1. Ernest Hemingway, "A Man's Credo," *Playboy* 10.1 (January 1963): 120.
2. Linda W. Wagner, "Introduction," *Ernest Hemingway: Six Decades of Criticism* (East Lansing: Michigan State University Press, 1987), 6–7; and see Linda Wagner-Martin, "Introduction," *Hemingway: Seven Decades of Criticism* (East Lansing: Michigan State University Press, 1998), 11–12.
3. Wagner-Martin, "Introduction," *Hemingway: Seven Decades of Criticism*, 10.
4. Ibid.
5. Miriam Marty Clark, "Hemingway's Early Illness Narratives and the Lyric Dimensions of 'Now I Lay Me,'" *Narrative* 12.2 (May 2004) [reprinted in this book].
6. "Invalid Masculinity: Silence, Hospitals, and Anesthesia in *A Farewell to Arms*" is an essay that is often referred to by critics.
7. "Hemingway and Cultural Geography: The Landscape of Logging in 'The End of Something.'"
8. Both the Beegel essay and that by John J. Fenstermaker appear here for the first time.

PART 1

New Critical Approaches to the Wound

Miriam Marty Clark
Diane Price Herndl
Dana Fore
Greg Forter
Marc Seals

Hemingway's Early Illness Narratives and the Lyric Dimensions of "Now I Lay Me"

Miriam Marty Clark

I want to begin with a claim so basic it scarcely needs to be made: Hemingway's early stories—those of *In Our Time* and *Men Without Women*—are full of sick and injured characters, from the laboring woman of "Indian Camp" to bullfighter Manuel Garcia Maera, drowning from pneumonia in "A Banal Story"; from boyish Nick with his shin barked, his eye banged, and his heart broken to war-wounded Nick, propped bleeding against a church wall or working his damaged leg every afternoon at the hospital or lying awake at night in a state that can only be called post-traumatic stress. There are more ill bodies than sexual ones in these stories, more characters in attitudes of suffering than in virtually any other state, of body or soul.

Reprinted with permission from *Narrative* 12.2 (May 2004). Copyright © 2004 by The Ohio State University. Published by The Ohio State University Press.

■ 3

There is Ole Andreson stretched on his bed in "The Killers" and Jack Brennan "all busted inside" at the end of "Fifty Grand"; there is William Campbell, concealed by a self-made shroud and talking through his riding nausea in "A Pursuit Race," and Joe Butler's father, "white and gone" by the side of the track in "My Old Man." There are boys holding their heads in their hands as though they were sick in one bar after another, and of course there is Nick himself, laid low in war. Treatment of illness also figures importantly in the development of plot and character. Doctoring is one way Nick knows his father. Like hunting—with which it is elided under the sign of the pocket knife and the arrowhead—it signifies power, responsibility, unsentimentality, even a "necessary" cruelty. Doctoring is the turf, if not terrain, of Nick's parents' conflict—he's a doctor, she's a Christian Scientist—where medicine's claims to power are always vitally at stake.

Through recurrent stories of illness and suffering, Hemingway marks several transformations. In the stories of Nick's boyhood, Nick believes that illness belongs to, even stigmatizes, the racially and socially other— the Indians in states of pneumonia, despair, or drunkenness. In time, first metaphorically, with his heart broken and his "feelings" sick, and then in the flesh, Nick comes to understand how illness and pain touch on—how they can, in a single moment, implode—his own life and the lives of others like him. Hemingway's accounts of medical care also trace the emergence of modern biomedicine, emphasizing in contrast to the primitive caesarian Nick's father performs in "Indian Camp" the medical technologies offered to the injured Manuel Garcia Maera—the anesthesia mask, later the tube in each lung—or to the boys at the hospital in Milan, the first ever to use machines for rehabilitation.

I want to go a step further here, arguing that to read Nick's *woundedness* as the central feature of these two volumes is to enable a reading of these stories as "illness narratives."[1] The usefulness of "illness narratives" within the field of bioethics is now well established by scholars including Arthur Kleinman, Kathryn Montgomery Hunter, Rita Charon, Arthur Frank, David Morris, and others. But my argument also takes part in a long conversation about wounds in Hemingway's fiction—one that runs from Malcolm Cowley's introduction to *Hemingway* and Philip Young's *Ernest Hemingway* to more recent considerations by Paul Smith, Michael Reynolds, Debra Moddelmog, and Margaret Sempreora, among others. Unlike many of these earlier discussions, my essay is not psychoanalytic in focus, arguing an original or primary trauma or tracing in images of woundedness a particular set of individual or cultural anxieties; nor are my aims historical or biographical. Instead, I want to consider the structural logic illness narratives bring to the stories, the generic complications they introduce—particularly in the relation of narrative and lyric passages—and the ethical imperatives they advance.

It may be useful to begin by contrasting Hemingway's early illness narratives with another set of modernist texts written at about the same time and also focusing on illness—William Carlos William's medical narratives.[2] Williams's are, in ways readily recognizable as "modern," epistemological narratives, following the doctor's paths of inquiry and the encounter—cure or care seeking—of doctor and patient. On the doctor's side there is medical knowledge, curiosity, human kindness tinged by impatience; on the patient's side there is the unknown, cloaked in medical mystery, alien speech or total silence, a sense of privacy or pride, personal and narrative otherness. The encounter is never perfect; the story always exceeds the doctor's ability either to elicit or interpret it; diagnosis and care—though only ever based on a partial knowledge of the patient's experience—do arise through listening, intuition, and interpretation of symptoms as symbols. It's in these forms of knowledge, and the discovery of their limits, that we as readers take part.

Hemingway on the other hand begins within the wounded body. If diagnosis takes place in and is a function of language, suffering—woundedness—exists first outside of and beyond speech. To read illness in Hemingway's early stories is not to seek a cause or to form a narrative of symptoms under the procedures of diagnosis, whether of a readerly or a medical kind, but rather to observe how, in Arthur Frank's memorable term, the body "begets" speech (27), how it finds a way "out of narrative wreckage" (55) produced by illness and into story. Trauma, Shoshana Felman writes in a definition Frank applies to illness, *exceeds* speech, story, and form, throwing them into a condition she describes as "in process and in trial." "As a relation of events," Felman writes, *testimony* is "composed of bits and pieces of a memory that has been overwhelmed by occurrences that have not settled into understanding or remembrance, acts that cannot be constructed as knowledge nor assimilated into full cognition, events in excess of our frames of reference" (5).

Such a definition—narrative wreckage followed by an unassimilated relation of events—seems at first a far cry from Hemingway's stringently crafted stories. But to read these stories as illness narratives and even as *testimony* of the kind Felman and Frank describe, turns out, I think, to be instructive. Trauma is registered *against* Hemingway's restrained forms and sentences, vital other to the spareness and clarity of the stories. Hemingway's omissions gain raw force not from the unsaid—the unspoken symptom or the not-yet-reached understanding in Williams' doctor stories—but from the unsayable, the bodily experience outside and in excess of language and story. In its sheer physicality, its brutally particular forms (drowning, pneumonia, shattered legs, disfigured limbs and features), and its lodgings in individual lives, illness in Hemingway exceeds modernist mythopoetic cultural metaphors: the chill abstractions of a "patient etherized upon a table," the sterile musings of the wounded Fisher King. It likewise exceeds modern biomedicine's narrative of cure. Both in individual stories and in a larger sense that extends among the stories, suffering exceeds medicine's diagnostic and curative powers. This is dramatically true in "Indian Camp," where Dr. Adams fails to attend adequately to the suffering of his patient's husband; but modern medicine—dualistic, mechanistic, and reductive[3]—likewise fails. In "In Another Country," even the novel technology of the rehabilitation machines cannot offer the major a remedy for his own profoundest suffering, which is not the injury to his hand but the loss of his young wife. His sadness—expressed to Nick in an angry warning against marriage for soldiers and later in his brief account of his desolation—turns the prominently displayed photographs of cured limbs into an ironic comment on the limits of medicine's power to cure or even to acknowledge suffering; it is also a mild reproach to Nick for his fascination with the machines. In a broader sense Nick's own cure—if it is a cure—takes place far beyond medical care, beyond civilization itself in the charred landscape of Seney and the natural terrain of "Big Two-Hearted River."

Most important to me here, Hemingway's illness narratives exceed chronological account, the generic boundaries of the short story, and the boundaries of a particular life story, fanning out both backward and forward from Nick's injury into multiple stories of injury, illness, and deformity, some touching Nick's life, others not clearly related to his own story. Arthur and Joan Kleinman argue that illness narratives, situated on the border between subjectivity and the symbolic order, allow us to trace otherwise hidden interconnections between social relations, institutions, and the body as "bodily processes outfold" into culture and "culture infolds the body" (710–11). "In their narratives," they write of a group of Chinese patients whose stories of illness following the Cultural Revolution are the subject of their study,[4] "remembrance of bodily complaints broadened into more general stories of suffering that integrated memories of menace and loss with their traumatic effects (demoralization, fear, desperation) and with their sources. . . . Bodily memory, biography, and social history merged" (714–15).

Hemingway's stories are similarly situated; as the central event of the stories, Nick's bodily experience—"being blown up at night" by a mortar shell—outfolds in lavish ways in these stories, incorporating both his own earlier physical and psychic wounds and the violence of the world all around him. Read in this way, "Now I Lay Me" marks the transfiguration of Nick's memories, revivifying the image of his embattled parents standing near dangerous, exploding fires or hovering, the snake between them, as the end of Eden. Suffering transfigures his desires as well, so that wives become dangerous as mortar shells. Even the landscape itself, full of undercurrents and deep holes, teeming with dangerous and endangered life, is transformed through the narrative outfolding of Nick's physical trauma. At the same time Nick's suffering becomes readable as the infolding of culture, his symptoms telling the deeply embedded violence of marriage, the outright violence of life among men, the brutal violence of war. Illness remains unresolved in the stories, represented though never fully contained in narratives of original sin, Freudian symbology, and masculine heroism; addressed but never fully remedied by ordinary measures such as prayer, talk, or medical care.

Though "Now I Lay Me" falls only little more than halfway through Philip Young's collection *The Nick Adams Stories,* and though it is followed there by stories of restoration, marriage, fatherhood, sexual knowledge, and power, it is forcefully situated as the last story of *Men Without Women,* the last of the first two volumes of stories in which most of the Nick Adams stories appear. Against the *bildungsroman* Young creates by setting the stories in chronological order stands a different narrative, an illness story that leaks into and echoes and shudders through the stories of childhood and war. The illness narrative advances and coheres *not* by contiguity or causality (the stories' chronological *disorder* makes this point) but by metaphors that mark—sometimes in the same moment—the outfolding of the body's traumas into cultural narratives and the infolding of cultural trauma into bodily symptoms. Sometimes these metaphors are circumstantial—the laboring woman of "Indian Camp" is associated with the woman laboring in wartime conditions in a cart outside of Adrianople in the italicized chapter that follows it, for example. Often the metaphors, whether they involve common circumstances or not, involve common postures of suffering—supine, crouching, propped. The birthing woman lies flat; her husband lies flat; Ole Andreson and Jack Brennan and Manuel Garcia Maera lie flat, resisting or resigned to death; an Indian lies face down in the sand on the Fourth of July. Joe Butler sees his old man, thrown and trampled in the steeplechase, "laying on the grass flat out with his face up and blood all over the side of his head" (*IOT* 171–72). Rinaldi falls face down against a wall after the explosion that wounds him and Nick. All of these instances make their way toward Nick's own fearful waiting—"While the bombardment was knocking the trench to pieces at Fossalta, he lay very flat and sweated and prayed, 'Oh Jesus Christ get me out of here'" (*IOT* 87)—and finally to those nights of fearful watching described in "Now I Lay Me."

Or another attitude: Prizefighter Ad Francis—now physically deformed and mentally deranged by blows in the ring—sits with his head in his hands looking at a fire in "The Battler"; Sam Cardinella has to be propped up in a sitting position in order to be hanged in chapter 15 of *In Our Time;* a cabinet minister, "sick with typhoid" and waiting to be shot by a firing squad in the rain, sits in the water "with his head on his knees" in helpless despair in chapter 5 (*IOT* 83). These accounts make their way, backward and forward, to Nick Adams' own suffering "sitting against the wall of a church where they had dragged him to be clear of machine gun fire" (81) and his post-traumatic memories of other fires, other battles, as far back as memory goes.

Nick's suffering is less profound than many of the other instances he encounters—the stories acknowledge this—and less profound than the collective suffering he sees on all sides of him in war. But the gravity and pathos of these other stories, witnessed rather than "lived" in the narrative, accrue to Nick's own story, *the* story of these two volumes. Their sheer number argues the fact that bodily experience exceeds the frame of a single narrative or life story; it takes many stories to tell *a* story of suffering. Nor, as William Carlos Williams also discovers, can narrative make a direct approach adequate to the deepest forms of suffering. *Woundedness* calls for metaphors, reiterations, silences—more than Nick's story alone will bear. The other stories—set in war or prison, the bull ring or the boxing ring—may be read as ways of saying, "it's as if . . . and as if . . . and as if." At the same time, Nick's injuries provide a metaphor for the sufferings of the world. The crouched, the dying, the traumatized become knowable by us through our engagement with Nick, not only in his narrative account but also in the emotional demands a story like "Now I Lay Me" makes on us.

How this happens leads me back to a question James Phelan has posed, one I alluded to earlier in this essay, about how *lyric* works in "Now I Lay Me." Phelan has long distinguished narrative from lyric by looking at the role of "judgments by readers." "Narrative," he notes, "requires audiences to judge its characters; lyric requires audiences not to judge its speakers," offering instead "the representation of a character (or speaker) who gives voice to a set of attitudes, thoughts, emotions, or choices that the audience is asked not to judge but to contemplate and imaginatively participate in" (1998, 47). Nick's story in "Now I Lay Me" is "ethically disconcerting," Phelan argues, "because in pulling us to sympathize with Nick, to share the feeling associated with his condition, it asks us to assent to some questionable values, especially those underlying the story's analogy between war and marriage, and, more particularly, between mortar shells and women" (48). Nick's gentle voice and his evident kindness and courage in this lyric mode lull us into accepting *without judgment* claims and analogies we would not assent to in narrative.

But here I want to draw on another way of thinking, one that frames lyric as "the entrance to another world of experience," a portal to a world outside of "our ordinary continuous experience in space and time" as Northrop Frye puts it (31, 36). This understanding of lyric may prove more useful in addressing the still-pressing question of how lyric works in this moving story. If the extraordinary experience that lyric touches here is *suffering*—the outfolding of the body's suffering into memory, metaphor, and attitudes, however disconcerting; the infolding of the world (its strife, its dangers) into the bodily experiences of pain, fear, silence—then it too makes its demands of its readers, and not just for sympathy but for a deeper engagement. Drawing on Levinas's work, as David Morris does, we might say that lyric in "Now I Lay Me" gives a *face*—ethically insistent—to Nick's suffering, which also registers a wider and deeper suffering in the world.

To say this, however, entails a pressing but often unacknowledged question of whether a book—fictional or nonfictional—can summon and command in the same way *the face* does for Levinas. However compelling Levinas's terms may be for an ethics of reading, the irreducibility of the face-to-face meeting to an ethical encounter, an act of moral reasoning, or the work of engaged reading present substantial resistance to such an approach. For Morris the face-to-face meeting functions as a metaphor for the ethical encounter that illness narratives call for. For Frank, as for Laub and Felman, the encounter with the other is, as I have already said, mediated by testimony; in such witness narrative the experience of suffering always exceeds any single accounts, and fixity of plot or fatedness of characters, any purely cognitive engagement, any clarity of meaning or response, even of genre, as Frank has noted (203). "The listener to trauma," Laub writes, "comes to be a participant and a co-owner of the traumatic event: through his very listening, he comes to partially experience trauma in himself. The relation of the victim to the event of the trauma, therefore, impacts on the relation of the listener to it, and the latter comes to feel the bewilderment, injury, confusion, dread and conflicts that the trauma victim feels. . . . The listener, therefore, by definition partakes of the struggle of the victim with the memories and residues of his or her traumatic past" (57). For Felman the demand such testimonies make is not only intellectual, aesthetic, and emotional but physical as well, restoring a noncognitive, bodily aspect to the face-to-face encounter; the role of testimony, she writes, "is to open up in that belated witness, which the reader now historically becomes, the imaginative capability of perceiving history—what is happening to others *in one's own body* with the power of sight (of insight) usually afforded only by one's own immediate physical involvement" (108).

But unlike many of the accounts Laub and Felman cite, and unlike the tentative and chaotic illness stories that are Frank's subject, Hemingway's stories do not advance under a strongly developed rhetoric of testimony. Their acknowledgement of suffering is swiftly, if never fully, offset by a rhetoric of bravery, violence, sexual mastery, and self-sufficiency, and by a narrative of artistic development highlighted in Young's chronological arrangement of the stories. Moreover, despite their testimonial aspects—that is, their relationship to events that overwhelm even repeated efforts to narrate and explain—the stories remain oriented first to the forms and aims of fiction; the immobility of fictional narratives marks them, in Levinas's words, as "wholly different from that of concepts, which initiates life, offers reality to our powers, to truth, opens a dialectic" (1989, 139). However human their summons seems to be, Hemingway's stories remain outside both the interhuman orientation and the order of revelation as Levinas defines them.

But even as I have raised serious questions about the idea of a face-to-face encounter mediated by Hemingway's stories, I want to suggest that these early texts constitute a meditation on the nature of suffering that is nevertheless illuminated by Levinas's thinking. I would like to focus on two closely related points. The first is Levinas's conviction that suffering cannot be talked about without reference to a future tense; the experience of suffering fuses the pain of the moment with a paroxysmal anxiety about what lies ahead—darker evil and death itself—as if, he writes, "there were something about to be produced even more rending than suffering" (1987, 69). The second is Levinas's argument that suffering and death do not lead, as Heidegger argues, to a supreme lucidity, virility, or heroism but that they stand as darkness or mystery, producing brutal exposure and paralysis of a kind we see movingly articulated in "Now I Lay Me."   .

To suffer, Levinas reasons, is to be not just in the midst of but *on the verge*. In ways the child's prayer half-perceives and half-creates, sleep shares with suffering a place at the verge of death, a fact Nick knows intimately. "I had," he says, "been living for a long time with the knowledge that if I ever shut my eyes in the dark and let myself go, my soul would go out of my body" (*MWW* 209). Nick's fear arises from his experiences in the war but it is focused on the present as it verges darkly into the future. "I had been that way for a long time," he notes, "ever since I had been blown up at night and felt it go out of me and go off and then come back. I tried never to think about it, but it had started to go since, in the nights, just at the moment of going off to sleep. I could only stop it by a very great effort" (209). For the sufferer there is no escape or retreat from this state, Levinas argues, and no illumination by way of it; death remains mysterious. Nick has suffered in war and has seen enormous suffering and death all around him but he is still alive both in the summer he describes and in the present tense of the story. In his wakefulness on those summer nights of "Now I Lay Me," he suffers both a stark knowledge of death instilled by the trauma of war and a sense of its inviolable mystery, signified by the darkness all around him.

In its paroxysmal form, suffering encounters not just the limits of experience but the radical suspension of agency. Death and the future refuse mastery through cognition, will, or force of action; they are, Levinas writes, "refractory to synthesis" operating "not as 'grasp' but as revulsion" (1988, 156). Unable to turn back from the verge or to seize what lies beyond, the sufferer sees his story is suspended in its fearful moment. Death announces itself in suffering, Levinas observes, away from light and activity; it "announces an event over which the subject is not master, an event in relation to which the subject is no longer a subject." By contrast, "in Heidegger's authentic existence," death "is a supreme lucidity and hence a supreme virility. It is *Dasein's* assumption of the uttermost possibility of existence, which precisely makes possible all other possibilities, and consequently makes possible the very fear of grasping a possibility—that is, it makes possible activity and freedom. Death in Heidegger is an event of freedom, whereas for me the subject seems to reach the limit of the possible in suffering. It finds itself enchained, overwhelmed, and in some way passive" (1987, 70).

Passivity is on the one hand the sum of losses—of mastery, of understanding, of subjectivity itself in the face of death—but it is also, for Levinas, the essential condition of responsibility. Stripped of all subjectivity, a person comes naked to the other, as keeper but also as hostage. This transaction is prior to language and law, beyond egoism and altruism, and remote from Hemingway's stories as from all fictions. Still, I think, the transformation of suffering into passivity and brutal exposure can be read as a crucial ethical moment for Hemingway. Nick's actions and attitudes in "Now I Lay Me" register in two significant ways the end of virility and heroism in suffering. The first is his indifference to the future, to love and work alike. "The girls, after I had thought about them a few times, blurred," Nick remembers form his wakeful nights, "and all became rather the same and I gave up thinking about them almost altogether" (*MWW* 222). Nick's thoughts of girls are simply memories, never erotically charged or deeply wishful. The last fact he notes about himself in the story is that "so far I have never married." Having come near ungraspable death, Nick grasps at almost nothing in the future tense; his statement to John—"I'll get a job on a paper" (219)—is the only claim he makes about the rest of his life, and he can't say whether the paper will be in Chicago or not, answering only "maybe" to John's question. In Nick's nights of post-traumatic insomnia—when his dread of death keeps him awake—the ego disintegrates and the future is effaced by death; hence, I think, the troubling association between women and mortar shells. "Death is never now," Levinas writes. "When death is here, I am no longer here, not just because I am nothingness, but because I am unable to grasp.

My mastery, my virility, my heroism as a subject can be neither virility nor heroism in relation to death" (1987, 72).

Such passivity in suffering and in the face of death produces what Levinas describes as a return to infancy. "When suffering attains its purity," he writes, "where there is no longer anything between us and it, the supreme responsibility of this extreme assumption turns into supreme irresponsibility, into infancy" (1987, 72). For Levinas this takes the form of "sobbing" and "shaking" in the midst of suffering. The second significant register of Nick's retreat and his losses are the shuddering prayers, not so far from sobbing, and the paroxysmal anxieties about being blown up. But his return to infancy also takes a metaphoric form in the memories he summons to keep himself awake—memories going back to the earliest recollection and to the time before recollections or speech, true infancy, to the house in which he was born. The return entails a descent into the dark, fraught family romance— mother, father, child, violence—where he is a helpless, passive watcher. It is given voice in his anxious dependence on a childhood prayer, "Now I Lay Me," and in literal infancy—a descent into speechlessness in prayer (of the Lord's Prayer), in conversation (with John), in courtship (of the Italian girls). In his recollections of his childhood Nick also sees the human race back to its own infancy, its evolutionary beginnings in fish and salamanders, and to its mythic and biblical infancy: mother, father, fraught by snakes, kept out of Eden by a burning fire. He himself becomes a belated Adam, restoring the war-shattered world as he restores the names of things. "So on some nights," he tells us, "I would try to remember all the animals in the world by name and then the birds and then fishes and then countries and cities" (215).

In this moment we may hear not the end but the return of virility, the subject's mastery and assimilation of the object—the world itself—through Nick's painstaking mental reconstruction. This renaming may seem, however subtly, to reverse the passivity, the infancy, the failure of heroism, and to signify a triumph both through and over suffering. But if we read with Levinas's conviction that the experience of suffering forbids a return to Adamic virility and egoism, Nick's nighttime labor—like a child's desolate effort to rebuild a city made of blocks or to remake the world from fact memorized at school—marks rather than reverses his passivity. Hemingway's story broods on the verge—broods lyrically—both disclosing and resisting the passivity that arises in the face of death. For Levinas this meeting of the will with the violence of death is the source of the profoundest of ethical encounters; whether death comes by God or enemy, by "blade of steel, chemistry of poison, hunger or thirst" he writes, "—solitude is broken and an opening"—a "half opening" is created for a relation with the Other. "My death," he writes in a sentence that seems applicable not only to the sleepless, shuddering Nick of "Now I Lay Me" but also to the stoic, haunted Nick of Hemingway's later story "A Way You'll Never Be," "comes from an instant upon which I can in no way exercise my power" (1969, 235). Death cannot be surmounted, endured, or integrated into life; its alterity cannot be assimilated. It breaks solitude and transforms the will so that it no longer "coincides with the I of need" but becomes "the desire that is for the Other" (1969, 236). Suffering, Levinas writes, "takes its place on a ground where the relationship with the other becomes possible" (1987, 76).

Much later, in an essay called "Useless Suffering," Levinas observes that pure suffering "is intrinsically meaningless and condemned to itself without exit" but that "a beyond takes shape in the inter-human." In this interhuman ethical perspective, he finds a radical difference between "*suffering in the Other,* which for *me* is unpardonable and solicits me and calls me, and suffering *in me,* my own adventure of suffering whose constitutional or congenital uselessness can take on a meaning, the only meaning to which suffering is susceptible, in becoming a suffering for the suffering—be it inexorable—of someone else." It is this attention to the Other, he adds, "which, across the cruelties of our century—despite these cruelties, because of these cruelties—can be affirmed as the very bond of human subjectivity, even to the point of being raised to a supreme ethical principle—the only one which it is not possible to contest" (1988, 159).

It would be a mistake, I think, to suggest that insight gained from suffering trumps or even substantially modulates the elements of mastery and bravado in Hemingway's fiction. Revisionist criticism has already demonstrated that those are challenged in many other ways in the stories and particularly in the displacement of the "self-styled macho man," as Cary Wolfe puts it, by a very different figured consumed by the "transgressive possibilities of gender performativity" (223). But Levinas's account of suffering provides new ways to think about Nick's situation in "Now I Lay Me" even as it transforms the ethical imperative the story advances. The lyric passages of this story situate *us* at the verge, where agency is suspended and grasp fails. Though they can never enact it, they imagine a moment that refuses both ethical stances and interpretive measures, one that cannot be assimilated or turned back from; they make us, however briefly, hostages to Nick's story. In this way "Now I Lay Me" does provide a half-opening to a world beyond the solitary self: to alterity, infinity, the Other. It is an opening that begins with Nick's own woundedness—useless suffering by every measure the stories offer. How directly and persistently it opens into the suffering of others and into that interhuman perspective explains, I think, the surprising ethical force of these stories—of *this* story, though it troubles our judgments to the end.[5]

NOTES

1. Illness is significant in Hemingway's later fiction as well. Paul Smith points out, for example, that "doctors, medicine, and the physical ills to which the body is vulnerable figure prominently" in *Winner Take Nothing* (13); of the later stories, several—including "A Way You'll Never Be," which finds Nick Adams, mentally exhausted and physically ill from the trauma of war, moving among the fly-swarmed bodies of the dead—hold particular interest for me. My emphasis in this essay, however, is on images and narratives of illness in *In Our Time* and *Men Without Women*. In these first two volumes, reckoning human vulnerability to violence in private worlds as in public, illness narratives lend coherence and frame an ethical encounter that continues through the short fiction of the 1930s.

2. Both poetry and prose, these medical narratives appear in various volumes of Williams's work, including *The Farmer's Daughters* and *The Autobiography;* Robert Coles has gathered them under the title *The Doctor Stories.*

3. Here I draw on David Morris's characterization of the modern "biomedical model" in *Illness and Culture in the Postmodern Age.*

4. Although the Kleinmans' study addresses a particular group of people and a set of specific political circumstances, it leads—like their other work—to a broader understanding of the sociosomatic process of everyday life and the role of illness narratives across cultures.

5. David Haney, Marc Silverstein, James Phelan, and Debra Moddelmog offered helpful commentary on earlier versions of this essay. I am grateful to them.

WORKS CITED

Cowley, Malcolm. Introduction to *Ernest Hemingway.* New York: Viking, 1944.

Frank, Arthur. *The Wounded Storyteller.* Chicago: U of Chicago P, 1995.

Frye, Northrop. "Approaching the Lyric." In *Lyric Poetry: Beyond the New Criticism.* Eds. Chaviva Hosek and Patricia Parker, 31–37. Ithaca: Cornell UP, 1985.

Hemingway, Ernest. *In Our Time.* New York: Scribner's, 1925.

———. *Men Without Women.* London: Jonathan Cape, 1928.

Kleinman, Arthur, and Joan Kleinman. "How Bodies Remember: Social Memory and Bodily Experience of Criticism, Resistance, and Delegitimation Following China's Cultural Revolution." *New Literary History* 25 (Summer 1994): 707–24.

Laub, Dori, and Shoshana Felman. *Testimony.* New York: Routledge, 1992.

Levinas, Emmanuel. *Totality and Infinity: An Essay on Exteriority.* Translated by Alphonso Lingis. Pittsburgh: Duquesne UP, 1969.

———. *Time and the Other.* Translated by Richard A. Cohen. Pittsburgh: Duquesne UP, 1987.

———. "Useless Suffering." In *The Provocation of Levinas.* Eds. Robert Bernasconi and David Wood, 156–67. New York: Routledge, 1988.

———. *The Levinas Reader.* Ed. Sean Hand. Oxford: Blackwell, 1989.

Moddelmog, Debra. *Reading Desire: In Pursuit of Ernest Hemingway.* Ithaca: Cornell UP, 1999.

Morris, David. *Illness and Culture in the Postmodern Age.* Berkeley: U of California P, 1998.

———. "Narrative, Ethics, and Pain: Thinking *With* Stories." *Narrative* 9 (2001): 55–77.

Phelan, James. *Narrative as Rhetoric*. Columbus: The Ohio State UP, 1996.

———. "'Now I Lay Me': Nick's Strange Monologue, Hemingway's Powerful Lyric, and the Reader's Disconcerting Experience." In *New Essays on Hemingway's Short Fiction*. Ed. Paul Smith, 47–72. Cambridge: Cambridge UP, 1998.

Reynolds, Michael. "*A Farewell to Arms*: Doctors in the House of Love." In *The Cambridge Companion to Hemingway*. Ed. Scott Donaldson, 109–27. Cambridge: Cambridge UP, 1996.

Sempreora, Margot. "Nick at Night: Nocturnal Metafictions in Three Hemingway Short Stories." *The Hemingway Review* 22 (2002): 19–33.

Smith, Paul. "Introduction: Hemingway and the Practical Reader." In *New Essays on Hemingway's Short Fiction*. Ed. Paul Smith, 1–18. Cambridge: Cambridge UP, 1998.

Williams, William Carlos. *Doctor Stories*. Ed. Robert Coles. New York: New Directions, 1984.

Wolfe, Cary. "Fathers, Lovers, and Friend Killers: Rearticulating Gender and Race via Species in Hemingway." *boundary* 2.29 (2002): 223–57.

Invalid Masculinity

Silence, Hospitals, and Anesthesia in *A Farewell to Arms*

Diane Price Herndl

It's evening now, and everybody's scribbling away.... And not just letters, either. Diaries. Poems. At least two would-be poets in this hut alone.

Why? you have to ask yourself. I think it's a way of claiming immunity. First-person narrators can't die, so as long as we keep telling the story of our own lives we're safe. Ha bloody fucking ha.

—Barker, *Ghost Road*

Between his own experience of being wounded in war and writing *A Farewell to Arms,* Ernest Hemingway wrote an essay called "How to be Popular in Peace Though a Slacker in War" for the *Toronto Star Weekly* (Reynolds 136). This essay will take up the question of "slackers" in World War I, specifically those who were thought to be malingering in war hospitals. Many critics have commented on the passage in which nurse Van Campen accuses Frederic Henry of using alcoholism to avoid going back to the front, but such comments almost always focus on his misogynist response to her, rather than on her accusation itself. I do not intend to echo her charge here, to take Frederic Henry to task for staying in the hospital longer than

Reprinted with permission from *The Hemingway Review* 21.1 (Fall 2001). Copyright © 2001 The Ernest Hemingway Foundation. Published by the University of Idaho, Moscow, Idaho.

he needs to, but to investigate questions about masculinity that arise from Hemingway's portrayal of the soldier as a suspect malingerer and a deserter. My investigation is going to look at Frederic Henry through the lens of Pat Barker's World War I trilogy—*Regeneration, Eye in the Door,* and *The Ghost Road*—not to offer a reading of Barker, but to use Barker's insights as a way of seeing Hemingway's.[1] I will be reading the wounded soldier as a performance of masculinity, to ask whether medicine in Hemingway's novel, as in Barker's, functions as a "technology of gender" that inscribes ideals of masculine behavior.

The Compulsion to Tell: Narration and Health

James Phelan describes the narrative paradox in *A Farewell to Arms* as one in which the narrator who is telling the story cannot be the same person who is experiencing the story. That is, the Frederic Henry who is the retrospective narrator already knows what the character Frederic Henry learns during the course of the story. I will articulate a different narrative paradox (but one that I think complements Phelan's): the narrator feels compelled to tell a story that the character cannot really articulate. The result is a novel focused on silence and stoicism. When Henry returns from the hospital, Rinaldi says to him, "Tell me all about everything." Henry responds, "There's nothing to tell" (*AFTA* 167). This interaction is representative of the narrative as a whole. Throughout, Frederic is torn between a compulsion to tell and his sense that he cannot, or should not, tell. Plenty of critics have diagnosed Catherine Barkley as insane, unbalanced, or crazy.[2] But critics almost always assume that Frederic Henry's malady is purely physical; he is the victim of shelling, in other words, but not shell shock.[3] To do so, I think, is to ignore one of the earliest commentaries on the war in the novel. Just before he is killed, the driver Passini comments: "Listen. There is nothing as bad as war. . . . When people realize how bad it is they cannot do anything to stop it because they go crazy" (50). I don't want to diagnose Frederic as insane, but I do want to cast some doubt on the precise nature of his malady, and raise the possibility that his *illness* is actually masculinity as it was presented to the World War I soldier.

In *A War Imagined,* Samuel Hynes, writing about the pioneering World War I psychiatrist W. H. R. Rivers (who is also one of Barker's main characters in her blend of fact and fiction), says of Rivers's method:

> He rejected the idea that men should suppress feelings, and helped his patients to accept and to express "unmanly" feelings; weeping, he told them, could be a help to grieving men, and there was no shame in breaking down under stress. War was an inherently traumatic experience, and fear was a natural response to it—the problem was a medical, not a moral one. (185–186)

In a novel like *Regeneration,* a late 20th-century feminist writer like Pat Barker can focus on Rivers and his methods and overtly articulate the crisis of masculinity brought about by the experience of World War I. But an author like Ernest Hemingway, caught absolutely in the bind of early-20th-century models of masculinity himself, cannot. Using Barker and World War I historians as a lens, however, we can read the dilemma and paradox of Frederic Henry's narration. On the one hand, he feels acutely the need to tell about his horrific experiences of war—watching his comrades Passini and Aymo die, his own suffering and wounding, the shooting of the sergeant, his forced desertion, and Catherine's death. On the other hand, he feels the code of manliness that requires that he not be perceived as complaining or weeping.

In an essay about *Regeneration,* Greg Harris argues that what Barker dramatizes in the narrative is the conflict men feel between telling and not telling, between what they are feeling and what they believe they should feel:

> . . . brutal experiences will be their reality, yet the most legitimate emotions that such anticipation might inspire—fear, angst, second thoughts—must be stifled. The men willingly suspend valid but invalidated emotions. . . . The gender codes, then, appear to the gendered subject as more legitimate than the private feelings they eclipse in the service of upholding a compulsory masculinity. (301)

Hemingway dramatizes this, too, but perhaps not in the self-conscious way that Barker does. Much of the narrative tension in the novel comes from Frederic Henry's simultaneous needs to tell and to keep quiet. This is exacerbated by Hemingway's style of narration, which Peter Schwenger identifies as explicitly masculine: "Plainly Hemingway's style is in one sense an extension of the masculine values he depicts: the restraint of emotion, the stiff upper lip, the *macho* hermeticism" (50). It is interesting that in employing a "masculine" style that resists the sentimentalism of a feminine style (one that would presumably focus on emotion) Frederic Henry may succumb to a different "female" problem—silence.

In her chapter on shell shock in *The Female Malady,* Elaine Showalter argues forcefully for reading shell shock as a kind of protest akin to the Victorian woman's use of hysteria as protest. "If the essence of manliness was not to complain," she argues, "then shell shock was the body language of masculine complaint, a disguised male protest not only against the war but against the concept of 'manliness' itself. . . . The heightened code of masculinity that dominated wartime was intolerable to surprisingly large numbers of men" (172). In *A Farewell to Arms,* Hemingway does not focus directly on the classic symptoms of shell shock—aphasia, memory loss, or paralysis. Instead, his focus is double—on a different form of silence (to which I will return), and on a form of self-medication, the very condition of which Nurse Van Patten accuses Frederic Henry, alcoholism. Drinking to excess, drinking to forget, drinking enough to be sick—these are repeated refrains. As he is convincing Henry to drink despite his recent jaundice, Rinaldi calls his own drinking "Self-destruction day by day . . . It ruins the stomach and makes the hand shake. Just the thing for a surgeon" (172). Ultimately, as we shall see, drinking as self-medication assists in silence.

Before we get to that, perhaps it would be useful to look directly at that interaction between Van Campen and Henry:

> "I suppose you can't be blamed for not wanting to go back to the front. But I should think you would try something more intelligent that producing jaundice with alcoholism . . . I don't believe self-inflicted jaundice entitles you to a convalescent leave." . . .

"Have you ever had jaundice, Miss Van Campen?"

"No, but I have seen a great deal of it."

"You noticed how the patients enjoyed it?"

"I suppose it is better than the front."

"Miss Van Campen . . . did you ever know a man who tried to disable himself by kicking himself in the scrotum?" . . .

"I have known many men to escape the front through self-inflicted wounds." (*AFTA* 144)

We should read this conversation in light of the novel's repeated hints at the prevalence of self-inflicted wounds. One of the very first things we see Henry do in the course of his duty is assist a man with his self-inflicted wounds. The soldier has deliberately left off his truss to make his hernia worse, but knows that his own officers will recognize this as self-inflicted.

Henry advises him to "fall down by the road and get a bump on your head" after thinking over the soldier's question: "You wouldn't want to go in the line all the time, would you?" (35). Even after Henry's legitimate wounding, the doctor needs to include "Incurred in the line of duty" in his report, telling Henry, "That's what keeps you from being court-martialled for self-inflicted wounds" (59). Hemingway repeatedly draws our attention to and then away from the question of self-inflicted wounds. Perhaps his point is to reassure us of Henry's masculinity—no "slacker," he—but we could also read it as a commentary on the whole self-destructiveness of wartime masculinity.[4] That is, masculinity itself becomes a self-inflicted wound.

We can read Frederic Henry against ideas of subjectivity and masculinity that would position him as destined to lose. Usually, these ideas are attributed to an unforgiving world: "If people bring so much courage to this world the world has to kill them to break them, so of course it kills them. The world breaks every one and afterward many are strong at the broken places. But those that will not break it kills" (*AFTA* 249). Such ideas often get posited in the novel not as "it" or "the world," but as "they": "You never had time to learn. They threw you in and told you the rules and the first time they caught you off base they killed you. Or they killed you gratuitously. . . . [But] they killed you in the end. You could count on that. Stay around and they would kill you" (327). Such sentiments are perhaps typical of a postwar modernist disillusionment, an alienation focused on the pointlessness of life and manifested later in existentialism.

It would be possible, though, to read these sentiments as figuring the condition of World War I masculinity, focused as it was on a particularly passive form of warfare.[5] Convinced by patriotic fervor to embrace military service as a path to masculine feats of heroism, most soldiers discovered that the war meant waiting in a trench to be shelled. That Frederic Henry doesn't engage in trench warfare doesn't obviate this point; most of his experience of war consists of waiting—waiting out bad weather, waiting for shelling to begin so that he can drive his ambulance, or waiting in the hospital to get well. He is wounded, in fact, while he is waiting. Sandra Gilbert has described World War I as "the apocalypse of masculinism": "paradoxically . . . the war to which so many men had gone in hope of becoming heroes ended up emasculating them . . . confining them as closely as any Victorian woman has been confined" (447–448). The novel depicts the war as anything but heroic; medals are awarded for nothing, wounds are sustained while eating spaghetti in a dugout, and death comes about randomly, without respect for one's manliness or bravery. Rinaldi explicitly wants Frederic to have been a hero:

> "Tell me exactly what happened. Did you do any heroic act?"
> "No . . . I was blown up while we were eating cheese."
> "Be serious. You must have done something heroic . . ." (*AFTA* 63)

Under such circumstances of passivity, randomness, irrationality, and meaninglessness, maintaining a faith in old models of manhood proves impossible. Indeed, several critics have recently examined the novel in terms of the dilemmas of masculinity that it presents. Ira Elliott, for instance, argues that in the gap between the narrating "I" and the "I" who experienced the war, the novel stages "the instability of the culturally-fixed categories male/female and homo/heterosexual, an instability in large measure engendered by the collapse of the pre-war social order." Elliott contends that "Frederic's narrative . . . retreats from 'truth' learned on the frontlines: gender, desire, and sex cannot be defined in oppositional binarisms" (292). Similarly, Charles Hatten argues that the novel represents a "crisis of masculinity," though he situates the crisis in "embattled sexual desire" and reads the misogyny in the novel as a failed attempt to resituate masculinity in physiology (77–78). Stephen Clifford reads Frederic as forced to choose between love for a woman and the homosocial world of masculinity. We can read Frederic Henry's narrative dilemmas, then, as a conflict between the very real need to tell about his experiences, and his finding that the story he has to tell does not tally with an early-20th-century masculinity. It should not be surprising then, if his experience of masculinity itself is threatened with invalidation.

The Compulsion to Stay Silent: Medicine as a Technology of Gender

Gerry Brenner argues that when we read the novel against the backdrop of the war's meaninglessness, "the thesis of *A Farewell to Arms* . . . is that no institution, belief system, value, or commitment can arm one against life's utter irrationality." Brenner sees the roles of medicine in the novel as "symptomatic of the failure of any system that offers or allows the illusion that it can give humankind health, order, meaning, or significance" (131). Brenner, Clifford, Elliott, and Hatten all seem to me to be right in their readings of the crisis of masculinity and rationality that the novel stages. I want to refract their insights, though, to reread the novel in terms of the way it stages a variety of "invalid masculinity"[6] and uses medicine as a technology of gender. Rather than reading the novel as a failure to reimagine gender roles, though, I will read it as a success of modern medicine, a success at constructing a modern, colonized masculinity that can perform in war.

I am borrowing the phrase "technologies of gender" from Teresa de Lauretis. She claims:

1. Gender is (a) representation—which is not to say that it does not have concrete or real implications, both social and subjective, for the material life of individuals. On the contrary,

2. The representation of gender *is* its construction—and in the simplest sense it can be said that all of Western Art and high culture is the engraving of the history of that construction.

It will not come as news that Hemingway is actively engaged in constructing masculinity. But I want to look at some of the specifics of how medicine is a part of that construction, especially when placed within a narrative that in some ways resists its own telling with strategic silences.

To look at silence in the novel is somewhat difficult, because, of course, silence simply *isn't there*. One has to look at moments when there *should* be something, when it makes the most sense that a narrator would want to describe an experience or a feeling, but doesn't. There are repeated instances of this. For example, after he is wounded, Frederic Henry never uses a metaphor or simile of any kind to describe his pain. He says "Good Christ" in response to questions about whether it hurts, and will comment that it "hurt badly" (*AFTA* 59–60), but there are no other descriptors. He once comments, "The pain had gone on and on with the legs bent and I could feel it go in and out of the bone" (83), but he does not comment on how he feels. In a conversation with Catherine, Frederic reinterprets the old adage that the brave man dies only once: "The brave dies perhaps two thousand deaths if he's intelligent. He simply doesn't mention them" (140). To this extent, Frederic maintains his image of the brave: he simply doesn't mention the pain. This accords with many other moments in the novel when we might expect some articulation of negative emotion or feelings—after he shoots the sergeant, after he is forced to desert the army, after Catherine dies—Frederic is repeatedly silent when it would seem healthiest to voice some reaction.

Frederic's silence, then, becomes a technology of gender, a representation that enacts gender as it represents it. To follow this line of thought is to concur with Judith Butler's insights about the performance of gender. If we cannot read the words, the language, then we have to read the action, the performance. If we take seriously Butler's claim that "gender is . . . an identity tenuously constituted in time—an identity instituted through a *stylized repetition of acts*" rather than "a stable locus of agency" (402, *emphasis mine*), then we can see Frederic's repeated silences as constituting a notion of masculinity as numbness, as lack of feeling, as a kind of dissociation from self.

He learns this dissociation, I would argue, from medicine. The discourses of medicine and masculinity in this novel join forces to colonize male subjectivity, to remake men as fighting machines. Rinaldi jokingly tells Henry that he will "get [him] drunk and take out [his] liver and put [him] in a good Italian liver and make [him] a man again" after his bout of jaundice (*AFTA* 168). The novel very clearly challenges the question of what kind of "men" medicine makes. Military medicine is an interesting oxymoron, since the goal of such medicine is to make men well enough to go back to potentially much greater harm. This is a theme that Pat Barker makes explicit in her trilogy, as Greg Harris argues: "Barker examines how patriarchal constructions of masculinity colonize men's subjectivity in ways that, especially in wartime, prove oppressive, repressive, and wholly brutal in their effects on the male psyche" (303). Barker herself puts it this way, in the voice of Billy Prior's character in *The Ghost Road*:

> We are [the hospital's] success stories. *Look at us.* We don't remember, we don't feel, we don't think—at least not beyond the confines of what's needed to do the job. By any proper civilized standard (but what does *that* mean *now?*) we are objects of horror. But our nerves are completely steady. And we are still alive. (200, *emphasis mine*)

In *A Farewell to Arms,* the patriarchal notions of masculinity are enforced through a medical narrative. Frederic Henry *tries* to tell his illness story, and tries to tell Catherine's illness story, but succeeds only in being told by that story. In his book on illness narratives, *The Wounded Storyteller,* Arthur Frank describes the shift into medical modernity as the moment when we are forced to surrender our "illness stories" to medicine itself:

> The *modern* experience of illness begins when popular experience is overtaken by technical expertise. . . . [A] core social expectation of being sick is surrendering oneself to the care of a physician. I understand this obligation of seeking medical

care as a *narrative surrender* and mark it as the central moment in modernist illness experience. (5–6, *emphasis mine*)

Frank describes the modern experience of medicine as colonizing; one becomes a subject of medicine and is spoken of or for, but one doesn't actually speak one's own illness narrative. Reading *A Farewell to Arms* within this framework, we see that Frederic is not really able to find a voice to describe his suffering: the stoicism that he embraces as an ideal (and that Hemingway employs as a style) keeps him from really being able to give voice to what he's thinking or feeling. He surrenders his own story that is culturally untellable; that is why his narration seems that of a "dumb ox" at times (as Wyndham Lewis called him). But being a "dumb," that is, silently, sufferer is exactly what the military and modernist medicine promoted as an ideal. The resulting narrative becomes a story of looking for anesthesia, of looking for a way to stop feeling, to stay quiet, but to continue on despite pain.

The ideal that colonizes him also, I think, finally separates him from himself. Early in his experience of hospital life, Frederic begins to dissociate himself from the self that feels pain.[7] As the doctor probes his leg for bits of shrapnel, he can occasionally feel sharp pain where the anesthetic has not taken complete effect. He writes: "[The doctor] used a local anaesthetic called something or other 'snow,' which froze the tissue and avoided pain until the probe, the scalpel or the forceps got below the frozen portion. The anaesthetized area was clearly defined by the patient" (*AFTA* 94). Such a shift seems almost literally a surrender to the medical narrative, if not to the medical case study; Henry ceases telling his story and tells, instead, "the patient's" story. This narrative shift to the third person is extended later on in the novel, when Henry begins to disclaim parts of himself:

My knee was stiff, but it had been very satisfactory. Valentini had done a fine job. I had done half the retreat on foot and swum part of the Tagliamento with his knee. It was his knee all right. The other knee was mine. Doctors did things to you and then it was not your body any more. The head was mine, and the inside of the belly. It was very hungry in there. I could feel it turn over on itself.

The head was mine, but not to use, not to think with, only to remember and not too much remember. (230)

Despite referring to it as "my knee" at the beginning of this passage, Henry concludes that "it was not [his] body any more." It should be no surprise, then, that he doesn't recognize himself in the mirror while he is boxing (311). Within Frank's terms, Henry has become a medical, colonized, subject, no longer "his own man," but the man that medicine has made him. As Gayle Whittier explains, "If the wound disconnects the perceiving and feeling self from the body, the clinical agenda encourages such disconnection, altering the patient from someone who is his body to someone who 'has' a body, the ownership of which is now under medical control" (8, *emphasis mine*). It is not his body anymore, and he can no longer use his head outside the confines that have been dictated to him by an outside narrative, a narrative of medicalized, anaesthetized masculinity.

Anesthesia as Model

If anesthesia becomes the model for masculinity in *A Farewell to Arms,* then we need to re-read the conclusion of the novel and re-read Catherine's death. Readings of her death have varied tremendously, though we could represent their range as running from Judith Fetterley's famous dictum, that the end of the novel shows that for Hemingway 'the only good woman is a dead one, and even then there are questions" (71), to Charles Hatten's conclusion that Catherine finally outdoes Frederic in a contest for masculine heroism: "dying stoically, she defeats Henry in the competition for status . . . she achieves exactly the story of heroic stature that persistently eludes Henry. . . . Barkley achieves her powerful subversion of Henry's masculinity precisely by imitating masculinity" (96). Rather than read Catherine in the end as either a triumph of a fully passive femininity or a fully stoic masculinity, however, I would suggest that we read her in terms of the importance of an anesthetized unconsciousness.

The last chapter of the novel is full of references to unconsciousness, pain, and anesthesia, and is, like much of the novel, set in a hospital. It opens with Catherine beginning to feel labor pains, and with Frederic's returning to sleep even though she is clearly lying awake next to him in pain:

> "Are you all right, Cat?"
> "I've been having some pains, darling."
> "Regularly?"
> "No, not very."
> "If you have them at all regularly we'll go to the hospital."
> I was very sleepy and went back to sleep. (312)

He registers that she is in pain and rather than doing anything to help alleviate it, he sleeps. I do not mean here to indict him for callousness toward her (there is little he could do anyway), but to point out that going to sleep in the face of pain becomes a motif throughout the chapter.

When Catherine's labor pains do become regular and they go to the hospital, she is moved into a room where there is "gas" to help with the pain, where she is put all the way under when the pains become too bad. Like Frederic throughout the novel, Catherine never describes her pain, doesn't really complain, and never uses metaphors for the pain. She will call the pains "good ones" or "big ones" (*AFTA* 314, 317), and she repeatedly asks for the gas, at times quite insistently (316, 319, 322, 323, 324). She does comment, "I'm awfully tired . . . And I hurt like hell . . . I hurt dreadfully," but that is as far as she goes in complaining. And in my ellipses here she is asking after Frederic and complimenting his performance: "Are you all right, darling? . . . You were lovely to me" (326).

It isn't Catherine's noble suffering, though, that interests me. It is the counterpoint the chapter sets up between Catherine's anesthesia and Frederic's. The chapter is punctuated by his excursions out of the hospital to the little café for breakfast, lunch, and dinner. At each meal, he drinks alcohol, and as Catherine's pain grows worse, he drinks more. For instance, with breakfast, he has two glasses of wine (*AFTA* 325), but Catherine has not even started using anesthesia. In other words, he begins anesthesia before she does. When he returns from breakfast, she has been moved to a room where she can be given gas. At this point, Catherine has become giddy on the gas, and comments, "It wasn't much . . . I'm a fool about the gas. It's wonderful." To which Frederic replies, "We'll get some for the home" (317). He begins giving her the gas, time passes, and then he goes out for lunch and beer. When he comes back, she tells him that "when the pain came too badly [the doctor] put [her] all the way out" and Frederic tells her, "You're drunk" (319). The connections Hemingway draws here between alcohol and anesthesia seem pointed: Frederic drinks, Catherine becomes drunk, and perhaps they should get some gas for the home. As the labor wears on, Catherine comes to complain as much as she ever does: "Oh, it doesn't work any more. It doesn't work!" (322). Frederic's response is to give her more gas, turning the dial on the machine higher and higher.

After the caesarian (during which Catherine is unconscious) and the baby's death, once again Catherine sends Frederic out for a meal. This time, he drinks a considerable amount: "I ate the ham and eggs and drank the beer . . . I drank several glasses of beer. I was not thinking at all . . . I ordered another beer. I was not ready to leave yet . . . I drank another beer. There was quite a pile of saucers now on the table in front of me" (*AFTA* 329). The point here isn't that he's drunk, but that the alcohol accompanies a refusal to think, a refusal to feel, and precedes his stoic response to Catherine's death. Like her, he uses an anesthetic, and the structure of the chapter emphasizes the comparison.

The other comparison Hemingway emphasizes in this closing is the usefulness of medicine to heal men to the extent that they can go and face death again; in Catherine's and the baby's case, medicine serves, again, only to precipitate death. Such a critique of medicine also calls into question the whole idea of "self-inflicted" wounds, of "malingering," or of "slackers." Catherine keeps insisting until almost the very end that she really will be all right, that she is making a fuss when she should be being brave. In being much worse than she seemed, or, more importantly, than the doctor has let on, Catherine may stand as a representative of other sufferers, who are really much worse than the doctors think. In suffering and dying from a "malady" as "self-inflicted" as pregnancy, she may also stand as a measure of the way that ideas of self-determination during the war, or during the modernist era, even, no longer make sense.

Critics frequently read the novel as ending with Catherine's death, but it seems to me that the novel in fact ends with Frederic's surrender of narration, which is itself a kind of death—certainly he becomes as silent as she. If we return to the quotation from Pat Barker that I used as an epigraph, we see that her character, Billy Prior, maintains that narration is "a way of claiming immunity. First-person narrators can't die, so as long as we keep telling the story of our own lives we're safe" (1995, 115). In stopping narrating, then, Frederic Henry ceases to claim immunity, ceases to try to keep safe. He not only stops feeling, but stops fighting against the "them" that would rule his life. The close of the novel therefore becomes emblematic for Frederic Henry's experience with medicine: he learns not to feel; he learns that it is not his body to do with as he pleases any more; he learns that he cannot really intervene or have any effect on outcomes. He can no more save Catherine than he could save his comrades. Colonized as a man, as a subject of military medicine, he has learned the lessons of World War I masculinity, and ceased to feel.

NOTES

1. Though it is outside the scope of this essay, one could draw interesting parallels between Wilfred Owen, Siefgried Sassoon, Ernest Hemingway, and Pat Barker, especially as they represent pain and masculinity. Adrian Caesar looks at the English World War I poets and argues that for them suffering becomes not only a mode of masculinity, but that "in [their] work [there is] a celebration of war as a vehicle of pain and suffering, which is shared by the voyeuristic reader who peeps at the horror through parted fingers and is consciously or unconsciously thrilled or excited by it" (2). This is particularly significant for a reading of Hemingway's representation of suffering, war, and masculinity in

light of Spilka's claim that Hemingway had developed much of his anti-war sentiments from reading Owen and Sassoon (among others) (1982, 352–353).

2. See Sandra Whipple Spanier's "Hemingway's Unknown Soldier" for the best survey of critical responses to Catherine (76–81).

3. Gerry Brenner and Stephen Clifford are exceptions. Brenner sees Henry as "disoriented" (138) and "a little out of his head" (139). Clifford points out that Frederic says to Catherine, "I'm crazy in love with you," and notes: "isn't it interesting that no critical readers have defined him as crazy." Clifford reads this as an indication of "narrative and gender bias in reading." (247)

4. Spilka reads Frederic Henry's wounding as less a testament to his masculinity than as a moment for Hemingway to experiment with androgyny. He points to Frederic's "manliness" in taking charge in the Milan hospital when they don't know what to do with him, but contrasts it to the "femininity" of his enforced passivity, and to gaining power through that passivity. He also points out that for Catherine and Frederic to have intercourse while he is wounded, Frederic would have to assume the "passive" position (1990, 212–213).

5. Spanier notes that *both* Catherine and Frederic are particularly passive and connects this to the effects of the war (89).

6. See Cohen, Elliott, and Hatten on the ways in which Hemingway seems to be using the novel as a kind of laboratory for exploring different modes of masculinity.

7. Though he never otherwise mentions anesthetic, Gerry Brenner comments that Frederic Henry holds off on mentioning Catherine Barkley until fairly late in the novel: "Sorely wounded, he avoids touching directly its most tender spot, Catherine. He keeps her offstage until his narrative is into its fourth chapter, enough time for its anesthetic, as it were, to take effect" (137).

WORKS CITED

Barker, Pat. *Regeneration.* New York: Plume, 1991.

———. *The Eye in the Door.* New York: Plume, 1993.

———. *The Ghost Road.* New York: Plume, 1995.

Brenner, Gerry. "A Hospitalized World." In *Critical Essays on Ernest Hemingway's A Farewell to Arms.* Ed. George Monteiro, 130–44. New York: G.K. Hall, 1994.

Butler, Judith. "Performative Acts and Gender Construction: An Essay in Phenomenology and Feminist Theory." In *Writing on the Body: Female Embodiment and Feminist Theory*. Eds. Katie Conboy, Nadice Medina, and Sarah Stanbury, 401–17. New York: Columbia UP, 1997.

Caesar, Adrian. *Taking it Like a Man: Suffering, Sexuality and the War Poets: Brooke, Sassoon, Owen, Graves*. Manchester: Manchester UP, 1993.

Clifford, Stephen. *Beyond the Heroic "I": Reading Lawrence, Hemingway, and "Masculinity."* Lewisburg: Bucknell UP, 1998.

Cohen, Peter. "'I Won't Kiss You. I'll Send Your English Girl': Homoerotic Desire in *A Farewell to Arms*." *The Hemingway Review* 15.1 (Fall 1995): 42–53.

Comley, Nancy R., and Robert Scholes. *Hemingway's Genders: Rereading the Hemingway Text*. New Haven: Yale UP, 1994.

Donaldson, Scott, ed. *New Essays on A Farewell to Arms*. Cambridge: Cambridge UP, 1990.

Elliott, Ira. "*A Farewell to Arms* and Hemingway's Crisis of Masculine Values." *LIT* 4 (1993): 291–304.

Fetterley, Judith. *The Resisting Reader: A Feminist Approach to American Fiction*. Bloomington: Indiana UP, 1978.

Gilbert, Sandra. "Soldier's Heart: Literary Men, Literary Women, and the Great War." *Signs* 8.3 (1983): 422–50.

Hatten, Charles. "The Crisis of Masculinity, Reified Desire, and Catherine Barkley, in *A Farewell to Arms*." *Journal of the History of Sexuality* 4.1 (1993): 76–98.

Harris, Greg. "Compulsory Masculinity, Britain, and the Great War: The Literary Historical Work of Pat Barker." *Critique* 39.4 (1998): 290–304.

Hemingway, Ernest. *A Farewell to Arms*. New York: Scribner's, 1929.

Hynes, Samuel. *A War Imagined: The First World War and English Culture*. New York: Atheneum, 1991.

Lewis, Wyndham. "The 'Dumb Ox' in Love and War." *Twentieth Century Interpretations of* A Farewell to Arms. Ed. Jay Gellens. Englewood Cliffs, NJ: Prentice Hall, 1970.

Phelan, James. "Distance, Voice, and Temporal Perspective in Frederic Henry's Narration: Successes, Problems, and Paradox." In *New Essays on* A Farewell to Arms. Ed. Scott Donaldson, 53–74. Cambridge: Cambridge UP, 1990.

Reynolds, Michael S. *Hemingway's First War: The Making of* A Farewell to Arms.
  New Jersey: Princeton UP, 1976.

Schwenger, Peter. *Phallic Critiques: Masculinity and Twentieth-Century Literature.*
  London: Routledge and Kegan Paul, 1984.

Spanier, Sandra Whipple. "Hemingway's Unknown Soldier: Catherine Barkley, the
  Critics, and the Great War." In *New Essays on A Farewell to Arms.* Ed. Scott
  Donaldson, 75–108. Cambridge: Cambridge UP, 1990.

Spilka, Mark. "Hemingway and Fauntleroy: An Androgynous Pursuit." In *American
  Novelists Revisited: Essays in Feminist Criticism.* Ed. Fritz Fleischmann, 339–70.
  Boston: G.K. Hall, 1982.

———. *Hemingway's Quarrel with Androgyny.* Lincoln: U of Nebraska P, 1990.

Whittier, Gayle. "Clinical Gaze and the Erotic Body in *A Farewell to Arms.*" *Studies
  in the Humanities* 23.1 (1996): 1–27.

Life Unworthy of Life?

Masculinity, Disability, and Guilt in *The Sun Also Rises*

Dana Fore

As Michael S. Reynolds and others have noted, the intense campaign of persona-building that Hemingway engaged in after being wounded in World War I makes it difficult to assess his level of anxiety over degeneration through disability. Even so, the cultural research of Joanna Bourke and Betsy L. Nies suggests that this fear would have been more than "in the air" for a wounded man returning from Europe. Bourke, for instance, notes that an increase of pension claims sensitized Britain to the literal costs of war-related disability and helped to re-energize debates over which veterans "deserved" charity and which did not (63–75). Nies, in turn, describes how similar financial concerns and the popularization of eugenic theories in the

Reprinted with permission from *The Hemingway Review* 26.2 (Spring 2007). Copyright © 2007 The Ernest Hemingway Foundation. Published by the University of Idaho, Moscow, Idaho.

United States combined to make the war-wounded body a site for particularly
intense fears about "degeneration."[1]

In addition to this body-obsessed cultural milieu, a seemingly minor
incident during Hemingway's recuperation in Italy may have helped cement
connections between disability and moral/physical breakdown in his mind.
Quoting from the writer's correspondence, biographer James Mellow reports
that not long after Hemingway's arrival at the hospital in Milan, "one of [his]
newly-acquired friends proved to be a problem" (70). The friend was the
wealthy Mr. Englefield, "an Englishman in his fifties, brother to one of the
Lords of the Admiralty":

> Mr. Englefield, who had been "younger sonning it in Italy for about twenty
> years," had adopted him, visited him often, made a practice of bringing him
> gifts—everything from eau de cologne to the London papers and bottles of
> Marsala. Later in life, however, Hemingway would remember Mr. Englefield in
> an acid sketch in a letter to a friend. On his visits to the hospital, Mr. Englefield,
> it seems, "got wet about wanting to see my wounds dressed. At the time I didn't
> know well-brought-up people were like that. I thought it was only tramps.
> I explained to him that I was not that way and that he couldn't come to the
> hospital anymore and that I couldn't take his Marsala." (Mellow 70)

This incident has been interpreted as contributing in a general way to Hemingway's awareness of sexual behaviors not acknowledged by his Midwestern
home town (Vernon 39). Critics such as Eby and Elliot concur that such an
incident would heighten Hemingway's interest in the idea of erotic variations
and help to move him past thinking about sexual desire in binary terms.
Yet while they recognize this subsequent interest in sexual variety, these
readings do not stray far beyond binarism themselves, ultimately situating
Hemingway's fascination within a familiar spectrum of either homosexual
or heterosexual behavior signified through a socially constructed gender.
(This is arguably true even in Eby's case, where Hemingway's hair fetish is
tied to his fascination with "effeminate" men and "boyish" women.)

If, however, Englefield's lapse of sexual decorum was indeed triggered by arguments over seeing Hemingway's "wounds dressed," it also serves as the young writer's introduction to a wider range of beliefs specifically tied to sexuality and disability. Mr. Englefield could, for instance, have been what disability researchers call a "devotee"—a species of fetishist whose erotic desires are triggered by the sight of people with disabilities. There exists today, for instance, a large community of devotees who seek out partners with amputations; others, however, are aroused by simply associating with disabled people (Bruno 1–10). The rapidly expanding field of disability studies has done much to create a fuller understanding of this kind of fetishism, as part of its wider research on the ways cultural stereotypes intersect with the realms of myth, psychology, pseudoscience, and medicine to impact the daily lives of people with physical and mental impairments.

The Sun Also Rises articulates ideas currently debated within the field of disability studies, especially those related to the concept of the "disabled identity" (Linton 8–32). An examination of these new concepts, in turn, allows a re-evaluation of Hemingway's attitudes toward wounds and masculinity. Specifically, the experiences of emasculated war hero Jake Barnes reflect Hemingway's awareness of what researchers call a "medical model" of disability—a worldview that equates disability with pathology and that forces disabled people continually to "prove" to the world at large that they are completely "cured" and therefore "normal."[2] The novel's downbeat ending suggests that a philosophy that continually denies bodily realities can be as physically and mentally destructive as a literal wound. In the end, Jake will never achieve the psychological stability he craves because he finally accepts prevailing social and medical philosophies about his injury—and these ideas, in turn, will always leave him vulnerable to the fear that he will "degenerate" into an invalid or a "pervert." The encounter with Englefield may have alerted Hemingway to the fact that merely having a disability made one vulnerable to a new range of sexual stereotypes and cultural assumptions—and especially to the idea that disability "turns" men into homosexuals or childlike, asexual beings (Shakespeare 10, 63–65).

The specters of the eunuch and the "queer" haunt Jake Barnes and drive his search for a viable identity. In the novel, Jake's struggle to define himself as a disabled man plays out in what Thomas Strychacz calls "theatrical representations," in which he exists on a continuum of behavior "between" male characters (8, 74–80). These are men whose behavior and physical characteristics seem like exaggerated aspects of Jake's own, at least potentially. Specifically, Jake occupies a psychological middle-ground between the disabled characters Count Mippipopolous and the bullfighter Belmonte—and as he accepts or rejects these characters, we are meant to understand that he is embracing or discarding the stereotypes of able-bodiedness or disability they represent.

Generally speaking, critics have glossed over the complexity of the relationship between Jake's identity and the stereotypes linking wounds, physical power, and masculine degeneration. This oversight is due largely to the influence of Freudian thinking even within more "modern" readings of the novel that move away from the older, blatantly "heroic" and masculinist interpretations of Philip Young, Carlos Baker, and Jeffrey Meyers.[3] And so while recent interpretations have established Hemingway's awareness of gender construction and varieties of erotic desire, they consider disability primarily as a catalyst alerting Jake in a general way to the existence of a "polymorphous" sexuality. The Freudian school either aligns Jake with the stereotypical figure of the disabled man who receives a compensatory "gift" of artistic or emotional sensitivity because of his impairment, or uncritically accepts the notion that he is "turning" gay because of his injuries.

Wolfgang Rudat's essay on the Count deserves a second look at this point. Rudat identifies Mippipopolous as the only psychologically healthy disabled man in the novel, situating him within an "inspirational" discourse crafted to show how a man with injuries arguably similar to Jake's might achieve a greater sense of mental stability. Rudat explains that Brett Ashley introduces the Count as a pawn in her quasi-sadomasochistic relationship with Jake, as yet another substitute for Jake himself, and as a target for her repressed frustration:

[When] Brett turns to Jake to assure him that the Count is one of them, that is, that the Count is also wounded, and then makes a show of telling the Count that she loves him and that he is a "darling," she is telling Jake that the Count too is sexually "wounded." . . . The Count, whom according to her own statement Brett has told that she was in love with Jake . . . knows . . . that Brett has now communicated to Jake that he, the Count, is sexually disabled. Not only does the Count take in stride the communication to another man of his own sexual status, but he actually confirms it in order to be able to explain to the other man his philosophy of life, that is, that he "can enjoy everything so well," including relations with women. (1989, 7)

This is a persuasive analysis of the sadomasochistic elements in Brett and Jake's relationship, but because it assumes without question that the Count is literally the best-adjusted disabled man in the novel, Rudat's reading gives a distorted picture of the disability experience that Hemingway wants to articulate.

Rudat does not recognize, for instance, that the strategies for psychic healing suggested by the Count's performance—the "subduing" of sexual desire and the transference of erotic energy into "symbolic gratification" (7)—amount to little more than a passive acceptance of the asexual status that non-disabled society considers proper for the disabled. Jake knows that the Count's solution amounts to a renunciation of his sexuality. He is familiar with this kind of "cure," and he has declared it useless; alone in his hotel room, he remembers that "the Catholic Church had an awfully good way of handling [his disability.] Good advice, anyway. Not to think about it. Oh, it was swell advice. Try and take it" (SAR 39).

Contrary to Rudat's reading, wherein Jake realizes the larger significance of the Count's advice only gradually, Jake is instantly aware that the Count is being presented to him as a "role" model, and he resents it for reasons that would be clear to a man like Hemingway, who had had a real brush with catastrophic injury. Jake's almost complete silence during this "playful" interlude between Brett and the Count may indicate his anger over having the Count paraded in front of him as a version of what Leonard Kriegel calls "the charity cripple"—a figurehead whose injuries are assumed by the non-disabled to represent the effects of all injuries, and whose typically devil-may-care attitude is held out as worthy of emulation by other "cripples" (36–37).

Jake is silent when Brett forces the Count to undress and expose his wounds, and when she declares. "I told you [he] was one of us" (*SAR* 67), Jake recognizes her condescension toward both the Count and himself. He knows that what Brett really wants to say is, "Look, the Count is like *you*" because he has suffered severe injury and survived; by implication, the Count's boundless ebullience is something Brett hopes Jake will adopt as well, simply because she cannot stand to be around depressing or gloomy people.

The Count, in turn, is also aware of what Brett is doing, and embraces the role of "supercrip" she has offered him. He parrots the inspirational drivel she wants to hear: "You see, Mr. Barnes, it is because I have lived very much that now I can enjoy everything so well. Don't you find it is like that?" To this utopian assessment of post-disability living, Jake responds curtly, "Yes. Absolutely" (*SAR* 67). Anger and embarrassment clip his sentences, and the affect is flat and mechanical because Jake wants to limit his participation in what is essentially Brett's own private freak show.

The banter ends with a significant exchange between Brett and the Count. During a discussion of the Count's values, Brett declares, "You haven't any values. You're dead, that's all." To which the Count responds, "No, my dear. You're not right. I'm not dead at all" (*SAR* 67–68). The concept of death here is more than a metaphor for *fin de siècle* malaise and ennui among the wealthy (Gaggin 95–99): it serves to expose the liminal nature of existence for the disabled male in this society. On the one hand, the fact that Brett can so glibly declare the Count as "dead" shows how close her thinking is to the eugenic/Social Darwinist stereotypes of the period. The Count's insistent and unequivocal response, in turn, gives the lie to his studied joviality and shows his own awareness of his marginalized status, revealing how desperately a disabled man must prove to others and himself that he is "worthy" to live. Hemingway's sensitivity to stereotypes of disability, rather than Jake's inability to interpret the Count's advice correctly, helps explain why the novel quickly casts such a "positive" role model into obscurity.

The next model of disability Jake encounters is the bullfighter Belmonte. This figure underscores the novel's ambivalence toward a worldview that valorizes traditional forms of masculine "performance" as "cures" for disability. The Belmonte character has been overshadowed, however, by the critical fascination with the relationship between Jake and the "damned good-looking" young matador Pedro Romero (*SAR* 170).

The tantalizing homosocial tension between Pedro and Jake diverts attention away from the dialectic that Hemingway created though the aging matador Belmonte—a dialectic that exposes the interplay between the wounded body and public/private constructions of "honor," "masculinity," and "disability." The general view of Jake's bullfighting adventures assumes that Hemingway wants the reader to identify most with the implicitly able-bodied spectators who clamor to see the new young bullfighter. This perspective reduces Belmonte to a foil for Pedro Romero, and the graphic details of the older man's corruption and decline simply underscore the beauty and potential for greatness embodied by the younger artist.

Through Belmonte, however, readers are again forced to consider the physical and psychological costs of "supercripism" and normality-at-any-price. The matador is described as a paradox, someone who had managed to live on past his real "life": "Fifteen years ago they said if you wanted to see Belmonte you should go quickly, while he was still alive. Since then he has killed more than a thousand bulls" (*SAR* 218). Driven to perform even though he is "sick with a fistula" (218), Belmonte is kin to the jovial, wounded, and "dead" Count Mippipopolous. The tone of these passages is significant: they spare Belmonte the kind of quiet disgust reserved for other macho failures, such as Robert Cohn. By reminding the reader that Belmonte cannot reach his former heights of greatness simply because he is "no longer well enough" (219), Hemingway acknowledges the burden of social expectations on disabled men, and discards yet another faulty role model, a matador who has crafted an identity based on negation—an attempt to purge the self of any trait associated with "the invalid."

How then might Jake Barnes achieve happiness in a world shaped by the limitations of his sexually mutilated body and by cultural narratives that stigmatize deformity? The novel suggests, at least initially, that Jake might achieve a sense of wholeness if he can correctly interpret the veiled truths conveyed by Brett Ashley and Bill Gorton. These are characters who, by virtue of their unconventional worldviews, serve not so much as role models but rather as guides to show Jake how he might thrive in his otherwise oppressive and limited environment.

For her part, Brett Ashley suggests what Jake might do in the realm of the physical. She recognizes intuitively what recent work on the sexual development of disabled men and couples has confirmed, that it is possible for severely disabled people to achieve sexual satisfaction by re-training their bodies to feel erotic pleasure in different ways, through different erogenous zones (Callahan 77–78, Brown 37–38, Milam 40–43).[4]

Critics have barely considered the idea that Jake could achieve sexual satisfaction in nontraditional ways. While Debra Moddelmog's analysis of lovemaking between mutilated heroes and their "normal" lovers in *Across the River and into the Trees* and *To Have and Have Not* acknowledges that Hemingway was willing to consider the possibility of such sexual behavior (122–123), Chaman Nahal's indignation over moments of "perverted sexual satisfaction" (qtd. in Rudat 1989, 2) between Jake and Brett Ashley constitutes the only critical recognition that Hemingway perhaps wanted to include the emasculated Jake in his pantheon of wounded but sexually active heroes.

However, the key moment that foreshadows the course of Jake's psychosexual development occurs not in the hotel room (as Nahal would have it), but rather in a Paris taxi when he finally gets a moment alone with Brett. Here we see how truly suitable Brett would be as a lover for Jake, because she is willing to entertain the possibility of a nontraditional erotic relationship. The meeting does not start well. "Don't touch me," she says. "Please don't touch me" (*SAR* 33). This reaction suggests a woman who knows about the nature of Jake's injury and is disgusted by thoughts of sex with a man whose penis has been mutilated. But the scene does not end there. Despite her protests, Brett finally admits that she "[turns] all to jelly" at Jake's touch. Thus she affirms a capacity to experience intense physical sensation from simple stimulation—which may translate into an ability to derive satisfaction from nontraditional sex. Descriptions of her eyes also proved a kind of silent response to Jake's question about what they can "do" as lovers: Brett has been a wartime nurse (46); she has proven her ability to withstand the sight of horrific wounds—to "look on and on after everyone else's eyes in the world would have stopped looking" (34). She would not be "afraid" to have sex with a deformed man, even though "she was afraid of so many things" (34).

Through this scene, Hemingway hints at what Jake must do in order to achieve happiness and psychological stability: he must re-evaluate the effects of his wound for himself, discarding former notions about "damaged" masculinity based on cultural stereotypes. He must, in other words, rid his consciousness of the idea that sexual mutilation can only trigger mental and physical "degeneration" into homosexuality or invalidism—an idea elegantly condensed in the words of the Italian colonel who tells Jake in the hospital that he has "given more than [his] life" (*SAR* 39). But such is the power of these cultural stereotypes that there can be no epiphanic moment when Jake suddenly "sees" the truth and decides to drastically change his life. Instead, he must grope his way toward solving the riddle of his new identity, trying the best he can to interpret the random hints he is given.

Some of these hints come from Bill Gorton, who emerges as a mentor for Jake during an odd shopping trip in Paris. During this interlude, Bill's eccentric banter makes connections between dead bodies and ethics in ways designed to establish that Bill, like Brett, is someone comfortable with non-standard bodies and perhaps able to help Jake on his journey toward psychological wholeness. When Bill and Jake are out walking in Paris, Bill stops by a taxidermist's shop and becomes strangely insistent that Jake buy something. "Want to buy anything?" he asks. "Nice stuffed dog" (*SAR* 78)

Jake declines, but Bill will not relent. "Mean everything in the world to you after you bought it," he says. "Simple exchange of values. . . . Road to hell paved with unbought stuffed dogs" (*SAR* 78). This odd joking appeals to Jake, who remembers it later when he introduces Bill to Brett as a "taxidermist."

To which Bill replies, "That was in another country. And besides all the animals were dead" (81). Bill's words have struck a chord with Jake, as well they might—by linking the notions of compromised (or "exchanged") values with "dead" bodies from "another country," Bill resurrects memories of the affable "supercrip" Count Mippipopolous and draws attention yet again to the question of how one can "overcome" or adapt to a catastrophic physical injury.

Bill's praise of out-of-place, nonstandard bodies and his certainty about their value seem to constitute a metaphorical expression of the same open-mindedness that led him to rescue a black Viennese boxer from a lynch mob earlier in the novel—a scene which Bill describes in similarly nonchalant, playful terms in order to downplay the mob's potential for violence (*SAR* 76–78). Taken together, these scenes establish Bill's importance to Jake's quest for wholeness as a disabled man. Specifically, these incidents show that Bill Gorton, like Brett Ashley, is committed to a nontraditional code of behavior allowing him to see values in bodies that the larger society would declare worthless or "dead." He seems eminently suitable as a friend for Jake: as a self-styled philosopher about what makes life worth living, Bill may be able to help Jake formulate his own principles for survival as a wounded man.

To see how Bill is only partially successful in healing Jake's psychic wounds, we must re-evaluate the quasi-erotic interlude between Bill and Jake that occurs during the Basque fishing trip in Chapter Twelve. As David Blackmore has elegantly explained, Jake's outdoor experiences foster an unexpected freedom of expression between the two men, to the extent that homoerotic desires rise "so near to the surface of Jake's personality as not to be latent" (59). Even so, I think Blackmore misses the mark when he concludes that the trip represents a victory for Hemingway's homophobia, as Jake finally falls back into "the trap of 'male homosexual panic'" (65). Like Blackmore, I believe Hemingway recognizes here that traditional concepts of masculinity—and especially *Freudian* concepts of masculinity—are too emotionally restrictive and in need of change. However, because the text links these norms and the same concepts of "normality" that stigmatize Jake's disability, I question whether the scene finally promotes the re-establishment of 19th century gender boundaries as Blackmore suggests (66).

To see the full range of ideas Hemingway presents here, it is necessary to reevaluate the psychoanalytical play that occurs between Jake and Bill in the woods. Analyses of Gorton's highly symbolic banter by both Blackmore and Buckley confirm, in essence, that Bill copies the tactics of a skilled psychotherapist, verbally creating a "safe" space for Jake to express hidden or taboo feelings without fear of censure. Thus, Bill's graphic admission that his "fond[ness]" for Jake would make him a "faggot" in New York (*SAR* 121) is an invitation for Jake to express similar feelings as part of the "talking cure" being constructed here.

What such analyses of this psychoanalytical session fail to see, however, is that Jake's same-sex desires may not be the only cause of his problems. For instance, the war-centered double entendres that initiate Bill's well-known repartee suggest the plight of disabled veterans. Even the famous scene where Bill teases Jake with the idea of "[getting it] up for fun" (Blackmore 60) is peppered with loaded questions that echo the standard phrases of a military recruiter: "Been working for the common good?" "Work for the good of all." (*SAR* 118). Thus the text introduces a narrative thread about military service/disability that parallels the homoerotic subtext and intensifies as the joking continues between the two men.

Bill's persistent invocation of "irony and pity" further enhances this disability subtext: the phrase is a poetic crystallization of the attitudes and experiences that shaped the lives of disabled veterans during this era. Joanna Bourke, for instance, describes an "early sentimentalization" of the war-wounded that lasted until the 1920s (56). She explains that the most bathetic public responses were reserved for men with obvious deformities and amputations: in this early period, "public rhetoric judged soldiers' mutilations to be 'badges of their courage, the hall-mark of their glorious service, their proof of patriotism'" (56). According to the popular mythology of the times, a severe wound inspired more than just intense patriotism: women were supposed to be especially attracted to men with obvious injuries; these men, in turn, "were not beneath bargaining pity for love" (Bourke 56). For a time, a distinction was made between men wounded in war and those born with birth defects: the former were "broken warriors," and poems singing their praises "adopted the ironic, passive tone of the newly-styled, modern poetry" (Bourke 57).

The decline of national fascination with the war-wounded was fore-shadowed by the concurrent stigmatization of veterans like Jake, whose disabilities were invisible to the public eye. Bourke reports: "The absent parts of men's bodies came to exert a special patriot power. In the struggle for status and resources, absence could be more powerful than presence. The less visible or invisible diseases that disabled many servicemen . . . could not compete with limblessness" (59). This bias in favor of amputees translated into a pervasive resentment against men who were "merely" diseased or invisibly injured: such men were more often considered to be of inferior stock, or literally less "important" than men with obvious wounds (Bourke 59–60). During the postwar years, as the novelty of wounded men wore off and disabled veterans began to compete for resources with the civilian unemployed, this kind of resentment would even be directed against "heroic" amputees (Bourke 63–75).

Given this historical context, there is a double irony at work in the novel. According to the new rules of this modern world, Jake could "pass" as one of the most heroic of heroes. He has suffered the all-important amputation of a "part"—one which most men would probably consider the most vital "limb" of all. And yet the injury cannot be paraded in front of the public for acclaim. Because his wound must remain hidden and unknown, it must also remain "shameful."

The other resonant moment of irony and pity occurs at the point were Bill's humorous play falters. The way Bill's lighthearted tone is broken intensifies the novel's focus on disability, revealing that Freudian therapy is ill-equipped to deal with the many problems associated with a physical impairment. In the midst of "defining" Jake, Bill explains,

You're an expatriate. You've lost touch with the soil. You get precious. Fake European standards have ruined you. You drink yourself to death. You become

obsessed by sex. You spend all your time talking, not working. You're an expatriate, see? You hang around cafes. . . . You don't work. One group claims women
support you. Another group claims you're impotent. (*SAR* 120)

On one level, this chatter reinforces the novel's well-known destabilization
of sexual stereotypes by lampooning the traditionally gay or bisexual figure
of the Wildean "Decadent." However, if we employ the psychoanalytical
perspective established by Blackmore, Rudat, and Buckley, this babble becomes
"empty speech"—the Freudian term for symbolic discourse designed to mask
unpleasant truths. Seen in this light, it becomes apparent that what Bill is
desperately trying—and trying *not*—to talk about is Jake's wound.

Consider first how the passage develops the character of the *expatriate*.
He or she is defined, ultimately, as someone who is "impotent." This seems
like an odd conclusion if one adheres to the literal definition of an *expatriate*
as someone who has left his or her homeland. However, the characterization
makes sense if one scratches the surface of the word to reveal the homonym
beneath—"ex-patriot," a euphemism for a discharged soldier. This hidden
concept exposes the wound-related anxiety here, because Jake's mutilated
penis is the reason he has become an "ex-patriot" and an impotent *expatriate*. All the flaws ascribed to this decadent character—alcoholism, laziness,
unemployment, sexual obsessiveness, and dependence on women—are
also weaknesses stereotypically ascribed to wounded men whose injuries
have supposedly destroyed all positive aspects of their former personalities
(Pernick 49–52).[5]

Jake's response to Bill's prompting is simple, yet significant: countering
the charge of impotence, he says, "No . . . I just had an accident" (*SAR* 120).
The matter-of-fact tone here suggests that Jake may finally be able to accept
his disability. He is on the verge of catharsis, of "coming out" as a disabled
man (Shakespeare 50–55).

Any potential recovery is thwarted, however, by Bill's response: "Never
mention that. . . . That's the sort of thing that can't be spoken of. That's what
you ought to work up into a mystery. Like Henry's bicycle" (*SAR* 120). The
joking is only half-hearted here: to some degree, Bill really *doesn't* want

Jake to talk about his wound explicitly because his amateur therapy session (and by extension, Freudian theory in general) cannot address this range of problems associated with physical impairment. Thus Bill, the advocate of irony and pity, becomes an ironic figure—a therapist asking his patient to repress inconvenient problems.

For his part, Jake intuits the opportunity for healing presented to him here, and wants to exploit it. He notes that Bill "had been going splendidly," and wants to "start him again" on a more in-depth discussion of Jake's wound (*SAR* 120). But the task is too daunting for Bill. After a brief discussion of the nature of Henry's wound, Bill declares, "Let's lay off that" (*SAR* 121), and the conversation turns to repressed homosexuality—a more familiar (and less threatening) realm for amateur psychoanalysts.

Interpreting *The Sun Also Rises* from a disability perspective leads to a dark view of human existence, but not for the reasons most critics have discussed. Jake's struggles to find a place for himself in the postwar world help Hemingway to show that a wide and unacknowledged range of social ideas attach to physical impairment, and these cultural narratives work unobtrusively and insistently to make disability into a "master trope for human disqualification" (Mitchell and Snyder 3). A disability reading of the novel centers the work in Bill Gorton's retain, "Oh, Give them Irony and Give them Pity" (*SAR* 118–119). Hemingway gives us a novel where the failed romance between the hero and his lady represents the day-to-day struggle for (and with) "normality" for a generation of severely wounded survivors.[6]

The final, terrible irony of the novel is that it supports the idea that Brett and Jake *can* end their torment and be together in all senses of the word: sex is not impossible between them. However, neither Jake nor any of his well-meaning friends can rid themselves of their ingrained prejudices about disability, and these social constraints become the real obstacles to Jake's rehabilitation. The furtive sexual pleasures that Brett gives Jake are few and far between, and expressed in the classic Hemingway modes of elision, understatement, and silence indicative of guilt; for his part, Jake has internalized the stereotype of the sexually mutilated man who would be better off dead—he finally believes that "there's not a damn thing [he can] do" (*SAR* 34).

Thus, at the novel's conclusion, when Brett declares "Oh, Jake . . . we could have such a damned good time together," he can only respond, "Yes . . . Isn't is pretty to think so?" (*SAR* 251). Although the use of "pretty" here is a "feminine" affectation, it is hardly, as Rudat has suggested (in "Hemingway on Sexual Otherness" and "Sexual Dilemmas"), the sign of Jake's life-affirming liberation from heterosexist prejudice. Rather, it is a sign that—despite occasional glimpses of his sexual potential—Jake has finally accepted the life society has mapped out for him as a disabled man. Jake will join Count Mippipopolous as a caricature of life and a toy for Brett's amusement, like one of the "pretty nice stuffed dogs" that stare at Bill Gorton from the window of a Paris taxidermy shop (*SAR* 78).

NOTES

1. Discussing how racist stereotypes from the 19th century carried over into the 20th, Nies describes how the growing presence of wounded veterans in postwar America engendered a paradoxical glorification of the "fighting Nordic male" even as it fostered a widespread "collapse in the belief in the sanctity of physical borders of white soldiers" (23). According to the Lamarckian logic behind this worldview, a wounded soldier had the potential to weaken the "national health" by transmitting his "defects" into the gene pool.

2. Simi Linton defines the "medical model" as a worldview that "casts human variation as deviance from the norm, as pathological condition, as deficit, and, significantly, as an individual burden and personal tragedy." This philosophy allows non-disabled people to ignore "the social processes and policies that constrict disabled people's lives" (11).

3. Young arguably provides the most sustained examination of disabled men in Hemingway's works, as well as the most influential material for defining the nature of disability issues in *The Sun Also Rises*. Young's analysis goes beyond subsequent critics in its clarification of the disability experience, insofar as it

resists the temptation to view Jake's mutilated penis as a metaphor for societal malaise. He recognizes that physical disabilities are never completely "overcome," and that they force individuals to view the world in different ways for a lifetime. Yet even Young falls back into the absolutist thinking that characterizes much Freudian thought regarding disability, suggesting that the disabled can never adapt to physical impairment that cannot be completely cured. Rather, disability becomes a totalizing flaw that causes the "primitivization" of personality (169), the core of an *idée fixe* that fuels a never-ending sense of "dis-grace" (41) and a dangerous "ambivalence" toward life.

4. In *Don't Worry, He Won't Get Far on Foot,* paraplegic author John Callahan describes achieving sexual satisfaction from a neck massage (77–78); in "Movie Stars and Sensuous Scars," Steven E Brown related the story of a disabled woman who trains herself to reach orgasm by rubbing her elbow (37–38); and in *The Cripple Liberation Front Marching Band Blues,* Lorenzo Milam describes a boyhood experience when he felt pleasure of sexual intensity by having a visitor lie next to him in a hospital bed (40–43).

5. Martin S. Pernick explains the basis for this totalizing view of disability in his analysis of eugenics and euthanasia. Specifically, he discusses the widespread belief in core genetic material known as "germ plasm" which, according to the science of the time, could be altered by environmental factors encountered after birth, such as poisons, illness, psychological shock, and wounds. Damaged germ plasm could drive a previously healthy organism into a state of physiological degeneration or "atavism" and transmit a variety of dangerous personality traits through a family bloodline (Pernick 49–52).

6. Tom Shakespeare eloquently summarizes the most common stereotypes of disabled sexuality:

   Stereotypes of disability often focus on asexuality, or lack of sexual potential or potency. Disabled people are subject to infantilization, especially disabled people who are perceived as being 'dependent.' Just as children are assumed to have no sexuality, so disabled people are similarly denied the capacity for sexual feeling. Where disabled people are seen as sexual, this is in terms of deviant sexuality, for example, inappropriate sexual display or masturbation. (10)

WORKS CITED

Baker, Carlos. *Ernest Hemingway: A Life Story.* New York: Scribner's, 1969.

———. "The Wastelanders." In *Modern Critical Interpretations: The Sun Also Rises.* Ed. Harold Bloom, 9–24. New York: Chelsea House, 1987.

Blackmore, David. "'In New York It'd Mean I Was A . . .' Masculinity Anxiety and Period Discourses of Sexuality in *The Sun Also Rises.*" *The Hemingway Review* 18.1 (Fall 1998): 49–67.

Bourke, Joanna. *Dismembering the Male: Men's Bodies, Britain and the Great War.* Chicago: U of Chicago P, 1996.

Brown, Steven E. "Movie Stars and Sensuous Scars." In *Male Lust: Pleasure, Power, and Transformation.* Eds. Kerwin Kay et al., 37–43. New York: Harrington Park, 2000.

Bruno, Richard L. "Devotees, Pretenders and Wannabes: Two Cases of Factitious Disability Disorder." *Journal of Sexuality and Disability* 15 (1997): 243–60.

Buckley, J. F. "Echoes of Closeted Desire(s): The Narrator and Character Voices of Jake Barnes." *The Hemingway Review* 19.2 (Spring 2000): 73–87.

Callahan, John. *Don't Worry, He Won't Get Far on Foot.* New York: Vintage Books, 1990.

Comley, Nancy R., and Robert Scholes. *Hemingway's Genders.* New Haven: Yale UP, 1994.

Eby, Carl P. *Hemingway's Fetishism: Psychoanalysis and the Mirror of Manhood.* New York: State U of New York P, 1999.

Elliot, Ira. "Performance Art: Jake Barnes and 'Masculine' Signification in *The Sun Also Rises.*" *American Literature* 67 (March 1995): 77–94.

Gaggin, John. *Hemingway and Nineteenth-Century Aestheticism.* Ann Arbor: UMI Research, 1988.

Hemingway, Ernest. *The Sun Also Rises.* 1926; New York: Scribner's, 2003.

Kriegel, Leonard. "The Cripple in Literature." In I*mages of the Disabled, Disabling Images.* Eds. Alan Gartner and Tom Joe, 31–46. New York: Praeger, 1987.

Linton, Simi. *Claiming Disability: Knowledge and Identity.* New York: New York UP, 1998.

Mellow, James R. *Hemingway: A Life Without Consequences.* New York: Houghton Mifflin, 1992.

Milam, Lorenzo. *The Cripple Liberation Front Marching Band Blues.* San Diego: MHO, 1984.

Mitchell, David T., and Sharon L. Snyder. *Narrative Prosthesis: Disability and the Dependencies of Discourse.* Ann Arbor: U of Michigan P, 2001.

Moddelmog, Debra A. *Reading Desire: In Pursuit of Ernest Hemingway.* Ithaca: Cornell UP, 1999.

Meyers, Jeffrey. *Hemingway: A Biography.* New York: Harper and Row, 1985.

Nies, Betsy L. *Eugenic Fantasies: Racial Ideology in the Literature and Popular Culture of the 1920s.* New York: Routledge, 2002.

Pernick, Martin S. *The Black Stork: Eugenics and the Death of "Defective" Babies in American Medicine and Motion Pictures since 1915.* New York: Oxford UP, 1996.

Reynolds, Michael S. *Young Hemingway.* New York: Basil Blackwell, 1986.

Rudat, Wolfgang E. H. "Sexual Dilemmas in *The Sun Also Rises:* Hemingway's Count and the Education of Jacob Barnes." *The Hemingway Review* 8.2 (Spring 1989): 2–13.

———. "Hemingway on Sexual Otherness: What's Really Funny in *The Sun Also Rises.*" In *Hemingway Repossessed.* Ed. Kenneth Rosen, 169–79. Westport, CT: Praeger, 1994.

Shakespeare, Tom. *Untold Desires: The Sexual Politics of Disability.* London: Cassell, 1996.

Spilka, Mark. *Hemingway's Quarrel with Androgyny.* Lincoln: U of Nebraska P, 1990.

Strychacz, Thomas. *Hemingway's Theaters of Masculinity.* Baton Rouge: Louisiana State UP, 2003.

Vernon, Alex. "War, Gender, and Ernest Hemingway." *The Hemingway Review* 22.1 (Fall 2002): 34–55.

Young, Philip. *Ernest Hemingway: A Reconsideration.* University Park: Pennsylvania State UP, 1966.

Melancholy Modernism

Gender and the Politics of Mourning in *The Sun Also Rises*

Greg Forter

The recent turn toward gender issues in Hemingway studies has made the author exciting and pressingly urgent once more.[1] This work has freed us from the myth of Hemingway as "He-Man of American literature";[2] it has made it possible to see in his writing more than the stylistic and representational embodiment of invulnerable manhood—a masculinity courageously asserting itself in the face of unmanning and life-threatening dangers. Instead, we have become attuned to the cracks in Hemingway's masculine armor. We have learned that manhood was for him a fraught and always fragile aspiration rather than an accomplished fact. For many of us, this has meant that what seems most moving in Hemingway now is his

Reprinted with permission from *The Hemingway Review* 21.1 (Fall 2001). Copyright © 2001 The Ernest Hemingway Foundation. Published by the University of Idaho, Moscow, Idaho.

persistent struggle, against enormous psychic odds, to resist his ossification into a man whose gynophobic self-loathing leads him to despise all feminine "softness"—both within and without him.

My essay contributes to an understanding of this struggle in several related ways. I argue that *The Sun Also Rises* records the battle with special intensity; it stages Hemingway's conflict between an autonomous and invulnerable masculinity on one hand, and an emotionally expressive and connected one on the other—a battle he resolves through the fetishization of style. This conflict is linked to the larger problem of loss in the novel. My broadest contention is that this loss records an external crisis that was not simply personal but social in character. I want, accordingly, to start by describing the social origins of the loss inscribed by the novel as Jake's wound, before moving on to theorize Hemingway's response to this loss, to link this response to American modernism more generally, and to offer a reading of *The Sun Also Rises* within the context thus elaborated.

The loss in question resulted from the crisis in masculinity that took place in the United States at the turn of the last century. Sociologist Michael Kimmel has chronicled that crisis with particular acuity. He suggests that the period from 1890 to 1920 witnessed the decline of a style of manhood by which men proved themselves as men in the volatile space of the market; to do so, they had to exert an almost obsessive control over the vagaries of their bodies, but could in the process wrestle a degree of autonomy, self-mastery, and power. According to Kimmel, the explosive spread of monopoly capitalism undermined this style of manhood. The opportunities for self-making afforded by small-scale capitalism began to disappear; men become increasingly reduced to parts in a bureaucratic machine, unable to achieve the sense of autonomy so central to the meaning of manhood they inherited. This transformation went hand in hand with challenges by women and ethnic minorities to middle-class male social power. And it gave rise to a widespread panic about the feminizing effects of modern urban living—a panic about the "feminization of American culture" produced by the shifts I've described. The result, according to Kimmel, was an intense nostalgia for rugged autonomy—the physical potency and virile self-mastery—being eclipsed by structural transformations in American life (81–188).

American modernism, at least in one of its most dominant strands, represents a relatively cohesive set of expressive responses to this crisis. Modernists as diverse as Eliot, Cather, Fitzgerald, Faulkner, and Hemingway responded to the loss of autonomous manhood in a melancholic manner. That is, they were unable to mourn or fully "work through" the loss, in part because of the nature of their attachment to the masculinity whose loss they lamented—an attachment that the psychoanalytic distinction between mourning and melancholia can help us describe.

The distinction was first proposed by Freud in "Mourning and Melancholia," whose title names two ways of responding to personal or social loss. Mourning is the process of healthy grieving. In it, the person experiencing loss comes gradually to relinquish his or her attachment to the lost object, and so to accept the necessity of remedial substitution: the need to displace desire and attachment from the dead onto the living, in the form of "good enough" replacements for what the self has lost. The condition of this capacity to mourn is a specific kind of object-relatedness. The mourner is able to relinquish lost objects because he or she has experienced them as separate all along. The ego has already come to grips with the painful reality of separateness—the experience of borders and edges, of an interval between "me" and "you," with all the dangers of loss, abandonment, and betrayal that this entails. Because the other exists in this way as a genuinely external object, its loss can be felt as real and fully integrated by the mourner, without a catastrophic confrontation with the limits to infantile narcissism.

Melancholia, by contrast, is a reaction to loss from within an attachment to objects that does not acknowledge their difference from the self. In one sense, the object here is not an "object" at all, but a kind of narcissistic extension or prolongation of the ego. Freud writes that the melancholic's "object-choice has been effected on a narcissistic basis, so that the object-cathexis, when obstacles come in its way, can regress to narcissism" (43). In other words, melancholia can result only when the attachment to an object is psychically archaic—when one loves in the other the image of oneself, because one has not learned to experience the other as having an independent existence outside of omnipotent fantasy. The melancholic responds to loss not by gradually relinquishing the dead in the name of substitutes, but, as Freud says, by "regress[ing] to narcissism": by identifying the self with the other, incorporating the other into the self, and keeping him or her alive as an internally differentiated part of the ego. "The shadow of the object [has fallen] on the ego," Freud writes (43). Entombing within itself the only "object" it deems worth having, the ego becomes existentially impoverished, unable to open up to new love, structurally inhibited and unresponsive.

The relevance of this process to Hemingway's biography seems clear. If Carl Eby is right that the author's masculine anxieties had their root in a failure of individuation—a difficulty in separating himself psychically from the maternal matrix—then Hemingway was perhaps almost clinically narcissistic. He defended himself against the trauma of loss entailed in separation/individuation by refusing to acknowledge the "otherness" of others, tending instead to treat them as narcissistic components of the self. One could in fact, with only slight distortion, rewrite Eby's thesis about fetishism as one about melancholia. Hemingway sought through fetishistic practice to "ward . . . off castration anxiety and disavow . . . the anatomical distinction between the sexes by paradoxically erecting a hypercathected monument to both" (Eby 73). The fetish, in this sense, is a melancholic object, precisely because it serves as a kind of narcissistic defense against loss, keeping alive a negated fantasy of maternal masculinity, and clinging to an inner image of the (m)other as essentially similar to the male self. The fetish thereby defends against the opening of that space separating self from not-self, masculine from feminine.

One might even speculate that Hemingway's suicide resulted from the failure of this fragile defense. Because fetishism contains a knowledge of the difference and separation it denies, and in Hemingway's case entailed a repeated identification with the fetishized female body (figured most insistently in his work by the tonsorial twinning of heroes and heroines), it's possible that the denial of such difference became increasingly difficult to sustain, and that the unmastered awareness of loss produced an equally un-masterable despair. A fetishist whose talisman loses its magic is, perhaps, a melancholy suicide.

In addition to biographical relevance, melancholia has here a cultural significance. At moments of profound social crisis, the melancholic process can become a general, collective condition, and this is what happened in American modernism's reaction to the loss of masculine authority and potency. It's crucial that this loss entails an ideal rather than a person. For ideals are, in some basic way, cathected narcissistically; they have to do with one's sense of self as much as one's relation to others. They speak to the self's constitution through incorporations of what a culture defines as valuable. The historical loss of a masculine ideal would seem almost inevitably to produce in men a narcissistic injury: a rupture between their actual selves and the exalted image from which history has severed them. The response to such loss would therefore be likely to develop along melancholic lines.

Such an injury *could*, of courses, be grieved and fully worked through. But the modernists who interest me did not pursue this opportunity. In response to social trauma, they sought neither to renounce nor to rescue a disappearing ideal of male autonomy and power, but rather to insist on its enormous value and its inevitable loss. These writers pay homage to a type of virility that can no longer be socially incarnated—that cannot withstand the onslaught of a destructed and emasculating modernity. These modernists could be said to remain melancholically fixated on a lost masculine ideal that is fundamentally toxic, and that they themselves show to be unlivable. This fixation makes it impossible to mourn or fully work through their losses—or to see in those losses an opportunity for reinventing masculinity in a less rigidly constrained, less psychically defensive, and less socially destructive fashion.[3]

I.

The Sun Also Rises offers an especially fruitful illustration of this process. It traces a *doubly* melancholic pattern, staging Hemingway's paralyzing identification with two different, lost, and incompatible forms of manhood, neither of which he is able to relinquish. These forms of manhood are the sentimental and the hard. The loss of each, paradoxically enough, is figured by the phallic wound at the book's center. The novel responds to their loss by celebrating highly fetishized codes of speech and ritualized modes of behavior—*styles*—which seek at once to memorialize and to deny the amputation around which the novel turns.

The war wound clearly stands as the psychic yet physical sign of a lost masculine potency. Precisely because he was once "whole," and precisely because he has lost that wholeness in a war dividing the old world from the new, Jake bears an emblematically modern male consciousness, haunted by the memory of a potency and plentitude it cannot recover. The wound defines him as fundamentally lacking, devoid of authentic substance; it suggests that the thing which once gave content to identity by differentiating men hierarchically from women—the penis—is now both literally and structurally inaccessible. This state of affairs makes it extremely difficult for modern men to *be* men; the wound cuts them off from the anatomical source of their own undoubted virility—a source that, in our cultural imaginary, is the root of male social power as well. It reconfigures masculine identity in terms of a restless and unfulfillable desire, with satisfaction definitively deferred in the absence of an enabling organ. And the wound leads to an experience of love as a kind of "hell on earth" (*SAR* 35), remaking even the city of romance—Paris—as a "pestilential" place (80) where the plague of unfulfillment plays itself out without mercy.

But the wound also carries an opposite meaning: the loss of a genteel, sentimental, and implicitly feminine masculinity. Jake's amputation and his knowledge of its consequences in this sense differentiate him from Robert Cohn, at once a kind of premodern anachronism and a "steer" who doesn't know he's a steer (145–146). The problem with Cohn, in other words, is that he *has not himself been wounded*. There are other characters in the novel of whom this is literally true—Mike, Bill, and Brett, for example. But they at least "know about" the wound; they have been metaphorically, if not literally, damaged, and have sufferance the kind of disillusionment the novel in part approves.

Cohn, in contrast, continues to behave as if a host of values that the wound renders hollow are still in fact live possibilities. Most significantly, he continues to *believe*—that's what makes him so distasteful and embarrassing to those who at least struggle to believe only in the impossibility of belief. He believes in "Literature" with a capital "L," substituting books for lived experience (18, 49), comparing Brett at one point to Circe (148), and seeking even to live what he thinks of as the writer's life of narcissistic unattachment (58). He believes in romance—the romance of faraway and exotic places, romantically described in turgidly romantic prose (17)—as well as the romance of mutually fulfilling love. He believed in outdated notions of chivalry, in a way that leads him to defend his "lady love" (Brett) against the corruption of her own promiscuity (182). And he believes, finally, perhaps above all, in traditional forms of meaningfulness, remaining oblivious to the wound that renders meaning something to be *made,* not inherited. This blindness makes Cohn unable to embrace the casual brutalities of modern sex, to see that his sexual encounter with Brett "didn't mean anything" (185).

Such a portrayal is clearly meant to convict Cohn of sentimentality. To be both sentimental and a man is to be at least implicitly feminized. So Cohn is caustically said to have been "moulded by the two women who trained him" (52). He's repeatedly shown to cry when he gets mad (57, 197, 206), to be incapable of drinking with the big boys (152), and to be essentially emasculated by both his evident pining for Brett and his willingness to "take" the verbal punishment dished out by the woman he's trying to abandon (Frances). Far from guaranteeing his manly success, then, the absence of a wound works to castrate Cohn.[4] The actual loss of a penis, in contrast, functions paradoxically as the sign of real manliness,[5] saving Jake from the related perils of sexual pleasure and affective connections, from the risk of sentimental softening that would render him, in Hemingway's eyes, insufficiently "hard," insufficiently modern—and therefore, insufficiently manly.

The wound thus carries the contradictory burden of two complex histories of loss—the loss of male power and potency on the one hand, and the apparently more beneficent rupture with sentimental manhood on the other. This contradiction results from Hemingway's inability to relinquish either male sentiment *or* male power, an incapacity intimately connected with the meaning of his modernism. As previously suggested, Hemingway's work responds not just to a personal, but to a social crisis of masculinity. That crisis led many we've come to call modernists to engage in an intense masculinization of artistic production, consolidating the borders between art and not-art along explicitly gendered lines, and rejecting direct expressions of emotion as flabby, artistically unauthentic, insufficiently ironic—in short, feminine.[6] Hemingway of course participated in this modernist cauterization of affect. His style of affective omission and *The Sun's* repeated injunction against talking about "it" are both good examples of this proclivity.

But Hemingway also felt this cauterization as a devastating loss to the capacity for creative living and self-making. He therefore *identified with* the forbidden form of manhood and lovingly internalized a sentimental masculinity, in order to keep alive in secret affective possibilities that could not be openly acknowledged or grieved. This internalized perpetuation of affect accounts for the repeated slide of his fiction into a discourse of sentimental attachment, a slide most notable, in *The Sun Also Rises,* in the case of Pedro Romero.

The bullfighter is clearly meant to stand as a kind of exemplary code hero: he turns the meaningless violence of modern life into meaningful aesthetic spectacle, and does so through a "maximum of exposure" to the dangers of that violence (172). The terms of this conquest are virtually synonymous with Hemingway's own aesthetic practice. There is, to begin with, an expressive rigor inseparable from the grace of its gestural economy. A balletic "smooth[ness]," an absence of "contortions," and a disinclination toward "waste[d]" motion all produce a "purity of line" that turns the ritualized action of the "show" into an expressive artistic performance. The *aesthetic* character of the bullfight, in other words, results from the matador's objectification of himself in a purely compositional pattern or configuration—a pictorial sequence of organized "lines." That sequence is rendered meaningful by the physical danger that it courts. "[S]omething that [is] beautiful done close to the bull [is] ridiculous if . . . done a little way off," because the condition of compositional beauty— the thing that makes the economy of gestures aesthetically powerful and significant—is the imminent and ceaseless pressure of the matador's literal death. This threat alone redeems Romero's beautiful self-objectifications, turning the bullfight into "something . . . with a definite end" instead of "a spectacle with unexplained horrors." The capacity to work always "close to the bull" (171), to dwell as much as possible in the bull's dangerous "terrain" (217), endows the otherwise "ridiculous" movements with beauty, meaning, and redemptive significance.

The ultimate logic of such a requirement is the physical fusion of man and bull, signaling the bullfighter's formal annihilation into the picture he composes. "Each time [Romero] let the bull pass so close that the man and the bull and the cape that filled and pivoted ahead of the bull were all one sharply etched mass" (221). Or again: "Romero's left hand dropped the muleta over the bull's muzzle to blind him . . . and for just an instant he and the bull were one. . . . Then the figure was broken. There was a little jolt as Romero came clear" (222). Frozen within this ecstatic embrace, "etched" together in a figure that crowns the bullfighter's pictorial sequence, bull and man become for a moment formally indistinguishable "objects" within the aesthetic totality of the spectacle. This happens, however, precisely at the moment where the matador exerts his greatest subjective agency. The figures fuse and the sword enters—and then the perfect fusion is broken by the opening of a chasm between master and mastered, killer and killed, living subject and dead object. The continued mobility ("jolt") of the man brings the spectacle to a "definite end" by setting him off from the sacrificial stasis of the now-definitively objectified animal. In this way Romero completes his artwork and exits his objective alienation into art—accomplishing both with an heroic gesture that is equal parts artistry and ritualized brutality. Such a feat embodies most fully "grace under pressure": the code hero courts objectifying dangers while transmuting them into sacrificial forms from which his masterfully orchestrating agency ultimately manages to free him.[7]

Such a pattern of action is only *necessary* in the modern world—a world of phallic woundedness where male identity must be made. But Hemingway chooses to locate his hero in a spectacle drawn from *pre*modern Spain. Because modernity has been cut off from masculine potency, one must return to the past to discover a manhood that can stave off chaos. Yet such a move risks contaminating Romero with some of the traditional forms of unmanliness the novel wants to reject. It risks, that is, making him resemble Robert Cohn too closely. The bullfighter's love is thus allowed to "mean something" that his status as code hero should prohibit. His romantic yearnings are hopelessly conventional in a way that makes him want to domesticate Brett (246). And his bullfighting is said to give "real emotion" through the "natural" "purity of [its] line," to express not just the "real thing" but the "old thing" that he was born with and no one else can ever learn (171–172)—to figure, in short, the romantic expressivity that *The Sun Also Rises* elsewhere consigns to a dead past and derides as a sentimental illusion.[8]

The bullfight could thus be said to enact the bind of Hemingway's relation to affect. Neither Romero nor anyone else in the novel is as unsentimental, as un-affected, as something in Hemingway wants to make them. Jake betrays the code of *afición* by essentially pimping Brett to Romero in the name of his sentimental attachment to her. Brett herself requires this pimping because she has "to do something [she] really want[s] to do" (187)—because she retains yearning for fulfillment that *The Sun Also Rises* elsewhere ridicules.[9] It may even be these sentimental lapses that make the novel appealing to us, saving it from Hemingway's proclivity toward the coldly dehumanized and austere. Without what the book reviles as sentiment, Romero's performance would be pure technique, incapable of eliciting the "real emotion" for which Jake and Hemingway value it. The bullfight itself would come close to embodying a fascist idealization of aestheticized violence. Jake would be little more than a callow and emotionally closed-down adherent of invulnerability. And Brett would be someone so scared of her feelings that she becomes involved only with those she can hurt because she will not risk loving them. What makes these characters likable is that they covertly perpetuate the yearnings they prohibit and revile as sentimental. To mourn this loss—to undo the prohibition—would recover the capacity to *be moved* in a way that need not to be disparaged, and so to feel fully vital and alive without inducing a self-humiliation that requires the reflex of emotional deadness and expressive self-paralysis.

II.

But the danger of even this unexpressed affect is apparently danger enough. Hemingway therefore seeks to resuscitate the phallic masculinity whose loss ought to be guaranteed by the fact of Jake's wound. The masculinity is not simply mourned as a lost illusion of the past. Nor is it openly celebrated as an authentic content for modern men—a move forbidden by the modernist redefinition of manhood in relation to lack and loss. Instead, phallic manhood is melancholically idealized *as lost,* enlisted in an endless battle against the longed for disturbance of affect, but only once it has been displaced from a psychic content or meaning to a style. *The Sun Also Rises* celebrates such style, not only by lauding the aesthetically formalizing tendencies of Romero's matadorial technique, but also by insisting repeatedly on the "how" as against the "what" ("I did not care what it was all about," says Jake. "All I wanted to know was how to live in it" [152]). The novel celebrates codes of speech and forms of ritualized behavior which compensate for the lack of content or meaning in modern life, while also protecting their adherents from the dangers of unfettered intimacy.

This dual function—compensation and protection—is crucial to the workings of style in the novel. For example, to be a "good drunk" (152) is to cultivate a "style" of drunkenness that avoids excessively emotional outbursts of an affectionate or violent kind, even while courting the alcoholic pressure to *succumb* to emotional expression.[10] Similarly, in the fishing episode, Bill and Jake both acknowledge the wound that ought to undermine at least Jake's professions of masculine prowess, and set about asserting that prowess by conquering the feminine waters and producing an aesthetic order from their chaos (120–125).[11]

The linguistic style of the novel and of its characters' speech likewise works to compensate for the emotion it omits yet continues to yearn for. Perhaps the most central example of this strategy is the book's refusal to specify the nature of Jake's injury:

Undressing, I looked at myself in the mirror of the big armoire beside the bed. . . . Of all the ways to be wounded. . . . I put on my pajamas and got into bed. . . . I read [*Le Toril*] all the way through, including the Petite Correspondánce and the Cornigrams. I blew out the lamp. Perhaps I would be able to sleep.

My head started to work. The old grievance. Well, it was a rotten way to be wounded and flying on a joke front like the Italian. In the Italian hospital . . . the liaison colonel came to visit me. . . . I was all bandaged up. But they had told him about it. Then he made that wonderful speech: "You, a foreigner, an Englishman" (any foreigner was an Englishman) "have given more than your life." What a speech! I would like to have it illuminated to hang in the office. He never laughed. He was putting himself in my place, I guess. "Che mala fortuna! Che mala fortuna!"

. . . I lay awake thinking and my mind jumping round. Then I couldn't keep away from it, and I started to think about Brett and all the rest of it went away. I was thinking about Brett and my mind stopped jumping around and started to go in sort of smooth waves. Then all of a sudden I started to cry. Then after a while it was better and I lay in bed and listened to the heavy trains go by . . . and then I went to sleep. (38–39)

This is a justly celebrated passage, one at the center of debates over whether Hemingway's depiction remains ironically detached or succumbs to senti-mentality. What strikes me about such debates is that critics rarely question the *value* of ironic detachment or of the omissions that enable it. The power of the scene derives in part from the fact that Jake declines to name the wound, as well as from his refusal to tell us what exactly he's feeling. Such omissions and understatements load his crying with an emotional intensity that resides in its very lack of specificity. He cries because of "it," and the Church tells him "Not to think about it," but the compulsively repetitive character of trauma requires him to return to "it," again and again. Attempts to name the wound, meanwhile, are rendered ridiculous by the Italian colonel's stumbling efforts to glorify it in words—efforts whose failure suggests that to name the injury is at once to trivialize and sentimentalize the unspeakable horrors of Jake's unmanning.

But at the same time, it is important to note the costs of this omission. There is a kind of gentility in the refusal to give the wound its name—a delicacy that Hemingway would seem to want explicitly to reject. This delicacy is less an expression of courage than a symptom of fear. To name the wound would be to give it a frightening psychic and physical specificity, raising the challenge of what it felt like to receive the wound, and what it feels like to have it. This would mean giving emotional content to Jake's illegible tears as well. Rather than linking those tears to Brett in some unspecified way ("I was thinking about Brett . . . Then all of a sudden I started to cry"), naming would require Jake to specify exactly what the wound has made impossible for him.

This in turn would undermine a central fantasy of the novel, that Jake is unable to satisfy Brett sexually, and therefore she can't help but "*trompe* . . . [him] with everybody" (62). Hemingway must have known that such a scenario is absurd. Sexual intercourse is not the prerequisite to female sexual satisfaction—for most women, penetration alone is insufficient for orgasm. Hemingway's commitment to masculinity as a principle of penetration—a version of manhood that the truth of Jake's wound has rendered increasingly difficult to sustain—prevents him from saying this. Instead, he and Jake engage in a melancholy taciturnity of style in an effort to make up for the loss of this masculine ideal. Left out of such a scenario is the possibility of a masculinity not committed to penetration as the sign of sexual mastery, one that can mourn the loss of phallic manhood in the name of a recovered capacity for receptivity, affect, and a sensuous pleasure unhampered by the will to power. Hemingway's fear of this receptivity leads him to romanticize unfulfillment—masculinity may not be unimpeachably hard anymore, but neither is it going to be soft. Instead masculinity must learn to tolerate a kind of perpetual if metaphorical hard-on. Desire cannot be satisfied in the absence of an organ to satisfy it, but this absence fails to compromise a phallic manhood imagined both as lost and psychically unrelinquishable.

In each of the cases I have described—drinking, fishing, speaking—a highly codified or stylized form of mastery invokes a knowledge it also disavows: knowledge of a phallic wound, knowledge of sentiment. The valorization of style thus functions precisely as a fetish, seeking to resolve the dilemmas of lost manhood by melancholically perpetuating what it pretends to grieve. Style defends against yet keeps alive the dual loss of sentiment and potency by serving as a kind of monument that ceaselessly speaks of the losses its erection seeks to silence. Style allows Hemingway and his characters neither openly to embrace lost affect nor to do without it, neither to lay claims to a hard masculinity nor really to renounce it.

In the case of phallic potency, the very irreparable character of loss bespeaks Hemingway's melancholic fixation. Because Jake is the victim of an amputation, his desire is *literally* unfulfillable. What he seeks but can never attain is less sexual satisfaction itself than a restoration of the penile object that cannot be recovered. The loss figured by his wound, therefore, can neither be forgotten nor mourned. It can't be forgotten because the penis remains absolutely constitutive of Jake's identity; the ultimate object of his desire is unforgettably inscribed as lost on his living body. And it can't be mourned because that would require the sober imperfection of displaced substitutes, and the *ideal* of phallic potency admits of no substitution.

Ideas by definition cannot be mourned—cannot be replaced with something like but different. Ambivalence is the prerequisite for productive grieving.[12] Although *The Sun Also Rises* offers a series of stylistic "substitutes" for the lost and idealized penis, the novel's fundamentally melancholic character results from the fact that these must fail. Style alone cannot fill the hole that constitutes modern masculinity, while filling that hole is, on *The Sun's* own terms, both the only way to set the world right and an unacceptably sentimental denial of historical and psychic reality.

III.

The canonization of Hemingway—and of the strand of modernism to which I've linked him—has had the effect of perpetuating this melancholic bind. Canonical culture and criticism remain committed to a masculinity of affectless mastery, often perpetuated in the same breath that proclaims it dead. Indeed, our commitment to such disavowal is partly responsible for the cultural authority invested in this strand of modernism. These texts repeatedly allow us to recover, through the fetish of their monumental forms, a heroic masculinity and social potency often described as lost or impossible at the level of content. The masculinism of such modernism thus inheres in a privileging of style over substance, a kind of mortality of form echoing the tendencies I have traced in Hemingway.

This is emphatically *not* to say that formal experimentation is inherently misogynist. Rather I'm suggesting that, for historically contingent but specifiable reasons, these modernists often honed their style as weapons against the perceived effeminacy of affect and emotional effusiveness. To create a distinctive linguistic *style* was to find a way of expressing oneself without the "sloppy sentimentality" of direct emotional expression. Modernist art thus sought to extinguish the affective content of authorial personality, sublating that content in objected forms memorializing their expressive origins.

These are contentious claims with complex histories of debate. A range of modernists do not fit into the account I've offered, particularly given the canon's expansion to include figures less fully invested in the binaries of gender (and race).[13] My point is less to offer categorical statements about what modernism "is," than to provide a speculative outline of what seems to me one of its dominant aesthetic ambitions—an ambition that contributed to its canonization in the 1950s, and that continues to govern our critical judgments today.

But even if such speculations about style turn out to be of limited interest, the melancholic *content* of many modernist texts seems indisputable. Time and again, our modernists elaborate a vision strikingly similar to Hemingway's, wherein the object of ultimate value is a lost and unmournable masculinity. One thinks of Faulkner's obsessive delineation of southern patriarchs, each of whom he at once critiques as destructive, anatomizes as dead, and idealizes as the last incarnation of a now historically impossible virility. Eliot also fits this paradigm, structuring *The Waste Land* around a mythically regal and regenerative masculinity, shown by the poem to be both necessary and inadequate to the task of shoring the self's fragments against ruin. Finally, both Cather and Fitzgerald contrast the destructive, commodified, and aesthetically tawdry present with a creative and expressively potent male past—a past that can no more survive in the modern world than it can be imaginatively relinquished [14]

An adequate account of modernist melancholia would entail more detailed treatment of these figures, as well as an attempt to think of them in relation to other, less melancholic authors. It would entail a more full account of the socially destructive character of the melancholic pattern—its misogyny and homophobia, for example. But it would also entail, as part of our collective engagement with Hemingway and other modernists, an attempt to locate moments in their work where something less defensive happens: moments when an authentic mourning shatters the affectless armor of masculinity, promising new forms of social being that embrace the connective potential of habitually disavowed affect. This is perhaps the most urgent task to which the new Hemingway studies needs to address itself.

NOTES

I'm grateful to the College of Liberal Arts at the University of South Carolina, Columbia for summer funding that enabled me to complete this essay.

1. The key texts here are Comley and Scholes, Eby, Lynn, Moddelmog, and Spilka.
2. From a Barnes and Noble catalogue, quoted in Moddelmog (2).
3. Work on modernism in relation to mourning is just beginning. I'm particularly indebted to Seth Moglen's *An Other Modernism,* which, though not centrally concerned with masculinity, argues that modernism in the United States contains two distinct strands—one fixating melancholically on loss, and one seeking more progressively to mourn and project lost aspirations into the future. Other significant contributions to the field include Breitwieser and Ramazani.
4. This view of Cohn's unmanliness in part reflects Jake's need to disparage a potent rival. But the fact that Hemingway lets us see this in no way undermines Jake's

judgments. The novel engages in strategies, particularly modes of second-person address, that construct readers as privileged insiders, seducing us into accepting both Jake's relatively benign evaluations and his more pernicious ones. See Wyatt 56–57.

5. See Moddelmog (129) and Schwartz (53–56).

6. Huyssen's essay is the classic statement concerning the modernist equation of sentimentality with a debased mass culture, and of mass culture with femininity. See also Clark, esp. 1–41.

7. The aesthetic Hemingway imagines here is a hypermasculinization of T.S. Eliot's "impersonality," wherein authorial personality is both eliminated and sublated into compositional forms.

8. Schwartz also notes the sentimentalization/feminization of Romero (64).

9. My argument here extends the Davidsons' claims concerning the circularity and groundlessness of the Hemingway code (86).

10. Mike is a "bad drunk" not only because alcohol makes him behave aggressively toward Cohn, but because it brings out his excessively affectionate behavior toward Brett. See *SAR* 84–85.

11. Blackmore offers an interesting account of how the fishing sequence at once destabilizes gender binaries and reconsolidates them in homophobic fashion (63–65).

12. This statement attempts to complicate Freud's assertion that, unlike melancholia, mourning springs from a relatively unambivalent relation to the lost object. Such claims need to be supplemented by Klein's insistence on the *centrality* of ambivalence to successful grieving (152, 156–158).

13. See Baker, Benstock, Boone, and Clark.

14. Examples include Fitzgerald's Gatsby, as well as Cather's Captain Forrester in *A Lost Lady* and Tom Outland in *The Professor's House*.

WORKS CITED

Baker, Houston A. *A Modernism and the Harlem Renaissance*. Chicago: U of Chicago P, 1987.

Benstock, Shari. *Women of the Left Bank: Paris, 1900–1940*. Austin: U of Texas P, 1986.

Blackmore, David. "'In New York It'd Mean I Was A . . .': Masculinity Anxiety and Period Discourses of Sexuality in *The Sun Also Rises*." *The Hemingway Review* 18.1 (Fall 1998): 49–67.

Boone, Joseph Allen. *Libidinal Currents: Sexuality and the Shaping of Modernism.* Chicago: U of Chicago P, 1998.

Breitwieser, Mitchell. "*The Great Gatsby*: Grief, Jazz and the Eye-Witness." *Arizona Quarterly* 47.3 (1991): 17–70.

Clark, Suzanne. *Sentimental Modernism: Women Writers and the Revolution of the Word.* Bloomington: Indiana UP, 1991.

Comley, Nancy R., and Robert Scholes. *Hemingway's Genders: Rereading the Hemingway Text.* New Haven: Yale UP, 1994.

Davidson, Arnold E., and Cathy N. Davidson. "Decoding the Hemingway Hero in *The Sun Also Rises*." In *New Essays on* The Sun Also Rises. Ed. Linda Wagner-Martin, 83–107. Cambridge: Cambridge UP, 1987.

Eby, Carl P. *Hemingway's Fetishism: Psychoanalysis and the Mirror of Manhood.* Albany: SUNY P, 1999.

Freud, Sigmund. "Mourning and Melancholia." In *Essential Papers on Object Loss.* Ed. Rita V. Frankiel, 38–51. New York: New York UP, 1994.

Hemingway, Ernest. *The Sun Also Rises.* 1926; New York: Scribner's, 1954.

Huyssen, Andreas. "Mass Culture as Woman: Modernism's Other." In *After the Great Divide: Modernism, Mass Culture, Postmodernism.* Bloomington: Indiana UP, 1986. 44–62.

Kimmel, Michael S. *Manhood in America: A Cultural History.* New York: Free Press, 1996.

Klein, Melanie. "Mourning and Its Relation to Manic-Depressive States." In *The Selected Melanie Klein.* Ed. Juliet Mitchell, 146–74. New York: Free Press, 1986.

Lynn, Kenneth. *Hemingway.* New York: Simon and Schuster, 1987.

Moddelmog, Debra A. *Reading Desire: In Pursuit of Ernest Hemingway.* Ithaca, NY: Cornell UP, 1999.

Moglen, Seth. "An Other Modernism: John Dos Passos and the Politics of Literary Form." Diss. UC Berkeley, 1999.

Ramazani, Jahan. *Poetry of Mourning: The Modern Elegy from Hardy to Heaney.* Chicago: U of Chicago P, 1994.

Schwartz, Nina. "Lovers' Discourse in *The Sun Also Rises:* A Cock and Bull Story." *Criticism* 26.1 (1984): 49–69.

Spilka, Mark. *Hemingway's Quarrel with Androgyny.* Lincoln: U of Nebraska P, 1990.

Wyatt, David. *Prodigal Sons: A Study of Authorship and Authority.* Baltimore, MD: Johns Hopkins UP, 1980.

Trauma Theory and Hemingway's Lost Paris Manuscripts

Marc Seals

In a 1934 letter to F. Scott Fitzgerald, Ernest Hemingway advised, "We are all bitched from the start and you especially have to be hurt like hell before you can write seriously. But when you get the damned hurt use it [. . .]" (*SL* 408). Hemingway often made use of his own painful and traumatic experiences in his fiction. A. E. Hotchner relates a conversation in which Ava Gardener asked Hemingway if he had ever had an analyst. Hemingway replied, "Sure I have. Portable Corona number three. That's been my analyst" (139). Rose Marie Burwell tells us that he often made this comment (162). For Hemingway, writing and trauma were inextricably linked; trauma provided material for his writing and writing provided a therapeutic outlet

Reprinted with permission from *The Hemingway Review* 24.2 (Spring 2005). Copyright © 2005 The Ernest Hemingway Foundation. Published by The University of Idaho, Moscow, Idaho.

for trauma. Hemingway repeatedly wrote about one particular traumatic experience—his first wife Hadley's loss of his early Paris manuscripts in 1922. He wrote about this incident in each of the major works published after his death—*A Moveable Feast, Islands in the Stream, The Garden of Eden,* and *True at First Light*—although Hemingway's editors have not always chosen to include the episode in the published versions of these works.[1]

Trauma accounts in literature present the reader with a rather peculiar economy of truth; Hemingway's posthumously published writing reveals aspects of his psyche that he was unable or unwilling to share publicly. In this article, I suggest that Hemingway's repeated writing about the loss of his Paris manuscripts might have served as a sort of creative flashback, allowing him to face and deal with the trauma of the loss.

In *Unclaimed Experience: Trauma, Narrative, and History,* Cathy Caruth defines trauma as "the response to an unexpected or overwhelming violent event or events that are not fully grasped as they occur, but return later in repeated flashbacks, nightmares, or other repetitive phenomena" (91). This definition certainly fits the disastrous events of December 1922. Hemingway was in Switzerland, covering the Lausanne Conference. Investigative journalist and editor Lincoln Steffens, whom Hemingway had met in Genoa, was also there. Steffens was apparently quite impressed with Hemingway's writing and expressed a desire to see more (Diliberto 131). As a result, Hadley packed up all of Hemingway's papers in a suitcase, intending to take his manuscripts to him in Switzerland (Reynolds 86). She left this suitcase unattended on the train while buying a bottle of Evian water for the trip, and the suitcase was stolen before the train even left the station. Unfortunately, Hadley had packed both the originals *and* their carbons, so the work was irrevocably lost. It is unclear how important the loss was to Hemingway at the time. Although Michael Reynolds maintains that Hemingway made a whirlwind return to Paris to check into the matter (86, 89), James Mellow disagrees (208–209). Nor did Hemingway bother to run a newspaper advertisement seeking the return of the manuscripts. When considering such an advertisement, he thought of offering a reward of just 150 francs—about ten dollars (Reynolds 86, 89–91).

In a 23 January 1923 letter to Ezra Pound, Hemingway wrote:

> I suppose you heard about the loss of my Juvenalia [*sic*]? I went up to Paris last
> week to see what was left and found that Hadley had made the job complete
> by including all carbons, duplicates, etc. All that remains of my complete
> works are three pencil drafts of a bum poem which was later scrapped, some
> correspondence between John McClure [editor, *Double Dealer*] and me, and
> some journalistic carbons. You, naturally, would say, "Good" etc. But don't say
> it to me. I ain't yet reached that mood. (*SL* 77)

Given this explicit statement of bitterness and distress, it seems odd
that Hemingway did not seek the return of the lost Paris manuscripts more
actively, regardless of the cost of even the chance for a successful resolution.
However, this does not necessarily mean that the event was not acutely
traumatic.[2] In fact, the relative lack of immediate concern fits neatly with
Caruth's psychoanalytic trauma-theory model, which states that the trauma
victim often may not note the significance of the event until years later.

Although other trauma theories also inform this study, Cathy Caruth's
model is most appropriate because it focuses on the writer of the traumatic
account. A writer-focused model is particularly suited to study of the loss
of Hemingway's Paris manuscripts because Hemingway never authorized
publication of the narratives relating this event; therefore, these were narratives with no author-sanctioned readers. Caruth follows a Freudian model,[3]
saying that a traumatic event is not "fully assimilated as it occurs" (5). She
explains that the trauma "is not locatable in the simply violent or original
event in an individual's past, but rather in the way that its very unassimilated
nature—the way it was precisely *not known* in the first instance—returns to
haunt the survivor later on" (4). In *Worlds of Hurt: Reading the Literature
of Trauma*, Kalí Tal says that such repetition of the traumatic experience is
the penalty for the initial repression of the trauma (7). In *Testimony: Crises
of Witnessing in Literature, Psychoanalysis, and History,* Shoshana Felman
and Dori Laub suggest that for a traumatic memory to lose its power, a form
of narrative construction and historical reconstruction must occur (69).

Thus, it seems quite possible that Hemingway was writing and rewriting about the loss of his manuscripts in an attempt, perhaps unconscious, at psychological discovery (or recovery) and perhaps even healing. Miriam B. Mandel observes that the events of Hemingway's early life provided the majority of material for his writing (240). What makes the loss of the Paris manuscripts *unique* is that the four treatments of the episode in his writing appear in works that he chose—for whatever reason—not to publish. Perhaps this event was just too personal to make public.

For this analysis, I will examine each of the four posthumously published works in chronological order according to the date when Hemingway appears to have *stopped* working on it. In *Hemingway: The Postwar Years and the Posthumous Novels,* Rose Marie Burwell reconsiders previously accepted dates of composition and attempts to reconcile inconsistencies in Hemingway's notes and letters. She concludes that *Islands in the Stream* was written from 1945 to 1952, *True at First Light* from 1954 to 1956, *The Garden of Eden* from 1948 to 1959,[4] and *A Moveable Feast* from 1957 to 1961 (xxiv–xxv). Writing about what she terms Hemingway's "flower narratives," Miriam Mandel says, "Although Hemingway uses the same material repeatedly, he does not repeat himself. The variations are indeed instructive" (254). Her point also applies to Hemingway's "suitcase narratives." Examined according to Burwell's chronological order, the variations are indeed instructive; a pattern of emotional healing emerges, as if Hemingway learned to accept the loss of the Paris manuscripts and perhaps even forgive Hadley for her carelessness (as well as seek *her* forgiveness for his own cruelty).

The relevant portion of *Islands in the Stream* is in the deleted "Miami" section, eventually published in short story form as "The Strange Country." Burwell tells us that this section of *Islands* was written in 1945 and 1946, making this the earliest fictional record of the loss of the manuscripts (217). Burwell also suggests that Hemingway did not intend to include the "Miami" section in the final version of *Islands.* By the time he finished working on *Islands,* he had already included many of its thematic elements in the manuscript of *The Garden of Eden,* including his loss of the Paris manuscripts (Burwell 58–59). Yet an examination of "The Strange Country" may reveal Hemingway's attitude toward this loss during the mid-1940s. Twenty-three years after the event, he had had ample time either to realize the true significance of the trauma or inflate its importance to mythic proportions in his mind, and he seems to have believed that the trauma of the experience was quite real.

Roger, the protagonist of "The Strange Country," is traveling from Miami to New Orleans with Helena, who is fourteen or fifteen years younger than Roger. Helena seems quite in love with Roger, and Roger is struggling not to hurt her, as he has so many other women. Helena tells Roger that she wants to write stories also, and this seems to disturb him greatly. When Helena asks what it was like when he started out writing, she inadvertently reopens an old wound. Roger confesses, "I thought I was writing the greatest stories ever written and that people just didn't have sense enough to know it. [. . .] Only I didn't think I was conceited. I was just confident." He tells Helena that the "first confident stories were lost" (CSS 645). Helena asks him to explain what happened, and Roger says that he'll tell her the story another time. She again asks him to tell her, and he again refuses, saying that it "still hurts like a bastard. No it doesn't really. It has a scar over it now. A good thick scar" (646). She continues to push, and he seems to relent. But after just three sentences, he stops. She pleads for him to continue.

Roger finally begins the story in earnest, but halfway through asks Helena if he really has to continue. She insists, and he then tells the story in great detail. The story that Roger tells is identical to the account in Michael Reynolds's *Hemingway: The Paris Years*. In fact, there is no detail in Reynolds's account that is not also in Hemingway's fictional treatment.[5] Whether Hemingway added fictional details to Roger's account is unclear (as is the complete veracity of Reynolds's biographical account). Perhaps most fascinating is Roger's reaction when he realizes that the work is truly and completely lost:

> I felt almost as though I could not breathe when I saw that there really were no folders with originals, nor folders with typed copies, nor folders with carbons and then I locked the door of the cupboard and went into the next room, which was the bedroom, and lay down on the bed and put a pillow between my legs

and my arms around another pillow and lay there very quietly. I had never put a pillow between my legs before and I had never lain with my arms around a pillow but now I needed them very badly. I knew everything I had ever written and everything that I had great confidence in was gone. (*CSS* 647–648)

Roger seems to regress into the womb, curled on his bed in a fetal position. Burwell observes that this passage might also evoke images of castration (217). Roger's assertion that he had lost "everything" that he "had great confidence in" may include his trust of the wife who lost the manuscripts. Roger goes on to say that although this was the first "true despair" he had ever experienced, he did not cry, for he was "all dried up inside" (*CSS* 648).

Roger further explains the reason for his extreme emotional shutdown:

Because I worked on newspapers since I was very young I could never remember anything once I had written it down; as each day you wiped your memory clear with writing as you might wipe a blackboard clear with a sponge or a wet rag; and I still had that evil habit and now it had caught up with me. (*CSS* 649)

Perhaps Hemingway was trying to accomplish the same thing here. By writing a (marginally) fictionalized account of the loss of the manuscripts, he may have been trying to "wipe his memory clear." If so, this effort to erase his memory was not successful, for Hemingway would revisit it again and again in his often barely fictional novels. Yet in each of the treatments of the manuscript loss that follow, some of the bitterness is lost, perhaps indicating a degree of psychological healing.

Hemingway's treatment of the lost manuscripts in *True at First Light,* written between 1954 and 1956, is more problematic. In the published version of this "fictional memoir," there is no obvious mention of the lost manuscripts. Hemingway waxes nostalgic about his year in Paris; he recalls this time with no apparent bitterness, mostly remembers the "secret cafés" (*TAFL* 147–148). He makes cryptic comments about love, fidelity, and marriage, calling love "a moveable feast" and asserting that "Fidelity does not exist nor ever is implied except at the first marriage" (262). Hemingway makes an even more obscure reference to the satisfaction of having someone steal from you, thinking they are undetected (267). Finally, he discusses his marriages, mentioning his present wife Mary, his second wife Pauline (who has died), and an unnamed wife whom no one would have liked (presumably Martha). Hadley is not mentioned.

However, in the original manuscripts of the African book, Hemingway does remember the loss of the manuscripts by the wife that he "loved first and best and who was the mother of my oldest son" (qtd. in Burwell xxv and Jenks 55). He then dreams that Hadley is with him in an inn (or *Gasthaus*) in the Swiss canton of Vaud:[6]

> [...] we were sleeping close together to keep warm and because that was the best way to sleep if both people love each other and it is a cold night. [...] My first and best wife was sleeping soundly, as always, and I could smell every scent of her body and the chestnut trees as well and she was warm in my arms and her head was under my chin and we were sleeping as close and trusting as kittens sleep. (qtd. in Mandel 246–247)

Hemingway remembers and records the traumatic event and the wife he blamed for it only in passing; perhaps this means he is a bit more healed. It is ironic that the loss of the Paris manuscripts (and the loving remembrance of Hadley) was cut in the final editing of the African book, making Hemingway the posthumous victim of a second manuscript "theft."

In *The Garden of Eden*, composed from 1948 to 1959, the trauma of the lost manuscripts receives its most creative and cathartic treatment when Catherine intentionally burns David Bourne's stories and press clippings leaving only his African narrative. Catherine initially tells David what she has done, but he cannot believe that it could be true. When David discovers that the suitcase is indeed empty, he too becomes "empty and dead in his heart" (*GOE* 219). Here writing is explicitly equated with life, and David has had more than just a brush with metaphoric death. He goes out to the metal drum that serves as a trash burner and stirs the ashes, just to make sure that it has really happened.

When Catherine wants to explain why it was necessary to destroy David's writing, he tells her, "All I want to do is kill you [. . .] And the only reason I don't do it is because you are crazy." When Catherine tells David that she'll kill him instead, he replies, "I wouldn't give a shit" (223). David does not fear death, because he has already been killed symbolically.

This account seems to treat the wife more harshly than the previous versions of the tale. Gioia Diliberto calls the *The Garden of Eden* account a "wicked, twisted version of what happened at the Gare de Lyon" (135). After all, Hadley did not *mean* to allow the suitcase to be stolen. However, *Garden's* vicious twisting of the actual events of 1922 must be tempered by David's fictional actions after Catherine leaves. Having neatly replaced Catherine with Marita, David determines to rewrite one of the missing stories—exactly what Roger in "The Strange Country" said was impossible. The reverse is true for David; not only can he remember the story clearly, he finds that "he knew much more about his father than when he had first written this story and he knew he could measure his progress by the small things which made his father more tactile and to have more dimensions than he had in the story before" (*GOE* 217). Not only can David remember the story, his memory—and thus his writing—is much improved.

The novel closes (at least in the form that Tom Jenks has given it to us) with a statement of absolute authorial confidence:

> David wrote steadily and well and the sentences that he had made before came to him complete and entire and he put them down, corrected them, and cut them as if he were going over proof. Not a sentence was missing and there were many that he put down as they were returned to him without changing them. By two o'clock he had recovered, corrected and improved what had taken him five days to write originally. He wrote on a while longer and there was no sign that any of it would ever cease returning to him intact. (247)

The trauma has been more than blunted; David's writing actually seems improved. Perhaps this was wishful thinking on Hemingway's behalf, but it may have reflected his own healing. Cathy Caruth, again following Freud's model, says that flashbacks of a traumatic event are expressed as "literal flashbacks" because the mind has not attached "psychic meaning" to the event (59). Thus, the mind might express the trauma in terms of abstractions only after psychological healing (or at least understanding) has begun. The fact that Hemingway had finally truly fictionalized the events of December 1922 may indicate yet another degree of healing.

The last book that Hemingway worked on was *A Moveable Feast*, composed from 1957 to 1961. *A Moveable Feast* is perhaps Hemingway's most direct account of the loss of the Paris manuscripts. Although the reader receives more detail in "The Strange Country," in *A Moveable Feast* the protagonist is (at least nominally) the author himself. Although this is also true in the manuscripts of the African book, the event receives only marginal attention there (and even less in the published version, *True at First Light*). In *A Moveable Feast*, Hemingway is not only able to write about the event, but also to speak of it in a way that suggests that he has learned to deal with it and move on.

Hemingway again details the events of that fateful day, but writes without bitterness. He acknowledges that the suitcase was stolen, perhaps indicating that he did not think Hadley lost it "accidentally on purpose" in a passive-aggressive attempt to destroy her "competition" for his attention, as some have suggested (Diliberto 135; Lynn 191). Hemingway says that she was bringing the stories and poems to him as a surprise, framing the event as a sweet gesture gone terribly wrong. He even describes Hadley's despair as she struggled to tell him about the theft. And Hemingway writes:

> That was over now and Chink had taught me never to discuss casualties; so I told O'Brien not to feel so bad. It was probably good for me to lose early work and I told him all that stuff you feed the troops. I was going to start writing stories again I said and, as I said it, only trying to lie so that he would not feel so bad, I knew that it was true. (74–75)

Gone are the bitterness and despair of the account from "The Strange Country"; gone is the desire to twist it into a vicious tale of a wife's revenge that surfaced in *The Garden of Eden*. All that remains seems to be forgiveness and a knowledge that the author must and will go on.

Apparently, Hemingway's treatment of Hadley in *A Moveable Feast* was intended to be even kinder. According to Gerry Brenner, a comparison of the unedited manuscript with the published text edited by Mary Hemingway reveals that Mary did far more than cut only "where repetitions and redundancies occurred," as she claimed (qtd. in Brenner). At the conclusion of the original manuscript's chapter sixteen, Brenner tells us, Hemingway absolves Hadley of any blame for the collapse of their marriage and proclaims he is glad that she was able to build a better life with a better man. Brenner searches for Mary's rationale for cutting Hemingway's apology to Hadley, but concludes that, regardless of the reason, Mary violated her own standard (539). Whether Mary excised passages that seemed kind to Hadley out of jealousy or out of concern for Hemingway's artistry is irrelevant; scholars wishing to analyze Hemingway's unexpurgated treatment of Hadley now have access to the manuscripts of *A Moveable Feast*.

It is probably significant that Hemingway chose to write about the theft of the suitcase containing the Paris manuscripts only in texts that remained unpublished during his lifetime. These were texts that he was unwilling or unable to finish. Perhaps this level of cathartic experience was too private to share knowingly, akin to selling transcripts of confidential sessions with a psychiatrist. Indeed, these books are Hemingway's attempts to expunge the pain and bitterness of this traumatic event. This fits well with the trauma theory proposed by Laurie Vickroy, who (adopting Suzette Henke's concept of "scriptotherapy") posits that trauma literature possesses an explicitly healing function (8).

In *The Garden of Eden*, as in *A Moveable Feast*, Hemingway equates writing with life. Late in the text, Hemingway tells the reader that when he is not working, he feels "the death loneliness that comes at the end of every day that is wasted in your life" (*AMF* 165–166). A day without writing is a day wasted, a day haunted by the spectre of death. If the failure to write is death, then the loss of completed writing may be considered a kind of psychological and symbolic murder. Laurie Vickroy calls this sort of loss "subjective death" (223); Hemingway faced it and survived. Kalí Tal writes, "Literature of trauma is written from the need to tell and retell the story of the traumatic experience [. . .]. Such writing serves both as validation and cathartic vehicle for the traumatized author" (21). A repeated literary representation of trauma may be seen as a triumphant statement of survival. Hemingway's writing about the loss of the Paris manuscripts serves these purposes.

In writing about the assault upon his literary "life," Hemingway shouts to the world that he is alive, like a man trapped under the rubble of a collapsed building—or a man blown up by a mortar shell who sees the soul go out of him. He has survived and bears witness to his ordeal. Through this testimony, Hemingway heals the wounds of the trauma, gaining strength each time he tells the story. Narration of the trauma is thus doubly therapeutic: if writing is life and loss of writing is death, then writing about his near-death experience is both a testimonial celebration survival and, by the very act of writing, an act celebrating life.

NOTES

1. I do not include *The Dangerous Summer* because much of it was published during Hemingway's lifetime (in three installments in *Life* magazine in 1960).
2. According to most Hemingway biographers, Hemingway's response can only be called mild when compared to the significance the event later appears to have taken in his mind (or at least in his writing).
3. Caruth acknowledges that her model is largely based on Freud's as outlined in *Beyond the Pleasure Principle*. For a similar model (albeit more inclusive of the narrative's audience), see chapter 2 of Felman and Laub.
4. John Leonard's "The Garden of Eden: A Question of Dates" does not change this general order of Hemingway's posthumously published works.
5. The basic facts of the manuscript loss are more or less consistent in each of the critical biographies examined. Reynolds' account does not differ significantly from Carlos Baker's 1969 "authorized" biography, *Ernest Hemingway: A*

Life Story (103). Reynolds simply provides greater detail and documents his sources even more carefully, drawing from numerous letters and interviews for his account. Reynolds' account also differs little from Kenneth Lynn's 1987 biography, *Hemingway* (187–188). However, James Mellow, in his 1992 biography, *Hemingway: A Life Without Consequences,* maintains that Hemingway may not have returned to Paris immediately to check on the carbons (209–213).

6. Though Mandel connects this dream to Hemingway's "flower narratives," the canton of Vaud is also the region of Switzerland where Lausanne is located.

WORKS CITED

Baker, Carlos. *Ernest Hemingway: A Life Story.* New York: Scribner's, 1969.

Brenner, Gerry. "Are We Going to Hemingway's Feast?" *American Literature* 54.4 (December 1982): 528–544.

Burwell, Rose Marie. *Hemingway: The Postwar Years and the Posthumous Novels.* Cambridge: Cambridge UP, 1996.

Caruth, Cathy. *Unclaimed Experience: Trauma, Narrative, and History.* Baltimore: Johns Hopkins UP, 1996.

Diliberto, Gioia. *Hadley.* New York: Ticknor & Fields, 1992.

Felman, Shoshana, and Dori Laub. *Testimony: Crises of Witnessing in Literature, Psychoanalysis, and History.* New York: Routledge, 1991.

Hemingway, Ernest. *The Complete Short Stories of Ernest Hemingway: The Fincia Vigía Edition.* 1987; New York: Scribner's, 1998.

———. *Ernest Hemingway: Selected Letters, 1917–1961.* Ed. Carlos Barker. New York: Scribner's, 1981.

———. *The Garden of Eden.* New York: Scribner's, 1986.

———. *Islands in the Stream.* 1970; New York: Simon & Schuster, 1997.

———. *A Moveable Feast.* 1964; New York: Touchstone, 1992.

———. *True at First Light.* New York: Scribner's, 1999.

Hotchner, A. E. *Papa Hemingway.* New York: Random House, 1966.

Jenks, Tom. "The Old Man and the Manuscript." *Harper's Magazine* (May 1999): 53–60.

Lynn, Kenneth S. *Hemingway.* New York: Simon and Schuster, 1987.

Mandel, Miriam B. "A Lifetime of Flower Narratives." In *Hemingway and Women.*

Eds. Lawrence R. Broer and Gloria Holland, 239–55. Tuscaloosa: U of Alabama P, 2002.

Mellow, James R. *Hemingway: A Life without Consequences.* New York: Houghton Mifflin, 1992.

Reynolds, Michael. *Hemingway: The Paris Years.* New York: Blackwell, 1989.

Tal, Kalí. *Worlds of Hurt: Reading the Literatures of Trauma.* New York: Cambridge UP, 1996.

Vickroy, Laurie. *Trauma and Survival in Contemporary Fiction.* Charlottesville: U of Virginia P, 2002.

PART 2

Wounds, Wars, Gender and *A Farewell to Arms*

Alex Vernon
Jennifer A. Haytock
Matthew C. Stewart
Linda Wagner-Martin
Gary Harrington

War, Gender, and Ernest Hemingway

Alex Vernon

> So much childbirth in Hemingway's stories.
> Especially in his war stories.
>
> —Susan Griffin, *A Chorus of Stones: The Private Life of War*

Ernest Hemingway's "Big Two-Hearted River" remains perhaps the most famous piece of fiction about war with no mention of the war in it. The absence of war is exactly the point of the story, as Nick Adams, a recently returned veteran of the Great War, attempts to forget the war, to recover his prewar adolescent self by engaging in his favorite prewar adolescent activity, fishing. Yet the very language of the story reveals Nick's soldierly self, and betrays his attempt to escape that self:

> Nick went over to the pack and found, with his fingers, a long nail in a paper sack of nails, in the bottom of the pack. He drove it into the pine tree, holding

Reprinted with permission from *The Hemingway Review* 22.1 (Fall 2002). Copyright © 2002 The Ernest Hemingway Foundation. Published by the University of Idaho, Moscow, Idaho.

it close and hitting it gently with the flat of the axe. He hung the pack up on the nail. All his supplies were in the pack. They were off the ground and sheltered now. (*CSS* 167)

This is the language of a soldier carrying out the physical tasks of soldiering, of getting down to his business. Ulysses S. Grant's mantra resonates here, and seems applicable to both Nick Adams and Ernest Hemingway: "I am a verb."

Nick manages over the course of this very long trip to suppress his memory and imagination almost entirely, except for one remembered prewar fishing trip with friends. Nick has mastered what Hemingway later calls "the greatest gift a soldier can acquire," the ability to "suspend your imagination and live completely in the very second of the present minute with no before and no after" (*MAW* xxvii). In "Big Two-Hearted River," besides war, the other significant absence from Nick Adams' consciousness is love. No women in Nick's life appear in the story, as if to suppress thoughts of one—war or women—he necessarily must suppress the other. Even the two trout he catches are both male.

Military and war experiences affect the soldier's sense of gender identity, which for the male veteran means his masculinity, his conception of himself as a man, and by extension his general conception and experience of gender relations. Thus even when a veteran avoids writing directly about his war and military experiences, we ought to be able, through textual performances of gender, to read the war in the text despite authorial intent. In speaking of war and gender relations we are not talking about romantic relations, but about the multiple possible relations the (male) veteran has with the gendered self and with gendered others—with, as an example, one's mother. For one of Hemingway's several literary biographers, Kenneth Lynn, "Big Two-Hearted River" addresses not Nick-Ernest's divided heart over the recent world war, but rather his divided heart over the "open warfare" he had more recently been engaged upon against his mother. Indeed, Lynn offers, "Not a single reference to war appears in the story," and its author's late-life commentary on the war's hidden presence represents a desperate "need of a heroic explanation for his life" as his writing career and mental stability suffered their painful breakdown (106).

Why must the story, however, be about *either* war *or* Nick-Ernest's mother? Why can't it be about both? This is the question Matthew C. Stewart poses in "Ernest Hemingway and World War I: Combatting [*sic*] Recent Psychobiographical Reassessments, Restoring the War" (2000). Stewart rightly challenges Lynn's excision of the war from the text. To Lynn's assertion that the story provides no explicit textual reference to the war, Stewart counters that "neither is there a single reference to Nick's conflicted feelings towards his mother [. . . nor] to familial strife of any kind" (210–211). Lynn's argument wants it both ways, to deny any intentional or unconscious connection with the war while positing an intentional or unconscious (he makes no distinction) connection with Nick-Ernest's mother. Even if Hemingway did come to the realization years later that the story was about the war, and regardless of whether his late-life commentary was accurate or revisionist, we readers can still understand the war as an unconscious motivation.

Stewart's conclusion offers us a way to read the story as about both the war in Europe and the war at home:

> But surely the war itself was an integral part of Hemingway's conflict with the old-fashioned, sanctimonious, emotionally coercive Grace. Surely it was doubly difficult in his particular situation to be treated like a kid. It was the summer of his coming of age, a stage of life when the final thrust towards independence and adult status is normal and necessary. But also, as a young man who had been to the war and a one-time city-beat reporter in Kansas City, he had already seen much more than someone his age would usually see, and had experienced things far beyond the ken of his suburban, essentially Victorian parents. The same mother who had initially doted on her son's war-hero status overlooked the deeper changes his experience had caused him. (209–210)

This resolution of Lynn's false *either war/or mother* dilemma feels half-hearted to me, a diplomatic compromise when read against the article's vitriolic attack on Lynn's interpretation and as Stewart participates in the very same muddling of character and author for which he criticizes Lynn. Nancy R. Comley and Robert Scholes's *Hemingway's Genders* (1994) only mentions "Big Two-Hearted River" once, and in passing, but in a way that does connect war and gender relations. "In that story there was no feminine element present, the feminine being one of those complications best avoided—like the swamp—by a man in Nick's delicate psychic condition" (71), or, I would add, by a vet in Harold Kreb's delicate condition in "Soldier's Home," a story written a month before "Big Two-Hearted River" (April and May 1924). Like Stewart, Comley and Scholes connect war and gender in Hemingway's fiction on the personal level of a returned veteran forced to relate to the women in his immediate environment.

In contrast, I believe we can connect war and gender through Hemingway both on and beyond the personal level, taking a cue from Comley and Scholes by "extending the interpretation beyond the bounds of individual works and into the larger text of the cultural codes that are active in the thought of any writer as alert and sensitive as Ernest Hemingway" (9). As does any major life experience, war contributes to the construction of one's identity, and doubtless does so in a gendered way, and thus in a way that must affect one's sense of gender dynamics. The Great War especially, as Sandra Gilbert concluded for literary critics, profoundly troubled gender constructions and relations. Gilbert's "Soldier's Heart," which first appeared in 1983, chiefly concerns the gender antagonism inspired by the war and its British literary response, because the experience of American combatants was significantly "less extended and less extensive" (269)—though she briefly connects Hemingway three times to this cultural gender antagonism (269, 287, 319).

Gilbert's essay appeared alongside a number of other feminist works in the early 1980s that delved into the relationship between gender and war.[1] This moment occurred contemporaneously with the important initial feminist reconsideration of Hemingway, yet the two critical movements never fully converged. As with Lynn, critics have tended to approach Hemingway through either war or gender. Comley and Scholes mention the war only once, in an introductory comment that was not pursued but that attributes his achievements "in part [to] the abrupt displacement of his youth that forced him to compare the culture of Oak Park with the cultures of Europe and of war" (4). Similarly, Jamie Barlowe's "Hemingway's Gender Training" urges us to continue the work of examining

> the complex web of forces and conditions into which Ernest Hemingway was born and in which he existed. [. . .] As I and others have argued elsewhere, Hemingway offers us a valuable site for studying the contested, fraught, and interesting late nineteenth- and twentieth-century history of gender in the United States, as well as in the other countries where he lived, fought, reported, and wrote. (147–148).

Yet Barlowe only mentions war as contributing to Hemingway's gender training in terms of the Spanish Civil War and World War II as mere backdrops for Hemingway's relationships with Martha Gellhorn and Mary Welsh, his third and fourth wives. Barlowe's short essay cannot include everything, of course, and she concentrates on the women and feminists who touched Hemingway's life. Still, for such an ambitiously titled essay to completely omit his formative war and postwar experience is striking. Discussions of gender and Hemingway can only be illuminated by consideration of Hemingway the veteran.

Man or Nurse?

The mature Hemingway's devotion to the infantry—"nobody has ever been anywhere that hasn't been with Infantry," he wrote to Colonel Charles "Buck" Lanham after returning from World War II (*SL* 586)—stands in stark contrast to the teenager's days driving Red Cross ambulances and delivering postcards, cigarettes, and candy to the Italian infantry. Real men did not join the Red Cross. While Teddy Roosevelt proclaimed in 1917 that "Red Cross work, YMCA work, driving ambulances, and the like, excellent though it all is, should be left to men not of military age or unfit for military service, and to women; young men of vigorous bodies and sound hearts should be left free to do their proper work in the fighting line" (Reynolds, 1986 22–23), war posters clearly depicted Red Cross work as a feminine endeavor. The threat of Red Cross service to a man's male image was widespread and persistent. Over a decade after the war, Dr. Magnus Hirschfeld's quirky *The Sexual History of the World War* (1930) reports how "feminine urnings," or homosexuals,

> evinced a strong disinclination to active [combat] service [. . . and] corresponding to their feminine constitution they desire to be used only for the care of the sick. [. . .] Immediately at the outbreak of the war, numerous homosexuals volunteered their services to the Red Cross, thus obeying the distinctive calling which, as the history of the homosexual problem informs us, urnings performed even among primitive peoples. (137)

The popularity of Hirschfeld's odd book certainly argues for its acceptance and authority in the popular imagination. Hemingway could only be acutely sensitive to the implication of his Red Cross days, could only feel his male self-image undermined by his mode of war service. Whether he worried more about his compromised public image or about his own potentially compromised virility (given the social codes) seems both unknowable and moot. Either way, surrounded by soldiers with real war stories, the young Hemingway began exaggerating his war record while still recovering from his wound in Europe. The nature of both his Red Cross service and his wounding—while delivering cigarettes, postcards, and chocolates to the entrenched Italian infantry—gave him cause to later mislead others about his service, all toward preserving a more manly and heroic image of himself.[2] After Frederic Henry's wounding, the surgeon Rinaldi visits him at the field hospital and jokingly accuses him and the priest of being "a little that way. You know"—by which he means a little homosexual (*AFTA* 65).

I do not intend to simply reiterate Philip Young's argument that Hemingway lived his postwar life asserting his manliness to compensate for the unmanly nature of his wound, much less that these assertions were expression of a deep homophobia. Rather, I want to return his war experiences to critical discussions of how gender is performed in his texts. Hemingway criticism has for so long and productively followed a trajectory away from Young's wound theory and from the war as the principal event of Hemingway's life that, for a feminist and gender studies approach, returning to the war would seem a backwards movement.

In terms of male homosexuality, if Hemingway had little to no awareness of it growing up in Oak Park, Illinois, he certainly learned about it in Europe during the war. A 1953 letter to Charles Poore intimates that while in the hospital in 1918, an Englishman made sexual advances toward him (Brenner 94),[3] and Reynolds confirms that "in Italy, he was propositioned by an older man and tested by a younger one" (1989 33). Hemingway's first published story featuring male homosexuality, "A Simple Enquiry," involves a major and his orderly in the Italian army, the army to which Hemingway was attached. The story appeared in *Men Without Women* in 1927, Hemingway having written it in 1926 and 1927, between *The Sun Also Rises* and *A Farewell to Arms*—the war and postwar experiences, and gender issues, were very much on his mind.[4] If it is only natural that Hemingway foregrounds "gay Paris" in *The Sun Also Rises*, it is just as natural that he suppress any homoeroticism in *A Farewell to Arms*, the novel most closely linked to his own war days and to the image of himself as a soldier, especially given that he already feels a degree of sexual ambiguity about his war service. His first three books, *In Our Time* (1925), *The Sun Also Rises* (1926), and *Men Without Women* (1927), already revealed Hemingway's curiosity about the variety of human genders and sexualities. In *A Farewell to Arms* (1929), Hemingway hides homoeroticism in the least likely place—within the famous heterosexual romance of Frederic Henry and Catherine Barkley.

I should perhaps state here, with Debra A. Moddelmog, that I am not asserting "a gay Hemingway," or even a 'queer' one, but instead am locating "Hemingway's sexual identity in the tension between the homosexual and the heterosexual" (1999 4–7). We can, in other words, discover an overlapping of the purely homosexual and the purely heterosexual encoded in the language and scenes of *A Farewell to Arms*, especially when we read it against his later, more explicitly gender-blurring novel, *The Garden of Eden*. In the process of tentatively proposing a homoerotic element in Frederic and Catherine's relationship, I am also, of course, associating Hemingway's various performances of gender with his war experience.

On the one hand, Catherine's position as nurse seems to confirm the staple wartime fantasy of the nurse as nympho. On the other hand, her position as a Red Cross nurse suggests a certain element of narcissistic mirroring in Frederic's attraction to her, given his own position as an ambulance driver (and Hemingway's as Red Cross volunteer). Catherine's mirroring of Frederic is also reflected in what Margot Norris calls the "echoic structure" of the dialogue whereby Catherine's responses frequently echo Frederic's lines (*AFTA* 68); she is his erotic double in both word and job. According to Moddelmog's summary of the early 20th century Western understanding of homosexuality as pathology, the term *homosexuality* "suggests sex with the same, love of the self" (1996 101). She quotes Michael Warner on this point:

> Having a sexual object of the opposite gender is taken to be the normal and
> paradigmatic form of an interest either in the Other or, more generally, in others.
> That is why in our century it has acquired the name of heterosexuality—a sexuality
> of otherness.... [A]ccording to this logic homoerotics is an unrecognized version
> of autoerotics, or more precisely of narcissism; both are seen as essentially an
> interest in the self rather than in the other.

According to this post-Freudian, post-Victorian modernist logic, Catherine's position as nurse and her echoic dialogue present the potential for a narcissistic homoerotic element in the heterosexual lovers' relationship.

This pair's mirroring, however, has a significant twist. Frederic falls in love with her in Book II only after his wounding, after he has found himself in her care. After, that is, he finds himself in a passive position, which in Hemingway's time was associated with the feminine and, in men, with the homosexual. As the letter to Poore tells us, Hemingway had homosexuality on his mind while in the hospital. Like Catherine, the highly sexual and gender-bending Brett Ashley served as a v.a.d. in the war, and ministers to

Jake Barnes in his hotel bed (Barnes, like Hemingway, can't have the nurse of his fantasies). As a v.a.d., Catherine is also in a position of skill, as Frederic is not. Dr. Valentini, the man who operates on Frederic and restores him to full masculinity, tells Frederic that Catherine is "a lovely girl" who will "make you a fine boy," by which he could mean she will nurse him back to manly health, or that she will bear him a fine son, or perhaps that she will play the role of a fine boy for Frederic, sexually speaking. "I will do all your maternity work free," the doctor offers, addressing not Catherine but the bed-bound, on his back, passive Frederic Henry (99).

The doctor takes his leave of Frederic by declaring that before the operation he "must be washed out" (99), referring to the enema Catherine administers to him prior to his operation. Nothing in the text suggests that he experiences the enema erotically, but still he is penetrated, just as another Catherine will anally penetrate her lover, David Bourne, in *The Garden of Eden*. Both scenes were edited to remove the most direct statements about what is transpiring,[5] yet despite the decorous omission of the word 'enema,' Hemingway still apparently needs to have it occur, just as he needs Catherine to need to do it because only she can touch her lover. The enema itself, however unerotic, nevertheless reinforces Frederic's relative position of passivity to Catherine, a position, in Hemingway's day, considered feminine—and for a man, queer. Even the dialogue between Frederic and Catherine, with his repeatedly calling her his girl—*my good girl, my lovely girl, my fine simple girl* (153)—her repetition of the idea, and the couple's insistence on their oneness intimates the dialogue to come, between Mary and Ernest and Catherine and David, in those future gender-bending, role-reversing love games. (Perhaps not coincidentally, that most exotic exploration of gender in Hemingway that is *The Garden of Eden* was begun in the burst of writing that occurred upon his return from World War II.)

According to this reading of *A Farewell to Arms,* Catherine's death in childbirth exposes the limitations of such male homoerotic projection onto a woman; as a mother, she can no longer be imagined (even subconsciously) into a man. Nancy Huston's argument in "The Matrix of War" that it is mothers, and not women, who are traditionally excluded from becoming warriors (think of Diana, the Amazons, and Joan of Arc), might apply here. If motherhood distinguished between men and women for the purposes of fighting, then a woman who isn't a mother, a woman in uniform, "passes" for a man—in Frederic Henry's case, for a version of himself (and/or his ambulance unit comrades). On the general association of non-mothers with men, Carl Eby summarizes Daniel Rancour-Laferriere's conclusion that "within a phallocentric signifying system [. . .] virgins are traditionally unconsciously regarded as phallic, since defloration is imagined as a symbolic 'castration.'" Eby quotes Rancour-Laferriere: "For a man, it is as if a virgin were another man (note that, in English, 'virgin,' 'virile,' and 'virago' are etymologically related). Not until he has deflowered her has he 'made a woman out of her.'" Eby uses this idea to assert that *For Whom the Bell Toll's* Pilar is "an icon of the phallic woman in her maternal aspect" (45), though I believe we should focus on Pilar's and Catherine's non-maternal status. Motherhood behind the only public evidence of a woman's lost virginity, it becomes, per Huston, the martial disqualifier—and Pilar and Catherine are, of course, every bit the soldiers that Robert Jordan and Frederic Henry respectively are. In *Farewell*, motherhood becomes the homoerotic disqualifier.

Scholars generally credit Europe as the source of Hemingway's discovery of unconventional sexual postures and behaviors during his 1920s Paris expatriation, yet it was in wartime and postwar Europe and Paris where such practices introduced themselves to him, at the very moment he was confronted by the "woman problem" and industrial revolution's challenge to his masculinity back home. Undoubtedly Ernest Hemingway lived through a particular historical moment and participated in its challenges to strict gender and sexual prescriptions, and this historical moment very much involved the war.

The Great War and the Gender War

Beginning with World War I, veterans of 20th century wars have a unique challenge to deal with in the combination of new forms of love—i.e., gender definitions and relations—with new forms of war. In addition to the profound technological changes and the total war strategy of the new warfare, one final distinct aspect of war for 20th century Americans is that it occurred entirely on foreign soil, that in every case it was an *over there* experience which (with some notable exceptions) has excluded American women, so that women and love become associated in the male psyche with a very distant home, the home they left behind and to which they will return, and the home that sent them to war in the first place. The "woman problem" came to a head, and the paradigm of gender confusion in 20th century warfare arose, during the First World War, and Hemingway could not but absorb its lessons.

One historical consensus about World War I is the unprecedented degree to which its soldiers were rendered passive by the new technology of machine guns, indirect fire artillery, and mustard gas. Soldiers rarely had the opportunity to fight the enemy, not in any classic sense in which one's own agency and skill might affect the outcome. Instead, bullets from great distance sprayed them, bombs dropped on them, and gas invaded their lungs, and they were powerless to prevent it. That male sufferers from shell-shock during the Great War were routinely characterized as exhibiting symptoms of hysteria, a purported mental affliction traditionally afflicting only women, reiterates the emasculating (and feminizing) nature of the war. Think of Jake Barnes, and of Sir Clifford Chatterley.

Alongside this disempowerment of the male soldier, this undermining of the very sense of active agency by which manhood in the Western world has long been defined, emerged an empowerment of women both at home and in service relatively near the front. This is the subject of Gilbert's "Soldier's Heart" essay—how in the British male literary response to the Great War, "the unmanning terrors of combat lead not just to a generalized sexual anxiety but also to an anger directed specially against the female" because women did not fight; because they entered the homefront workforce, took financial control over their lives, and loosened conventional gender restrictions on their behavior; and because they remained ignorant of the facts of the front while enthusiastically supporting the war. Women, according to Gilbert, appeared to men to celebrate and enjoy images of the self-sacrificing male soldier so that "the words of woman propagandists as well as the deeds of feather-carrying girls had evidently transformed the classical Roman's noble *patria* into an indifferent or avaricious death-dealing *matria*" (285).

On the personal level of our subject, and setting aside the well-known tensions between Hemingway and his mother, we can read Nick-Ernest's mother as embodying the American version of the Great War's *matria fatale*. My resolution of the false dilemma of reading "Big Two-Hearted River" as a story about either war or the mother but not both sees Nick's mother as inextricably connected with the war. Reynolds quotes a letter that Hemingway's mother wrote him on the occasion of "his nineteenth birthday, as he lay wounded in the Milan hospital." In the letter Grace Hall Hemingway "rejoiced 'to know that in the eyes of humanity my boy is every inch a man. . . . God bless you, my darling. . . . It's great to be the mother of a hero'" (1986 33). The young veteran might very well feel some resentment toward his mother's celebration of the event that nearly killed him, and her characterizing her son as a man and hero because of it sat at odds with his own experience of the event as decidedly unmanly and unheroic—blown up delivering candy and tea to 'real' soldiers.[6] It only makes sense that, to forget the war and its effect upon him during the fishing trip, Nick Adams must also forget his mother. "Don't you love your mother, dear boy?" asks Mrs. Krebs in "Soldier's Home" of her son the veteran. "'No,' Krebs said" (*CSS* 116).

Although written over a decade after the war, "The Short Happy Life of Francis Macomber" offers another possible expression of the male psyche's postwar anxiety of having been figuratively unmanned by the war, coupled with a fear of what Gilbert labels "the deadliness of female [sexual] desire" (291). Having already unmanned her husband by sleeping with their hunting guide, Robert Wilson, did Margot Macomber intentionally kill her husband, as Wilson suspects? Did she intend to shoot the buffalo but, unconsciously perhaps, desire and bring about the death of her husband? Or was the shooting really just an accident? Hemingway leaves the story ambiguous, put perhaps in terms of his own status as a veteran of the Great War the story's final answer is irrelevant. What matters is this veteran's expression of a protagonist first unmanned on a foreign expedition and subsequently killed by his promiscuous wife.

A chain of associations connects Mrs. Macomber with the Great War, specifically with woman-sponsored pro-war propaganda. Margot Macomber was drawn from Jane Mason, and both the fictional and the actual woman appeared in a magazine beauty-product advertisement; that magazine, in Jane Mason's case, was *The Ladies' Home Journal,* a publication which unabashedly supported the war effort in World War I.[7] According to Joanne L. Karetzky's *The Mustering of Support for World War I by The Ladies' Home Journal* (1997), *The Journal* deliberately participated in the transformation of the American public's "traditional isolationism to a new willingness to become actively involved in world affairs"—in, that is, the First World War (1). In January 1917, *The Journal*'s editor, Edward William Bok, met with President Woodrow Wilson to offer his magazine's service in the patriotic cause: "Not only did the President outline *The Journal*'s wartime mission, but Bok credited him with suggesting specific topics as well" (20). Despite its male editorship, the magazine appeared to voice women's encouragement of the war and their menfolk's manly duty to fight. It even printed letters identical in spirit to the one Grace sent her son after learning of his wounding.

For male soldiers and front-line volunteers, like Hemingway, who passively suffered the new technology, the war paradoxically made men of them and unmanned them. Like the soldiers motivated by the same ideology behind *The Ladies' Home Journal,* Francis Macomber goes after the lion to assert his maleness, to defy his woman's challenge of it, and suffers in the extreme. That Wilson is not only a veteran but also a machine-gunner (*CSS* 8, 26), an agent of one of the new mass-casualty technologies, underscores his emasculating effect on Macomber and the story's potential resonance with the Great War. The ambiguity of Margot's volition also resonates with the war; no woman directly wished death on any man in her life, even as her collective message compelled him to be manly and placed him in front of the enemy gun.

I do not claim that Hemingway intentionally wanted us to read "Macomber" as a war story, nor that he consciously associated the Jane Mason advertisement with *The Journal's* pro-war ideology (though it seems plausible enough). But he most decidedly had the war on his mind while finishing the story in early 1936, as evidenced textually by Wilson's past and contextually by contemporary events. Only a few months earlier, Hemingway had joined some two hundred volunteers to help clean up the over six hundred bodies of World War I veterans killed during a hurricane that overswept their makeshift camps in the Florida Keys. Later that month, September 1935, Hemingway's article "Who Murdered the Vets?" appeared in *New Masses*, and his "Notes on the Next War" appeared in *Esquire*. Memories of the past war with Germany and talk of the next one were significant presences during the composition of "Macomber."

War, Marriage, and Childbirth

Writes Judith Fetterley in 1978 about *A Farewell to Arms:*

> If we weep reading the book at the death of soldiers, we are weeping for the tragic and senseless waste of their lives; we are weeping for them. If we weep at the end of the book, however, it is not for Catherine but for Frederic Henry. All our tears are ultimately for men, because, in the world of *A Farewell to Arms* male life is what counts. And the message to women reading this classic love story is clear and simple: the only good woman is a dead one, and even then there are questions. (71)

Fetterley's book arrived during the salad days of feminist literary criticism, and the deep misogyny she finds in Hemingway has since been somewhat ameliorated in the criticism. One still finds, however, such antagonistic assertions as Margaret Higonnet's, that Hemingway's image of soldiers appearing pregnant when "protecting their cartridges under their capes" in *A Farewell to Arms* is an "aggressive masculinist metaphor" (215) that wrongly appropriates feminine imagery. Following Nancy Huston, who essentially argues that men turn to hunting and soldiering out of venus envy, Jennifer

Haytock's recent essay in this journal concludes that the novel's opening imagery symbolizes how the "soldiers will give birth not to a living being but to violence and death" (70).

Images and talk of pregnancy, childbirth, and marriage in Hemingway have received much critical attention. As generally interpreted, they indicate Hemingway's male characters' fear of losing independence, freedom, and the pleasures of male camaraderie—their refusal, in other words, to grow up and accept adult responsibilities. I would like to suggest that these images and this discourse can also be directly linked to war.

One way to read the scene of the soldiers marching with "the two leather cartridge boxes on the front of their belts, gray leather boxes heavy with the packs of clips of thin, long, 6.5 mm. cartridges, bulged forward under the capes so that the men, passing on the road, marched as though they were six months gone with child" (4), is as an expression of their experiencing the military and war as emasculating and thus feminizing insofar as the soldier's losing agency. His story becomes one of "being done to," to use Samuel Hynes' phrase in his book *The Soldiers' Tale*, with its apt subtitle, *Bearing Witness to Modern War* (3; emphasis added). The male soldier is "done to" not only by the enemy and by the new technology, he also becomes an instrument for and an object of the warmakers on his own side, a victim bearing the burden for empowered others, as the image depicts. Here Reynolds summarized Hemingway's experience of childbirth through 1922:

> Hemingway grew up with an unusual awareness of a woman's painful and bloody birthing process. Early, before he understood sex and death, he was marked by birth's pain and its accompanying screams. His mother, Grace, continued bearing children until she was forty-three and he was fifteen; at age eleven, Ernest was present when Grace bore his sister Carol at the summer cottage. His father specialized in obstetrics in his home office; all his early life Ernest lived in the presence of pregnant women who carried the secret and suffered the pain. That woman [he saw] birthing on the Adrianople road brought it all back to him, the mystery and the pain. Nowhere in his later fiction would babies ease gently into this world. (1989 77)

To depict a soldier six months gone with child, then, is hardly an envious appropriation of the feminine, hardly a male soldier's empowerment through violence; it is instead a rendering of the man's position as soldier as one of severe suffering—of the suffering to come as their metaphoric burden approaches term in range of the enemy's guns.

If pregnancy and childbirth for women signify and embody their social bonds, military service signifies a man's social bonds. Paradoxically, military service—and especially for American men headed to the Great War—serves as a liberation from domestic, economic, and social obligations, and a reassertion of manly autonomy, but also as the ultimate tie to society, one that demands the selfless sacrifice of the individual for society. If, as Nina Baym and other feminist scholars have maintained, woman for the male psyche represents social integration, responsibility, and self-sacrifice for community (through marriage),[8] then she also embodies that very social contract which got him to the battlefield—a symbolic fact which, again, must affect his relations with her. War poster after war poster depicted women (and children) as the motivating spirit calling the soldiers to arms; the woman figure was often draped in the American flag. In the foreground of a 1918 poster from the Liberty Loan Committee of Washington, troops in various uniforms bearing their rifles with bayonets fixed at port arms march toward the viewer, and above them the image of a mother holding a child merges into the American flag.[9] Another poster features such a female figure pointing to a roll call of dead soldiers. But for two transposed letters, *marital* and *martial* are the same word.

Thus Nick Adams in "Night Before Landing," on a ship on his way to war, discusses marriage, and the story ends the night before landing with Nick's pronouncement about his girl, "We're going to get married" (*NAS* 142). In "Now I Lay Me," Nick in a tent during the war remembers his wounding and fights sleep to fight death, the story concluding with his conversation with another soldier, again, about marriage. And in that originating Nick Adams story, "Indian Camp," the young Nick associates childbirth with the husband's death and with a crippling leg injury similar enough to Hemingway's own war wound; to the degree that Hemingway volunteered for ambulance duty, his wound too, like the Indian husband's wound and subsequent death, was self-inflicted. Frederic Henry too conceives a child with Catherine Barkley on his hospital bed, once again suggesting an association between fatherhood and war wounds.

"Rather than being a study in war, love or initiation," wrote Michael Reynolds in *Hemingway's First War: The Making of A Farewell to Arms,* the novel "is more properly a study in isolation. Frederic's progression in the novel is from group participation to total isolation" (271). Nick Adams' solo journey in "Big Two-Hearted River" portrays another veteran seeking escape from social allegiance. For an American male to escape war, he must escape social ties. He must, like Harold Krebs and Frederic Henry, desire to relinquish love. Elsewhere Reynolds reports on a correspondence between Owen Wister, the father of the Western genre, and Hemingway's editor Max Perkins. *Farewell's* "flaw," as Reynolds paraphrases Perkins, "is that the war story and the love story do not combine. [. . .] If only the war were in some way responsible for the nurse's death in childbirth" (1997 4–5). The war, I contend, is entirely responsible. Catherine Barkley and the baby both must die at the end of *A Farewell to Arms* not because "for Hemingway the only good woman is a dead one" as Fetterley argues (71), but because for Frederic Henry to have a final farewell to arms, he must lose all obligatory social ties, must escape the social contract embodied in wife and child, just as in an older American tale, Rip Van Winkle escapes his henpecking wife and, simultaneously and ironically, the Revolutionary War.

Another source, then, for a misogynist or misogamist strain in Hemingway and in other veterans is this symbolic association of women and wives with society and therefore as the cause for the soldier's wartime suffering. The association of children with social responsibility also contributes to a misopedist strain, so that the presence of childbirth in Hemingway's war stories signifies what sends the male soldier to war as well as what the emasculated soldier must bear during war. Publications like *The Ladies' Home Journal* and posters and articles exhorting men to defend their homes, their women and children, reinforce the association. The male soldier, especially during World War I, finds himself—to use a literary metaphor from World War

II—in a Catch-22. To escape the emasculating nature of the industrializing, bureaucratic new 20th century world, he escapes in literature to the Western frontier and to Tarzan's Africa, and in life to the war—but the military and the war actually subvert the possibility for autonomous agency and self-definition. One is subject to the desires of the chain of command, and subjected to the guns of the enemy. One is bound to the military family as well as to the social family which the military serves. Hemingway, with his ambiguous soldierly status and his wounding, with his confrontation with male homosexuality and the dissolution of women's gender roles and prescriptions, hardly discovers in war a buttress for his masculine sense of self.

Conclusion

I conclude this study on war and gender in Hemingway with a discussion of two related stories rarely commented upon as war stories, "Cross-Country Snow" and "An Alpine Idyll." The first story appeared in *In Our Time;* the second in *Men Without Women.* Both stories, to quote Joseph Flora on "Cross-Country Snow," move "from action to dialogue, from outdoors to indoors" (192). Both stories also invite us to ask questions about the two main male characters' attitudes toward women—in the first case, to a pregnant waitress and Nick's pregnant wife, and in the second case to a local man's dead wife.

For Shelley Fisher Fishkin, "Cross-Country Snow" is very much a war story, or rather a postwar story:

It is only after Nick has confronted death and pain firsthand in the war that he can truly appreciate the miracle of that which is peaceful and beautiful and good in life. It is significant that "Cross-Country Snow," an idyll permeated by friendship, trust, and exhilaration with living, is placed after the chapters dealing with the war. It is not an innocent's idyll. It is a reverie of two men fully aware of the impermanence of life, and thus the value of the present; of two men familiar with the world's imperfections savoring the perfect moment.

[...] One must confront a world of chaos and war to understand the value of order and peace. (152)

My reading of the relationship between war and pregnancy works well with Fishkin, because the pregnancy of the waitress and Nick's wife Helen suggests the impermanence not of undomesticated male camaraderie, but of the world at peace and of the male citizen's respite from his social obligation as a soldier. The other story, "An Alpine Idyll," reiterates this message through the presence of the local man with the dead wife, as the man happens to be a veteran of the Great War.

The idylls of both stories remain a Swiss ski trip, but they also imply a larger idyll, the one between the wars. Though Hemingway wrote the stories in the 1920s, he was fully aware that the First World War had satisfactorily solved nothing, and that another war was likely. Writing in hindsight, Paul Fussell in *The Great War and Modern Memory* reminds us of the historical continuity between the wars, as essentially the same event separated only by a generation. Fussell's seventh chapter, "Arcadian Recourses," offers an interesting interpretive strategy for "Cross-Country Snow" and "An Alpine Idyll." In that chapter Fussell describes how narratives of the Great War often have a seemingly standardized inclusion of "pastoral oases," moments of pause between the fighting, moments of peace. In British texts such pastoral reference "is a way of invoking a code to hint by antithesis at the indescribable," at the war; "at the same time, it is a comfort in itself" (235–236).[10]

Using an essay by Erwin Panofsky, Fussell explores the English tradition of the *memento mori*, of for example juxtaposing skulls among pastoral roses "as an emblem of the omnipotence of Death, whose power is not finally to be excluded even from the sequestered, 'safe' world of pastoral," a tradition which adds "a special resonance of melancholy to wartime pastoral." This tradition understands the classical line *Et in arcadia ego* as "Even in Arcadia I, Death, hold sway" (246)—an apt epigraph for "An Alpine Idyll," which provides a *memento mori* in the figure of the local veteran's dead wife, and the image of her husband Olz hanging his lantern from her mouth, frozen in rigor mortis, when he needed to cut wood in the shed where he stored her until the snow cleared and he could bring her to town. The two Hemingway stories are idylls, pastoral oases between the world wars, but ones in which war and death also hold sway, reminding us of such idyll's transience.

If the unnamed narrator of "An Alpine Idyll" is Nick Adams, then the story offers us a sympathetic position toward a fellow veteran, Olz, a man alone and utterly misunderstood by his own community. Several times the innkeeper refers to Olz as a beast, while the narrator and John hardly blanch at Olz's tale because veterans of the Great War's Western Front wouldn't. If Hemingway did not experience in Italy the horrible conditions of trench life on the Western Front, we can safely assume that he would have known about them from storytelling veteran friends and strangers, and from his reading. It was not rare for corpses, unable to be removed for any number of reasons (bad weather being one), to linger in the trenches for some time. And not only linger, but be used. Where duckboards ran short, soldiers walked on corpses to keep their boots out of the standing water and mud. Where trench walls threatened to collapse, corpses were used to buttress them until better materials could be brought forward. For the millions of troops who over the course of four years lived such a life with corpses, it would not be difficult to imagine a corpse as the best place for hanging a lantern for lighting a nighttime task—and most work in the trenches took place at night. Soldiers living so much around corpses soon enough become inured to their presence; they learned to separate the person they knew from the heap of flesh now holding up sandbags, a necessary separation that helped distance them emotionally from lost friends and psychically from their own too-vulnerable bodies. The narrator and John, read as veterans, would not give Olz's tale a second thought.

The character whom the narrator and John (read as veterans) would most dislike is the innkeeper, the civilian who didn't go to the war, living in a country that didn't go to war, the civilian who so misunderstands trench life that he considers it "beastly." Fussell and others have remarked on the intense aversion for civilians—indeed for anyone not at the front line—felt by soldiers of the First World War—for not suffering, for not understanding, for allowing the inhumanity to continue. The grotesque part of Hemingway's story isn't what Olz does with his wife's corpse, but the innkeeper's reaction, or rather his failure to appreciate the veteran's life. The presence of women in both "Cross-Country Snow" and "An Alpine Idyll" keeps us aware of the past war and warns us of the next one. The dead woman in "An Alpine Idyll," instead of supporting the argument that the only good woman for Hemingway is a dead one, underscores the passive, suffering, 'feminine' nature of soldiering in World War I, and in effect shows us a veteran, Olz, who treats his wife's body exactly as he might have treated a male comrade's in the European trenches.

While Hemingway's warring and wounding are an essential element of the man he afterward became, to ascribe anyone's complex gender sensibilities to a single factor, such as wartime experience, would be to commit a serious critical oversight. In the case of Ernest Hemingway, so many other factors contribute: the general crisis of manhood and the vexing "woman problem" of the beginning of the 20th century; Hemingway's boyhood spent mostly among sisters and under the example of his independently-minded suffragette mother and his rather domesticated and mentally troubled father; the conventional morality and gender ideas of his Midwest, middle-class upbringing in Oak Park, Illinois; the heritage of nineteenth century self-reliant frontier manliness, of which Theodore Roosevelt was the last great champion; the heritage of 19th century literary gender constructions in some American but primarily in Victorian novels written by both men and women; and the sexual psychology of the day, as chiefly professed by Havelock Ellis, whom Hemingway read.

But we cannot afford, if we want to understand Hemingway's gender troubles, to ignore the war's impact. Judith Fetterley has asserted that "war simplifies men's relation to women" (49). I disagree. War simplifies nothing; it complicates everything.

NOTES

1. 1982: Jean Bethke Elshtain's "Women as Mirror and Other: Toward a Theory of Woman, War, and Feminism" and Nancy Huston's "Tales of War and Tears of Women." 1983: Sandra Gilbert's "Soldier's Heart: Literary Men, Literary Women, and the Great War," Cynthia Enloe's "Does Khaki Become You? The Militarization of Women's Lives." 1984: Nancy C. Harsock's "Prologue to a Feminist Critique of War and Politics."

2. Reynolds doubts that Hemingway's heroic carrying of a wounded Italian soldier while he was himself wounded ever happened (1986 18–21).

3. One of the purposes of Brenner's essay is to present the lack of convincing evidence of James Gamble's homosexuality—though if Brenner is incorrect, Gamble's position as Hemingway's Red Cross commander reinforces the association of the Red Cross with homosexuality, and Hemingway's exposure to homosexuality during the war.

4. In *The Sun Also Rises,* Bill Gorton says the Civil War was about homosexuality. "Abraham Lincoln was a faggot. He was in love with General Grant. So was Jefferson Davis" (121).

5. See Moddelmog on *Garden* (1996 98); Norris on *Farewell* (67).

6. Hemingway was perhaps (if unconsciously) responding to his mother in *Farewell* when he has various characters talk to Frederic Henry as if he were a little boy: "Be a good boy" (98), "You're such a silly boy" (102), "you sleep like a little boy" (104).

7. Hemingway had the clipped ad in his files (Reynolds, 1997 224).

8. Baym's "Melodramas of Beset Manhood." See also Laura Mulvey's idea of the "split hero" motif in the Western film genre in *Visual and Other Pleasures.*

9. Used by permission of The Provincial Museum of Alberta, with grateful thanks to Maurice F.V. Doll, Curator of Government and Military History. Visit the museum's on-line exhibit at "The Poster War: Allied Propaganda Art of the First World War" (© 1999) http://www.pma.edmonton.ab.ca/vexhibit/warpost/english/post29.htm.

10. Irwin Shaw's 1948 WWII novel *The Young Lions* begins before the war, in 1938, at a ski hotel in the Austrian mountains, where a young American woman's idyll is shattered when a young Nazi soldier attempts to rape her.

WORKS CITED

Barlowe, Jamie. "Hemingway's Gender Training." In *A Historical Guide to Ernest Hemingway.* Ed. Linda Wagner-Martin, 117–153. New York: Oxford UP, 2000.

Baym, Nina. "Melodramas of Beset Manhood: How Theories of American Fiction Exclude Women Authors." In *The New Feminist Criticism: Essays on Women, Literature, and Theory.* Ed. Elaine Showalter, 63–80. New York: Pantheon, 1985.

Brenner, Gerry. "'Enough of a Bad Gamble': Correcting the Misinformation on Hemingway's Captain James Gamble." *The Hemingway Review* 20.1 (Fall 2000): 90–96.

Comley, Nancy R., and Robert Scholes. *Hemingway's Genders: Rereading the Hemingway Text.* New Haven: Yale UP, 1994.

Eby, Carl P. *Hemingway's Fetishism: Psychoanalysis and the Mirror of Manhood.* Albany: SUNY, 1999.

Fetterley, Judith. *The Resisting Reader: A Feminist Approach to American Fiction.* Bloomington: Indiana UP, 1978.

Fishkin, Shelley Fisher. *From Fact to Fiction: Journalism & Imaginative Writing in America.* New York: Oxford UP, 1985.

Flora, Joseph M. *Hemingway's Nick Adams.* Baton Rouge: Louisiana State UP, 1982.

Fussell, Paul. *The Great War and Modern Memory.* New York: Oxford UP, 1975.

Gilbert, Sandra M. "Soldier's Heart: Literary Men, Literary Women, and the Great War." In *No Man's Land: The Place of the Woman Writer in the Twentieth Century,* vol. 2: *Sexchanges.* Sandra M. Gilbert and Susan Gubar, 258–323. New Haven: Yale UP, 1988.

Haytock, Jennifer. "Hemingway's Soldiers and their Pregnant Women: Domestic Ritual in World War I." *The Hemingway Review* 19.2 (Spring 2000): 57–72.

Hemingway, Ernest. *The Complete Short Stories of Ernest Hemingway: The Finca Vigía Edition.* New York: Simon and Schuster, 1987.

———. *Ernest Hemingway: Selected Letters, 1917–1961.* Ed. Carlos Baker. New York: Scribner's, 1981.

———. *A Farewell to Arms.* New York: Scribner's, 1929.

———. *The Nick Adams Stories.* Preface by Philip Young. New York: Scribner's, 1972.

————. *The Sun Also Rises.* New York: Scribner's, 1926.

————, ed. *Men at War: The Best War Stories of All Time.* New York: Crown, 1942.

Hirschfeld, Magnus. *The Sexual History of the World War.* New York: Falstaff Press, 1937.

Huston, Nancy. "The Matrix of War: Mothers and Heroes." In *The Female Body in Western Culture.* Ed. Susan Rubin Suleiman, 119–136. Cambridge: Harvard UP, 1986.

Hynes, Samuel. *The Soldier's Tale: Bearing Witness to Modern War.* New York: Penguin, 1997.

Karetzky, Joanne. *The Mustering of Support for World War I by The Ladies Home Journal.* Lewiston: Edwin Mellen, 1997.

Lynn, Kenneth S. *Hemingway.* New York: Simon and Schuster, 1987.

Moddelmog, Debra A. "Protecting the Hemingway Myth: Casting Out of Forbidden Desires from *The Garden of Eden.*" In *Prospectus: An Annual of American Cultural Studies* 21. Ed. Jack Salzman, 89–122. Cambridge: Cambridge UP, 1996.

————. *Reading Desire: In Pursuit of Ernest Hemingway.* Ithaca: Cornell UP, 1999.

Mulvey, Laura. *Visual and Other Pleasures.* Basingstoke: Macmillan, 1989.

Norris, Margot. *Writing War in the Twentieth Century.* Charlottesville: U of Virginia P, 2000.

Reynolds, Michael. *Hemingway's First War: The Making of* A Farewell to Arms. Princeton, NJ: Princeton UP, 1976.

————. *The Young Hemingway.* New York: W.W. Norton, 1986.

————. *Hemingway: The Paris Years.* New York: W.W. Norton, 1989.

————. *Hemingway: The 1930s.* New York: W.W. Norton, 1997.

Stewart, Matthew C. "Ernest Hemingway and World War I: Combatting Recent Psychobiographical Reassessments, Restoring the War." *PLL: Papers on Language and Literature* 36.2 (Spring 2000): 198–217.

Hemingway's Soldiers and Their Pregnant Women

Domestic Ritual in World War I

Jennifer A. Haytock

The connection between the world of the domestic and that of war has seldom been explored. Yet the structure of the two kinds of experience is remarkably similar: both are marked by a need for ritual to keep chaos in check. If, as Ann Romines suggests, the housekeeper cleans to keep nature under control and to gain a sense of power within her confined life, the soldier sets up his own rituals to keep the random forces of death at bay. Technological advances made during World War I in particular shocked soldiers with the randomness and impersonality of their violence; shells and gas appeared with no apparent connection to an identifiable enemy. While the domestic world is inhabited by two sexes, the military world

Reprinted with permission from *The Hemingway Review* 19.2 (Spring 2000). Copyright © 2000 The Ernest Hemingway Foundation. Published by the University of Idaho, Moscow, Idaho.

■ 115

has historically been inhabited, theoretically, by only one. Therefore, in the military men have taken on such traditionally female tasks as cooking, nursing, and even homemaking—the imbuing of a space with emotional significance. And, of course, the world of war has often included women, whether they are prostitutes, refugees, volunteers, or nurses.

This essay addressed two issues: Hemingway's use of domestic ritual in his writings about World War I, and the relationships in those texts between soldiers and pregnant women. To explore these issues I will use two related but different frameworks. Ann Romines' *The Home Plot: Women, Writing, and Domestic Ritual* explains the significance of domestic ritual in literature, a presence that might be overlooked by readers not trained to see it. Nancy Huston's "The Matrix of War" discusses the relationship between war and childbirth; she explores the anthropological and mythological connections between the two. While feminist critics have demonstrated the importance of female domestic writers within the body of American literature, few critics have examined domesticity and its significance in works by male writers. Using the work of Romines and Huston directs attention toward elements less fully explored in Hemingway's writing, especially the tension and attraction to domesticity in his works about World War I.

Romines locates the origins of domestic writing in works by Sarah Orne Jewett, Mary Wilkins Freeman, and other nineteenth-century American writers and explores its significance in works by Willa Cather and Eudora Welty. She defines domestic rituals as those "performed in a house"; these rituals are marked by regular recurrence, emotional significance, group bonding, and symbolic meaning (12). Domestic ritual, Romines argues, fights nature's power to decay; it is women's way of taking control of their lives. Part of the importance of domestic writing lies in the connections it shows between the home and the public sphere; women's work and their attitudes toward it reveal the nature of broader social forces that create the home and that the home in turn reproduces.

Huston's essay "The Matrix of War" provides a framework for exploring relationships among men, women, and war. She explains that "the symbolic equivalence between childbirth and war might be said to be one of the rare constants of human culture" even as she acknowledges that the experiences "have traditionally been perceived as mutually exclusive" (127). Huston examines a variety of myths and rituals to argue that while women, mothers in particular, are excluded from the realms of hunting and combat, the glory men achieve on the battlefield is described in terms similar to those describing the pain women experience in childbirth.[1] She uses the term "reciprocal metaphorization" to describe the back and forth linkage between depictions of fighting and those of childbearing (131). That is, the language used to describe one of those experiences is also used to describe the other. Even though Huston argues that it is women's ability to have children that causes men to fight, the term reciprocal metaphorization tends to imply a lack of cause and effect. From Huston's work it appears that the ways in which the two activities have been discussed deny a causal relationship. Rather, ideas about war and childbirth circle each other, taking on different meanings as one or the other takes on different symbolic significance.

Hemingway's *In Our Time* (1925) foregrounds male experience before, during, and after World War I, but domesticity, imaged in part by pregnant women, forms the necessary context for this experience. Critics have suggested various strategies for understanding the relationship of the stories to the interchapters; Jackson J. Benson, for example, points out repeated images of violence, screams, sex, birth, and death in the collection. Similarly, Richard Hasbany argues that *In Our Time* is united by the techniques of imagism: a focus on words and images that leads to an interplay between those images. I believe that awareness of the domestic images—those of eating, cooking, childbirth, and relationships—can lead to an understanding of both the disruptions and continuities that thread the pieces of *In Our Time*. For example, in the opening story, "On the Quai at Smyrna," the narrator comments on the women giving birth, in particular on the women whose babies died. "You couldn't get the women to give up their dead babies. They'd have babies dead for six days" (*IOT* 12). The dead babies both reflect the destruction of the present and suggest darkness in the future. Yet while masculine concerns with war and military occupation fill the consciousness of the narrator, the women are moving forward with life apart from the war. Wayne B. Stengel points out that

> Ultimately, it is [the narrator's] isolated vision of childbirth that undermines the complete devastation of this refugee encampment and yet makes it doubly grisly. Something still lives or struggles to live amidst this masculine vision of destruction. Throughout *In Our Time*, one male voice attempts to cover, evade, or effect these views of female fecundity. (90)

This story establishes a context through with which men view pregnant women throughout the rest of the collection, as these women signify men's loss of control amidst chaos and violence. *In Our Time* only marginally touches on the actual fighting of World War I; in fact the war is much less present than the domestic world. The text offers glimpses of war in the early interchapters, and at the same time some of these interchapters describe domesticity and its disruptions at the front. For example, in Chapter I the narrator is the kitchen corporal, and he describes how "the adjutant kept riding up alongside my kitchen and saying, 'You must put it out. It is dangerous. It will be observed.' We were fifty kilometers from the front but the adjutant worried about the fire in my kitchen" (13). Here, domestic tools have become a source of danger for soldiers. In the same chapter, "women and kids were in the carts crouched with mattresses, mirrors, sewing machines, bundles. There was a woman having a kid with a young girl holding a blanket over her and crying" (21). The evacuation has displaced the home and domestic activities; by Chapter VI, when Nick is wounded, the home is physically destroyed: "The pink wall of the house opposite had fallen out from the roof, and an iron bedstead hung twisted toward the street. Two Austrian dead lay in the rubble in the shade of the house" (63). In Chapter VII, Nick mocks domesticity by going upstairs with a prostitute. After Chapter IX, the war and the domestic disappear from the interchapters entirely, replaced by the bullfighting vignettes. But the early interchapters remain images that are juxtaposed with and against the stories.

The stories of *In Our Time* show domestic life to be, at least for men, entrapping and stifling. In "The Doctor and the Doctor's Wife," the wife is a passive-aggressive woman who controls her entire house with her sighs of pain and her penetrating voice that traps the doctor in conversations he does not wish to have. He and his son feel the need to escape his wife's control by retreating outdoors. In "The End of Something," Marjorie represents domesticity by bringing the blanket and the picnic food; later in "The Three-Day Blow" Bill tells Nick how lucky he is to escape marriage with Marjorie: "Once a man's married he's absolutely bitched. . . . He hasn't got anything more. Nothing. Not a damn thing. He's done for" (47). He claims Nick would have to marry Marjorie's whole family: "Imagine having them around the house all the time and going to Sunday dinners at their house, and having them over to dinner and [Marjorie's mother] telling Marge all the time what to do and how to act" (47). Bill imagines domestic life to be entrapping, for Nick and for Marjorie.

But despite Nick's experience of his parents' unhappy marriage, Bill's image of Marjorie and domestic life is not necessarily Nick's. In "'Nothing Was Ever Lost': Another Look at 'The Marge Business,'" H. R. Stoneback argues that Marjorie displays great dignity in response to Nick's rejection and that Nick feels her loss profoundly. Linda Wagner comments that Marjorie has already achieved the "semi-stoic self awareness which Hemingway's men have, usually, yet to attain" (63). Indeed, Marjorie is competent in outdoor activities, not merely domestic ones: she rows the boat, sets up fishing lines, and cleans fish. And despite Nick's claim that "I've taught you everything," he now feels that "you know everything. That's the trouble" (*IOT* 34). He has nothing further to teach her and thus the relationship is no longer "fun." While at first he may have been drawn to Marjorie's difference from his mother, he comes to feel that her competence in both indoor and outdoor matters leaves him with no role, and thus, like his father, he is powerless in the relationship. At the end of "The Three-Day Blow" Nick is comforted by the thought that he and Marjorie might get back together; subsequent stories, however, reveal that this does not happen. The brush with domesticity proves to be both comforting and frustrating for Nick.

After the war, the home becomes even more a structure of confinement and disorientation. As Stengel argues, "'Soldier's Home' . . . is one of the central stories in American literature about shell-shocked return to false domestic tranquility by an aesthetic sensibility that has deeply confused the rites of war and American gamesmanship with how to avoid feminine control" (93). Krebs' mother has received harsh treatment from critics, who claim that her religious mania and her selfish love prevent her from understanding the needs of her son; Robert Paul Lamb, for example, points to "scenes that seem to demonstrate Mrs. Krebs' unsuitability as a mother" (25). Yet if Mrs. Krebs is, for Harold, a confining force, that role is not her fault. She knows about war, she says, from her father's experience in the Civil War, and if, as is the case, this knowledge is irrelevant to the events of World War I, she is no more ignorant of the horrors of technological warfare than were most soldiers when they went to war. She tries to reach out to her son: she cooks his breakfast, a gesture of love even if linked to demands that cause Krebs' feelings of guilt; she runs interference with his father to get him access to the car. Further, she is aware that she cannot understand her son. When Krebs apologizes for saying he does not love her, she responds with a choky "all right" (*IOT* 76); although she says she believes him, her "all right" indicates a willingness to allow the fiction that she believes him rather than expresses true belief.

Lamb argues that the story has a "larger cultural significance" (29) than simply the mother-son relationship. He discussed Krebs' reaction to the girls at home who have changed during his absence and the social "anxieties, pervasive by the mid-1920s, that the American family . . . was on the verge of collapse" (31). But it is important to connect the two phenomena. While Mrs. Krebs recognizes changes in her son, she has also seen changes in the young women about her. If she has spent her life defining herself as a wife and mother, she may feel threatened by the bobbed hair and apparent sexual promiscuity the young women exhibit. The foundations of her domestic life have been rocked by changes that occurred in the States while Harold was being changed by the war. Social change as well as the war have separated mother and son.

For soldiers who lost their sense of autonomy during the war, pregnant women add to and complicate an already-present fear of powerlessness. As a soldier in World War I, Nick discovers his lack of control over the future; the violence of war refuses logic. And for Nick, whose first experience with childbirth in "Indian Camp" involves the death of the father, Helen's pregnancy must also signify a threat to himself. Further, the figure of the pregnant woman invokes fear of the loss of (male) independence, especially through memories of the controlling mother; the domineering and manipulative Mrs. Adams is the figure against which both Nick and his father assert their independence in "The Doctor and the Doctor's Wife." The narrative style of *In Our Time* forces the reader to place Helen's pregnancy against the background of the first story; images of pregnant women on the pier in Chapter 1, juxtaposed with Nick's memories of childhood, suggest that pregnancy involves violence, for the father and for the soldier.

How the father and soldier handle such insecurity and threat of violence is integral to the stories of *In Our Time;* the pregnant woman requires her husband to reconcile anxiety about the future with a loss of control. On the illegal fishing trip in "Out of Season" the young, possibly pregnant wife[2] taunts her husband, "Of course you haven't got the guts to just go back" (100); she herself leaves and in so doing forces her husband to consider the consequences of his actions. She demands that he re-evaluate his definition of manhood, because what is masculine in a single, childless man is no longer masculine in a man with children to provide for. As a prospective father, he cannot risk breaking the law and spending time in jail. For Nick, too, pregnancy requires that he face a loss of personal autonomy. George asks, "It's hell, isn't it?" (111), referring to the upcoming changes in Nick's life. Nick, however, answers, "No. Not exactly" (111). Although his later remarks convey his expectation of reduced independence, he seems to have found some compensations in Helen's pregnancy, such as the satisfaction of love and family. Perhaps these compensations also take the form of Nick's relief at not having been rendered impotent during the war (luckily avoiding the fate of Jake Barnes). In this case, pregnancy has the power to affirm manhood. As David J. Ferrero argues, Nick does not rebel against Helen and the baby but accepts his upcoming fatherhood with an understandable sadness at the loss of his more carefree youth (26). Significantly, Helen also apparently has mixed feelings about the pregnancy and the changes the baby will cause, suggesting that anxiety about the future produced by pregnancy is not limited to men.

If homes with women are fraught with tension, homes without them seem, on the surface, to be an attractive alternative. In "The Three-Day Blow," Nick and Bill fall into a domestic routine in which Nick warms his feet while Bill brings him dry socks. The house, occupied by only Bill and his father, is a retreat for Nick, who sometimes sleeps there too. In "The Battler," Nick stumbles into an outdoor domestic setting, where the former fighter and his friend have set up camp. The dinner Bugs cooks is described in detail: "Into the skillet he was laying slices of ham. As the skillet grew hot the grease sputtered and Bugs . . . turned the ham and broke the eggs into the skillet, tipping it from side to side to baste the eggs with the hot fat" (*IOT* 57). After Ad Francis tries to attack Nick, Bugs asks Nick to leave, in the politest terms: "I wish we could ask you to stay the night but it's just out of the question. Would you like to take some of that ham and some bread with you?" (62). The homeless men have their own system of domesticity and hospitality. In "Cross-Country Snow," George daydreams about getting away from a settled life:

> "Gee, Mike, don't you wish we could just bum together? Take our skis and go on the train to where there was good running and then go and put up at pubs and go right across the Oberland and up the Valais and all through the Engadine and just take repair kits and extra sweaters and pyjamas in our rucksacks and not give a damn about school or anything." (*IOT* 110)

He wishes to trade in home for pubs and replace entrapping domestic accoutrements with "repair kits and extra sweaters and pyjamas." This desire for male mobility, however, does not seem to appeal to Nick. Underneath the above scenes of male domesticity lies a sense of impermanence, tension, and unfulfillment.

Instead, "Big Two-Hearted River" shows Nick's desire for a solitary male home. He sets up his camp with detailed care:

> Already there was something mysterious and homelike. Nick was happy as he crawled inside the tent. He had not been unhappy all day. This was different though. Now things were done. There had been this to do. Now it was done. . . . He had made his camp. He was settled. Nothing could touch him. It was a good place to camp. He was there, in the good place. He was in his home where he had made it. (*IOT* 139)

Nick does not like being unsettled; the need to set up the camp had been hanging over him. Once the camp is made, however, he is safe within his own handiwork, responsible to no one else within his own domestic sphere. The description of his cooking, like that in "The Battler," is detailed and extensive, telling what he cooks and how he cooks it. In his mind he runs over an argument he once had with a friend about the best way to make coffee. The rituals of domesticity have a soothing power, whether the actions are performed by men or by women; in this way *In Our Time* shows the arbitrary nature of the assignment of gender roles and the constriction caused by social enforcement of female-centered domesticity.

While *In Our Time* ends with isolated male domesticity, *A Farewell to Arms* works in the other direction, from male domesticity to restructuring domestic heterosexual relationships in the context of World War I. In the time between writing the two works, Hemingway left his first wife, Hadley Richardson, and married Pauline Pfeiffer; for Hemingway, Pauline's dangerous pregnancy and Caesarean delivery as well as guilt at abandoning Hadley were prominent issues. *A Farewell to Arms* shows a domesticity beset by outside forces rather than by individual suffocation as in *In Our Time*. The later novel also focuses more on World War I itself; thus domesticity and domestic ritual at the front stand in comparison to his treatment of domesticity behind the lines of battle.

A Farewell to Arms emphasizes the importance of home places. As Frederic Henry travels from station to station and from the front during the retreat, he often describes houses, and the military and medical personnel are quartered in the houses of evacuated citizens. He enjoys "a house in Gorizia that had a fountain and many thick shady trees in a walled garden and a wisteria vine" (5). He is pleased too that "the Austrians seemed to want to come back to the town some time, if the war should end, because they did not bombard it to destroy it but only a little in a military way" (5). During his scenic drive to the front, too, Frederic notices damaged homes, the "broken houses of the little town that was to be taken" (45). During the retreat, Frederic pays attention to the farmhouses they pass, and he protects one house from looting by the two sergeants one of the drivers has picked up. As they leave, he looks back: "It was a fine, low, solid stone house and the ironwork of the well was very good" (*AFTA* 202). Noticeably, Frederic does not comment on the people who must have lived in these houses or on their fates. It is the shell of the domestic world that he sees, not the soul.

The novel does, however, evoke the central issues of domesticity by describing the ritual of eating in great detail. The text often mentions specifically what the characters eat and how they eat it; during dinner at the mess Frederic relates how the men eat by "lifting the spaghetti on the fork until the loose strands hung clear then lowering it into the mouth, or else using a continuous lift and sucking into the mouth, helping ourselves to wine from the grass-covered gallon flask" (*AFTA* 7). Just before he is wounded, Frederic caters to the demands of his men for food, bringing them macaroni and cheese; as a result from an earlier conversation with his drivers about socialism, Frederic here dispenses with military hierarchy: "No. . . . Put it on the floor. We'll all eat" (53). They sit about the pot as a group, "all eating, holding their chins close over the basin, tipping their heads back, sucking in the ends" (54). Later, during the retreat, the soldiers complain about the lack of food, and Frederic comments: "[Food] can't win a war but it can lose one" (184). He refers both to the practical, physical needs for food in order for soldiers to work and to fight and also to the psychological need for food in order for soldiers to feel that their country supports them in their efforts and to bond with their fellow soldiers in the ritualistic eating of it. The eating of food at the front is a communal act, just as it is in the home. This point is emphasized by the soldiers finding and drinking wine they assume has been saved for a wedding (217). The drinking of the wine shows the easy translation of family ritual into military ritual. The fact that the wine has gone bad may reflect the darkness behind the ritual of eating and drinking during a time of violence and upheaval.

For the novel shows that eating during war has become a dangerous activity as well as a ritual. Frederic is wounded when the dugout in which he is eating is bombed. Critics have pointed often to the impersonality of death in World War I; the shells can hit at any time. Stanley Cooperman comments that Frederic is frightened by "the horror of male passivity" (182), and indeed technological warfare has made the soldiers into helpless targets. Frederic is specifically affected by being wounded during a domestic ritual; when Rinaldi tries to say Frederic is a hero, Frederic denies any heroism with the comment: "I was blown up while we were eating cheese" (*AFTA* 63). Although Rinaldi and others try to make any wounding a cause for heroism precisely because of their "horror of male passivity" in the war, Frederic is not afraid to face facts and even seems to find a kind of satisfaction in the circumstances of his injury. He seems to be comforted by the knowledge that he was not wounded during a foreign activity like killing the enemy but rather during a familiar activity, one he can understand.

Frederic equates war and the reasons for fighting with the protections of the domestic world. With his drivers, who are socialists and resent the war, he argues that fighting is necessary:

"What is defeat? You go home."
"They come after you. They take your home. They take your sisters."
"I don't believe it," Passini said. "They can't do that to everybody. Let everybody defend his home. Let them keep their sisters in the house." (*AFTA* 50)

The drivers challenge the propaganda that brings America into the war and in which Frederic still needs to believe. He desperately desires a safe place for himself and for the performance of rituals that create a sense of comfort and familiarity.

Throughout *A Farewell to Arms* Frederic sets up and lives in a number of temporary homes. Critics often discuss the housekeeping he sets up with Catherine Barkley, but before he lives with Catherine he lives with his friend Rinaldi. They share a room in their house behind the lines, a room described in a mixture of domestic and military terms:

> The window was open, my bed was made up with blankets and my things hung on the wall, the gas mask in an oblong tin can, the steel helmet on the same peg. At the foot of the bed was my flat trunk, and my winter boots, the leather shiny with oil, were on the trunk. My Austrian sniper's rifle with its blued octagon barrel and the lovely dark walnut, cheek-fitted, schutzen stock, hung over the two beds. (11)

This home shows a fusion of domestic comfort with military necessity. With Rinaldi Frederic shares a home and a close relationship; Rinaldi, referring to his professional ability to doctor soldiers, speaks to Frederic in markedly sexual language: "I would take you and never hurt you" (64). This homoerotic tension between the two men is deferred by their continual references to women, especially prostitutes. Before Frederic leaves on the retreat he spends his last night in the room that he shared with Rinaldi but sleeps in Rinaldi's bed rather than his own. Whether or not Rinaldi has sexual feelings for Frederic (and vice versa), Frederic finds with Rinaldi a sense of home and of family, with Rinaldi as both brother and mother.

With Catherine, Frederic shows a simultaneous desire for and resistance to setting up a truly domestic existence. On leave before meeting Catherine, Frederic sleeps with a number of women, but those experiences always leave him feeling empty:

> I had gone . . . to the smoke of cafés and you needed to look at the wall to make it stop, nights in bed, drunk . . . sure that this was all and all and all and not caring. Suddenly to care very much and to sleep to wake with it sometimes morning and all that had been there gone and everything sharp and hard and clear and sometimes a dispute about the cost. (*AFTA* 13)

At first he sees Catherine as only a diversion from the prostitutes and has no intention of falling in love with her, but when she arrives at the hospital he finds himself immediately in love. Judith Fetterley sees this reaction as evidence of Frederic's selfish immaturity: "it seems clear that he falls in love when he needs to and with whom" (56). Yet Frederic's need for Catherine goes beyond a simple need for someone to take care of him and, as Cooperman argues, to comfort his "horror of male passivity." Catherine helps Frederic create a home place, as Rinaldi did at the front; Frederic says repeatedly that he goes "home to the hospital" (117, 118, 134). But this domestic space has even less legitimacy than his room with Rinaldi, for in the hospital the lovers are together only in secret and would be separated if it were publicly known they were sharing a room.

Part of Frederic and Catherine's strength as a couple is their ability to create a home wherever they are. They have the hospital, various hotel rooms, even Frederic's cape. After his desertion from the Italian army, Frederic and Catherine create a home in the hotel at Stresa:

> That night at the hotel, in our room with the long empty hall outside and our shoes outside the door, a thick carpet on the floor of the room, outside the windows the rain falling and in the room light and pleasant and cheerful, then the light out and it exciting with smooth sheets and the bed comfortable, feeling that we had come home, feeling no longer alone. (*AFTA* 249)

When they arrive in Lausanne for the birth of their child, Catherine comments:

> "I have to try and make this room look like something."
> "Like what?"
> "Like our home."
> "Hand out the Allied flags." (309)

Frederick jokes that the war has been their home; the source of their domesticity is not a place but an event.

Frederic and Catherine's relationship is a ritual displaced, a marriage made in the new circumstances of war. In pre-war times, a love affair might take a "natural" course to marriage and then to sex and children. During war, however, marriage postpones sex and children, since, as Catherine points out, if they were to get married they would be separated immediately. Catherine's friend Fergy's comment that "you'll fight before you marry" (*AFTA* 108) is telling; she may be suggesting that the two lovers are incompatible, but she may also be referring to an interruption of traditional courting and marriage rituals. That is, in the normal course of events couples fight after they marry, but by rushing their sexual relationship and disrupting expected patterns Frederic and Catherine may fight before they marry, hence permanently breaking off the path to marriage.

Frederic has mixed feelings about actually being married, but he does not seem to realize that Catherine may not be eager to be married either. Catherine is a VAD, meaning, as she says, that she works hard but no one trusts her until there is a crisis (*AFTA* 25). In "Corpus/Corps/Corpse: Writing the Body at War," Jane Marcus explains the social ramifications of being a VAD: well-bred women volunteered to go to the front to do the dirty work of war—dealing with blood, guts, and shit—much to the embarrassment of others, whose sensibilities were offended by middle- and upper-class women doing such work (124–5). Sandra Whipple Spanier argues that Catherine already knows about the war when she meets Frederic; her lover has been killed at the Somme so she knows about technological warfare and its impersonality. Catherine has seen the pointlessness of maintaining the old standards; she refused to sleep with her first lover because "I didn't know about anything then. I thought it would be worse for him. I thought perhaps he couldn't stand it and then of course he was killed and that was the end of it" (*AFTA* 19). She also had the "silly idea" that her fiancé would show up at her hospital with a saber cut; instead "they blew him all to bits" (20). When Frederic, her replacement lover, shows up at her hospital with a blown apart leg, Catherine cares for him calmly and efficiently. Catherine takes responsibility for the pregnancy, mentioning that she has done something to prevent or get rid of it and failed, and telling her friend Fergy that "I get in my own messes" (246). With the new world of war, Catherine realizes, she cannot count on anyone else to keep her out of messes; she knows, as Frederic does not, that men are not fighting for her honor but rather to protect and restore their own manhood. She herself must take responsibility for protecting her honor, if she wants to protect it, which she sees no point in doing.

Despite Catherine's much-documented selfless love for Frederic and her comfort in domestic spaces, she is not really a domestic woman. On the boat trip to Switzerland, Frederic cautions her not to let the oar hit her in the stomach, but Catherine responds, "If it did . . . life might be much simpler" (*AFTA* 275). Like Helen in "Cross-Country Snow," she is not pleased about the implications of having a child for herself and her lifestyle. She worries that "she won't come between us, will she? The little brat" (304), expressing a fear of family life and of the mothering role that will divert her availability from Frederic. She also shows her ignorance of what a baby's needs are:

"There aren't many people reach my time without baby things."
"You can buy them."
"I know. That's what I'll do tomorrow. I'll find out what is necessary."
"You ought to know. You were a nurse."
"But so few of the soldiers had babies in the hospitals." (308)

Catherine disproves any idea that women automatically know how to mother or even that nursing is directly connected to domesticity.

Frederic and Catherine's relationship shows the weakness of social institutions to provide structure and security during the upheaval of war. During Catherine's labor, Frederic reflects on Catherine's suffering for their nights of passion: "This was what people got for loving each other. . . . You never got away with anything. Get away hell! It would have been the same if we had been married fifty times" (*AFTA* 320). The ritual of marriage is no protection from the dangers of nature. Society might disapprove of their relationship, but, as Michael Reynolds argues, the ultimate judge is biology and poor doctoring. Domesticity is what the lovers desire, not marriage, for domesticity brings comfort and security while marriage, in war, brings separation, anxiety, and greater enforcement of gender roles.

The violence that war does to domesticity and social institutions is anticipated by the novel's opening image of soldiers as pregnant women: "the men, passing on the road, marched as though they were six months gone with child" (*AFTA* 4). What causes this visual effect is the accoutrements of military necessity: rifles and ammunition. The soldiers will give birth not to a living being but to violence and death—foreshadowing the bloody and fatal end of Catherine's pregnancy. Significantly, for both the soldiers and for Catherine, "pregnancy" signifies not hope for the future but entrapment and danger. Death for soldiers can come at any time, unsuspected, just as for women, especially before medical advances of the later twentieth-century, death can accompany childbirth.[3]

Many critics have speculated on the narrative necessity that Catherine die, as well as on the implications of her death for Frederic. Cooperman suggests that Catherine's death castrates Frederic (183); Fetterley claims, "Frederic needs to feel betrayed and Catherine serves this need" (63). Spanier points out that it is Catherine who acts with a true soldier's ability to live in the moment, Catherine who is the real "Hemingway hero," showing Frederic how to die with little fuss. But Catherine's death also suggests Hemingway's failure to imagine a new role for women, a way to transform the liberated Catherine into a mother. How could she be transformed from a "Hemingway hero" to a wife and mother?

As the system of signification described in Huston's "Matrix of War" shows, the hero and the mother cannot be combined in a single person. The tensions of domesticity laid out in *In Our Time* are explored further in *A Farewell to Arms,* but the latter novel, like the former work, still ends with a solitary male figure. The war has brought changes in women as well as in men, and correspondingly the nature of domesticity changes. It is this mutable domesticity that Hemingway seems to find so unsettling. World War I, it is argued, showed the world the fragility of Western civilization and the instability of its foundations; for Hemingway this exposure of civilization's cracks includes the revelation of an inconstant domesticity, leaving men to find and create home places for themselves. For women, this mutable domesticity ultimately means their erasure from Hemingway's world; as Catherine Barkley shows, the collision of the stoic hero with the mother figure creates, simply, absence—a literary black hole.

NOTES

1. In ancient Greece and Rome, Huston points out, burial rituals expressed greater honor for men who died in battle and women who died in childbirth than for people who died of other causes (131).

2. Thomas Strychacz suggests that Tiny may be pregnant because of "her misapprehension of 'Tochter' (daughter) for 'Doctor' and the many references in the story to 'carrying'" (85n.). I would add that the tension between the couple and the husband's simultaneous concern for his wife's health suggest an unplanned pregnancy.

3. Hemingway's father Clarence wrote a medical essay entitled "Sudden Death That May Come to a Recently Delivered Mother" that discusses case histories of women who died unexpectedly after giving birth. Hemingway would have been aware of this essay; see Reynolds on Hemingway's familiarity with medicine, particularly obstetrics.

WORKS CITED

Benson, Jackson J. "Patterns of Connection and Their Development in Hemingway's *In Our Time*." In *Critical Essays on Ernest Hemingway's In Our Time*. Ed. Michael S. Reynolds, 103–119. Boston: G. K. Hall, 1983.

Cooperman, Stanley. *World War I and the American Novel*. Baltimore: Johns Hopkins UP, 1967.

Ferrero, David J. "Nikki Adams and the Limits of Gender Criticism." *The Hemingway Review* 17.2 (Spring 1998): 18–30.

Fetterley, Judith. *The Resisting Reader: A Feminist Approach to American Fiction*. Bloomington: Indiana UP, 1977.

Hasbany, Richard. "The Shock of Vision: An Imagist Reading of *In Our Time*." In

Ernest Hemingway: Five Decades of Criticism. Ed. Linda Welshimer Wagner, 224–240. East Lansing: Michigan State UP, 1974.

Hemingway, Clarence. "Sudden Death That May Come to a Recently Delivered Mother." *The Hemingway Review* 18.2 (Spring 1999): 43–45.

Hemingway, Ernest. *A Farewell to Arms.* New York: Scribner's, 1929.

———. *In Our Time.* New York: Scribner's, 1930.

Huston, Nancy. "The Matrix of War: Mothers and Heroes." In *The Female Body in Western Culture.* Ed. Susan Rubin Suleiman, 119–136. Cambridge: Harvard UP, 1986.

Lamb, Robert Paul. "The Love Song of Harold Krebs: Form, Argument, and Meaning in Hemingway's 'Soldier's Home.'" *The Hemingway Review* 14.2 (Spring 1995): 18–36.

Marcus, Jane. "Corpus/Corps/Corpse: Writing the Body at War." In *Arms and the Woman: War, Gender, and Literary Representation.* Ed. Helen M. Cooper, Adrienne Auslander Munich, and Susan Merrill Squier, 124–167. Chapel Hill: U of North Carolina P, 1989.

Reynolds, Michael. "A Farewell to Arms: Doctors in the House of Love." In *The Cambridge Companion to Hemingway.* Ed. Scott Donaldson, 109–127. Cambridge: Cambridge UP, 1996.

Romines, Ann. *The Home Plot: Women, Writing and Domestic Ritual.* Amherst: U of Massachusetts P, 1992.

Spanier, Sandra Whipple. "Hemingway's Unknown Soldiers: Catherine Barkley, the Critics, and the Great War." In *New Essays on* A Farewell to Arms. Ed. Scott Donaldson, 75–108. New York: Cambridge UP, 1990.

Stengel, Wayne B. "Strength of the Mothers, Weakness of the Fathers: War, Sport, and Sexual Battle in Hemingway's *In Our Time.*" *Publications of the Arkansas Philological Association* 20.1 (1994): 87–103.

Stoneback, H. R. "'Nothing was ever lost': Another Look at 'That Marge Business.'" In *Hemingway: Up in Michigan Perspectives.* Ed. Frederic J. Svoboda and Joseph J. Waldmeir, 59–76. East Lansing: Michigan State UP, 1995.

Strychacz, Thomas. "*In Our Time,* Out of Season." In *The Cambridge Companion to Hemingway.* Ed. Scott Donaldson, 55–86. New York: Cambridge UP, 1996.

Wagner, Linda W. "'Proud and Friendly and Gently': Women in Hemingway's Early Fiction." In *Ernest Hemingway: The Papers of a Writer*. Ed. Bernard Oldsey, 63–71. New York: Garland, 1981.

Ernest Hemingway and World War I

Combatting Recent Psychobiographical Reassessments, Restoring the War

Matthew C. Stewart

"Napoleon taught Stendahl how to write."

—Ernest Hemingway

To ask whether or not the First World War had a profound effect upon Ernest Hemingway would, not so long ago, have been considered a rhetorical question. It can no longer be considered so, since the influential critics Kenneth S. Lynn and Frederick Crews have sought to dismiss the importance of World War I from Hemingway's life and fiction.[1] The mainstream interpretation, which held sway well into the 1980s, has been advanced in most detail by Philip Young, whose breadth of analysis and psychoanalytical bent amplified the theory of the wound first advanced by Edmund Wilson. Although he did not speak as extensively of the wound theory, Malcolm Cowley had already

Reprinted with permission from *Papers on Language & Literature* 36.2 (Spring 2000). Copyright © 2000 by The Board of Trustees, Southern Illinois University. Published by Southern Illinois University, Edwardsville.

marked out Hemingway's First World War experiences as a turning point in his life as early as 1945.

Following Cowley and Young, many a teacher taught many a student that Hemingway was badly wounded at the war—wounded inside as well as outside. That war left him with a fear of night, a fear said to relate to his abrupt confrontation with his own mortality. It gave him insight into the fragility of the world, and it fostered a deep skepticism towards the grand abstractions that the First World War rendered bitterly ironic. For a generation of critics, the war was not only the obvious subject matter, the *sine qua non,* of certain stories and novels, it also undergirded the entire *oeuvre,* and lurked below the surface of certain important stories that never mentioned the war. But times have changed, and as Susan Beegel puts it in her recent bibliographic essay on Hemingway criticism, in the 1980s "it became clear that the 'wound' and the 'code' were about to be muscled off the stage of Hemingway studies" (289). Because the psychobiographical version elaborated by Lynn and supported by Crews inaccurately reappraises Hemingway's life and work in relation to the war, and because this erroneous version has gained considerable currency—indeed, much outright acceptance—among general readers and academics alike, I would like to consider anew the importance of the First World War in Hemingway's life and work.

I am not concerned here with clarifying the events surrounding Hemingway's wounding at Fossalta di Piave, for Robert W. Lewis, Michael Reynolds, and, most skeptically, Jeffrey Meyers have thoroughly examined this episode. In a study co-credited to Henry S. Villard, James Nagel has constructed the most convincing say on the matter, countering to a degree the more skeptical scholarly opinions. They have shown the necessity of questioning biographical sources and interpretations that have hardened into "facts," and, more importantly, their discussions of Hemingway's war experiences rid this portion of his life of a critical one-dimensionality that may have begun to cling to it. But Lynn and Crews have subsequently substituted one sort of unidimensionality for another. They make it seem as if the war slid off Hemingway like water off a duck's back and have asked us to understand that some of his most admired war stories are not really war stories after all.

Such stories as "Now I Lay Me" and "Big Two-Hearted River," they argue, do not have a wounding nor even the generalized trauma of war at their center, perhaps not even at their periphery. From the demythification of Hemingway's own wound, these critics have extrapolated a Hemingway profoundly unchanged by what he experienced in Italy. Thus Frederick Crews on Hemingway: "Nothing in his subsequent conduct suggests that he returned from Italy with a subdued temper, much less a revulsion against killing or a grasp of the issues and ironies behind the war" (95). Thus Kenneth S. Lynn on "Now I Lay Me," a story set seven kilometers from the front in Italy and whose two main characters are hospitalized soldiers: "What counts supremely in the story is not the northern Italian frame that has made so many readers regard it as a tale of war, but the childhood memories within the frame" (1987 48).[2]

Writing on the publication of Hemingway's *Selected Letters* in 1981, Lynn argued that the war played no part in "Big Two-Hearted River," a story he describes as "a sun-drenched, Cézannesque picture of a predominantly happy fishing trip" (1981 26). In the process of laying out his surprising version of Hemingway's famous story, Lynn rakes Malcolm Cowley over the coals. Attaching anti-American motives to Cowley, he excoriates his introduction to *The Portable Hemingway*, wherein he sees Cowley "shoveling much more war-victim material into 'Big Two-Hearted River'" (1981 25). In 1984 Cowley responded to Lynn's attack, reiterating his belief in the importance of Hemingway's war experience and offering as new testimony a previously unpublished letter from 1948 in which Hemingway directly states that Cowley was correct about the war wound: "Big Two Hearted River [sic] is a story about a man who is home from the war" (Cowley, 1984 230). In 1985, R. W. B. Lewis thought that the argument had been put to rest, with Cowley winning the day. Not so, however. In his subsequently published biography, Lynn devotes over four pages to refuting the war-trauma interpretation of "Big Two-Hearted River" and asserts that Hemingway's letter was one of several posthumously published pieces which make Hemingway to be "a master manipulator . . . making fools of [critics] from beyond the grave" (*Hemingway* 106). Thereafter Frederick Crews joined ranks with Lynn, specifically countering both Cowley and Lewis and asserting the wholesale claim that Hemingway returned from the war unchanged. The rest of this essay will be a direct refutation of the revisionists' interpretation of the war's influence on both Hemingway's life and fiction, using "Big Two-Hearted River" as a case in point.

Crews in particular makes much of the cheery, jocular tone found in the young Hemingway's letters home from the Italian hospital where he was recuperating. These letters prove, he claims, that Hemingway couldn't have been much hurt: "the adeptness of his sprightly rhetoric sits poorly with the conventional idea of his thoroughly unnerved, shell-shocked condition" (95). Setting aside the caricature of "the conventional idea" as holding that Hemingway was immediately and absolutely psychically altered by his wounding, what Crews too easily dismisses is the rhetorical context of these letters home. Very likely Hemingway did as millions of war veterans have done and adopted the uncomplaining, kidding stoicism expected of him under the circumstances. The manly thing, the adult thing, the heroic thing was not to let on to those at home. Besides putting on the brave and happy face, the later letters could well constitute a bid for public attention, as James R. Mellow has asserted (63–64). Hemingway's early letters were delivered to the local press by his parents, and Hemingway's subsequent letters were surely written under the apprehension that they might well find a public audience.

No doubt Hemingway did find things in his wounding and in his hospital stay in which he could take comfort. Even this sort of ordeal, with all its attendant pains and fears, had its compensations in social status and new experience. But about his wounding and convalescence, several factors are not in dispute. He underwent surgery, he picked many pieces of shrapnel from his legs, and, thanks largely to his drinking, he was hit with a case of jaundice. Hemingway was, by several accounts, the life of the party on the hospital floor, full of still adolescent vigor, and his letters home are indeed chipper, but he was not a fool incapable of comprehending the gravity of his situation or of feeling his injuries.[3]

Crews and Lynn do not mention Agnes von Kurowsky's statement that, while hospitalized, Hemingway "was worried about his leg. He was afraid they'd amputate" (qtd. in Reynolds, "Agnes Tapes" 269) nor that as late as 22 April 1920, he straightforwardly explained to his parents that although his leg was in pretty good shape, it still bothered him after a hard day—a long recovery time for a young and active man. An early attempt at a fictionalized version of his wounding develops a decidedly unspritely rhetoric. Writing longhand on Milan Red Cross stationary, Hemingway sketches the downfall of Nick Grainger of Petoskey, Michigan. Like Hemingway, Nick has been struck in the legs by a mortar on the Italian front. Yet, his case is worse than Hemingway's in that he apparently has lost both his legs and his left arm to amputation. The war over, peace celebrants noisy in the streets, Nick bitterly fingers his medals and remains uncomforted by the florid citation that accompanies them. The sketch ends before he swallows the poisonous bichloride solution he has filched for the clear purpose of committing suicide (JFK 604). As a piece of fiction—corny dialogue, unrealized ironic potential—this sketch provides a baseline from which to measure Hemingway's growth as a writer during his subsequent Paris apprenticeship. And the sketch is an early instance of the suicide theme that would become central in Hemingway's life and fiction. Most to the point here, this particular piece of writing directly refutes the revisionists' thesis that the war contained no dark dimension for the young Hemingway. And nowhere in the revised version of Hemingway does one see mention of his confidences to his wife Hadley about his recurrent battle nightmares—this in 1923, five years after his wounding (Reynolds, *Paris Years* 203). Rather than recognize the mixed nature of Hemingway's wounding, Crews and Lynn insist on depicting a sort of dumb (but cheerful) ox, all the while ignoring the cultural context of his behavior as well as much evidence that would necessitate a less one-dimensional portrait of Hemingway.

There is indeed a great deal more evidence that indicates Hemingway was profoundly influenced by the war. Both his life and his fictions show that the wounding had its serious effects. Members of Hemingway's family who observed him upon his return from the war would agree. His brother Leicester has written that "not all of Ernest's wounds were physical. Like hundreds of thousands of other soldiers before and since, he had received some psychic shock. He was plagued by insomnia and couldn't sleep unless he had a light in his room" (48).[4] It could be argued that Leicester, a young boy when Hemingway returned from Italy, must be judged a second-hand source in regards to this event, perhaps even that he is only giving a version of events fed to him at some later date by brother Ernest. However, Leicester was actually an early debunker of some of Earnest's Italian war tales, and in regards to this particular portion of his brother's life is not gullible (*My Brother* 46–47, interviewed in Brian 22). Furthermore, Marcelline, who was twenty-one at the time, also relates her brother's troubled mental state in her memoirs. "In between [his] extrovert activities Ernie had quiet, almost depressed intervals," she writes (Sanford 183). But she actually proceeds to betray her protect-the-family-name use of word *almost,* for she describes her brother as staying in bed for long periods of time, drinking on the sly to ease his pain, retreating from family activities and showing little inclination to forge an adult identity for himself (173–199).

A reading of Hemingway's letters also reveals a change in his state of mind after the war. With an oddly narrow selectivity and tendentious emphasis, Crews examines Hemingway's 1948 letter to Cowley, wherein Hemingway states, "In the first war, I now see, I was hurt very badly; in the body, mind, and spirit; and also morally" (qtd. in Cowley, "Wound" 229). Crews emphasizes the clause *I now see* to declare that Hemingway "belatedly claimed to have adopted this poignant" war-wound reading (96). As I have already shown, there is a great deal of evidence apart from this one letter with which to counter Crews's mis-emphasis, but a different reading of the letter also presents itself as plausible. It is more tenable to emphasize the words *very badly,* so that we see the older Hemingway not belatedly claiming a wound he never felt, as Crews would have it, but better understanding the dimensions and profundity of that wound. This interpretation is bolstered when the next sentence from the letter is not omitted from consideration: "The true gen is I was hurt all the way through" (qtd. in Cowley, "Wound" 229–30). *All the way through,* Hemingway particularizes, and, more tellingly, he uses a favorite phrase of his at the time—*the true gen*—which he used to signify the transcendent, core truth adhering to an event.[5] The gen, the mere fact, has always been that Hemingway was wounded; the true gen was that he had been wounded deeply, quite probably so deeply that his trauma found itself in his stories in a way that he was only partially conscious of and only partially but not totally in control of as an author. Such slowly arrived-at self-understanding, the gradual (or eventual) coming to terms with the sort of trauma suffered by Hemingway should not be difficult to imagine.

Lynn and Crews undermine their arguments by staging false dilemmas. Either Hemingway immediately and constantly showed the profound effects of the war upon him, or he came out of the war untouched. Either the psychic germ of "Big Two-Hearted River" is World War I or it is Hemingway's conflicts with his mother (Lynn's argument, as we shall see), but not both. But those who have known or worked with veterans know that the effects of trauma may surface only after the passage of time, sometimes gradually, sometimes by fits and starts, sometimes all at once upon actuation by a particular stimulus, sometimes after the passage of many seemingly trouble-free years.[6] Likewise, understanding the effects of one's wounding is a process, often one that transpires over many years, even decades. There is no single, exclusive paradigm that invariably governs the effects of traumatic experience.[7] It is certainly reasonable to conclude that Hemingway suffered the effects of his wounding at first (and I wish to re-emphasize to a greater degree than acknowledged by Crews or Lynn), and that with the passage of time he came to a deeper awareness and a better understanding of the war's effects upon him. It is reasonable to accept that the reaction to a wounding need not come in a simple either/or form, that a wounding survived can leave victims feeling alternatively vulnerable and indestructible, and that the balance between these two feelings is quite capable of shifting over the course of one's life.

It is true that in the 1950s Hemingway actually denied the war-wound interpretation of his work as put forth by Philip Young. But Hemingway's objections in this instance were partly strategic. He wished to hold prying biographers and critics—of whom there were beginning to be a substantial number—at bay, and he was not about to encourage any public version of himself that did not conform to the hairy-chested hero regularly depicted in the pages of national magazines. In his letters of the period he repeatedly asserts his desire to retain his privacy and to have his fictions read on their own terms, without reference to facts from his own life. In part these assertions stem from sincere beliefs about his art and in part they stem from Hemingway's heavy investment in the macho myth that adhered to his life in the fifties.[8]

On the subject of his own biography, Hemingway had mixed feelings and was capable of combining subtle encouragement with openly expressed discouragement in his letters to would-be biographers and critics.[9] In Young's particular case, Hemingway does not deny that he was traumatized in WWI, but rightly sees the critic as oversimplifying the *oeuvre* and overplaying his critical thesis. There had been "plenty [of] trauma in 1918," he admitted to Harvey Breit, complaining that Young dwells on the trauma, rather than the fact that he had managed to overcome it (*Selected Letters* 865–67). By this time, too, the public Hemingway, "'fraid o' nothing," had firmly seized hold of a large segment of the casual public's imagination and of its subject's own self-conception as well. The truths Hemingway told in his fictions battled with the *Life*-magazine myth, which was to a large extent of his own making. Hemingway's letters do demonstrate his ability to prevaricate, pose, and manipulate. They also show him to be sincere and straightforward in many instances. Hemingway's 1948 assertion of war trauma to Cowley should be taken at its word. For one thing, what he says in his letter runs counter to the public persona he had participated in building, and, as we shall see, there is a great deal of evidence to be gathered from his statements and fictional works of the twenties that supports his retrospective self-assessment.

In his quest to prove that Hemingway's "'post war disillusionment,' such as it was, proved to be a belated and derivative manifestation," (97) Crews ignores a great deal of very early evidence, including a 1926 letter to Maxwell Perkins. Writing twenty-two years earlier than the letter to Cowley that Crews picks at, Hemingway complains that Allen Tate has been unfair to him by creating a sort of critical dipstick with which to measure the depth of his alleged hardboiledness: "As a matter of fact I have not been at all hard boiled since July 8 1918—on the night of which I discovered that that also was Vanity" [*sic*] (*Selected Letters* 240). The date Hemingway mentions, of course, is that of his wounding at Fossalta di Piave. It is difficult to posit a motivation for Hemingway to lie gratuitously to Perkins in 1926 about his reaction to being wounded.

Neither are Hemingway's early war poems taken into account by the revisionists, including one entitled "Killed Piave—July 8—1918," in which a female speaker expresses her longing for her dead lover, who appears metaphorically as "A dull, cold, rigid bayonet" (*Complete Poems* 35). Written in Paris (all before 1923), the war poems offer little by way of literary achievement but do comprise more evidence that Hemingway thought seriously about the war and felt its wasteful, destructive nature early on, not belatedly. Lynn makes nothing of the poems but chooses to summarize Hemingway's many later assertions that the war had injured him as an obdurate old man's "effort[s] to account for his imperiled sense of himself, as well as to preserve his macho reputation" (*Hemingway* 106).

Finally, neither Crews nor Lynn adequately deals with the imposing fact that so many of Hemingway's protagonists—including those in his earliest stories—are men wounded in war: Nick Adams, Jake Barnes, Frederic Henry, Robert Jordan. Sticking with his posthumous psychoanalysis, insistently returning to the sites of supposed childhood trauma, positing Hemingway as always and ever the victim of himself, Lynn ignores the recurrent presence of fictional protagonists wounded by war. This is not to say that Lynn does not delve into the psyches of these characters; rather, it is to say that he fails to come to terms with the fact that out of an infinite number of causes available with which to wound his main characters, Hemingway consistently chose war.

It is obviously impossible to disprove the centrality of the war in stories set at the front, such as "Now I Lay Me"; therefore Lynn's and Crews's arguments need to be discussed no further in relation to these stories. However, both men have also examined "Big Two-Hearted River," and this story's relationship to the war is admittedly much more indirect. Predictably they have found that this story is not concerned with the war either, though many readers have seen it as depicting a war-traumatized Nick Adams returning to familiar territory for camping, fishing and psychic, perhaps spiritual, recovery. Not so, says Lynn. The story is really about Hemingway's rebellious squabbles with his mother Grace. For two consecutive summers after returning from the war, Hemingway and his mother fought an escalating series of battles that culminated in his banishment from the family summer home in July of 1920. Lynn deduces that this familial acrimony is the true psychic germ of Hemingway's famous story:

> Perhaps, then, the "other needs" Nick feels he has put behind him include a need to please his mother, while his talk of his tent as his home may represent a reaction to being thrown out of his parents' summer cottage. Perhaps, too, the burned-over country and the grasshoppers that have turned black from living in it constitute tacit reminders to him of his mother's penchant for burning things. And finally, the activity of his mind that keeps threatening to overwhelm his contentment could be his rage [towards his mother]. (*Hemingway* 103–04)

This argument is consistent with a dominant tendency in Lynn's study: that the conflicts in Hemingway's stories have their source in his own psychic turmoil, that he had little understanding of, often little awareness of, the nature of his rages and inner torments. Lynn's method is at once subtle and mechanical. It is subtle in that it combines detailed biographical research with sophisticated readings of the works and exhibits the critic's high powers of inference. Yet Lynn too often uses his subtle insights less than responsibly. Lynn's conditional rhetoric here ("perhaps," "may," 'perhaps,' "could be") would seem to indicate that his reading of this enigmatic story is as speculative as any other, as indeed it is. But in the course of his argument, Lynn actually treats his speculation as if it were a fact beyond dispute—witness his excoriation of those whose speculations are not in line with his own. Lynn's method becomes mechanical in that it insists upon the equation *inner torment equals content of the story*, while assertive, consciously controlled, fictive imagination is relegated to the end of the bench.

In the light of the vitriolic opinions expressed about his mother by Hemingway as an older man, it is perhaps difficult to judge that his 1920 fights with her are merely typical of a twenty-year-old's desire to be granted autonomy and adult status. Lynn clearly does not judge them so, but rather presents them as being manifestations of a mind already abnormally conflicted in regards to his mother. But surely the war itself was an integral part of Hemingway's conflict with the old-fashioned, sanctimonious, emotionally coercive Grace. Surely it was doubly difficult in his particular situation to be treated like a kid. It was the summer of his coming of age, a stage of life when the final thrust towards independence and adult status is normal and necessary. But also, as a young man who had been at the war and one-time city-beat reporter in Kansas City, he had already seen much more than someone his age would usually see, and he had experienced things far beyond the ken of his suburban, essentially Victorian parents. The same mother who had initially doted on her son's war-hero status overlooked the deeper changes his experiences had caused him.[10] In an unpublished letter to Charles Poore, Hemingway relates that after being home from the war for some time "I was having a pretty bad time and my mother started to eat me out for drinking and not taking things seriously etc. and I told her that I had had a sort of bad time some of the time in the war and that if she would leave me alone I would work out of it okay." In his description of Hemingway's summers of familial discontent, Lynn again presumes a false dilemma—it was either the war (wrong interpretation) or his mother (correct interpretation) that was at the root of Hemingway's—and hence Nick's—restlessness and moodiness. That the two problems could be mixed together, as they skillfully are in fictional form in "Soldier's Home," for example, is an idea that Lynn never entertains.

But another problem confronts the reader. Lynn, who too readily formulates biographical statements about Hemingway based on material in the stories, seems to be operating with two sets of standards. Those who interpret "Big Two-Hearted River" to be a story about a war-wounded Nick are admonished three times in the space of two pages that there is no *textual* evidence for this interpretation—as indeed there is not (*Hemingway* 104–106). Yet Lynn remains unruffled by the fact that neither is there a single reference to Nick's conflicted feelings towards his mother. The story certainly contains no reference to Nick's "being thrown out of his parents' summer cottage," as Lynn states, conferring a fact from Hemingway's life onto his protagonist. Indeed, there are no explicit references to familial strife of any kind.

Not only can Lynn be hoist on his own critical petard, he often engages in a sort of circular logic that too readily muddles Hemingway's characters with himself. It is often very hard to discern whether or not Lynn is basing a textual interpretation on Hemingway's life or an interpretation of Hemingway using a story as evidence. He moves back and forth without drawing careful distinctions between these procedures. While using biographical evidence to suggest (though it can never prove) a certain textual interpretation is legitimate criticism, to work in the other direction, to draw conclusions about the author's life based upon his characters is a more dubious approach, and one from which Hemingway has too often suffered. While Lynn is a subtle reader, his readings are often much more an exploration of Hemingway's frame of mind (invariably angry, guilty, depressed or sexually confused in his version of things) during composition than they are textual interpretations. Lynn's criticisms of his war-wound predecessors, then, prove nothing aside from his willingness to engage in a critical double standard.[11]

What sort of textual evidence can be brought to bear on the story qua wound story? Its placement in the context of *In Our Time* strongly argues in favor of its interpretation as a story informed by the war. This volume contains seven stories and one vignette wherein Nick Adams is indisputably the protagonist. The stories occur in chronological order and trace various stages in Nick's development. In the sole vignette he is a soldier on the Italian front and has been hit in the spine. He is dragged to safety amidst the wreckage of a war-ruined town (later recalled in the imagery of Seney's obliteration in "Big Two-Hearted River") and addresses his comrade in arms with the words "not patriots" (63). In "Cross-Country Snow," which is the penultimate Nick Adams story, Nick refers to having a bad leg that interferes with his ability to ski. From these clues alone it is not reckless to hypothesize that Nick's unspecified problems in the ultimate story may have their origins in the war. Moreover, the reader has already also read "Soldier's Home" before reading "Big Two-Hearted River," and this story is a quintessential, explicit portrait of a traumatized veteran, a portrait that paves the way for the reader to conjecture similar causes for the wounded veteran Nick's problems. Yet Lynn, as he does with "Big Two-Hearted River," analyzes "Soldier's Home" *only* in terms of family dynamics (*Hemingway* 258–60). Clearly mother-son dynamics are of great importance in "Soldier's Home," but the story's *sine qua non* is the depiction of a war veteran struggling to readjust to post-war civilian life. The family tensions cannot be seen as an issue somehow distinct from Krebs' status as a returned soldier. Thus, when the reader comes to the next story about a man he knows to be, like Krebs, both troubled and a veteran, he is surely justified in hypothesizing a thematic unity between the two stories and in positing the war as the underlying cause of the veteran's troubles.

Crews goes so far as to assert that in "Big Two-Hearted River" Nick is not even troubled: "Nick Adams neither moves about nor thinks like a man who has recently undergone a physically and spiritually crippling trauma. His escape, through the satisfactions of expert camping and fishing, from an unstated preoccupation is all but complete" (96). While it is true that the source of Nick's inner turmoil is never explicitly revealed, Hemingway's rendering of Nick's delicate mental state and his evocation of the precarious balance Nick strives to maintain are among Hemingway's finest achievements. To miss them is to miss the story. And as for Nick's "escape" being "all but complete," Crews avoids any mention of the swamp, an obvious and dominant symbol, which Nick does not feel up to challenging at the end of the story.

Finally, it should be stated that the imagery of "Big Two-Hearted River" is consistent with the war-trauma reading. As he did in the earlier Nick Adams story "The End of Something," Hemingway beings "Big Two-Hearted River" with a descriptive paragraph which does not advance the action of the story in the least, but which serves as an objective correlative for the story's emotional landscape. In the former story, Hemingway prepares the reader for the breakup of Nick and Marjorie in his opening paragraph, which is devoted entirely to a description of the ghost town Hortons Bay. In the opening paragraphs of "Big Two-Hearted River," Hemingway similarly focuses his attention on the burned-over landscape through which Nick walks on his way to a better place. This imagery is consistent with other post-war literary wasteland imagery and touches the cultural memory of the devastated landscapes of the First World War.

In stories written subsequent to "Big Two-Hearted River," Nick's career as a soldier receives further amplification. If literary quality is a register of how deeply an author has felt the subject matter about which he writers, then Hemingway felt very deeply about his war experiences, for these are some of his finest stories. They are "In Another Country," "Now I Lay Me," and "A Way You'll Never Be." The first story very clearly anticipates *A Farewell to Arms* in its opening paragraph, its setting and the theme it raises. It depicts the ruined lives of wounded soldiers in a hospital, in particular the physical therapy of the American narrator and an Italian major.[12] It is clear that the physical therapy is useless and that some sort of metaphysical, perhaps spiritual, therapy would be more fundamentally valuable for the physically battered men. The second story, as stated above, depicts Nick and an Italian soldier lying awake at night near the front, unable to sleep. The American narrator dreads sleeping because he fears that his soul will leave his body. The final story depicts Nick Adams returning to the Italian front as a would-be morale booster, but he has been shot, receiving a head-wound that has rendered him barely able to control himself at the front. Indeed, his principal task is to hold onto his sanity.

These three war stories are remarkable for their literary quality, for their high degree of autobiographical resonance, and for the way they illuminate *A Farewell to Arms* and each other. Most to the immediate purpose, however, is to assert that they constitute additional early evidence that Nick Adams was severely traumatized by the war. Lynn and Crews build a version of Hemingway as a world-renowned, middle-aged author pulling the wool over the eyes of friends and critics during the forties and fifties. Twenty-five years after the fact, they maintain, Hemingway fabricates the idea that the war affected him. Yet "In Another Country" and "Now I Lay Me" were composed only two years after "Big Two-Hearted River," and "A Way You'll Never Be" was composed in mid-1932.[13] These are Nick Adams stories; they are set at the war; they show Nick as physically and psychically wounded.

The opening pages of "Now I Lay Me" even echo many particulars of "Big Two-Hearted River," including the central action of trout fishing as psychic restoration. Clearly these stories cast what Cowley called "a retrospective light" on "Big Two-Hearted River" ("Nightmare" 41).[14] Lynn and Crews require us to assume that these stories, some of Hemingway's finest explorations of the human consequences of war, were written so that he would have the means to delude English professors twenty-five years later. And if we are asked to accept this, would we then also be asked to assume that Hemingway discussed his war nightmares with his first wife in the 1920s for the same reason? Hemingway as both young and middle-aged man undoubtedly kidded, exaggerated, misled, pulled legs, manipulated, hoaxed, and lied. But the existence of these early war stories and their high degree of interconnectedness with "Big Two-Hearted River" argues strongly against the idea that Hemingway decided to lay claim to the importance of the war in his work belatedly and factitiously.

In viewing Hemingway's life, Lynn and Crews have noted his blind spots and his ability to deceive and manipulate but have then gone on to see blindness and manipulation where they do not exist. In the fictions they have sought in some instances to deny the seemingly obvious, and instead of contenting themselves with opening up additional avenues of criticism have tried to do so at the expense of closing down entirely legitimate interpretations already in existence. It must be emphasized in the face of this recent and much discussed and much-believed-in psychobiographical criticism that the First World War had a profound effect upon the life and work of Ernest Hemingway, and that the war looms large below the surface of "Big Two-Hearted River."

NOTES

1. While a more balanced set of views exists within the small community of experienced Hemingway scholars, wherein Lynn was greeted with more skepticism and wherein the more traditional view of the war's impact on Hemingway was

not so readily abandoned, outside this small community of scholars one observes Lynn's considerable influence. Invariably if the graduate students I have taught have read any secondary literature on Hemingway, it has been Lynn, and just as invariably they are much taken with his conclusions. At conferences, in the faculty lounge, out of the mouths of those who are teaching Hemingway in survey classes, one hears the new version of Hemingway according to Lynn. Even within the ranks of modernist scholars, not only does Lynn's insistently psychoanalytical approach attract its supporters, but a good many of his specific conclusions, including those arrived at through a tendentious methodology, are apt to be referred to approvingly. The readiness to accept Lynn's version of Hemingway can be seen partly as a sign of the scholarly times, which for some years has been much in favor of debunking and chopping the author down to size. Certain scholarly methodologies and not a few critical careers have been built upon the attitude that the critic is every bit as wise as the author—indeed, wiser. When critics and their readers do not consider or are not aware of all the pertinent facts, this sort of spurious wisdom becomes entrenched if allowed to go unchallenged.

2. This sort of either-or rhetoric too frequently mars Lynn's provocative study. Not content to shed light on an underemphasized aspect of the story, he typically overstates the case, denying the obvious importance of the war.

3. The most up-to-date and thorough account of this portion of Hemingway's life is to be found in Villard and Nagel; see especially James Nagel's chapter entitled "Hemingway and the Italian Legacy," 197–270. Reynold's *First War* retains scholarly value as well.

4. Later in life, Hemingway himself wrote to Arthur Mizener that out of concern for him after he returned from the war his younger sister Ursula would wait up for him and sleep with him (*Selected Letters* 697).

5. In 1945 Hemingway wrote to Cowley, "The gen is RAF slang for intelligence, the hand out at the briefing. The *true* gen is what they know but don't tell you" (*Selected Letters* 603, emphasis in original).

6. See especially Lansky; Peterson and Solomon.

7. Observations on the effects of trauma and the behavior of trauma victims are elaborated in a large and still-growing body of professional writings about

reactions to stress in combat and to other forms of posttraumatic stress disorder. For example, see Blank, Clipp and Elder, Laufer, and McFarlane.

8. For discussion of Hemingway and fame and for an elaboration of the Papa myth and the depiction of the macho Hemingway see Donaldson and Raeburn.

9. All the major biographies treat Hemingway's relationship with Arthur Mizener, Philip Young and Charles Fenton. James R. Mellow gives the most concentrated consideration of this subject, drawing upon Hemingway's unpublished letters to Carlos Baker (562–78).

10. In any number of war veterans' oral histories and in case studies of young war veterans, one repeatedly reads of their resentment at having adult status thrust upon them all at once in war only to return home to families, employers, indeed to a society in general that ignores or tries to retract that adult status conferred *in extremis* during their military service.

11. In his role as Lynn's bulldog, Crews lauds Lynn's proclamations that the critic ought "to be guided by the story itself rather than by the retrospective gloss" (Crews 96). Lynn's problem is that he himself does not stick to this method, and Crews's problem is that he seems not to have noticed that Lynn does not follow his own advice. It is also interesting to note that in his biography Lynn spends four and a half pages arguing against the war-wound interpretation but only devotes one paragraph to sketching out his own mother-conflict interpretation.

12. While the narrator is never named, there are so many similarities between him and Nick Adams that many critics have accorded "In Another Country" the status of literally being about Nick Adams, and most have, at the very least, accorded it the status of being what Joseph DeFalco has termed a "generic Nick Adams" story.

13. For the dating of the stories' composition, see Paul Smith's extraordinarily thorough guide (85–86, 164–65, 172–73, 268–71). There is also good evidence that Hemingway wished to write "A Way You'll Never Be" in the twenties, made several attempts to write it then, but simply could not do so until more time had passed. In light of the various war stories written by Hemingway several years after the end of the war, one scarcely knows what to make of Crews's claim that "Hemingway's 'postwar disillusionment' . . . proved to be a belated and

derivative manifestation" (97). One might also question the rather odd critical standard by which the worthiness of a piece of fiction is judged according to the length of time its author required for creative germination.

14. Besides Cowley, critics who have linked the later war stories with "Big Two-Hearted River" include Young, DeFalco, Waldhorn and Flora.

WORKS CITED

Beegel, Susan F. "The Critical Reputation of Ernest Hemingway." In *The Cambridge Companion to Hemingway*. Ed. Scott Donaldson, 269–299. New York: Cambridge UP, 1996.

Blank, Arthur S. "The Longitudinal Course of Posttraumatic Stress Disorder." In *Posttraumatic Stress Disorder: DSM-IV and Beyond*. Ed. Jonathan R. T. Davidson and Edna B. Foa, 3–22. Washington, DC: American Psychiatric Press, 1993.

Brian, Denis. *The True Gen: An Intimate Portrait of Ernest Hemingway by Those Who Knew Him*. New York: Grove, 1988.

Clipp, Elizabeth Colerick, and Glenn H. Elder. "The Aging Veteran of World War II: Psychiatric and Life Course Insights." In *Aging and Posttraumatic Stress Disorder*. Ed. Paul E. Ruskin and John A. Talbott, 19–52. Washington DC: American Psychiatric Press, 1996.

Cowley, Malcolm. "Nightmare and Ritual in Hemingway." In *Hemingway: A Collection of Critical Essays*. Ed. Robert P. Weeks, 40–51. 1945; Englewood Cliffs, NJ: Prentice-Hall, 1962.

———. "Hemingway's Wound—And Its Consequences for American Literature." *The Georgia Review* (Summer 1984): 223–39.

Crews, Frederick. *The Critics Bear it Away: American Fiction and the Academy*. New York: Random House, 1992.

DeFalco, Joseph. *The Hero in Hemingway's Short Stories*. Pittsburgh: U of Pittsburg P, 1963.

Donaldson, Scott. "Introduction: Hemingway and Fame." In *The Cambridge Companion to Hemingway*. Ed. Scott Donaldson, 1–15. New York: Cambridge UP, 1996.

Flora, Joseph M. *Hemingway's Nick Adams*. Baton Rouge: Louisiana Sate UP, 1982.

Hemingway, Ernest. *Complete Poems*. Lincoln: U of Nebraska P, 1983.

———. *88 Poems*. Ed. Nicholas Gerogiannis. New York: Harcourt, 1979.

———. *Ernest Hemingway: Selected Letters, 1917–1961*. Ed. Carlos Baker. New York: Scribner's, 1981.

———. *In Our Time*. 1925; New York: MacMillan, 1970.

———. Letter to Charles Poore. 3 April 1953. American Heritage Center, University of Wyoming.

———. Letter to Clarence and Grace Hall Hemingway. 22 April 1920. Hemingway Room, John F. Kennedy Library.

———. *The Short Stories of Ernest Hemingway*. 1938; New York: MacMillan, 1986.

———. Unpublished manuscript #604. Hemingway Room, John F. Kennedy Library.

Hemingway, Leicester. *My Brother, Ernest Hemingway*. 1962; New York: Fawcett, 1967.

Lansky, Melvin R., and Carol R. Bley. *Posttraumatic Nightmares: Psychodynamic Explorations*. Hillsdale, NJ: The Analytic Press, 1995.

Laufer, Robert S. "The Serial Self: War Trauma, Identity and Adult Development." In *Human Adaptation to Extreme Stress*. Ed. John P. Wilson et al., 33–53. New York: Plenum, 1988.

Lewis, R. W. B. "Who's Paper?" [Review of *Along With Youth: Hemingway the Early Years*, by Peter Griffin, and *Hemingway: A Biography*, by Jeffrey Meyers.] *The New Republic* (2 December 1985): 31–34.

Lewis, Robert W. Jr. "Hemingway in Italy: Making it Up." *Journal of Modern Literature* 9 (1981): 209–36.

Lynn, Kenneth S. "Hemingway's Private War." *Commentary* 72.1 (1981): 24–33.

———. *Hemingway*. New York: Simon and Schuster, 1987.

McFarlane, Alexander C. "Resilience, Vulnerability, and the Course of Posttraumatic Reactions." In *Traumatic Stress: The Effects of Overwhelming Experience on Mind, Body and Society*. Ed. Bessel A. van der Kolk et al., 155–181. New York: Guilford, 1996.

Mellow, James R. *Hemingway: A Life Without Consequences*. New York: Houghton Mifflin, 1992.

Meyers, Jeffrey. *Hemingway: A Biography*. New York: Harper, 1985.

Nagel, James. "Hemingway and the Italian Legacy." In *Hemingway in Love and*

War: The Lost Diary of Agnes von Kurowsky, Her Letters, and Correspondence of Ernest Hemingway. Eds. Henry S. Villard and James Nagel, 197–270. Boston: Northeastern UP, 1989.

Peterson, Kirtland, et al. "Subtypes and Course of the Disorder." In *Post-traumatic Stress Disorder: A Clinician's Guide,* 3–23. New York: Plenum, 1991.

Raeburn, John. *Fame Became of Him: Hemingway as a Public Writer.* Bloomington: Indiana UP, 1984.

Reynolds, Michael. *Hemingway's First War: The Making of* A Farewell to Arms. Princeton: Princeton UP, 1976.

———. "The Agnes Tapes." *Fitzgerald-Hemingway Annual* (1979): 251–77.

———. *The Young Hemingway.* Oxford: Blackwell, 1986.

———. *Hemingway: The Paris Years.* Oxford: Blackwell, 1989.

Sanford, Marcelline Hemingway. *At the Hemingways: A Family Portrait.* Boston: Little, Brown, 1961.

Solomon, Zahava. *Combat Stress Reaction: The Enduring Toll of War.* New York: Plenum, 1993.

Villard, Henry S., and James Nagel. *Hemingway in Love and War: The Lost Diary of Agnes von Kurowsky, Her Letters, and Correspondence of Ernest Hemingway.* Boston: Northeastern UP, 1989.

Waldhorn, Arthur. *A Reader's Guide to Ernest Hemingway.* New York: Farrar, 1972.

Wilson, Edmund. "Hemingway: Gauge of Morale." In *The Wound and the Bow: Seven Studies in Literature,* 214–42. New York: Oxford UP, 1947.

Young, Philip. *Ernest Hemingway: A Reconsideration.* 1952; New York: Harcourt, 1966.

A Farewell to Arms

Reconsiderations

Linda Wagner-Martin

Most of the thematic emphases of literature the world over are incorporated in Hemingway's mixture of romance and war novel. Within the American literary tradition of using as subject a man's inner quest for a meaningful self—whether that quest took the character to the frontier, as in James Fenimore Cooper's novels, or to the ocean, as in Herman Melville's, or to another country, as in Henry James's—Hemingway's *A Farewell to Arms* establishes Frederic Henry as a true, and somewhat conventional, American Hero.

To be engaged in war may be the ultimate test of manhood. The outcomes of performance in either battle or as a noncombatant in the military

Reprinted from *Ernest Hemingway's A Farewell to Arms, A Reference Guide* (chapter five). Copyright © 2003 by Linda Wagner-Martin. Published by Greenwood Press, Westport, Connecticut.

are stark: death or life. Life after war might be a limited one, however, marred by either physical or psychological debility. Either way, the odds are indisputably high.

Frederic Henry, in the milieu of war, almost unconsciously becomes the prototype of the twentieth century existential figure. In a world of confusion, with military events hostile to any individual's well-being, the person alone has no philosophic star to guide by. His duty is to take orders. Privileging himself as a thoughtful, knowledgeable person has no place in the soldier's arena: he must recognize that he is only a small bit of fodder for the machinery of war.

Soldiers cannot even think about any kind of personal health, much less the concept of self-actualization. Serving one's country becomes the single, and primary, goal.

Such a goal, however, is usually directionless. Mandated by the circumstances of "serving" in the military, a person's own choices are severely limited: the very point of military discipline is to replace one's personal choice. The notion of courage, then, is also dramatically changed. To follow a superior's order may wipe out any volition. It was this dilemma that so attracted Hemingway to Stephen Crane's Civil War novella, *The Red Badge of Courage*. To call a fearful boy's behavior "courage" is to insist on more realistic definitions—or, more appropriately, to insist that courage under someone else's command is very different from personal courage.

In *A Farewell to Arms*, Hemingway deals with this impossible situation through the use of metaphors and hesitant stream-of-conscious passages. Except for the paragraph about inflated language, he seldom gives his reader lessons in either social studies or psychology: he writes about the characters he fashions as human, and gives them words that seem germane to the situation. The only passages in which he treats the issue of courage and/or bravery comprehensively are in the scenes of Frederic's leaving Catherine, when he mediates during their night together, "we were never lonely and never afraid when we were together. . . . If people bring so much courage to this world the world has to kill them to break them, so of course it kills them. The world breaks every one and afterward many are strong at the broken places. But those that will not break it kills. It kills the very good and the very gentle and the very brave impartially. If you are none of these you can be sure it will kill you too but there will be no special hurry" (249). Earlier, in a dialogue between the two, Frederic had reassured Catherine that "they" wouldn't get her "Because you're too brave. Nothing ever happens to the brave." When she points out that the brave also die, he responds that they die only once—a tautology that might sound poetic but is only nonsense. Catherine also points that out to him, ending with the last word: "He knew a great deal about cowards but nothing about the brave. The brave dies perhaps two thousand deaths if he's intelligent. He simply doesn't mention them" (139–140).

It is noticeable that Hemingway uses these words about the brave to refer to Catherine. For a male speaker surrounded by men in battle, such a shift in reference comes as a surprise. Inherent in the concepts of courage and bravery is the gendered consideration of manliness. In days of earlier American literature, the military was the province of men; women were excluded entirely. The military was one of the safely male areas where men might choose to serve, in part as a way to escape the domestic—the home and family, church, and community that were increasingly in the twentieth century becoming areas of women's control. (In fact, in the late nineteenth century, the phrase "separate spheres" grew up to connote the kind of division of power in middle- and upper-class families, and in the cultures those families dominated.)

It is this gendered allocation of power that gave rise to some of the more recent questioning of the military (seen during our history with the Vietnam War). If to be a man is to make your own situation, then to voluntarily relinquish such decision making is to act—in effect—against oneself. Frederic Henry's attempt in *A Farewell to Arms* to adjudicate his own "separate peace" as he deserts and flees with Catherine (and as the wounded Nick Adams character in the *In Our Time* vignette had coined the phrase initially) is one means of bridging the seemingly wide division between obeying military orders and making decisions personally.

Hemingway's narrative strategy in *A Farewell to Arms* is to put the outright criticism of war into the mouths of the young Italian mechanics, rather than attributing the criticism to Frederic Henry. Even though he later deserts, Henry seems a bit incredulous at the harshness of Passini's judgments (it is Passini, who here shows no belief at all in the war effort, who is killed in the shell explosion that wounds Henry):

> "Tenente," Passini said. . . . "Listen. There is nothing as bad as war. We in the auto-ambulance cannot even realize at all how bad it is. When people realize how bad it is they cannot do anything to stop it because they go crazy. There are some people who never realize. There are people who are afraid of their officers." (50)

When Henry tries to get Passini to blame the wealthy ammunitions manufacturers, or other war profiteers, by responding "Also they make money out of it," Passini shatters his liberal beliefs by saying simply, "Most of them don't. . . . They are too stupid. They do it for nothing."

Immediately juxtaposed with this somewhat elevated discussion (though Passini avoids the ultra-patriotic words that Henry despises) is the scene of Henry's going to a headquarters building in search of food for his men. There is only cold macaroni and hard cheese, but there is also the atmosphere of relief inside the building that the attack is starting. As if to foreshadow that attack, the major notices, "Outside something was set down beside the entrance" (52). When the major says, "Bring *him* in," the reader has the same kind of disbelief that Henry experiences: a wounded man became a "something" in the day-to-day business of running the war. And immediately following this brief scene is the description of both Henry's wounding, and its accompanying out-of-body consciousness, and Passini's death.

Paul Fussell writes about what he calls "military memory":

> Everyone who remembers a war first-hand knows that its images remain in the memory with special vividness. The very enormity of the proceedings, their absurd remove from the usages of the normal world, will guarantee that a structure of irony sufficient for ready narrative recall will attach to them. And the irony need not be Gravesian and extravagant: sometimes a very gentle irony

emerging from anomalous contrasts will cause . . . "certain impressions [to] remain with one—a sunrise when the Huns are quiet, a sunset when they are raising a storm, a night made hideous by some distant cannonades. . . ." One remembers with special vividness too because military training is very largely training in alertness and a special kind of noticing.[1]

Like the "something" deposited outside the door of the tent, Hemingway's *A Farewell to Arms* is filled with slight details that open out only later in the novel, making readers return to their first introduction as if to process these details anew.

One of these is the quick mention of "the new graves in the [hospital] garden" that Henry—now hospitalized in Milan—observes as he goes for his walks and for his physical therapy, generally conducting himself as a person in recovery (75). Just a few feet from his room, however, lie the buried bodies of fellow soldiers who have died on the other side of the curtain that shrouds his bed. Another is the equally brisk mention of his going to sleep in Milan, watching "the beams of the search-lights moving in the sky," and his subsequent waking—"sweating and scared and then went back to sleep trying to stay outside my dream" (88). Italy is clearly a country at war, vigilant in keeping watch for any impending bombing. And Frederic Henry is clearly a man traumatized by his near-death wounding, a horrifically surprising attack that came in the darkness. Another is the ambulance major's description of the war (on Henry's return to action), which he consistently calls "very bad. . . . You couldn't believe how bad it's been" (167) and in the midst of the description, saying simply "we lost three cars."

Drawing on the author's careful planting of the assumptions people bring to war—and in his assumptions the character Frederic Henry was no less naïve than the other young soldiers or drivers—here Hemingway punctures another of those assumptions—that driving ambulances was not dangerous. Three of the fewer than a dozen ambulances under the major's jurisdiction were lost—the cars' men, presumably, dead. Just as Henry himself was blown up by a mortar shell, whoever was on the lines—regardless of which uniform he wore or what his responsibility was—was in danger of dying.

Hemingway uses this fallacy of assumption twice in the novel. One assumption is that ambulance personnel are, somehow, safe. Yet he gives us the deaths of Passini and Aymo, and Henry's wounding, to counter that public knowledge. Another is the fallacy that women no longer die in childbirth. Frederic thinks about these assumptions in almost the same language (the Catherine-dying-in-childbirth scene is another of the stream-of-consciousness passages): "And what if she should die? She won't die. People don't die in childbirth nowadays. That was what all husbands thought. Yes, but what if she should die? She won't die. . . . [W]hat if she should die? She can't die. Yes, but what if she should die? She can't, I tell you. . . . [B]ut what if she should die? She can't die. Why would she die? What reason is there for her to die?" (320). With the changing of insistent verbs, the quick repetition of short sentences, the blunted effect of the somber pattern of repetition as the reader begins to see how sure, even if implausible, Catherine's death is becoming, Hemingway builds toward the character's actual (quiet and gentle) death with all the bravado Frederic Henry can muster. But to the last question, "What reason is there for her to die?" the reader knows that such reasonlessness is precisely the point.

Catherine's death almost takes the fall for the fact that Hemingway writes very little unpleasant description of the battles of war per se. One of the problems with marketing war novels was that the readers did not want to know what trench warfare or the scenes on the hillsides of the Marne were like. As Fussell notes,

> One of the cruxes of the war, of course, is the collision between events and the language available—or thought appropriate—to describe them. To put it more accurately, the collision was one between events and the public language used for over a century to celebrate the idea of progress. Logically there is no reason why the English language could not perfectly well render the actuality of trench warfare: it is rich in terms like *blood, terror, agony, madness, shit, cruelty, murder, sell-out, pain* and *hoax,* as well as phrases like *legs blown off, intestines gushing out over his hands, screaming all night, bleeding to death from the rectum,* and the like. . . . The difficulty was in admitting that the war

had been made by men and was being continued *ad infinitum* by them. The problem was less one of "language" than of gentility and optimism; it was less a problem of "linguistics" than of rhetoric. Louis Simpson speculates about the reason infantry soldiers so seldom render their experiences in language: "To a foot-soldier, war is almost entirely physical. That is why some men, when they think about war, fall silent. Language seems to falsify physical life and to betray those who have experienced it absolutely—the dead."[2]

In both Fussell's book and in *A Farewell to Arms,* the soldier's reliance on communicating with relatives and friends back home by sending the Field Service Post Card illustrates the failure of civilized language—and the soldier's reluctance to invade his family's private and safe space with the language that could do justice to his experiences. On the postcard, categories are harmless yet reassuring:

I am quite well.
I have been admitted into hospital
> sick and am going on well.
> wounded and hope to be discharged soon.[3]

At two points in Hemingway's novel, Henry sends these postcards to avoid being in touch with his family. Each time he checks only "I am quite well." The first time he relies on these "official language" messages is when he has begun to learn what war is really about. The second time, however, is used to provoke the reader into assessing Frederic's state of mind once he has deserted. He uses the Field Service card during the idyllic months that he and Catherine live as a couple complete in themselves, awaiting the birth of their child. That the second instance seems to be as inexpressible as the first gives the reader the same kind of concern as does the dialogue between Catherine and Frederic when they reassure each other that they will never need to meet the other's father. In the scene where they talk about Catherine's past craziness and look ahead to the birth of their child, Catherine comments that wine had given her father the gout.

"Have you a father?"

"Yes," said Catherine. "He has gout. You won't ever have to meet him. Haven't you a father?"

"No," I said. "A step-father."

"Will I like him?"

"You won't have to meet him."

"We have such a fine time," Catherine said. "I don't take any interest in anything else any more. I'm so very happy married to you." (154)

The enormity of the couple's pretense—why does Hemingway give Frederic a step-father rather than a father, since it was his father he loved and that father still lived—and, more startlingly, Catherine's valorizing of their withdrawal from all the world, even their own families, under the guise that they have married, which they have not, creates more than irony: it clearly signals the readers that the "craziness" thought to be long in the past may still be with them, only this time, that it may be infecting both of them. The wages of war, the distillation of what war means—complete and utter separation from the known world, the world that makes a person human—impacts the reader here with first puzzlement and then despair. The least reconcilable dialogue is yet to come, however. Frederic Henry asks Catherine:

"Where will you have the baby?"

She replies, "I don't know. The best place I can find."

Operating now, as Henry says, in his "clear and cold" factual mode, he continues, "How will you arrange it?" And Catherine replies, as much in a fantasy of denial as he,

"The best way I can." (153–154)

Serving in a wartime army, living in a foreign country, unmarried and illegitimately pregnant, Catherine has nothing but a fantasy power. She has no rights, no way of providing for her hospitalization, no reason to be abroad but to serve in the hospital staff—and once her pregnancy becomes advanced, she will lose that sinecure. Juxtaposing these scenes as Hemingway does, the reader sees the necessity for Henry's using the Army Zona de Guerra postcards, "strange and mysterious" though he finds them (36). As Hemingway makes clearer and clearer, nothing is stranger and more mysterious than this illusory romance that Catherine and he have created.

To return to Frederic Henry as he is nearer the start of *A Farewell to Arms*, however, is to show how illusory was his first conception of war. He admits, "It seemed no more dangerous to me myself than war in the movies" (37). Henry's behavior strikes the reader accordingly: this is a young American who goes out with his friends, drinks too much, chases whores, and amasses statistics after a week-long leave that makes him one of the cocks of the walk. He is also something of a United States nativist: he has moments of wishing he were with the British forces rather than the Italian (after all, in Oak Park and other parts of the States, the men he serves with would be designated "wops"). He wonders about the Italian stereotypes and thinks about the difficulty of learning their language. He thinks of them as being marked by their Catholicism (the reason for the continued appearance in the novel of the young priest), by their wine drinking, by their lustiness (which the confessional in the Catholic church makes amends for), and by their hail-fellow-well-met characteristics. Even in the midst of learning to know Italians, he wishes for the English, "big and shy and embarrassed and very appreciative together of anything that happened. I wish that I was with the British. It would have been much simpler" (37). (Hemingway's nativism also prompts the dialogue about how comic the Japanese are, "a wonderful little people fond of dancing and light wines" [76], and much of the pidgen English kind of quality of his prejudicial statements might be ignored under the guise of translation problems.)

Wendy Steiner sees World War I as the most powerful of forces shaping American literature early in the twentieth century. She speaks particularly to the polite and patriotic phrasing of the fiction and essay intended to be polemic, to draw the United States into the war conflict, and to the way that expression jarred against the voicing of "the shattered despair of younger novelists," whose naturalistic mode gave the reader lines such as Henry Miller's "the boys from the north side and the boys from the south side—all rolled into a muck heap and their guts hanging on the barbed wire. . . . The whole past is wiped out." In Steiner's words, the younger writers' "bitter analysis polarized the generations, the sexes, and the aesthetic orientations of everyone concerned. The parents who had proudly sent their sons to die for their country, the women who rejoiced in the nobility of soldiers' blasted experience, and the traditionalists who eagerly embraced the war as a lesson in morality and propriety were equated with the cause of the war itself.[4]

In one of his earliest stories, "Soldier's Home," Hemingway had exploded the myth that a soldier—one who had seen any war at all—*could* return home. The story begins with the dilemma that Harold Krebs, who had seen action and was full of honest accounts of battle, faced when other men prided themselves on recounting inflated narratives. The language of his war had already been usurped—and dishonestly so. While he focused his enmity toward his mother and the complacent community, Harold Krebs knew at heart that the anger was within himself, was somehow his fault. Steiner notes that writers who dealt with the subject of World War I were implicitly drawn to the topic of such guilt. She says, "The dislocation brought on by World War I, the fact that even the winners came home to a world they could not live in, provoked a profound analysis of the phenomenon of victimization. Woodrow Wilson's argument for neutrality had been based on the need to avoid the dynamic of physical battle, on the grounds that the difference between winner and loser was too slight. The United States, he claimed, could not 'fight Germany and maintain the ideal of government that all thinking men share. . . . A ruthless brutality will enter into the very fibre of our national life'" (850).

Hemingway's handling of this problem within *A Farewell to Arms* was to create the character of Ettore, the American of Italian descent who is fighting in the Italian army. Even the glamour of Ettore's living in San Francisco—though a buddy calls him "just a wop from Frisco"—cannot keep his reprehensible qualities from Henry's and Catherine's criticism. Ettore Moretti is a man on the make, regardless of national characteristics. He wants all five of the medals he says he has been awarded ("But the papers on only one have come through") because they enhance his womanizing power. He comments to

Frederic that with his silver medal, "[T]he girls at the Cova will think you're fine then. They'll all think you killed two hundred Austrians or captured a whole trench by yourself." Tactless and offensive, Ettore shows Frederic (whom he calls "Fred" twice in this scene, the only time anyone in the novel deviates from Frederic Henry's chosen name) the "deep smooth red scar" on his arm. He boasts about his other two wounds that will make the three "wound stripes" on his sleeve almost as eye-catching as his medals. Ettore is the soldier who fights only for booty, of whatever kind (119–123).

In this negative definition of war hero, Hemingway posits everything objectionable to those who understand the horrible process of battle. He also gives the reader a contrast to the braggart Ettore (and the much more passive, but perhaps not any more heroic, Frederic Henry). In the character of Gino, the ambulance driver who explains to Frederic that "it really had been hell at San Gabriele," Hemingway gives the reader an observer of war who presents facts truthfully, with no self-aggrandizement. Instead, Gino uses his narrative in order to admit to his fear.

> He said the Austrians had a great amount of artillery in the woods along Texnova ridge beyond and above us, and shelled the roads badly at night. There was a battery of naval guns that had gotten on his nerves. I would recognize them because of their flat trajectory. You heard the report and then the shriek commenced almost instantly. They usually fired two guns at once, one right after the other, and the fragments from the burst were enormous. He showed me one, a smoothly jagged piece of metal over a foot long. It looked like babbitting metal.
>
> "I don't supposed they are so effective," Gino said. "But they scare me. They all sound as though they came directly for you. There is the boom, then instantly the shriek and burst. What's the use of not being wounded if they scare you to death?" (182)

Gino's discourse echoes that of the major, who is not afraid to tell Frederic Henry upon his return from the Milan hospital how bad things have been over the summer and fall. The Italians had lost 150,000 men on the Bainsizza Plateau and on the San Gabriele, and another 40,000 on the Carso. He said bluntly, "If they killed men as they did this fall the Allies would be cooked in another year. He said we were all cooked but we were all right as long as we did not know it. We were all cooked. The thing was not to recognize it" (133–134).

In a kind of counterpoint, a weary and visibly "thinner" Rinaldi tells Frederic Henry matter-of-factly, "This war is killing me. I am very depressed by it. . . . All summer and all fall I've operated. I work all the time. I do everybody's work. All the hard ones they leave to me" (167). But eventually Henry goes back to the front and—despite the verbal warnings he has had— is stunned by what he sees: the destruction of the forests and the ground where the troops have been shelled, the "many iron shrapnel balls in the rubble of the houses and on the road beside the broken house where the post was" (185). The physical waste is bringing the bludgeoning character of war closer to Henry.

It is when Henry sleeps at post during the night that the full force of the possibility of enemy attack hits him; the fear that Gino had described takes over.

> The wind rose in the night and at three o'clock in the morning with the rain coming in sheets there was a bombardment and the Croations came over the mountain meadows. . . . They fought in the dark in the rain and a counter-attack of scared men from the second line drove them back. There was much shelling and many rockets in the rain and the machine-gun and rifle fire all along the line. They did not come again. . . .
>
> The wounded were coming into the post, some were carried on stretchers, some walking and some were brought in on the backs of men that came across the field. They were wet to the skin and all were scared. We filled two cars with stretcher cases as they came up from the cellar of the post and as I shut the door of the second car and fastened it I felt the rain on my face turn to snow. The flakes were coming heavy and fast in the rain.
>
> When daylight came the storm was still blowing but the snow had stopped. It had melted as it fell on the wet ground and now it was raining again. There

was another attack just after daylight but it was unsuccessful. We expected an attack all day but it did not come until the sun was going down. . . . We expected a bombardment but it did not come. It was getting dark. (186)

Hemingway's emphasis here is not on the damage done by the shelling and the attacking, but rather on the state of mind of Frederic Henry and the others, whose job was to wait, to keep watch, to convey the wounded, to try to save lives.

After this scene, with its countless examples of brave men doing their jobs with no thought of medals or wound stripes, Hemingway juxtaposes the scene of Frederic Henry nervously preparing for the evacuation and asking his superior officer what the policy is for using the ambulances during a retreat. What he is told shocks him. The ambulances will be used to carry hospital supplies and equipment, not to save the wounded. The wounded are left behind. When a country has a chance to be a winner, human life is worth saving. But when the country is on the run, its armies in retreat, all human life can be extinguished—with no guilt or repercussions. The people in charge of humanitarian efforts are intent on saving only themselves and their equipment.

In some ways, this context makes the decision of Catherine Barkley, V.A.D. who was brought to Italy to aid the wounded, somewhat more understandable. Once a country was losing, even the medical personnel saved themselves first. Fergie would be transferred out, and no matter how badly the wounded needed aid, the hospital would provide no human comfort—perhaps shelter, but not personnel.

It seems fair to say that what Frederic Henry learns in the process of becoming a military man is that one acts primarily to save himself. In contrast to the rules and lessons of the service, Hemingway shows the less educated (in this novel, the ambulance drivers and mechanics) and people separate from the military forces as the only true observers of the horrors of warfare. Positioning Frederic Henry between those two camps, Hemingway allows his protagonist a range of legitimate behaviors. In James Phelan's reading of Henry, for example, the character illustrates what Phelan sees as *A Farewell to Arms*'s primary plot, "a coherent process of growth and change in Frederic Henry that culminates, tragically and ironically, in the moment of his greatest loss. Furthermore, I believe that Hemingway's representation of this process cannot be appreciated until we combine our attention to style, character, and structure with careful attention to voice" (Phelan 60). In Phelan's discussion of the novel, he draws parallels between the way Hemingway makes the reader identify, first, with the naïve Henry—albeit with some criticism for his egotism and machismo—and the way that somewhat critical identification changes into understanding as the novel goes its carefully drawn way.

Phelan sees immense distance between Hemingway as author and Frederic Henry as character, particularly at the novel's start. "For all the authority of his voice at the beginning of the narrative, Frederic Henry is strikingly ignorant; the implied presence of Hemingway's voice, which gives the sentence its pointed irony, makes Frederic's voice naïve. This gap between Frederic and Hemingway is arguably the most important revelation of the first chapter. It established a tension between author and narrator that is one major source of our continued interest in the narrative, and it helps define the major initial instability of the narrative: Frederic's situation in a war whose effects and potential consequences he is ignorant of" (64).

By concentrating on the style of the way the character's voice interacts with the unnamed, third-person, authorial voice, Phelan is able to enrich the reading of Henry that summarizes his sorrowful learning experiences throughout the narrative as "maturing." Surely a man does not need to escape being killed (several times), become a killer himself, and lose both his child and his wife in order to mature. Hemingway may have thought of himself as a realist, but he was never aiming for martyrdom—for either Frederic Henry or himself.

One of the most-detailed presentations of the role of "retrospective narration" in Hemingway's characterization of Frederic Henry is James Nagel's essay, in which he argues that the Henry the reader knows is not conveyed through a realistic, chronological description of the man enduring World War I: "*A Farewell to Arms* is fundamentally not a realistic novel about World War

I narrated by Ernest Hemingway; it is, rather, a retrospective narrative told by Frederic Henry a decade after the action has taken place for the purpose of coming to terms emotionally with the events."⁵ Enriched with the 1990s critical interest in self-narration, Nagel's is the current view of reading Henry so that the obvious moral impasses of the novel can be assessed in fairly complex ways. Frederic Henry during the war was a young man, relatively inexperienced. The Frederic Henry who narrates the novel has learned from both the war and his great love: he is a different character.

Phelan's analysis gives us a more complex approach to voice and figuration, as he points out, to counter the ease with which this retrospective view can be assimilated:

> The rub in seeing Frederic as the victim rather than the source of irony is that if unselfconscious Frederic has learned about the war and the world at the time of the action, then his knowledge should always be a part of his perspective as he retells the story. In other words, Frederic writes as if he does not know what he in fact knows. (82)

Phelan's approach is also one of the few that focuses on the interaction between Henry and the young priest. While Hemingway's triangular design—Rinaldi, the priest, and Catherine as Henry's objects of value—is clearly set up from the start, little critical attention has been paid to his friendship with the priest. It is almost as though the critics have adopted the pose of the officers at the mess, and see the priest as an object of ridicule rather than a spokesperson for one whose life is directed toward a goal.

The character of the priest—young himself, and intentionally unnamed except by profession—in many ways establishes the innocence of Frederic Henry as young soldier: even as he is being corrupted by drink and sex, his higher motivation (his military service) is idealistic. Why else has he volunteered for any involvement in the war at all?

As Phelan points out, it is in Henry's conversations with the priest after he has returned from this convalescence in Milan that the reader sees how disillusioned the young American has become.

[Priest] "I had hoped for something."
  "Defeat?"
  "No. Something more."
  "There isn't anything more. Except victory. It may be worse." (179)

Phelan notes that "Frederic's voice here now echoes Passini's; the conventional wisdom has been replaced by the values of the Italian peasant. Furthermore, as Frederic voices values more in line with Hemingway's, the authoritative quality of the voice is softened to some extent" (71).

It can be said that, throughout *A Farewell to Arms,* the presence of the priest has a reassuring, almost tranquilizing, effect. But it is also from the priest that Frederic is given permission to value his love for Catherine. As the priest tries to understand how Henry, whom he likes and admires, can deny any love for the God who is his very life, he confirms Henry's potential for loving: "When you love you wish to do things for. You wish to sacrifice for. You wish to serve" (72). But Henry—even in the midst of his passion for Catherine—says flatly, "I don't love." The priest maintains his reassuring role by saying, "You will. I know you will. Then you will be happy." Henry, however, in one of the cruder moments of nonfeeling that Hemingway gives the character, replies complacently, "I'm happy. I've always been happy." The interchange is strange in what Henry might think is the expression of his brutal honesty, but in effect, he robs the priest of parts of his own belief system. Frederic Henry may be a person with no illusions, but he also shows himself incapable of appreciating the kindness of friendship. To ameliorate this cynical impression, Hemingway closes the scene by showing the wounded Henry going off to sleep, thinking of the priest's Abruzzi—"what was lovely was the fall to go hunting through the chestnut woods"—rather than fearing either attack or his own customary nightmares (73). This scene, coupled with the one referred to earlier, when the priest tells Henry how terrible the summer has been, is the end of Hemingway's use of the young priest. From then on, reliance on language gives way to the efficacy of action.

Robert Lewis points to Hemingway's belief that words are treacherous. Several scenes "link the motif of talking with that of thinking. The former language activity is open; the latter, closed within the head of the thinkers. Throughout Hemingway's other work (as well as throughout *A Farewell to Arms*), nonthinking is a valid, even valuable state. . . . [A] way of coping with irrational and absurd reality" (Lewis 134).

It is the priest who cuts through the brash language Rinaldi has used to welcome Frederic back. . . . "How are you really?" Lewis calls their ensuing conversation a "minidrama in epistemology applied to their understanding of the war" (135). Incomprehensible though it may be to outsiders, the war demands Hemingway's cryptic and restrained choices of words, many of which are negatives. When the priest asks Frederic—who has just commented that any belief in victory is impossible—what he does have belief in, he answers, "In sleep" (179).

Effectively cutting the priest and his conversation off, Frederic yet reaffirms their friendship, promising "We'll have a walk and talk together" when he again returns (180). The language of war has ceased to bridge the distance between people caught in the travesty of fighting other human beings, but the human beings themselves remain valuable.

Whenever he appears in *A Farewell to Arms,* the nameless priest prompts the reader's reference to Frederic Henry's belief system. There are many scenes in the novel ostensibly "about" religion. As Lewis contends, "religion is significant throughout the novel, whether in the character of the priest or in the absence of religion in the lives of most of the other characters" (38). Even while these characters seem irreligious, however, the text is filled with both religious objects and religious vocabulary—the Saint Anthony medal and the prayers of the supposed Catholic Italian ambulance drivers; the references to souls, belief systems, and various threats of death. Count Greffi, for example, looks back from his near century of life to comment on the soul, and the priest, in his urging Frederic to go to the Abruzzi, creates a place that seems to serve as a spiritual refuge, "the homeland where nature and human beings cohere, where life is good"—and, by implication, pure. As Hemingway uses the mention of the land, in fact, it is seen to be (in Lewis's description) "an area isolated in both time and place, a pastoral haven remote from both the war and the cities of the plains that attract the profane" (110).

If *A Farewell to Arms* were intended to be only a war novel, or even only the combination of war novel and romance that most readers see it as being, Hemingway's emphasis on the spiritual would be less necessary. But to write the quest story, the narrative of Frederic Henry as pilgrim, Hemingway had to provide the clear, sweet moments of spiritual possibility as contrast to the urban, mechanized, blood-soaked landscape of war.

To break into the convention of the war novel frees Hemingway from a number of constraints. It allows him to draw a hero who in his conflicted state deserts his military duty rather than losing his life by upholding it. Individual life is thus privileged above any common, nationalistic good. The primary plot of a war novel is usually the account of battles that, all too inevitably, lead to either victory or death—sometimes both. In contrast, Hemingway's reader comes to the close of *A Farewell to Arms* relatively ignorant of World War I's outcomes. In fact, Hemingway's breaking out of the paradigm of war novel has allowed him to emphasize the domestic narrative over that placed on the battlefield. As Margaret Higonnet and her coeditors write in the introduction to *Behind the Lines, Gender and the Two World Wars,*

> Even when women writers describe the wartime losses that they have suffered as women—as wives, mothers, and lovers—they are displaced, for the primary loss in war literature is inevitably death; mourning is secondary. (Higonnet, Jenson, Michel, and Collins 14)

What Hemingway does in *A Farewell to Arms* is make mourning primary: the structure of the book, and therefore its impact, depends on the well-being of Catherine and the child. That Hemingway also reverses the character of the bereaved—as well as the character lost—is another surprise. Lament as the reader does the known losses of life during the First World War, the only scenes of death in *A Farewell to Arms* give him or her the deaths of Passini and Aymo, modest figures dead through random and therefore meaningless acts. Hemingway does not tell the stories of men who perform valiantly in the fields of war. His characters either die accidental deaths, or else—like Bonello and Frederic Henry—desert.

Because of Hemingway's scenes of dialogue between Henry and the ambulance drivers, as well as between Henry and Rinaldi, the officers, and the priest, the reader remains conscious of war and all its philosophical justifications. But because none of these passages of discourse ever praises the war, the author succeeds in debunking the rhetoric of patriotism. As the introduction to *Behind the Lines* remarks, "Much of the strength of men's literature of war derives from the tension between patriotism and criticism" (15). *A Farewell to Arms* comes down hard on the side of criticism of war. Unrelieved in his censure of World War I, Hemingway crafts a book that never posits so much as a shimmer of glamour, romance, or honor in men's activities in the field.

Given the literary fact that the war novel is held to be a male-dominated genre, with men of war serving as protagonists and adversaries, what Hemingway achieves in *A Farewell to Arms* is a moving story of people caught in the unreasonableness of war who are yet intent on creating a world that is balanced, honorable, and even guided by rational principles.

Jane Marcus points to Hemingway's uncharacteristic choice of the humble ambulance drivers and mechanics—foreign and undistinguished military people, not officers leading a charge—as a signal of how different even the war segments of the novel are from the expected. In the growth to maturity of Aymo and the others, she sees a parallel with the changes in Frederic Henry. As she notes,

> The ambulance drivers are equally made into "men" by the requirements of their jobs. They must overcome their fear of open spaces and the dark and drive long distances in the night with their cargo of maimed men. (Marcus 142)

In their service to aid and transport the wounded, these figures can be identified as more feminine than masculine. They care for others; they—for the most part—are armed to protect themselves and their vehicles rather than to fight as aggressors in the lines. Indeed, it is unexpected that the male characters in *A Farewell to Arms* are *not* fighting men.

Yet, in what Marcus defines as an important sexual pattern, Hemingway's characters do fit an expected gender pattern. Marcus points out, "In wartime, the impotent male is a vampire. . . . [M]en must be potent. Women must be maternal" (131). There is no question that Catherine and Henry play out these established sexual roles: for all the inconvenience of an unexpected pregnancy, in fact, Henry might be said to have proved his potency beyond question.

In Hemingway's skillful structuring, there are implied changes in Henry's virility. At several points in the book, his whole being is traumatized. The most important of these places is Book III, which serves as the novel's pivot. The massively disillusioning events of the war that seems in the process of being lost causes the same kind of shock to Henry's psychological system that the mortar shell injuries did to his physical body. Once back in the lines, he assumes command of the ambulances and their drivers, but his judgment is shaken. He had volunteered for neither retreat nor defeat.

As simply as the language Hemingway chooses to describe it, the former began:

> The next night the retreat started. We heard the Germans and Austrians had broken through in the north and were coming down the mountain valleys toward Cividale and Udine. The retreat was orderly, wet and sullen. In the night, going slowly along the crowded roads we passed troops marching under the rain, guns, horses pulling wagons, mules, motor trucks, all moving away from the front. There was no more disorder than in an advance (188).

With the incremental repetition he often used to achieve tone, Hemingway's next paragraph established the pervasive rain, mud, and hopelessness. About the crush of refugees, the hysteria, the bundles of life's treasures, he says nothing. Only the stifled push of evacuation, and finally, "The column stalled again in the night and did not start" (195). And of course, "It was still raining" (198).

Frederic Henry and his drivers—Bonello, Piani, and Aymo—maintain their stoic composure. They give rides to two pairs of people—two "sergeants of engineers" separated from their Italian unit and two adolescent sisters who fear for their lives, and their virginity. It is through Henry's interactions with both pairs that Hemingway charts his character's disintegration.

With the young sisters, who speak so little English that they are dependent on body language rather than words, the ambulance personnel need to make them understand they are in no danger. Hemingway's attention falls first on this pair, because their fearfulness adds a kind of dark comedy to the good-hearted efforts of the men to transport, feed, and comfort them. When Aymo mistakenly touches the thigh of the older sister, a gesture of assurance, she "drew her shawl tight around her and pushed his hand away. . . . The girl looked at me fiercely" (195). In a paragraph describing the fear of what Henry calls these "two wild birds," Hemingway plays on the shock value of coarse language—whatever its dialect.

> [Aymo] turned to the girl. "Don't worry," he said. "No danger of ———," using the vulgar word. "No place for ———." I could see she understood the word and that was all. Her eyes looked at him very scared. She pulled the shawl tight. "Car all full," Aymo said. "No danger of ———. No place for ———." Every time he said the word the girl stiffened a little. Then sitting stiffly and looking at him she began to cry. I saw her lips working and then tears came down her plump cheeks. Her sister, not looking up, took her hand and they sat there together. The older one, who had been so fierce, began to sob (196).

In a later interchange, the men ask the girls if they are virgins (which they are), and the girls seem cheered by receiving acknowledgment. Their predicament, and their virginity, sends Frederic Henry into a reverie about Catherine, their great love, and the stream-of-consciousness tapestry of lines from the lyric "Western wind." The condition of human love is itself drastically changed in the presence of war—and what war does to its practitioners.

The scenario of the two sergeants of engineers seems meant to illustrate how corruptible men at war can become. On the second day of the retreat, conditions worsen. The drivers make the young sisters leave them and join the populace at large, where they will be more anonymous and perhaps safer. The sergeants, however, will be useful once the ambulances leave the main roads and try to reach Udine by crossing the countryside. When the sergeants try to bolt, seeing that the ambulances will never make the trek, Frederic Henry shouts his orders:

"Get busy," I said, "and cut brush."

"We have to go," one said. The other said nothing. They were in a hurry to start. They would not look at me.

"I order you to come back to the car and cut brush," I said. The one sergeant turned. "We have to go on. In a little while you will be cut off. You can't order us. You're not our officer."

"I order you to cut brush," I said. They turned and started down the road.

"Halt," I said. They kept on down the muddy road, the hedge on either side. "I order you to halt," I called. They went a little faster. I opened up my holster, took the pistol, aimed at the one who had talked the most, and fired. I missed and they both started to run. I shot three times and dropped one. The other went through the hedge and was out of sight. I fired at him through the hedge as he ran across the field. The pistol clicked empty and I put in another clip. I saw it was too far to shoot at the second sergeant. He was far across the field, running, his head low. I commenced to reload the empty clip. Bonello came up.

"Let me go finish him," he said. I handed him the pistol and he walked down to where the sergeant of engineers lay face down across the road. Bonello leaned over, put the pistol against the man's head and pulled the trigger. The pistol did not fire.

"You have to cock it," I said. He cocked it and fired twice. He took hold of the sergeant's legs and pulled him to the other side of the road so he lay beside the hedge. He came back and handed me the pistol.

"The son of a bitch," he said. He looked toward the sergeant. "You see me shoot him, Tenente?"

Hemingway's style intensifies the impersonality of this execution. Bonello's bragging, Henry's demand for authority (and the long-recognized penalty for disobeying an officer, even though—as the sergeant had said—Henry was not their officer), the sense that killing was what a person had to do in wartime all jar against the very humane treatment these same men had just given to the young Italian girls. But in each case, the military men are following the prescriptions of their "duty"—to protect women and children, to create military order. The double-bind of following orders, even if those orders are not one's own and serve no purpose (especially in the light of a retreat that cannot salvage much), traps Frederic Henry here, despite his sense of himself as a fair person.

Hemingway's description works to make the reader question Henry's act. The spareness of Henry's orders to the men—to cut brush, to halt—seems intended to shortcut the phrase the sergeants might have anticipated. At no time does Henry threaten to shoot them, and never has his gun been in evidence.

The word choice "dropped one" also places the killing into the realm of sport shooting, as does Piani's kidding that Bonello "killed him on the sit. . . . He wasn't flying very fast when you killed him" (207). The sense of the impersonal continues as the sergeant's body is undressed to provide material to put under the ambulance wheels, leaving him clothed only in his long underwear; whatever dignity remains is to death lost. And Bonello's sense of accomplishment—"all my life I've wanted to kill a sergeant"—also chills the reader.

Even though Hemingway may be trying to balance whatever scales of justice exist in war, the fact that the sergeants eat before the drivers, try to steal a clock from the abandoned farmhouse, and dislike the ambulance drivers hardly stacks up beside the death of one of the sergeants (unnamed, unmourned, distinguished only as the one who talks the most).[6]

After the killing of the sergeant, Frederic Henry is hit with guilt about what he has done to his own men. He seems never to think about the execution. But about the ambulance drivers, he says, "It was my fault. I had led them up here" (205) and he feels much worse when Aymo is shot by a sniper (who may be an Italian). Hemingway shows Henry's rational military thinking ("We could avoid the main line of the retreat by keeping to the secondary roads beyond Udine. I knew there were plenty of side-roads across the plain. I started down the embankment").

But as soon as Henry calls for his men to follow, a shot hits the embankment. His command "Come on" is immediately changed to "Go on back," but Aymo, "as he was crossing the tracks, lurched, tripped and fell face down. We pulled him down on the other side and turned him over. 'His head ought to be uphill,' I said. Piani moved him around. He lay in the mud on the side of the embankment, his feet pointing downhill, breathing blood irregularly. The three of us squatted over him in the rain. He was hit low in the back of the neck and the bullet had ranged upward and come out under the right eye. He died while I was stopping up the two holes" (213).

That both Bonello and Piani question Federic Henry's leadership comes out clearly as the three of them sit together, mourning their friend. Bonello asks, "Who's dead next, Tenente? Where do we go now?" (214) Later that rainy night, when they stop to rest, Bonello deserts and Piani covers for him, saying that he was afraid to die. He would rather be a prisoner. (In the novel itself, having witnessed—and been a part of—the killing of the sergeant surely made Bonello tentative about his own desertion. Who could be sure that Frederic Henry would not draw on him?) The context of war that Hemingway has pictured makes Bonello's—and, as a foreshadowing, Frederic Henry's—choice understandable.

Hemingway returns the reader to the concept of bravery, by interrogating the relationship between living and dying, and being brave, being a patriot. None of the dead was brave, but neither did the dead do any harm. One of the reasons the ambulance drivers are apt characters for this novel is that they have so little to gain by being courageous: they instead have jobs to do, and they try to do them. They do not give orders; they are on the humanitarian side of conflict. Yet of the three drivers Frederic Henry had started his journey with, only one remained. The novel also returns the reader to the echo of Henry's explaining to Catherine that he is not a brave man. Using the metaphor of a baseball hitter, Henry says, "I know where I stand. I've been out long enough to know. I'm like a ball-player that bats two hundred and thirty and knows he's no better" (140). Being a mediocre player is better, at that, than killing people—either intentionally as he did with the sergeant or accidentally as he did with Aymo.

To view Henry's aggressive act as evidence of the military right, if not of machismo, is to call into question Scott Donaldson's reading that Frederic is at heart passive, if not cowardly, able to get others to either suggest what should be done or to take action themselves (as Bonello finished off the sergeant).[7] Thomas Strychacz contributes a more complex assessment of Hemingway's early male characters, people Strychacz sees as driven by their need to perform in manly ways. As he says, "Performance itself does not guarantee manhood; but manhood does require successful performance. Fashioning manhood 'while the crowd hollers' and looks on is the crucial drama men undertake in Hemingway's early work: the moment when his characters undergo their most intense experiences of authority or humiliation."[8] (As an aside to the use of the world *manly* is novelist Jim Harrison's comment in the *New York Times Magazine* that the concept of being "manly" differs. For Harrison, who grew up in mid-Michigan, men who "fished and hunted strenuously" might not consider those activities particularly masculine. Rather, according to Harrison, "That idea seemed to derive from writers of city origin like the tortured Hemingway, who, though a very great writer, seemed to suffer from a prolonged struggle with his manhood."[9])

This kind of self-dramatization Strychacz names occurs regularly in Frederic Henry's relationship with Catherine, and is one of the reasons Fergie mistrusts him. There are the initial evenings when he drinks too much and arrives late, so that he cannot be with Catherine. There is his overweening confidence in the Milan hospital when he pulls her into his bed as soon as she arrives, and his disruptive insistence that she work the night shift so that they can make love. (Hemingway gives us the charming "Come back to bed, Catherine. Please" to endear Henry to the reader as well as to his lover [102]; he works hard to show how effective Henry's charm is, not only in Milan but throughout their Switzerland escape.) Ironically, it is in the

midst of Henry's passion for Catherine that when the priest describes to
him what love is, Henry denies ever having loved. Perhaps it should not be
such a surprise when he responds as he does to Catherine's admission of
her pregnancy. In a scene that serves as culmination of her self-effacement,
her wanting to be him, for them to be the same person, she apologizes for
having become pregnant from their frequent bouts of intercourse.

> "Nothing. Nothing's the matter."
>> "Yes there is."
>> "No nothing. Really nothing."
>> "I know there is. Tell me, darling. You can tell me."

The outcome of their conversation proves that Catherine's assessment was
right—Frederic is not happy about the pregnancy, despite his protestations,
and she is made to be the apologizer after all. "I'm going to have a baby,
darling. It's almost three months along. You're not worried, are you? Please
please don't. You mustn't worry. . . . I did everything. I took everything but
it didn't make any difference." Rather than empathize with what she has
been through during the last months, however, Frederic replies inanely,
"I'm not worried."

Later, when the conversation resumes, Frederic shows his true feelings
as Catherine asks,

> "You aren't angry are you, darling?"
>> "No."
> "And you don't feel trapped?"
>> "Maybe a little. But not by you."
> "I didn't mean by me. You mustn't be stupid. I meant trapped at all."
> "You always feel trapped biologically."
> She went away a long way without stirring or removing her hand.
> "'Always' isn't a pretty word."
>> "I'm sorry."

"It's all right. But you see I've never had a baby and I've never even loved any one. And I've tried to be the way you wanted and then you talk about 'always.'"

"I could cut off my tongue," I offered.

"Oh, darling!" she came back from wherever she had been. "You mustn't mind me."

We were both together again and the self-consciousness was gone. "We really are the same one and we mustn't misunderstand on purpose." (137–139)

The assault readers feel in this scene stems from Frederic Henry's utter lack of sympathy for Catherine, a lack of sympathy that is clear form his stiffly withheld emotions. His response is not only monosyllabic ("No") or terse ("I'm not worried," "I'm sorry") or glib ("I could cut off my tongue") but some lines are insulting: "You always feel trapped biologically. . . . Maybe a little. But not by you." What Hemingway carefully omits is any evidence that Frederic is happy about the baby—or even accepting of it. This collective response erases earlier evidence of his charm, or of his genuine caring for this woman. On her own in foreign countries, and those countries at war, Catherine knows better than to involve him into her necessary planning. His quip about cutting off his tongue hardly serves any serious apology, just as *his* feeling of "being trapped" hardly compares with *her* situation.

It is this scene that has angered women readers (and some men) through-out the last thirty years. Yet Sandra Whipple Spanier reads Catherine as the code hero in this novel, and pays tribute to her ability to lose herself within the relationship. Spanier acknowledges that the character of Catherine offends some readers; she notes that "it is hard for them to see the subordination of the individual ego to a personal relationship as a mark of maturity. Rather than being respected for her self-knowledge and clear-eyed pragmatism as she attempts to construct a sane context for her existence in an insane world, Catherine has been perceived as lacking in character because she has chosen to define herself in terms of a relationship."[10] While Spanier builds an impressive case for Catherine as a wise and surviving lover, as does Ernest Lockridge, *A Farewell to Arms* provides too many instances of Frederic Henry's immaturity, his habit of using Catherine, even to creating the grieving facade as he does at the end of the novel's narrative. If Catherine Barkley were alone in the novel, Spanier's case might be stronger.

In a recent essay about language in *A Farewell to Arms,* Gary Harrington notes that seldom in the novel does the reader find any warmth in Frederic's "love" for Catherine. He uses as examples the frequent references to prostitutes, the notion that neither of the lovers will ever meet each other's families, and the naming of Catherine as "your English" and the "English you go to see every night at the hospital." Harrington's point is that this novel, too, like *The Sun Also Rises,* is filled with puns, puns that when read correctly add to the unpleasantness of the tone of the great love relationship:

> However, whether Frederic likes it or not—and he does not—Catherine carries the child to term. After the delivery, Frederic goes to the restaurant where he "read[s] the paper of the man opposite" (329). The news provides details of "the break through on the British front," a somewhat graphic pun relating both to the Caesarean operation and to the resultant hemorrhaging which at that moment afflicts Catherine. Not coincidentally, early in the novel both Frederic and Rinaldi refer to Catherine as "the British" (32). . . . A closely related play on words occurs in Frederic's description of the weather after his lunch on the day of the delivery. Frederic reports that "The day was cloudy but the sun was trying to come through" (318), just as the couple's son is at that moment trying unsuccessfully on his own to "come through." (Harrington 70)

Harrington's note to this commentary is itself pertinent, as he refers to another of those pieces of information about pregnancy that Frederic simply blotted out—Catherine's narrow hips. He refers to another play on words during the retreat, when Frederic tells Aymo to let the sisters leave because "they won't be very useful. . . . You ought to have some one that could push. . . . Pick up somebody with a wide back" (199).

Another of Harrington's points is that even as Catherine is struggling for her life, Frederic asks the doctor only "Will that scar flatten out?" as if only her appearance matters to him. Harrington continues, "the remark anticipates Frederic's own emotional wound being reduced in the future to an affectless reminiscence; considering his atonal narration throughout *A Farewell to Arms,* he seems to have arrived at some approximation of this condition by the time that he begins to tell their story. This emotional leveling finds an analogy in Frederic's recounting late in the novel his memory of the ants on the log in the fire" (71).

To view Frederic Henry as emotionally stymied goes against the grain of most extant criticism, which wants to find him changed—for the better— because of his involvement with Catherine. The very fact that he can narrate his mournful story (his narration becoming *A Farewell to Arms*) bespeaks his comparative health. For Jamie Barlowe-Kayes, however, the whole matrix of narration—Hemingway's craft and intention, Frederic Henry's ostensible meanings, Catherine's words as a part of that composite—is suspect. Barlowe-Kayes suggests a more comprehensive way of reading the character of Catherine in relation to that of Frederic Henry when she insists that both figures exist in an unstabilized space. The crux is, according to this critic, that Catherine must be read as "a subject, not an object."[11] The reader must see that Catherine Barkley's supposedly superior knowledge as it relates to war—and which she uses to educate Henry—is of little value in saving her own life. Readers may accept the idea that Catherine has superior knowledge as a way of giving her character a superior position. But it remains Hemingway's role to decide what kind of knowledge is valued:

> [H]er "knowledge" about war is not finally attachable to her experience, other than vicariously. She knows no more about dying in war (even as a nurse) than Frederic knows later about dying in childbirth. Thus, whatever subjectivity might seem to be implied in her articulation of the text's privileged information is instead undermined when she is re-read as Hemingway's version of an attractive puppet who speaks knowingly about what he does not allow her to know (179).

Barlowe-Kayes also points out that Catherine's willingness to both "'educate' Frederic Henry and to subordinate herself to his desires—almost to the point of abandoning her responsibilities—[provides] yet another screen behind which Barkley's objectification is hidden to Hemingway himself and to many Hemingway critics." Catherine therefore cannot be read, or judged, outside of the cultural context that has itself shaped the kinds of responses a good, and particularly a loving, woman would be allowed to make.

Barlowe-Kayes concludes that "Hemingway's text, as a representation of the traditions of gender relations, repeats that tradition's inherent, unacknowledged objectification of women. As a metaphor, Barkley also iterates Hemingway's praise for acquiescent, self-sacrificing, fully supportive women" (180).

For the general reader, however, it is hard to deny the supposed reality of Catherine and Frederic: characters exist in fiction not to provide practice in applying reading theory, but to capture the imaginations of readers. One of the main problems with Catherine Barkley as heroine, or as hero, is that she wants so desperately to lose herself in Frederic Henry's identity. Where is the incipient feminist, the courageous woman who cares for the wounded in war? Where is the twentieth century's "new woman"?

Some of these issues are hard to decipher because a great many segments of *A Farewell to Arms* borrow from the patterns of classic romance. Once the reader meets Catherine, all elements of conventional romance are introduced. The meeting occurs in a garden. Catherine—dressed in white, aristocratic, educated, later described as a "goddess"—is protected by a nurse, her friend Fergie; and Rinaldi as the magical introducer suggests the French epic, *The Song of Roland*'s second of the same name. Catherine herself calls attention to the "game" of romance, with its rituals; and we are given the phallic object of the stick and the beauty of her long, uncut hair as well as her tall blondness to complete the romantic trope.

Lisa Tyler's important essay comparing Emily Brontë's *Wuthering Heights* and *A Farewell to Arms* describes borrowings—women named Catherine, each carrying a fetus named Catherine; both Englishwomen with the same physical characteristics; both trying to reclaim a lost adolescent love. Rain shrouds both books; dialogues are symbolic (and redolent, in the Hemingway novel, of lines from *Heights*); the love relationships are exclusive. The passion of the lovers is also unholy: neither woman is religious, neither recognizes life after death.[12]

John Cawelti's definition of romance underscores the use of one or the other (or both) of the lovers' deaths to reveal the level of their passion. He cites the stories of Tristan and Isolde, and Romeo and Juliet, to show that readers believe that "the intensity of the lovers' passion is directly related to the extent to which their love is doomed" (Cawelti 39–42). Hemingway plants a number of signals throughout *A Farewell to Arms* that doom, not joy, is the tone of the love affair. And while many readers might attribute the somberness of the book to its being set during a brutal war, others would recognize the dark risks that the experience of great passion carries.

Many of these signals can also be read as indicating that *A Farewell to Arms* is meant to be a courtly love story. (Even as Hemingway is writing the sexual descriptions for everything except Frederic's and Catherine's love making, he reminds his readers of the chastity, of the abstinence typical of the court romance.) Hemingway had grown up reading the Arthurian legends, and his use of the wounded Jake Barnes in *The Sun Also Rises* draws partly from the wounded Arthur, king whose land will be barren unless he is rescued by a virgin knight bearing a bloodstained lance—the young matador Pedro Romero.

Then, too, as early as 1924, Hemingway's friend Eric Dorman-Smith remembers discussing the French "Arthur" story, *Chanson de Roland,* with an excited Hemingway.[13] The story of Roland (sometimes called "Orlando") threads under *A Farewell to Arms,* as it does Hemingway's later novel *For Whom the Bell Tolls* and Virginia Woolf's 1928 *Orlando.*

Roland's tale has become legend. In it the man of integrity must survive and prosper even though his family betrays him. Orphaned or abandoned, the hero finds his role of service with the Emperor Charlemagne. With his cousin Rinaldo, Roland/Orlando does numerous great deeds as the emperor's paladin, but his most memorable is sacrificing himself and his troops to save Charlemagne. That battle occurs at the monastery of Roncesvalles, where sacrifice and purity are the marks of nobility.[14]

To transfer this skeletal outline to the themes of *A Farewell to Arms* is not difficult. Rinaldi, the other officers, and Frederic Henry are the paladins of the Allies: they are men given to compassionate service (Rinaldi as physician, Henry as ambulance driver). They are not in the business of conquering people and land for their own benefit. Both see the value in Catherine, though Rinaldi (usually the more successful lover) loses out in this instance.[15]

Hemingway adds a dimension of sexual tension to his novel by making Rinaldi less chaste, more avaricious. His sexual appetite for women is clear, and he consistently flirts with Henry as well. As roommates, Rinaldi and Henry share an intimacy that the protected Oak Park Hemingway had never known. "You're dirty," Rinaldi tells Frederic as he returns from his leave. "You ought to wash" (11). In the midst of asking for sexual details of his various exploits, Rinaldi makes Henry aware of his body. Notice this contradictory descriptive entrance: "We shook hands and he put his arm around my neck and kissed me. 'Oughf,' I said" (11).

The pattern is repeated nearly every time Henry returns to their room: the American relates nonphysically to the Italian man's advance-which-might-not-really-be-advances: "You have that pleasant air of a dog in heat. . . . Good night, little puppy" (27); Rinaldi calls Henry "baby" (41), "Poor dear baby" (64), "We won't quarrel, baby. I love you too much. . . . We are war brothers. Kiss me good-by" (67). After Henry is wounded, Rinaldi "came in fast and bent down over the bed and kissed me" (64); "Rinaldi kissed me. You smell of Lysol. Good-by, baby. Good-by" (77). As Rinaldi admits during the first visit to the hospital:

> I wish you were back. No one to come in at night from adventures. No one to make fun of. No one to lend me money. No blood brother and roommate. Why do you get yourself wounded? (65)

He uses a sexual image to tell Henry he is jealous of his friendship with the priest:

"Sometimes I think you and he are a little that way. You know." And when Henry is angry, Rinaldi continues, "you are just like me underneath. . . . You are really an Italian. All fire and smoke and nothing inside. . . . We are brothers and we love each other." (65–66)

Like the novel published twenty-five years after Hemingway's death, *The Garden of Eden*, *A Farewell to Arms* has a texture that allows more sexual readings than the primary heterosexual pairing of Catherine Barkley and Frederic Henry. But it is the romance plot, with that couple's great love, that has received the most critical attention. Judith Fetterley's now-famous criticism of the book, "Hemingway's 'Resentful Cryptogram,'" ascribes what she calls the structural "deviousness and indirection" of the narrative to Hemingway's hostility toward strong women. She challenges his verbiage about "idyllic union," "their Swiss idyll," and "genuine commitment" when such language is set against the fact that Catherine dies, and dies because she is female (Fetterley 61).

Fetterley places the pair within the context of war, noting that for men to die in battle is noble, but for Catherine to die in childbirth is willfulness that she somehow might have controlled.

The difference between what men deserve in the world which produces these doctors and soldiers and priests and what women deserve can be seen in the disparity between the treatment of Catherine's death and the treatment of the deaths of men at war. "You will not do any such foolishness,' the doctor said. 'You would not die and leave your husband'"; "'You are not going to die. You must not be silly.'" The tone here is appropriate to a parent addressing a recalcitrant child and the remarks are at once a reprimand and an implicit command which at some level assumes that Catherine is in control of whether she lives or dies. Indeed, Catherine herself has internalized the attitude of her doctor. She presents that *reductio ad absurdum* of the female experience: she feels guilty for dying and apologizes to the doctor for taking up his valuable time with her death—"I'm sorry I go on so long." (63)

Fetterley's point is that the soldier who has hemorrhaged to death in the ambulance above Henry was not apologizing; Catherine's death is, however, accompanied by guilt because "As long as there is a man around who needs her, she ought not to die" (64)

So far as the argument that Catherine instructs Frederic, making him into a better man, Fetterley sees that role of providing wisdom to be another kind of trap. "On the simplest level, Catherine allows Frederic to avoid responsibility and commitment. But in so far as this allows him to avoid growing up, she has failed him and is thus subject to hostility on this account. She is equally subject to hostility for having complicated his life and come so close to thrusting responsibility on him. . . . Catherine has betrayed Frederic. . . . The point is that whatever way you look at it, Catherine is bad news. Thus we might finally see her death as the unconscious expression of the cumulative hostilities which Frederic feels toward her. Essentially, she gets what is coming to her" (72).

Frederic Svoboda draws this consideration of the self-sufficiency of romance into a larger context when he mediates that "the Hemingway protagonist often seems to exist like Hemingway in a moment after: after the nineteenth century, after wilderness, after innocence, after loss" (Svoboda 169). Of all the themes that can be defined, particularly in connection with the male protagonist, perhaps the most pervasive is that of loss, loss that often produces a great effect upon the reader. *A Farewell to Arms* becomes one of Hemingway's great works because in it, according to Svoboda, "That essential sense of the seriousness of life—and sometimes of its joy—is underscored by its occurring against a backdrop of love and war, certainly two of the world's most serious undertakings" (171).

If many of the themes of the novel can be drawn from the military and war-linked parts of the novel, it is partly because such conflict is so clearly gendered. Men's roles in war are predictable, just as they are predictive of the character of the person involved with the conflict. Accordingly, to comment on the themes of such a narrative from the perspective of its women characters means realizing that the women in the novel will of necessity play the responsible roles assigned to women during wartime. Catherine Barkley is as surely trapped by her role as Frederic Henry is by his.

Catherine's role in her life with Frederic Henry is to love and support him. As Hemingway had written to F. Scott Fitzgerald about the ways he tried to work romance into much of his writing, "Love is also a good subject as you might be said to have discovered."[16] As numerous critics have also understood, the traditional place of the woman in love is a subordinate one.

NOTES

1. Fussell, 326–27; the quote includes words from Stephen Hewett's *A Scholar's Letters from the Front*, 46.
2. Ibid., 169–70; Louis Simpson's comment from *The Poetry of War*, 172.
3. Quoted in Fussell, 184. *See also* Leed, *No Man's Land,* and Angela Smith, *The Second Battlefield.*
4. Steiner, 848–49. See Trout, "'Where Do We Go From Here?'" and McKenna and Raabe, "Using Temperament Theory."
5. Nagel, "Catherine Barkley"; see also Balbert, who comments on the way Frederic's "practical, soldierly, but delimiting brand of merely 'survivalist' ideology" becomes broader and richer once he loves Catherine ("From Hemingway to Lawrence").
6. Among critics who discuss Henry's killing the sergeant are Bell, "Pseudoautobiography and Personal Metaphor"; Lewis, *A Farewell to Arms;* Paul Smith, "The Trying-Out of *A Farewell to Arms*"; and several essays in Gary Wiener's *Readings on* A Farewell to Arms.
7. Donaldson, "Frederic Henry's Escape."
8. Strychacz, "Dramatizations of Manhood."
9. Harrison, "First Person Female."
10. Spanier, "Catherine Barkley"; hereafter cited in text. See also Lockridge, "Faithful in Her Fashion."
11. Barlowe-Kayes; hereafter cited in text.

12. Tyler, "Passion and Grief."

13. As noted in Reynolds, 93; see also Fuchs's "Ernest Hemingway."

14. The best description of Hemingway's interest in this theme is Moreland's *Medievalist Impulse.*

15. Early Hemingway writings suggest that he was more intrigued with Rinaldi than his role in *A Farewell to Arms* shows. The character appears in the vignettes of *In Our Time,* as well as in a manuscript titled "The Mercenaries" at the John F. Kennedy Library Hemingway collection. Set in Petoskey, Michigan, and Chicago, the story has as the "I" protagonist a character named "Rinaldi Rinaldo."

16. Ernest Hemingway to F. Scott Fitzgerald, *Letters,* 177.

WORKS CITED

Balbert, Peter. "From Hemingway to Lawrence to Mailer: Survival and Sexual Identity in *A Farewell to Arms.*" *Hemingway Review* 3.1 (Fall 1983): 30–43.

Barlowe-Kayes, Jamie. "Re-reading Women: The Example of Catherine Barkley." In *Hemingway: Seven Decades of Criticism.* Ed. Linda Wagner-Martin, 171–84. East Lansing: Michigan State UP, 1998.

Bell, Millicent. "Pseudoautobiography and Personal Metaphor." In *Modern Critical Views of Ernest Hemingway's* A Farewell to Arms, 113–29. New York: Chelsea House, 1987.

Cawelti, John G. *Adventure, Mystery, and Romance.* Chicago: U of Chicago P, 1976.

Donaldson, Scott. "Frederic Henry's Escape and the Pose of Passivity." In *Modern Critical Interpretations of Ernest Hemingway's* A Farewell to Arms, 97–112. New York: Chelsea House, 1987.

Fetterley, Judith. "Hemingway's 'Resentful Cryptogram.'" In *Modern Critical Views of Ernest Hemingway's* A Farewell to Arms, 61–75. New York: Chelsea House, 1987.

Fuchs, Daniel. "Ernest Hemingway, Literary Critic." In *Ernest Hemingway: Five Decades of Criticism.* Ed. Linda Welshimer Wagner, 39–56. East Lansing: Michigan State UP, 1974.

Fussell, Paul. *The Great War and Modern Memory.* New York: Oxford UP, 1975.

Harrington, Gary. "Partial Articulation: Word Play in *A Farewell to Arms.*" *Hemingway Review* 20.2 (Spring 2001): 59–75.

Harrison, Jim. "First Person Female." *New York Times Magazine*, May 16, 1999, 100–101.

Hemingway, Ernest. *Ernest Hemingway: Selected Letters, 1917–1961*. Ed. Carlos Baker. New York: Scribner's, 1981.

———. *A Farewell to Arms*. New York: Scribner's, 1929.

———. *In Our Time*. New York: Boni & Liveright, 1925.

———. "The Mercendaries." Item 572–73. Hemingway Archive, John F. Kennedy Library.

Higonnet, Margaret Rudolph, Jane Jenson, Sonya Michel, and Margaret Collins, eds. *Behind the Lines: Gender and The Two World Wars*. New Haven: Yale UP, 1987.

Leed, Eric. *No Man's Land: Combat and Identity in World War I*. Cambridge: Cambridge UP, 1979.

Lewis, Robert W. A Farewell to Arms: *The War of the Words*. New York: Twayne, 1992.

Lockridge, Ernest. "Faithful in Her Fashion: Catherine Barkley, the Invisible Hemingway Heroine." *Journal of Narrative Technique* 18.2 (Spring 1988): 170–78.

Marcus, Jane. "Corpus/Corps/Corpse: Writing the Body in/at War." In *Arms and the Woman: War, Gender, and Literary Representation*. Ed. Helen M. Cooper, Adrienne Auslander Munich, and Susan Merrill Squier, 124–67. Chapel Hill: U of North Carolina P, 1989.

McKenna, John J., and David M. Raabe, "Using Temperament Theory to Understand Conflict in Hemingway's 'Soldier's Home.'" *Studies in Short Fiction* 34.2 (1997): 203–13.

Moreland, Kim. *The Medievalist Impulse in American Literature: Twain, Adams, Fitzgerald and Hemingway*. Charlottesville: UP of Virginia, 1996.

Nagel, James. "Catherine Barkley and Retrospective Narration in *A Farewell to Arms*." In *Ernest Hemingway: Six Decades of Criticism*. Ed. Linda W. Wagner, 171–85. East Lansing: Michigan State UP, 1987.

Phelan, James, *Narrative as Rhetoric, Technique, Audience, Ethics, Ideology*. Columbus: Ohio State UP, 1996.

Reynolds, Michael S. *Hemingway's Reading, 1910–1940*. Princeton: Princeton UP, 1981.

Smith, Angela. *The Second Battlefield*. New York: Palgrave, 2000.

Smith, Paul. "The Trying-Out of *A Farewell to Arms*." In *New Essays on* A Farewell to Arms, Ed. Scott Donaldson, 27–52. Cambridge: Cambridge University Press, 1990.

Spanier, Sandra Whipple. "Catherine Barkley and the Hemingway Code: Ritual and Survival in *A Farewell to Arms*." In *Modern Critical Interpretations of Ernest Hemingway's* A Farewell to Arms, 131–48. New York: Chelsea House, 1987.

Steiner, Wendy. "The Diversity of American Fiction." In *Columbia Literary History of the United States*. New York: Columbia UP, 1988.

Strychacz, Thomas. "Dramatizations of Manhood in Hemingway's *In Our Time* and *The Sun Also Rises*." In *Hemingway: Seven Decades of Criticism*. Ed. Linda Wagner-Martin, 45–59. East Lansing, MI: Michigan State UP, 1998.

Svoboda, Frederic J. "Great Themes in Hemingway." In *A Historical Guide to Ernest Hemingway*. Ed. Linda Wagner-Martin, 155–72. New York: Oxford UP, 2000.

Trout, Steven. "'Where Do We Go From Here?': Ernest Hemingway's 'Soldier's Home' and American Veterans of World War I." *Hemingway Review* 20.1 (Fall 2000): 5–22.

Tyler, Lisa. "Passion and Grief in *A Farewell to Arms*: Ernest Hemingway's Retelling of *Wuthering Heights*." In *Hemingway: Seven Decades of Criticism* Ed. Linda Wagner-Martin, 151–69. East Lansing: Michigan State UP, 1998.

Wiener, Gary, ed. *Readings on* A Farewell to Arms. San Diego: Greenhaven Press, 2000.

Partial Articulation

Word Play in *A Farewell to Arms*

Gary Harrington

As many commentators have observed, Hemingway's title *A Farewell to Arms* involves a play on words relating both to Frederic Henry's desertion from the Italian army and to his later leave-taking of Catherine Barkley after her death in Switzerland.[1] Largely overlooked, however, is the extent to which Hemingway deploys double meanings elsewhere in the novel. They relate most frequently, of course, to Frederic Henry, and serve to challenge his integrity both as narrator and as Catherine's companion.[2] Except in a few instances when he deliberately and explicitly plays on words, Frederic remains unaware of the puns that reside in his narration. Hemingway's wordplay may consequently register Frederic's subconscious at work, and thus may be seen

Reprinted with permission from *The Hemingway Review* 20.2 (Spring 2001). Copyright © 2001 The Ernest Hemingway Foundation. Published by the University of Idaho, Moscow, Idaho.

to accord generally with "Lacan's theory of the repressed. . . . [in which] the unconscious reveals itself through verbal play," to borrow a phrase from Ben Stoltzfus's analysis of *A Farewell to Arms* (124). In this same vein, Paul Smith comments, "it may be that the persuasive force of [*The Sun Also Rises* and *A Farewell to Arms*], more Jamesian than we once thought, depends on their narrators *not* understanding the implications of their narratives" (28). Further problematizing the narrative is the fact that Frederic deliberately shades his story, foregrounding some aspects and glossing over others, to present himself as favorably as possible under the circumstances; in short, he is, as Gerry Brenner observes, an "untrustworthy" narrator (4). Smith succinctly sums up Hemingway's narrative strategy for his first two novels: "Both Frederic Henry and Jake Barnes say less than they know and, at times, know less than Hemingway wrote" (28).

Certainly, the wordplay that constitutes so prime a component of Hemingway's narrative procedure in *A Farewell to Arms* is not unique in his career. James Hinkle has cannily discerned many puns in *The Sun Also Rises* and Craig Kleinman has noted what he terms "wordy jokes" (a punning phrase itself) in *A Farewell to Arms*. Hemingway also uses wordplay in the short stories. To mention just two well-known examples: in conversation with Francis in "The Short Happy Life of Francis Macomber," Robert Wilson uses the rather brutal pun "Topping" (*CSS* 23) to allude to his evening activities with Margot, and the older waiter in "A Clean Well-Lighted Place" voices perhaps the most famous pun in Hemingway when he responds "Nada" to the barman's question, "What's yours?" (*CSS* 383).

One highly revealing play on words in *A Farewell to Arms* involves Frederic's returning to the front before his knee is completely healed. He has only "partial articulation" in the wounded leg (96), a pun that captures his reticence and failings as a narrator. Upon examining Frederic's leg, Rinaldi comments, "Is that all the articulation you have? . . . It's a crime. . . . They ought to get complete articulation" (166). By "they" Rinaldi means the doctors; Hemingway may well be indicating that the readers of *A Farewell to Arms* might expect a more "complete articulation." Similarly, while making their diagnosis, the doctors in Milan "[t]est [Frederic's] articulation" (96), which matches the reader's task in working through this intricate text.

Frederic also influences others to distort or disguise their communications: Catherine, for example, declares that she will intentionally make the letters she writes to him at the front "'very confusing'" (155), and Helen Ferguson agrees to follow Frederic's advice, "'Don't write anything that will bother the censor'" (25). Frederic himself employs a related practice when writing back to the States. On the *Zona di Guerra* postcards he mails home, he "cross[es] out everything except, I am well," remarking to himself, "That should handle them. Those postcards would be very fine in America; strange and mysterious" (36). An analogy may be drawn between his attitude concerning the postcards and the intentions governing his narration: the sole message transmitted in the postcards—"I am well"—suggests the ethical fitness Frederic ultimately attempts to claim in the novel, and he is willing to manipulate his narration in order to do so. By his own admission, Frederic is "anxious to please" (94) the doctors in the hospital and lies to them (94, 97) in order to do so, a strategy that may underlie his presentation of himself to the reader.

One of the novels mentioned by Count Greffi during the billiards game in Stresa further accentuates that readers should treat Frederic's narration with caution. Greffi mentions "*Mr. Britling Sees Through It*," and Frederic responds, "No he doesn't. . . . He doesn't see through it" (261). Frederic is presumably poking fun at Greffi's mistake in recalling the title of H. G. Wells' *Mr. Britling Sees It Through*.[3] By having Greffi transpose the last two words of the title, though, Hemingway himself may be suggesting that a close inspection of *A Farewell to Arms* would enable the reader to "see through" the self-serving aspects of Frederic's narration. Additionally, Frederic himself does not "See through" to the hollow core of his relationship with Catherine nor does he "see through" to the possible disastrous consequences of their wartime relationship, although she with a conscious prescience does.

Significantly, Frederic equivocates in his discussion with Greffi, telling him that he has been reading "nothing" (260) and only upon Greffi's insistence amending this statement to "'nothing any good'" (261), a judgment that of course includes Wells' novel. Frederic's derogatory assessment of *Mr. Britling Sees It Through,* a tale treating the early years of World War I on England's home front, may derive from the fact that the title reminds Frederic of his own failure to "see it through." The other text Frederic and Greffi discuss, Barbusse's *Le Feu,* vitriolically condemns "shirkers." Frederic has previously been accused by Nurse Van Campen of shirking by means of "a self-inflicted jaundice" (144), and prior to encountering Greffi, has deserted from the army altogether, so his lack of enthusiasm regarding the Barbusse work may also stem from personal considerations.

Another figure Frederic meets after his desertion is the failed American opera singer, Ralph Simmons, whose stage name, Enrico DelCredo, obliquely impeaches Frederic's reliability. Frederic himself is referred to as "Enrico" by the major (172, 175) and during the drinking about Bassi facetiously asks whether Frederic's name is "Frederico [*sic*] Enrico or Enrico Frederico?" (40). The fact that Frederic's first and last names can easily be reversed might suggest that he is, to borrow Falstaff's phrase, a "double man" (*1 Henry IV,* 5.4.138), a possibility reinforced by the fact that those significant silhouettes of Frederic produced by the street vendor in Milan are achieved by "separate[ing] the two thicknesses and past[ing] the profiles on a card" (135). From another perspective, Frederic's seeming to others to lack a surname might indicate that his presentation of himself is incomplete.

The name Simmons adopts, Enrico DelCredo, roughly translates as "Henry's faith" or perhaps "I believe Henry." On the surface, this might seem to affirm Hemingway's correlation of Frederic and Simmons. However, the fact that Enrico DelCredo is merely a stage persona, that Simmons is less than galvanizing as a performer, and that he tries to pass as a native even though he has difficulty with Italian pronunciation, all combine to prevent our accepting without reservation any favorable implication of his stage name as it relates to Frederic.[4] Like Simmons, Frederic lacks native fluency; his wearing one of Simmon's suits further associates the two, particularly so in that Frederic hopes the suit will deceive others into believing him to be a civilian. This hope is thwarted, however, when the Italian authorities "see through" his disguise.

Frederic's deceptions also appear in the wordplay generated by his relationship with Catherine. Hemingway implies that Frederic fools not only Catherine but also perhaps himself regarding his frequently averred love for her. Frederic seems more interested in Catherine physically than emotionally, as may be indicated by Hemingway's reference to the novel in progress as his "tale of transalpine fornication" (Baker 199). Recording potential titles for the nearly-completed novel on a sheet of paper, Hemingway jotted down a paraphrased quotation from Marlowe's *The Jew of Malta* in which Barabas reveals his callous attitude regarding sexual relationships: "I Have Committed Fornication But that was *In Another Country And Besides* the wench is dead" (Oldsey 19).[5]

At least according to Carlos Baker (199), the title Hemingway finally settled upon, *A Farewell to Arms,* derives from another Renaissance writer, George Peele.[6] Hemingway held Renaissance authors, and especially Shakespeare,[7] in high esteem, and *A Farewell to Arms* more explicitly than any other Hemingway work reflects this attraction. As Shakespeare's plays amply demonstrate, Renaissance literature brims with puns; consequently, Hemingway's frequent punning in *A Farewell to Arms,* his most "Shakespearean" text, should come as no surprise. Indeed, a play on words that specifically depends upon an Elizabethan context surfaces in Rinaldi's comment that Frederic needs "'a good Italian liver'" to "'make [him] a man again'" (168). According to Elizabethan beliefs, the liver was the repository of passion, as when Ferdinand in *The Tempest* refers to "the ardor of [his] liver" (4.1.56), and when Benedick in *Much Ado About Nothing* says of Claudio, "Then shall he mourn, / If ever love had interest in his liver" (4.1.230–231). Rinaldi's joking offer to replace Frederic's liver surgically thereby hints that Frederic's relationship with Catherine lacks true devotion. However, in a different sense Frederic himself is in fact "a good Italian liver" in that he lives well, if not very responsibly, while in Italy.

Even while recuperating from his injury, Frederic indulges in the good life, managing for example to attend a horse race with Catherine and some others. One of the winners embodies the proverbial horse of a different color, since he has apparently been dyed "a purplish black" (128), a fact so obvious that even a blind man, or one nearly so—Crowell Rodgers—can detect the duplicity. The utter transparency of this hoax prefigures to some extent Frederic's later ineffectual disguise as a non-commissioned soldier and as a civilian. On this same occasion, Catherine and Frederic whimsically back a horse named "Light for Me" (131). If the world "light" in the horse's name might pertain to Catherine's weight, then the couple's betting on Light for Me points to Frederic's concentrating upon the physical aspects of the relationships. Significantly enough, Light for Me loses the race, finishing fourth in a field of five (131). As the pregnancy proceeds, Catherine of course becomes progressively heavier, remaining neither "light" in weight nor sexually available for Frederic. Late in the pregnancy, Catherine tells him, "'I know I'm not fun for you, darling. I'm like a big flour barrel. . . . I'm just something very ungainly that you've married'" (309). The couple, of course, are not actually married, and in Switzerland Catherine states that she will go through the ceremony only after she is "'thin again'" (293), only after she is one more "light" for Frederic.[8]

Catherine's desire to visit that traditional honeymoon venue, Niagara Falls, ironically underscores the fact that they are unmarried. This choice reflects her romantic perspective, as does her desire to see the Golden Gate. One of Frederic's suggestions of potential sites tends much less toward the picturesque. As Catherine fumbles in recalling the name Golden Gate, Frederic proposes that they might visit, among other locations, the stockyards, a bizarre joke on Frederic's part that unwittingly forecasts Catherine's being butchered on the operating table.[9] This remark also intertwines the novel's strands of love and war by recalling Frederic's description of "sacrifices" in war as "like the stockyards at Chicago if nothing were done with the meat except to bury it" (185).

Just prior to Frederic's return to the front, the novel highlights his personal responsibility for Catherine's tragic end. Shortly before Catherine announces her pregnancy in the Milan hotel room, she and Frederic go to the armorer's to purchase a pistol. Frederic informs Catherine that hunters use "'the little mirrors set in wood'" (149) to trick larks into the open. Shortly thereafter, he repots that the room they briefly occupy at the hotel has "many mirrors"

(152), aligning Catherine with the hunted birds and by extension implying that Frederic considers their relationship to be simply a "lark."[10] After asking the hotel waiter what sort of "game" is available for dinner, Frederic orders woodcock. The overt phallic resonance of this choice emphasizes his cavalier involvement with Catherine, especially so in that they have only a bit of time before Frederic rejoins the troops, leaving the pregnant Catherine behind to fend for herself. Frederic's choice of woodcock also summons up Polonius's memorable phrase when warning Ophelia of the stratagems of potential male seducers as "springes [traps] to catch woodcocks" (*Hamlet* 1.3.115).[11]

Catherine's being associated with the woodcock as "game" also puns on Frederic's casual attitude toward their relationship, which he describes early on as a "game" (30), an outlook he arguably maintains throughout. Not long after they meet, Frederic tells Catherine that he loves her, but he then confides to the reader:

> I knew I did not love Catherine Barkley nor had any idea of loving her. This was a game, like bridge, in which you said things instead of playing cards. Like bridge you had to pretend you were playing for money or playing for some stakes. Nobody had mentioned what the stakes were. It was all right with me. (30–31)

Catherine also refers to their relationship on this occasion as a game, although in less complacent terms: "This is a rotten game we play, isn't it?" (31). After Catherine slaps Frederic during their second meeting, he comments, "I felt I had a certain advantage. . . . I was angry and yet certain, seeing it all ahead like the moves in a chess game" (26). Frederic's statements with regard to their relationship as a game, in combination with the couple's actually playing "many two-handed card games" (290) and chess (300) late in the novel, may indicate that Frederic's attitude does not change substantially. The chess references could also allude to Ferdinand and Miranda's chess game in Act Five of Shakespeare's *The Tempest,* a scene employing puns such as Miranda's "Sweet lord, you play me false" (5.1.172) to provide an inauspicious prediction for the young Italian couple's future.

Frederic and Catherine's own future initially seems in some ways roseate. Even Frederic's injury proves a felicitous mishap, bringing the two back together for a time. The doctor who performs the operation upon Frederic in Milan is named Valentini, suggesting romance. The procedure, in an evident phallic wordplay, for a time makes Frederic's leg "'stiff as a board'" (166),[12] a pun adding an extra dimension to Frederic's comment to Nurse Gage that his leg is full of "'old screws and bedsprings'" (85).

The nature of Frederic's injury, however, anticipates his later negative attitude regarding the pregnancy: according to one doctor, Frederic's wounded leg had been penetrated by "foreign bodies [which] were ugly, nasty, brutal" (94). Frederic likewise views the pregnancy as invasive; he sees the fetus as an unwelcome "foreign body" that has infiltrated Catherine's system and encroached upon the convenience of their relationship. Frederic's description of the moments after the disclosure of the pregnancy insinuates the presence of an interloper: "We were quiet awhile and did not talk. Catherine was sitting on the bed and I was looking at her but we did not touch each other. We were apart as when some one comes into a room and people are self-conscious" (138). When Frederic does speak, he declares, "'You always feel trapped biologically'" (139). Clearly, Frederic's perspective upon fathering the child is less than enthusiastic, a jaundiced attitude punningly reflected in his actually contracting jaundice shortly after Catherine informs him of the pregnancy. In his rancorous dispute with Nurse Van Campen, Frederic compares the experience of jaundice to being kicked in the scrotum. Hemingway thereby associates Frederic's physical malady both with sexual activity and its anticipated interruption—the pregnancy prompting his currently dour state of mind.

Van Campen's report on Frederic's alcohol consumption during his recuperation causes him to lose his leave. The original date for his return to the front, 25 October, one of the very few specific dates mentioned in *A Farewell to Arms,* nonetheless bears much significance—its importance in the narrative further underscored by Frederic's actually doing the math to calculate the date (135). The twenty-fifth of October, St. Crispin's Day, was made famous in history as the date of the battle of Agincourt, where vastly outnumbered English forces defeated the French in 1415. But Frederic does not return to the front on 25 October, a fact that like the novel's title, derived from a poem celebrating martial and patriotic virtue, suggests that epic military action may no longer be possible in the modern age, or at least not for Frederic.[13] By choosing and then rejecting 25 October, Hemingway presumably was thinking of the memorable speech delivered displaying the same opulent rhetoric which Frederic disparages in his famous commentary on nationalistic diction:

> I was always embarrassed by the words sacred, glorious, and sacrifice and the expression in vain. We had heard them . . . and had read them . . . now for a long time, and I had seen nothing sacred, and the things that were glorious had no glory . . . (184–185)

In the play, Henry V proclaims five times that the battle will occur on St. Crispin's Day, thereby implying that the English cause is indeed "sacred."[14]

The loss of a sense of the sacred in the modern age appears in Frederic's losing the St. Anthony medal which Catherine had given him; ironically, in the Christian tradition one prays to St. Anthony for help in finding lost objects (Delaney 63). When taking into consideration Frederic's rather hedonistic gratification of his assorted appetites, his losing the medal is appropriate. St. Anthony (1195–1231), an ascetic Franciscan, spent most of his brief life preaching in northern Italy, the setting for much of A Farewell to Arms, and "work[ing] ceaselessly and untiringly with heretics" (Delaney 63).[15] Far from converting nonbelievers, Frederic himself has grave doubt concerning the existence of God. In conversation with Count Greffi, Frederic remarks that he has religious belief only at night (261). Greffi maintains that love is "a religious feeling" (263); by transference, then, Frederic's devotion to Catherine is generally confined to their nights together in the bedroom.

Frederic's feeling more lust than love for Catherine is exhibited in her being associated time and again with prostitutes in his narration. Shortly after meeting Catherine, Frederic comments that seeing her was "better than going every evening to the house for officers" (30), and in the hotel in Milan

Catherine says that she feels like a whore. Frederic has told Catherine that they can enter this hotel without luggage (151); this of course alerts the hotel staff to their purpose in being there, and implies Frederic wants a relationship without baggage, in essence, one without responsibility. Frederic's quoting "To His Coy Mistress" in this episode unintentionally displays his carnality, since Marvell's speaker, as Catherine notes, is intent on seduction. Similarly, during Frederic and Catherine's time together at the hospital in Milan, Catherine's willingness to "do night duty indefinitely" (108) contains an implication of sex-as-profession not unlike that signified by the name "Jane Nightwork," a prostitute mentioned by Shallow in 2 Henry IV (3.2.198–199).

When pregnancy hinders Catherine's "night duty," she employs other methods in an attempt to solidify her union with Frederic. In Switzerland, for example, Catherine wants to have her hair cut so that she might more closely resemble Frederic, with the potential result, as she puts it, of their becoming "'all mixed up'" (300). She and Frederic do indeed seem mixed up in the sense of "confused," particularly with regard to their future as a couple, and even to their status as such. Incredibly enough, it is nearly midway through the novel before Frederic ascertains that Catherine's father is alive. Catherine pledges that Frederic will never have to meet her father; Frederic reciprocates by promising that she will never have to meet his stepfather (154). This exchange hardly represents the mature commitment of two people who consider themselves bound to one another for life. Catherine at another point makes an inadvertently revealing comment by saying, "'Thank God I'm not your family'" (304), thereby signaling a greater emotional distance between the two than either of them would admit.

The indeterminacy of their status also emerges in their frequent remarks about marriage. Frederic and Catherine remain unmarried, despite having told themselves and others, such as the doctor and the hairstylist, that they are husband and wife. And although Frederic frequently asserts his desire to marry Catherine, after one such avowal he tells the reader, "I suppose I enjoyed not being married, really" (115).[16] When he and Piani come upon some wine during the retreat, Frederic concludes, without any particularly compelling evidence, that "It must have been wine they had saved for a wedding," but the future celebrants "had kept it too long and it had gone to pieces and lost its quality and color" (217–18). This implies that for Frederic, actual marriage to Catherine would finally have been anticlimactic.

Catherine intends the phrase "mixed up" to indicate a convergence of appearance and consequently identity, a variation of her often stated longing to "become" Frederic, as when she remarks, "'Oh, darling, I want you so much I want to be you too'" (299). In Book 5 generally, and especially after she enters the hospital, Catherine's behavior does in fact come to resemble Frederic's. For example, her craving more and more of the anesthetic rivals Frederic's own prodigious yearning for alcohol. Frederic early in the process describes her as "a little drunk from the gas' (318). Later, and just after one of those instances when Catherine lavishes extravagant praise upon the doctor, Frederic bluntly—and unfairly, since she is merely reacting to the anesthetic—tells her "'You're drunk,'" to which she replies "'I know it. . . . But you shouldn't say it'" (319).

In Milan, Frederic spent much of his time genuinely drunk in a hospital bed, and his veiled flirtation with Nurse Gage while awaiting Catherine's arrival is mirrored in the sexual subtext of Catherine's interaction with the doctor who administers the anesthetic in the operating room; with regard to Catherine's experience in the hospital room, then, Hemingway intertwines the motifs of sex and death. Shortly after describing the doctor as "wonderful" three times in a brief period, Catherine exclaims to the doctor, "'*Give it to me. Give it to me,*'" after which the following description occurs: "She clutched hold of the mask and breathed short and deep, pantingly. . . . Then she gave a long sigh. . . . 'That was a very big one,' Catherine said. Her voice was very strange" (319). Just afterwards, Catherine says "'There it comes'" adding "'*Give it to me*'" yet again (319), and a moment later the doctor sends Frederic, apparently against his wishes, out of the room. Even more telling is this passage:

> "I want it now," Catherine said [to the doctor]. . . . I watched Catherine breathing deeply and rapidly. . . . "had a very big one a while ago. The doctor made me go clear out, didn't you, doctor?" Her voice was strange. It rose on the word doctor. The doctor smiled. "I want it again," Catherine said. . . . I heard her moaning

a little. . . . "That was a big one," she said. "That was a very big one. Don't you worry, darling. You go away. Go have another breakfast." (316–317)

Frederic's terse response here speaks volumes: "'I'll stay,' I said" (317).

Earlier in *A Farewell to Arms,* Catherine has paraphrased Shakespeare in describing Frederic as "'Othello with his occupation gone,'" to which Frederic gave the ugly response, "'Othello was a nigger. . . . Besides, I'm not jealous'" (257).[17] To the contrary, and despite the fact that Frederic may remain unaware of the full range of his feelings, he does indeed seem envious of Catherine's ardent appreciation of the doctor's ministrations, and so his motives are mixed in giving Catherine ever higher doses of gas. Presumably, Frederic wants to relieve Catherine's pain, but he also, consciously or not, wants to match or outdo the doctor in what appears in the narrative as a sublimated sexual competition. When he takes over for the doctor the second time, Frederic's application of the anesthetic causes her to cry out, "*Oh, it doesn't work* . . . [I]t doesn't work any more. . . . [I]t doesn't work at all. . . . It doesn't work. It doesn't work. It doesn't work'" (322). Feeling inadequate in more ways than one, Frederic declares, "'I'll make it work. I'll turn it all the way'" (322). Frederic is perhaps even seeking revenge upon Catherine for her esteem for the doctor. Judith Fetterley goes so far as to contend that Catherine's death "is in fact the fulfillment of [Frederic's] own unconscious wish, his need to kill her" (53), and that her dying "is the logical consequence of the cumulative hostilities Frederic feels toward her" (62).

Be that as it may, Frederic's behavior in the hospital at best demonstrates poor judgment, as he continually gives Catherine doses of gas in excess of the doctor's instructions to "'turn [the dial] to the numeral two'" (317). As the ordeal continues, Frederic becomes more conservative in the amount of gas he administers: after turning the dial to "three and then four" Frederic remarks that he "was afraid of the numbers above two" (323), an unintentional pun which, as Robert Lewis observes, manifests Frederic's fear of the child's disrupting his idyll with Catherine (53).

The number two figures prominently elsewhere in the novel, and, as in the hospital, the references betoken the couple's desire to isolate themselves from others. Shortly after relaying the news of the pregnancy, Catherine stipulates, "'We mustn't [fight]. Because there's only us two and in the world there's all the rest of them. If anything comes between us we're gone and then they have us'" (139). In this same exclusionary mode, although Frederic and Catherine regularly pass through three villages on their walks from the Guttingens' to Montreux, in his narration Frederic can only recollect the names of two of them. When describing the view from the Guttingens', Frederic mentions that the island on the lake has two trees, in essence a paradigm of Frederic's concept of an ideal relationship: he and Catherine "alone together," separated from the world at large. Frederic's attraction to the surname of Archbishop Ireland exhibits this same sentiment. He remarks, "What made it pretty was that it sounded like Island" (38). However, to paraphrase the Donne passage which was later to supply the title for *For Whom the Bell Tolls,* Hemingway's point is that no couple is an island, entire of itself.

Two islands also figure in the couple's escape from Italy. The names of these islands, Isola Bella and Isola Madre, hint that for Frederic beauty and motherhood remain separate and distinct from one another. Prior to the couple's seeking refuge in Switzerland, the barman in Stresa who jokes about Catherine's not actually being Frederic's wife declares that while fishing recently he "'caught some beautiful pieces. Trolling this time of year you catch some beautiful pieces'" (244). For the reader, the word "pieces" carries a decidedly sexual undertone, especially given its peculiar ostensible meaning here. Notably, when the barman and Frederic go trolling for "beautiful pieces," Frederic relates that he rows them to Isola Bella but does not even mention Isola Madre.

However, whether Frederic likes it or not—and he does not—Catherine carries the child to term. After the delivery, Frederic goes to the restaurant where he "read[s] the paper of the man opposite" (329). The news provides details of "the break through on the British front" (329), a somewhat graphic pun relating both to the Caesarean operation and to the resultant hemorrhaging which at the moment afflicts Catherine. Not coincidentally, early in the novel both Frederic and Rinaldi refer to Catherine as "the British" (32). Rinaldi calls her "'your English'" and the "'English you go to see every night at the hospital" (77).[18] A closely related play on words occurs in Frederic's description of the weather after his lunch on the day of the delivery. Frederic reports that "The day was cloudy but the sun was trying to come through" (318), just as the couple's son is at that moment trying unsuccessfully on his own to "come through."[19]

The baby's final delivery by Caesarean section pertains to Frederic's earlier paraphrasing of a memorable passage from Shakespeare's *Julius Caesar*. Frederic states, "'The coward dies a thousand deaths, the brave but one'" (139). He claims that he does not know the origin of the aphorism, but Catherine observes that "'probably a coward'" (140) said it, implying, intentionally or not, that Frederic is a coward. The paraphrase also associates Frederic with the original speaker of the line, Julius Caesar, whose insistent professions of courage in Shakespeare's play to some degree convey the opposite impression. So Catherine, who elsewhere seems remarkably conversant with Elizabethan literature, is intuitively right regarding a text she has not read. Catherine also maintains that "'the brave dies perhaps two thousand deaths if he's intelligent'" (140). Although she claims in this episode not to be brave, her envisioning herself as dead in the rain, according to her own criterion, might suggest otherwise, as does her fortitude when facing death in the novel's final chapter.

As she becomes aware that she is dying, Catherine elicits a pledge from Frederic not to "'do our things with another girl, or say the same things,'" and vows, in a phrase containing perhaps as much menace as promise, "'I'll come and stay with you nights'" (331). This is somewhat like Caesar's ghost telling Brutus "thou shalt see me at Philippi" (4.3.283) and also resembles Hostess Quickly's threat to Falstaff to "ride thee a' nights like the [night] mare" (*2 Henry IV* 2.1.76–77).

When it earlier appears that Catherine will survive, Frederic's rather offhand question to the doctor, "'Will that scar flatten out?'" (325), exemplifies his fixation upon Catherine's appearance. Additionally, the remark anticipates Frederic's own emotional wound being reduced in the future to an affectless reminiscence; considering his atonal narration throughout *A Farewell to Arms,* he seems to have arrived at some approximation of this condition by the time that he begins to tell their story. This emotional leveling finds an analogy in Frederic's recounting late in the novel his memory of the ants on the log in the fire. Although most of the ants are burned or steamed to death, which punningly connects to that recurrent description of soldiers in the war being "cooked," as in "doomed," a few ants escape.[20] Frederic reports, "Some got out, their bodies burnt and flattened, and went off not knowing where they were going" (327), a condition aptly corresponding to Frederic's own in the novel's final paragraph. Frederic feels emotionally "burnt and flattened" by Catherine's death, and he wanders aimlessly back to the hotel with no clear direction for the future. Brenner notes that "[w]hether caused by war, family, or accident, and whether physical, emotional, spiritual, or psychological, wounds define the world of this novel: injury ridden." Hospitals and doctors cannot "cure the wounds that accompany Frederic when he walks from the hospital at the novel's end" (Brenner 28).

Earlier in *A Farewell to Arms,* the "house doctor" had told Frederic that to make a complete recovery he would have to expose his wounds to the sun (97). Frederic's retrospective narration of his time with Catherine exposes his psychological wounds to the light and effects a sort of confessional cleansing. Unfortunately, Frederic's quest for emotional rehabilitation meets with only marginal success because he suppresses as much as he reveals. Yet, for the reader, the wordplay in *A Farewell to Arms* reveals even more than Frederic attempts to suppress.

NOTES

1. Stoltzfus detects in the title "homonyms that slide into the novel's themes. The world treats Frederic and Catherine harshly. . . . The world is not *fair,* and neither protagonist *fares* well" (127). Malcolm Cowley sees this "symbolic title" as constituting "Hemingway's farewell to a period, an attitude, and perhaps to a method" (qtd. in Oldsey, 10).

2. While opinions of Frederic Henry and the reliability of his narration continue to vary, many now dispute the notion that Frederic's attitudes are fully endorsed

by Hemingway. For example, see Donaldson, *New Essays*.

3. Based upon Frederic's apparent knowledge of the actual title, I am assuming that the mistake here is Greffi's rather than Hemingway's. The manuscript at the Kennedy Library renders the title *Mr. Britling Sees Through It,* as in the published text. My thanks to Stephen Plotkin of the Kennedy for providing this information. Lewis also notes the transposition and attributes it to Greffi (1995, 164).

4. In one of his discarded conclusions to *A Farewell to Arms,* Hemingway subtly calls attention to Simmons's using a different name for performance by having Frederic refer to him as "whatisname [*sic*]" (Reynolds, 1976, 46).

5. Although he ultimately rejected the phrase from Marlowe in favor of *A Farewell to Arms,* Hemingway titled one of his short stories "In Another Country." The Marlowe quotation figures in a surprising number of twentieth century texts. Bartlett provides a valuable, if brief, discussion of this matter.

6. Sylvester asserts, rather unconvincingly I think, that *Othello* "is the primary literary antecedent of the novel's title" (177). Lockridge, apparently following Sylvester's lead, calls *Othello* "the camouflaged source of Hemingway's title" (73).

7. Among much other evidence of his admiration for Shakespeare, Hemingway told George Plimpton in 1958, "I read some Shakespeare every year, *Lear* always. Cheers you up if you read that" (Bruccoli 119). Reynolds in *Hemingway's Reading* lists thirteen Shakespearean plays (181). Not only does Hemingway paraphrase Shakespeare's *Othello* and *Julius Caesar* in the novel, but in his introduction to the 1948 illustrated edition he referred to *A Farewell to Arms* as his version of *Romeo and Juliet* (Reynolds, 1981, 25). Reynolds adds, however, "I suspect that [Hemingway] got [this] idea from the critics after the fact" (*Reading* 25).

8. In naming the horse Light for Me, Hemingway might also be punning on "light" as standard Elizabethan terminology for sexual promiscuity; Shakespeare employs "light" in precisely that sense time and again. To cite just one of a multitude of examples, Portia in *The Merchant of Venice*—a text from which Hemingway quotes in "God Rest You Merry, Gentlemen"—quips, "Let me give light, but let me not be light, / For a light wife doth make a heavy husband" (5.1.129–130).

9. Adventurous speculation might detect in Frederic's other two suggestions—the

Woolworth Building and the Grand Canyon—a self-complimentary phallic innuendo and a derogatory vaginal reference.

10. The association of the visit to the armorer's and the exchange in the hotel is reinforced by what Stoltzfus identifies as the "phallic connotations" of the pistols in the novel (123 and *passim*).

11. In *Twelfth Night*, Shakespeare again uses the terms "woodcock" to imply sexual deception. As Malvolio spies the forged letter supposedly registering Olivia's desire for him, Fabian remarks "Now is the woodcock near the gin [trap]" (2.5.83).

12. Significantly enough, Frederic uses the exact phrase "stiff as a board" as he is drifting into an erotic dream about Catherine during the retreat: "If there were no war we would probably all be in bed. . . . Bed and board. Stiff as a board in bed. Catherine was in bed now. . . . Maybe she was lying thinking about me. Blow, blow, ye western wind" (197).

13. Brenner notes "Hemingway's borrowing the novel's title from that of George Peele's poem, then, is ironic, for he rejects the poem's conviction that 'duty, faith, love are roots, and ever green'—that they offer meaningful value" (29). Certainly Frederic rejects some of these virtues; whether or not Hemingway does so is open to discussion.

14. The prominence of 25 October in both *A Farewell to Arms* and *Henry V* presents the tantalizing possibility of a source for the names of the two main characters in the novel: in Act 5 of *Henry V*, *Henry* becomes betrothed to *Katherine* of France. It should be noted, however, that other possibilities exist: for example, Lynn posits one of Hemingway's correspondents, Barklie Henry, as the source for "the last name of both his principals" (389), a thesis supported by Hemingway's comment in a letter to Henry, "By god I did name all the characters after you didnt [*sic*] I?" (*SL* 255, n.1). Stoneback maintains that "Maybe [Hemingway] really named Frederic Henry after . . . the famous Martini-Henry rifle, creation of *Frederic* Martini and A. *Henry*" (37). Also worth remembering is that the central figure in Peele's poem is named Henry Lee.

15. Reynolds lists Rose Fyleman's *Book of Saints* in the inventory of Hemingway's books in Key West in 1940 (1981, 128). Although Fyleman's book appeared in 1939, ten years after the publication of *A Farewell to Arms*, Hemingway's owning

Book of Saints may indicate an abiding interest in the subject.

16. Perhaps noteworthy in this context is that Falstaff in *2 Henry IV* cynically promises marriage to both Mistress Ursula and Hostess Quickly, and, interesting, to the latter as she bathes his wound (2.1.91–92).

17. For an extended discussion of the influence of *Othello* on *A Farewell to Arms* see Wilson, "Bidding Goodbye." Although I find much to admire in his essay, Wilson and I come to very different conclusions about the significance of the allusion. For additional commentary on *Othello* and Hemingway, see Lockridge, "*Othello* as Key," and Sylvester, "The Sexual Impasse."

18. Frederic uses similar phrasing to explain to Piani his muttering while experiencing that erotic dream about Catherine: "'I was having a dream in English'" (198).

19. One of the major problems with the delivery is the narrowness of Catherine's hips, a situation anticipated by what ultimately may be recognized as a play on words during the retreat. After Aymo picks up the two Italian girls, Frederic tells him, "'They won't be very useful. . . . You ought to have some one that could push. . . . Pick up somebody with a wide back to push'" (199).

20. The most prominent use of the word "cooked" occurs on 133–134, where the British major employs the term thirteen times in a single paragraph. The Captain at the post who relays the Brigade's contradictory orders provides another example: "'If those bastards let them through we are cooked'" (187).

WORKS CITED

Baker, Carlos. *Ernest Hemingway: A Life Story.* New York: Scribner's, 1969.

Bartlett, Phyllis. "Other Countries, Other Wenches." *Modern Fiction Studies* 3 (1958): 348–349.

Brenner, Gerry. *Concealments in Hemingway's Works.* Columbus: Ohio State UP, 1983.

Bruccoli, Matthew. Ed. *Conversations with Ernest Hemingway.* Jackson: UP of Mississippi, 1986.

Delaney, John J. *Dictionary of Saints.* Garden City: Doubleday, 1980.

Donaldson, Scott, ed. *New Essays on* A Farewell to Arms. Cambridge: Cambridge UP, 1990.

Fetterley, Judith. *The Resisting Reader: A Feminist Approach to American Fiction.*

Bloomington: Indiana UP, 1978.

Hemingway, Ernest. *Ernest Hemingway: Selected Letters, 1917–1961.* Ed. Carlos Baker. London: Granada, 1981.

———. *A Farewell to Arms.* New York: Scribner's, 1929.

———. *The Short Stories of Ernest Hemingway.* New York: Scribner's, 1938.

Hinkle, James. "What's Funny in *The Sun Also Rises?*" *The Hemingway Review* 4.2 (Spring 1985): 31–41.

Kleinman, Craig. "Dirty Tricks and Wordy Jokes: The Politics of Recollection in *A Farewell to Arms.*" *The Hemingway Review* 15.1 (Fall 1995): 54–71.

Lewis, Robert W., Jr. *Hemingway on Love.* Austin: U of Texas P, 1965.

———. "Manners and Morals in *A Farewell to Arms.*" In *Hemingway: Up in Michigan Perspectives.* Ed. Frederic J. Svoboa and Joseph J. Waldmeir, 157–165. East Lansing: Michigan State UP, 1995.

Lockridge, Ernest. "*Othello* as Key to Hemingway." *The Hemingway Review* 18.1 (Fall 1998): 68–77.

Lynn, Kenneth S. *Hemingway.* New York: Simon and Schuster, 1987.

Oldsey, Bernard. *Hemingway's Hidden Craft: The Writing of* A Farewell to Arms. University Park: Pennsylvania State UP, 1979.

Reynolds, Michael S. *Hemingway's First War.* Princeton: Princeton UP, 1976.

———. *Hemingway's Reading 1910–1940: An Inventory.* Princeton: Princeton UP, 1981.

Shakespeare, William. *The Riverside Shakespeare.* 2nd ed. Ed. G. Blakemore Evans. Boston: Houghton Mifflin, 1997.

Smith, Paul. "The Trying-Out of *A Farewell to Arms.*" In *New Essays on* A Farewell to Arms. Ed. Scott Donaldson, 27–52. Cambridge: Cambridge UP, 1990.

Stoltzfus, Ben. "A Sliding Discourse: The Language of *A Farewell to Arms.*" In *New Essays on* A Farewell to Arms. Ed. Scott Donaldson, 109–136. Cambridge: Cambridge UP, 1990.

Stoneback, H. R. "'Lovers' Sonnets Turn'd to Holy Psalms': The Soul's Song of Providence, the Scandal of Suffering, and Love in *A Farewell to Arms.*" *The Hemingway Review* 9.1 (Fall 1989): 33–76.

Svoboda, Frederic J., and Joseph J. Waldmeir, eds. *Hemingway: Up in Michigan Perspectives.* East Lansing: Michigan State UP, 1995.

Sylvester, Bickford. "The Sexual Impasse to Romantic Order in Hemingway's
Fiction: *A Farewell to Arms, Othello,* 'Orpen,' and the Hemingway Canon." In
Hemingway: Up in Michigan Perspectives. Ed. Frederic J. Svoboa and Joseph J.
Waldmeir, 177–187. East Lansing: Michigan State UP, 1995.

Wilson, Andrew. "Bidding Goodbye to the Plumed Troop and the Big Wars: The
Presence of *Othello* in *A Farewell to Arms.*" *The Hemingway Review* 15.2 (1996):
52–66.

Out of the Picture

Mrs. Krebs, Mother Stein, and "Soldier's Home"

J. Gerald Kennedy and Kirk Curnutt

Brother, brother, here is mother.
We are all very well.

—Gertrude Stein, "Accents in Alsace"

To preface the story of Harold Krebs, the alienated veteran of World War I, Hemingway opens "Soldier's Home" with a brief description of two photographs. One portrays Krebs at a Methodist school in Kansas, among his fraternity brothers, each wearing "exactly the same height and style collar" in a scene of male solidarity. The other captures him in Europe, presumably after the Armistice: "There is a picture which shows him on the Rhine with two German girls and another corporal. Krebs and the corporal look too big for their uniforms. The German girls are not beautiful. The Rhine does not show in the picture" (*CSS* 111). Intended as a generic war photo of victorious troops posing with comely women in a vivid foreign

Reprinted with permission from *The Hemingway Review* 12.1 (Fall 1992). Copyright © 1992 The Hemingway Society. Published at the University of West Florida, Pensacola, Florida.

setting, the picture fails to produce the intended effect. None of the visual signs quite conveys the notion of military or romantic conquest. Instead, the picture betrays Krebs's chronic inability to live up to expectations or to play the role of hero: the uniforms are ludicrously small, the girls are less than ravishing, and the legendary river—calculated to certify the landscape as foreign—is nowhere to be seen. The juxtaposition of the two photos subtly implies a change in Krebs himself from a conventional, Midwestern college boy to a clownish figure posturing with "German girls" in a parody of male dominance.

Hemingway's wry comment about the Rhine indeed epitomizes the bathetic quality of Krebs's personal dilemma in "Soldier's Home." The young man has come home "years after the war was over," a circumstance that townspeople find "rather ridiculous." The photo in which the Rhine "does not show" metaphorizes Krebs's ongoing inability to represent and validate his war experience in a small town that has "heard too many atrocity stories to be thrilled by actualities" (CSS 111). His lack of recognition within the community parallels the more humiliating situation that he faces at home: his failure to be accepted as an adult by his suffocating parents. He has returned from the bloodiest battles of the war to have his mother ask him not to "muss up" the newspaper because his "father can't read his Star if it's been mussed." The inadvertently comic photo of Krebs in uniform exemplifies his awkward struggle to be regarded *at home* as a good soldier, a Marine who has endured the slaughter of the Western front.

The clever sentence summing up Krebs' predicament must have occurred to Hemingway in 1924 in a moment of complex irony, for he conjured it up not from his own sardonic imagination but from Gertrude Stein's "Accents in Alsace," an experimental composition in *Geography and Plays* (1922). Since March 1922 Stein had been functioning as Hemingway's Parisian mentor, communicating (as he later conceded) "many truths about rhythms and the uses of words in repetition" (*MF* 17). He had reviewed *Geography and Plays* in 1923 for the Paris *Tribune* and so presumably recalled (or referred back to) the closing section of "Accents in Alsace," which reads:

Sweeter than water or cream or ice. Sweeter than bells of roses. Sweeter than winter or summer or spring. Sweeter than pretty posies. Sweeter than anything is my queen and loving is her nature.

Loving and good and delighted and best is her little King and Sire whose devotion is entire who has but one desire to express the love which is hers to inspire.

In the photograph the Rhine hardly showed. (Stein 1922, 415)

Like Stein, Hemingway calls attention to a picture in order to note what has eluded the photographer; in "Soldier's Home," the river indeed no longer shows at all. But what is the object of this esoteric allusion to *Geography and Plays?* Is Hemingway thus acknowledging a debt or, conversely, indulging in parody? Or does he mean by this subtle revision of Stein's line to call attention to something else just out of sight in "Soldier's Home": the increasingly strained relationship between the brash young Hemingway and garrulous female writer old enough to be his mother? When we reconsider the circumstances under which he composed the story and reexamine those fictional traces of Stein's style, the narrative takes on a new aspect, indicative of Hemingway's determination in the spring of 1924 to throw off the influence of his mentor.

The salient facts of the Hemingway-Stein friendship, familiar to most scholars, require only brief summary here. Suffice it to say that when Hemingway arrived in Paris in 1921, a letter of introduction from Sherwood Anderson enabled him to make the acquaintance of Stein and her companion Alice B. Toklas. During the spring of 1922, Hemingway must have paid several visits to the famous atelier on the rue de Fleurus, admiring the paintings, tasting the liqueurs, and receiving instruction from the author of *Three Lives* and *Tender Buttons*. Like Anderson, Stein initially treated Hemingway as a protégé and (according to *A Moveable Feast*) lectured him on money, food, clothing, art, literature, and sex. She read his early stories and offered blunt criticism; she let him read her own compositions to illustrate the effects that she was trying to create. For a while, Hemingway welcomed this attention.

Stein's ideas about writing challenged him, and his regard for her literary opinion persisted into 1923 when he confessed to her: "I've thought a lot about the things you said about working and am starting that way at the beginning" (*SL* 79). As he learned his craft and began to publish stories, however, he grew impatient with Stein's imperious manner and looked to establish his literary independence.

As Michael Reynolds remarks, by early 1924, Hemingway "no longer needed Gertrude Stein," since his stories were virtually writing themselves (Reynolds 1989, 41). When Ford Madox Ford invited him in February to lend a hand at the editorial office of the *transatlantic*, Hemingway suddenly found himself in a position to do Stein a favor, persuading Ford to publish sight unseen part of her long narrative, *The Making of Americans*. If Hemingway admired the work (as he professed to do), he also recognized an opportunity to twit Ford for his stuffiness, to repay Stein for her tutelage, and to demonstrate his own professional ascendancy. That winter he spent precious hours retyping and copyediting the manuscript for serialization in Ford's little magazine. But he carried out this labor, it would appear, less to promote Stein's work than to amass the necessary credit to cancel his own debt. His letter of 17 February 1924 manages to be both deferential and patronizing: addressing her (as usual) as "Miss Stein," he assumes the role of agent as he lightly counsels her to accept Ford's offer of thirty francs per magazine page. "Be haughty but not too haughty," he admonishes, hinting that she should not question the terms that he himself has negotiated. Hemingway further implies that he has manipulated Ford to gain her this royalty: "I made it clear it was a remarkable scoop for his magazine obtained only through my obtaining genius" (*SL* 111). But we know that Hemingway talked Ford into publishing *The Making of Americans* only by suppressing the fact that the manuscript ran to nine hundred pages, even as he allowed Stein to believe that the entire work would be serialized. By stretching the truth to both parties, he brokered a deal that (in his mind) enabled him to settle his account with Stein.

But as "Soldier's Home" attests, other tensions complicated the situation. Although Hemingway needed to break away from Stein to assert his autonomy and mark the end of his apprenticeship, psychic attachments made the process difficult. Recent biographers agree that he had discovered in Stein both a teacher and a surrogate for Grace Hemingway, the strong-willed mother from whom he had revolted during the angry summer of 1920. Kenneth Lynn characterizes Stein as "Grace's most encompassing replacement," noting similarities in age, weight, voice, and manner (168); Reynolds calls Stein "the Paris mother" whom Hemingway needed (Reynolds 1989, 35). Jeffrey Meyers notes that both women "were frustrated artists who felt irritated by their thwarted careers and lack of recognition" (76). To both, Hemingway attributed an emotional instability linked to menopause. Estranged from Grace, he felt a peculiar need for Stein's approval and affection, yet the very resemblance that drew him to her produced a recurrent, subconscious resentment of her solicitude.

From the outset, Stein's androgynous manner provoked in Hemingway an uncertain gendered response. "Gertrude Stein and me are just like brothers" he wrote to Sherwood Anderson in March 1922, asserting a fraternal bond. By the summer of that year, however, a physical attraction had moved Alice B. Toklas to jealousy; Stein acknowledged a "weakness" for Hemingway, while the younger writer toyed with the outrageous notion of seducing his ponderous lesbian preceptor (SL 62, 79, 650). With Stein, Hemingway felt something very like a masculine bond; yet he also wanted to bed her, perhaps in his mind to feminize her. He moreover felt a filial affection, having discovered a nurturing mother to foster and validate his literary work. But the relationship cooled during the four months that Hemingway and his wife spent back in Toronto for the birth of their son. Perhaps the writer's brief visit to his Oak Park home in December 1923 allowed him to recognize the Oedipal tug in his attraction to Stein; or, perhaps, the birth of Bumby gave him a different perspective on the relation of mothers and sons. Whatever the reason, when he returned to Paris in January, he began to redefine his friendship to Stein.[1]

As if to rehearse a scene he now anticipated, he began in late March or early April to write "Soldier's Home," a story about a son's need to escape from parental authority and domestic routine. If the events were fictional, many of the specific details derived, of course, from Hemingway's uncomfortable return to Oak Park in early 1919 after his own war service as an ambulance driver in Italy. Although he had not fought on the Western Front like his protagonist, he had seen the effect of war, sustained a wound, and developed a cynical outlook. Back home he too had trouble readjusting to civilian life: he quarreled with his mother, pored over books about the war, and somewhat ironically entertained his admiring sisters. There he also stooped to misrepresenting his wartime activities and felt the shame of exaggerating an entirely respectable record.[2]

But whatever imaginative grist Hemingway salvaged from those troubled months in Oak Park five years earlier, his situation in Paris gave immediacy to the story. While preparing Stein's text for the *transatlantic,* he conceived a narrative about a son too confused to remain obedient and respectful, a son who deliberately hurts his mother by telling her that he does not love her. With Stein's prose rhythms and repetitions filling his head and perhaps still scrolling out of his typewriter, Hemingway developed the confrontation between the prescriptive Mrs. Krebs and the disaffected Harold, who feels the emptiness of her language and feigns contrition to avoid a scene. Throughout "Soldier's Home," echoes of Stein's rhythms and repetitions infuse Hemingway's style. These are nowhere more apparent than in the paragraph depicting Krebs's voyeuristic interest in the local girls:

> He liked to look at them from the front porch as they walked on the other side of the street. He liked to watch them walking under the shade of the trees. He liked the round Dutch collars above their sweaters. He liked their silk stockings and flat shoes. He liked their bobbed hair and the way they walked. (*CSS* 112)

Hemingway subsequently works variations on a more revealing phrase: "He did not want any consequences. He did not want any consequences ever again. He wanted to live without consequences." Krebs wants to protect himself from emotional wounds, to escape ridicule. The same passage introduces an antiphonal phrase: "He did not want to tell any more lies. It wasn't worth it ... It was not worth the trouble. ... But it was not worth it ...

It was not worth it" (*CSS* 113). Hemingway learned from Stein that repetition with variation could convey the insistence of a fixed idea without invoking psychoanalytic terms. He had heard her talk about repetition many times, and typing *The Making of Americans* clarified for him the possibilities and excesses of her method.[3]

While he thus emulated her prose effects in a seeming act of stylistic homage, Hemingway also explained, through the dilemma of Harold Krebs, why a son might need to throw off a stifling maternal influence. As if to signal a private project, he inserted into the opening paragraphs of "Soldier's Home" the photo reference that would have had peculiar significance for Stein. Among contemporary readers, perhaps she alone recognized the sentence as a reformulation of her own ironic line in *Geography and Plays*. An equivocal gesture, Hemingway's allusion calls attention to what is now out of the picture, to what has been excluded by the very act of rewriting that it signals. What the author seems intent to show is his capacity to move beyond or away from the stylistic influence of Stein through a parodic appropriation that at once simulates and subverts the language of an influential text.

The composition evoked by Hemingway in fact has some relevance to the subject of "Soldier's Home," for "Accents in Alsace" also explores (in its fashion) the effects of the Great War upon family relationship. Set in the Rhineland, this experimental pseudo-drama (Stein divides the piece into acts and scenes) loosely reflects the clash between French and Germanic cultures in Alsace during and after the war. The opening section introduces the Schemils and their son, who has run away to join the French Foreign Legion.[4] Learning of this defection, the Germans decide "to embrew his mother and sister and father too," but the family avoids reprisal by paying off "the Boche." The rest of the composition mixes general perceptions of Alsatian life with glancing references to the war ("It is an occasion. / When you see a Hussar.") and bits of intimate talk, presumably between Stein and Toklas. Much of the composition defies explication, however, and the story of the Schemils fades from view after two lines that possibly refer to a photograph the sister has sent to her soldier-brother: "Brother brother here is mother.

/ We are all very well." Anticipating the son's desire to carry a picture of his mother, the sister presents the photo and reports on the domestic scene in the banal language of wartime censorship.

Another photograph forms the likely subject of the final section of "Accents," "The Watch on the Rhine," which portrays a post-war euphoria in which conflict has yielded to sweetness and pleasure. This closing passage declares Stein's love for her "queen," Alice B. Toklas, and points to the autobiographical basis of the work. Stein and Toklas had toured Alsace in 1919 and served in a civilian relief program in Mulhouse; "Accents" registers the sights and sounds of the local scene as it commemorates their volunteer work. James R. Mellow suggests that the closing section marks Stein's attempt to capture the "burgeoning" mood of "The first spring of the peace" (286). Stein here observes that "in the photograph the Rhine hardly showed," probably alluding to an actual picture of herself and Alice, contented and indifferent to the strategic significance of the Rhine (then being guarded by Allied troops).[5] Indeed, she closes the composition by announcing that "in the midst of our happiness we were very pleased."

Hemingway's revision of this scene with Krebs, the other corporal, and the German girls thus turns an image of lesbian felicity into a putative sign of heterosexual desire. In this way Hemingway seems to locate the action of "Soldier's Home" within the domain of conventional, middle-class mores; yet he does so only to cast doubt on the sexual prowess implied by the photo of Krebs. After returning home (presumably from the 1919 "Watch on the Rhine"), Krebs sits on the porch watching local girls, but he discovers that "their appeal to him was not very strong"; he even convinces himself that "he did not really need a girl" (CSS 112–13). He also remembers boasting, however, that "he could not get along without girls, that he had to have them all the time." Caught between desire and denial, Krebs decides (in a line taken from Anderson's "The Untold Lie") that "it was all a lie both ways": he both does and does not need women. His conflict apparently stems from a fear of being emotionally wounded, for he suspects that women cannot understand what he has been through: "The world they were in was not the world he was in" (CSS 113).

At the same time, Krebs's anxiety and apparent confusion may betray another sort of nervousness: Hemingway's uncertain response to Stein's lesbianism. If he has in mind an actual photo of Stein and Tolkas on a riverbank in Alsace, what he also leaves out of the picture in "Soldier's Home" is his simultaneous fascination and discomfort with sapphic relations. Hemingway must have recognized in "Accents" Stein's covertly androgynous passion for Toklas, figured in the "devotion" of the king for his queen. Lynn suggests that Hemingway viewed the bond between Stein and Toklas as a "bolder, Parisian variation" of his mother's relationship with Ruth Arnold, the vocal student whose open affection for Grace sparked so many rumors in Oak Park that Clarence Hemingway finally banned her from the family home (168).[6] Through a curious pattern of association perhaps tied to the gender ambivalence precipitated (we now suspect) by his mother, Hemingway worked his way from the photo of Stein and Toklas to an exploration of the young soldier's sexual uncertainties. The picture in which the Rhine "does not show" anticipates the latent gender anxiety that complicates Krebs's relations with local girls, with the sister who calls him her "beau," and with the mother who wants him to find a "nice girl" and marry.

In yet another sense, Hemingway's reaction to the picture of Stein and Toklas in Alsace may betray his perception that playful compositions like "Accents" tended to trivialize the war. While Stein regarded many pieces in *Geography and Plays* as "political compositions" (*Autobiography* 188), war typically provides a pretext for what Richard Bridgman calls the "rhymed gaiety" of the poetry (158). Although Stein and Toklas performed wartime service for the American Fund for French Wounded (distributing care packages to wounded "doughboys"), the author kept a careful distance from the fighting. Only once, during her post-armistice visit to Alsace, did she actually observe a battlefield. In *The Autobiography of Alice B. Toklas* she recalls that spectacle with disbelief: "To anyone who did not see it as it was then it is impossible to imagine it. It was not terrifying it was strange. We were used to ruined houses and even ruined towns but this was different. It was landscape. And it belonged to no country" (187). For Stein, the war was "strange," unreal, and literally unimaginable. Even her later narrative *Wars I*

Have Seen (1945) displays her relative innocence of the horrors of battle. On the other hand, Hemingway's service on the Italian front in 1918 produced a lifelong preoccupation with warfare. His professional identity emerged from that violent episode, and he developed a proprietary attitude toward combat that informed his fictional program. In 1925 he argued that for the writer "war is the best subject of all. It groups the maximum of material and speeds up the actions and brings out all sorts of stuff that normally you have to wait a lifetime to get" (*SL* 176). Stein's elision of brutality in her writing must have struck him as willful escapism, a refusal to confront the harshness of life and death. Hemingway later observed that Stein always "wanted to know the gay part of how the world was going; never the real, never the bad" (*MF* 25).

In fact, Hemingway had reason to suspect that Stein found his preoccupation with war not only distasteful but ludicrous. In December 1923 she published in *Ex libris* the verse fragment now known as "He and They, Hemingway," which Hemingway surely saw upon his return to Paris that winter.[7] Like "Accents," the poem is a collage of conversational gambits, the most intelligible of which perhaps alludes to Hemingway's arrivals and departures ("How do you do and good-bye. Good-bye and how do you do"). The piece also pokes fun at the young writer's pretensions, including a ponderous line that he possibly uttered in conversation: "Is there any memorial of the failure of civilization to cope with extreme savagedom?" (Stein 1923, 193). The poem prefigures Stein's later comment that Hemingway "went the way so many other Americans have gone before. He became obsessed with sex and violent death" (Preston 191). Though Hemingway's response to the portrait is unknown, Stein's barely concealed parody suggests that she took a dim view of "savagedom" as a literary subject.

The widening rift between Stein and Hemingway thus places the conflict between mother and son in "Soldier's Home" in a new light. Reynolds claims that the story projects the inability of Hemingway's parents to understand his work: "By that spring of 1924 he was writing stories that he knew his parents could not read without being deeply hurt. Deep within him he needed their approval and support, but a part of him continually raised barricades to prevent the possibility" (Reynolds 1989, 191). Similarly, "Soldier's Home" may represent Stein's inability to appreciate narratives informed by the savagery of battle: "His mother asked him to tell her stories about the war, but her attention always wandered' (CSS 114). Hemingway could cut loose symbolically from Grace's expectations by portraying her as a one-dimensional "devouring mother" (DeFalco 143); yet he could not quite imagine complete liberation from Stein. Krebs tries to declare his independence by telling his mother that he does not love her. But when Mrs. Krebs breaks into tears, Harold recognizes that his strategy has failed: "It wasn't any good. He couldn't tell her, he couldn't make her see it. It was silly to have said it" (CSS 116). What Krebs cannot make his mother see it that he is no longer her little boy; combat has changed him. In this sense, "Soldier's Home" is not only the story of a soldier's struggle to recuperate from battle; it also portrays a son's need to achieve autonomy and respect. What nauseates Krebs is not his mother's piety but the ease with which she reduces him to a child who promises his "Mummy": "I'll try and be a good boy for you." Krebs's capitulation reveals a dependence on his mother that persists despite his efforts to deny it.

After Mrs. Krebs prays for Harold, he plans to leave home, thinking that he can escape to Kansas City with "one more scene maybe." The brave tone of the conclusion masks its irony, for though Krebs believes that the scene has not touched him, he lies to himself. His mother's reminder that she held him as a baby has evoked nausea and shame. His ambivalence may betray Hemingway's anxiety that no matter how rapidly his writing developed or how coolly he posed as Stein's agent, he remained dependent upon her approval.[8]

Such a recognition may explain why he chose an esoteric allusion to his mentor to signal his independence. Elsewhere in In Our Time, Oedipal conflicts with artistic predecessors reveal Hemingway's struggle to establish his "vocational integrity" against the stifling expectations of literary tradition (Renza 674).[9] The most obvious of these encounters, "My Old Man," projects a revolt against his first patron, Sherwood Anderson, in a story that literally culminates with the death of the father. An explicit allusion to

"The Untold Lie" likewise associates Anderson with Mr. Krebs, the patriarch of "Soldier's Home"; the father's absence may imply that Hemingway had already thrown off the weight of Anderson's expectations by the spring of 1924. Yet, unprepared to defy Stein's authority, Hemingway perhaps dreaded the impending scene that would produce a break with her.

What finally compelled Hemingway to declare his independence were reviews of *In Our Time* that exaggerated the influence of Stein and Anderson, lumping the three of them into an "expatriate school." During a hurried ten days in late 1925 he wrote *The Torrents of Spring,* a travesty of Anderson's *Dark Laughter* that also lampooned his mentor's style: "All that in Paris. Ah, Paris. How far it was to Paris now. Paris in the morning. Paris in the evening. Paris at night. Paris in the morning again. Paris at noon, perhaps. Why not?" (*TS* 116). The jibe is curious, for recently Hemingway had praised Stein's technique, telling one friend that she could "take [language] apart and see what makes it go. Maybe she don't get it together again. But she's always getting somewhere" (*Letter* 4). The contradiction suggests that, though he had rehearsed the break with Stein in "Soldier's Home," his conflicted feelings toward her remained. Wanting to be regarded as an original, he perhaps feared that Stein would leave the imprint of her style on every line he wrote. In this sense, "Soldier's Home" prefigures an action Hemingway would repeat throughout his career—trying to push Stein out of the picture because he could not get her out of his prose.

NOTES

1. Hemingway did, however, ask Stein and Toklas to stand as godmothers for the March 1924 christening of his son, a gesture which underscores Stein's maternal function in Hemingway's Paris life. It is worth mentioning the odd coincidence that long before meeting Stein, Hemingway had assumed the nickname "Hemingstein" or simply "Stein," and that he also referred to his mother as "Mrs. Stein." See Lynn (64).

2. See Reynolds, *The Young Hemingway* (36–64). For Hemingway's lies, see

especially 55–57.

3. For an insightful examination of the contrast between the two, see Perloff, who argues that Stein uses abstract repetition as a means of analyzing changes in feeling. She contends that this technique is fundamentally unlike the concrete, "natural" language used by Hemingway (682–83).

4. Toklas recalls how she and Stein met this family in *What is Remembered* (103).

5. Many thanks to Noreen O'Conner of Yale University Press for locating the 1919 picture of Stein and Toklas at the Beinecke Rare Book Library, Yale University.

6. Lynn (168). See also Reynolds, *Hemingway: The Paris Years* (36–37), for insight into Hemingway's interest in lesbianism.

7. The poem's original title was "Hemingway: A Portrait." Stein added the new title in 1934 for publication in *Portraits and Prayers*. In a February 1924 Letter to Anderson, Stein claims to have shown the poem to Hemingway before he returned to Toronto in the fall of 1923. If so, Hemingway did not mention it in the published correspondence. See White (36).

8. *The Autobiography of Alice B. Toklas* suggests that Hemingway's fear of being the eternal pupil was not unfounded: Stein claims that her "weakness" for him arose because "he takes training and anybody who takes training is a favorite pupil" (216). Hemingway retaliated with a snide portrait of Stein in *Green Hills of Africa* (23–28), but his most honest response may appear in an unpublished fragment called "The Autobiography of Alice B. Hemingway" where he admits that Stein "makes some good cracks" but is undisciplined about her art: She "invents a way of writing that she can do every day and feel good. It doesn't have to mean anything and it doesn't have to please anybody but her and she can do two thousand to five thousand words of it every day of her life" (2, 3–4).

9. Among the writers that Renza finds Hemingway challenging are Twain, Thoreau, Henry Adams, and Anderson. Stein is mentioned only in biographical asides, and her absence from the list of misprisioned figures exemplifies the paternal biases of Renza's Bloomian model.

WORKS CITED

Bridgman, Richard. *Gertrude Stein in Pieces.* New York: Oxford UP, 1970.

Brinnan, John Malcolm. *The Third Rose: Gertrude Stein and Her World.* Boston: Little, Brown and Co., 1959.

DeFalco, Joseph. *The Hero in Hemingway's Short Stories.* 1963: Folcroft Library Editions, 1978.

Hemingway, Ernest. "The Autobiography of Alice B. Hemingway." Item #256. Hemingway Collection. John F. Kennedy Library.

———. *The Complete Short Stories of Ernest Hemingway: The Finca Vigía Edition.* New York: Scribner's, 1987.

———. *Ernest Hemingway: Selected Letters, 1917–1961.* Ed. Carlos Baker. New York: Scribner's, 1981.

———. *Green Hills of Africa.* New York: Scibner's, 1935.

———. Letter to William B. Smith, 26 February 1925. The William B. Smith Collection, Princeton University. Unpublished.

———. *A Moveable Feast.* New York: Scribner's, 1964.

———. *The Torrents of Spring.* New York: Scribner's, 1926.

Lynn, Kenneth. *Hemingway.* New York: Simon and Schuster, 1987.

Mellow, James R. *Charmed Circle: Gertrude Stein and Company.* New York: Avon, 1974.

Meyers, Jeffrey. *Hemingway: A Biography.* New York: Harper and Row, 1985.

Perloff, Marjorie. "'Ninety-Percent Rotarian': Gertrude Stein's Hemingway." *American Literature* 62 (December 1990): 668–83.

Preston, John Hyde. "A Conversation." *Atlantic* 156 (August 1935): 187–94.

Renza, Louis A. "The Importance of Being Ernest." *South Atlantic Quarterly* (Spring 1989): 661–90.

Reynolds, Michael S. *The Young Hemingway.* Oxford: Basil Blackwell, 1986.

———. *Hemingway: The Paris Years.* Oxford: Basil Blackwell, 1989.

Stein, Gertrude. *Geography and Plays.* Boston: Four Seas, 1922.

———. "He and They, Hemingway." *Portraits and Prayers.* New York: Random House, 1923. Originally published as "Hemingway: A Portrait" in 1923.

———. *The Autobiography of Alice B. Toklas.* New York: Random House, 1933.

———. *Wars I Have Seen.* New York: Random House, 1945.

Toklas, Alice B. *What is Remembered*. 1963. San Francisco: North Point, 1985.

White, Ray Lewis. Ed. *Sherwood Anderson/Gertrude Stein: Correspondence and Personal Essays*. Chapel Hill: U North Carolina P, 1972.

Hemingway's Senses of an Ending

In Our Time and After

Paul Smith

At the end of a life we expect that the last thing said or the last act performed will be revealing, the last look at the past or the first at some other future. At the end of a story, the end of its world and the people who lived there, we expect as much. And more, for some latter-day critics say that the end of the story is the end of us, the readers who have lived a sort of life in that fiction and die with its last word; except, perhaps, for those critics who are left, drifting like Ishmael, to tell the tale again.[1]

In this apocalyptic mood, I have reread the endings of Ernest Hemingway's forty-nine short stories, especially the seventeen written between 1922 and 1925,[2] and it should come as no surprise that I have found a pattern—I think.

Reprinted with permission from *The Hemingway Review* 12.1 (Fall 1992). Copyright © 1992 The Hemingway Society. Published at the University of West Florida, Pensacola, Florida.

To describe that pattern I have drawn, lightly, on Kenneth Burke's dramatistic theory and J. L. Austin's theory of speech-acts. From Burke I have used the concept of the *pentad:* the "ratio" or relationship between two of the elements of *scene, act, agent,* and *agency* that reveal *purpose;* and I do so because the ratio Burke seems to favor is the most common in Hemingway, the relationship between *scene* and *act:* between the cold wind from the bay, the early morning on the lake, the dark swamp and a character's *purposive* action.

From Austin I have used the concept of speech as action, performatives spoken more than literally and following the tacit rules that inform our social speech: Nick to his father in "The Doctor and the Doctor's Wife," "I know where there's black squirrels" (*SS* 103); or to his skiing friend in "Cross-Country Snow," "There isn't any good in promising" (*SS* 188); or to George in "The Killers," "I'm going to get out of this town" (*SS* 289)—all are more than statements; they are social acts of *inviting, predicting,* or *judging* performed in saying something—in Austin's terms, illocutionary acts.

With those two rudimentary critical concepts, a pattern becomes apparent in the endings of all but a few of the seventeen stories before 1925:

First, an *associative act,* one in which a character moves or gestures toward another in an act of agreement or reconciliation—some gesture of inclusion;

Then, a *dissociative act,* one in which a character moves away from another, in an act of disagreement or separation—some gesture of exclusion;

And finally, an act, often a speech-act by a character or narrator, referring to an aspect of the scene that conjoins with the previous acts in a Burkeian ratio. This third element usually serves a prospective or retrospective function, predicting the character's future or commenting on their final moments together and apart.

The example of "Up in Michigan" may have some unusual significance since it was the first story Hemingway finished in Paris in the early months of 1922. Liz Coates's penultimate act is to take off her coat and "tuck it around [Jim] neatly and carefully"—an act of (almost maternal) *association.* Liz's second act is to "Walk across the dock and up the steep sandy road to go to bed"—an act of *dissociation*. And in the story's last sentence the narrator, who has earlier assumed her view and at times her voice, tells us that "a cold mist was coming up through the woods from the bay" (*SS* 86). That cold mist had been mentioned before, and it made Liz feel "miserable and everything felt gone" (*SS* 85). The sandy road, the bay, the mist, all had been scenic elements waiting in the story to say something to her and to us of her life and prospects and, in concert with her acts, they do.

Of the other sixteen endings there are nine (some 56 percent) that follow a similar, sometimes more complex, pattern: an associative act, a dissociative act, concluded with one which predicts or reviews those acts or implications: "Out of Season," "A Very Short Story," "The Revolutionist," "Indian Camp," "Soldier's Home," "Mr. and Mrs. Elliot," "Cross-Country Snow," "Big Two-Hearted River," and "Banal Story"; and with a little ingenuity one might add "Cat in the Rain." "The End of Something," and its companion, "The Three-Day Blow."[3]

I'll take the time to argue for this pattern in three stories. In "Out of Season" Peduzzi happily promises to bring minnows, salami, everything together for "You and I and the Signora. The three of us." To which the young gentleman replies, "*I* may not be going . . . very probably not," and with the singular pronoun he dissociates himself not only from Peduzzi but also from his wife. That speech act in itself both recalls the ominous dialogue earlier with his wife at the *Concordia* Hotel—a name Burke would say was "rotten with perfection"—and predicts the dissolution of the marriage. So the young gentleman's final remark, "I will leave word with the padrone at the hotel office" (*SS* 179) is close to redundant, and that redundancy is a salient feature of the story's ending.

"A Very Short Story" seems at first to resist this analysis and might be dismissed to the genre of the sketch, the vignette, and interchapter—anything to get rid of it. But then it becomes clear that the sketch, like many of the 1924 *in our time* chapters, was an ending in itself and followed the pattern in most of the 1925 *In Our Time* stories. Its first three paragraphs celebrate the intimacy of the narrator's love affair with the nurse; the second three predict and finally recount her infidelity; and in the last, as Robert Scholes has nicely noted, the narrator projects the nurse's fate into eternity with a punitive speech act, she did not marry "in the spring, or any other time" (SS 142).

Then there is "Big Two-Hearted River" with its fugitive ending read as apocryphal commentary on the gospel of his published text. It may seem that there are no acts of association or dissociation between characters; but in a perfect Burkeian scene-act ratio, Nick is neither alone nor talking to himself, for he is in an intimate ritualistic relationship with the swamp and its local deities, the mink he had noticed in the morning and to which he offers the trout's offal. Clearly an act of association, it is followed by Nick's return to camp, and his decision not to fish the tragic swamp. But the story ends with the narrator's prediction that "there were plenty of days coming when he *could* fish the swamp" (SS 232).

I have selected these three stories not because they demonstrate the pattern, but because that pattern raises interesting questions about the stories. For example:

Were the early sketches of 1923, like "A Very Short Story," exercises Hemingway set himself to test his skill at the writer's ultimate task, how to end a story? Is it a very short story, only because it is the end of one?

Does the redundancy of the ending of "Out of Season" reveal an uncertain hand? If a writer doubts the force and effect of his newly-discovered ending pattern, is it not likely that in his *second* try he might italicize it, as he does here, with Peduzzi's and the young gentleman's repetitive remarks? And is this uncertainty similar to that which seems to have led him to invent the story of Peduzzi's suicide?

There is no end of talk on the original ending of "Big Two-Hearted River," for it raises the question of why Hemingway wandered so far for so long from the pattern that had served so well in eight other stories written before the summer of 1924. That ending, published as "On Writing,"[4] forecast Hemingway's judgment three months later than its "mental conversation . . . is the shit" (SL 133). He had utterly misread Joyce's *Ulysses* and, in that misreading, inadvertently condemned himself for what he called the "weakness of Joyce," that "Daedalus . . . was Joyce himself, so he was terrible" (NAS

238); for his own Daedalus, Nick Adams in the original beginning, was too close to himself—and was, indeed, terrible. Gertrude Stein had said as much when she dismissed the early ending as "a little story of meditations" and reminded the young writer that "remarks are not literature" (Stein 219).

In a lucky last minute, he rewrote the ending, and with it paid silent homage to Joyce, to the one book of his he rarely mentioned, *Dubliners,* and to its last story, which he knew he must try to match, "The Dead." Gabriel Conroy's communion with the falling snow seems distant from Nick Adams's contemplation of the cedared swamp, but the force of Joyce's story was immanent and profound. The two stories end with an approach to "that region where dwell the vast hosts of the dead" and at a moment when "the time had come to set out on [a] journey westward" (Joyce 223).

The journey for Hemingway led in the summer of 1925 to Spain and *The Sun Also Rises,* his first and, I suspect, the only novel for which ending it was nearly effortless.[5] Its only variation on the dominant pattern in the earlier stories is to place the scenic event between the associative and dissociative speech acts: between Brett's witless "we could have had such a damned good time together" and Jake's ironic "Isn't it pretty to think so," the policeman raises his baton, and the car slows, pressing the forlorn couple together.

In the next decade, the ending pattern that dominated *In Our Time* and so immediately concluded *The Sun Also Rises* diminished dramatically in *Men Without Women* (1927) and *Winner Take Nothing* (1933) and virtually disappeared in the four stories included in *The First Forty-nine* (1938). Between May 1926 and May 1927, in a year nearly as miraculous at 1924, Hemingway finished another eleven of the fourteen stories in *Men Without Women,* but the earlier pattern appears in less than half of them (46%): "An Alpine Idyll," "The Killers," "A Canary for One," "Ten Indians," "Hills Like White Elephants," and "On the Quai at Smyrna" published later.[6]

Two exceptions to the pattern are the two stories of the woe in war and wedding, "In Another Country" and "Now I Lay Me," that led him at long last to write *A Farewell to Arms.* The forty-one manuscript attempts to end that novel are evidence of the difficulty Hemingway faced at the novel's conclusion. In the eight categories of endings Bernard Oldsey has noted

(101–110), Hemingway ventured three types of conclusions: a moralistic note on suffering and death, a summary continuation of the story, and brief authorial notes on when and how a story should end. The impulse toward a dark preachment, a synopsis, and—most significantly—a self-reflexive comment on the nature of an ending, all bespeak his troubled search for an appropriate conclusion.

But when he wrote the novel's last three sentences, he settled for what he had learned in *In Our Time*. Frederic dismisses the nurses, "But after I got them out and shut the door and turned out the light it wasn't any good."[7] His last blessing and farewell fails, for it was "like saying good-by to a statue," and he leaves the hospital to walk "back to the hotel in the rain," the once prophetic and now memorial rain (*FTA* 332).

From 1928 to the fall of 1933, Hemingway wrote another fourteen stories for *Winner Take Nothing,* and the *In Our Time* ending appears in only five stories (36%): "The Sea Change," "The Mother of a Queen," "A Clean, Well-Lighted Place," "The Gambler, the Nun, and the Radio," and "Fathers and Sons."[8]

Those five years began with *A Farewell to Arms,* a fiction that some still read as fact. Four of the fourteen stories apparently are drawn close to the life; another four are derived from the accounts of others. And one began as a story but appeared at the end of this period in *Death in the Afternoon,* a book teeming with fact and now read as fiction.[9] For this tentative exploration along the boundary between fiction and nonfiction, Hemingway found little direction in the patterned endings of *In Our Time*.

So, too, with the last four collected stories written between 1936 and 1938: the earlier ending pattern is so complicated by irony in "The Capital of the World" and so ambivalently rendered in the two African stories, "The Short Happy Life of Francis Macomber" and "The Snows of Kilimanjaro," that it seems to have lost its interest or usefulness as Hemingway ventured into those last bright experiments in narrative and narration.

But the last story collected in his lifetime, "Old Man at the Bridge," followed precisely the old pattern from his first collection. First cabled as a dispatch after an exhausting day on the road between Ebro Delta and

Barcelona on Easter Sunday 1938, the story's ending suggests that in that bone-weary state Hemingway drew one last time on the pattern he knew so well. In what I take to be a "representative anecdote," the narrator urges the old man to join him in the retreat from the Ebro. The old man tries to rise, falls again, and—speaking to no one—says "I was only taking care of animals." The narrator looks to the overcast skies, thinks to himself that the old man's cats "know how to look after themselves," predicts that "that was all the good luck the old man would ever have," and then leaves (*SS* 80).

That last dispatch was Hemingway's hail-and-farewell to the pattern he discovered writing the stories of *In Our Time* and, at last, to the art of the short story.

I would claim little for this pattern of endings that informed the fictions of *In Our Time* and then diminished and disappeared in the later collections, were there not other issues that history illuminates.

In those fifteen remarkable years, Hemingway exhausted a relatively limited conception of the art of the story, and then was exhausted in turn when it did not serve his reaching vision of the boundaries of fiction, a vision beyond the grasp of his imaginative art. The history of this early pattern, then, documents the rise and fall of his art of the story.

But the pattern served him well in the endings of his first two novels, and so helped him begin what was for him the necessary career of the novelist.

Nor would I make much of this pattern of endings without the manuscript evidence of seven of Hemingway's stories: "Up in Michigan," "Indian Camp," "Big Two-Hearted River," "An Alpine Idyll," "Ten Indians," "Hills Like White Elephants," and "The Sea Change." In each of these stories, Hemingway did *not* immediately arrive at this pattern for his endings. However, in each he reworked the ending to approximate that pattern, and then revised the preceding pages to lead into it. And most connoisseurs would agree, I think, that these seven stories are vintage Hemingway.

At least three questions remain:

When did Hemingway discover this pattern? I wager it came to him as he wrote the "Paris 1922" sentence. In most of them a dispassionate narrator tells of an event he witnessed that both associates and dissociates two characters, like the "beefy red-faced Episcopal clergyman holding an umbrella" over a "one-legged street-walker who works the Boulevard Madelaine."[10]

What does it say of his art? If these early stories are quintessential Hemingway, it is fitting that with them he claimed his place among the modern ironists. And he did it with the ironic strategy Northrop Frye has described: one that opposes and so cancels out both the archetypal comic mode that ends with inclusion, the festive marriage that affirms life and continuity, and the tragic mode that ends with exclusion, the mournful funeral that re-affirms the law of nature and reminds us of our own end (223–239). That ironic opposition leaves us, as always, with the weather, the rain that falls on the bishop and the street-walker, not because one or the other is just or unjust, but because it simply falls.

And last, why did this pattern start so soon and then diminish? Wallace Stegner, who knew the story well, had it right when he said that short fiction was always the younger, not the older, writer's province, because "it uses up so many beginnings and endings."[11]

NOTES

1. Like Frank Kermode in *The Sense of an Ending* (New York: Oxford UP, 1967).
2. All but two, "The Undefeated" and "Banal Story," were published in *Three Stories and Ten Poems* (1923) or *In Our Time* (1925).
3. The remaining four, "My Old Man," "The Doctor and the Doctor's Wife," "The Undefeated," and "The Battler," reverse the pattern with a dissociative act followed by an associative act.
4. In *The Nick Adam Stories* (New York: Scribner's, 1972).
5. He rewrote Jake Barnes's last remarks only twice: "It's nice as hell to think so" and then "Isn't it nice to think so" before he settled on "Isn't it pretty to think so."
6. More of those six have been critically favored than those eccentric to the *In Our Time* pattern: "Fifty Grand," "Today is Friday," "A Pursuit Race," "A Simple

Enquiry," "Che Ti Dice la Patria," "In Another Country," and "Now I Lay Me."

7. In a manuscript version of this ending Hemingway identified Frederic's thin hope: "I thought if . . . we could be alone we would still be together."

8. Again, in all but recent studies, these five have received more critical attention than "Wine of Wyoming," "A Natural History of the Dead," "After the Storm," "God Rest You Merry, Gentleman," "Homage to Switzerland," "The Light of the World," "A Way You'll Never Be," "One Reader Writes," and "A Day's Wait." Susan Beegel's recent collection of critical essays, *Hemingway's Neglected Short Fiction: New Perspectives* (Ann Arbor: UMI Research P, 1989), corrects the conventional assessments of several of these stories.

9. The four "close to the life" are "Wine of Wyoming," "The Gambler, the Nun, and the Radio," "A Day's Wait," and "Fathers and Sons"; those from others' accounts are "After the Storm," "The Mother of a Queen," "God Rest You Merry, Gentlemen," and "One Reader Writes"; "A Natural History of the Dead" began as a story, appeared in the bullfighting book, and then as a story in *Winner Take Nothing*.

10. These six "Paris 1922" sentences are reprinted in Carlos Baker, *Ernest Hemingway: A Life Story* (New York: Scribner's, 1969), 90–91.

11. Quoted in Anne Tyler's review of *The Collected Stories of Wallace Stegner*, p. 2.

WORKS CITED

Austin, J. L. *How To Do Things With Words*. New York: Oxford UP, 1965.

Baker, Carlos. *Ernest Hemingway: A Life Story*. New York: Scribner's, 1969.

Beegel, Susan F. Ed. *Hemingway's Neglected Short Fiction: New Perspectives*. Anne Arbor: UMI, 1989.

Burke, Kenneth. *A Grammar of Motives and A Rhetoric of Motives*. Cleveland and New York: Prentice-Hall, 1945, 1950.

Frye, Northrop. *Anatomy of Criticism: Four Essays*. Princeton: Princeton UP, 1957.

Hemingway, Ernest. *Ernest Hemingway: Selected Letters, 1917–1961*. Ed. Carlos Baker. New York: Scribner's, 1981.

———. *A Farewell to Arms*. New York: Scribner's, 1929.

———. *The Nick Adams Stories*. New York: Scribner's, 1972.

———. *The Short Stories of Ernest Hemingway*. New York: Scribner's, 1938.

Joyce, James. *Dubliners*. New York: Viking Press, 1958.

Kermode, Frank. *The Sense of an Ending*. New York: Oxford UP, 1967.

Oldsey, Bernard. *Hemingway's Hidden Craft: The Writing of* A Farewell to Arms. University Park: Pennsylvania State UP, 1979.

Scholes, Robert. *Semiotics and Interpretation*. New Haven: Yale UP, 1982.

Stein, Gertrude. *The Autobiography of Alice B. Toklas*. New York: Random House, 1933.

Tyler, Anne. Rev. of *The Collected Stories of Wallace Stegner*. *The New York Times Book Review*, 18 March 1990, 2.

Hemingway's *In Our Time*

Cubism, Conservation, and the Suspension of Identification

Lisa Narbeshuber

An emblematic moment in *In Our Time* occurs in the first paragraph of that strange preface[1] of sorts, "On the Quai at Smyrna." Describing a refugee population at Smyrna, the narrator, a British officer, says,

> We were in the harbour and they were all on the pier and at midnight they started screaming. We used to turn the searchlight on them to quiet them. That always did the trick. We'd run the searchlight up and down over them two or three times and they stopped it. (*IOT* 11)

The powerful light destroys the shelter of darkness and brings a violent clarity. An artificial extension of the human eye, the searchlight for Hemingway also

Reprinted with permission from *The Hemingway Review* 25.2 (Spring 2006). Copyright © 2006 The Ernest Hemingway Foundation. Published by The University of Idaho, Moscow, Idaho.

■ 241

possesses a peculiarly tactile quality, as if to emphasize the physical force of this technology, and reverse the conventional associations of light with objectivity and enlightenment. Moving "up and down over them," the glare seems to touch the screaming people, forcing them to silence.[2]

Throughout *In Our Time*, Hemingway explores the destructive power of touch and human presence. Human beings in Hemingway's text have been transformed into dangerous creatures, with a domineering stance toward the world and physical capacities radically enhanced and extended by 20th century technology. When discussing *touch*, then, I refer not just to a certain kind of physical contact, but to all forms of human impact on other people, things, and creatures, especially in the machine culture of Hemingway's time.

In Our Time offers a critique of and a tentative solution to a culture of domination, as Hemingway suggests the necessity of caution, of withholding touch, and of refusing to bring darkness and absence to light, except after much consideration—if at all. From Hemingway's viewpoint, the sense of caution—understood as caring and conserving—demands a certain quality of perspective, as well as a circumspect attitude towards touch. I will argue that much of *In Our Time* considers how to approach people, things, and creatures without objectifying them. My argument conflicts with an important strain of Hemingway criticism that compares the structure of *In Our Time* with the radical modernist styles of Cubist painting. Such comparisons are interesting. But behind the spirit of the original Cubists working between 1907 and 1914, when Cubism was a unique way of seeing the world, rather than just a set of techniques, is an attitude towards reality that Hemingway decidedly rejects.

Ever since Paul Rosenfeld described *In Our Time* as a Cubist work in a 1925 review, many critics have pointed out what they see as Cubist elements in the book. For example, Jacqueline Vaught Brogan argues that the fragmentation of the narrative in *In Our Time* parallels the visual fragmentation in a Cubist painting, while Elizabeth Dewberry Vaughn points out that Hemingway's repetition of words parallels Picasso's repetition of geometrical forms. For Vaughn, both Hemingway and Picasso emphasize form over content; because of this emphasis the audience discovers meaning by looking both at the work as a whole and at the relationship among the individual parts of the text or painting. For A. Carl Bredahl, the "divided narrative" of *In Our Time* mirrors the work of Cubist painters who visually dismantle "formally considered integrated units" (16). But Bredahl goes on to explain that "Picasso, Panguin [*sic*? Paquin?], and Duchamp took apart in order to discover new ways to integrate" (16). Bredahl argues, then, that this concern with a new integration in a world of disunity also drives Hemingway's divided narrative.

However, I would argue that *In Our Time* is more interested in maintaining the moment of *disintegration*—in refusing to enter into modernity's desire to totalize and dominate the world. "New ways to integrate" sounds too positive, too optimistic—like the early Cubists themselves, as we shall see. Rather than looking at connections, Hemingway attends to the spaces in between. Rather than bringing the multiple facets of people, things, events, ideals, and ideologies together on his textual canvas, he tends to dismantle any such powerful gatherings, and, with them, power as domination. Furthermore, family, fatherhood, and marriage, as well as other cultural myths and institutions, either fail altogether or are held in a state of suspension. At the end of the book, we are presented with something other than communal or individual unity.

To clarify this understanding of *In Our Time,* we must take a detour through John Berger's influential essay, "The Moment of Cubism," fleshing out more precisely the techniques and spirit of the age. Berger argues that Cubism as a movement was characterized by a revolutionary optimism about perception, social organization, and the individual's potential. Of the spirit of the time, Berger writes, "[t]here was a startling extension through time and space of human power and knowledge. For the first time the world, as a totality, ceased to be an abstraction and became *realizable*" (163). Cubism's nerve-center, as defined by Berger, included painters such as Picasso, Braque, Léger, and Juan Gris, as well as poets such as Cendrars and Apollinaire, themselves energized by the shattering technological and scientific changes taking place. In this vital context, these artists forged a radically new understanding that consciousness is not detached from its objects, that people are embedded in the world, and that empty space and traditional perspective are illusions. The Cubist techniques of flattened surfaces, positive spaces, and multiple angles create a sense of the object's availability, its simultaneity of presence. As one critic vividly puts it, far from creating the experience of alienation and fragmentation often associated with Cubism, "[Braque and Picasso's] paintings of 1911 have very little air in them, and the continuous vibration and twinkling of brush-strokes against the discontinuous geometry of their structure is set forth, not as light, but as a property of matter—that plasma. . . . of which the Cubist world was composed" (Hughes 29–32). To achieve this sense of fluidity and plenitude, the conventions of perspective, which gave the viewer a detached, God's-eye view of reality, had to be destroyed.

The pre-war Cubist vision, while rejecting perspective and its illusory promise of a God-like view of reality, makes its own promise, namely, that the world might appear as immediate and available: "now man was able to extend *himself* indefinitely beyond the immediate: he took over the territory in space and time where God had presumed to exist" (Berger 164). According to Berger, a new sense of secular unification informs Cubism's technical innovations, opening up the entire globe to human control. Berger's essay captures the excitement over Faraday's "concept of field," speed of travel (airplane, train, streetcar, automobile), speed of communication (telegraph, radio, newspapers, cinema), mechanical modes of reproduction, and modern architecture. Such technological advances mark a progressive, transformative critical mass: "Imperialism had begun the process of unifying the world. Mass production promised eventually a world of plenty. Mass-circulation newspapers promised informed democracy. The aeroplane promised to make the dream of Icarus real" (167). Modern technologies fundamentally altered the ordinary experience of the world and one's place in it. Affirming Berger's vision of the modern "machine age" and its effects on Cubism and beyond, art critic Robert Hughes observes that the view from the train "was not the view from the horse" (12). To Hughes, "the machine meant the conquest of horizontal space. It also meant a sense of that space which few people had experienced before—the succession and superimposition of views, the unfolding of landscape in flickering surfaces as one was carried swiftly past it, and an exaggerated feeling of relative motion" (12).

In effect, for both Berger and Hughes, Cubism is a kind of realism, accurately registering the new urban landscape. For Berger, though, what matters most is the rapid unfolding of a utopian moment envisioned by the pre-war affiliations of Cubists, who found a way to gather up all the seemingly disparate elements of the cosmos, showing that these elements could be grasped as a whole ("The Cubists were the first artists to attempt to paint totalities rather than agglomerations" [181]).

> In a Cubist picture, the conclusion and the connections are given. They are what the picture is made of. They are its content. The spectator has to find his place *within* this content whilst the complexity of the forms and the 'discontinuity' of the space remind him that his view from that place is bound to be only partial. (180)

"Partial" yes, but according to this vision and in the spirit of plenitude, the self *is* deeply interconnected to everything else: "In an entirely original sense, which remains at the basis of modern consciousness, a man *was* the world which he inherited" (164).

It would not be surprising if *In Our Time* paralleled the spirit, characteristics and techniques of Cubist artists. William Carlos Williams, Gertrude Stein, and William Faulkner,[3] to list a few, explored Cubist practices after the war, and critics, as we have seen, find parallels in *In Our Time*. But I deviate from such readings in two ways. First, Hemingway preserves what looks like perspective in form and theme, and second, *In Our Time,* recognizing the impulse to dominate inherent in any totalizing practice, whether utopian or not, attempts to sabotage the urge to dominate characteristic of the machine age. In this respect Hemingway is closer to the notoriously negative Theodor Adorno (who stubbornly abhorred any forms of identity, possessiveness, or totality)[4] or to the anarchic Marcel Duchamp, not in his integrative mode but with his dysfunctional machines ("their mechanisms often providing no clue to their function and thereby presenting a scandal to the pragmatic intelligence" [Nicholls 232]). With precision and commitment—without the broadness of gesture or detached irony of Duchamp and his impossible machines—*In Our Time* is equally wary of the modern. The collection values respectful distances and mediation rather than the promise of immediacy or accessibility. In other words, while it could be argued that Cubist techniques transplanted into the post-war era take on a different meaning, I argue instead that Hemingway rejects not only the original Cubist techniques but also their utopian spirit, form, and content.

Nevertheless, it might seem strange to speak of Hemingway as an exemplar of the negative. His style appears to relish surface description, a feature often parodied. He is known for his paratactic arrangements of evidence. Moreover, Hemingway, although in an apparently essentialist way, seems to present a kind of "collage" of elemental images. The cumulative effect suggests simultaneity or at least an atemporal synthesis—putting *In Our Time* on the side of the immediate, of presence. In "Indian Camp," for example, which parodies a rite-of-passage tale,[5] mythic images of mother, father, infant, water, and blood occur together, giving that sense of simultaneity and plenitude celebrated by many pre-war European intellectuals and artists, including the Cubists.

On one level, "Indian Camp" does indeed capture all at once a surplus of images, a fullness of time's movement, and a sense of the complexity of experience. But whereas Cubism strives for an immediate grasp of the whole, the spaces between fragments facilitating an easy movement of energy, *In Our Time's* spaces resist the passage of energy. Instead, the collection's insistence on blockages and gaps reintroduces the ideals of reflection, distance, and negative space. This is less obvious in the breaks between vignettes and stories proper, which act as hinges joining Cubist fragments, but for the most part the breaks in *In Our Time* stress the destruction of the object, rather than greater unity.

The start of "Indian Camp" offers the promise of fulfillment with images of the father in apparent control, reassuring his son on their journey to rescue the woman in distress: "The two boats started off in the dark. Nick heard the oarlocks of the other boat quite a way ahead of them in the mist. . . . Nick lay back with his father's arms around him" (*IOT* 15). Hemingway presents such images only to immediately undermine them. The next sentence ("It was cold on the water") undercuts the warmth provided by Nick's father. More seriously, the story will subvert both the atmosphere of assurance and the glow of authority over the doctor by exposing his treatment of the pregnant woman and the death of her husband.

There are a number of elements to consider here. We do not yet know much about Doctor Adams. We learn more in the following stories. But at this point he connotes authority; he represents colonial power, Western science, and the pioneering spirit of the Wild West (with his handy medical improvisations). Hemingway underscores the doctor's desire for control over himself and others with a brief sketch of his behavior in the shanty at the camp:

> "Those must boil," he said, and began to scrub his hands in the basin of hot water with a cake of soap he had brought from the camp. Nick watched his father's hands scrubbing each other with the soap. While his father washed his hands very carefully and thoroughly, he talked. (*IOT* 17)

The doctor goes on to explain the medical necessity for a caesarean birth ("You see, Nick, babies are supposed to be born head first . . ." [17]). In the attitude of his scientific discipline,[6] the doctor is split off from the patient's screams, the patient's husband's distress, and his own child's inability to deal with the crisis. The passage also suggests Nick's own perceptual disassociation. Sinking under the strain of the traumatic situation, he sees his father not as a whole person but as "hands scrubbing each other."[7]

Hemingway depicts the doctor—writ large, as an embodiment of imperialism—unable to connect with the whole, violently confining his "object" to the terms of his discourse. When the "object" screams, the doctor puts aside both her agony and Nick's distress:

> Just then she cried out.
> "Oh, Daddy, can't you give her something to make her stop screaming?" asked Nick.

"No. I haven't any anaesthetic," his father said. "But her screams are not important. I don't hear them because they are not important." (*IOT* 16).

Critics have had various responses to this exchange. Some defend the doctor's matter-of-fact, impersonal approach as a medical necessity. Others regard it as a sign of callousness, or even inhumanity and racism.[8] On one level, the doctor completes the task set out for him: he delivers the infant, presumably saving the baby's life along with the mother's. Nevertheless, the story complicates this "success" as the doctor's interaction with his son unfolds. What begins for Nick as an enlightening rite of passage quickly unravels. The more Nick witnesses, the more Hemingway underscores a traumatic blockage of energy, knowledge, and perception. What does Nick witness? He sees his father detached from the person he is supposed to care for, having transformed her into a dehumanized object.[9] In herself, the woman seems to be nothing—either as a subject ("'her screams are not important'") or in the particularity of her flesh ("'That's one for the medical journal George,' he said. 'Doing a Caesarian with a jack-knife and sewing it up with nine-foot, tapered gut leaders" [*IOT* 18]). Nick's desire to learn more about his world evaporates after he sees more of his father's cavalier attitude toward the patient: "Nick did not watch [his fathering sewing up the incision]. *His curiosity had been gone for a long time*" (my emphasis 17).

Thematically, Hemingway gives a sense of time slowing down and moving in reverse, opposing the dynamic, forward-looking spirit of the pre-World War I Cubists. Nick's world moves in slow motion and arrives at something like temporary stasis.[10] The plot of the story moves from the promises of pregnancy, adventure, and initiation to death and disassociation; Hemingway stops the movement of Nick's desire ("curiosity") and transforms the living patient into a reified body. *In Our Time* also sets up blockages through formal juxtapositions. The deadening of Nick's interest follows his father's subtly aggressive invitation to look ("You can watch this or not, Nick, just as you like. I'm going to sew up the incision I made" [*IOT* 17]), as well as his attempt to engage Nick in identifying with him ("How do you like being an interne?" [17]).

Later in the story, Hemingway juxtaposes the sentence, "Nick, standing in the door of the kitchen, had a good view of the upper bunk when his father, the lamp in one hand, tipped the Indian's head back" with "It was just beginning to be daylight . . ." (*IOT* 18). The relationship between these two sentences is negative, undoing the progression from dark to light. The husband's death casts a distinct pall over the dawning day. Earlier, the sentence explaining the doctor's deafness to the woman's screams ("because they are not important") was juxtaposed with her husband's fatal withdrawal ("The husband in the upper bunk rolled over against the wall" [16]). Now we learn that the husband has cut his own throat (because of her screams?). This scene does more than simply present a facet of the husband's character, as would be the case in Cubist art. Instead, it accentuates what the doctor does not know, and in so doing accentuates the unavailability of the experience of the whole. At the same time, the story continues to dismantle the hero-doctor-father image.

While Cubist painting moves faithfully from layers of facets to unified wholes, Hemingway throws the impetus in reverse. The stories in *In Our Time* begin with complete words, or rather play on readers' assumptions of complete words. In "The Doctor and the Doctor's Wife" and "Soldier's Home," for instance, the background is an ideal (pre-war) family life; in "The End of Something," the world of romance. The remnants of ideal worlds subtly inhabit most of these stories; they can be intuited from the moments of tragedy or the parody of tragedy ("A Very Short Story") or the sense of irony with regard to proper behavior ("Mr. and Mrs. Elliot," "Cat in the Rain," "Out of Season"). Sometimes Hemingway approves of the hidden ideal ("Cat in the Rain") and sometimes he ridicules it ("The Three-Day Blow"), but in each case he starts with a whole and shatters it. "Indian Camp" is the first full-length story in the collection and not surprisingly offers the fullest version of a lost universe. It combines "universal" images of fathers and mothers, new life and new death, night and day, nature and culture; it suggests the genres of romance, adventure, and creation myth. Of course "Indian Camp" also depicts the very same worlds unglued—conflicts of race, class, gender, and generation; the imposition of Western cultures on nature. This latter point appears quietly in the contrast of the open meadow and water with the reeking enclosure of the shanty ("The room smelled very bad" [*IOT* 16]), and the contrast of a natural childbirth with a crude caesarean. The overwhelming dominance of modern culture over nature also appears powerfully in the vignettes, where a "war machine" dominates nature, and in "Big Two-Hearted River," where Nick rethinks the meaning of human action. "Indian Camp" begins with the promise of a rich and meaningful cosmos, but ultimately trauma and the disorienting effects of trauma shatter the desired unity, returning the cosmos back to the audience piece by piece as wreckage.

If trauma essentially causes the breakdown of the world, *In Our Time* brings the reader not to a utopian construction (the moment of Cubism), but to a confrontation with *the hole*. Readers admire Hemingway for his sensitivity to psychological devastation, but he is equally adept at portraying physical vulnerability. The pre-war fascination with technology and speed sought to leave the vulnerable body behind and extend *being* into the machine. This was the dream of the Italian Futurists, under the leadership of Fillipo Tomaso Marinetti ("Time and Space died yesterday. We already live in the absolute, because we have created eternal, omnipresent speed" [Caws 187]). The Cubists too celebrate the collective body, wherein an older, essentially bourgeois individualism is exploded. Hemingway, however, maintains the importance of individual subjectivity and insists upon the value and the radical particularity of the flesh. Once again, this emphasis involves trauma. "Indian Camp" gives us intimate images of the pregnant body cut open and stitched up—a closure almost immediately undone, in a way, by the opening up of another wound, the husband's cut throat. The *In Our Time* vignettes show suffering bodies in a collectively psychotic world, wherein the very structures for making meaning collapse. The world ceases to mean, connect, or move. It blacks out, retracts into itself, or flies about senselessly. Hemingway's *In Our Time* provides a cognitive frame for exploring such a devastated world, ironically finding in collapse a starting point for investigating old meanings and creating new ones.

In keeping with the theme of disorientation, the vignettes appear like fragmented cuts from a movie. The scenes are brutally concrete, but often lack adequate contexts for orienting the reader. Chapter I thematically underscores the disappearance of context with images of a lieutenant in a stupor ("Oh, I am so soused" [*IOT* 13]), riding his horse and surrounded by drunken soldiers moving through the night ("Everybody was drunk. The whole battery was drunk going along the road in the dark" [13]). The second vignette completes the frame of "Indian Camp," depicting the chaos of an "evacuation" filled with strangely out of place animals ("water buffalo and cattle," "camels bobbing along" [21]), objects, and people ("women and kids were in the carts crouched with mattresses, mirrors, sewing machines, bundles"). It is as if the basic fabric of a village had been suddenly torn apart and randomly flung through space. The portrayal seems particularly psychotic, with displaced creatures and people unmoored in time as well as space: "No end and no beginning. Just carts loaded with everything they owned . . . jammed solid on the bridge. . . . Greek cavalry herded along the procession" (21). In the midst of this procession, Hemingway includes an image of human vulnerability that echoes "Indian Camp": "There was a woman having a kid with a young girl holding a blanket over her and crying. Scared sick looking at it" (21).[11] Both the focus on pain (the girl frightened and crying, the pregnant woman in labor) and the attempt to find a safe place (huddling under the blanket) when the world is being uprooted on a mass scale suggest a need to withdraw from the world. Almost every vignette draws attention to such withdrawal, implying a need to arrest the speed of mass mobilization (technological culture) and to return to the body as the source and end-point of meaning.

Nothing interferes with the capacity to produce a meaningful world more than pain.[12] Chapter IX depicts a matador badly gored through the belly ("the bull rammed him wham against the wall"), losing both his mind and body: "the horn came out, and he lay in the sand, and then got up like crazy drunk and tried to slug the men carrying him away and yelled for his sword but he fainted" (*IOT* 83). The vignettes provide an anatomy of trauma, detailing the fragility of the body against the modern, totalizing machinery of a world war. Hemingway temporarily sets aside human-produced systems of meaning—jobs, patriotism, languages, gender, codes, territory, and so on—taking us to the animal level underlying such productions. The vignettes focus on the trauma of soldiers *and* animals. Both suffer. Both appear aware, on some level, of their bodies and psyches on the verge of disintegration. Chapter X presents in gruesome detail a horse being "whacked . . . on the legs," its "entrails hung down in a blue bunch," "Blood pumped regularly from the horse's front legs" (89). Such details are found throughout the vignettes. Most striking are the moments when Hemingway captures a *particular life* teetering on or dragged to the verge, such as the horse "cantering jerkily along the barrera." At the end of the vignette, the animal's movements are "nervous and wobbly" (89).

The most agonizing scenes of human bodies in distress include the executions of the sick cabinet minister ("When they fired the first volley he was sitting down in the water with his head on his knees" [*IOT* 51]) and Sam Cardinella ("When they came toward him with the cap to go over his head Sam Cardinella lost control of his sphincter muscle" [143]). Perhaps most dramatically, Hemingway takes the reader behind the eyes of a dying bullfighter:

> Maera lay still, his head on his arm, his face in the sand. He felt warm and sticky from the bleeding. Each time he felt the horn coming. . . . They laid Maera down in a cot and one of the men went out for the doctor. . . . Maera felt everything getting larger and larger and then smaller and smaller. Then it got larger and larger and larger and then smaller and smaller. Then everything commenced to run faster and faster as when they speed up a cinematograph film. Then he was dead. (131)

Paralleling the chaos of the "external" world, the dying Maera's perception of space and time breaks down. Arguably, this portrayal of life winding down like a broken machine suggests the need for perspective, for the structural play of vignettes and stories in a binary pattern: back and forth, near and far, figure and ground.

At any rate, the vignettes are shocking. As we consider the woman in labor, Nick's wounded spine, or the myriad images of death and maiming,

Hemingway invites us to pause over the body, over how bodies are organized, conceptualized, touched. These painful images cause the world to recede and the body to obtrude. Thematically, they represent paralysis, for in a way the wounded, immobilized body blocks movement, representing a productive refusal to objectify, crystallize, or accede to the ordinary meanings of the world.

Hemingway values the pause that comes before movement. Unlike James Joyce in *Portrait of the Artist as a Young Man,* he does not trace the victory of individuation over paralysis. On the contrary, *In Our Time* values a frame of mind that ceases to individuate or identify and that resists the optimistic flow encouraged by progressive narratives or by Cubism's utopian visions of immediacy and availability. The vignettes and some of the short stories (in particular "Indian Camp" and "The Battler") show the dangerous powers of the human hand transformed by technology (the doctor's jack-knife, Bugs's blackjack), as it touches and damages other beings. In the face of unprecedented power to destroy, Hemingway looks for hesitation. In "The End of Something" and "The Three-Day Blow," Nick hesitates before a conventional relationship and conventional adolescent masculinity. In other words, instead of seeing Nick's rejection of Marjorie as merely pathetic, I see it as consistent with the moment of crisis and stillness that Hemingway seeks to preserve and offers to the reader as a mode of perception. Crisis, suspension, refusal of identity. This sequence, cognitive and emotional, is an opportunity to perceive and evaluate the construction of meaning.

Krebs, in "Soldier's Home," also stands still before a similar turning point. Home from the war, Krebs does not want to take on the roles available to him, much to his mother's dismay:

"Have you decided what you're going to do yet, Harold?" his mother said, taking off her glasses.

"No," said Krebs.

"Don't you think it's about time?" His mother did not say this in a mean way. She seemed worried.

"I hadn't thought about it," Krebs said.

"God has some work for every one to do," his mother said. "There can be no idle hands in His Kingdom."

"I'm not in His Kingdom," Krebs said.

"We are all of us in His Kingdom."

Krebs felt embarrassed and resentful as always. (*IOT* 74–75)

Kreb's mother, well-meaning but finally thoughtless, imposes on her son an oppressive set of goals, underwritten by the patriarchal Kingdom of God, and therefore unquestionable.

In the pre-war universe adeptly pictured by Berger, the Cubists are able to perceive the building blocks of the world and understand how the world comes together structurally. In the vignettes, Hemingway shows how that very same material world, sturdily engineered, can be systematically and violently demolished. More subtly, "The End of Something," in an extended description, recalls the dismantling of the lumbering town, Hortons Bay. Piece by piece, the lumber schooner loaded up all the heavy machinery: "Its open hold covered with canvas and lashed tight . . . it moved out into the open lake, carrying with it everything that had made the mill a mill and Hortons Bay a town" (*IOT* 31). For Marjorie, the mill's ruin evokes fantasies of a romantic kingdom ("'There's our old ruin, Nick,'" "'It seems more like a castle'" [32]), but Nick remains unresponsive to this opening into an older world. Krebs likewise declines either to take on conventional roles or make new meanings for himself, even though his mother insists upon the existence of worlds both material ("Charley Simmons has a good job;" "The boys are all settling down") and immaterial ("His Kingdom") (75). The stories of *In Our Time* always start with the presumption of a model world and then proceed to undo it. Ruins, kingdoms, towns, neighborhoods—worlds are put into brackets. Krebs and Nick stand on the brink, refusing *in their very beings,* rather than with any conscious intention, to be turned on and set into motion.

The First World War crystallized both the West's will to dominate and its newfound capacity to transform and destroy. The vignettes capture the global effects of the modern *zeitgeist*. The stories capture the individual

hand objectifying the body and operating accordingly. Against the expanding networks of power, *In Our Time* suggests a return to a human scale,
appreciating the limits of the body and mind. This is why I prefer to see
the interplay between the vignettes and the stories as analogous to, but not
identical with *perspective* rather than the Cubist style, associated as it is with
the collective, the social-as-vast-machinery, and the availability of nature
(and everything else) to the modern technological imprint. Hemingway
wrote that *In Our Time*'s structure of stories divided by vignettes "give[s]
the picture of the whole between examining it in detail. Like looking with
your eyes at something, say a passing coastline, and then looking at it with
15× binoculars" (qtd. in Wilson 122–23). Emily Watts argues that this statement accords with Cubism's technique of "looking at a similar image from
several different points of view and from several different angles" (87). But
the styles of Braque's or Picasso's pre-war paintings do not simply provide
different points of view and multiple angles; their Cubism provides these
angles simultaneously. The vignettes and stories on the other hand exist as
separate perspectives that one cannot inhabit simultaneously. When one
looks through binoculars, the magnified view displaces the ordinary view,
and vice versa. Hemingway's style is more humble than the Cubist style. He
gives up the demand for speed and conquest, and accepts a human pace and
human limits when it comes to assimilating reality. Consider, for instance,
the disjunction between Krebs' war experience and his post-war struggle to
construct a history of those experiences. Yet even a proto-Cubist like Cézanne,
whom Hemingway deeply admired, creates a sense of the simultaneity of
facets. As Stephen Kern put it, "[Cézanne] wrestled with them until, as
Merleau-Ponty believed, he created 'the impression of an emerging order,
of an object in the art of appearing, organizing itself before our eyes'" [142]).
If one respects the actual workings of the medium, such an impression of
emerging order is impossible to recreate in textual forms, especially linear
works like *In Our Time*.[13]

I prefer to think of the relationship between vignette and story as a
relationship between the available and the unavailable, the near and the distant,
the conscious and the unconscious, the precise and the ambiguous. To view

multiple facets of an object all at once, in Cubist fashion,[14] is to attempt to possess or master it totally. My angle on *In Our Time* finds a positive stress on the unavailable, the absent, and the quality of time *before objects become objects* at all. While Cubism and other movements, including Futurism, dream of an end to otherness, Hemingway wants to allow the other to remain other: not yet possessed or mastered by the human will to power. But he also wants to preserve some semblance of the self and its own immanent viewpoints. Characters such as Nick Adams, then, view any dispersal of selfhood—either that implied by Berger's utopian simultaneity or seen by art critic Peter Fuller in the Cubist vision—as "depersonalisation, the shattering of the individual subject, and the cultural debasement of spiritual, affective and sensual experience" (Fuller 110). Whether taken as utopian (Berger) or as continuous with the will to power erupting in the war (Fuller), Cubism disperses the self into the field. In contrast, Hemingway wants to experience and rethink the post-war cosmos from specific locations, particular points of consciousness, unique sensing beings. Fuller suggests that even Picasso had to reject his pre-war style in order to respect the self and the other more fully, otherwise "how could he have said anything through cubism about a sense of the other as a full, autonomous and complete person in the world? How could he have affirmed through it those sanguine and curvaceous properties of flesh . . . ?" (110).

The return to a human scale (not the superhuman scale of modern culture) as well as a rethinking of the relationship to the other is, appropriately, given greatest weight in "Big Two-Hearted River." We observe Nick scaling down; he retreats from the intense activity of modern civilization and enters into more marginal spaces, resisting the allure of modernity and its will to stamp everything in its own image. Nick enters the woods not to build a stronger identity—some new version of the rugged individual, for instance—or to recover more authentic objects. He enters *the other of the woods* to inhabit a pre-objective, pre-egoistic moment. The whole thrust of *In Our Time* leads to this point, where one must reconsider how to approach objects, how to live with them, and how to touch them while causing the least amount of harm and perhaps even some good.

Traditionally, the woods have haunted the imagination as a magical space, external to "civilization." Significantly, though, Nick's camp maintains connections to culture. After the train—that most potent symbol of "civilizing" machinery—drops Nick off and vanishes "up the track out of sight," he sees the remains of Seney:

> There was no town, nothing but the rails and the burned-over country. The thirteen saloons that had lined the one street of Seney had not left a trace. The foundations of the Mansion House hotel stuck up above the ground. The stone was chipped and split by the fire. It was all that was left of the town of Seney. Even the surface had been burned off the ground. (*IOT* 133)

Like Thoreau, who moved only a small physical distance from Concord down the road to Walden Pond, Hemingway lets the signs of town and back-country play off each other. For Hemingway, however, the industrialization feared by Thoreau has scorched the earth (the historic logging town of Seney was destroyed by slash fires kindled in the clearcut forests). The town remains only as a trace, a ghost, a reminder that Nick is not running away, but productively waiting and meditating. Nick withdraws from Seney, perhaps, to consider new objects and how to approach them.

Before touching a trout, Nick wets his hands, "so he would not disturb the delicate mucus that covered him" (*IOT* 149). An improper touch destroys life, and as he does in the vignettes, Hemingway zeros in on the particulars:

> If a trout was touched with a dry hand, a white fungus attacked the unprotected spot. Years before when he had fished crowded streams, with fly fishermen ahead of him and behind him, Nick had again and again come on dead trout, furry with white fungus, drifted against rock, or floating belly up in some pool. Nick did not like to fish with other men on the river. Unless they were of your party, they spoiled it. (149)

Nick's treatment of the fish offers a sharp contrast to his father's treatment of the mother-to-be in "Indian Camp." Although Nick's approach to "Mother

Nature" leaves an imprint, his attitude is reverential, especially when we compare him to the remembered crowds of fly fishermen whose presence feels like an invasion, an insensitive trampling over the landscape. Nick sets out to fish the river. He baits his hooks with worms, guts the fish and eats them, and yet he approaches the process with striking care and sensitivity, making sure, for example, that he does not taint the fish he returns to the water.[15] The mood takes us back to Doctor Adams' approach to another mother's body and the deadly after-effects of the "operation." Hemingway seems to remind us of the doctor's failures, but at the same time to recover and transfer the lost potential for elation to "Big Two-Hearted River."

The negative effects of touch extend beyond "Indian Camp." They spread throughout *In Our Time,* from the doctor's objectification of the Indian woman's body, to the tanks and bombs that devastate the landscape, to the boxer's wounded face, to the fires razing Seney and affecting the surrounding life (the blackened grasshoppers of "Big Two-Hearted River," symbols of the trauma visited upon the victims of war, must be seen in this larger light). Stressing the importance of approaching the world from a new position, *In Our Time,* while not imposing a new metaphysics, does suggest that any new relationship between humans and *the other* must take into account the specific qualities of the other (in the case of "Big Two-Hearted River," the fish).

Even as Nick intrudes upon the fish, he acts with special care for the fish's well-being: "He held the trout, never still, with his moist right hand, while he unhooked the barb from his mouth, then dropped him back into the stream" (*IOT* 149). Hemingway describes Nick's relation to the trout in sensuous rather than merely visual terms. As an object the trout's presence is ambiguous, partly available and partly withdrawing from perception: "The trout was steady in the moving stream, resting on the gravel, beside a stone. As Nick's fingers touched him, touched his smooth, cool, underwater feeling he was gone, gone in a shadow across the bottom of the stream" (*IOT* 149). The image of the slippery fish and the various qualities of the stream—fluid, murky, clear, shallow, deep, near, remote—suggest the inherent ambiguity of matter, an ambiguity which Hemingway accepts rather than trying frantically to objectify. The other does not appear in

In Our Time as an object to be subsumed by human definitions. Instead, Hemingway seems more interested in giving the other back to the shadows, to its own perhaps imperceptible qualities, imperceptible at least from a human viewpoint. As his style with its sometimes ethereal quality reveals, Hemingway values the immaterial as much as the material, and prefers the ambiguous to the objectified. Nick himself takes on a sort of fluidity, fishing half-submerged in the river:

> Holding the rod far out toward the uprooted tree and sloshing backward in the current, Nick worked the trout, plunging, the rod bending alive. . . . Holding the rod, pumping alive against the current . . . the spring of the rod yielding to the rushes, sometimes jerking under water, but always bringing him in. (*IOT* 152)

Here, Nick partly fuses with the river, connected to the depths by the living current of the rod. Rather than describe Nick physically as a precisely demarcated, objectified human shape, Hemingway transforms him into a non-visual life current.

Earlier, in a long description of Nick as he prepares a meal, Hemingway divests Nick of his hyperactive, mechanical reactions. In several pages detailing Nick's careful preparation of his beans, spaghetti, bread, and coffee, Hemingway goes beyond mere reportage to show Nick approaching an object of another kind—his own pleasure. As Nick learns to enjoy himself, care for his senses, and generally attend to the particular rhythms of his body, he develops a consciousness able to resist the speed of modern life: "He knew the beans and spaghetti were still too hot . . . he was not going to spoil it all by burning his tongue. For years he had never enjoyed fried bananas because he had never been able to wait for them to cool" (*IOT* 140). While Cubist ideas and practices break down, reconstitute, and attenuate the individuality of the body, transforming people into abstractions or machinery when not absorbing them into a field or into the anonymity of the masses, Hemingway snatches the body back from its dispersal into the frenzy of the technological world, pointing out that the flesh has its own specific, limiting qualities: "His tongue was very sensitive" (140). *It burns*—a fact that must be seen alongside the other fires occurring throughout the collection.

Nick, aligning with his body's sensitivity, connects with the other of nature, his flesh learning how to refuse to move at the speed of the machine. Hemingway's style acts as a cognitive frame, demanding a new kind of attention, a halting and more human pace than that of the new mass media. From the perspective of an urban pace, the following paragraph must appear absurd:

> Nick ate a big flapjack and a smaller one, covered with apple butter. He put apple butter on the third cake, folded it over twice, wrapped it in oiled paper, and put it in his shirt pocket. He put the apple butter jar back in the pack and cut bread for two sandwiches. (*IOT* 146)

Such a style is itself a form of attention, a style centered on a sensuous and caring relationship with things. Its pace allows a careful perceptual encounter with the world, as advocated, not surprisingly, by Henry David Thoreau in *Walden:* "The finest qualities of our nature, like the bloom on fruits, can be preserved only by the most delicate handling. Yet we do not treat ourselves nor one another thus tenderly" (3). I think Hemingway would approve. *In Our Time* struggles to achieve just such a "delicate handling," and sometimes that means not handling at all, not stamping, accumulating, or possessing (even if only perceptually), but retracting, undoing, and respecting the unavailability of the other.

NOTES

1. Hemingway originally entitled it "Introduction by the Author" (Stewart 58).
2. Matthew Stewart observes that "[t]his is a strange and guilt-induced manner of describing the use of the searchlights, centered on the victims ('to stop *their* screaming'), rather than on the perpetrators, whom the searchlights were actually intended to expose" (65).

3. Both Williams (particularly in *Spring and All*) and Stein—with their exploration of surfaces, the purity of the word, and the continuous present—arguably share some of the formal and thematic concerns of Berger's utopian Cubists. Faulkner, particularly in *The Sound and the Fury*, creates a textual canvas designed to hold multiple temporalities in a single framework. His sentence structure, unlike Hemingway's, is characterized by fullness, endless qualifications packing the tensions and complexities of entire histories into single sentences.

4. See, for example, *Minima Moralia* for a taste of Adorno's philosophical negativity as well as his scathing tone.

5. As Amy Strong has pointed out (citing Paul Smith, Joseph M. Flora, Philip Young, and Joseph DeFalco) "Indian Camp" traditionally has been read as a tale of initiation (19). Some recent critics have acknowledged Hemingway's blatant critique or parody of the initiation story. James Mulvey in "Failed Fathers in Hemingway's 'Indian Camp,'" for one, writes that "[i]n 'Indian Camp' Hemingway, with 'modern' irony and pessimism, has turned the traditional nineteenth century 'initiation' story on its head" (75).

6. Bridging the gap between the scientific and the human persists as a serious problem in the medical profession, and in the sciences in general. See, for example, Evelyn Fox Keller's *Reflections on Gender and Science* (1958), Ed Rosenbaum's *A Taste of My Own Medicine* (1988), or Neil Postman's *Technopoly: The Surrender of Culture to Technology* (1993).

7. Before the woman begins to scream, Nick tries to imitate his father's coolness, responding "I know" and "I see" to medical explanations (*IOT* 16). His shaky attempt to emulate his father's detachment fails when the screaming begins.

8. Thomas Strychacz describes the "mercy mission" as "a form of Manifest Destiny upon the Indian camp. [Dr. Adams and Uncle George] play the role of the Great White Father, bring to birth a child/nation supposedly deficient in civilized attributes" (55).

9. In her discussion of racial power relations in "Indian Camp," Amy Strong argues that "Dr. Adams chooses to envision [the Indian woman's] body as a territory without agency or voice, a kind of uninhabited land he takes possession of and must get under control" (22).

10. In the face of the Indian woman's suffering and his own trauma, time slows for

Nick. While the events of the short story unfold quickly, for Nick the caesarean seems to take an unendurably long time: "Nick held the basin for his father. It all took a long time" (*IOT* 17).

11. While detecting different voices in the vignettes, we are unable to identify narrators or characters except as embodiments of different speech patterns. This reinforces the feeling of disconnection.

12. As Elaine Scarry writes in *The Body in Pain*, "Physical pain does not simply resist language but actively destroys it, bringing about an immediate reversion to a state anterior to language, to the sounds and cries a human being makes before language is learned" (4).

13. Despite Hemingway's spiritual affinity with Cézanne, the writer's forms in my opinion have virtually nothing to do with the artist's techniques. To say otherwise is to ignore the radical differences of media, although there are cases where such comparisons between literature and art make sense, especially where typographical play is central as in Pound's *Cantos* or Williams's *Spring and All*. However, even Hemingway's characteristic repetitions do not seem to create fragments, multiple facets, or alternative and disruptive experiences of a scene. Instead, they unfold in a linear way, creating a consistency of character, mood, or attitude that is very unlike the blossoming facets of Braque, Picasso, or Cézanne. On the other hand, Cézanne and Hemingway converge in their concern for the sensuousness of nature as well as for the role of an immanent consciousness "moving in the picture" (as Nick says in a version of "Big Two-Hearted River" that pay homage to Cézanne ["On Writing" 240]).

14. Unlike Hemingway, whose prose has a strangely ethereal or elemental quality, writers such as William Carlos Williams, Gertrude Stein, and Ezra Pound explicitly incorporated other material into their works, playing with Cubist technique of collage. Pound's incorporation of letters, Chinese ideograms, and other forms of quotation offers a dramatic example. Such inclusions, as many critics have pointed out, enact the objective presence of the other in the text, just as Cubist painting draws attention to the material dimensions of the canvas, to the paint, or to objects attached to the canvas (newspaper, for example). The canvas itself becomes the focus, more than the object being represented.

15. Nick's interaction with the fish is arguably similar to Native American rituals of respect and reverence for game killed for food or ritual.

WORKS CITED

Adorno, Theodor. *Minima Moralia: Reflections on a Damaged Life*. 1951. London: New Left Books, 1974.

Berger, John. "The Moment of Cubism." *The Sense of Sight: Writings by John Berger*. Ed. Lloyd Spencer. New York: Pantheon, 1985. 159–188.

Bredahl, A. Carl. "Divided Narrative and Ernest Hemingway." *The Literary Half-Yearly* 24.1 (January 1983): 15–21.

Brogan, Jacqueline Vaught. "Hemingway's *In Our Time*: A Cubist Anatomy." *The Hemingway Review* 17.2 (Spring 1998): 31–46.

Caws, Mary Ann, ed. *Manifesto: A Century of Isms*. Lincoln: U of Nebraska P, 2001.

Fuller, Peter. "Under Picasso." *New Society* (16 July 1981): 109–111.

Hemingway, Ernest. *In Our Time*. New York: Scribner's, 1925.

———. "On Writing." *The Nick Adams Stories*. New York: Scribner's, 1972. 233–241.

Hughes, Robert. *The Shock of the New: Art and the Century of Change*. London: Thames and Hudson, 1980.

Keller, Evelyn Fox. *Reflections on Gender and Science*. New Haven: Yale UP, 1985.

Kern, Stephen. *The Culture of Time and Space 1880–1918*. Cambridge: Harvard UP, 1983.

Mulvey, James. "Failed Fathers in Hemingway's 'Indian Camp.'" *Eureka Studies in Teaching Short Fiction* 4.2 (Spring 2004): 71–77.

Nicholls, Peter. *Modernisms: A Literary Guide*. Berkeley: U of California P, 1995.

Postman, Neil. *Technopoly: The Surrender of Culture to Technology*. New York: Vintage, 1993.

Rosenbaum, Edward E. *A Taste of My Own Medicine: When the Doctor is the Patient*. New York: Random House, 1988.

Rosenfeld, Paul. "Tough Earth." *New Republic* (November 1925): 22–23.

Scarry, Elaine. *The Body in Pain: The Making and Unmaking of the World*. New York: Oxford UP, 1985.

Stewart, Matthew. "It Was All a Pleasant Business: The Historical Context of 'On the Quai at Smyrna.'" *The Hemingway Review* 23.1 (Fall 2003): 58–71.

Strong, Amy Lovell. "Screaming Through Silence: The Violence of Race in 'Indian Camp' and 'The Doctor and the Doctor's Wife.'" *The Hemingway Review* 16.1 (Fall 1996): 18–32.

Strychacz, Thomas. *Hemingway's Theaters of Masculinity.* Baton Rouge: Louisiana State UP, 2003.

Thoreau, Henry David. *Walden and Civil Disobedience.* 1854 and 1849. Ed. Sherman Paul. Boston: Houghton Mifflin, 1957.

Vaughn, Elizabeth Dewberry. "*In Our Time* and Picasso." In *Hemingway Repossessed.* Ed. Kenneth Rosen. Westport, CT: Praeger, 1994. 3–8.

Watts, Emily Stipes. *Ernest Hemingway and the Visual Arts.* Urbana: U of Illinois P, 1971.

Wilson, Edmund. *The Shores of Light: A Literary Chronicle of the Twenties and Thirties.* New York: Farrar, Straus and Young, 1952.

Recurrence in Hemingway and Cézanne

Ron Berman

Words and also forms in Hemingway have second lives; especially those motifs (trees, rocks, roadways) deriving from visual art. Hemingway himself identified Paul Cézanne as an influence on his work. For Hemingway, the main issue was Cézanne's ability to interpret landscape. Neither was concerned with documentary accuracy—although recent scholarship comparing photographs of Cézanne's scenes to his painted versions of them makes useful inferences about the way that depiction changes as well as represents facts (Machotka 1–7). Meyer Schapiro wrote that "the visible world is not simply represented on Cézanne's canvas. It is recreated through strokes of color, among which are many that we cannot identify with an object and yet

Reprinted with permission from *The Hemingway Review* 23.2 (Spring 2004). Copyright © 2004 The Ernest Hemingway Foundation. Published by the University of Idaho, Moscow, Idaho.

are necessary for the harmony of the whole" (qtd. in Kelder 386). But that phrase "recreated" needs to be examined with respect to Hemingway's work. It means seeing things in a particular way; and also making more than one interpretation of the same thing.

A number of critics have tried to deal with Hemingway's ideas about visual and verbal art. One attempt concludes that "Indian Camp" is constructed around "cyclical events" and repeated motifs (Hagemann 108). Another, that the reiteration of natural forms in "Big Two-Hearted River" can be traced to specific work like Cézanne's "The Poplars" and "Farmyard at Auvers" (Johnston 29–30).[1] A basic book on Hemingway and the arts has a chapter on landscape and writing. It too notes the quality of reiteration. Certain landscapes "remain a constant" in the fiction (Watts 44).

Hemingway acknowledged connections between his own work and visual art, especially the painting of Cézanne. The Lillian Ross interview at the Metropolitan Museum of Art in 1949 is often adduced:

> After we reached the Cézannes and Degas and the other Impressionists, Hemingway became more and more excited, and discoursed on what each artist could do and how and what he had learned from each. . . . Hemingway spent several minutes looking at Cézanne's "Rocks—Forest of Fontainebleau." "This is what we try to do in writing, this and this, and the woods, and the rocks we have to climb over," he said. "Cézanne is my painter, after the early painters. . . . I can make a landscape like Mr. Paul Cézanne by walking through the Luxembourg Museum a thousand times." (Ross 36)

Reiteration and sequence dominate the statement. Hemingway addresses a painter and also painters before him. He implies familiarity with the way that a particular school of painting turns and returns to its subjects. There is even reiteration in his language, although Ross does not pursue a definition of "this . . . this and this." When Hemingway says he walked through the museum "a thousand times" the repetition—which is fairly startling—draws no blood. She treats the statement as an exaggeration, but it is meant to be evidence that he saw the same thing in necessarily different ways.

Cézanne often reiterated or recast the subjects of his paintings. The rocks of Fontainebleau were part of an immense body of work redone in order to capture as many aspects of the landscape as possible. Here are some titles keyed to the catalogue of John Rewald: *Rochers à L'Estaque, Dans le Parc du Château Noir, Rochers et Branches à Bibémus, Sous Bois Devant Les Grottes Au-dessus du Château Noir, Rochers et Arbres, Intérieur de Forêt, Pins et Rochers, Arbres et Rochers dans le Parc du Château Noir, Rochers Près des Grottes Au-dessus du Château Noir.* This list does not include related subjects like the rock formations of the Mont Sainte-Victoire paintings. The forms of "the woods, and the rocks" were constantly reworked by Cézanne. These forms and certain others were continuously reinvented by Hemingway (Watts 146–149). Cézanne redrew and repainted an unending series of versions of landscapes in pencil, oils, and watercolors. Landscape scenes are variations on a central subject—and even titles are reiterations. This could not have been unknown to Hemingway.

Hemingway did not specify the immense number of versions of Cézanne's most essential element of landscape, the trees that provide vertical forms for the Fontainebleau painting. There are, for example: *L'Estaque, L'Estaque—Rochers, Pins et Mer, Marroniers et Ferme du Jas de Bouffan,* the many versions of *Sous-Bois; Les Grandes-Arbres, Le Grand Pin, L'Allée à Chantilly, Dans la Forèt de Fontainebleau.* However, one reiterated subject in Cézanne—curves in the road—can be traced because Hemingway invoked it a number of times and made it recognizably part of his own *language* as well as landscape.

The Cézannes that I have in mind among many others are *Maisons Au Bord d'une Route, La Route Tournante* (1881), *Le Tournany de Route Près de Valhermeil, La Route Tournante à La Roche-Guyon, La Montagne Sainte-Victoire au Grand-Pin, La Route en Provence, La Route Tournante en Sous-Bois, La Route Tournante* (1904), *Matinée des Printemps à Saint-Antonin,* and *La Route Tournante en Haut du Chemin des Lauves.* To these must be added numerous views of farms and towns, and, always, the series of paintings of Mont Sainte-Victoire. Cézanne's late landscapes—his "curves in the road"—have been called new visions of nature (Novotny 110–111).

Perhaps the issue left unpursued by the Ross interview—what, after all, was Hemingway referring to when he said that he had "learned" something of immense importance?—can be clarified. Evidently, one thing learned was the art of reiteration: "In the . . . *Mont Sainte-Victoire* series. . . . variations, studied like successive geological strata, grew out of Cézanne's ceaseless experimentation with the theme. They stem also from the different centering of the subject, which Cézanne insisted upon considering from every possible angle (left, right, forward, backward, high, low), according to the position in which he placed himself. The theme became a pretext for variations whose multiplicity distanced him from the concrete object" (Monnier 116).

The central location for these ideas is in Hemingway's work of the 1920s. Here is the opening of "The Three-Day Blow":

> The rain stopped as Nick turned into the road that went up through the orchard. The fruit had been picked and the fall wind blew through the bare trees. . . . The road came out of the orchard on to the top of the hill. There was the cottage, the porch bare, smoke coming from the chimney. In back was a garage, the chicken coop and the second-growth timber like a hedge against the woods behind. The big trees swayed far over in the wind as he watched. It was the first of the autumn storms. (*SS* 115)

The passage has embedded in it a number of allusions to the landscape of Cézanne. The phrase "on top of the road" translates part of the title of *Le Mont Sainte-Victoire Au-dessus de la Route du Tholonet* and also of *Maison Près d'un Tournant en Haut du Chemin des Lauves* (Rubin 400, 414). The phrase "the road came out of the orchard on to the top of the hill" not only contains the language of many titled paintings but is seen from their perspective. The phrase "the big trees" that "swayed far over in the wind" is literal Cézanne as in the pencil and watercolor *Les Grands Arbres,* the oil *Les Grandes Arbres au Jas du Bouffon,* and a number of drawings. As for the second part of Hemingway's line, Lionello Venturi gave his own title to *Les Grandes Arbres: "Bare Trees in the Fury of the Wind"* (qtd. in Rubin 412). That may be because Cézanne himself had in 1863 written a poem, "The

Great Pine," in connection with this subject and containing the line "The tree shaken by the fury of the winds" (qtd. in Schapiro 108).

Hemingway's opening lines are about more than one subject. In 1957, he completed a group of chapters for the book that was to become *A Moveable Feast*. He gave them to his wife Mary for typing—one of them told "how it was to be writing 'The Three-Day Blow' at a table in a café on the Place St.-Michel." But she was "disappointed to discover that the sketches contained so little that was straightforwardly autobiographical" (Baker 352). There is also very little that was straightforwardly documentary. In the section of *A Moveable Feast* that Baker describes, Hemingway writes that "in Paris I could write about Michigan." He meant that literally: "I was writing about up in Michigan and since it was a wild, cold, blowing day it was that sort of day in the story." Scholars are aware that he links the writing of the stories of this period to Paris and especially to Impressionism, but it will be useful for all readers to get his own sense of connection: "I could walk through the gardens and then go to the Musée du Luxembourg where the great paintings were that have now mostly been transferred to the Louvre and the Jeu de Paume. I went there nearly every day for the Cézannes and to see the Manets and the Monets and the other Impressionists that I had first come to know about in the Art Institute of Chicago. I was learning something from the painting of Cézanne that had made writing simple true sentences far from enough to make the stories have the dimensions that I was trying to put in them" (MF 7, 13).

Possibly more than technique was involved. Hemingway came to Cézanne at a time when his stock was very high. Roger Fry had in 1914 called him "the Christopher Columbus of a new continent of form" (qtd. in Osborne 215–216). By 1927, when Fry's book on Cézanne appeared, he was understood to be not only the leading post-Impressionist but also a world-historical figure. Fry himself was seen to be such a figure.[2] Fry wrote about Cézanne from 1906 on, organized exhibitions of his work in 1910, bought his paintings for J.P. Morgan and the Metropolitan Museum, and coined the term "post-Impressionism." Virginia Woolf's biography of Roger Fry makes a number of important observations: she believes that Fry's book on Cézanne was his most significant work, and that it was significant both for its author and its subject. Woolf states that the theme of this book is the definition of artistic identity opposed to received opinion. She cites Fry on "the double story" of Cézanne, i.e., his creating a technique and then becoming "the great protagonist of individual prowess against the herd" (Woolf 284–286). So, when we say that anyone might have been influenced by Cézanne or ideas about him in the first decades of the twentieth century, we necessarily mean that viewers such as Hemingway came to the painter through ideas generated by his leading critic. What were some of those ideas? First, that the painter's intellectualism was an important part of his total effect. Second, that he provided a new kind of technical language for art. Third, that the artist was himself a model for independent thought. Here is Fry on the late work, those landscapes so much admired by Hemingway:

> A picture belonging to M. Vollard . . . represents a road plunging from the immediate foreground into a wood of poplars, through which we surmise the presence of a rock face, which rises up behind and dominates the tree tops. . . . the more one looks the more do these dispersed indications begin to play together, to compose rhythmic phrases which articulate the apparent confusion, till at last all seems to come together to the eye into an austere and impressive architectural construction, which is all the more moving in that it emerges from his apparent chaos. It is perhaps in works like these that Cézanne reveals the extraordinary profundity of his imagination. He seems in them to attain to heights of concentration and elimination of all that is not pure plastic idea, which still outrange our pictorial apprehension. . . . the completest revelation of his spirit may be found in these latest creations. (Fry 78–79)

There are certain essentials: the motif of the road, the organization of detail into harmony, the warning that there are elements in his work that outrange our "pictorial apprehension." Above all, there is the conception of landscape as a dominant idea.

Pavel Machotka has gone to archives and also, so far as they can be known, to Cézanne's locations. He has collected photographs of the sites, and taken

new ones from approximate perspectives. His reconstruction tries to account
for the season and time of day of the original; change, damage, and natural
cycles in the sites; differing versions of the same scene. The reasons he gives
for the project are helpful for Hemingway's own reiteration: chief among
them that "more than one painting" is needed to produce coherence of idea
or motif—and also to be faithful to the variations of nature (Machotka 1–2).
A single motif requires many versions, an idea often restated in Cézanne's
letters and interviews. Hemingway scholars have tried to examine his
landscape in terms of fidelity to "place." R.W.B. Lewis sees "place" first of all
as a recognizable terrain. He concentrates on Hemingway's local knowledge
and on the primacy of fact in any given description of city or country. But he
acknowledges also that such description is not a matter of documentation.
"Place" is always modified by idea (Lewis 119–121, 143).

That is a useful context for the opening of Hemingway's "The Three-Day
Blow" in which the *route tournante* comes over a hill to a particular terrain.
Getting there, we see the scene—but in a delimited way: "There was the
cottage, the porch bare, smoke coming from the chimney. In back was the
garage, the chicken coop and the second-growth timber like a hedge against
the woods behind" (*SS* 115). The usual descriptives are not there. There are
no colors in this most important part of the opening. There is form but no
draftsmanship—a trait in Cézanne much criticized by those who came after
Roger Fry. Two things become apparent, the first that this passage is about
perception not place; the second that it is seen in black and white. This is a
drawing, not a painting, pencil without the usual watercolor. There is another
perspective: "They stood together, looking out across the country, down over
the orchard, beyond the road, across the lower fields and the woods of the
point to the lake. The wind was blowing straight down the lake. They could
see the surf along Ten Mile point." Here too there is the total absence of
color—and no attempt to differentiate, describe, or compare objects within
the scene. The curving road has taken us to a familiar but at the same time
an unexpected place, a Michigan landscape seen in Impressionist terms.[3]

The terrain in Hemingway's stories and novels of the 1920s is seen from
the viewpoint of "curves in the road" arriving at (even, to borrow Fry's

phrasing, plunging into) landscapes of the mind (Novotny 111). "Indian Camp" begins by following a road that winds through the woods, arriving, finally at a point in back of the hills. In order to get where they are going, which is both a real and a metaphorical place, Nick and his father have to come "around a bend" towards an equivocal light (*SS* 92). In "The Battler" Nick starts along a smooth roadbed "going out of sight around the curve" (*SS* 129). In "Big Two-Hearted River," he walks along a road "climbing to cross the range of hills" that separates two realms (*SS* 211). "The Three-Day Blows" begins with a road that appears and disappears, going up through an orchard then "to the top of the hill" (*SS* 115). "In Another Country" the roads wind across land and water, but recurve to meet and "always . . . you crossed a bridge across a canal to enter the hospital" (*SS* 267). The road in "An Alpine Idyll" stops at a cemetery, then climbs and twists into the hills where anything can happen. The motif is at its most dominant in the middle chapters of *The Sun Also Rises* where the *route tournante* takes us not only into the Spanish Pyrenees but into Cézanne's world of color and forms: "For a while the country was much as it had been; then, climbing all the time, we crossed the top of a Col, the road winding back and forth on itself, and then it was really Spain" (*SAR* 93).

There have been different kinds of histories of the *route tournante* in visual art and literature. Sometimes they coalesce. In art history, roads have a technical function of separating the planes of a landscape. One example—startling in its delineation of limits—is Armand Guillaumin's "The Outskirts of Paris," done about 1874. If ever one wants to see a road "winding back and forth on itself" while fragmenting nature into parcels, this is the oil painting to look at. Yet here technique and meaning shade into each other: about half the painting is taken up by the recurved road, which speaks either to a pleasing sense of geometry or to a baffled sense of the segregation of things natural behind barriers (Chatelain 108–109). The sense of a division of realms is strong: between men and nature, between the artist and the object before him. In Hemingway, the winding road is by no means a still, formal part of a described scene. It is an entry into a divided realm. The point has been strongly made: in his analysis of "Rocks at Fontainebleau" Meyer Schapiro points out that "there is a similar landscape in the writing of Flaubert. . . . In his great novel, *The Sentimental Education,* he describes the same forest of Fontainebleau as the setting of two lovers who have left Paris for the peace of nature during the convulsions of 1848: "The path zigzags between the stunted pines under the rocks with angular profiles. . . . But the fury of their chaos makes one think rather of volcanoes, deluges and great forgotten cataclysms" (118).[4] Schapiro says that this scene from the novel is even more disturbing than Paris. It reminds us of natural disorder—which becomes coupled with our own sense of inevitable human disorder.

The openings of both "Indian Camp" and "The Battler" are illuminated by the following passage about the "limited access" into some of Cézanne's *routes tournantes:* "A clear visual path is frustrated, in the first composition, by the restless violence of the overlapping planes formed by the rocks; in the second, by the aggressive jutting of the rock at the framing edge and by the densely grouped, multi-colored foliage, which forms another barrier across the road and denies the eye a place to rest; in the third, by the ominously insistent intrusion of the trees and their branches into the line of sight" (Kelder 390–391). "Indian Camp" has this kind of topography, with its access going "through a meadow that was soaking wet with dew" along a trail that first "went into the woods" and then to a "road that ran back into the hills" (91). The words replicate Cézanne's titles, the terrain replicates his scenes. Hemingway uses the road—which, in order to arrive in the frame, even "came around a bend"—to repeat motifs of Impressionist perception. Boundaries are in fact barriers. Volumes are in sharp contrast, with the shapeless and organic completely unclarified.[5] The road, which is after all a figure of more than one kind of perspective, does not grant "access" to the meadow, woods, or hills. It would appear as if the geometry of culture does not have "access" to the irregularity of nature, so that the burden of the story has been prefigured.

In this story, Hemingway raises a larger question about the separation of things knowable and those not knowable. He works with the conflict of visual components. His mountains and forests are not only volumes and planes but lines of limitation. Isaiah Berlin was later to use the concept of "access" in a related way. In a skeptical essay on the possibility of shaping reality, he concluded that there was no possibility of doing so. There would always be unreachable areas in the world, and also within the mind: "The belief that somewhere there exists a solution for every problem, though it may be concealed and difficult of access . . . is the major assumption that is presupposed in the whole of Western thought. Moral and political questions, in this respect, did not differ from others." Berlin thinks that while everything is open to inquiry, few things are permeable to it (170, 173–74). Wittgenstein set the rules about discovering meaning in experience. Here is his opinion—it is a memorable one—of Bertrand Russell's confusion of certainties: "Russell's works should be bound in two colours . . . those dealing with mathematical logic in red—and all students of philosophy should read them; those dealing with ethics and politics in blue—and no one should be allowed to read them" (qtd. in Glock 207). Explanation has its limits, and they are quickly reached. That matters greatly as a context for a story full of questions without answers.

The idea of "access" denied applies to Hemingway. The premise of roads and also of inquiries is that they go somewhere. *Routes tournantes* invariably fail to reach certain symbolic objects on their horizon. They reach but cannot penetrate the barriers of rocks, woods, mountains. In "Indian Camp" Nick asks the question "Where are we going?" and the answer is necessarily qualified. Perhaps it can be provided from "The Battler," in which we are "a long way off from anywhere." There is always "the curve" and, as usual, it goes "out of sight" from foreground to background (*SS* 129). Once again there are the undefined volumes of woods and swamp. These make their own demands on interpretation. (A recent history of the novel makes the point that "the place between water and land functions . . . as a threshold. Its presence signifies the necessity of passing from one state to another").[6] In "The Battler," the roadway devolves from track to trail to a path "at the edge of the trees" (*SS* 130). We move from perspective to a point beyond viewing, and from technique to meaning—we now know the tendency of the story, from known and unknown. It is characteristic in Hemingway to begin on a straight road or roadway, then to experience an entirely different kind of locus of movement—and also of the mind.

"The Battler" begins with Nick being thrown off a freight train, and walking, tired, cold and hungry, along the railroad tracks. We begin with straight lines, which is to say within the Western mind. But Nick is surrounded by dark woods and impenetrable swamps, the psychic meanings of which are sufficiently clear. When Nick gets to the campfire that he has seen from the railroad tracks he finds a man called Ad who has been wrecked by life. Ad has been in the ring, and he took a good punch. The trouble is, he took too many of them. But it may not have been the ring that broke him. The meeting is something so different from Nick's orderly middle-class past that it makes such a past itself unreal. He expects logic in experience; Ad Francis is there to show that chaos is as likely as order. He has been a heroic figure—"I could take it" he says, "Don't you think I could take it, kid?"—but the ring has deformed him, made him, as he says, "crazy" (SS 131). He has been married, or pretended to be married, to a woman who may—or may not—have been his sister. He welcomes Nick to the fire, then transparently tries to take Nick's knife in order to stab him. So, we have Ad being crazy, incompatible reasons for it, and Ad wanting to kill Nick. It's often been remarked that in these stories Nick always learns something, but what he learns here is that there may not be any answers.

In the middle of it all, Bugs heats a skillet, and ham, eggs, and bread materialize: "As the skillet grew hot the grease sputtered and Bugs . . . turned the ham and broke the eggs into the skillet, tipping it from side to side to baste the eggs with the hot fat" (SS 133). One kind of detail belongs to the constancy of nature: there is precise description of things—fire heats, ham slices are held on bread by gravity, bread picks up gravy by osmosis, eggs run because liquids seek their own level. The laws of mechanics are working, but a second kind of detail seems less Newtonian: Bugs tells a wonderful story-within-the-story about how Ad Francis went mad, gives Nick more food and coffee, then calmly hits Ad with an antique blackjack that has seen a lot of use. He is precise, just putting Ad to sleep with a well-placed tap.

Nick leaves the camp, looks backward, sees Bugs waking his friend up and giving him some more coffee. The story moves relativistically from one set of boundaries to another. They have no intersection.

The most sustained of Hemingway's landscapes of the 1920s are those in *The Sun Also Rises*. All are approached from railroad tracks, roads, trails, and paths that circle and rise and then disappear:

> There were wide fire-gaps cut through the pines, and you could look up them like avenues and see wooded hills way off. . . . then we were out in the country, green and rolling, and the road climbing all the time. . . . then the road turned off and commenced to climb and we were going way up close along a hillside, with a valley below and hills stretched off back toward the sea. . . . then, climbing all the time, we crossed the top of a Col, the road winding back and forth on itself. . . . and the road ran down to the right, and we saw a whole new range of mountains. . . . and the road went on, very white and straight ahead, and then lifted to a little rise. . . . away off you could see the plateau of Pamplona rising out of the plain, and the walls of the city, and the great brown cathedral and the broken skyline of the other churches. . . . the road slanting up steeply and dustily with shade-trees on both sides, and then leveling out. . . . And as we went out along the road with the dust powdering the trees and down the hill, we had a fine view, back through the trees, of the town rising up from the bluff above the river. . . . The road climbed up into the hills and left the rich grain-fields below . . . and the hills were rocky and hard-backed clay furrowed by the rain. We came around a curve into town, and on both sides opened out a sudden green valley. . . . Far back the fields were squares of green and brown on the hillsides. Making the horizon were the brown mountains. They were strangely shaped. As we climbed higher the horizon kept changing. As the bus ground slowly up the road we could see other mountains coming up in the south. Then the road came over the crest, flattened out, and went into a forest. It was a forest of cork oaks, and the sun came through the trees in patches . . . and ahead of us was a rolling green plain, with dark mountains behind it. (*SAR* 88–108)

Hemingway's *routes tournantes* are more allusive than we may think. I have by no means covered all his versions of the road winding through Spain—while it simultaneously traverses the landscapes of Cézanne. It goes through a particular part of Cézanne—I think that the best way to get at Hemingway's reiterations of the *route tournante* is through the Mont Sainte-Victoire paintings.

Arguing from technique, Pavel Machotka calls the ten canvases on this subject done between 1902 and 1906 Cézanne's culminating work. They provide the volumes and also the green and brown (ocher) in Hemingway's own version. They provide the translations from planes of entry and of view. They have, as Cézanne himself noted, the property of never having colors "join at the edges." They alternate "meadows" and "full sun." Above all, they create a succession of views with new understanding of a landscape reached at different points. But the consideration of technique inevitably reaches a point of meaning, and Machotka concludes that just as his own photographs of the scene are inadequate so is the argument from technique. This is a culminating series of works because nothing else has managed in this way to translate space on to canvas (119).

The "space" in question is the distant view of the mountain made accessible, *but only to a limited extent*, by roads that rise and curve and disappear. Towards the end of his life, in 1901, Cézanne bought a modest property halfway up the hill of Les Lauves north of Aix. Here is where he spent the days making the last paintings of Mont Sainte-Victoire. He rarely changed his perspective on the mountain, but kept on painting it from different angles, at different times, and in different colors. No single image represents a final view of the subject. None of these paintings is ever able to resolve—and none of them care to provide—any final interpretation of the scene. The components of these views are invariably earth and sky: The entry into these components is invariably through *routes tournantes* like those "countless gently climbing, descending, and curving roads with hills in the background" around Les Lauves.[7] The roads are everywhere, yet there are in all these canvases areas that cannot be fully explained. On this, the painter was adamant, even stating that a blank space would be preferable to inserting something that would fake comprehension. Landscape was by no means open to visual understanding—we recall Fry's statement that it might "outrange our pictorial apprehension."

In a letter to his son in 1906 Cézanne remarked "that as a painter I am becoming more clear-sighted before nature, but with me the realization of my sensations is always painful. I cannot attain the intensity that is unfolded before my sense. I do not have the magnificent richness of coloring that animates nature" (qtd. in Rewald 1977, 104). The solution is to keep repainting certain motifs at different times and from different angles. The same subject needs to be repeated in the hope that at some point its meaning will reveal itself. During an interview in the same year, 1906, Cézanne took out a number of paintings from all over this house and "followed the limits of the various planes on his canvases. He showed exactly how far he had succeeded in suggesting the depth and where the solution had not yet been found" (Rewald 1996, 1: 539–540). Implicit is the idea that a painting is not simply exposition. It concerns information withheld. Another interview conducted by Joachim Gasquet (printed in Paris in 1926) finds Cézanne discoursing at some length about the point at which description may—or may not—be adequate to the subject:

> You see, motif is this. . . . (He put his hands together . . . drew them apart, ten fingers open, then slowly, very slowly brought them together again, clasped them, squeezed them tightly, meshing them). That's what one should try to achieve. . . . If one hand is held too high or too low, it won't work. Not a single link should be too slack, leaving a hole through which the emotion, the light, the truth can escape. You must understand that I work on the whole canvas, on everything at once. With one impulse, with undivided faith, I approach all the scattered bits and pieces. . . . Everything we see falls apart, vanishes, doesn't it? Nature is always the same, but nothing in her that appears to us lasts. . . . What is there underneath? Maybe nothing. Maybe everything. Everything, you understand! So I bring together her wandering hands. . . . I take something at right, something at left, here, there, everything, her tones, her colors, her

nuances, I set them down, I bring them together. . . . They form lines. They become objects, rocks, trees, without my planning. They take on volume, value. . . . But if there is the slightest distraction, if I fail just a little bit, above all if I interpret too much one day, if today I am carried away by a theory which runs counter to that of yesterday, if I think while I paint, if I meddle, whoosh! Everything goes to pieces" (qtd. in Rewald 1996, 1: 546)[8]

To be aware of this interview is to put the Ross interview into perspective. There is the relentless empiricism that marks both Cézanne's work and Hemingway's. Iteration means the discovery of an identity more complex than any single given statement about it. As expected, Cézanne is concerned with two main issues: constant reinterpretation, and the extraction of meaning from technique. We are prepared to think of the rocks and trees in their landscapes as real and also as symbolic entities. There is the conclusion that one may find either "everything" or "nothing" in a scene. The remark, like Hemingway's observation to Ross about "what we try to do" is elliptical: writing and painting can succeed and also fail in depiction. And even when they do succeed in their statement there are barriers for cognition.

Gasquet took down Cézanne's opinion that the issue of painting a landscape finally becomes one of adequate "language." Painting, according to Cézanne, was the "deciphering" of a "text." The process, in fact, is that of establishing "two parallel texts" of visualization and the statement of meaning. In the Ross interview Hemingway talks about paintings and motifs, here Cézanne talks about language and texts. Both imply that the study of terrain and composition exceeds the mastery of topography. I have not cited everything stated or claimed by Cézanne, but the more one looks at this interview (published in 1926), the better Hemingway looks at the Met.

In summarizing the last landscapes, Meyer Schapiro begins with technique, emphasizing the importance of changing colors from point to point, and making sense out of separated details. Then he adds that "the distant landscape resolves to some degree the strains of the foreground world. . . . dualities that remain divided, tense, and unstable in the observer's space" (74). This conclusion makes sense when applied to *The Sun Also Rises*. As

Schapiro points out, there is a kind of double drama in process, that of the eye's movement through terrain, and that of building a kind of intellectual "harmony." The scene has "externalized" something not easily articulated. Momentarily there has been control achieved over experience (Schapiro 74). Both Machotka and Schapiro—and the many art historians cited by Rewald in his definitive study—find the Mont Sainte-Victoire iterations to have considerable spiritual depth; even unstated religious feeling. When Jake and Bill finally reach water in the mountains they make an embarrassed but effective iteration of their own, retelling Genesis within a landscape by the banks of a stream. In the scene, a road rises into the woods, then turns in its curving way across the fields. Schapiro states of "Road at Chantilly" that the path through the trees seems to be "a modest, unlikely theme" (80). But it is everywhere in Cézanne and Hemingway.

NOTES

1. Beginning with this article, I have cited many titles of Cézanne. These titles, whether in English or French, exist in variant forms. Whenever a title is cited it is in the form used by the source. Different publications are cited because of variations in the reproduction (color, size, detail, quality) of paintings or drawings.

2. See Pavel Machotka (xiii, 1–7). Jakob Rosenberg states that Fry's critical understanding of Cézanne has not been surpassed (101). For a full treatment of Fry's standing see Alfred Werner's introduction to Fry's *Cézanne: A Study of His Development* (i–xiii).

3. The Hemingway scene should be compared to Cézanne's *Route tournante en Haut de Chemin des Lauves* which is reproduced in Machotka (114). I have used the term "Impressionism" as Hemingway used it, as a kind of shorthand including post-Impressionism.

4. See Hemingway's letter "To Henry Strater, Nordquinst Ranch, 14 October 1932": "A man can be a hell of a serious artist and not have to make his living by it—see Flaubert, Cézanne and Co" (*SL* 369). The remark is enigmatic without knowing

the conclusion of Roger Fry's *Cézanne: A Study of His Development*. According to Fry, Flaubert and Cézanne were connected by romanticism, technique, "infinitely laborious" reconstructions of their work—and by their financial independence which allowed them to do their work without kowtowing to critics (87–88).

5. See Meyer Schapiro's discussion of "Turning Road at Montgeroult" (112).

6. A number of modern novels begin "on a shore, strand, bank, or marsh," including those of Conrad, Flaubert, Joyce, and Woolf (Doody 321).

7. Rewald points out that these roads, which were "all over the region of Aix," became part of the paintings of Mont Sainte-Victoire (Rewald 1977, 1:545).

8. Rewald alludes in his elaborate notes to E.H. Gombrich, Max Raphael, Lionello Venturi, and other historians of art. My discussion of the Mont Sainte-Victoire paintings relies on these citations. See *Paintings* I: 539, 545–547. Note especially Rewald's judgment of the reliability of the Gasquet interview.

WORKS CITED

Baker, Carlos. *Hemingway: The Writer as Artist*. Princeton: Princeton UP, 1973.

Berlin, Isaiah. *The Sense of Reality*. New York: Farrar, Straus and Giroux, 1996.

Chatelain, Jean et al. *Impressionism: A Centenary Exhibition*. Paris: Metropolitan Museum of Art, 1974.

Doody, Margaret Anne. *The True Story of the Novel*. New Brunswick: Rutgers UP, 1997.

Fry, Roger. *Cézanne: A Study of His Development*. New York: Farrar, Straus & Giroux, 1970.

Glock, Hans-Johann. "Wittgenstein and Reason." In *Wittgenstein: Biography and Philosophy*. Ed. James C. Klagge. Cambridge: Cambridge UP, 2001. 195–220.

Hagemann, Meyly Chin. "Hemingway's Secret: Visual to Verbal Art." *Journal of Modern Literature* 7.1 (February 1979): 87–112.

Hemingway, Ernest. *Ernest Hemingway: Selected Letters, 1917–1961*. Ed. Carlos Baker. New York: Scribner's, 1981.

———. *A Moveable Feast*. New York: Scribner's, 1964.

———. *The Short Stories of Ernest Hemingway*. New York: Simon and Schuster, 1995.

———. *The Sun Also Rises.* New York: Scribner's, 1970.

Johnston, Kenneth G. "Hemingway and Cézanne: Doing the Country." *American Literature* 56.1 (March 1984): 28–37.

Kelder, Diane. *The Great Book of French Impressionism.* New York: Cross River, 1980.

Lewis, R. W. B. "Hemingway's Sense of Place." In *Hemingway In Our Time.* Ed. Richard Astro and Jackson R. Benson. Corvallis: Oregon UP, 1974. 113–43.

Machotka, Pavel. *Cézanne: Landscape into Art.* New Haven: Yale UP, 1996.

Monnier, Geneviève. "The Late Watercolors." In *Cézanne: The Late Work.* Ed. William Rubin. New York: Museum of Modern Art, 1977. 113–18.

Novotny, F. "The Late Landscape Paintings." In *Cézanne: The Late Work.* Ed. William Rubin. New York: Museum of Modern Art, 1977. 107–11.

Osborne, Harold. Ed. *The Oxford Companion to Art.* Oxford: Clarendon Press, 1970.

Rewald, John. "The Last Motifs at Aix." In *Cézanne: The Late Work.* Ed. William Rubin. New York: Museum of Modern Art, 1977. 83–106.

———. *The Paintings of Paul Cézanne: A Catalogue Raisonné.* 2 vols. New York: Harry N. Abrams, 1996.

Rubin, William. Ed. *Cézanne: The Late Work.* New York: Museum of Modern Art, 1977.

Rosenberg, Jacob. *On Quality in Art.* Princeton UP, 1967.

Ross, Lillian. "How Do You Like It Now, Gentleman?" In *Hemingway: A Collection of Critical Essays.* Ed. Robert P. Weeks. Englewood Cliffs: Prentice-Hall, 1962. 17–39.

Schapiro, Meyer. *Cézanne.* New York: Abrams, 1952.

Watts, Emily Stipes. *Ernest Hemingway and the Arts.* Urbana: U of Illinois P, 1971.

Woolf, Virginia. *Roger Fry: A Biography.* London: Hogarth, 1940.

Men without Women
as Composite Novel

Joseph M. Flora

Ernest Hemingway's *In Our Time* (1925) has long been counted among the definitive texts of literary modernism. Highly experimental, it seems intent on being new while probing the world being born as the values of the 19th-century (literary and otherwise) were crumbling. Some observers have judged *In Our Time* Hemingway's most experimental work. Most often it has been linked with James Joyce's *Dubliners* (1914), Sherwood Anderson's *Winesburg, Ohio* (1919), and—in the last two decades—Jean Toomer's *Cane* (1923).

Dubliners, Winesburg, Cane, and *In Our Time,* often taught as novels, are made up of individual segments that can stand alone but work together to

Reprinted with permission from *North Dakota Quarterly* 68.2–68.3 (Spring–Summer 2001). Copyright © 2001 by The University of North Dakota. Published by University of North Dakota Printing Center.

make an effective collage with its own integrity and larger meaning. Critics have emphasized their novelistic effect and considered them as a subgenre. Maggie Dunn and Ann Morris have recently traced an impressive lineage of the short-story cycle. They posit that the form, reflective of modern and postmodern assumptions, proved especially genial throughout the 20th century and offer *composite novel* as a more descriptive term for such works. Not surprisingly, Dunn and Morris highlight *In Our Time* as among the seminal composite novels.

What is surprising is that they do not include any other Hemingway title in a fairly extensive annotated appendix of composite novels—although both *Men without Women* (1927) and *Winner Take Nothing* (1933) exemplify traits characteristic of the genre. Hemingway typically thought a great deal about the unity of his short-story gatherings. As Paul Smith has emphasized, Hemingway gave uncommon attention to the placement of a story in a book, frequently reversing an earlier decision.[1] He expected that the placement of a story would influence a reader's understanding of the story and of the book that held it. As the very titles of Hemingway's "collections" emphasize, he saw thematic unity in each book. Typically, writers of short stories title a collection for a major story in it, as Eudora Welty did with *A Curtain of Green* (1941) or Doris Betts with *The Astronomer and Other Stories* (1965), but Hemingway has no story called "Men without Women" or "Winner Take Nothing"—as there is none called "In Our Time." For him, the book title was an opportunity to underscore a larger concept. In "The Art of the Short Story," Hemingway observed that stories "read differently in a book anyway."[2] No writer was ever more aware than he of this truth, nor of the interplay collected stories provide.

Perhaps critics would be more conscious of *Men without Women* and *Winner Take Nothing* as modernist texts if interchapters again threaded the larger narrative. Hemingway was, however, not tempted in that direction. Probably he would assent to the statement of Tim O'Brien, a writer who learned much from him and invited inevitable comparisons when he constructed from his Vietnam experience his own composite novel, *The Things They Carried* (1990): "I feel I'm experimenting all the time. But the difference is this: I am experimenting not for the joy of experimenting, but rather to explore meaning and themes and dramatic discovery . . . I don't enjoy tinkering for the joy of tinkering, and I don't like reading books merely for their artifice. I want to see things and explore moral issues when I read, not get hit over the head with the tools of the trade" (269).

Kenneth Lynn has called attention to the relative neglect of *Men without Women*: "If *Men without Women* was not destined to become the most widely influential book of short stories ever published by a twentieth-century American author, that was only because it followed *In Our Time*" (366). Following the lead of Hemingway's title, this essay explores the merits of considering *Men without Women* as a composite novel. Do the men become a collective or emerging protagonist, such as O'Brien provides in *The Things They Carried* or Gloria Naylor in *The Women of Brewster Place?* Do they lead us to consider other unities? Interchapters absent, can we discover other ways in which *Men without Women* is experimental or shows Hemingway turning in new directions?

Hemingway links his second collection to his first by bringing to the fore possibilities anticipated in the short bullfighting interchapters of *In Our Time*. "The Undefeated," the lead story, studies the sport, replacing the brief interchapters of the earlier work with a story that builds on duration. Bullfighting, virtually an exclusively male sport, takes the bullfighter into the terrain of the bull; the possibility of the man's death becomes real—as in no other sport. The opening words of the story name the bullfighter of the story, Manuel Garcia. The first word recalls one of the names for Christ, the most celebrated of men who lived without women.[3] Building on the Christ analogy (his first major use of that imagery), Hemingway establishes an important motif for *Men without Women*.

Hemingway had completed "The Undefeated" before *In Our Time* was published. He might have placed it in that work. After Scribner's refused to let him include "Up in Michigan," Hemingway needed another story for the book. Rather than use "The Undefeated" he wrote "The Battler." Perhaps the length of "The Undefeated" (long by Hemingway standards, it is the longest story of *Men without Women*) dissuaded him, but likely theme influenced him. *In Our Time* accents youth and uncertainty; *Men without Women*—as the title clarifies—puts the emphasis elsewhere.

Early in his life Hemingway took a special interest in the aging male—and Manuel becomes the first of a gallery of "old" men who populate Hemingway's fiction. Manuel's exact age is not given, but certainly in terms of his profession he is an old man; his career is behind him. A pitiful figure as the story opens, he humbles himself in Don Miguel Retana's office to plead for a fighting slot. "I want to work," he says (183).[4] In this scene, Manuel anticipates Arthur Miller's Willy Loman, who also wearily sets down his suitcase, pleads for work, tries to hold on to his dignity and identify as salesman. For both men, only their deaths restore a measure of that dignity.

In gentler times, as Miller's play makes clear, Willy might have been a carpenter or a farmer, but he was not inevitably a salesman. For Manuel, profession is a calling. It is what he is, exclusively. There are no women in "The Undefeated"—nor in Manuel's life. He has, apparently, never married. As he lies dying at the end of the story, he does not think of any woman, indeed of any human being—only his professional identity.

> "Wasn't I going good, Manos?" he asked, for confirmation.
> "Sure," said Zurito. "You were going great."
> The doctor's assistant put the cone over Manuel's face and he inhaled deeply. Zurito stood awkwardly, watching. (205)

Hemingway ends his story emphasizing no triumphant victory, but rather self-delusion or, more affirmatively put, the power of illusion. Ambiguity abounds. The picador Zurito, another older man, helps us see it. Although readers may admire the determination, the dedication of Manuel, his price for the conviction of being "undefeated" has been high. Rather than his victory, readers may be more haunted by his loneliness. His dedication to his profession appears to have cut him off from family and the companionship that for most people make life worthwhile. In any deep sense, Manuel has lived a life without women. In the longest story of the book, there is not a single woman nor a memory of a woman.

Concern with profession—and its relationship to marriage—emerges as a dominant theme of *Men without Women*. Hemingway's biography makes clear why this should be so. Treating other professions in his work, Hemingway was invariably also reflecting on the profession that mattered most to him—writing. "The Undefeated" directly juxtaposes the two professions. On one level, the sportswriter on duty on the night of Manuel's last fight (Hemingway's word for him is "critic") allows Hemingway to satirize that guild and to uphold the honor of the *aficionado*, but if we read the collection as a composite novel, we receive notice of the considerable extent to which *Men without Women* is also metafiction. How does the story of a Manuel get told? By an artist—who likely pays a similarly great price for his art.

The theme of writers and writing—and truth-telling—is inherent in several stories of the collection. It is a part of the texture of "Today is Friday" in which Hemingway recounts the crucifixion story in the modern idiom of a boxing contest—drama waiting to be rendered as narrative. Written at a time (as were several other stories of the collection) when Hemingway was experiencing much guilt over the demise of his own marriage to Hadley and was briefly a man without a woman, the story deals with the varying reactions of three Roman soldiers to the death they have just witnessed and what that death means. Hemingway's depiction of that aftermath reminds us of other accounts of that life of a man who made his mark as a storyteller but wrote none, told in three synoptic gospels and one other. Through those accounts, the stories of the crucified Nazarene continue to have their impact. "Today Is Friday" might also have been called "The Undefeated," and at least Zurito might have been willing to grant the appropriateness of the first soldier's insistent view of Jesus at Calvary: "I tell you, he was pretty good in there today" (272). Who will tell his story? What story?

Following "Today Is Friday," Hemingway tucked the slight "Banal Story," continuing the high art of sharp contrasts that is a key tool of the entire book. From consideration of the divine, Hemingway plunges readers to the banal—from echoes of the four gospels to the flatulence of *Forum* magazine as an unnamed writer smugly surveys the "warm, homespun, American tales" of the popular journal. A little goes a long way, and Hemingway moves quickly to end the piece with portrayal of another death, that of the bullfighter Manuel Garcia Maera. The reader's mind may jump back to the Manuel of "The Undefeated" as well as to the crucified Jesus of the preceding story. Unlike the Manuel in the lead story, this Manuel dies from pneumonia (a banal ending?). Like Jesus, he is, however, transformed in death. "Men and boys bought full-length colored pictures of him to remember him by, and lost the picture they had of him in their memories looking at the lithographs" (275). It will take the writer to bring alive Maera's work in the bullring that earned him a tomb next to Joselito.[5]

By the time readers of *Men without Women* come to "Banal Story," they have found the death of a sports figure to be a recurring motif: bullfighter Manuel in "The Undefeated," boxer Ole Andreson in "The Killers," Jesus (metaphorically a boxer) in "Today Is Friday." These stories play against each other in surprising ways, and echoes of the Christ story are present in each. Titles might easily be interchanged.

Sheridan Baker and Arthur Waldhorn have both called attention to the many similarities between "Today Is Friday" and "The Killers."[6] As they recognized, the title of "Today is Friday" could easily be "The Killers." Because of the sinister force of evil that Hemingway portrays in "The Killers," the title "Today Is Friday" has great applicability to it. Considering *Men without Women* as a composite novel, we discover the important extent to which this famous story also contributes to the force of the book as metaficton—for "The Killers" also becomes a story about writing or not writing, telling or not telling.

Most readers of "The Killers" have considered Nick Adams its protagonist. Readers familiar with *In Our Time* immediately recognize certain traits of his character—his vulnerability and his resolve to throw off that vulnerability. But there is something surprising about the first acknowledged encounter with Nick in *Men without Women*. In the many Nick Adams stories, Hemingway often veils Nick's identity—hides him until late in the story (as in "The Doctor and Doctor's Wife") or makes minimal use of his name (as in "Now I Lay Me," the last story of *Men without Women*, only twice and late) or (as in "In Another Country," the second story of *Men without Women*) using no name at all for the first-person narrator. But here in the fourth story of the book early in the story, the reader encounters him with full name. He is sitting at a lunch counter in Henry's lunchroom talking to his friend George when the killers Al and Max, looking like characters from a B movie, enter and take seats. The narrator reports, "Nick Adams watched them" (215). Only Ole Andreson, the target of the killers' assignment, is also identified with two names.

The dominant reading that Nick is protagonist of the story was eventually challenged by R. S. Crane, who focused on the plight of Andreson, seeing Nick as serving an expository function. For him, Andreson is the athlete-hero, who—having apparently violated some code—makes a choice to accept his fate. When Nick talks with him, Ole is in his Gethsemane. But Andreson will soon make the departure to his Calvary, his *coleta* metaphorically still there. He is certainly alone, certainly a man without a woman.

Nick, by contrast, is on the threshold of manhood. About to move beyond the world that formed him, in Henry's lunchroom he encounters fearful intimations of what is out there in the world. At Mrs. Bell's boarding house as he warns Andreson (a warning not needed or heeded), he finds an important example of determination, perhaps foolishness. At the end of the story, Nick is back at Henry's talking with George, planning to get out of town.

> "I can't stand to think about him waiting in the room and knowing he's going to get it. It's too damned awful."
> "Well," said George, "you'd better not think about it." (222)

The question at the end of "The Killers" is not what Andreson will do, but what Nick will do. He will, of course, continue to think about Andreson and his fate. But the totality of *Men without Women* suggests he will do more. He will eventually write about this event—and perhaps already has.

There is good evidence for such a conclusion. A reader of *In Our Time* knows from its final story that Nick has become a writer. "The Killers," however, presents a Nick younger than the one who emerges at the end of

"Big Two-Hearted River." But here I am interested in the sense of Nick that we find in *Men without Women*, present by first name only in two other stories of the book, "Ten Indians" and "Now I Lay Me." The first is a third-person story of Nick's boyhood, just as he emerges into sexual awareness. His name (first only) is used several times, by the narrator and by other characters. In "Now I Lay Me," a first-person story set on the Italian front of World War I, Nick is the narrator, and his name (again, first only) is not heard until mid-story, used twice by his father as Nick recollects moments that define the marriage that made him; his father's use of his name may carry something of the force of accusation as Nick relives the telling scene of his father's return from hunting (that primal male activity) to find his wife burning prized arrowheads and other artifacts her husband has kept stored in the basement. Nick has been present for his mother's great cleaning. If he did not actively aid her effort, he did not protest it either.[7] As Nick lies in the hospital, he often relives the painful episode, but he does not talk about it with John his orderly, who was apparently wounded in the same attack that caught Nick and lies on the bed next to his. The flashback echoes of Nick's name are all the more effective in the narrative because John (who is from Chicago, married, and a father) addresses Nick only as "Signor Tenente." The first-person narrative of the story is not interior monologue. Nick's report is very controlled and comes some time after the events "in another country" are related. Narrator Nick has opted for the profession that puts extreme strains on its practitioners and has become one of the men without women. "Now I Lay Me" ends with words appropriate to all of *Men without Women*:

> But I kept on with my prayers and I prayed very often for John in the nights and his class was removed from active service before the October offensive. I was glad he was not here, because he would have been a great worry to me. He came to the hospital in Milan to see me several months after and was very disappointed that I had not yet married, and I know he would feel very badly if he knew that, so far, I have never married. He was going back to America, and he was very certain about marriage and knew it would fix up everything. (282)

If John had advised Nick that marriage would take care of everything, the unnamed narrator of "In Another Country," whom the reader confronted many stories earlier, has received the opposite advice. In the manner of the composite novel, the final story reminds the attentive reader of the first. Manuscript evidence suggests how closely allied they were in Hemingway's mind: a working title for "Now I Lay Me" was "In Another Country—Two: A Story" (Smith 172). But readers scarcely needed this evidence to link the two, or to suspect that the narrator of the final story, reluctant to let his name into the narrative, is the same as the narrator of the first. Neither narrative voice is tough and hardened, but rather sensitive and perplexed. Characterization, structure, setting, and theme all link the two stories. The first-person point of view also speaks about some need to tell a story and its usefulness to the confessional mode and understanding of oneself—especially one's defects and demons. Even if the reader of "In Another Country" chooses not to identify the narrator with Nick, the story's effect on the metafictional emphasis of *Men without Women* is substantial. The Italian major tells the young American that marriage should be avoided because one can "lose" it: a man "should find things that he cannot lose" (209). The major, recently married, has lost his wife to pneumonia. The Nick listening to him already knows that there are other ways of losing in marriage than through death, other—more compelling—reasons for being wary of taking the step.

"Now I Lay Me" is famous for its images of a threatening and destructive female presence. "Ten Indians" provides further evidence that Nick has good reason to hesitate about marriage. In that story, Nick's mother is present only through her telling absence. It is the Fourth of July, a time when families often picnic and celebrate together—as the Garner family is doing—but Nick's mother is not at home. Nick has spent Independence Day with the Garners. His father has spent the day by himself. Although the story ends with emphasis on Nick's self-pity (and recovery) as he reflects on his father's report that in the woods he had come across Nick's Indian girlfriend "thrashing around" with Frank Washburn (256), in later years Nick may come to see his father, as the reader does, as a man without a woman.

The Garners, with whom "Tens Indians" begins, provide the major example of a successful marriage to be found in *Men without Women*. They have been married for many years (about as long as Nick's parents have), and the marriage will surely last. Circumstances seem right. The Garners live in the early years of the century—not summer people, but year-round residents in northern Michigan. They travel by horse and buggy and will never ride on the *rapide* as the Americans traveling abroad do in other stories of *Men without Women*. The Garner parents may never even see Chicago, or its suburb Summit where the reader finds Nick in "The Killers." Farmers, the Garners work together. This family provides the most coherent "we" of the book. The men of Hemingway's book are fundamentally alone although they sometimes travel together, as in "Che Ti Dice La Patria?" and "An Alpine Idyll." Alliances are typically brief—occasioned apparently by a business assignment in the first instance, a recreational trip in the second. Not even in the war stories is there a sense of community purpose—a larger "we." In "In Another Country" the narrator's use of "we" in the opening half of the story emphasizes temporary alliances.

The other enduring "we" of the book also comes in a marriage, Jack Brennan's in "Fifty Grand." Since Jack is a boxer, his profession—like that of the bullfighter—is not conducive to duplicating what the Garners have. Jack has been able to maintain his integrity as a boxer over many years. But unlike Manuel Garcia of "The Undefeated," he has struggled mightily to have a life aside from his profession. Indeed, he is eager for the last fight and the financial means that will allow him to immerse himself in the domesticity that his work interrupts so frequently. Waiting for that fight, he is—again unlike Manuel—realistic about where he is in his career, what age has done to him, what he can reasonably expect. As he endures the training and the waiting before the final bout—and the separation from his family that the training entails—he thinks mainly about his wife and daughters. On the surface the essence of the hard-boiled fighter, he writes his wife regularly and worries about the effect of his profession on his daughters and the kind of lives he wants them to have. He also cares about his integrity as a boxer, as he proves in his drunken struggle after he has been visited by the gangsters Morgan and

Steinfelt, who are rigging the fight. He assents to their plan because he believes that his losing is the only possible outcome of the fight. Realizing in the ring that he has been double-crossed, he quickly reacts to bring about the outcome that will earn him the money he had intended for his family. Jack loses the fight, but he is "undefeated."[8] He can now experience more of those things his profession has kept from him, most especially the company of his wife.

Among the large number of first-person stories of the book, "Fifty Grand" has an unusual narrative stance. Though he is gifted at the one-liner, Jack Brennan does not tell his own story—narration is not his trade. That task is undertaken by his trainer Jerry, who knows boxing and realizes what matters most to Jack. No "critic," his voice is the right one to convince us that Jack was "pretty good in there today," to reveal what the newspaper writers have missed.

"Fifty Grand" furthers the metafictional subtext of the book, a subtext noticeably present in the first-person stories. Attention to the profession of writing pervades the book, often with implications for the gender theme stressed by the title. The theme of writing is, in fact, central to "An Alpine Idyll," one of those first-person stories; the story's title accents the art of story telling. Is the unnamed narrator Nick Adams? The skiing, the location, the need for male camaraderie all suggest the possibility. So does the attention to detail, the keen narrative eye. But Nick or not, the thrust of "An Alpine Idyll" is to portray the narrator dealing with story: reports about the peasant Olz, who is unable to bring his dead wife down from the mountains until the spring thaw and has meanwhile propped her body in the shed and regularly used her open mouth to hang the lantern when he cuts wood. The narrator and his friend John encounter different perspectives from the innkeeper (who finds the husband a beast) and the sexton (who is amused). The priest's reaction is different from both. What and where is the truth? Although John falls asleep as the accounts unfold, the narrator remains keenly interested. We sense his pictorial skill and his delight in the senses—and his search for meaning.

What the narrator might make of the macabre story is only implied. Coming down from the mountains (as Olz has) and the skiing retreat, the narrator returns to a world of obligations, symbolized in the substantial gathering of mail the innkeeper has given him. The single female presence in the story is the girl who waits tables—visually a compelling image, echoing the separation highlighted in the book's title.[9] The story contains no direct references to the circumstances of the narrator's life. Does he have a wife? A fiancée? "Did you love your wife?" the priest had asked the peasant. "'*Ja*, I loved her,' Olz said. 'I loved her fine'" (266). The disturbing question reaches far beyond Olz, certainly to the narrator as he ponders the human question of how people mistreat those they love most.[10]

That question is certainly applicable to "A Canary for One," a story that surprises readers when they discover that it is a first-person story. The narrator (an American in post-war France) hides himself until he reaches the middle of the story, and he never lets his name enter the story, which becomes confession. Although he is in a train compartment with his wife, we come to realize that they are not speaking—the presence of the other is torment. The husband has preferred to look outside the train, recounting with precise skills the specifics of what he has been seeing—with special attention to a burning house. He declines the opportunity to enter into conversation with the talkative American lady who shares the compartment and chatters about her purchase of a canary to assuage the pain of their daughter, whose courtship with a Swiss the mother has halted because, she says, "American men make the best husbands" (260). (Whereas the narrator of "An Alpine Idyll" was eager for story, the narrator of this story is not eager for details.) More than the burning house, the canary becomes a symbol for the ending of the marriage. The wife's pain—and the narrator's—becomes palpable by the end of the story. Ever finding symbols, the husband enters the conversation only once: "'Look,' I said, 'There's been a wreck'" (261).

Is this narrator Nick Adams? Critics have been reluctant to so identify him, probably because there are few links to specific circumstances of stories clearly about Nick. Although no circumstance of the story would rule out the possibility that the narrator is Nick, it is not necessary to so view him. Instead, we find him part of a composite protagonist who relates uncertainly to women, who suffers because of that uncertainty or isolation.

Hemingway's noticeable turning to first-person stories in *Men without Women* (a single story in *In Our Time* is told in the first person) furthers both the metafictional aspect of the book and the sense of a collective protagonist. Six stories are in the first person in the second collection; in three of them the narrator does not let his name enter the script. "Che Ti Dice La Patria?" might also be a Nick story. The narrator is again a keen observer, noting carefully the countryside through which he and his friend, Guy, travel. He renders precisely the unpleasant episodes that transpire "in another country"—his purpose to give his reader a basis for answering the question posed in the tile, revealing the realities of Fascist Italy. Attention to circumstances of his own life are minimal. He is eager to return to France. Neither he nor Guy is tempted by the kind of "love" that now pervades Italy. Although information about his life is minimal, the narrator does have purpose—as the first-person narrative implies. Following "The Killers," the story at least carries a suggestion that Nick has gotten out of town, has seen something of the world, and now flaunts that worldly wisdom. The narrator's dialogue and his prose reflect a toughened front. But, again, Hemingway took no pains to give exact circumstances that would indicate that the narrator is Nick. But clearly "Che Ti Dice" takes on force as a unit of *Men without Women* that it did not have as "Italy, 1927" in its original publication as a travel report in the *New Republic*.

The American man of "Hills Like White Elephants," also traveling in post-war Europe, makes a vivid contribution to the collective protagonist. His presence is highlighted from the start of the story. He and the American "girl" (we come to know her as Jig, a name that eventually comments on the insignificance of her place in the man's life—as does the narrative's keeping her "girl" and him "man") discuss their future, complicated now by the fact of her pregnancy. "Hills Like White Elephants" is almost exclusively dialogue—almost as much a "play" as "Today is Friday." Although the real issue of the story is the man's strong wish that Jig get an abortion, the word is never once used in the story. Noticeably absent also is the word *baby* or any of the words suggesting long-term commitment: *home, family, husband, wife*. Love is Jig's word, and comes first from her lips.

"And if I do it you'll be happy and things will be like they were and you'll love me."

"I love you now. You know I love you."

"I know. But if I do it, then it will be nice again if I say things are like white elephants, and you'll like it?"

"I'll love it. I love it now but I just can't think about it. You know how I get when I worry." (213)

The avowal of love does not carry much conviction. The story is titled for the girl's metaphor, and the action of the story is to make clear to her that her pregnancy reveals just how weak her partner's love for her is. If the story avoids certain words, it accents others, chiefly the word *know*. Jig has discovered painful knowledge in a twenty-minute train stop. She realizes that she has purchased a white elephant, an item of great cost that now has little value.

"You know how I get when I worry," the man has said. Although the pronoun *we* occurs several times in the story, the man is an "I" person, not ready, perhaps not able to participate deeply in a "we." His wishes dominate the scene. The "girl" is expected to accede to them. He makes it clear that the expanded "we" a baby entails is not what he wants.

Alert to the impact of profession, especially the profession of writing, in Hemingway's work, Joan Didion and John Gregory Dunn sensed the metafictional possibilities of "Hills Like White Elephants."[11] In the movie script they wrote for dramatization of the story, the man becomes a writer (one very like Ernest Hemingway) who, like the alert Jig, is envisioning the story that becomes "Hills Like White Elephants" even as it is happening. The story by itself has no clues that the man is a writer, but the context of *Men without Women* might indeed suggest the possibility. Writer or not, Nick or not, the story about an American man traveling in Europe with a girl carrying the baby he doesn't want becomes even more trenchant when juxtaposed with "In Another Country"—the story that precedes it. "A man must not marry," the major had advised the young American (209).

For most of the men of *Men without Women,* amatory desires lead to pain. In "A Simple Enquiry," the major's inquiry to his orderly is anything but simple. The major's questions imply a preference that dare not speak its name. He asks his orderly, nineteen-year-old Pinin, if he has ever been in love with a girl. The intent of the major's question is clear. In the context of the entire book, the question reverberates even more hauntingly: "You are in love with this girl now? You don't write her. I read all your letters" (251). The major—though his position in a profession of men is high—obviously suffers a good deal. He seems doomed to the isolation in which we find him. He is not without compassion and conducts himself with noticeable dignity; in a story set in wartime, he is obviously at war with himself. The story also invites reflection on the other males of the story—the smiling adjutant who sits outside the major's private quarters, quite aware of the propositioning of Pinin. The adjutant has doubtless been propositioned himself and may hold his soft war-time station for reason. Hemingway wishes to make the reader wonder with the major about the final question of the story: "The little devil, he thought, I wonder if he lied to me" (252). Pinin may not know the answer to the question yet, even if he is heterosexual: "You are in love with this girl now?"

Four stories later, "A Pursuit Race" also addresses the question of sexual identity, but much more subtly and more ambiguously. Both stories show a man in bed talking with another man, talking around or over the real issues. Although the title of the later story seems to promise depiction of athletic activity, the pursuit race of the story is internal. William Campbell, advance man for a burlesque show, lies in a hotel room in Kansas City comforting himself with alcohol and drugs, but not with a woman. When the burlesque manager arrives and confronts him about his neglect of duty, Campbell affirms his resignation from his job and his decision not to "race" any longer. Heterosexuality (the burlesque show) will no longer pursue him, as he declares that he has his "wolf" back.[12] Campbell tongues his sheet and declares his love for it. He gives much advice to Mr. Turner, who is also a William.

"But listen, Billy, and I'll tell you a secret. Stick to sheets, Billy. Keep away from women and horses and, and—" he stopped "—eagles, Billy. If you love horses you'll get horse-shit and if you love eagles you'll get eagle-shit." He stopped and put his head under the sheet.

. . . .

"If you love women you'll get a dose." (270)

If D. H. Lawrence's "The Prussian Officer" is the primary literary influence on "A Simple Enquiry," Sherwood Anderson's "The Man Who Became a Woman" may well lurk beneath Hemingway's strange tale. In any case, Hemingway's story portrays a man tormented by his sexual identity and unable to function in a world with or without women.[13]

L. P. Hartley observed that readers prefer novels to short story collections because of the psychic jarring that accompanies reading a collection. His metaphor is driving in stop-and-go traffic. A novel gives a smoother ride. Readers stay with characters longer, get to know them better (Hartley 157–59). The composite novel makes the stop-and-go method less wearing, insisting on unities while emphasizing disjuncture and variety. In the modernist composite novel, disjuncture is part of the larger meaning. But the work also pulls the other way.

Men without Women is a "nervous" book, more nervous than *Winesburg, Ohio* or *In Our Time.* Like much literature to emerge in modernism, it embodies strenuous effort at articulation: J. Alfred Prufrock's "It is impossible to say just what I mean" or Benjy Compson's "I was trying to say." Hemingway's use of Nick Adams in *Men without Women* is in marked contrast to the use of him in *In Our Time.* In Hemingway's first composite novel, Nick's presence is as constant as that of George Willard's in *Winesburg, Ohio.* In *Men without Women* Nick's presence becomes more tentative, more veiled—as if it has become more difficult for Hemingway to portray him. In several stories, Nick might or might not be the narrator. Always with Nick Adams, but much more pronounced in this book than in *In Our Time,* is a sense that there is more to tell, but that it cannot be told. Nick's nighttime fishing in "Now I lay Me" suggests something of what that drama might be. We sense the material for a Nick Adams work with the plenitude of *Look Homeward, Angel,* but the method of the book indicates it will not come—though we sense story wanting to break out, like Benjy's "trying to say."

Writing and not writing, telling or not telling—these become major themes in a work that highlights isolation and the difficulty—often the impossibility—of finding love and lasting commitment, the loneliness of a world of men without women. The very title—with its long preposition taking a commanding position as the middle word—emphasizes negation and carries the force of verb. Sexual tragedy is the powerfully insistent theme that is repeatedly operative in individual stories, but also suggestive of the ambiguity of the collective protagonist—especially as he emerges as Nick Adams, the recurring presence of the book and the last man we view in the book.

NOTES

1. Smith's *A Reader's Guide to the Short Stories of Ernest Hemingway* provides for each story a summary of composition and publication history as well as consideration of sources, influences, and critical studies.

2. Written in 1959, "The Art of the Short Story" was intended for a students' edition of Hemingway's favorites among his stories. The project was abandoned, and in spring 1981 an edited version of the essay was published in the *Paris Review*. My *Ernest Hemingway: A Study of the Short Fiction* (1989) publishes Hemingway's final draft of the essay, which was edited only for correction of obvious typographical errors and standardization of punctuation pertaining to story titles. Notes provide significant variant material appearing in earlier drafts but omitted later by Hemingway. The reference cited here appears on page 132.

3. Matthew 1:23 would have been familiar to Hemingway: "Behold, a virgin shall be with child, and shall bring forth a son, and they shall call his name Emmanuel, which being interpreted, is God with us." The opening words and scene of the story seem to say, "Behold, the man" (*Ecco Homo!*). Hemingway grew up on

the King James Version of the Bible, the version cited here. Joseph DeFalco says that in Western culture the "journey toward individuation is best personified in the life of Christ" (186) and that Hemingway made the Christ story a major trope.

4. Although *Men without Women* remains in print as a paperback Scribner Classic, page references in this essay are to *The Complete Short Stories of Ernest Hemingway*, Finca Vigía Edition. Like *The First Forty-nine* (1938), it retains the structures of *In Our Time*, *Men without Women* (stories from "The Undefeated" through "Now I Lay Me"), and *Winner Take Nothing*. There are slight variations in the 1927 text. "To-Day Is Friday" becomes "Today Is Friday," as it had in *The First Forty-nine*. In the Finca Vigía edition, "s—" in "The Pursuit Race" produces the word Hemingway wrote.

5. Hemingway highlights a male phenomenon here. Women and girls do not buy the pictures, but their lives will certainly be impacted by the male obsession. In contrast, "Today Is Friday" notes the presence of women at the crucifixion scene. When the first soldier asks, "What became of his gang?", the second soldier replies, "Oh, they faded out. Just the women stuck by him" (273).

    Finding the emphasis on male experience so dominating in *Men without Women*, Virginia Woolf famously felt excluded.

6. Sheridan Baker, 59; Arthur Waldhorn, 89.

7. Paul Smith presents the manuscript evidence for Nick's culpability (173).

8. Length alone may invite juxtaposing "Fifty Grand" and "The Undefeated"; they are by far the longest stories of *Men without Women*. Both treat aging athlete protagonists. (Well over half of the stories make reference to the domain of sports—in addition to bullfighting and boxing, the men of the book have participated in hunting, fishing, football, fencing, skiing, bicycle-racing—giving another thematic unity to the totality.)

9. The image of the serving female is a haunting one for the story—and for most of Hemingway. Even in death, Olz's wife serves him. The other duty for women—implicit in "An Alpine Idyll"—is to wait.

10. Although Nick's mother seems to resent or refuse the burden of serving ("Ten Indians"), and although she performs destructive acts in "Now I Lay Me," we need not doubt that she loves her husband and son. The man in "Hills Like

White Elephants" professes his love for Jig. Self-love rather than serving love may be dominant in both cases. As Hemingway reveals, love sometimes takes strange shapes and is sometimes unwise and destructive. As Oscar Wilde put it, "Each man kills the thing he loves."

11. "Hills Like White Elephants" was paired with Mary McCarthy's "The Man in the Brooks Brothers Shirt" and Dorothy Parker's "Dusk before Fireworks" for a film presentation called *Women and Men: Stories of Seduction* (1990). The films, made for HBO, premiered on Public Television. The Hemingway story starred Melanie Griffith and James Wood. Joan Didion and John Gregory Dunn adapted Hemingway's story.

12. Ernest Fontana has identified *wolf* as slang for an older male lover and suspects that William Campbell has contracted a venereal disease from this lover.

13. In Anderson's story, the narrator recounts his youthful love for a race horse and his fantasizing that the horse is a girl or he a boy and the horse a man.

WORKS CITED

Baker, Sheridan. *Ernest Hemingway*. New York: Holt, 1967.

Crane, R. S. *The Idea of the Humanities and Other Essays Critical and Historical.* Chicago: U of Chicago P, 1967.

DeFalco, Joseph. *The Hero in Hemingway's Short Stories*. Pittsburgh: U of Pittsburgh P, 1963.

Didion, Joan, and John Gregory Dunn. "Men without Women." In *Women and Men: Stories of Seduction*. 1990. HBO film available on video.

Dunn, Maggie, and Ann Morris. *The Composite Novel: The Short Story Cycle in Transition*. New York: Twayne, 1995.

Flora, Joseph M. *Ernest Hemingway: A Study of the Short Fiction*. Boston: Twayne, 1989.

Fontana, Ernest. "A Pursuit Race." *Explicator* 42 (1984): 43–45.

Hartley, L. P. "In Defence of the Short Story." In *The Novelist's Responsibility*. London: H. Hamilton, 1967.

Hemingway, Ernest. "The Art of the Short Story." In *Ernest Hemingway: A Study of the Short Fiction*. Ed. Joseph M. Flora. Boston: Twayne, 1989.

———. *The Complete Short Stories of Ernest Hemingway*. Finca Vigía Edition. New

York: Scribner, 1987. It reprints *Men without Women,* New York: Scribner, 1927, with slight textual variations.

Lynn, Kenneth S. *Hemingway.* New York: Simon and Schuster, 1987.

O'Brien, Tim. "Interview with Tim O'Brien." In *Anything Can Happen: Interviews with Contemporary American Novelists.* Ed. Tom Leclair and Larry McCaffery. Urbana: U of Illinois P, 1983.

Smith, Paul. *A Reader's Guide to the Short Stories of Ernest Hemingway.* Boston: G. K. Hall, 1989.

Waldhorn, Arthur. *A Reader's Guide to Ernest Hemingway.* New York: Farrar, 1972.

Woolf, Virginia. Review of *Men without Women, New York Herald Tribune Books* (October 9, 1927) reprinted as "An Essay in Criticism." In *Granite and Rainbows: Essays.* New York: Harcourt Brace, 1958.

In Our Time

Women's Presence(s) and the Importance of Being Helen

John J. Fenstermaker

In *Our Time* (1925) comprises thirty narratives: sixteen chapters or vignettes, and fourteen stories.[1] Emphasizing the moral/ethical effects upon the individual and the larger culture of the violence, miscommunication, and loss of control that characterize "our time," it presents disturbing events particularly related to World War I, the Bolshevik Revolution, and the Greco-Turkish conflict. Action at home and abroad is continually darkened by the deterioration of pre-war values—community, domestic, legal, patriotic, political, and religious. While the collection conspicuously investigates masculinity and manhood, especially in its eight Nick Adams narratives, issues touching women's presences, voices, and roles are ubiquitous. These thirty narratives individuate more than forty female characters, the most

---

Previously unpublished essay, used by permission of the author.

important of whom appear, speak, and act (Marjorie, Mrs. Krebs); appear, do not speak, but function importantly (Krebs's female peers, Mrs. Elliot's girlfriend); do not appear, are merely referred to, but function critically (Ad's wife; Helen, Nick's wife). The others have only inconsequential roles but mention brings them whole to the mind's eye—the nurse from St. Ignace, Hopkins' Blonde Venus. In this collection, often praised for its various experiments, no stylistic initiatives are more original and none more comprehensive than Hemingway's complex presentations of women.

. . . . .

Chapters I–VIII document war and its aftermath, and alternate with the first seven stories, five highlighting Nick. The overture story "Indian Camp" presents a series of violent moments and loss of control emanating from an improvised Caesarian and rolling over the child Nick: his father's carelessly telling Nick within earshot of the expectant mother and her newly invalided husband—"I haven't any anaesthetic. . . . But her screams are not important. I don't hear them because they are not important" (16), leaving unarticulated the pressing medical truth that this complicated emergency will brook no distractions; destruction of the family by the father's suicide; and from the pregnant woman herself, the first communication in the volume by a female character—no voice, only impotent, piercing screams and a lone violent act, these collectively registering both her pain and her humanity.[2]

The other initial Nick Adams stories continue the focus on miscommunication and loss of control. In "The Doctor and the Doctor's Wife," Nick's parents' dysfunctional marriage, compromising his father's role, stagnates beyond the reach of the wife's Christian-Scientist pieties, here effecting his father's silent capitulation following her defense of a half-breed Indian who manipulated and humiliated the doctor: "Dear, I don't think, I really don't think that any one would really do a thing like that" (26).[3] In "The End of Something" and "The Three-Day Blow," a confused and guilt-ridden young Nick cannot explain why love "isn't fun any more" (34) as he withdraws from Marjorie, his equal in boating and fishing, and a self-possessed, potentially apt life partner, who, along with her mother, believes the young couple engaged.[4] In "The Battler," Nick, riding the rails, escapes serious injury in the Michigan woods despite failing to anticipate life-threatening danger from a railroad brakeman and from an unstable ex-boxer and his black companion, the latter two dependent upon the fighter's ex-wife, who underwrites the bond uniting this extraordinary mixed-race pair.

In these five stories, young Nick's introduction to the broad world develops in an environment where non-whites and women occupy central, and for him, often confusing roles. At one time or another, Dr. Adams, Uncle George, Nick, and Ad appear morally or ethically flawed or otherwise ineffectual—in details compared unsympathetically with the non-white males. Interactions with the pregnant Indian reveal character flaws in Nick's father and uncle. An unpaid debt for Dick Boulton's wife's medical care leads to Dr. Adams being temporarily compromised by the Indian Boulton and by another wife—the doctor's own. And Nick fails to apprehend the real in the bizarre: he is thrown from a moving train; he joins at their campfire a black man with a criminal past who routinely restores to reality a "not quite right" white fighter through a blackjack blow to the head, this partnership surviving wholly through the unaccountable largess of the fighter's ex-wife.[5] Finally, Nick's own search for love finds him uncertain about his feelings and conception of a woman's place in his life, causing him to behave with unintentional cruelty toward Marge when dissolving their relationship.

The positive portrayals or occasional triumphs of the non-white males over the white men uniformly track to women—the pregnant Indian, Boulton's wife, Mrs. Adams, Marjorie, Marjorie's mother, Ad's wife. Although, like the non-white males, they act from conventionally subordinate roles, these women consistently effect major action, and they shape the domestic subject at the heart of each story: "Indian Camp"—family (husband, wife, child); "The Doctor and the Doctor's Wife"—marriage and family (Adamses, Boultons); "The End of Something" and "The Three-Day Blow"—marriage and family (Marjorie and Nick, Marjorie's mother); "The Battler"—marriage and unconventional male/female pairing (Ad and former wife, former wife and Ad/Bugs). Regardless, the miscommunication, violence, and loss of personal control ubiquitous "in our time" threaten the fortunes of all these characters.

Those characters coping best in these early stories are not the obvious principals—Dr. Adams and Nick. The most successful (empowered) characters are Dick, Marjorie, Bugs, and Ad's wife. Key among them are Marjorie and Ad's wife: Marjorie, a member of Nick's generation, speaks and acts effectively, although unsuccessfully pursuing a traditional marriage and family with Nick; Ad's wife, broader in her comprehension of male/female relationships, shares with Marjorie the domestic as her chosen field for effective action (compromised, of course, because Bugs and Ad must live outside society's conventional borders). Each of these initial stories concludes with Nick in the outdoors, re-emphasizing Nick's maturation as a staple concern of the collection. When young, he idealizes his father, but increasingly Nick embraces only what is invariably sound in his father's beliefs—the codes and rituals opening up the natural world, specifically, rites grounded in fishing and hunting.

Away from home, adult Nick faces a male-dominated world destabilized by the chaos, ethical compromises, and suffering characterizing, particularly, modern warfare, as seen in the vignettes framing these early stories. Only three of the fifteen vignette chapters contain female characters; significantly, none speaks. Chapters I–VIII expose corruption of pre-war beliefs—patriotic, political, civil, legal, religious, and domestic—in a world of men without women and largely without honor (Stewart 93–98). Valor among modern warriors has widely degraded into the ignoble—producing fear, failure, even death: in Chapter I, a drunken officer frets about light from a fire in a rolling kitchen 50 kilometers from the front, ignorant that his troops travel towards wholesale slaughter at the Champagne (Hagemann 53); in Chapter II, a humiliated Greek army herds its dislocated civilian population in retreat, providing a touchstone image linking a birth in this story to that in "Indian Camp" in ways as simple as pain and as complex as racial prejudice: women and children "in the carts [crouching] with mattresses, mirrors, sewing machines, bundles. . . . a woman having a kid with a young girl holding a blanket over her and crying. Scared sick looking at it"; in

Chapters III and IV, British Tommies "pot" German soldiers; in Chapter V, a firing squad executes scapegoated government ministers; in Chapter VI, Nick, seriously wounded, willingly abandons war: the Austrian dead in the street, the impotence of the Church whose wall he lies against, the pain of his comrade Rinaldi, and, not least, the devastating cost of war conveyed by the pink bedroom wall of a house revealed in an exploded opening, where a young girl's "bedstead hung twisted toward the street"; in Chapter VII, a frightened soldier calls for Jesus until the shelling quits, the following evening abandoning Jesus when bedding a prostitute; in Chapter VIII, a prejudiced cop needlessly kills two thieves.

Despite emphasis in these first eight vignette chapters on military action and, thus, primarily on male characters and issues, conventional ideals broadly have become coarsened, compromised, corrupted "in our time." As in the previous stories, these latter values surface through female characters and the developing male/female subtext in the collection, specifically here through the silent presence of two women and two girls: in Chapter II, the woman giving birth during the evacuation, an act endured amid human and animal detritus, and traumatic for the young girl breaking down trying to help; in Chapter VI, the unseen girl whose home and intimate space have been violated, leaving her wounded, dead, missing, or in flight; in Chapter VII, a government-funded prostitute available to servicemen, a woman merely mentioned, who embodies, on demand, succor more tangible than that of Jesus. These girls and women, manipulated and humiliated as was the pregnant woman of "Indian Camp," are without voice or agency. The prostitute, for example, is simply alluded to, and the child of the exploded pink bedroom exists only in her absence. Their soundless fates do not obscure the powerful meaning of their stories, however: beyond honor on the fields of war, other traditional ideals have become debased "in our time"—particularly those religious and domestic values protecting home, family, and conjugal rights and relationships.

Nick is absent in stories 6, 7, and 8 where, the war over, male/female and marriage/family relationships at home begin to emerge more fully as subjects. Unfortunately, domestic ironies prove as brutalizing as had the

Front. In "A Very Short Story," a wounded soldier in Italy loves his nurse, who shares his hospital bed with the full knowledge and cooperation of the other patients (male) and despite her embracing traditional ideas about love and marriage—prayers in the Duomo and church banns, love letters, commitment and fidelity, and, for him, a full-time job at home. Even so, while her soldier is in the States arranging their marriage, she yields to an Italian major, who proves false—producing through this sexual license a second failed relationship for her and, for the American, beyond the failed relationship, gonorrhea from a chance encounter with a salesgirl in a Chicago taxicab.[6] The third of these stories, "The Revolutionist," features a post-war Hungarian idealist committed to communist world revolution. No actual women or family appear, but metaphorically the narrator serves the young man as father, Italian comrades as brothers, and the Catholic Church as "mother," the latter in the reproductions of medieval and early Renaissance religious paintings that release the young man's fervent political/spiritual aspirations. Each fails, and, last seen, the revolutionist is imprisoned in a real world overwhelmed by betrayal and untruth.

"Soldier's Home" is critical for understanding *In Our Time*.[7] This story follows the seventh of fifteen chapters; it is seventh of fourteen stories and exactly halfway through the volume by page count. Moreover, the importance of Nick Adams as a representative of his generation—its race, class, and gender—begins to come into focus here in the family and community of Harold Krebs (hand in glove parallel to Nick's parents and community values) at his return from the War. The longest series of sustained miscommunications within *In Our Time* occurs between mother and son. Krebs's mother (highly suggestive of Mrs. Adams), a woman steeped in pre-war expectations regarding community, domesticity, patriotism, and religion, "knows" that wartime "temptations" reveal "how weak men are," that "there can be no idle hands in [God's] Kingdom," that "all work is honorable," that other boys are becoming "really a credit to the community" while Krebs lacks "ambition" (75). She wraps her most powerful arguments against his inertia and emotionlessness in the rhetoric of religion and motherhood, putting herself forth directly: "Don't you love your mother, dear boy?" His ill-considered, "No," and explanation, "I don't love anybody" (75, 76), leave him feeling guilty and no match for her tears and manipulative sentimentality: "I'm your mother.... I held you next to my heart when you were a tiny baby." "I know, Mummy.... I'll try and be a good boy for you" (76). He cannot kneel and pray as she wishes; regardless, on this domestic battlefield, Krebs's emotional forces are completely overrun.

At this nadir moment midway through the volume, pre-war American values anchored in religion, patriotism, domesticity (male/female relationships, marriage, family), and community (ambition, work)—largely ineffectual throughout the preceding Nick Adams stories—are specifically recalled in this non-Nick Adams piece and again seen collapsing. Now Krebs must flee his home and beliefs that nourish him no longer: "He had felt sorry for his mother and she had made him lie. He would go to Kansas City and get a job and she would feel all right about it" (77). Yet the story does not conclude at this point nor on this note. Its final sentence takes the reader back to the subject of an earlier conversation with his younger sister, Helen: "He would go over to the schoolyard and watch Helen play indoor baseball" (77).[8]

To this point, Krebs has made no positive contact with any female in the story—not abroad with the French and German women, not at home with the local girls, his mother, or Helen. Indeed, he has made no serious effort at a meaningful relationship with anyone. Now Krebs, a man who abhors lying, is being driven from his home to avoid living falsely. Nevertheless, the final emotion in this story describing a veteran's wounding on the home front is affection for a person of the opposite sex, albeit a safe feeling because bestowed upon a sibling child. One can imagine Harold watching Helen pitch with uncomplicated pre-war enthusiasm.

More important, however, taking up an interest in Helen and Helen's ball playing energizes, even if only minimally, the heretofore passive Krebs. Acting for Helen may initiate a first step in a largely unpremeditated plan of action, but one already including the portentous decision to depart for Kansas City to find work. An emotionally stunted veteran, Krebs, for the first time after the war, makes an effort on another's behalf, achieves genuine human contact, and, moreover, continues a tenuous link with his family.

Krebs yields to his mother's wishes in planning to leave for Kansas City, but without enthusiasm. Helen's agency, on the other hand, is life-giving, getting Krebs on his feet, breathing a degree of purpose into the resolve initiated by his mother. The child Helen is the first female character to use her agency to produce unquestionably positive action by a previously ineffectual white male.

. . . . .

The concluding eight vignettes continue to image a male world of violence, dishonor, and death, despite war's ceasing to be their subject. No women appear in Chapters IX–XIV, where codes dictate the stylized violence of the bullfight. In Chapter XII, "the bull charged and Villalta charged and just for a moment they became one." This symbolic ideal moment exists nowhere else among the sixteen vignettes. Indeed, in the remaining five bullfight chapters, formal rituals cannot control even acceptable violence nor mitigate human failure, uniformly embodied in compromised male characters.[9] And this grim vision embraces America. In Chapter XV, the final chapter, the state's hanging of Sam Cardinella exposes inhumanity within American civil, legal, and religious institutions. Capital punishment is dehumanized: state authorities brutalize Cardinella and five prisoners forced to watch his execution; the priest fails as "father," ignoring sacerdotal comfort, then challenging Cardinella's manhood for showing fear at the hour of death: "Be a man, my son." This concluding chapter, like the previous fourteen, stresses violence, miscommunication, and loss of control in a general context of dishonor and, often, death.

. . . . .

The final six stories of *In Our Time* differ dramatically from the concluding vignette chapters, introducing a world of men *with* women, a focus on marriage and family, a limited optimism. The first three marriage tales involve Americans traveling in Europe after the war. In "Mr. and Mrs. Elliot," middle-aged, bisexual Cornelia ensnares wealthy, young, naive Hubert— impotent on his wedding night. Drifting aimlessly about France, he, a bad poet, is bested for his wife by her girlfriend from Boston. Initially stressing traditional family values, the story closes in sterile tableau: "Mr. and Mrs. Elliot tried very hard to have a baby . . . as often as Mrs. Elliot could stand it" (85); later, the women "now slept together in the big mediaeval bed. . . . Elliot drank white wine and Mrs. Elliot and the girl friend made conversation and they were all quite happy" (88).

In "Cat in the Rain," the couple traveling in Italy also faces childlessness, the conflict focused on marriage roles. The hotel padrone furthers the young wife's quest to rescue a cat, stirring domestic yearnings: "I want to pull my hair back tight and smooth. . . . I want to have a kitty to sit on my lap and purr when I stroke her. . . . I want to eat at a table with my own silver and I want candles" (93—94). Her insensitive and impatient husband fails to "hear" her—"Oh, shut up and get something to read" (94). She is attracted to pre-war family roles—wife, mother, homemaker—and distinctly uninterested in the modern accoutrements of her class touching upon hairstyle and dress, travel, seemingly even role or purpose in life. Her desire to hold and stroke a cat signals the wish for a baby. At story's end, the padrone finds her a "big tortoise-shell cat" (94). The symbolism is ominous, however: virtually all male tortoise-shell cats are sterile, and the female cannot reproduce a tortoise-shell (Bennett 255).

"Out of Season" also features an American couple in Italy. The husband inadvertently engages the town drunk as a guide for illegal fishing. The couple argues at lunch, increasing tension over the fishing. During that expedition, he attempts conciliation, addressing her by nickname. Tentatively, Tiny accepts. Soon appalled by the guide, the husband urges her to leave. Coolly, she asserts togetherness: "If you go to jail we might as well both go" (100). Even this weak affirmation of unity continues to clear the air and affirms their togetherness. Thus encouraged, he insists that she return to the hotel, and she yields, leaving without fanfare. The husband's final words to the guide regarding the next day's fishing register the couple's progress: "I may not be going . . . very probably not" (103).

A husband's acting in accord with his wife's wishes provides direct connection to "Cross-Country Snow." This first post-war Nick Adams tale, particularly in its parallels with "The Three-Day Blow," emphasizes Nick's maturity generally and specifically his growth regarding male/female relationships.[10] Nick accepts his marital responsibilities. He intends to become a family man. Nick thinks, speaks, and acts regarding Helen's pregnancy as she would wish—even before George, his close friend. Moreover, we understand that Nick enjoys with Helen the rituals of skiing, a bonding like his with George but free of the competitive jealousy he may have felt with Marjorie. Answers to questions about Nick's growth in grasping the complexities of his world are realized here as they are not in the pre-war stories. He is stronger and more self-aware, willing to chance a permanent relationship with a woman. He has a close friendship with George, which both men articulate the need to keep: "Maybe we'll never go skiing again, Nick." "'We've got to,' said Nick. 'It isn't worthwhile if you can't'" (112). Yet for the immediate future, Nick understands, his family responsibilities and his love for Helen necessarily subordinate the relationship between the men. Most important within the context of the marriage tales, Helen's pregnancy—and their joint resolution to return to the States for the birth—reintroduces the desirability of having a child and demonstrates successful male/female communication.

"Mr. and Mrs. Elliot" moves from a traditional to a modern footing, but the couple ignores disruptive issues. Although the husband in "Cat in the Rain" never addresses his wife by name and does not apprehend her unhappiness, she articulates it, a positive sign. In both marriages, tension between pre-war and post-war domestic values complicates establishing common ground for communication. In "Out of Season," the wife cleanses her husband's moral lenses. She protests successfully; he addresses her by nickname, an affectionate gesture, and listens, apologizes, and acts—canceling further fishing. Bonding between the sexes, unlikely for the Elliots—possible for the couple of "Cat in the Rain," incipient for the pair in "Out of Season"—is realized in Nick and Helen. Among the four young men in the marriage tales, Nick is the most aware, realistic, and accepting of the world in which he finds himself, the most functional male in the volume. He is not alone but partnered with a worthy woman and lines of communication between them appear open.

"My Old Man" extends the marriage group, the family focus shifting to father/son (Joe's mother is dead). This subject recalls the opening movement of *In Our Time*, where Nick experiences the best in his father's philosophy, ideals grounded in the natural world. Young Joe also learns about life under his father's tutelage—in the natural world of beautiful racehorses. Joe is emotionally attached to a flawed but loving father engaged in corrupt horse-racing in post-war Italy and France. Butler loves Joe and wants more for his son—such as an American education—but he continues with race fixing. Finally, breaking clean, he buys Gilford, a steeplechase racer. Father and son are owners. Butler is honest, Joe happy. Gilford shows promise. The return home looms. Then following a "crash" at a water jump, Butler is dead, and Joe hears the gunshot that destroys Gilford. Worse, Joe overhears two gamblers: "Butler got his, all right" "I don't give a good goddam if he did, the crook" (129). The gamblers threaten Joe's future, making this boy, like Nick, a victim of the violence, miscommunication, and loss of control destroying or maiming throughout *In Our Time*. Highlighting a father/son relationship like Nick's and ending with the son scarred and alone, but armed with his father's love of nature, anticipates "Big Two-Hearted River"—a father/son story in which no woman appears, but in which the woman's role proves stunning.

Nick's story ends as it began in "Indian Camp," among his father's timeless rituals in nature. Images opening "Big Two-Hearted River," however, suggest a war zone, vividly recalling battle scenes throughout *In Our Time* and specifically Nick's painful experiences: "There was no town, nothing but the rails and the burned-over country" (133). Nick has returned to the Michigan woods to reclaim his roots, and focused on his own stability, he is not distracted. Nick effects order through his father's wordless rites—domesticating a camp site, and fishing, professional in both equipment and guile: "Nothing could touch him" (139), not even potentially painful memories of Hopkins, a long-lost fishing buddy. Only when a ritual fails do Nick's emotions surface. A large trout breaks his line: "Nick's hand was shaky. . . . He felt, vaguely, a little sick" (150). Later, the swamp threatens: "in the fast deep water . . . the fishing would be tragic. . . . a tragic adventure"

(155). A self-controlled Nick avoids the swamp and fishes well, exercising craft, honoring the past.

Taught by his father to find pleasure and pattern in nature, Nick also has participated in the violence, miscommunication, and loss of control representative of his generation. He understands that even timeless rituals in nature can fail: the Indian father kills himself; Nick loses Marjorie, only barely avoids harm from the ex-prizefighter, is wounded; Seney burns; Hopkins disappears; the trout gets away, and the swamp threatens. Codes and traditions governing war, religion, patriotism, politics, the law, the corrida, even the rites of marriage carry no guarantees. By the time he reaches "Cross-Country Snow," Nick knows these truths. A sophisticated Nick now faces down the uncertain future through a personal value system anchored in self-awareness, self-discipline, personal integrity—arguably even courage.

"Big Two-Hearted River" concludes the evolution begun with the marriage tales. The Elliots' union is weak, but the women in "Cat in the Rain" and "Out of Season" are strong and talk, the latter producing agreements with her husband. In "Cross-Country Snow," Nick and Helen share interests—regarding the baby and their immediate future, consensus. The child/family subtext of the marriage tales culminates with Nick and Helen, becoming focused on fathers/sons in "My Old Man" and "Big Two Hearted River."

Distinct from the vignettes, the fourteen stories focus on the individual and present a different vision. In the opening eight stories, traditional values broadly, especially religious and domestic ideals centered in women, appear weakened. Increasingly, however, male/female relationships grow more important. Traditional women's roles—centering on family in the desire for a child and, in "My Old Man" and "Big Two-Hearted River," on mentoring the child—renew focus on Nick, the volume's most complete male. "L'Envoi" returns him to mind.

"L'Envoi," a postscript and the last vignette of *In Our Time*, touches upon now-familiar themes of violence, dishonor, and death. Greek King George II is "very jolly" albeit under house arrest with the Queen. Traditional values—from divine right through the fundamental responsibilities of government, law, politics, and social justice—are compromised in this tableau featuring a now powerless symbolic "Father" wistfully dreaming of America. Collectively, then, the vignettes offer a dark picture, a world where the principal institutions—state, military, church—are dysfunctional or corrupt, and conducted exclusively by men.

The fifteen vignette chapters contain no women's voices. Ironically, in "L'Envoi," the Queen, the king's closest family member, speaks. Her conventional greeting to the narrator—"Oh how do you do?"—is wonderfully suggestive: i.e., how do we do? go on? live in this brutal world?

Entrusting the volume's critical question to a woman recalls other women: those depicted positively—Marjorie, Ad's wife, the child Helen, and the wives in "Cat in the Rain" and "Out of Season"; those with similar agency but depicted less positively—Mrs. Adams, Mrs. Krebs, and Mrs. Elliot; and no less memorably, those victims of the age's violence—the pregnant Indian wife, the woman giving birth before the terrified young girl, the female child of the pink bedroom, the prostitute with the faithless soldier. Regardless of agency, women's lives in the first eight stories and, especially, in the concluding six center in male/female relationships, often involving family. Highlighting this pattern in the concluding vignette suggests that the fruitful male/female relationship is not a lost pre-war value; rather, such relationships are crucial—for both the individual and the culture—and a partial response to, how do we do?

And Nick? His love for his father begins and ends the stories of *In Our Time*. His embracing marriage and family responsibilities first develops in "Cross-Country Snow," where a self-aware Nick chances a permanent relationship with Helen. Later, in "Big Two-Hearted River," is he happily married to Helen? No evidence exists to the contrary. It is notable that neither the loss of a child nor the failure of a marriage threatens Nick's fishing idyll—only briefly the memory of Hopkins.

In Our Time broadly investigates masculinity and manhood—in soldiers, police officers, government officials, clergymen, bullfighters, criminals, husbands, fathers—even a king. In his valuing women and family, in his stressing self-knowledge and self-discipline, and in his successfully surviving the age's violence, adult Nick Adams emerges a model of male wholeness.

He splashes ashore ending "Big Two-Hearted River, Part II" happy and stronger than earlier: "There were plenty of days coming when he could fish the swamp" (156). This hopeful image consequentially reduces the darkness of the vignettes and lingers positively in the mind's eye beyond the close of *In Our Time*.

· · · · ·

Thematically, Helen is the paramount woman of *In Our Time*. Like Marjorie, she shares a deep sports interest with Nick; like the women in "Cat in the Rain" and "Out of Season," she can undoubtedly speak forcefully: convincing Nick to forego their carefree lifestyle and return to America for the baby's birth. Like Tiny in "Out of Season," she carries her point without weakening the relationship: asked whether he is glad about Helen's pregnancy and their decisions, Nick responds, "Yes. Now." As wife, Helen confirms Nick's maturity, and her fertility helps initiate and define his domestic life as family man— both spouse and father. Indeed, Helen is every bit as important for Nick as his "need for thinking, the need to write" (134). Nick represents his age and class; Helen images hope for this generation by helping realize a desideratum long sought in these tales—a fruitful male/female relationship.

Moreover, as an experiment in fictional technique, Helen is a brilliant creation. She is "the thing left out," which, in Hemingway, possesses an understood and critical existence and presence. Helen never physically appears; merely spoken of in "Cross-Country Snow," she, like the war, goes unmentioned in "Big Two-Hearted River." Unseen and unheard, Helen has no warts; she exists only and exactly as Nick comprehends her. Their meaningful male/female relationship, realized as family, includes considerable agency for Helen in "Cross-Country Snow," and provides a major positive image considering the various pregnant or wishing-to-become-pregnant women throughout the narratives who are ignored, misunderstood, or otherwise victimized.

The major character of *In Our Time* is Nick. The collection's principal woman, Nick's equal and his incomparable mate, and Hemingway's brilliant technical experiment, is Helen. Despite her apparently subordinate position—physical absence—Helen has a palpable presence, a forceful voice, a critical role.[11]

NOTES

1. This essay examines the first edition of *In Our Time* (New York: Boni & Liveright, 1925). It ignores, therefore, "On the Quai at Smyrna," a story added as an introduction by Hemingway to the first Scribner edition of *In Our Time* in 1930, the standard edition of this collection since that date. Page numbers cited here refer to Simon and Schuster's 1996 Scribner Paperback Fiction reprint.

2. The incapacitated father, himself wracked by her cries and concerned about wife and child in light of his serious injury, may misunderstand or comprehend too starkly the white man's dismissal of her pain, possibly providing impetus to his own fatal act. The mother, who does not speak (and is not spoken to by the doctor even after the successful birth, simply left not knowing "what had become of the baby or anything" [18]), perhaps responding to the doctor's words to Nick and in pain during the sans-anesthetic operation, rises and bites George, the sole white man of four restraining her. The doctor's failed communication and poor judgment (would he have asked the child to assist with a Caesarian on a white woman back home?) raise manifold race, class, and gender issues. Moreover, among the Indians, George's exclamation when bitten—"Damn squaw bitch!" (17)—could reflect, gloss, even amplify the objectionable in the doctor's remarks.

3. Conventionally assessed, Mrs. Adams appears negative: in a lakeside cabin she withdraws to a darkened room, finding solace primarily in religious texts she confidently quotes despite their unresponsiveness to the reality angering her husband: "Remember, that he who ruleth his spirit is greater than he that taketh a city" (25). In "Indian Camp," the doctor effects life and death. Here his mastery and masculinity are eclipsed. He suffers humiliation retreating from, after threatening, the half-breed Dick Boulton: "I'll knock your eye teeth down your throat" (25). Shortly thereafter, Mrs. Adams' words drive him from the house, the woods affording comfort to father and son. After exercising fateful

power over the Indian mother and father, Dr. Adams is unmanned by an Indian in his debt for "pulling his squaw through pneumonia" (26) and by a white woman—the doctor's wife, at the domestic center of his household.

4. His parents' marriage may make Nick wary. Regardless, Marjorie's rough parity at fishing and friend Bill's contemptuous "once a man's married he's absolutely bitched" (46) effectively destroy this relationship. Marjorie neither cries nor argues; refusing Nick's help with the boat, she departs completely composed, and "The End of Something" concludes as Nick, a victor without spoils, dismisses Bill. In "The Three-Day Blow," Bill, fearing Nick's loss to marriage, risks hyperbole: "Imagine having them [Marge's parents] around the house all the time and going to Sunday dinners at their house, and having them over to dinner and her telling Marge all the time what to do and how to act" (46). Bill's images derive from basic Midwest family traditions and centered in Marjorie lose much of the negative force he intends, especially as Bill's exaggerations and other "profundities" shared between the young men are capped off in the final scene by their immaturity, now turned dangerous—after drinking heavily, Nick and Bill hunt in a heavy gale (unknown to Bill's father, also there hunting): "Outside now the Marge business was no longer so tragic. It was not even very important. The wind blew everything like that away" (49).

5. Ad's wife is nameless, speechless, absent, and unnecessary to the basic storyline: Ad's former earnings could be assumed to fund the two men, or their exact means of support could be ignored in the fast-paced action generated by Nick's arrival. Thus her presence as prime mover is purposeful. It keeps a woman central to the action: "one day she just went off and never come back. . . . He just went crazy" (61). Further, it develops the sinister sexuality in this tale of inversions and taboos: an inter-racial, same sex (homosexual?) relationship becomes, at least symbolically, a ménage a trois given her direct participation. (Bugs is clearly taken with her and the male/female twinning: "She was an awful good-looking woman. Looked enough like him to be twins. He wouldn't be bad-looking without his face all busted. . . . She's a mighty fine woman. . . . She looks enough like him to be his own twin" [61]).

6. This first of the non–Nick Adams stories shares much with previous Nick Adams narratives: male/female relationships are the subject; the male character is

ineffectual, and the women possess agency and move events in unconventional directions. Traditional trappings abound: commitment, banns, church, marriage, fidelity—love intended to last. Nevertheless, love-making unchecked even by routine responsibilities and carried out on a male hospital floor where all know and thus partake at some level in this drama represents, at best, a loosening of traditional standards. Similarly, an encounter in a taxi with a liberated sales clerk is not government-sponsored prostitution, but assuredly its heart is carnality, not commitment.

7. Returning to Oklahoma later than most local vets, Krebs finds no one to talk with honestly about his experiences. The lies he must tell to hold attention ruin first his actual experiences and then the truth that he had been a first-rate soldier. Unable to re-establish male friendships, he is unwilling to speak the altogether different lies required to enter complicated male/female social groupings among his female peers, grown now into attractive young women. Alienated thus, and not wanting to face any consequences, Krebs contents himself with merely watching the girls at home, occasionally recalling French and German women after the war with whom he spent time and how language barriers simplified a casual, essentially impersonal physicality. But it is the lies and betrayals within the domestic fabric at home that finally threaten to smother him.

8. While Helen cannot offer Harold an adult male/female relationship, her affection for him comes without reservation. When she asks him if he couldn't be her "beau" were she older, her fondness is unrelated to his war record, his plans to be a credit to the community, or his religious beliefs. She really wants him to come watch her play indoor. He knows baseball, a sport in which she excels beyond the reach of her peers. He answers her questions about being his beau—"Am I really your girl?" "Do you love me?"—with seemingly rote responses: "Sure," "Uh, Huh" (74). But by the end of the story, an unquestioning admiration like hers, free of the emotional baggage of religious, domestic, and community obligations, must seem attractive, especially given his predilection: "He liked her. She was his best sister" (73).

9. The young torero in Chapter IX unexpectedly must kill five bulls, causing him to collapse, puking. In Chapter X, the picador's horse's "entrails hang down in a blue bunch"; the bull freezes at the sight. In Chapter XI, the bull simply lies

down "from so much bad sticking"; crowd members attack the torero, cutting off his pigtail. In Chapter XIII, a drunk Luis fights bulls with Maera. In Chapter XIV, Maera is gored and dies. These bullfight chapters recapitulate the collapse of pre-war values: i.e., age-old corrida rites, both aesthetic and spiritual, cannot stay modern violence, dishonor, and death.

10. In this later idyll, Nick and George ski in the Swiss Alps, and we see the enjoyment of each in this sport. They share drinks and nicknames, as in the earlier story, but briefly carefree, they are not careless and do not wish to get drunk. Both have responsibilities. They conclude their conversation as Nick and Bill had earlier, with the role of a woman in Nick's life. George suddenly asks, "Is Helen going to have a baby? Nick's "Yes" is immediately forthcoming, and, more important, he responds additionally, "Yes. Now," to George's question, "Are you glad?" (111). Assuredly, we are in a story far different from "The Three-Day Blow"; accepting the responsibilities of marriage and fatherhood, Nick overtly repudiates Bill's keystone belief: "once a man's married he's absolutely bitched."

11. For whatever reason, Hemingway repeats certain names in his works. In *In Our Time*, for example, we find Uncle George in "Indian Camp," husband George in "Cat in the Rain," and good friend George in "Cross-Country Snow." The exact import of the name Helen is unclear. Indisputably, however, the importance of being Helen in this collection is remarkable: at the nadir moment in the fourteen stories, the child Helen gets to his feet and moving with some resolve, her brother Harold, whose alienation from everyone and from the values of his community threatens to overwhelm him. Because of the representativeness of Harold and Nick within their generation, the role of the two identically named females in helping these males to stability—despite the violence of their recent pasts—underscores for the reader the positive potential "in our time" of recognizing, tolerating, and supporting male/female relationships of every description—a primary theme of the collection. (Interesting to consider in this regard is the range represented by two of the most empowered women of *In Our Time*, Ad's wife and Helen, Nick's wife—neither of whom appears in the text.)

WORKS CITED

Bennett, Warren. "The Poor Kitty and the Padrone and the Tortoise-shell Cat in 'Cat in the Rain.'" In *New Critical Approaches to the Short Stories of Ernest Hemingway*. Ed. Jackson J. Benson, 245–56. Durham: Duke UP, 1990.

Hagemann, E. R. "'Only Let the Story End as Soon as Possible': Time-and-History in Ernest Hemingway's *In Our Time*." In *Critical Essays on Ernest Hemingway's* In Our Time. Ed. Michael S. Reynolds, 52–60. Boston: G. K. Hall, 1983.

Hemingway, Ernest. *In Our Time*. Scribner Paperback Edition. New York: Simon and Schuster, 1996.

Stewart, Matthew. *Modernism and Tradition in Ernest Hemingway's* In Our Time. Rochester, NY: Camden House, 2001.

The Holograph Manuscript
of *Green Hills of Africa*

"and if you fail you may simply write good prose and that is worth doing"

Critical neglect of *Green Hills of Africa* has gone hand in hand with neglect of its handwritten manuscript, languishing over the decades at the University of Virginia. This 491-page text, written on newsprint in pencil and ink, represents *Green Hills* before transcription to typescript. The Alderman Library came to possess this manuscript through a circuitous route which reveals the generous side of Hemingway's nature. Hemingway entrusted the typing of *Green Hills* to Jane Armstrong, wife of journalist-photographer Richard Armstrong. As Hemingway explains in the fragment of a 1947 letter (probably written to Charles Scribner) which accompanies the manuscript and attests to its authenticity, in 1934 he lacked funds to pay Mrs. Armstrong

Reprinted with permission from *The Hemingway Review* 12.2 (Spring 1993). Copyright © 1993 The Hemingway Society. Published at the University of West Florida, Pensacola, Florida.

■ 323

adequately for her work, so he gave her the manuscript. In 1947, Jane Armstrong's daughter negotiated its sale to Scribner's. In the fragment of the letter Hemingway writes: "please don't try to buy it for nothing, but get her all you can for it and take your percentage" from the resale.

The *Green Hills* manuscript is a treasure both for those who relish Hemingway gossip and for those with a deeper interest in his literary artistry. The manuscript reveals juicy digs at Gertrude Stein, Scott Fitzgerald, John Dos Passos, and Archibald MacLeish which were later deleted from the published 1935 text. More importantly, it reveals that Hemingway's intriguing Foreword in which he announces his intention "to write an absolutely true book to see whether the shape of a country and the pattern of a month's action can, if truly presented, compete with a work of the imagination," was added after the manuscript was written. Indeed the volume's four-part, thirteen-chapter structure was also "imposed" on it after this handwritten draft was completed. The manuscript has no structural divisions at all.

But first, the gossip. Pages 65 and 66 of the 1935 published *Green Hills* text contain Hemingway's famous retort to Gertrude Stein. In the Alderman manuscript, he actually wrote "he doesn't have to read books written by some *bitch* he's tried to help get published" rather than "some *female* he's tried to help get published." The manuscript continues:

"She's just jealous. She knew that would make you angry" [says P.O.M.].
"I'll say it. She's skillful when she's malicious."

Then the manuscript shows this rather weak disparagement which Hemingway or his editors wisely deleted: "Homme des letters. Woman of letters. Salon woman with a lousy, stinking life."

In fact, much of what appears in the *published* passage on Stein was inserted after this manuscript draft was written. P.O.M.'s assertion: "You never should have helped her. Some people never forgive that" was added later, as was Hemingway's long speech on page 66 which begins "It's a god-damned shame" and ends "You would have liked her then, really."

Between the completion of the manuscript and its publication, Hemingway would seem to have decided that Stein's motive for attacking him was her unwillingness to acknowledge that he had taught her to write dialogue. He thus turned his initial contempt into a calculated pity—a more clever rhetorical stance. He was not, however, compassionate enough to retain this original sentence on Stein in his famous passage paying homage to *Huckleberry Finn:*

> But from that comes all that is American in a woman called Stein that you will hear of as long as she is alive, from it comes what another writer called Anderson started with, and what I knew to start with.

The Maxwell Perkins correspondence in the Hemingway Collection at the Kennedy Library suggests that Hemingway's revision of his Stein remarks came late—and as a result of Perkins's prodding. *Green Hills* was published in October 1935, and in a letter to Hemingway dated 30 August 1935, Perkins writes:

> I'll send on the page proof next week. I *request* that you consider what you say of Gertrude Stein. I'm not afraid of libel & I don't care a hang about her, but what she has said was plainly spiteful & jealous & not worth so much notice from you, & almost all readers will not know what she said anyway but will sympathize with a bitch because she gets called a bitch. I simply submit this for your consideration.

Hemingway also deleted two long passages, one written over the other, which refer to Fitzgerald, Dos Passos, and MacLeish. The manuscript reveals that Hemingway was particularly preoccupied with the subject of cowardice from April to 16 November 1934, the period of *Green Hills'* composition. On page 281 of the published version of *Green Hills,* after Hemingway compares Captain Eric Edward Dorman-Smith to Pop (Philip Percival), he first wrote, then deleted:

Of the others that I saw the most of since, except for Dos there was something wrong with all of them. The charming ones were cowards and so you were never really comfortable with them and they were never really comfortable with themselves.

Hemingway crossed this out, and tried again:

Of the others that I saw the most of since, Archie [MacLeish] had the most charm and we had had good times together. But he was really a coward so you were never completely comfortable with him just as he was never completely comfortable with himself. Dos was a damned fine guy but right now he was perhaps a little over-married. That would pass or get worse, I thought. But Dos was a good friend and as brave as a charmed buffalo. The oldest friends I had were the best ones. Chink, Hickok and Mike Ward. Except Karl [Charles Thompson]. Karl was a damned good guy. He could be better than anyone. I wondered what he'd done down there. He was no coward. Hickok was the most intelligent and one of the best. Scott was a coward of great charm. I wondered why the cowards all had so much charm. Maybe Archie wasn't a coward. Maybe it was just caution.[1] What the hell was a coward anyway? A coward was a man who was afraid when there was nothing, as yet, to be afraid of. We're all afraid. Plenty afraid. But if you feared things before they got bad. Oh what the hell. That definition did not hold. A really brave man feared nothing for himself. It was a question of dignity. A brave man had a certain pride. A coward said this pride was of no importance. Perhaps it wasn't but it was of great importance to whoever had it. It made things so bloody much easier. A man without inner dignity is an embarrassment. The cowards had the charm though. Not all of the charming ones were cowards tho. Look at Tunney. There was a very brave man and he had great charm. Charm is of two kinds, I thought. Either a trick, or it comes from modesty.

Hemingway then shifts abruptly to his father:

My father was a coward. He shot himself without necessity. At least I thought so. I had gone through it myself until I had figured it in my head. I knew what it was to be a coward and what it was to cease being a coward.[2] Of course it was easy now because I no longer cared what happened. I knew it was better to live it so that if you died you had done everything that you could do about your work and your enjoyment of life up to that minute, reconciling the two, which is very difficult, so that you had no outstanding debts. So that you were paid up to that time. That's all you could do and you were all right.

During this time Hemingway had been criticized for not lending his support to Depression relief efforts; however, in a forceful passage on the artist and the state which he later also deleted from *Green Hills,* he suggests it was courage of principle, not cowardice or lack of sympathy, which caused him to refrain. On page 28 of the published version, before the line "Pop never drank before lunch," is a deleted passage in the manuscript in which Kandisky inquires of Hemingway: "What do you think a writer's relation to the state should be?" Hemingway replies:

"A writer if he is good should be against the state no matter what it is. There will always be plenty of bad writers who will work for the state. A good writer has something that is not for sale. That he has no right to sell or to loan. Like the standard meter that is kept in Paris. He can fight for the state, or for any employer, or any organizations, as a man, if he chooses, but if he writes for them he is a whore."
"What can he believe?" [asks Kandisky]
"Anything he finds to be true."
"Can he put his beliefs in his writing?"
"Only if he is sure they are true. A man's beliefs, if he learns in life, change many times."

Hemingway's beliefs about his volume *Green Hills of Africa* apparently underwent a change over time, a change which might be described as a deepening appreciation of the volume's possibilities. As noted earlier, it seems likely that the Foreword declaring Hemingway's intent was not written until *after* the work itself was completed. Similarly, the four parts which so suggestively organize the month's African safari into "Pursuit and Conversation," "Pursuit Remembered," "Pursuit and Failure," and "Pursuit as Happiness" were late artful structural markers. In the Alderman manuscript Hemingway's narrative simply flows without structural pause from page 1 to the work's last lines on page 491. Originally there were not even *paragraph* breaks between what we know as Chapters Five and Six and Eleven and Twelve. At some later reading, Hemingway penciled in paragraph signs. After the full manuscript was written and typed, he must then have decided on the chapter breaks. These were added before the serialization of *Green Hills* in *Scribner's Magazine* May through November of 1935.

The seven-part *Scribner's* serialization clearly was not structurally to Hemingway's liking. When the book appeared in October, the seven *Scribner's* parts had become four, and thirteen chapters headed by Roman numerals were titled simply Chapter One, Chapter Two, etc.[3] In fact, only the titles of the first and last parts, "Pursuit and Conversation" and "Pursuit as Happiness," were used in the magazine serialization. The opening install-ment in May printed the Foreword and the two "Pursuit and Conversation" chapters. It ended with the editorial come-on: "'First of the Hills and the Trophy of Jealousy,' the second part of Ernest Hemingway's 'Green Hills of Africa,' will be in the June *Scribner's*." This June installment, however, only presented half of what Hemingway would later call "Pursuit Remembered" (Chapters Three through Nine in the published volume). It stopped after the first section of Chapter Five, with Hemingway's confession that "The next day I found that I was all wrong about that country" (93).

The July 1935 issue completed the long Chapter Five. It was titled "In Droopy's Country" and was marked Part III. Chapters Six, Seven, and Eight were printed in the August *Scribner's* under the awkward title "Hide Hunters Bird Shoot. Toward the Coast with Conversation." With this fourth installment *Scribner's* unaccountably began to give each new *chapter* a heading as well. This practice was inaugurated with Chapters Seven and Eight which were headed "No Kudu and the Unseen Lion. Under Way Again," and "Toward the Coast with Conversation. First View of Garrick. The Bitterness About the Salt." Such titles and headings invite readers to approach the chapters as diary or journal entries.

The September *Scribner's* printed, under the title "Defeat on the Salt. The Rains Move Up," the final chapter of the book's "Pursuit Remembered" section (Chapter Nine) and the two chapters which comprise the volume's "Pursuit and Failure" section (Chapters Ten and Eleven). Chapter Nine is headed "Karl Kills On The Salt"; Chapter Ten, "The Rains Move Up"; and Chapter Eleven, "Failure of the Salt—Disgust with M'Cola—Return Of The Scouts. We Set Out." The book's final two chapters, which comprise its "Pursuit as Happiness" section, are printed respectively in the October and November issues and are titled "Pursuit as Happiness" and "The End of Pursuit as Happiness." Chapter Twelve is headed "The New Country" and Chapter Thirteen bears no heading at all.

It seems likely, therefore, that Hemingway did not determine the titles of the two central parts, "Pursuit Remembered" and "Pursuit and Failure," until after May 1935. He also recognized that the seven chapters which comprised the volume's flashback (Chapters Three through Nine) belonged together as one temporal unit. If the two opening "Pursuit and Conversation" chapters provided the prologue to the dramatic action, the long "Pursuit Remembered" section supplied the exposition and rising action of his African drama. They prepared for his "Pursuit and Failure" anti-climax and for his "Pursuit as Happiness" climax and denouement. I am trying to suggest that Hemingway himself saw his African trip in greater dimension *after* his initial narration of it. Perhaps he saw the need to suggest the deeper aesthetic and philosophical implications of his work, and he chose to do so with a Foreword which (like Twain's foreword to *Huckleberry Finn*) spurs us to pay attention to the book's declaredly artless artistry. He does it as well with the titles of his four sections. As I have argued elsewhere, these function to set the philosophical and aesthetic stage ("Pursuit and Conversation"); to demonstrate the expansive power of memory (the long "Pursuit Remembered" section); and to challenge us (in the final two sections) to appreciate the intangible over the tangible.[4]

Green Hills is as much about the elusive dimensions of art as it is about Africa. Hemingway's structural divisions work to encourage the recognition that "pursuit" means artistic pursuit of truth (the artist's role in the state) as much as pursuit of kudu and sable. But perhaps this point is too subtle. This dimension was certainly missed by that sophisticated reader Edmund Wilson, as well as by a legion of subsequent readers.[5] Perhaps Hemingway did not allow himself enough time between the completion of the handwritten draft of *Green Hills* on 16 November 1934 and its subsequent sale to Charles Scribner's Sons in February 1935 to enhance this dimension sufficiently. Both the *Green Hills* manuscript and Hemingway's letters suggest that he believed the extra dimensions he was seeking to capture in writing were of greatest importance. Deleted lines in *Green Hills'* provocative passage on the fourth and fifth dimensions reveal the value Hemingway attached to his artistic experiment. In this passage, Papa is speaking to Kandisky of:

> "The kind of writing that can be done. How far prose can be carried if any one is serious enough and has luck. There is a fourth and fifth dimension that can be gotten."
>
> "You believe it?" [asks Kandisky]
>
> "I know it."
>
> "And if a writer can get this?"
>
> "Then nothing else matters." (26–27)

In the Alderman manuscript, Hemingway then wrote: "All other writing will be judged by that no matter what it is about." In the published text, Kandisky then asks if Hemingway is speaking of poetry, and Papa replies:

> "No. It is much more difficult than poetry. It is a prose that has never been written. But it can be written, without tricks [EH first wrote *distortions* but crossed it out] and without cheating. With nothing that will go bad afterwards."
>
> "And will it endure?" [Kandisky asks in a deleted passage]
>
> "Forever." [Papa replies]

Faith in this elusive artistic dimension is vital, and thus the religious analogy which begins with the first spoken words in the volume, Garrick's dramatic "It is finished," and ends with Papa's tested (and proven) faith in the memories of his African "pursuit" and his ability to transform them into an enduring work of art. A comparison of manuscript and published versions of *Green Hills of Africa* reveals that Hemingway later added lines to underscore the importance of faith. During the hunt for the disappearing sable bull, Hemingway later added these lines lamenting the ordinary hunter's quick abandonment of the intangible: "You could not hunt them against that unbelief. I had had no chance to train them; no power to discipline" (264). These lines are not in the handwritten manuscript.

Hemingway's own formidable grasp of the intangible, we must recognize, was the result not only of his personal faith and discipline, but of his superior memory. He had no difficulty recalling a lost sable, or a lost time. In Chapter Five of *Green Hills,* when he is tracking the buffalo, Hemingway writes: "I was *thinking* of the buff the way I had seen them when we had gotten the three that time" (115). Revealingly, he first wrote "I was *picturing* the buff the way I had seen them." He then changed *picturing* to *thinking.* I submit that thinking, to a large degree, was picturing to Hemingway. And picturing meant remembering. In the final, thirteenth (hour) chapter of *Green Hills,* when Hemingway writes his definition of "good country," he first wrote: "Here there was game, plenty of birds, and I liked the natives. Here I could shoot and fish. That, and writing was all I cared about doing" (285). After 16 November 1934 and before publication, he added two phrases and a sentence to this testimonial: "That, and writing, *and reading, and seeing pictures* was all I cared about doing. *And I could remember all the pictures.*"

It is ironic that in a book underscoring the importance of taking one's time, of not being hurried, Hemingway allowed himself so little time to enhance this extra, aesthetic dimension of *Green Hills* between the completion of his manuscript draft and the sale of the work. He might, for example, have done more to contrast his two "plains": the more rugged and thus difficult highlands which he preferred, and Karl's flat, prosaic lowlands. He might have clarified and enhanced his passage on the fourth and fifth dimensions and expanded the aesthetic and philosophical dimension of his narrative until such a tension was created between Africa and art that it would rival that between Alabama and art in James Agee's *Let Us Now Praise Famous Men.* "But dollars damn me, and all my works are botches," Herman Melville cried in anguish about his similar money woes, and it appears that financial pressures impelled the rapid sale of Hemingway's manuscript.[6]

Despite my lament for less haste, for more time, study of the holograph manuscript of *Green Hills of Africa* confirms one truth about Hemingway's artistry: the wholeness of his imagination when it was functioning in good form. The African experience is delivered whole by Hemingway. His characteristic method of revision—adding prepositional phrases—reveals that composing for Hemingway was largely a matter of memory, of recalling further parts of the picture and adding them in. Questions, however, still remain about the editing of *Green Hills of Africa*. What happened to the Jane Armstrong typescript in December 1934 and January 1935? How and when did Hemingway hit upon his book's Foreword and structure?[7] Did Maxwell Perkins encourage Hemingway to temper his criticisms of Fitzgerald, Dos Passos, and MacLeish, as well as those of Gertrude Stein?

It seems clear that the changes Hemingway made between manuscript and published version overwhelmingly were improvements in the text: deletion of petty personal vendettas; creation of a suggestive structure and an intriguing Foreword; and small enhancements of aesthetic and philosophical speculation. If he did not quite achieve the tension between art and Africa which he was seeking, Hemingway surely fulfilled this assertion which can be found on the back of an inserted manuscript page: "and if you fail you may simply write good prose and that is worth doing."

NOTES

I wish to thank the Alderman Library at the University of Virginia, the Hemingway Collection of the John F. Kennedy Library in Boston, and the Hemingway Foundation for so generously making manuscript materials available to me.

1. While writing the manuscript from April to November 1934, Hemingway was clearly still piqued at MacLeish for declining the African trip. Page 65 of the published text originally included another deleted passage on cowardice. In it Hemingway compares MacLeish unfavorably to Karl (Charles Thompson):

    "But Karl is brave." [says P.O.M.]

    "As brave as anybody ever could be."

    "He's like Hamlet."

    "Yes, he really is and Archie *thinks* he is. Archie's not like Hamlet. He's like a man who studied Hamlet. He's studied a lot of things."

    On page 95, Hemingway cut the line "the righteous are always wrong" following his admission of being ashamed "at being a four-letter man [originally "a *shit*"] about boots, at being righteous against pain, at being righteous at all." Seven clauses later, the published text reads "hating all righteous bastards now, one absent American friend especially" while the manuscript reads "*MacLeish* especially." Time clearly tempered Hemingway's ire at his friend.

2. This sentence is substituted for these deleted sentences: "I knew how, truly, in actual danger. I felt a clean feeling as in a shower."

3. The serialization does, however, present more of the beautiful Edward Shenton "decorations" than appear in the book, and fuller borders of those that are duplicated. Shenton's black-and-white sketches are impressionistic in brush strokes and invite the reader to collaborate in filling-in each scene.

4. See my "*Green Hills of Africa:* Hemingway's Celebration of Memory." *The Hemingway Review* 2.2 (Spring 1983): 23–31.

5. Edmund Wilson, "Hemingway: Gauge of Morale" (1947); rpted. in John K. M. McCaffery, ed. *Ernest Hemingway: The Man and His Works* (New York: World Publishing, 1950). 236–257.

6. Evidence of Hemingway's tenuous financial condition is suggested by his inability to pay Jane Armstrong all he wished for typing the manuscript; by a letter from Max Perkins to Hemingway dated 18 December 1934 which begins: "I am enclosing herewith the five hundred, and I am enclosing a statement about the interest on the loan"; and by the flurry of letters and telegrams exchanged in mid-February 1935 regarding the price Scribner's would pay for *Green Hills*. In *Earnest Hemingway: A Life Story* (New York: Scribner's, 1969), Carlos Baker

indicates that *Cosmopolitan* had offered to buy *Green Hills*—if Hemingway would cut it to 45,000 words. Hemingway angrily refused. Hemingway hoped for much more than the $5,000 Scribner's finally paid for serialization, and he received that much only after expressing great anger and placing considerable pressure on Perkins.

7. The Maxwell Perkins correspondence in the Hemingway Collection at the Kennedy Library reveals that chapter titles were being discussed as late as July and August 1935. In a telegram to Hemingway dated 31 July 1935, Perkins inquired if Hemingway planned chapter titles and stressed that Shenton's illustration scheme depended on it. He asked Hemingway to hold chapter titles to five or six words. Hemingway's reply is lost, but a letter from Perkins to Hemingway dated 5 August 1935 begins: "I think you are dead right about not having chapter titles, and about having the three part titles. As soon as you know exactly where they go—I suppose they will go where they did in the original manuscript, but I haven't got it—let us know." This suggests that the original typescript Hemingway sold to Scribner's in February 1935 had *three* part titles—not four as appear in the published version. A partial carbon typescript of *Green Hills* in the Hemingway Collection at the Kennedy Library (Item 89) which was found with the partial typescript of the setting copy of *Green Hills* (Item 88) reveals a title page containing the title *Green Hills of Africa*; the Foreword now included; and three Parts also typed:

PART ONE. . . . Pursuit and Conversation

PART TWO. . . . Pursuit Remembered

PART THREE. . . . Pursuit as Happiness.

On this typescript page Hemingway has crossed out THREE and changed it to FOUR, and written in PART THREE . . . Pursuit and Failure. Thus naming Chapters Ten and Eleven "Pursuit and Failure" was a late decision. The chapter numbers are also written in hand in both the carbon typescript (where they are written in *words*: Chapter One) and the setting copy (where they become Roman numerals: Chapter I). Even more startling is a never before discovered title of *Green Hills*. The title written in Hemingway's hand in the setting copy is *Africa is Cold*. It is crossed out and *The Green Hills of Africa* is rendered in pencil.

WORKS CITED

Agee, James and Walker Evans. *Let Us Now Praise Famous Men: Three Tenant Families*. New York: Houghton Mifflin, 1941.

Baker, Carlos. *Ernest Hemingway: A Life Story*. New York: Scribner's 1969.

Hemingway, Ernest. *Green Hills of Africa*. Decorations by Edward Shenton. New York: Scribner's, 1935.

———. "Green Hills of Africa." *Scribner's Magazine* 97.5 (May 1935), 257–268; 97.6 (June 1935), 334–344; 98.1 (July 1935), 14–21; 98.2 (August 1935), 74–83; 98.3 (September 1935), 157–165; 98.4 (October 1935), 200–206; 98.5 (November 1935), 262–273. Decorations by Edward Shenton.

———. Manuscript. *Green Hills of Africa*. Ernest Hemingway Collection (#6250), Clifton Waller Barrett Library, Manuscripts Division, Special Collections Department, University of Virginia Library. Used by permission.

———. Partial Typescripts. *Green Hills of Africa*. Items 88 and 89. John F. Kennedy Library. Boston, Massachusetts. Used by permission.

Lounsberry, Barbara. "*Green Hills of Africa*: Hemingway's Celebration of Memory." *The Hemingway Review* 2.2 (Spring 1983): 23–31.

Perkins, Maxwell to Ernest Hemingway. 18 December 1934, 31 July 1935, 30 August 1935. John F. Kennedy Library. Boston, Massachusetts.

Wilson, Edmund. "Hemingway: Gauge of Morale." 1947. In *Ernest Hemingway: The Man and His Work*. Ed. John K. M. McCaffery. New York: Cooper Square, 1950. 236–257.

Money and Marriage

Hemingway's Self-Censorship In *For Whom the Bell Tolls*

Robert W. Trogdon

F or most of his career as a professional writer, Ernest Hemingway fought a war against what he called "genteel writing." In a letter to Maxwell Perkins, his editor at Charles Scribner's Sons, he defended his use in *A Farewell to Arms* (1929) of certain words considered obscene at the time: "There has always been first rate writing and then American writing—(genteel writing)" (Bruccoli 102). Discussions of what words he could and could not use in his books dominated the correspondence between Hemingway and his editors from 1925 to 1950. An examination of his career, from the 1925 publication of *In Our Time* to the 1938 publication of *The Fifth Column and the First Forty-nine Stories,* reveals that with every book he published Hemingway

Reprinted with permission from *The Hemingway Review* 22.2 (Spring 2003). Copyright © 2003 The Ernest Hemingway Foundation. Published by the University of Idaho, Moscow, Idaho.

enjoyed greater freedom in his use of words generally considered to be obscene by Perkins and others. This greater freedom of expression, however, did not extend to Hemingway's biggest commercial success, *For Whom the Bell Tolls* (1940). This novel is unique due to the conspicuous absence of "dirty" words in English, not only in the published version but in the manuscript as well. Hemingway wrote the novel without using any of the obscene words he had fought to include in his previous works. While on the surface this seems to be a relatively minor point—one of only limited, prurient interest—answering the question of why Hemingway wrote in this way reveals an important aspect of his career and how his personal life influenced the style and content of his art. When writing *For Whom the Bell Tolls,* he gave in to commercial pressures that came not from his publisher but from events in his personal life. He exercised self-censorship in writing the novel to increase the chances of serializing it or of selling it to a book club. Hemingway wanted the extra income to achieve financial independence from his second wife, Pauline Pfeiffer. Quite directly, *For Whom the Bell Tolls* was shaped stylistically by Hemingway's divorce from Pfeiffer and his desire to marry Martha Gellhorn. The novel provided Hemingway with the money to maintain the lifestyle he had grown used to in the 1930s, but which he would have lost without the use of the Pfeiffer family fortune.

One thing must be made clear before beginning this examination— Hemingway's modification of his usual writing style in no way detracts from the artistic merits of the novel. *For Whom the Bell Tolls* remains a moving novel with some of his best characters, best descriptions of action, and most memorable passages. As Allen Josephs puts it, "Long after the politics and the particulars of the war itself are forgotten, readers will still be moved by the story of Robert Jordan and Maria and the band of guerillas who attempt to blow a bridge on which the future of the human race could turn" (11). The following analysis does not deal with the artistry of the novel. Rather, it is an attempt to show how other, non-artistic considerations affected how Hemingway wrote. This approach is best articulated by William Charvat in *The Profession of Authorship in America:*

The terms of professional writing are these: that it provides a living for the author, like any other job; that it is a main and prolonged, rather than intermittent or sporadic, resource for the writer; that it is produced with the hope of extended sale in the open market, like any article of commerce; and that it is written with reference to buyers' tastes and reading habits. The problem of the professional writer is not identical with that of the literary artist; but when a literary artist is also a professional writer, he cannot solve the problems of the one function without reference to the other. (3)

This essay deals with how the problems of Hemingway the professional writer influenced the creation of Hemingway the literary artist.

During the first part of his career, Hemingway had a considerable reputation as a writer who realistically presented material of a violent and sexual nature. While the violent material presented few problems for him or his magazine and book publishers, his use of what many considered to be obscene language and his depiction of sexual intercourse did cause problems. Boni & Liveright, his first American publisher, asked that he remove the phrase "tried to have a baby" and its variations from the 1925 publication of "Mr. and Mrs. Elliot" in *In Our Time*. (Hemingway restored the original language when the collection was reissued by Scribner's in 1930). He could not publish "Up in Michigan" in the United States until 1938, fifteen years after it had been published in Paris as a part of *Three Stories and Ten Poems*. His discussions with Perkins and the editors of *Scribner's Magazine* about the magazine serialization of *A Farewell to Arms* were primarily focused on obscenity and sexual content; despite the fact that the editors removed many of the obvious references to Frederic and Catherine's sex life, the second installment was declared "salacious" in Boston and seized by the police (Bruccoli 93–107).

Hemingway's reputation as an uncompromising or obscene writer (depending on one's view of the matter) was promoted by some critics. For example, Hemingway reacted angrily when Harry Hansen, in his "First Reader" column for the *New York World Telegram*, called him "Naughty Ernest" (Bruccoli 111–112). Even H. L. Mencken, normally unstinting in his opposition to censorship, disparaged Hemingway's use of certain words. In his *American Mercury* review of *Death in the Afternoon* (1932), Mencken wrote:

> Only too often he turns aside from his theme to prove fatuously that he is a naughty fellow, and when he does so he almost invariably falls into banality and worse. The reader he seems to keep in his mind's eye is a sort of common denominator of all the Ladies' Aid Societies of his native Oak Park, Ill. The way to shock this innocent grandam, obviously, is to have at her with the ancient four-letter words. (123)

As Michael Reynolds has shown, some common readers shared this view of Hemingway, canceling their subscriptions to *Scribner's Magazine* to protest the serialization of *A Farewell to Arms* (82–83).

For Hemingway, the use of what he referred to as "dirty words" by his characters served an important artistic purpose. He believed that in order to create realistic dialogue he had to use the words that real people used, a belief he articulated several times in print. In 1932, he wrote a form letter for Scribner's to use in answering complaints from readers about obscene language in *Death in the Afternoon,* perhaps anticipating a reaction similar to the one that greeted the publication of *A Farewell to Arms.* (There is no evidence that the letter was ever used.) In the letter, Hemingway writes:

> The fundamental reason that I used certain words no longer a part of the usual written language is that they are very much a part of the vocabulary of the people I was writing about and there was no way I could avoid using them and still give anything like a complete feeling of what I was trying to convey to the reader. If I wrote any approximation even of the speech of the bull ring, it would be unpublishable. . . . My use of words that have been eliminated from writing, but which persist in speech has nothing to do with the small boy chalking newly discovered words on fences. I use them for two reasons. 1st as outlined above. 2nd when there is no other word which means exactly the same thing and gives the same effect when spoken. (Bruccoli 179–180)

Two years later, Hemingway made a more thorough and public statement of this artistic principle in "Defense of Dirty Words," one of his *Esquire* essays. In response to columnist Westbrook Pegler's statement, "'Ring Lardner never wrote a dirty scene or line or even a dirty word, although he produced some pieces dealing with acts of misconduct by very unpleasant characters,'" Hemingway wrote:

> Take the matter of dirty words. I doubt if a day has passed in my life in which I have not heard what Mr. Pegler calls dirty words used. Therefore how could a writer truly record any entire day and not use dirty words?
>
> On certain days and in certain places I have heard no sentences which did not contain at least one of the words which both the Latin races and ourselves use in times of stress. (19)

But while Hemingway clearly wanted as much leeway as possible in the use of obscene language, he did understand that he had to conform to the laws and the standards of the day. A magazine that published material deemed obscene by the U.S. Post Office would lose its second-class mailing rate, thereby making it unprofitable to publish (Paul 38). "Defense of Dirty Words" contains one word that could give offense, but only in its French form: "merde." Hemingway was also willing to compromise with his book publishers. He readily agreed to the exclusion of "Up in Michigan" and to the revision of "Mr. and Mrs. Elliot" in the Boni & Liveright edition of *In Our Time*. In *The Sun Also Rises* (1926), he emended Mike Campbell's statement that "the bulls have no balls" to "the bulls have no horns" when Perkins objected to that "particular adjunct" (Bruccoli 42–44). (Hemingway's original language was restored in the 1954 Scribner's edition.) After extensive discussions of what could be printed in *A Farewell to Arms,* Hemingway was willing to do as his publisher wanted. As he was revising *Death in the Afternoon,* he wrote Perkins, "About 4 letter words—See your lawyers—If you are unwilling to print them entire at least leave 1st and last letters—You say that's legal—" (Bruccoli 169). Later, when preparing *Green Hills of Africa* (1935) for book publication, he revised at his editor's request a passage in which he called Gertrude Stein a "bitch," even though the passage had appeared in the serialized version of the safari narrative (Bruccoli 225–228). In short, for most of his career as an author Hemingway understood his publishers' concerns and agreed, although not always cheerfully, to certain demands.

As his career advanced, Hemingway was, for the most part, allowed ever more latitude over what words he could print in his books. In *A Farewell to Arms,* he had been made to accept dashes in the place of expletives. In *Death in the Afternoon,* Scribner's had allowed him a bit more freedom, printing "F—k" in "A Natural History of the Dead" (143–144). However, when the story was printed in *Winner Take Nothing* the next year, the word appeared as "F—" (151–153). In Harry Morgan's death speech in *To Have and Have Not* (1937), Hemingway for the first time was allowed to spell out the word: "No matter how a man alone ain't got no bloody fucking chance" (225). The novel was the first Scribner's title in which this expletive was printed complete; no doubt the importance of the speech convinced Perkins that the word should be printed without any missing letters.

However, there were no discussions between Hemingway and Perkins about dirty words in *For Whom the Bell Tolls* because there were no strong expletives in English in any version of the novel. Hemingway stated that he started work on what would be his fourth novel on 1 March 1939 (Baker 339). In his study of the manuscript of *For Whom the Bell Tolls,* Thomas Gould has shown that Hemingway did not use any profane words, even during the early stages of composition:

> The first draft of the manuscript indicates that Hemingway was still unsure about how to present the offensive language in his story. Often in the manuscript, when one of his characters utters a profane word or phrase, the author used the vague term "obscenity." Later, in the revision stage, he substituted a more specific word. For example, in chapter 9 he changed "obscenity" to words such as "besmirch" and "vileness" (MS 198–99, 200). Also, in chapter 25, "obscenity thyself" was changed to "defile thyself" (MS 566). (76)

Gould also explicates other strategies Hemingway employed: using the Spanish translation for the English profanity (78–79) and the slight alteration of a profane word, i.e., replacing "fuck" with "frig" or "muck" (79–80). Gould argues that Hemingway made these changes in order to avoid confrontation with his publisher because Scribner's, after the Boston ban of the serialization of *A Farewell to Arms,* "was wary of publishing material that might lead to banning or seizures, in which they could lose their investment or face legal suits" (71). Gould's conclusion, however, ignores the use of expletives in the works Hemingway published in the 1930s.

A better explanation develops when Hemingway's marriage, finances, and publishing plans for the novel are considered. The composition of *For Whom the Bell Tolls* coincides with the end of Hemingway's marriage to Pauline Pfeiffer, his second wife, and his developing relationship with Martha Gellhorn, the woman he would marry in November 1940. In order to gain freedom from Pauline, Hemingway had to produce a best-seller, a work which would replace the income he would lose after his divorce.

To understand Hemingway's self-censorship, one must first understand his personal and financial situation during the 1930s. The decade was Hemingway's most prolific as a writer. Between 1930 and 1938, Scribner's published or reissued six books by Hemingway: *In Our Time, Death in the Afternoon, Winner Take Nothing, Green Hills of Africa, To Have and Have Not,* and *The Fifth Column and the First Forty-nine Stories.* In addition, he was also writing articles for the magazines *Fortune, Esquire,* and *Ken,* as well as for the North American Newspaper Alliance, and publishing stories in *Esquire, Scribner's Magazine,* and *Cosmopolitan.* But this prolific output did not translate into an equally large monetary reward. Compared to sales of the 1929 edition of *A Farewell to Arms* (101, 675 copies), none of the books of the 1930s sold well. From 1930 to 1938, Scribner's printed only 4,275 copies of *In Our Time;* 22,080 copies of *Death in the Afternoon;* 20,300 copies of *Winner Take Nothing;* 15,580 copies of *Green Hills of Africa;* 41,085 copies of *To Have and Have Not;* and 15,100 copies of *The First Forty-nine.* The combined total was 118,420 copies—a mere 16,745 more than for the edition of *A Farewell to Arms.* Hemingway's contracts for these books called for a royalty of 15% of the book's list price on the first 25,000 copies sold and 20% thereafter. Therefore, his earnings for these six books would have been only $49,357.63 over an eight year period.[1] In reality, his earnings from these books would have probably been much less since payments were made only on books sold, not printed. Sales of his work to magazines, of course, brought in additional income, but except for the *Esquire* "Letters" Hemingway's sales to periodicals were sporadic at best.

While Hemingway's income during the 1930s was large by the standards of the day, his lifestyle was more expensive to maintain than that of most Americans. Hemingway had his own cabin cruiser, the *Pilar;* he had accepted the *Esquire* assignments in part out of his desire to purchase the boat. Between 1930 and 1938, he made four trips to the American West to hunt and fish, five trips to Europe, and eighteen trips to New York City. For months at a time he resided in Havana and Bimini. Hemingway also took his first trip to Africa during this decade, going on a three-month safari in 1933–34. Hemingway traveled so much during the 1930s that *Vanity Fair* called him and Pauline "America's Favorite Gypsy Couple" (Raeburn 49). Added to these expenses was the upkeep of his family; he had earlier assigned all of the royalties from *The Sun Also Rises* to his first wife, Hadley Richardson, and part of the earnings from *A Farewell to Arms* went into a trust fund for his mother, Grace Hall Hemingway. His political beliefs also caused him to spend money. A supporter of the Loyalist cause during the Spanish Civil War, in 1936 Hemingway contributed $1,500 to buy ambulances and paid for the transportation of two volunteers (Baker 296–297). And of course Hemingway's earnings would be further reduced by the inevitable income tax.

During the 1930s, Hemingway made a lot of money, although not as much as might have been expected, and spent a lot of money. Without the financial support of his wife's family, especially that of her uncle, Gus Pfeiffer, he could not have afforded to live as he did. It was Uncle Gus who gave Hemingway money while he waited to divorce Hadley Hemingway in 1926, who paid the rent on Ernest and Pauline's first Paris apartment, who bought the couple a Model A Ford in 1928, who financed the African safari, and who bought the couple a home in Key West (Baker 178–226, *passim*). In addition, Gus Pfeiffer, as Reynolds puts it, "directed his minions in Spain" to gather the material Hemingway needed while writing *Death in the Afternoon* (*The 1930s* 9). The resources of the Pfeiffer family were great, and during her marriage Pauline, according to Bernice Kert, "shared her money with [Hemingway], generously and discreetly" (344). While it would be presumptuous to state that Hemingway married Pauline Pfeiffer for her money, its effects cannot be overlooked when examining his literary productions of the 1930s. During that decade, instead of attempting to write another novel to capitalize on the success of *A Farewell to Arms,* Hemingway explored other genres, as evidenced by *Death in the Afternoon* and *Green Hills of Africa.* The treatise on bullfighting and the safari memoir are good books, but at the time of publication they appealed to far smaller audiences than that available for novels. This is clearly seen in the sales of *To Have and Have Not,* which had nearly twice the number of copies printed as *Death in the Afternoon.* Simply stated, during the 1930s Hemingway was as close as he ever would be to being a truly independent writer, one who wrote exactly what and how he wanted.

The situation changed rapidly when Hemingway's affair with Martha Gellhorn began eroding the foundation of his marriage. The two met in December 1936 in Key West, and Hemingway pursued her, but their affair does not seem to have begun until they both went to cover the Spanish Civil War in April 1937 (Kert 297). Pauline confronted him about the liaison in Paris in January 1938 (Kert 312). For the rest of the year they quarreled (Kert 316–318, 322). By the end of 1938 the marriage was over in all but a legal sense, and in April of 1939, one month after commencing work on *For Whom the Bell Tolls,* Hemingway had essentially moved to Havana, where he and Martha began living together at the Finca Vigía (Baker 340–341). Martha's charms were obvious, but the disintegration of his marriage to Pauline meant a substantial financial loss to Hemingway—in more ways than were immediately clear. In the summer of 1940, as a condition for granting him a divorce, Pauline demanded and got a monthly payment of $500 from Hemingway (Baker 349).

In order to gain the needed money, Hemingway hoped to sell the serial and book club rights to his new novel. In writing *For Whom the Bells Tolls,* therefore, he was careful not to include material that could be considered obscene by any postmaster. His correspondence with Perkins indicates that Hemingway was considering serialization as he was working on the novel. On 3 March 1940, he wrote to Perkins: "Harry Burton of Cosmo came down to see me about serialization." By 13 May, however, the possibility of selling the serials rights to *Cosmopolitan* had disappeared:

> Harry makes me sick. I interrupted my work, paid $150 to a mother and daughter to type the Mss. day and night on his promise to give me an instant and absolute decision on 28 chapters and then he tries to jew me down to a 30,000 serial price and no decision until he has it all so as to know about cutting.

But in the conclusion of this unpublished letter to Perkins, Hemingway raises a new possibility for an extra source of income:

> Have you gone into Book of Month business and thought how that would affect us both and whether would be better to or not to (always provided they wanted it). I hate to put that many copies out for such a chickenshit sum.

Hemingway had never previously considered serializing a book until he had finished writing it. For example, in 1927 when another Hearst representative approached him for the serial rights for his next novel, Hemingway had turned down the offer of $12,000, responding:

> I write this so that you will see that I am not trying to hold things up in order to get a better offer somewhere else on the strength of this one. There are only two difficulties in the way of signing the contract. The first that I would not wish to serialize against Scribner's wishes. The second that, after consideration, I do not want to take an advance which might even unconsc[i]ously affect the writing of a novel because of the necessity of submitting it for serialization. (Bruccoli 62–63)

The idea of placing a novel with a book club was even more unusual for Hemingway. In 1929, he accused the Book-of-the-Month Club of forcing Little, Brown to cut the obscene material from the American edition of *All Quiet on the Western Front*. When Perkins suggested submitting *Death in the Afternoon* to the Book-of-the-Month Club, Hemingway, in a letter of 4 April 1932, responded:

> If the publisher needs a sure 7,000 from that source all right—but I have to see that two things are not imperilled; the further sale, which helps you as much as it does me, and the integrity of the book which is the most imp[o]rtant thing to me. If anyone so acts as to put themselves out as a book of the month they cannot insist in ramming the good word shit or the sound old word xxxx down the throats of a lot of clubwomen but when a book is offered for sale no one has to buy it that does not want to—and I will not have any pressure brought to bear to make me emasculate a book to make anyone seven thousand dollars, myself or anyone else. (Bruccoli 163)

For a commercial author in 1940, the advantages of serializing a novel or publishing it with a book club were great. Both strategies would of course do much to publicize the work; the word-of-mouth exposure *For Whom the Bell Tolls* eventually received from the Book-of-the-Month Club is incalculable. Both would also bring in a large sum of money immediately, without Hemingway having to wait for six months after publication to get his first royalty, as was customary with Scribner's and other trade publishers. He wanted more than $30,000 for serial rights from *Cosmopolitan*. Placing the book with the Book-of-the-Month Club was an obvious second choice. That firm took an initial printing of 135,000 copies, according to Scribner's printing records. Hemingway got a royalty of fifteen cents a copy from the Book-of-the-Month Club, or only $20,250 for their first order. But by 1945, the club had taken a total of 398,600 copies, paying Hemingway in all $59,790. During the same time, Scribner's had printed 294,886 copies for itself, making Hemingway's royalty for the trade edition $158,749.80 (Royalty statement).

There are other indications that Hemingway wanted to make a lot of money quickly on the novel. The proof copy submitted to the Book-of-the-Month Club ends as the published version of the novel does, with Robert Jordan waiting to open fire on the Fascist patrol, but Hemingway had Perkins insert a typed page stating that the author had plans to add two chapters explaining what happened to Golz and describing Andrés' return to the now abandoned partisan camp (Bruccoli 285). Hemingway may have believed that the club's judges would like to see all of the sub-plots wrapped up. In any event, this did not seem to make any difference.[2] While Hemingway and Scribner's were working on revising the novel and wooing the Book-of-the-Month Club, Maurice Speiser, Hemingway's lawyer, was trying to sell the movie rights. On 7 October a request for twenty-five copies to be sent to Donald Friede, a former publisher turned agent in Hollywood, was made to Perkins. Soon thereafter, Paramount purchased the film rights for $110,000 (Reynolds 1999, 33). This was the first time Hemingway had actively sought to sell a work to Hollywood.

There are other clues in Hemingway's letters and in the pre-publication versions of the novel to indicate that the end of his second marriage and his need for a best-seller influenced the composition. In January 1940, six months before he had finished the first draft, Hemingway wrote Perkins,

> Of course I suppose people have to praise a book when the author lets them read it. They can't just say 'It's horse[s]hit' probably even no matter what they th nk [sic]. But have let various people that I trust read this one and they think it's the best I ever wrote. Hope to God so. People like Esther Chambers, Joris Ivens, Chris LaFarge, Otto Bruce . . . (Bruccoli 277)

In April he reported that he had let adventurer Ben Finney read the first 32 chapters (Bruccoli 281). Prior to this, Hemingway usually let very few people read his works in progress. As Watson and Zylstra have suggested, he may have been soliciting ideas for revision from these readers (55–56). The one reader who could not or would not offer suggestions was Pauline.

In the January 1940 letter to Perkins, Hemingway writes, " . . . Pauline hates me so much now she wouldn't read it and that is a damned shame because she has the best judgement [sic] of all" (Bruccoli 277).

Hemingway's thoughts on marriage also surface in a passage from Chapter Thirteen that Perkins asked him on 14 August 1940 to delete, as he thought that it confused the reader about Jordan's marital status. Hemingway had written:

> But what was the other thing that made as much for bigotry as continence? Sure. Being married to an unattractive woman and being faithful to her. Being married to such a woman and work at it was twice as strong a force for bigotry as continence. Twice as strong. Sure. But look at that old one from home with a beautiful wife who seemed, when you talked to her, twice as bigoted and witch-hunting as he was. Sure, he told himself. You'll have quite a time writing a true book. You better confine yourself to what happens.
>
> Now, back to Maria. (Bruccoli 287–288)

While it is impossible to state with certainty, the above passage may be a veiled reference to Pauline and Hemingway's feelings toward her. In any event, he followed Perkin's advice and deleted the passage.

Although Hemingway probably wrote the novel in the manner he did to gain Book-of-the-Month Club acceptance, this does not diminish it as a work of art. *For Whom the Bell Tolls* is a fine novel, and whether the lack of obscene words in English weakens the work is a matter for each reader's judgment. What an awareness of the pressures surrounding the composition of the novel does show is how Hemingway attempted to balance the demands of art and commerce. Although he was first and foremost a literary artist, Hemingway was also a professional. Accepting the fact that he wrote for money gives us a more complete view of Hemingway and perhaps a greater appreciation for what he accomplished.

NOTES

1. The list prices for Hemingway's titles of the 1930s were *In Our Time*, $2.50; *Death in the Afternoon*, $3.50; *Winner Take Nothing*, $2.00; *Green Hills of Africa*, $2.75; *To Have and Have Not*, $2.50; and *The Fifth Column and the First Forty-nine Stories*, $2.75. For each copy sold, Hemingway's royalty would have been *In Our Time*, .375 cents; *Death in the Afternoon*, .252 cents; *Winner Take Nothing*, .30 cents; *Green Hills of Africa*, .413 cents; *To Have and Have Not* .375 cents for the first 25,000 copies printed and .50 cents for the remaining 14,038 copies sold by 1945; and *The Fifth Column and the First Forty-nine Stories*, .413 cents.

2. The epilogue has been located among the papers at the Finca Vígia (Phillips 12).

WORKS CITED

Baker, Carlos. *Ernest Hemingway: A Life Story*. New York: Scribner's, 1969.

Bruccoli, Matthew J. Ed. with the assistance of Robert W. Trogdon. *The Only Thing That Counts: The Ernest Hemingway-Maxwell Perkins Correspondence*. New York: Scribner's, 1996.

Charvat, William. *The Profession of Authorship in America, 1800–1870*. 1968. New York: Columbia UP, 1992.

Contract for *For Whom the Bell Tolls*. 15 July 1940. Charles Scribner's Sons Archive. Princeton University Library. Princeton, NJ.

Gould, Thomas E. "'A Tiny Operation with Great Effect': Authorial Revision and Editorial Emasculation in the Manuscript of Hemingway's *For Whom the Bell Tolls*." In *Blowing the Bridge: Essays on Hemingway and For Whom the Bell Tolls*. Ed. Rena Sanderson. New York: Greenwood, 1992: 67–81.

Hemingway, Ernest. *Death in the Afternoon*. New York: Scribner's, 1932.

———. "Defense of Dirty Words: A Cuban Letter." *Esquire* 2.4 (September 1934): 19, 158b, 158d.

———. *For Whom the Bell Tolls*. New York: Scribner's, 1940.

———. Letters to Maxwell Perkins. 3 March 1940 and 13 May 1940. Charles Scribner's Sons Archive. Princeton University Library. Princeton, NJ.

———. *To Have and Have Not*. New York: Scribner's, 1937.

Josephs, Allen. *For Whom the Bell Tolls: Ernest Hemingway's Undiscovered Country.* New York: Twayne, 1994.

Kert, Bernice. *The Hemingway Women.* New York: W.W. Norton, 1983.

Mencken, H. L. Rev. of *Death in the Afternoon* by Ernest Hemingway. In *Ernest Hemingway: The Critical Reception.* Ed. Robert O. Stephens. New York: Franklin, 1977. 123.

Paul, James C. N. and Murray L. Schwartz. *Federal Censorship: Obscenity in the Mail.* New York: Free Press of Glencoe, 1961.

Perkins, Maxwell. Letter to Ernest Hemingway. 13 May 1938. Charles Scribner's Sons Archive, Princeton University Library. Princeton, NJ.

Phillips, Jenny. "The Finca Vigía Archives: A Joint Cuban-American Project to Preserve Hemingway's Papers." *The Hemingway Review* 22.1 (Fall 2002): 8–18.

Raeburn, John. *Fame Became of Him: Hemingway as Public Writer.* Bloomington: Indiana UP, 1984.

Reynolds, Michael S. *Hemingway's First War: The Making of A Farewell to Arms.* Princeton, NJ: Princeton UP, 1976.

———. *Hemingway: The 1930s.* New York: W.W. Norton, 1997.

———. *Hemingway: The Final Years.* New York: W.W. Norton, 1999.

Royalty statement for *For Whom the Bell Tolls.* 22 January 1941. Charles Scribner's Sons Archive. Princeton University Library. Princeton, NJ.

Scribner Press. Printing Cards for *IOT, DIA, WTN, GHOA, THHN, First 49,* and *FWTBT.* Charles Scribner's Sons Archive, Princeton University Library.

Watson, William Braasch and Eric J. Zylstra. "Ben Finney's Bad Advice to His Good Friend: Hemingway's Vulnerability While Writing *For Whom the Bell Tolls.*" *The Hemingway Review* 16.2 (Spring 1997): 51–60.

PART 4

Places of Continuing Reassessment

Marc Hewson
Blythe Tellefsen
Anthony E. Rebollo
Laura Gruber Godfrey
H. R. Stoneback

A Matter of Love or Death

Hemingway's Developing Psychosexuality in *For Whom the Bell Tolls*

Marc Hewson

The recuperation of Ernest Hemingway as a writer sensitive to problems of gender and sexuality has become almost a critical commonplace in the last decade or so. Increasingly, his work is investigated as evidence that the macho public image he cultivated—and that remains the most widely held impression of him as a man and writer—hid a more troubled soul from view. While the important posthumous novel *The Garden of Eden* has been at the forefront of this scholarly interest, given its twin concerns of female sexual liberation and resultant masculine fear of lost power, the recovery process has also been extended to include almost all of Hemingway's other fiction. That fact notwithstanding, some earlier novels and stories have been less

Reprinted with permission from *Studies in the Novel* 36.2 (Summer 2004). Copyright © 2004 University of North Texas. Published by the University of North Texas Press.

instrumental in this revaluation, not because they are not exemplary of the author's mixed feelings about social constructions of human identity, but because they have been seemingly more difficult to fit into a new conception of his work. This is particularly—and unfortunately—true of *For Whom the Bell Tolls,* a novel that demands revisiting as evidence of the maturation of theme Hemingway's writing underwent as the author approached mid-life.

For example, two of the three most recent book-length studies of gender in Hemingway's fiction rather discount *Bell* by devoting less space to it than to many of his other works, both earlier and later. In *Hemingway's Genders: Rereading the Hemingway Text* (1994), Nancy Comley and Robert Scholes offer few more than a handful of references to *Bell* in their examination of a Hemingway they call the "anti-Papa" visible "beneath the patriarchal mask" (145). Without question, their focus on the crucial relationship between Pilar and Maria is useful in furthering our knowledge of the book. Their suggestion, for instance, that the lesbian overtones in the novel provide a richer sense of sexual and love relationships than Hemingway had earlier examined contributes to the trend of revaluating his views on sexuality. By underplaying the novel as a whole, however, Comley and Scholes possibly underemphasize its important place in the author's difficult gender development. Similarly, Debra Moddelmog's analysis in *Reading Desire: In Pursuit of Ernest Hemingway* (1999) is rather spare in its discussion of *Bell,* allowing it little space in her description of Hemingway as a writer at once dissatisfied with and trapped by cultural prescriptions (of sexual and other sorts).[1] Moddelmog succeeds in making us realize that the long-held ideas about Hemingway's life and fiction need to be rethought, but her confining of *Bell* to a brief discussion of Robert Jordan's and Maria's respective physical and psychical wounds fails to offer the nuanced picture of that book that could help to demonstrate Hemingway's changing and complex psychosexuality.

The exception to this trend of dismissing *Bell* overly quickly is Carl Eby's recent psychoanalytical investigation, *Hemingway's Fetishism* (1999), which makes extensive use of the novel to establish its case that Hemingway was a deeply conflicted but ultimately patriarchally grounded man and writer.[2] Eby's study of *Bell,* along with his arguments about most of Hemingway's other texts, offers us a writer who, from start to finish, was concerned with the establishment and maintenance of a solid, masculine sense of self. Yet, Eby's work is accomplished at the expense of some fairly important differences that are visible between Hemingway's earlier work and the ideas evident in *For Whom the Bell Tolls*. One of the main discrepancies Eby fails to credit is the fact that in tone and theme *Bell* is not the same novel as *The Sun Also Rises* and *A Farewell to Arms*. By this point in his career, at least in terms of his approach to sexuality and human-identity creation, Hemingway appears to have moved beyond the more simplistic definitions that governed those books.

In an essay assessing Hemingway's tendency to view love as an ultimate impossibility between men and women, Pamela Boker explains that "[w]hat is fundamentally lacking in Hemingway's inner experience of love, as it is portrayed in his novels, is a sense of basic trust and object constancy which could allow his hero to retain the feeling of intense love even after the beloved object is lost" (97), imputing to the author an understanding of love as transitory and finite because always incomplete. The irony and pity of Jake and Brett's relationship in *The Sun Also Rises* result from each partner's discomfort with socially defined roles and their inability to establish identities by way of their love for one another. That is to say, love does not offer them an answer to the confusion of modern life but, instead, becomes an extension of it precisely because Jake and Brett cannot trust themselves or each other. A similarly reductive, though finally not so bleak, view of male-female relationships is also evident in Hemingway's next novel. The game of love that both Catherine and Frederic play early on in *A Farewell to Arms*—he by calculating his chances for a sexual union, she by forcing him to act the part of her dead fiancé (and later on by subordinating her desires to his)—suggests a continuing inability on the writer's part to recognize that love can be mutually beneficial, mutually rewarding on a physical and spiritual level. Admittedly, Hemingway had matured in his understanding of love by the time of *Farewell,* and it would be unfair to suggest that it does not present a more balanced relationship than exists in *Sun*. It is impossible, moreover, to ignore the strongly voiced opinion of many scholars that it is

Catherine's influence on him that engenders Frederic's "commitment to love, life, and family responsibilities" (Balbert 31). Spanier, for one, gives Catherine "credit as the exemplary figure of the novel," declaring her the embodiment of "courage and honor that many have called the 'Hemingway code'" (80). That Catherine "teaches [Frederic] the value of love" does move the novel somewhat away from a conception of sexual relations that pits masculine against feminine and argues for a more complex view of love, sexuality, and gender on Hemingway's party by 1929 (Wexler 121). Yet, the persistent ambivalence in the novel, demonstrated by Catherine's unceasing focus on Frederic's wants, and the resulting lack of a relationship completely free of gender antagonism suggest the author's continuing distrust in the chance for reciprocal love. By the writing of *Bell,* however, Hemingway's suspicion on this front seems to have dissipated.

What we find in the later novel appears to be an older, more tempered and more accommodating Hemingway, a Hemingway more willing to believe in the possibility of love's positive place in the twentieth century. What Eby and other recent gender critics overlook are the more complicated attitudes evident in this novel, written as Hemingway was enduring the collapse of his second marriage and, perhaps more relevantly, as he approached middle age. If nothing else, it is a book that helps to explain the more ruminative writer behind posthumously published texts such as *Islands in the Stream* and *The Garden of Eden.* It thus marks an important turning point in Hemingway's career as he began more systematically to expose his uncertainty about the patriarchal social situation of which he was so much a part. In fact, we might profitably view this novel as the result of Hemingway's growing need to reassess, through writing, his interaction with stereotypical conceptions of masculinity and femininity—his own and others'—and therefore as a rehearsal ground for the more conscious experiments he would undertake in those later manuscripts which are not considered to be primary evidence of his conflicted feelings about gender and sexuality. In the move *Bell* makes beyond the negativity of *Sun* and the ambivalence of *Farewell,* it is possible to discern a Hemingway increasingly open to positive relations between sexes and genders. We might accordingly note how close the main themes of his fifth novel are to contemporary feminist ideas about love's place in the creation of human identity and, more specifically, to the concepts of *écriture feminine* and gender bisexuality that French feminist Hélène Cixous began to theorize a little more than a decade after Hemingway's death in 1961.[3]

Cixous's sense of the need to depoliticize gender differences between men and women through open communication and loving relationships, as well as her argument that writing becomes a site for people to expose and embrace their femininity, matches quite closely with *Bell*'s exploration of male-female sexual relations and Hemingway's focus, through Robert Jordan, on the positive—Cixous would say feminine—aspects of life rather than on the negative (or masculine) ones. The affirmations of life and love that Jordan makes as he experiences emotional commitment for the first time with Maria appear symptomatic of Hemingway's desire to move beyond a restrictive system of sexuality or gender to one that approaches a Cixousian embrace of otherness and togetherness. And, by exploring the developing sensitivity to questions of personal, sexual, and even artistic identity in this novel, we can begin to see how crucial *Bell* is as a mid-point in his career and thereby recognize how much it has to tell us about "*el nuevo Hemingway*" whom so many scholars are currently investigating (Comley and Scholes 146).

Cixous's part in this is made clearer once we understand that she does not preclude male writers from the exposure of femininity in their texts. Furthermore, like Hemingway's depiction of heterosexual love in *For Whom the Bell Tolls,* her theory about relationships is one of inclusiveness rather than of exclusivity. To combat the masculine tendency toward divisiveness along gender lines, she envisions a *rapprochement* between male and female, "a recognition of each other," and the creation of a society that admits both genders and sexes without fear of discrimination. "Each would take the risk of *other,*" she goes on to explain, "of difference, without feeling threatened by the existence of an otherness, rather, delighting to increase through the unknown that is there to discover, to respect, to favor, to cherish" (Cixous 1986, 78). Significantly, for our connection of her ideas with Hemingway's novel, it is through writing that Cixous understands this to be possible, for she believes that it is in writing that the political hierarchies inherent in gender relations are left behind:

> Everyone knows that a place exists which is not economically or politically indebted to all the vileness and compromise. That is not obliged to reproduce the system. That is writing. If there is a somewhere else that can escape the infernal repetition, it lies in that direction, where *it* writes itself, where *it* dreams, where *it* invents new worlds. (Cixous 1986, 72)

The newly invented world Cixous envisions comes about through writing that is sensitive to gender difference's not being a means to power, in other words, through writing that is feminine in nature.

This feminine writing is unfazed by difference, does not try to co-opt difference for political ends. Rather, it allows a freedom between the sexes that negates the cultural ranking of male and female, masculine and feminine. Such writing becomes for Cixous "a having without limits, without restriction; but without any 'deposit,' a having that doesn't withhold or possess, a having-love that sustains itself with loving, in the blood rapport, . . . in the assault of love on nothingness" (Cixous 1991, 4). Pleasure and love—often sexual love—are, indeed, integral to Cixous's system of *écriture féminine* since it is partly by means of love and sexual enjoyment (*jouissance*) that a reciprocity or openness to the other is possible. Pleasurable activities stimulate love, she argues, which in turn stimulates generosity, thus countering appropriation and enslavement. This focus on love and pleasure leads Cixous to emphasize the importance of love relationships in works of fiction as indicators of the writers' thoughts about gender and sexual identity. She urges a study of such relationships: "it's on the couple we have to work if we are to deconstruct and transform culture, . . . on the question, for example, of what a completely different couple relationship would be like, what a love that was more than merely a cover for, a veil of, war would be like" (Cixous 1981, 44). Not surprisingly, she therefore views sexual relations both as a metaphor for the differing economies of masculinity and femininity and as an arena for effecting social change. That is to say, sexual excitement shows how men

and women are different, but by bringing them together it also offers a clue
to destroying the phallocentric manipulation of their differences.

The importance of this idea to our interpretation of Hemingway is
easily gauged when we remember that in much of his writing he, too, seems
eager to complicate the typical (and simplistic) gender distinctions made by
masculine cultural practice. In *For Whom the Bell Tolls,* this translates into
Jordan's decision not to let his and Maria's love be overshadowed by the fear
of their (or at least his) impending death, as well as his assurance to Maria
that they are a part of one another even in death. If we acknowledge that for
Cixous "writing [of a feminine sort] . . . represents a fundamental birth drive
which will destroy the old order of death" (Stanton 78), the possibility that
Hemingway used *Bell* to work out—or at least come to terms with—his own
feelings about loving and dying becomes all the more intriguing. For example,
Ben Stoltzfus has argued that Jordan and Maria's love and lovemaking are
"concretizations of feeling and emotion . . . that . . . resist the erosion of time
and the corrosive forces of death" (20), which is suggestively similar to the
equation of love and life that Verena Conley makes in her discussion of how
feminine writing acts as a rejuvenating force: "Cixous's endeavor . . . has been
to push back the limits of death in and through writing. She . . . rearticulates
life and death in such a way as to privilege life and love . . . , continuously
urging a discourse of deliverance with resonances of coming onto life and
love" (93). Linking these two ideas together, we can begin to recognize that
through the love affair that lies at the center of *Bell* and through its focus
on life over death Hemingway was opening himself to ideas about gender
and identity in ways he had not in the past.

For the most part, Jordan ignores anything that might take his attention
away from his mission. But, even as he forces himself to concentrate on
the objective of blowing the bridge and repeatedly returns to a contemplation of the death he believes will accompany it, he chides himself for this
habit, reminding himself time and again not to let these morbid thoughts
interfere with the relationship he is developing with Maria. Though Jordan
is destined to die and though Hemingway was working the novel toward a
tragic conclusion from the outset, we must recognize that both author and

protagonist want to emphasize life and love, even in the face of death. That, certainly, is the implication of Jordan's thoughts about the importance of enjoying his time with Maria while it is still possible.

Lying with her after their first experience of mutual orgasm in chapter thirteen, Jordan realizes that his feelings for Maria differ from any he has felt for a woman before. He further understands that the depth of that emotion necessitates his concentration on it and his commitment to it: "if your life trades its seventy years for seventy hours I have that value now and I am lucky enough to know it. And if there is not any such thing as a long time, nor the rest of your lives, nor from now on, but there is only now, why then now is the thing to praise and I am very happy with it" (166). Jordan comes to realize that he and Maria are "making an alliance against death" (264) through their love for each other. Whenever his thoughts wander from her back to the likely deadly result of his mission, he reproaches himself for focusing on the wrong thing: "Til death do us part. In two nights. Much more than likely. Much more than likely and now lay off that sort of thinking. You can stop that now. That's not good for you. Do nothing that is not good for you" (168). Instead, he determines that he will "take what [he has], and do [his] work," with the result that he "will have a long life and a merry one" (169). It is important that Hemingway should highlight the length of Jordan's life here since it returns the novel to a Cixousian idea of love's power. While it defies temporal logic that two nights or seventy hours might represent a long life, Jordan's determination demonstrates that he is thinking in terms not of chronological time but of psychological time: his life will be a long and a merry one because he will spend his remaining hours confirming the meaningfulness of his existence through his love for Maria.[4]

Hemingway's emphasis on a qualitative rather than a quantitative view of life is made clearest in the passages describing the couple's lovemaking, in which the overwhelming sense is one of tenderness and communion—both emotions that Cixous views as being feminine in nature. Indeed, the very phrasing Hemingway employs to describe Jordan's feeling while lying naked beside Maria might intimate a feminine model of relating:

Now as they lay all that before had been shielded was unshielded. Where there had been roughness of fabric all was smooth with a smoothness and firm rounded pressing and a long warm coolness, cool outside and warm within, long and light and closely holding, closely held, lonely, hollow-making with contours, happy-making, young and loving and now all warmly smooth. . . . (70–71)

It is important to note the similarities here to Cixous's understanding that female love involves openness and commitment. In her words, "love necessarily means opening up another" (Cixous 1979, 81); and the correlation between Jordan and Maria's divestment of clothes and simultaneous dropping of emotional restraints—the unshielding of all that has previously been shielded—suggests just such an openness, an instance of almost Cixousian understanding and sharing.

This supposition is made all the more plausible by the sense it makes of Pilar's comments to the two lovers after they first experience mutual ecstasy: the earth "never moves more than three times in a lifetime" (174). The implication is that Hemingway wants to underline the importance, even the sacredness, of what Maria and Jordan have just shared; though Jordan is skeptical about Pilar's gypsy "wizardry" (175), the author's attitude towards the efficacy of the union is far less cynical. The description Hemingway offers of their lovemaking itself, though perplexing, indicates his belief in the positive nature of Maria and Jordan's experience. Even before they begin to make love, a force seems to bind the two together:

in his hand, he felt the girl's hand firm and strong, the fingers locked in his. From it, from the palm of her hand against the palm of his, from their fingers locked together, and from her wrist across his wrist something came from her hand, her fingers and her wrist to his that was as fresh as the first light air that moving toward you over the sea barely wrinkles the glassy surface of a calm, as light as a feather moved across one's lip, or a leaf falling when there is no breeze; so light that it could be felt with the touch of their fingers alone, but that was so strengthened, so intensified, and made so urgent, so aching and so strong by the hard pressure of their fingers and the close pressed palm and

wrist, that it was as though a current moved up his arm and filled his whole
body with an aching hollowness of wanting. (158)

The almost electric energy passing between them argues in favor of
Hemingway's wish to explore the positive power of desire and love. That
he will go on shortly to depict their sexual union in terms that call to mind
Cixous's rules of *écriture féminine* further supports the contention that, at
least in this novel, Hemingway was exploring a view of sexuality that differed
substantially from the model he typically followed.

In discussing the treatment of sexuality in Cixous's novel *Le livre de
Promethea*, Emma Wilson claims that Cixous "almost exclusively narrates and
creates a text of the interior and of metaphor, only loosely related to social
reality . . . , an interior realm of consciousness, perception and imaginary
scenarios" (129). A similar argument could be made in connection with the
methods Hemingway employs to express Jordan and Maria's initial sexual
relationship. In fact, he characterizes their respective responses to pleasure
in terms that Cixous herself might be expected to use in differentiating
masculine sexuality from feminine, and it is intriguing, to say the least, that
he appears to favor Maria's *jouissance*. Lying beneath Jordan, Maria first feels a
sensuous attachment to the world around her: "there was the smell of heather
crushed and the roughness of the bent stalks under her head and the sun
bright on her closed eyes. . . . [F]or her everything was red, orange, gold-red
from the sun on the closed eyes, and it was all that color, all of it, the filling,
the possessing, the having, all of that color, all in a blindness of that color."
The attempt Hemingway makes here to describe Maria's feelings—his very
entry into her consciousness—offers an important clue to his developing
desire to explore femininity and to bring female sexuality to life. The light
and warmth associated with Maria's sexual response are markedly different
from the way Jordan first feels during intercourse:

> For him it was a dark passage which led to nowhere, then to nowhere, then
> again to nowhere, once again to nowhere, always and forever to nowhere, heavy
> on the elbows in the earth to nowhere, dark, never any end to nowhere, hung

on all time always to unknowing nowhere, this time and again for always to nowhere, now not to be borne once against always and to nowhere, now beyond all bearing up, up, up and into nowhere. (159)

The terms Hemingway uses to express his protagonist's response are much more somber, making the usual phallocentric equation of femininity with nothingness and the threat of male absorption. Yet by the end of the scene, it is the female attitude that reigns supreme as Jordan's feelings of fear during the couple's lovemaking are alleviated by the burst of pleasure he and Maria share at their simultaneous climax.

As the world moves for both of them, Hemingway shows that the experience changes Jordan's way of thinking: "suddenly, scaldingly, holdingly all nowhere [was] gone and time [was] absolutely still and they were both there, time having stopped and he felt the earth move out and away from under them" (159). At the moment of orgasm, Jordan's senses once more come into play. The feeling of holding Maria, the sensation of warmth from their bodies, and, particularly, the metaphorical notion of being transported off the earth—all refocus the scene on the sensory perception after Jordan's intervening experience of sensory deprivation. Through their combined *joussance,* Hemingway seems to imply, Jordan has arrived at a response similar to Maria's: pleasantly aware of their togetherness rather than fearful of it. That time and place also regain importance additionally suggests the author's movement away from a negative sense of female sexuality. Nowhere vanishes and time stops, possibly indicating a symbolic staying of death through Jordan's concentration on being at the height of ecstasy and implying that, however inadvertently, Hemingway was engaging with a feminine model of sexual relations.

When we turn our attention to the couple's second and final earth-moving paroxysm two nights later, Wilson's description of how Cixous envisions sexuality in *Le livre de Promethea* might once again be used to explain Hemingway's attitude. Like Cixous's novel, *Bell* seems to be "a novel which seeks to enact the birth of a new eroticism which is . . . freed from . . . binary oppositions, yet also explores conflict and difference within identity" (130).

By their third night together, though, Hemingway has developed Jordan and Maria's relationship beyond simple physical chemistry, insisting instead upon the importance of their psychological closeness. That is surely one of the implications to be derived from the terms with which he describes their lovemaking in chapter thirty-seven:

> Then they were together so that as the hand on the watch moved, unseen now, they knew that nothing could ever happen to one that did not happen to the other, that no other thing could ever happen more than this; that this was all and always; this was what had been and now and whatever was to come. This, that they were not to have, they were having. They were having it now and before and always and now and now and now. Oh, now, now, now, the only now, and above all now, and there is no other now but thou now and now is thy prophet. Now and forever now. Come now, now, for there is no now but now. Yes, now. Now, please now, only now, not anything else only this now, and where are you and where am I and where is the other one, and not why, not ever why, only this now; and on and always please then always now, always now, for now always one now; one only one, there is no other one but one now, one, going now, rising now, sailing now, leaving now, wheeling now, soaring now, away now, all the way now, all of all the way now; one and one is one, is one, is one, is one, is still one, is still one. (379)

Given what she considers to be the novel's focus on the altered human perception of time during love and war and her explanation of Gertrude Stein's use of such a subject years before, Jacqueline Vaught Brogan makes the supposition that this passage might possibly be Hemingway's attempt at matching and surpassing the stylistic proclivities of his one-time mentor. Whether we accept Brogan's argument that the "passage achieves not mere parody, but at the very least a parity with his authorial precursor" (89), Hemingway's emulation of Stein's style here is important in recognizing his movement beyond the sort of writing and thinking he had earlier employed in creating his love scenes.

One of the overwhelming difficulties in reading Stein is her frequent refusal to abide by common literary and grammatical conventions, a tendency that, according to theorist Luce Irigaray, often marks woman's position in male society:

> she is called . . . incomprehensible, perturbed, capricious—not to mention her language in which 'she' goes off in all directions and in which 'he' is unable to discern the coherence of any meaning. Contradictory words seem a little crazy to the logic of reason, and inaudible to him who listens with ready-made grids, a code prepared in advance. (103)

Though Stein's style can more generally be equated with the Irigarayan ideal of feminine language than Hemingway's, perhaps a connection is possible in the case of *For Whom the Bell Tolls*. Recourse to Cixous's notions of sexual pleasure, which entail the importance of union and mutual gratification for sexual partners and which thus extend beyond Irigaray's more narrowly female-centered arguments, can also help to demonstrate just how far Hemingway is in this passage from a masculine sense of sexuality. As Barbara Freeman contends, "[s]exual and inscriptional expenditure . . . function in tandem" for Cixous (65), meaning that writing of the body and of sexual pleasure allows for a freedom from the oppressive hierarchization of masculine and feminine genders and male and female sexualities. While this is generally understood in the context of women writers, we may plausibly adapt the idea to explain how the lovemaking passage in chapter thirty-seven evidences Hemingway's changing approach to sexuality.

We should first note the expansiveness of his description of Maria and Jordan's sexual enjoyment. The clearly effusive nature of the language—the attempt Hemingway makes to extend beyond a rational explanation of their pleasure by means of the repetition of key words and phrases—might be taken as a man's attempt to move beyond socially prescribed masculinity, beyond stereotypically masculine codes of grammar and sense-making. We must also acknowledge that the possessiveness and divisiveness that characterized the couple's lovemaking in chapter thirteen has disappeared. While he earlier emphasized Jordan's and Maria's individual responses, here Hemingway is careful to declare their unity ("they knew that nothing could happen to the one that did not happen to the other, that no other thing could happen more than this;" "one and one is one"). This extension of each lover into the other, as Gerry Brenner comments, evidences a "lack of phallic regionalization" and "suggests an antiphallocentric text that Hélène Cixous might well find deserving of comment" (137). Unlike a masculine approach to sexuality, with its attendant fears about expenditure, a feminine sexual understanding is based on just the sort of shared experience that Maria and Jordan appear by now to have enjoyed.

Between the moment they climb into his sleeping bag one final time in chapter thirty-one and the instant of their orgasm together six chapters later, then, Jordan makes a final conversion from retentiveness to a belief in mutual expenditure. Maria's complaint of pain after two successive evenings of lovemaking (and Jordan's attempt to initiate a third) apparently denies him the possibility of further sex before the bridge-blowing the following morning. Feeling guilty about depriving him, Maria offers to masturbate him instead. Jordan refuses, though, on the ground that he will need all of himself for the attack the next day. The clear connection Hemingway makes here between his protagonist's sexual and physical potential would seem to indicate that the author himself understands sexuality in terms of retention. The fact, too, that this would be wasted vitality cannot be overlooked. Squandering the sexual-physical manifestation of his manhood definitely worries Jordan:

> I'll keep any oversupply of that for tomorrow. I'll need all of that there is tomorrow. There are no pine needles that need that now as I will need it tomorrow. Who was it cast his seed upon the ground in the Bible? Onan. How did Onan turn out? he thought. I don't remember ever hearing any more about Onan. He smiled in the dark. (342)

Interestingly enough, though, his fear over the depletion of himself only colors Jordan's thoughts about masturbation. When Maria later suggests that they make love, his anxiety quickly disappears. The reason for this may not appear readily visible; however, it is perhaps not too far-fetched to suggest that Jordan's conversion has something to do with his creator's understanding of the importance of sexual union in the discovery of personal identity.

If, as Cixous suggests, woman's difference from man is indicated in part by her more liberated and liberating approach to sexuality, it might be the case that for Hemingway only interaction with a non-masculine sexual principle could allow for potential male liberation and self-definition—the conclusion to which Earl Rovit inadvertently comes when he calls Maria "the vessel of Jordan's complete self-realization; in his mergence with her, he has achieved the immortality of becoming 'other'" (134). More importantly, though, Jordan's musings about ecstasy after their final lovemaking, and after Maria has confided that she has once more experienced orgasm, might be thought of as Hemingway's own questions about sexual union and what it means:

> How little we know of what there is to know. I wish that I were going to live a long time instead of going to die today because I have learned much about life in these four days; more, I think, than in all the other time. I'd like to be an old man and to really know. I wonder if you keep on learning or if there is only a certain amount each man can understand. I thought I knew about so many things that I know nothing of. (380)

If it can be suggested that Hemingway's interpretation of sexuality to this point in his career had been a stereotypically masculine one, we might view this passage as a veiled or unconscious admission of doubt as to the validity of patriarchal sexual identities and as an indication of the writer's desire to explore other avenues of sexual and gender self-expression than those he had previously walked. The implication, therefore, of Jordan's final climax with Maria, especially its oddly feminine mathematical equation of "one and one is one" (379), might be that Hemingway was experimenting not simply with how to express sexual pleasure but with how to define it.

It is reductive of the novel, however, and of *Bell*'s complex themes to imply that Jordan and Maria's relationship is simply a modulation of the author's ideas about male and female sexual responses. While their physical compatibility does lead to an almost symbiotic connection between the two lovers, it is important to recognize that Hemingway does not limit this closeness to the time of their mutual orgasms. Rather, the attachment they feel, though it begins in sexual contact, develops beyond intercourse—a fact that is integral to our viewing the novel as something more than Hemingway's description of good sex. He is, in fact, at pains to demonstrate that sexual enjoyment reaches past the confines of physical togetherness, that it can foster other, non-sexual, connections between partners. That is why, when Jordan is to be left behind at the end of the novel because of his broken leg, Hemingway indicates the extent to which his and Maria's lives have become intertwined beyond the mere fact of mutual physical enjoyment. While the inevitable death that has been in the air since the opening pages of the book is almost upon him, Jordan chooses again to focus on life, on the life that will continue through Maria's ongoing love for him, assuring her that his death does not mean the end of him: "We will not go to Madrid now but I go always with thee wherever thou goest. Understand? . . . Thou wilt go now, rabbit. But I go with thee. As long as there is one of us there is both of us. Do you understand? . . . If thou goest then I go, too . . . Whichever one there is, is both . . . I am thee also now" (463). As Robert Gajdusek explains, by such attitudes "Hemingway's protagonist . . . argues for . . . self-transcendence and empathetic projection into the 'other'" (19). And it is important that the argument should be voiced by a man in this novel. In attributing these words to his hero rather than to that man's female partner, Hemingway has begun to move beyond the type of male stoicism that marked his earlier protagonists. While in previous books his heroes often accept their lovers' self-abnegation (as when Catherine declares that she has no existence outside of Frederic), by *For Whom the Bell Tolls* Hemingway's fantasy of the subsumed woman has changed quite a bit.

Admittedly Maria does at times appear the submissive and passive woman many readers feel Hemingway specialized in creating. The links, for instance, to such patriarchally constructed women as Mary Magdalene or the Virgin Mary—with both of whom Maria shares a name—are not to be denied, and her drying of Jordan's shoes and fetching him clean socks do implicate her creator in a re-establishment of typically hierarchized male-female relationships, as does her ignoring her pain to offer her lover a final sexual experience. In this sense, Maria can be regarded as a logical extension of earlier help-mate partners in Hemingway's fiction, a conclusion further prompted by her determination to become a perfect wife for Jordan if they escape the war: "I will make thee as good a wife as I can.... Clearly I am not well trained but I will try to make up for that.... I will make mistakes but you will tell me and I will never make them twice, or maybe only twice.... I will go to school to learn to be a wife, if there is such a school, and study at it" (348). It is wrong, though, to suggest that Maria's submissiveness to Jordan marks the totality of Hemingway's ideas about sexuality and gender relations in *For Whom the Bell Tolls*. We must also acknowledge that Jordan is against Maria's becoming a subservient and dutiful wife, just as he is against her servicing his sexual needs in forms other than intercourse: "[w]hat we have we have together and we will keep it and guard it.... We will have our necessities together. I have no necessities apart from thee" (349). This refusal of Maria's offer of masturbation and his understanding of their relationship as something more than mere sexual compatibility seems to offer some evidence that Hemingway, too, had begun to imagine relationships that were based on reciprocity and not on subjugation.

Despite Boker's claim, then, about the lack of trust shown by Hemingway's lover-heroes, by the time Jordan convinces Maria to leave him to die on the Spanish hillside he has indeed come to see that love can move beyond mutual sexual gratification and that he and she are joined not merely by lust but by love. As Cecelia Farr rightly points out, by the conclusion of the book we have witnessed Jordan's "shift from an arrogant to a loving perception . . . [by way of his] awareness of difference from Maria and his (apparently new) willingness to acknowledge reciprocity in his relationship with her. After all, the earth moves for both of them, and he seems to need Maria's love just as she does his" (157). Needless to say, such a revelation for a Hemingway hero is just short of miraculous. It can help, though, to prove just how far the author had come toward a new and different sensibility by the end of the

1930s. If we acknowledge Jordan's regret over dying without passing on his new outlook on life and love as an indication of Hemingway's determination not to leave his own revelations unspoken, we may begin to understand how important a book *Bell* is in the development of his ideas about gender and sexual identity. "You've had just as good a life as grandfather's though not as long," Jordan tells himself. "You've had as good a life as any one because of these last days. You do not want to complain when you have been so lucky. I wish there was some way to pass on what I've learned, though. Christ, I was learning fast there at the end" (467). Reminiscing about the three days he has lived with Maria makes him want to teach his new-found knowledge to others, something Hemingway is arguably doing by presenting the novel to the reading public.

In the end, the importance that Hemingway places on love in his novel can aid our recognition of his desire—conscious or otherwise—to rethink his previous ideas on sexuality and gender. Rather than the failed or self-interested affairs we find in some earlier works, *Bell* provides us with one of the few positive relationships Hemingway created, and the feelings that Jordan and Maria share act as a barometer for the less guarded and more optimistic, more Cixousian, view of love he began to evince in his middle age. Though their relationship, like almost all of his fictional affairs, is doomed to death (and by death), Hemingway makes a step forward in this book that indicates an increasing unease with the gender and sexual definitions available to men and women in a patriarchal society and suggests a desire to find an alternate means of self-identification through openness, commitment, and love. Admittedly, *For Whom the Bell Tolls* is a far less clearly articulated example of Hemingway's growing concern with gender issues than the books he would work on after World War II. However, it does rank as an important part of our recuperation of his literary reputation. If *The Garden of Eden* and the other post-war manuscripts are touted as a departure for Hemingway from his previous work, we must understand that it was a departure forecast by the themes present ten years earlier in *Bell*. Given this, it is imperative that we allow this novel equal importance with the more provocative texts of his later middle age and register it as a watershed in his writing as Hemingway moved toward a more confessional, more honest, approach to his art and his questions about gender, sexuality, and identity.

NOTES

1. In offering such an analysis, Moddelmog follows in the footsteps and builds upon the ideas of Mark Spilka, whose book *Hemingway's Quarrel with Androgyny* (1990) began the trend of lengthy studies into the writer's difficulties with sexuality and gender by suggesting that his work was a defensive reaction against a fear of his innate femininity and an attempt to proclaim the dominance of his masculinity. While Spilka's work remains an integral part of the recovery of Hemingway now taking place, his essentializing of the differences between men and women without recognizing those differences as culturally controlled or stereotyped has the effect of downplaying Hemingway's own knowledge of this reality and desire to combat it in his fiction.

2. As with Moddelmog, Spilka's claims, as well as those of early Hemingway scholars such as Cowley and Young, are evident at the foundation of Eby's ideas. While his work is far more theoretically based, it continues the tradition of seeing Hemingway as a wounded soul using writing to shore up his damaged (masculine) identity.

3. The possible connection between Cixous's theories and Hemingway's later writing has been noted by Willingham in her examination of gender in *The Garden of Eden,* the only published work so far to bring the two authors together.

4. This was apparently a favorite theme for Hemingway in the 1930s. Stories like "The Short Happy Life of Francis Macomber" and "The Snows of Kilimanjaro" also explore the male attitude towards love, particularly as the hero's life is waning. That he should write a number of texts addressing this point suggests that Hemingway was trying hard at this time to come to some conclusions as to how men (and artists) are expected to interact with women and with life. This would become an even more urgent need for him in coming years as the themes of the artist's duty to art and the man's duty to human relationships began to take over in such manuscripts as *Islands in the Stream* and *The Garden of Eden.*

WORKS CITED

Balbert, Peter. "From Hemingway to Lawrence to Mailer: Survival and Sexual Identity in *A Farewell to Arms.*" *The Hemingway Review* 3 (1983): 30–43.

Boker, Pamela A. "Negotiating the Heroic Paternal Ideal: Historical Fiction as Transference in Hemingway's *For Whom the Bell Tolls.*" *Literature and Psychology* 41 (1995): 85–112.

Brenner, Gerry. "Once a Rabbit, Always a Rabbit? A Feminist Interview with Maria." In *Blowing the Bridge: Essays on Hemingway and* For Whom the Bell Tolls. Ed. Rena Sanderson. Westport: Greenwood P, 1992. 131–42.

Brogan, Jacqueline Vaught. "Parody or Parity: A Brief Note on Gertrude Stein and *For Whom the Bell Tolls.*" *The Hemingway Review* 15 (1996): 89–96.

Cixous, Hélène. "Rethinking Differences: An Interview." In *Homosexualities and French Literature: Cultural Contexts, Critical Texts.* Ed. George Stambolian and Elaine Marks. Ithaca: Cornell UP, 1979. 70–86.

———. "Castration or Decapitation?" Trans. Annette Kuhn. *Signs* 7 (1981): 36–55.

———. and Catherine Clément. *The Newly Born Woman.* Trans. Betsy Wing. Minneapolis: U of Minnesota P, 1986.

———."Coming to Writing." In *Coming to Writing and other Essays.* Ed. Deborah Jenson. Cambridge: Harvard UP, 1991. 1–58.

Comley, Nancy R., and Robert Scholes. *Hemingway's Genders: Rereading the Hemingway Text.* New Haven: Yale UP, 1994.

Conley, Verena. "Saying 'Yes' to the Other." *Dalhousie French Studies* 13 (1987): 92–99.

Eby, Carl. *Hemingway's Fetishism: Psychoanalysis and the Mirror of Manhood.* Binghamton: SUNY P, 1999.

Farr, Cecelia Konchar. "Moving Earth: Ecofeminist Sites in Hemingway's *For Whom the Bell Tolls* and Gellhorn's *A Stricken Field.*" In *Hemingway and the Natural World.* Ed. Robert E. Fleming. Moscow, ID: U of Idaho P, 1999. 153–64.

Freeman, Barbara. "'*plus corps donc plus écriture*: Hélène Cixous and the Mind-Body Problem." *Paragraph* 11 (1988): 58–70.

Gajdusek, Robert. "Pilar's Tale: The Myth and the Message." *The Hemingway Review* 10 (1990): 19–33.

Hemingway, Ernest. *For Whom the Bell Tolls*. New York: Charles Scribner's Sons, 1940.

Irigaray, Luce. "This Sex Which is Not One." Trans. Claudia Reeder. In *New French Feminisms*. Ed. Elaine Marks and Isabelle de Courtivron. New York: Shocken Books, 1981. 99–106.

Moddelmog, Debra. *Reading Desire: In Pursuit of Ernest Hemingway*. Ithaca: Cornell UP, 1999.

Rovit, Earl. *Ernest Hemingway*. New York: Twayne Publishers, 1963.

Spanier, Sandra Whipple. "Hemingway's Unknown Soldier: Catherine Barkley, the Critics, and the Great War." In *New Essays on A Farewell to Arms*. Ed. Scott Donaldson. Cambridge: Cambridge UP, 1990. 75–108.

Spilka, Mark. *Hemingway's Quarrel with Androgyny*. Lincoln: U of Nebraska P, 1990.

Stanton, Domna C. "Language and Revolution: The Franco-American Dis-Connection." In *The Future of Difference*. Ed. Hester Eisenstein and Alice Jardine. Boston: G. K. Hall, 1980. 73–87.

Rewriting the Self Against the National Text

Ernest Hemingway's *The Garden of Eden*

Blythe Tellefsen

Then the Lord God said, "Behold, the man has become like one of Us, knowing good and evil; and now, lest he stretch out his hand, and take also from the tree of life, and eat, and live forever"—therefore the Lord God sent him out from the garden of Eden. . . .

When Ernest Hemingway entitled his last, posthumously published, unwieldy behemoth of a novel *The Garden of Eden* and described the book's theme as "the happiness of the Garden that a man must lose" (Baker 460), he inserted it into a long tradition of Christian mythology to which America's own history is most intimately connected. Hemingway's explicit connection of his novel to the story of man's expulsion from Paradise indicates the major themes of his novel: creation, love, temptation, desire for forbidden knowledge, longing for eternal life, evil, destruction, and loss. Such a catalog of themes describes most of Hemingway's major works—*The Sun Also Rises,*

Reprinted with permission from *Papers on Language & Literature* 36.1 (Winter 2000). Copyright © 2000 by The Board of Trustees, Southern Illinois University. Published by Southern Illinois University, Edwardsville.

A Farewell to Arms, In Our Time, For Whom the Bell Tolls—all of which focus on the frustration of his major characters' most basic desires, a frustration almost always connected intimately with love and death.

To describe Ernest Hemingway as an author of stories primarily about love that draw on a long tradition of Christian mythology would be, perhaps, somewhat surprising to readers more familiar with Ernest Hemingway as the author of action novels with the "Code Hero" as the central character. And yet, the obstacles faced by all these famous American Heroes—Robert Jordan, Jake Barnes, Frederic Henry—are obstacles posed by love (of a woman, country, humankind), knowledge (of good, evil, fate) and death (emotional, physical, spiritual). Hemingway's work breaks with Christian mythology, however, in suggesting that death is not the door to new life but the end of life. And so Hemingway's texts, although permeated with death, remain focused on the question of how to live.

That question emerges in Hemingway's work as an exploration of identity; a subset of the primary question is formed by questions about sex, gender, nationality, race, nature, art, and the family. These questions usually, although not exclusively, are faced by a white American male who must define himself through his actions. The constant strife in the Hemingway novel, the continual struggle to "live the Code," does not seem to me to valorize unquestioningly the American Hero as represented in national myth, but rather to evince a profound sense of the instability of the category of white, male American and a deep ambivalence about that identity.[1]

Thus, although Hemingway's texts exploit and valorize the authority vested in white, Protestant males, a subversive subtext undercuts such authority, founded in an intense ambivalence about, and manifested in an equally intense examination of, the identity of that subject.[2] In fact, a subtext to Hemingway's primary plot seems always to be an obsessive reiteration of the question "What does it mean to be a white male American?" The exploration of that question culminates in the highly controversial and heavily edited novel entitled *The Garden of Eden,* which seems to me to be both the culmination of his long career and a kind of repetition of it.[3] *The Garden of Eden* can be read as Hemingway's attempt to construct a new garden—a new America, if you will—by reimagining the categories of race and gender, the structure of the family, and the meaning of artistry. All of these categories are deeply imbricated in one another: race and sexuality intertwine in provocative, productive, destabilizing ways (as does the most repressed element, class); the role and the work of the artist are examined and emerge as stabilizing entities that work against the reinvention of identity; Africa functions in a multitude of highly unstable ways throughout the text; and a ghostly America shadows the entire novel with a haunting, proscriptive presence.

In this novel, the Hemingway male is split into two people who struggle to reshape their identities against cultural norms. Catherine Bourne is David Bourne's dark double, and her desperate struggle for self-definition and empowerment serves not only as an exploration of the peculiar problems facing a certain class of woman, but also as a catalyst for and a counterpoint to David Bourne's own struggle for mastery of self. As its title suggests, the novel retells the Biblical story of the Fall: a man and a woman seek knowledge and, as a result, lose innocence and Paradise. The Serpent's identity is ambiguous; many critics argue for Catherine Bourne as the incarnation of evil, others argue for Marita, some locate true evil in David himself. I suggest, however, that the Serpent is embodied, or disembodied in this case, not by the character, but by the overriding power of the Nation—by the legal demands of the state and the social demands of its predominant culture—that lures the Bournes (particularly Catherine) to attempt to reinvent their selves against that culture's dictates and causes those attempts to fail.[4]

What makes *The Garden of Eden* so interesting is that the instability of identity, the mutability of sexuality and race, the intimate, generative connection between art and "reality," and the exorbitant pressures of mythology and ideology on human subjects are not repressed or contained, relegated to the subtext, emerging only as the cracks and fissures of the main narrative, but instead form the primary story. *The Garden of Eden* is the mirror-image of a more typical Hemingway text—what is usually repressed is foregrounded here. Here, the usual fear of becoming the Other becomes instead a direct attempt to do so: Catherine and David Bourne attempt to transfigure themselves through complex experiments in which race and sexuality intermingle to produce new subjects who are, in a twist of the colonial project, "white but not quite" and, additionally, neither female nor male, hetero nor homosexual, the self nor the Other. The interpellation of race, gender, sexuality, art, religion, and death is so complicated, however, so entangled and twisted, that explicating them is exceedingly difficult. What follows is an attempt to trace the figurations of these factors as they intersect and collide throughout the text and to link those figurations to the national project as it intersects with and collides with Hemingway's.

The novel opens in an Edenic honeymoon scene. The Bournes' idyllic holiday, however, is soon threatened by Catherine's "dangerous" cutting of her hair. The danger lies in what the haircut signifies; in bed that night Catherine claims that she is male, asking David to become her "girl." The sex/gender transformations are soon followed by racial ones—Catherine becomes obsessed with tanning—and transformations along "self/other" lines—she asks that David cut and bleach his hair exactly like her own, and that he, too, tan as dark as possible. Finally, Catherine engages in a sexual relationship with another woman and encourages David to engage in a relationship with that woman as well.

At first, these experiments seem to emerge from the desire to violate relatively standard cultural taboos for mere excitement; Catherine, desiring to eroticize her relationship with her husband, chooses to dally with Africanness that she and her culture equate with heightened, primitive sexuality, and dally as well with forms of sexuality that she and her culture equate with titillating sexual deviance.[5] Such dalliances could be read as an exploitation of Otherness while holding fast to one's privileged position, an explanation that garners further merit when one considers that the tanning is always accompanied by an obsessive blonding, resulting in two contrasting racial figurations. Catherine never renounces her racial affiliation (if, indeed, that were possible), declaring, for instance, "I'm the darkest white girl in the world" (169), and there is never any question of Catherine losing her status as a rich, white, heterosexual American. Her new race and gender are experiments with which she plays but which remain transitory embodiments for her.

Catherine's wish to become an "African girl" is most certainly not a desire to emulate Africans (29). Indeed, Catherine is repulsed by David's African stories, and her hysterical outburst against them is imbued with racist assumptions:

> [The honeymoon narrative is] certainly much more interesting and instructive than a lot of natives in a kraal or whatever you call it covered with flies and scabs in Central Africa with your drunken father staggering around smelling of sour beer and not knowing which ones of the little horrors he had fathered. (189)

Catherine's dehumanization and denigration of Africans and her insistence that her life provides superior material for a story give credence to the argument that her racial experiments are nothing more than an exploitation of an imaginary otherness;[6] I argue, however, that this reading oversimplifies a more complex problem. Although Catherine is racist and exploitative, she is not simply playing at embracing Otherness. She truly feels that she is both dark and male, although what she means by that is unclear. This, for instance, Catherine asserts, "I'm a girl. But I'm a boy too and I can do anything" (15); "Take a good look because this is how I am" (46); "I really am this dark. The sun just develops it" (64); and, in a desperate attempt to explain her pain to David and Marita, cries out. "I broke myself in pieces in Madrid to be a girl and all it did was break me in pieces. . . . Now all I am is through. You're a girl and a boy both and you really are. You don't have to change and it doesn't kill you and I'm not. And now I'm nothing" (192). Her racial and sexual metamorphoses *are* much more than titillating experiments with Otherness for Catherine; they are attempts to fashion a self as whom she can live. She finds the identity into which she is born unbearable and in desperation turns to manipulation of the kinds of identity categories with which she had been imbued by her culture in order to invent a different, more bearable, self.

When she fails to create and inhabit that self, she becomes "nothing"—a self in danger of losing identity altogether. Such loss of identity reflects not only the power of "natural" identity markers—the pressure exerted on selves by society to force them into conformity with cultural expectations—but also the real difficulty involved in constituting oneself as a new being. Catherine's difficulty, in other words, is related to the difficulties experienced by all subjects who experiment with the transformation of self, whether it be a temporary, long-term, or even permanent "strategy" such as racial or sexual passing, or a "real change" such as that undergone by transsexuals. How can one change the self (whether that original self is constructed and shaped by the discursive power of the state or is a "natural," biologically produced entity) and still exist in a world in which identity markers (which are "read" and interpreted by other selves) are what constitute the self?[7]

Catherine has assumed that by effecting outward transformations—by declaring herself to be male, dressing in a masculine fashion, cutting and dyeing her hair, tanning her skin, kissing a woman in public—in short, by performing herself differently, she can overcome her constitutive self and, through an effort of will and imagination, invent a new self, not simply a new image. The "madness" that overtakes her, her increasingly destructive and joyless behavior, and the emptiness and loss with which she repeatedly identifies herself suggest, however, that she can't.[8]

The reasons for that failure are complicated and interwoven. Certainly, her failure stems in part from the sheer difficulty of sustaining a self that does not conform to cultural expectations. Catherine's difficulty also emerges, however, from her inculcation with Christian ideology and with the modernist replacement of religion with art. In fact, the substitution of Artist for God and Art for Religion is a significant reason for Catherine's destructive behavior that, in fact, results from the frustration of her creative drive. Catherine longs to be an artist but believes that she cannot be one. She tells David,

> The whole way here I saw wonderful things to paint and I can't paint at all and never could. But I know wonderful things to write and I can't even write a letter that isn't stupid. I never wanted to be a painter nor a writer until I came to this country. Now it's just like being hungry all the time and there's nothing you can ever do about it. (53)

Catherine's constant self-fashioning can be understood as a result of this frustrated artistry; unable to create more traditional forms of art, she turns to her body as the one palette available to her. Indeed, Catherine's language reflects this understanding of her body-fashioning; she speaks of her haircuts in terms of a project that she has carefully considered, planned, and executed, saying, "First I had the idea on the road somewhere after Aix en Provence. . . . But I didn't know how it would work or how to tell them how to do it. Then I thought it out and yesterday I decided . . ." (47). Her efforts to include David in this refashioning, too, are exercises in artistry—she is "creating" a new person out of the material of her husband. When, under her direction, David suntans with her and cuts and bleaches his hair exactly like hers, Catherine becomes the creator and David her creation—she is the Artist/God and David the Art/Being created in her own image.

Catherine's artistry and her destruction of David's stories are often read by critics as a feminist response to the pressures of the patriarchy—a patriarchy that dictates art's parameters and constituents, establishes men as creators, and defines women as their creations, muses, or often, as obstacles to their artistic fulfillment. Thus, for instance, Kathy Willingham argues that

> Catherine's suffering and presumed descent into madness relate directly to her
> debilitating insecurities in the face of the patriarchal dominance of the arts. . . .
> Throughout the novel Catherine struggles heroically to legitimize her creativity,
> and she does so by using her physical body. . . . She literally embraces the avenue
> of artistic expression which "l'ecriture feminine" advocates. (47)

In such a reading, Catherine's unhappiness is a direct result of the patriarchy's refusal to grant legitimacy to her artistry, an oral, not written, artistry (she insists repeatedly that David let her "tell" it), and her experiments with the body as an art form. Willingham asserts, "In every respect Catherine's personal actions signify the larger political revolution that Cixous maintains results inevitably from a woman's liberation" (59); thus, destroying David's stories is a triumphant assertion of woman's freedom from the "art" that would constrain her. Indeed, the story burning prompts the final break between Catherine and David, which can be read as the achievement of female independence.

And yet, such readings fail to consider Catherine's ever deepening unhappiness throughout the novel. They also overlook her reasons for wanting to be an artist and the reasons her body is not serviceable enough to embody those artistic endeavors. Why, if she is proudly challenging patriarchal artistry, does Catherine tell David "I was getting impossible again, like a painter and I was my own picture. *It was awful*" (54, emphasis added)? One could argue that *Hemingway* has failed to live up to his creation, has abandoned "feminine" or androgynous writing for the "masculine text"[9] when he ensures that his character, Catherine, remains unfulfilled despite her creative experiments and descends into "madness" at the novel's end. But I think Catherine's unfulfillment is linked more closely to her own, modernist confusion of Art with God.

The essential question is "Why does Catherine want to be an artist?" One answer is that Catherine is afraid of death and the loss of all she has seen, felt, heard, and *been* that death brings. When Catherine complains that she can't write or paint and David reassuringly says, "The country is here. You don't have to do anything about it. It's always here. The Prado's here," Catherine responds, "There's nothing except through yourself. . . . And I don't want to die and it be gone" (53). When David again reassures her, saying, "You know what you saw and what you felt and it's yours," Catherine again responds, "But what about when I'm dead?" (53) and, a moment later, "I can't stand to be dead" (54). Death obliterates transitory human experience, but Art—paintings, sculptures, novels—can commemorate, preserve, represent, and immortalize those experiences and, to some degree, the artist himself/ herself. Thus Catherine's creative body-fashioning will never be enough for her because the mortal body cannot immortalize experience; therefore, so it is essential to Catherine that David, by writing the honeymoon narrative, preserve her experience for her.[10]

That fear of death, and the desire for art to preserve her, is deepened by Catherine's and David's continued investment in the religious mythology that sees their sex/gender experimentation as sinful; as Comley and

Scholes note, they "quickly begin speaking of their new sexual adventures in a language drawn from cultural and religious discourses that regard such activities as abhorrent" (56). Although David attempts to draw on rational, liberal, modern thought to explain away his feelings of guilt, he fails to do so, thinking after one encounter, "You're lucky to have a wife like her and a sin is what you feel bad after and you don't feel bad. *Not with the wine you don't feel bad, he told himself, and what will you drink when the wine won't cover for you?*" (21, emphasis added). Catherine, nicknamed Devil by David, looks for reassurance after her sexual experiments, asking him, "You don't think I'm wicked?" (17), but what is clear is that not only does David think so, but *she* does as well. Indeed, her attempts to twin with David are intended to bind them in sin; after David, once again, cuts his hair like hers, she tells him, "[W]e're damned now. I was and now you are. Look at me and see how much you like it" (178).

Catherine's and David's failure to sustain a new garden is also linked to the importance of gender and family to the national project. In *Imperial Leather,* Anne McClintock explores the constitution of the nation through the interworkings of race, class, and gender, and her revelations clarify what is at stake for both the Bournes and America. McClintock suggests that national, political, and imperial structures are established and justified through the manipulation of the idea of the traditional, gendered family:

> [T]he family offered an indispensable figure for sanctioning social hierarchy within a putative organic unity of interests. Because the subordination of woman to man and child to adult were deemed natural facts, other forms of social hierarchy [such as those based on race and class] could be depicted in familial terms to guarantee social *difference* as a category of nature. The family image came to figure *hierarchy within unity* as an organic element of historical progress, and thus became indispensable for legitimizing exclusion and hierarchy within nonfamilial social forms such as nationalism, liberal individualism and imperialism. The metaphoric depiction of social hierarchy as natural and familial thus depended on the prior naturalizing of the social subordination of women and children. (45)

Such ideological standbys as "The Family of Man," "The Father of Nations," and "The White Man's Burden" are examples of such use of the familial trope to justify nationalism and imperialism. In order to recognize *what* makes Catherine's sexual experimentation dangerous, and *for whom,* we must consider that Catherine and David Bourne are clearly meant to represent young Americans abroad. Their honeymoon in Europe is a kind of reverse colonization—the richer, whiter, younger Americans, fresh from the victories of World War I (which, one may recall, began America's ascent to world power) return to the old country that has been devastated by the same war that has, perversely enough, empowered their own nation. In fact, David Bourne directly associates his and his wife's activities with such reverse colonization, stating, "The Russians are gone, the British are beginning to be poor, the Germans are ruined, and now there is this disregard of the established rules which can very well be *the salvation* of the whole coast. *We are pioneers* in opening up the summer season which is still regarded as madness" (167, emphasis added). As modern pioneers, engaged in an errand of salvation into the wilderness of old Europe, the Bournes are always distinguished from their surroundings. They are never depicted as the naïve, brash, or classless Americans in confrontation with the European aristocracy (as such American are, for instance, in much of Henry James's work). Instead, the Bournes are always a commanding presence: rich, white, and leisured, empowered to order whatever they like from the surrounding "villagers" who seem to exist primarily to serve them. For instance, while in France, the Bournes apparently buy forgiveness for their unconventional attire:

> They gave twenty francs which was more than a dollar then and since the priest took up the collection himself their attitude toward the church was known and the wearing of shorts in the village regarded as an eccentricity of foreigners rather than an attempt against the morality of the ports of the Camargue. (6)

Later, in Spain, the Bournes are the sole occupants of a small hotel whose proprietors literally cater to their every whim: stocking their preferences in wines and food; speaking deferentially at every encounter; complimenting the Bournes on their eccentric hairstyles; and, with the introduction of Marita to their company, even overlooking the menagé-à-trois taking place before their eyes. As Catherine puts it, rather wryly, "We're good clients. What the good client does is très bien" (83). *The Garden of Eden* is permeated with references to race and gender, but *class* is the element that enables experiments with race and gender *and* that must be absolutely repressed throughout the novel. Class is *necessarily* reduced to economic power—the Bournes are richer, therefore of higher class, therefore able to command their surroundings—because to acknowledge *another* form of class would be to undercut the foundation on which the Bournes's (and America's) power is based.

Money and class are deeply imbricated in the problems that confront the Bournes as they attempt to transform themselves. It is because the Bournes represent American—America as white, rich, and young—that Catherine's attempts at gender transformation are dangerous—they are dangerous to the National Myth that is based on a strict, familial gender pattern. In fact, Catherine's entry into the family matrix, her transformation from single girl to *wife*, is rooted in economics; as she reminds David, the big checks deposited in her account are "because I'm married. I told you it was the best thing for us to be married" (26). Catherine is rewarded financially for performing the role prescribed for her by her society, but she must continue to fulfill that role in order to function as a legitimate representation of The State. Thus, the *outward* signifiers of her *inward* transformation—masculine dress, hair, and later, a female companion whom she kisses openly—threaten not only David's masculinity but also the America she, as a good wife and potential mother, must represent. Catherine's experimentation with her sexuality and gender is actually a challenge to the social role prescribed for her by that sex/gender assignment and thus a challenge to the familial structure upon which national mythology depends.

Catherine's desire for David to join her in the gender-bending, tanning, hair-cutting and coloring experiments are based in part on her recognition that her society will exert tremendous pressure against the changes she wishes to effect. She attempts to forestall that pressure by getting David to join forces with her against society; thus, for instance, she tells David "We're not like other people" (27), and "I want us to get darker . . . [because] that takes us further away from other people. You see why it's important" (30). Catherine's urgent desire to separate herself from society, a society that reads her as "white, married female," is accompanied by a desperate need for David to embark on that project with her, in part because she senses that she cannot undertake the journey alone. These shared sex/gender experiences are also a way of giving David access to and sympathy for female experience. Thus, Catherine tells David, "You know it isn't so easy to be a girl if you're really one. If you really feel things," and when David replies, "I know," she stresses, "Nobody knows. I tell you so when you're my girl" (86).

The ghostly "America" haunting this novel, however, always means something quite different for Catherine than for David, despite their shared experiences, because David remains attached, however, ambivalently, to his nation in a way that his wife is not. His ambivalence is suggested by his reaction to a letter from his publisher that assures him that he has "validated his promise" as a writer. He thinks, "The hell with how it was in New York and the hell with that thin-lipped bastard Coolidge fishing for trout in a high stiff collar in a fish hatchery in the Black Hills we stole from the Sioux and the Cheyenne and bathtubbed ginned up writers wondering if their baby does the Charleston" (59–60). David's bitter diatribe emerges from the stark contrast between the ideal and actual America. The President, leader of a great nation, man of courage and honor, engaging in the manly activity of fishing in the beautiful natural world, is actually a cheat, fishing in a well-stocked commercial hatchery, and leading a nation of thieves. As a young, white American male, David presumably once believed the myth of America, and the discovery that reality diverges quite sharply from that myth disgusts and disheartens him in a different way than it would for someone who never believed that myth.

The implicit criticism of commercialism here, however, belies the fact that economics ties David firmly to his nation. His purchase, while abroad, of both the New York Herald and the Chicago Tribune, his careful perusal of letters from his publishers, and his press clippings demonstrate his continued attachment to America. The gulf dividing David from Catherine is located in the economic sphere and is best illustrated by their different attitudes toward the press clippings David receives from his American publishers. David reads his clippings and his letters and immediately proceeds to calculate how much money his new book will earn; for him, the United States, whatever else it may represent for him, is the locus of both his fame as a writer and his income—an income that saves him from depending on his wife. Catherine, however, is terrified of the clippings. They represent a dangerous intrusion into her marriage and a threat to the new identities she is designing for herself and for her husband: she tells David, "I'm frightened by them and all the things they say. How can we be us and have the things we have and do what we do and you be this that's in the clippings?" (24).

The "David Bourne" represented in the clippings presents a powerful antithesis to the "David Bourne" Catherine is creating, and the arguments between David and Catherine about the clippings foreshadow the issues that will destroy their marriage. For Catherine, any intrusion from the past, from America, from others, is a threat to her attempt to reconstruct new identities for herself and her husband. For David, however, the clippings represent his identity as a newly-famous American writer, an identity he intends to keep. Thus, when Catherine declares, "If the reviews had said it was worthless and [the book] never made a cent I would have been just as proud and just as happy," David thinks "I wouldn't," although, ominously enough for their marriage, "He did not say it" (25).

In fact, another reason for the failure of the Bournes' experiment is that David remains deeply invested in his art and his identity as an artist. Whereas sex for Catherine is a way of crossing boundaries and binding people together in love or damnation, sex for David has always been a catalyst for his art, an art created in solitude. With Catherine, however, David does not "have that sudden deadly clarity that had always come after intercourse" (13) to generate his art, and, thus, she poses somewhat of a problem for him. She does not want to be a catalyst for art; she wants to be the subject of art and, indeed, the artist herself. Thus, even in the earliest weeks of their relationship, David is already considering how and when he will "get back to work" in terms that emphasize the sharp division David makes between work and love, writing and Catherine:

> It would be good to work again but that would come soon enough as he well knew and he must remember to be unselfish about it and make it as clear as he could that the enforced loneliness was regrettable and that he was not proud of it. He was sure she would be fine about it and she had her own resources but he hated to think of it, the work, starting when they were as they were now. *It never could start of course without the clarity* and he wondered if she knew that and if that was why she drove beyond what they had for something new that nothing could break. (14, emphasis added)

Catherine's insistence that David write about them is an attempt to combine love and the art—to make love (and herself) the focus and fruit of work. But David has an almost Puritan devotion to his work—it is a separate, holy enterprise, the preserver of self and sanity that defends David from the onslaught of Catherine's demands. David thinks of his work as the real, important, serious business against which Catherine is first a pleasant distraction, and later a deadly enemy. At first, he thinks, "When I have to work I will. Nothing can stop that. The last book is good and I must make a better one now. This nonsense that we do is fun although I don't know how much of it is nonsense and how much is serious" (31), but, as Catherine's "nonsense" begins to interfere increasingly with David's life, he retreats into his work: "You better get to work, he told himself. . . . You better get to work. You have to make sense there. You don't make any in this other" (146); "She understands it [the work] less and less. But you've worked well and nothing can touch you as long as you can work" (211); "He cared about the writing more than about anything else, and he cared about many things" (211). Catherine attempts to compete with the work (each time David works, she cuts her hair or experiments sexually with a woman, etc.), but when David stops writing the honeymoon narrative, she realizes she has failed. Catherine's burning of David's African stories is a last-ditch effort to seize control of the work and join it to their relationship; she succeeds, however, only in destroying the last remnants of their marriage.

That destruction has caused critics to read the relationship between the African or "elephant" story and the honeymoon narrative or "Catherine's story" as competing narratives, whether they favor the novel or the short story contained within it.[11] These readings have made several important connections between the two competing stories but have overlooked what I see as the most important connection between them. That connection is located in David's investment in his identity as a white, male American author and the part Africa plays in the construction of that identity. Although, like Catherine, David's identity is intimately connected to Africa, the "Africa" of David's imagination, unlike Catherine's, is a real place—David has been there and had experiences he transforms into stories that represent the continent, the people, and his own history. They are works of fiction based in reality, what Catherine calls "historical" stories.

These stories are not representative of anything so much as they are of David's struggle for self-mastery (mastery of his own identity, of his ability to create/sustain/present that identity) and mastery of the text, both the "fictional" text and the "real" text of history. David's Africa is as imaginary as Catherine's but more dangerous because it is an illusion represented as truth—a truth that suppresses and denies the deeper truth of the roles blackness, whiteness, and violence play in the construction of personal and national identity.[12] In fact, narrative control is essential to historical representation, and thus the struggle for mastery of the text is a prevalent theme in American literature that seeks, in part, to tell the story of America. By returning to Africa, the place of his childhood, David seeks to seize control of his own story and, implicitly, America's. David's African stories are his *bildungsroman*—through enduring hardship, learning the ways of the wilderness, persevering to reach a goal, gaining knowledge, and, finally, rejecting his father, David becomes an American man. David's identity as a white, American male is thus formed from the African jungle and against, in part, the nameless "natives" whose stories are never told.

The "blackness" that enables David to become a man is acknowledged cursorily by the inclusion of a second, African father figure in the text—his father's friend Juma, a man who "had always been David's best friend and had taught him to hunt" (171). Juma speaks only Swahili, which must be interpreted for David and the reader by David's father's American voice. Such necessary interpretation, however, as Toni Morrison points out, also silences the African's voice and increases the white man's authority.[13] To have Juma's story told for him by a white American is to enable the American to shape not only his own story, but the African's as well.

Juma, in fact, is saddled with being the victim of violence—the elephant wounds him badly—and the perpetrator of it—he kills the elephant's "askari" and administers the final death blow to the elephant. Thus the violence and killing taking place in Africa, most likely at a white man's behest, are finally located in the African himself. However guilty are David and his father, the real guilt is laid at Juma's doorstep. American innocence, if not preserved entirely, is at least partially upheld through transference of the guilt to an African.

The violence of this story indicates that David Bourne also participates in the "regeneration through violence" that Richard Slotkin documents as a prevalent theme in American literature, although this violence is transformed, transferred, and projected throughout David's stories.[14] There are two African stories in *The Garden of Eden*, both violent, but only one is represented in the text.[15] In the story we are given, David accompanies his father and Juma on an exhausting trek through the jungle that culminates in the elephant's slaughter and David's realization that he hates not only elephant hunting, but his father(s) as well. After this experience, David decides that he must remember to "Never tell anyone anything ever. Never tell anyone anything again" (181).

Such willful silence is the weapon of the powerless—a withholding of truth so damaging to oneself, or potentially damaging to one's people, that it must remain unspoken. Silence, too, according to Doris Sommer, may be a willful resistance to interrogation, a protection of self from the would-be-interrogator. Sommer has carefully explicated moments of such silence in what she calls "resistant texts" where information is deliberately withheld and attention called to that withholding.[16] Such silence is a strategy, a deliberate refusal to reveal all for an unspoken purpose, concomitant with a declaration that information is being withheld. There is danger involved in comparing the silence of an angry white child to that of a disempowered, oppressed adult; certainly, their positions, status, experiences, and suffering are not to be equated. At the moment when David decides to be silent, however, he *is* suffering intensely from his own disempowerment. David's inability to protect the elephant that he knows he betrayed by "telling" not only frustrates and saddens him, but causes him to retreat to the only defensive weapon he has at hand—a decision not to tell anyone anything ever again.

What is remarkable, however, is that the silent child becomes a writer of semi-autobiographical stories, narrating his experiences as a child in Africa, as a wartime pilot, and as a lover on his honeymoon. When David becomes an adult, he does tell the story—because he, not his deceased father, now has control. David's writing, his investment in his identity as an author, can therefore be linked to his will-to-power: power to shape his own identity, to re / present his father and his father's story, and narrate/create history. What is significant is the difference between the history David chooses to tell and the one that he ostensibly tells but which remains unrepresented in the text. The story that David tells, the slaughter of the elephant, is a story of his own disempowerment and decision to silence himself. In effect, by retelling the story, he reclaims the voice he lost as a child (and claims the right to tell not only his own father's story, but Juma's as well). What he chooses not to tell, at least in the text, is more significant: the story of the slaughter of human beings by his father. Unlike the elephant story, in which the tracking, shooting, injury to Juma, and the elephant's death are represented in graphic detail, this story remains a blank space. We have snippets, references, opinions voiced, just enough to pique the reader's interest, such as Marita's declaration that it's a "terrible story and it's wonderful" (154), and Catherine's counter-assertion that "It's horrible. . . . It's bestial" (157). David states matter of factly, "It's a story about Africa back before the 1914 War. In the time of the Maji-Maji War. The native rebellion of 1905 in Tanganyika. . . . It's a story that happens in Africa when I was about eight years old" (157). Finally, we have Catherine's description of it as "that horrible one about the massacre in the crater and the heartlessness of your own father" (223).[17]

The Maji-Maji revolt of 1905–1907 is perhaps the most significant African rebellion of the early twentieth century, an event that not only threatened German control over its African colonies and forever changed colonial rule in East Africa, but also destroyed huge expanses of African land and nearly erased whole African peoples. The revolt was sparked when the German authorities began "the forced cultivation of cotton by peasant farmers in German East Africa" (Roberts 126), and soon spread throughout many diverse peoples, all of whom rose up against the whites and their African soldiers. The final result of the rebellion was mass slaughter, mostly of Africans: "On the German side, some 400 were killed, including 15 whites; in retaliation the Germans laid waste large areas and starved whole peoples into submission. Over 200,000 people may have died as a result of the rising, and much of the south-east was permanently depopulated" (654). Still, the specter of African revolt haunted colonial Africa from that point on, and many changes in policies were made as a result of that violent uprising.[18]

This East-African history is distant from the United States; after all, it was the *Germans* who plundered and destroyed Tanganyika. It is linked, however, to the history of the United States by two rather salient points. The first one is that David's father, an American, clearly participated in the retaliatory slaughter. The second point is that this uprising was a revolt of Africans against the forced growing of *cotton*—the one crop that remains most closely associated with slavery in the United States. The history that David writes, but which remains silenced in the text we have, is, in a sense, a transference of the violence at the heart of America's own history. The colonization and slaughter of Africans in German East Africa is substituted for the enslavement and often murder of Africans at the hands of Americans—deeds excused and justified in the name of "King Cotton."

The sense of empowerment that David gains from his status as a writer, his ability to shape and tell a story according to his own needs and desires, and, in fact, his ability to narrate history, explains why Catherine has become so dangerous to him—she wants to control the story by dictating what stories he tells. He is similarly threatened by the identity, or identities, Catherine wants him to assume. Catherine wants David to be a dark female; in fact, usually she wants him to become her—calling him, for instance, "My sweet dearest darling Catherine . . . my sweet my lovely Catherine" (56). Catherine is obsessed with her own *inability* to write; thus, for David to become black, female, and especially Catherine, to become a person without control of the narrative and history. A change in David's identity, however temporary, is also a change in status—a change from the status of master/subject (of himself, of history, of the text) to slave/object.

There is another reason, however, even more deeply obscured, for David's fear of becoming Other—a fear linked to his father's African children. This fear is so deeply repressed as to be scarcely represented in the text—but it is there, nonetheless, and I believe it is perhaps the deepest reason for David's final rejection of Catherine's project. Acknowledgment of these black children consists of interlinked, vague, almost buried references: David's assertion that "It [the story] started with the evil in the shamba" (93); the referral to "his Kamba servant and brother who shared with him the guilt and knowledge of the delay . . ." (129); his oblique statement that "he wondered why there was no drumming from the shamba. Something was strange if his father was there and there was no drumming" (160); and Catherine's description of the story as depicting his "drunken father . . . not knowing which ones of the little horrors he had fathered" (189). Taken together, these statements indicate, at the very least, that David's father engaged in interracial sexual relations and, most likely, that David discovered this fact, perhaps even witnessed the act. Thus, there is the possibility that David has part-African brothers and sisters. David's reference to his "Kamba brother and servant" is most likely meant to alleviate potential criticism of David for having a "servant" by making their relationship fraternal (*i.e.,* friendly). But such a characterization not only raises the specter of "miscegenation," but also recalls the very real historical fact that white children often played with their black brothers and sisters while, at the same time, exercising the power of master over their enslaved siblings.

David's having African siblings reveals not only the lie at the heart of the myth of America, but also the tenuous nature of one's own status as "white," and thus, the almost arbitrariness of the benefits accorded to one by that status. If "they" are black, and thus inferior, semi-human, and enslaved (or colonized, in this case), and you are white, and thus superior, fully human, and free (the colonizer, in this case), but you all share the same father, on what "fiction of law and custom" is your status based (Twain 29)? On the status of your different mothers? But how, in fact, can you be absolutely certain that a slight taint of the "tarbrush" hasn't swept over your maternal line? How do you know that you will never be revealed as something other than you think you are?[19]

David Bourne's nearly absolute repression of the existence of his black siblings, as well as his apparently overwhelming need to remember them, is part of the larger national story. The categories of whiteness and blackness, so fundamental to the structure of American identity and society, are fictions presented as fact for the convenience and empowerment of one at the expense of the other. David's assertion, then, that "They [his father and Juma] would kill me and they would kill Kibo too if we had ivory," although immediately followed with the declaration that he had "known it was untrue" (198), indicates, again however subtly, that the white child (and reminiscing adult) sensed the dangerous tenuousness of one's position—especially when economic gain or loss is involved.

The troubling suggestion of "miscegenation" and loss of one's identity that is entwined with the possibility/probability of having mixed-race, unacknowledged siblings is further complicated in this text by the fact that Catherine's insistence of "twinning" with David is also faintly incestuous in nature. Their natural resemblance to each other is marked from the onset of the novel: "Most people thought they were brother and sister until they said they were married. Some did not believe that they were married and that pleased the girl very much" (6). Their matching haircuts, clothes, suntans, and hair color, all acquired at Catherine's behest, serve to heighten this natural resemblance to the point of twinship, and Catherine, at one point, calls David her "good lovely husband and [her] brother too" (29). Thus,

Catherine's desires touch upon David's deepest fears, fears with which he has been obsessed for many years. To enter into an incestuous, racialized relationship with Catherine is, in a sense, to re/enter into a kind of displaced relationship with those lost, African siblings—even, in fact, to (at least momentarily) become one of those siblings.

David is attracted to the possibility of being black, female, homosexual, and even incestuous; he admits that to himself as he contemplates his new haircut/color:

> "So that's how it is," he said to himself. "You've done that to your hair and had it cut the same as your girl's and how do you feel?" He asked the mirror. "How do you feel? Say it."
>
> "You like it," he said.
>
> He looked at the mirror and it was someone else he saw but it was less strange now.
>
> "All right. You like it," he said. "Now go through with the rest of it whatever it is and don't ever say anyone tempted you or that anyone bitched you." (84)

David not only decides that he does, indeed, like his new, feminized/twinned appearance, but that he will accept responsibility for liking it. His gazing into the mirror for confirmation of his identity marks his entry into a feminine space for a moment in that his contemplation of his mirror image echoes those multiple moments of mirror gazing by women documented by Jenijoy LaBelle, who argues that the mirror wields crucial power over women in the construction of their identities.[20]

Both Catherine and Marita gaze into mirrors at various points for solitary moments in apparent efforts to re/gain a sense of self. Catherine does so right before she cuts her hair for the first time, the moment marking her (supposed) entry into masculinity, and again, immediately after her entry into "lesbian" sexuality: "When she came back to the room David was not there and she stood a long time and looked at the bed and then went to the bathroom door and opened it and stood and looked in the long mirror. Her face had no expression and she looked at herself from her head down to her feet with no expression on her face at all" (115). Marita, too, gazes into Catherine's mirror when she replaces Catherine in the role of "Mrs. Bourne," again, in what seems to be a moment of contemplation of self-identity: "She went over to the door of the bathroom and looked at herself in the full length mirror. Then she smiled at the mirror" (244). There are also several instances of Catherine and David looking at themselves in the mirror; for instance, Catherine tells David, "Look at us in the mirror on the bathroom door" (43), and again, "Look at us together" (175), which they do. Indeed, the one purchase Marita, Catherine, and David make for the hotel in which they live is a mirror for the bar so that, according to Catherine, "We can all see each other when we talk rot and know how rotty it is. You can't fool a bar mirror" (103). The mirror, by reflecting one's physical appearance, offers a confirmation of identity: "See," the mirror says, "that's who you are." Thus, when David first cuts his hair like Catherine's, he tells himself, while looking in the mirror, "You like it. Remember that. Keep that straight. You know exactly how you look now and how you are" (85). David equates how he looks with who he is.[21]

In fact, all this mirroring and remirroring indicates David's and Catherine's increasing uncertainty about their identities. The more David and Catherine experiment with their appearances in an effort to reshape their identities, the more vulnerable they become to the mirror's/society's gaze. In other words, dependence on refashioning one's image to refashion one's self renders that self increasingly vulnerable—one becomes dependent on the mirror, the Other, society, to tell one who one is. In attempting to break free of the society that has produced them by changing their appearances, David and Catherine have only cemented their dependence upon that society more firmly. They have accepted the "fact" that one's exterior (one's color, features, genitalia) signifies who one is and, consequently, what status one will occupy.

David's increasing vulnerability to the mirror's reflection is in direct conflict with his desire to wield power and shape his own story; thus, he becomes increasingly uncomfortable with Catherine's project. His decision to break with Catherine is signified by his refusal (after he has again acceded

to her request to bleach his hair) to look in the mirror. That refusal to look is
a refusal to become Catherine's double, to become the feminized, Africanist
subject/object of her desires:

> "I wish you could see yourself," Catherine said.
> "I'm glad I can't."
> "I wish you'd looked in the glass."
> "Just look at me. *That's how you are and I did it and there's nothing you can
> do now. That's how you look.*"
> "We couldn't really have done that," David said. "I couldn't look that way
> you do."
>
> · · · · ·
>
> David looked at her eyes that he loved and at her dark face and the incredibly
> flat ivory color of her hair and at how happy she looked and he began to realize
> what a completely stupid thing he had permitted. (177–78, emphasis added)

The "incredibly stupid thing" David has permitted is the abdication of his
status as the powerful, white, male author and the concession of that power
to Catherine. Catherine, at this moment, has become the Artist and David
the Artist's object. But David Bourne is too invested in his identity as a
writer and the power that identity gives him to accept this new status, and
a short while later he signals his impending break with Catherine by telling
her "I'm through with the narrative" (188). From this point on, David rejects
Catherine's behavior as madness and bonds with Marita. Catherine burns
David's stories and leaves, ostensibly to find artwork and publishers for the
honeymoon narrative. Marita and David become "the Bournes," and David
rewrites the African stories and "there [is] no sign that any of [them] would
ever cease returning to him intact" (247).

Critics have read this ending in a variety of ways. Nagel, for instance,
sees it as a happy ending in which David has achieved artistic power, arguing, "What is most significant about the conclusion . . . is . . . that David has
been able to transform the difficulties of his present life into significant art
by using present emotions to capture the feelings of the past" (337). Jones

also approves the novel's ending as evidence of David's return to his rightful place, writing, "David Bourne's resolve to put aside the honeymoon narrative and write the elephant story symbolizes the reclamation of his identity as a man and as a writer" (6). Other critics, however, reject the ending as inappropriately optimistic, preferring Hemingway's alternative manuscript ending in which Catherine returns and she and David agree to commit suicide together; Comley and Scholes argue that

> The published novel also offers this sanitized relationship [David and Marita] as a happy ending in which innocence has been recaptured and the serpent Catherine banished so that Eden may be Eden once more again. . . . It is, then, a great pity that Scribner's has treated us as if we were Kurtz's "Intended" instead of allowing us to come to grips with the complexity of sea changes and tribal things in Hemingway's unfinished novel. (102–03)

Burwell also sees the ending both as inappropriate and, in fact, as evidence of David's *failure* to grow as an artist, arguing, "His ability to rewrite the African stories rapidly . . . [is] not a triumph over his writer's block; [it is] a crystallization of his resistance to a feminine mode of experience, resistance that for a time the androgynous experience threatened to dissolve" (1973, 213).

Although I agree with Burwell that this ending does represent a failure on David's part, I believe that to read the published ending as happy, whether or not one agrees with it as an appropriate choice, is a misreading of the text. In order to read the ending as David's reassertion of independence, whether one applauds or bemoans that act, one must first overlook Marita's role in the Bourne family drama. Marita intends from the onset of her relationship with the Bournes to claim David for her own. When David and Marita are first alone, she tells him, "Your wife is wonderful and I'm in love with her," quickly adds, "I'm in love with you also" and then makes a rather curious comment, stating, "I'm glad I'm smaller [than Catherine]" (98). Marita represents herself as the truly feminine woman—the small one, the blushing one, the appreciative and supportive one who claims that "Nothing I do is important" (112). She is also the "true woman" sexually who, immediately after she seduces Catherine, claims that "perversion" is "overrated and silly. . . . It's only something girls do because they have nothing better" (120) and later tells Catherine, "I'm . . . more of a woman than you are" (192). She compounds this hypocrisy by playing "hard to get" with David, telling him "I love to kiss you. . . . But I can't do the other" (126), performing the role of "virtuous female"—the Madonna to Catherine's whore.

At every opportunity, Marita pretends to defend Catherine while insinuating herself into David's confidences, playing on his anger and bewilderment at Catherine, telling him, for instance, "Poor David. What women do to you" (140), while declaring her real intention to "find things to do that will hold you" (141). She holds him, in fact, by being a better wife than Catherine. She tells Catherine (in front of David) that she must leave David alone because "he's in the middle of a story," asking her "Haven't you any conscience at all?" (152). Later, in bed with David, Marita signals her superiority to Catherine and her intention to replace her by asking David, "You don't want me to do her things? . . . *I can do them better than she can*" (185, emphasis added). Finally, after Catherine leaves, David tells Marita "We're the Bournes. It may take a while to have the papers. But that's what we are" (243), and Marita "looked at herself in the full length mirror. Then she smiled at the mirror" (244). That smile is a smile of triumph at her success in ousting Catherine.[22]

By deciding to divorce Catherine and marry Marita, David abandons all attempts to reconfigure identity and erase boundaries delineating traditional concepts of gender, race, and sexuality. As I read it, David Bourne thus abandons all attempts to write a new America in which whiteness, maleness, and heterosexuality, as represented by the patriarchal family, no longer constitute American national identity. Catherine, the generative spirit of that reconstitution of identity, is rejected and dismissed—she will not fill the role of white wife and mother and thus she must be cast out of the (national) story. She is replaced by a new Mrs. Bourne who is eager to fill the role of supportive wife to the creative male artist. Marita Bourne will make sure that David will "have [his] men friends and friends from the war and to shoot with and to play cards at the club" (245). She will also ensure, however, that he will not have "any women friends. . . . Fresh, new ones who will fall in love and really understand you and all that" (245). Marita, unlike Catherine, is taking no chances.

"The papers" David refers to are, of course the divorce papers from Catherine and marriage license for the Bournes—the legalization of their relationship by the state. David's impending divorce from Catherine and proposed marriage to Marita (if consummated) represent reentry into proper matrimony, sanctioned by the state and, in fact, the basic structure upon which the state is formed. David's abandonment of the honeymoon narrative and his rewriting of the African stories are also a return to the proper story: the story of the white American boy gaining mastery of himself and the text—and the narrative of history in which whiteness emerges out of the darkness of Africa. David's return to that story, his decision to rewrite the old stories rather than write new ones, represents his renewed commitment to, and entrapment by, the same old mythology, the same old story of America.

A final note: After David Bourne introduces Catherine to the blustering Colonel, the Colonel says, enigmatically, "The get's no good" (63). David assumes the Colonel is referring to their potential children and tells the Colonel, "There's isn't any get yet" (63). In fact, the only "get" that David and Catherine produce is the honeymoon narrative—the book that Hemingway wrote but never published. In a sense, then, Hemingway's "get," *The Garden of Eden,* must have remained, for him, "no good." Why it was no good for Hemingway remains open to speculation, but I would like to suggest that its existence proves that David Bourne's failure was not Ernest Hemingway's. *The Garden of Eden* may have, in the end, only reentered the circle of American consent/dissent/consent/dissent, but it does offer momentary glimpses of other gardens, and other potential configurations of self and, implicitly, the nation to which those selves belong. That it ultimately reconfigures the same old relationships and tells the same old story evinces more than anything else, the strength and power of American mythology over its citizens.

NOTES

1. That ambivalence inspires me to turn to Homi Bhabha's brilliant theorizing of the colonial situation, which I find to be useful in exploring Hemingway's work. According to Bhabha, in the colonial situation authority is always constituted by, with and through the *ambivalence* the wielder of that authority feels when confronted by the object / (subject) against which that authority is exercised. That ambivalence arises, in part, out of the inherent paradox involved in the command "Be like us but not too much alike" given to the colonized subject. Much of Bhabha's work focuses in some manner on the results of that ambivalence: in "The Mimic-Man," for instance, Bhabha locates resistance in the colonized subject simply in that subject's existence—the appearance of a man (Bhabha does not contemplate the difference gender may make in this schema) who is "almost but not quite white," whose very presence testifies to the inherent lie at the heart of the colonizing mission (which purports to want to "civilize" the colonized, make him/her "another (English) man," and yet, when such a transformation more or less occurs, refuses to grant equal status to that subject). Thus, as Bhabha states in "Signs Taken For Wonders," "colonial discourse has reached that point when, faced with the hybridity of its objects, the presence of power is revealed as something other than what its rules of recognition assert" (112); confronted by the colonized who has fulfilled the command, "Be like us," but is still excluded from becoming "one of us," the colonizer must simultaneously recognize and repress the knowledge of the "civilizing mission."

   This suppressed knowledge on the part of the colonizer results in a space of resistance for the colonized; as Bhabha states, "The ambivalence at the source of traditional discourses on authority enables a form of subversion, founded on the undecidability that turns the discursive condition of dominance into the grounds of intervention" (112). That subversion can manifest itself in various forms; what interests me here is the *possibility* that such ambivalence and subversion can exist, as I read it, in the *absence* of the colonized subject's *presence*—that the *knowledge* of the lie at the heart of *one's own society* can be enough to produce a sense of ambivalence toward that society and result in subversion of it on the part of the *colonizer*.

2. It is not my purpose to reconstitute Ernest Hemingway as a sensitive, politically correct individual who has been wrongly accused of sexism, racism, and so forth. Hemingway's abuse of others is well documented and is not my concern here. Rather, I am interested in locating the stresses apparent in Hemingway's fiction that arise out of his position as a privileged white male and his recognition, no matter how repressed, of the problems inherent in the constitution of his self and his power in his society.

3. I am aware of the continuing controversy over the Scribner's heavily edited edition of the novel. I have not had the opportunity to review the manuscripts, but I gather from the reports of others that while the differences in major themes are not significant, the edited version of Hemingway's work differs from the original manuscripts in very important ways. A most insightful analysis of the significance of such differences has been written by Debra Moddelmog in "Protecting the Hemingway Myth: Casting Out Forbidden Desires from *The Garden of Eden*." Moddelmog argues convincingly that Jenks' version of the novel is "written in effect by a cultural myth" (93) in an attempt to preserve and protect the public Hemingway for his readership. The result is a version of *The Garden of Eden* that meets the "psychic, social, and sexual needs of a segment of the American public," primarily, of course, readers invested in the mythical figure of "Papa," a man's man among men (93). For the purposes of my argument, the most significant difference (among many) is perhaps the chosen ending of the novel. If, for instance, the novel had ended with the provisional ending of Catherine's and David's proposed mutual suicide, *The Garden of Eden* would not read as such a complete reinscription of the national myth. By focusing on the published version of this work, although done out of necessity, I think my article contributes to the ongoing debate over how and why texts are produced for a reading public. Indeed, an underlying question posed by my argument is, Is it possible to write against a tradition, one often (certainly in Hemingway's case) created and reinforced by one's own past work, and thereby imagine and construct a very different kind of "America" and "American"? Given the "collaborative" nature of this posthumously published novel, one that Hemingway either could not, or would not, finish, it would seem that in Hemingway's case, it most certainly was not possible. For discussion

of the issues involving the editing of the novel, see Carl Eby's "'Come Back To The Beach Ag'in, David Honey!': Hemingway's Fetishization of Race in *The Garden of Eden* Manuscripts"; several articles in *The Hemingway Review* 10:2 (Spring 1991) including Jenks's defense of his work; Nancy R. Comley's and Robert Scholes's, *Hemingway's Genders: Rereading the Hemingway Texts;* and, of course, Moddelmog's article. I am deeply indebted to Moddelmog for her incisive comments on my earlier reading of *The Garden of Eden.*

4. Obviously an underlying tenet of this reading is that "selves" are constructed, *at least partially,* in and through the community, that web of social desire and control in which those selves are born, live, and die. Indeed, the power of that state and culture is not "present" in the novel in the sense that it is openly discussed or examined; rather, that power shadows the novel as a ghostly presence, hovering on the verge of embodiment at moments when the characters evince a sense of shame, guilt, or fear. Thus, "the Nation" as I read it in this text reflects Michel Foucault's conception of society as a vast web of elusive but interrelated and co-productive elements that exert hidden but powerful pressure on the individuals who exist within it.

5. For fascinating explanations of these two general claims, please see Toni Morrison's *Playing in the Dark: Whiteness and the Literary Imagination* and Eve Sedgewick's *The Epistemology of the Closet.*

6. Of course, it could also be argued that Catherine's outburst is against a racist story in which Africa and Africans are represented in derogatory ways by a white man.

7. The problem of conforming one's outward appearance to reflect one's inward identity is complicated further by the recognition that such "inward identity" may be a fiction.

8. Catherine's dilemma seems closely related to the one faced by Judith Butler who (in the wake of criticism of *Gender Trouble,* in which she reads gender as "performative") answers the question, "What about the materiality of the body?" (1993, ix). Butler suggests that perhaps "certain constructions of the body [are] constitutive in this sense: that we could not operate without them, that without them there would be no 'I,' no 'we.' . . . We might suggest that bodies only appear, only endure, only live within the productive constraints of

406   Rewriting the Self Against the National Text

certain highly gendered regulatory schemas" (xi). In fact, to assume that one can change one's gender like a change of clothes not only ignores the process of gendering itself, the incorporation of such gender *as* one's self, but also the fact that without such "constitutive construction" there may be no self at all. When one adds the difficulty of gender performativity to the multitudinous difficulties surrounding arguments about "race," Catherine's dilemma becomes clearer.

9. See Rose Marie Burwell's "Hemingway's *Garden of Eden*: Resistance of Things Past and Protecting The Masculine Text." Burwell puts the blame on the character, David Bourne; yet one senses that David's failure, in Burwell's eyes, is really Hemingway's, particularly after reading her longer study of four Hemingway novels entitled *Hemingway: The Postwar Years and Posthumous Novels*. She writes, "The androgynous honeymoon narrative now threatens to mingle with the masculinist African stories. . . . Because Catherine enters the writing through the honeymoon narrative on which she insists he work, she, like the old elephant, must be removed . . ." (121). Who, after all, "removes" Catherine from the text but the author? Although Burwell's work offers much insight, I think Toni Morrison is perhaps a better reader of Hemingway when she writes of *The Garden of Eden*: "The inner story [African stories] Catherine despises and eventually destroys. She thinks it boring, irrelevant. David ought to be writing about her instead. The reader is made to understand and be repelled by her selfish narcissism. But in fact she is right. At least Hemingway thinks she is, for the story we are reading and the one he has written *is* about her" (89, emphasis in the original).

10. Despite her insistence on the importance of finishing the narrative, Catherine's despair may not be assuaged by the narrative's completion; she tells David, "I'm older than my mother's old clothes and I won't outlive your dog. *Not even in a story*" (163, emphasis added). Statements such as these, I believe, bolster my contention that Catherine is ultimately a tragic, not triumphant, figure.

11. See, respectively: Rose Marie Burwell's *Hemingway: The Postwar Years and the Posthumous Novels*: "When Catherine, whom David has begun to see in images of ivory, and who wants David to focus his critical energy on the honeymoon narrative which gives her a voice, comes too close to the African

stories, David symbolically kills her by abandoning the honeymoon narrative"
(107) and "The androgynous honeymoon narrative now threatens to mingle
with the masculinist African stories. . . . Because Catherine enters the writing
through the honeymoon narrative on which she insists he work, she, like the old
elephant, must be removed" (121); Robert B. Jones's "Mimesis and Metafiction
in Hemingway's *The Garden of Eden*": "Within this Eden, under Catherine's
domination, Bourne produces dully prosaic, mannered melodrama; and his
loss of artistic integrity follows from his loss of selfhood. Contrastingly, the
elephant story is symbolically Bourne's text, the product of an authentic selfhood" (11); James Nagel's "The Hunting Story in *The Garden of Eden*": "What
is most significant about the conclusion, however, is not that the marriage has
come to its predictable end but rather that David has been able to transform
the difficulties of his present life into significant art by using present emotions
to capture the feelings of the past" (337).

12. In order to see how this representation of Africa functions in the construction of
    David's personal and national identity, it is useful to recall the racially entangled
    weave of American history. Although black and white were constructed as
    entirely separated races, there was a vast and profound intermixing of not only
    cultures, but people, which resulted in the birth of children who, denied the
    status of legitimate inheritors of their white father's rights, privileges, wealth
    and identity, enriched their fathers as chattel. The myth-makers of American
    culture were hard pressed to explain those children, and that pressure emerges
    in American literature as the fear of (and very real possibility of) becoming the
    Other. That fear is sometimes repressed, as in Edgar Allen Poe's *The Fall of The
    House of Usher* or *The Narrative of Arthur Gordon Pym*, sometimes exploited,
    as in Herman Melville's *Moby Dick* or Mark Twain's *The Tale of Pudd'nhead
    Wilson*.

13. See Morrison's discussion of the implications of the silence of Harry Morgan's
    black companion in *To Have And Have Not*.

14. For further discussion of the theme of the regeneration of violence in America,
    see Slotkin's *Regeneration Through Violence*.

15. Burwell refers to *three* such stories; unless one counts the novel entitled *The
    Rift*, however, I cannot find a third story.

16. Sommer discusses such moments of silence throughout her article "Resisting The Heat: Menchu, Morrison, and Incompetent Readers."

17. A suggestive note: David's first novel is referred to only by the title, *The Rift*; no mention is made of the content of that novel. In reading about the Maji-Maji rebellion, however, I came across this notation: "All these [certain tribes who fought in the revolt] lived in the highland area south east of Lake Victoria and west of the Rift Valley" (Iliffe 1969, 9). Perhaps, then, this first novel was also about the rebellion; if so, it would indicate that David Bourne has been obsessed with the events of this revolt for a very long time. Burwell also makes an astute connection between this novel and David's past:

> What little can be discerned about the link between David's memories of life in Africa and his vocation as a writer is suggested by the title of his autobiographical first novel, *The Rift*, that indicates the geological depression of Africa (the Great Rift Valley) as well as the breach between David and his father that the African stories develop. (*GOE* 205)

Burwell, however, does not continue to develop that link further.

18. For a detailed examination of the Maji-Maji revolt, see John Iliffe's *Tanganyika Under German Rule 1905–1912*. In this text Iliffe argues, interestingly enough, that the "Maji Maji became a mass movement because it acquired an ideological content which persuaded people to join and fight. The ideology was religious" (24). Africans were evidently convinced that an important religious leader could protect them from German bullets through the ingestion of magic water, or maji. See also, John Iliffe. *A Modern History of Tanganyika,* in which he details the results of the uprising throughout colonial Africa.

19. Of course, such speculations may seem slightly paranoid, yet many nineteenth-century texts explored those very questions. Kate Chopin's short story, "Desiree's Baby," links paternal power and authority to whiteness and then reveals the awful consequences when that power is exercised against the wife of the plantation owner whose child's features evince "tainted blood"—only to have it revealed that it is the plantation owner himself who bears that blood. Mark Twain, in his critical exploration of slavery, *Pudd'nhead Wilson,* creates a world in which it is revealed, after all, that black is white and white is black—and that the purportedly white son of the master can, in fact, be sold down the river. Both

stories not only evince the real arbitrariness underlying racial designations, but forcefully undercut the white, paternal authority on which the American nation, and her story, is based. In an instant, both stories say, the master can become a slave. The white American's most fearful nightmare can thus become reality—one could, literally in a moment, be revealed as an imposter and become the disempowered and dehumanized Other.

20. Drawing on Lacan's famous conception of the mirror stage, LaBelle argues that although ". . . the mirror stage . . . is for Lacan a single, originary event . . . I have found that, for women, mirroring is not a stage but a continual, ever-shifting process of self-realization" (10). In a society where women, all too often, *are* their face and form—defined and valued in terms of their physical appearance—the mirror is instrumental in the construction and recognition of the self. The mirror reflects not just the physical woman, but society's definition of her personhood—the mirror, a representative of society's (male) gaze, tells a woman who she is. LaBelle states:

> . . . In European culture for at least the last two centuries a female self as a social, psychological, and literary phenomenon is defined, to a considerable degree, as a visual image and structured, in part, by continued acts of mirroring. Many women have accepted such definitions, and as a result their self-identities have an exteriority—and hence a vulnerability—greater than masculine egos. (9)

21. The narrator, however, contradicts David's presumption, adding, "Of course he did not know exactly how he was. But he made an effort aided by what he had seen in the mirror" (85).

22. Of course, all of Marita's machinations and David's apparent helplessness against them can also be read as evidence of Hemingway's famous tendency to blame his marital infidelities on other women, and thus exculpate himself from his own guilt. For documentation of this tendency, see any biography of Hemingway, especially Mark Spilka's.

The Taxation of Ernest Hemingway

Anthony E. Rebollo

I happen to have worked hard all my life and made a fortune at a time when whatever you make is confiscated by the govt. That's bad luck.

—Ernest Hemingway (SL 537)

Introduction

Ernest Hemingway's comment about the "confiscation" of his fortune refers to the federal taxes he was required to pay on the income generated by his literary works. Viewed in isolation, the comment could be viewed as ordinary griping or cynical exaggeration. But it should not be so easily dismissed. Taxpayers of Hemingway's era, particularly writers and others with fluctuating income, were hit hard by tax rates that seem unbelievably high by today's standards. As a result of those rates, which approached and then exceeded 90 percent, federal income taxes were an ever-present concern for high-income earners

Reprinted with permission from *The Hemingway Review* 26.2 (Spring 2007). Copyright © The Ernest Hemingway Foundation. Published by the University of Idaho, Moscow, Idaho.

■ 411

of the 1930s, 1940s, and 1950s. It should come as no surprise, therefore, that tax and tax-related issues were regularly discussed in Hemingway's private correspondence, and even crept into some of his novels.[1]

Why are these tax matters of any significance to Hemingway scholars? The answer, quite simply, is that they fill a gap in the existing biographical accounts of Hemingway's life and his literary career. Those accounts, while exhaustive on many levels, do not discuss the fundamental tax principles which came to occupy so much of his time, thoughts and efforts. To be sure, many of the scholarly accounts of Hemingway's life address aspects of taxation, particularly Michael Reynolds's *Hemingway: The Final Years,* which recounts insightful facts and figures about certain tax matters and discusses Hemingway's frustrations with one of his tax attorneys, Alfred Rice. But, for the most part, existing biographies contain little information about taxes beyond references to how much tax Hemingway paid during certain years.

Intended to assist in filling the information gap, this article will demonstrate that Hemingway personally dealt with, or wrote about, most of the major tax concepts embodied in the *Internal Revenue Code.* That was no mean feat because concepts in the *Code* range from ordinary civil issues, to criminal issues, to core questions about what will or will not be taxed, how earnings are taxed, and when they are taxed.

Hemingway's written observations about such concepts establish that taxes played a surprisingly prominent role in his professional and personal life. The question of how best to describe that role is complicated, however, by the broad and varied principles covered by the tax laws. Here, I will follow the general framework and sequence of the tax concepts addressed in the *Internal Revenue Code.*

Using the *Code* as a guidepost, this article commences with a brief overview of the basic tax issues that Hemingway had to consider during the early- to mid-20th century, followed by a discussion of some of the common methods he employed to lessen the impact of taxes. Throughout the article, Hemingway's written observations and comments about such tax matters are noted, including his curious late-life remarks about the state of his tax affairs and possible investigations by the Internal Revenue Service. Finally, the article concludes with an overall assessment of Hemingway's outlook on and approach to dealing with crushing federal taxes.

The "Infernal" Revenue Code

> Am over-due in Cuba now the way things are going and when I get there must do my income tax. I wish the bastards in addition to taking all your money (or only 90%) did not have to take two weeks to a month out of your working life. . . .
>
> —Ernest Hemingway (*SL* 893)

Although Hemingway was born in 1899, when there was no federal income tax in force in the United States, his first earnings from full-time employment were generated less than five years after the 1913 enactment of the income tax laws. As Hemingway progressed as a writer and his income increased over time, Congress seemingly kept pace with him by continually increasing both income tax rates and the complexity of the tax laws. The increases were a by-product of Depression-era legislation and the need to fund three wars that happened to be fought during Hemingway's lifetime (World Wars I and II and the Korean War). What started out in 1913 as a base income tax of 1% eventually rose to an all-time high of 91% during the 1940s.

In the early part of Hemingway's career, his lower income and the relative simplicity of the tax laws undoubtedly kept the administrative burden and aggravation of dealing with taxes to a minimum. But at the years passed and the tax rates increased, tax matters became more and more of a distraction, especially because Hemingway took an active role in preparing his own tax returns. In the 1940s, he found himself in the 90% tax bracket (Reynolds 162), and ultimately came to view the tax season as "the bastardly income tax epoch that comes to interrupt and bitch work just at the best working time" (*SL* 881).

Until 1955, tax returns were due in March, which meant that the time spent on tax matters was especially substantial during the fall and winter of each year. In addition, mandatory income tax withholding laws did not take effect until 1943; before the enactment of those laws, the only reliable method of ensuring that there would be sufficient funds at year-end with which to pay taxes was periodically to plan for and track income and expenses. Consequently, mid-20th century taxpayers actually devoted considerable time and energy to tax issues throughout the entire year. As evidenced by his personal letters, this was true for Hemingway as well.

In addition to spending time on preparing his tax returns, Hemingway was forced to pay periodic installments on his taxes. Frequently, this meant making arrangements to borrow money to pay taxes and then making arrangements to repay those loans. His comment to Harvey Breit, found in a 29 June 1952 letter, is typical: "Have to pay back the money I borrowed for income tax and have set aside other money for this year's income tax. It leaves damned little with the over-head here" (SL 773).

The basic tax considerations for professional writers at the time were as follows. First, were the earnings from writing subject to tax in the first place, or could they fit within a statutorily defined "exclusion" from income? If not, the next question to be considered was *when* the income was subject to tax. Because of the way tax rates were structured, pushing income into future years, or spreading the income back into prior years could make a big difference in the bottom-line tax dollars owed. Another key consideration was whether the income was "ordinary," and therefore taxed under the usual set of tax rates, or whether it could be characterized as "capital gain," which was taxed under a set of much lower rates. Finally, whenever the earnings were reported as income, the taxpayer had to consider whether there were deductions that could be claimed to minimize the "net income" and thereby reduce the tax.

In dealing with these tax issues, Hemingway was assisted by Maurice Speiser, an actual "Philadelphia lawyer" whom he met in Hendaye, France at a barbershop in the late 1920s (Scott). For two decades, Speiser handled a variety of legal issues for Hemingway, as evidenced by the correspondence preserved in the Speiser and Easterling-Hallman Foundation Collection of Ernest Hemingway at the University of South Carolina. With respect to tax matters, Speiser not only provided advice regarding the computation and payment of periodic income tax installments, he also assisted Hemingway with engineering amendments to the tax laws in 1942, following the critical and commercial success of *For Whom the Bell Tolls.*

After Speiser's death in 1948, Alfred Rice took over primary tax assistance responsibilities for Hemingway. Rice, who has been described as "inexplicably maladroit," could turn the annual preparation of income tax returns into a "marathon event" (Reynolds 303). In some instances, Hemingway's frustration with Rice's handling of certain tax matters was palpable. In a 7 December 1957 letter to A. E. Hotchner, for example, Hemingway complained bitterly about an unexpected tax liability from years past, which he attributed to "what at best could be overall ignorance" on the part of Rice (qtd. in DeFazio 230). Nevertheless, Rice remained with him to the end and, even after Hemingway's death, Rice continued to represent Mary Hemingway.

Despite the professional assistance Hemingway received (or in some cases, because of it), he took an active role in trying to understand and address each of the tax issues listed above.

Exclusions for Foreign-Earned Income

> What with war and all last year now find have to pay tax on around 30,000 income. Been figureing that business all day. Fortunately don't have to pay on money earned outside the country because was away over six months so won't have to pay on all that.
>
> —Ernest Hemingway (*SL* 477)

While the tax laws broadly define what types of receipts will constitute taxable income, there have always been at least a handful of "exclusions from income." One such exclusion provision, which still exists and was present in Hemingway's time, involved the receipt of "earned income" generated while working outside of the United States. The provision was a bit tricky, however, and was a narrowly defined exception to the general rule that United States citizens are subject to tax on their worldwide income.

In essence, taxpayers of Hemingway's era were permitted to exclude "earned income" generated from work performed while residing, for a certain required amount of time, outside of the United States. Beginning in 1926, individuals who were "bona fide residents" of a foreign country (or countries) could qualify for the exclusion by living and working outside the United States for a period of six months. In 1942, however, the six month period was lengthened to one year. Because the definition of "bona fide resident" was difficult to meet, in 1951 Congress implemented an alternative "physical presence" test, allowing an exclusion of foreign "earned income" if an individual could show that he or she was physically present in a foreign country or countries for seventeen months out of a consecutive eighteen month period.[2]

Hemingway referenced this test in a 10 March 1953 letter to A. E. Hotchner, his agent and an attorney. In the letter, Hemingway disparagingly described individuals who claimed the exclusion from income under the eighteen-month physical presence test (because they could not meet the bona fide residence test) as follows: "Probably all those 18 month non tax guys will be the founders of the next great American Fortunes. The former ones were founded by the people who didn't fight in the Civil war (1861–1865)" (qtd. in DeFazio 142). The "non tax guys" were individuals who had no real interest in living outside the United States, apart from the tax benefits that their presence in foreign countries may have secured.

Because Hemingway lived and worked so much of his adult life outside of the United States, one might expect that the exclusion provision provided him with a steady, reliable method of reducing, if not eliminating, his United States income taxes. That was not the case, however, because the definition of "earned income" hinged on working for someone else, either as an "employee" or under a contract for certain specified services. As a result, royalties from book sales by a self-employed author, even if a United States citizen with a bona fide year-round residence outside the country, generally did not qualify for the beneficial tax treatment.

However, Hemingway could avail himself of the benefits of the exclusion provision in some circumstances. It applied, for example, to pay he received while working on assignment as a war correspondent during World War II. His wife at that time, Martha Gellhorn, was similarly employed and, according to Hemingway, she was motivated (perhaps too motivated) by the fact that the exclusion applied to pay she received for her work as a journalist. Writing to Charles Scribner on 29 October 1947, Hemingway remarked that he "used to wonder in 1944–45 how long Martha would have stayed at the wars if her Colliers dispatches had suddenly been ruled taxable rather than tax free and if she had not had an expense account and the hospitality of the Generals" (*SL* 630).

When the exclusion for foreign earnings did apply, the tax savings to Hemingway were substantial. In June 1948, Hemingway used the exclusion provision to his advantage when he agreed to A. E. Hotcner's request to write two short stories for *Cosmopolitan* for the sum of $15,000. A nontaxable payment of that amount was the equivalent of a $75,000 payment subject to tax—a function of the high tax bracket that would have applied to Hemingway's earnings for that work had the exclusion not been applicable under the circumstances (Reynolds 174).

Actors and motion picture companies made liberal use of the foreign-earned income exclusion provision, particularly in the 1950s. With the adaptation of Hemingway's novels and short stories into movies and television programs, there was even consideration given to whether Hemingway could qualify for the exclusion by claiming at least a portion of his payments for services as an "actor." But while Hotchner mentioned this idea on at least one occasion,[3] it is clear that, for Hemingway, trying to fit himself in to the exclusion provision as an actor, a researcher, or some other type of Hollywood employee was not a priority and, for that matter, had never been.

While the extraordinarily high tax rates of the mid-20th century were undoubtedly a motivating factor for the decision by some celebrities to live and work in foreign countries, that simply was not true for Hemingway. Early on, he had decided to live and work abroad and, while incidental tax benefits were a bonus, they were certainly not the reason for Hemingway's choice of residences. For instance, as early as 3 March 1919, Hemingway wrote to Jim Gamble that "I'm patriotic and willing to die for this great and glorious nation. But I hate like the deuce to live in it" (*SL* 21). At that time, his income was very modest and tax considerations were not a factor in his desire to live outside of the country. Some thirty years later, even after his income had increased substantially, his outlook was the same. The reasons that Hemingway gave for choosing to live in Cuba—the favorable working conditions there, the fact that cockfighting was legal, the proximity of the Gulf Stream, and the live-pigeon matches held at the shooting club–had nothing to do with tax or financial matters (*BL* 403–404).

In the final analysis, Hemingway did not choose to live in France, or Cuba, or anywhere else, in order to escape the effects of "confiscatory" United States taxes. Even if he had been so motivated, the exclusion for foreign earned income could never have provided a complete fix because his royalties did not qualify as "earned income." Accordingly, Hemingway had to consider questions about when and how the proceeds from the sales of his works would be taxed.

The Effect of the Annual Accounting Concept and "Progressive" Tax Rates

> It has been considered a hardship to tax fully the compensation of writers, inventors, and others who work for long periods of time without pay and then receive their full compensation upon the completion of their undertaking.
>
> —Maurice Speiser

The federal income tax system, both now and during Hemingway's time, is based on an annual accounting period and "progressive" tax rates. The concept of an "annual accounting period" basically means that an individual taxpayer pays tax based on net income or gains that are received in a given tax year, usually from 1 January up to and including 31 December. A system with a "progressive" tax rate structure is designed so that a high-income individual, such as an actor or entertainer, will pay a larger percentage of tax on his or her annual income than an individual with much less income.

Successful writers like Hemingway were especially hard-hit by the taxes due to a combination of factors—the nature of their work as writers and the interplay between the annual accounting period and progressive tax rates. For example, several years of work on a novel would probably mean that there was very little income during those years. While deductible expenses over the same period may have been high, their usefulness was limited, because they could be claimed for the year in which the expenditures occurred and were therefore capped by the limited income generated during that year. As a result, expenses from one year could not be netted out against the eventual profits in a later year, when the novel was released for sale to the public. Both the nature of the profession and the annual accounting system combined to produce problems like these.

The progressive tax rate structure further compounded difficulties for a writer who had several years of little or no income followed by a sudden, dramatic increase in income (for instance, during the year that a novel was released). The tax paid by such a writer during the year of the spike in income would ordinarily be much higher than the tax he or she would have paid had the same amount of income been received in equal installments during the several years it took to write the novel. Within a tax system with progressive rates, two individuals with exactly the same income and deductions over the same multi-year period can pay substantially different amounts of tax, depending on the timing and receipt of income within that same multi-year period.

Methods of avoiding the effects of this unfortunate set of circumstances were few, but important. They largely consisted of attempts to "time" the receipt of income, so that an otherwise large influx of income could be "unbundled" to reduce taxes by "pushing" income into future years, or by "spreading back" the income into previous tax years. This could be accomplished legitimately under some circumstances and, when they could, Hemingway and his attorneys attempted to do just that.[4]

Pushing Income into Future Years

> May have to come after the first of the year on some tax business. I wish you
> wouldn't pay me any more money the rest of this year if you can help it. Can't
> you pay it next year?
>
> —Ernest Hemingway (SL 530)

To take advantage of "timing" issues, contracts or payment schedules could
be drafted in a way that would ensure receipt of funds in a later year or
years, as opposed to bunching the receipt of the income in the then-current
year. To do this properly, careful advance planning was required, usually
in the context of contract negotiations. It also required careful monitoring
afterwards, to ensure that the terms of agreements on the timing of payments
were followed. This explains statements like the following, from a letter
Hemingway wrote to Maxwell Perkins in November 1943: "Charley suddenly
cabled asking if I wanted all of some 29,000 now or next year. I want it as it
was promised in the contract or agreement between Grosset [and] Dunlap,
yourselves and me and not suddenly in a lump sum upsetting my estimate
and declaration of expected income according to contracts made" (SL 553.
Bracketed insertion by Carlos Baker).

    Without a contract requiring future payments according to a pre-
determined schedule, an old tax principle called "constructive receipt"
prohibited taxpayers from refusing income payable in one year simply so
that it could be received and reported as income in the next. The doctrine of
"constructive receipt" essentially provides that when a "taxpayer has the power
to receive but voluntarily does not receive a receipt it shall be considered as
if it were received" (Kragen 423). Even if the doctrine of constructive receipt
posed no problem, however, attempting to "push" the receipt of income
into the future could only help so much. At some point, it would become
impractical and have the effect of the "tail wagging the dog."[5]

    A second approach to dealing with timing issues, though not without
its own drawbacks, was an early form of "income averaging," which allowed
certain taxpayers to spread back income from one year over several prior

years in order to smooth out the tremendous tax liability that otherwise would have been caused by a sudden spike in income.

The Need to "Spread Back" Income Into Prior Years

To illustrate the point, an outstanding American book, recently completed after a 7-year period of research and preparation, was offered for sale to the public in December 1940, but it was not until 1941 that the author received the great bulk of his compensation in the form of royalties and proceeds of motion-picture rights.

—Maurice Speiser

A tax statute enacted in 1939 provided a crude mechanism by which certain taxpayers could "spread back" income earned in one year over more than one prior tax year, provided that (a) the work undertaken to generate that income had been in progress for at least a five-year period and (b) 95 percent of the income from those efforts was received in a one-year period. Unfortunately, the law was far from adequate and was difficult to apply.

While the categories of income qualifying for the "spread" were limited, it was clear from the beginning that Congress intended the law to cover income generated by writers. Nevertheless, the actual language of the statute was unclear and gave rise to questions about whether its beneficial effects applied to writers who were self-employed (as opposed to those working for others). There were also questions about whether the time periods and other criteria used to determine whether income could be "spread" made any sense, or were simply arbitrary.

The intricacies of the income-averaging provision were not lost on Hemingway's attorneys, who wished to ensure that the benefits of the spread back would be available to self-employed writers like their client. In 1942, following the success of *For Whom the Bell Tolls*, Hemingway's attorney, Maurice Speiser, along with attorney G. Campbell Becket, weighed in with a memorandum to the United States House of Representatives Committee on

Ways and Means, then considering legislation to amend certain provisions of the Internal Revenue Code.

In their memorandum, which is part of the legislative history of the Revenue Act of 1942, Speiser and Becket summarized the main tax problem for writers and artists as follows:

> Under existing law, such persons [*i.e.,* writers who work for long periods of time without pay and then receive their full compensation upon the completion of their undertaking] have their income for the whole period aggregated into the final year. This results in two inequities: First, only the deductions, expenses, and credits of the final year are changeable against the compensation for the full period; second, under our graduate surtax, the taxpayer is subjected to a considerably greater burden because of the aggregation of his compensation. (3401)

In essence, Speiser and Becket urged Congress to remedy the then-existing law because it did not fit well with the actual financial realities of many writers. Without naming the author or the novel, they illustrated their concerns about the law by referring to "an outstanding American book," which "was offered for sale to the public in December 1940, but it was not until 1941 that the author received the great bulk of his compensation in royalties and motion-picture rights" (3402).

Concerns like those expressed by Hemingway's attorneys resulted in amendments and clarifications to the tax laws. After enactment of the Revenue Act of 1942, the new "spread back" provision made it clear that independent authors, or self-employed writers, could qualify for its beneficial effects. Second, the requirement that the work in question had to have been conducted over a five-year period was shortened to a much more realistic three-year period (and shortened again in 1954 to a two-year period).

The 1942 amendments to the law did not fix every problem. For one thing, the computation required to "spread" the income could be tremendously detailed and time-consuming. This is evidenced, in part, by Hemingway's "tax prep" documents for tax years 1940–1945, maintained by the Department of Rare Books and Special Collections at Princeton University.

"Ordinary Income" Versus "Capital Gain"

> Also, there is a strong possibility that in selling a block of stories like this it can
> be regarded as a capital transaction which means that tax can't disturb it. I'm
> going to see Al [Rice] today and give him this gen.
>
> —A. E. Hotchner (qtd. in DeFazio 97. Bracketed insert by DeFazio)

The characterization of income as ordinary income versus capital gains could also have a dramatic effect on the amount of tax paid. While the top-end tax rate for ordinary income soared during Hemingway's lifetime, the rate of tax for gain on the sale or exchange of property was substantially lower. In 1954, for example, the top rate of tax on capital gains was 25 percent, more than 60 percent *lower* than the top rate of tax imposed on ordinary income.

As the name implies, "capital gain" arises from the sale of "capital assets," which basically includes all property held by a taxpayer. There was an important exception to the general definition of that term, however, which specified that the term "capital asset" did not include "property held by the taxpayer primarily for sale to customers in the ordinary course of his trade or business."[6] Accordingly, the sale of literary works by professional writers did not qualify for capital gain treatment; a professional's literary output was viewed as property held for sale to others in the ordinary course of the author's business of writing.

Amateur writers, on the other hand, were not viewed as being "in the business" of writing, and *could* sell literary works and receive capital gain treatment. That particular loophole was eliminated in 1950, after negative publicity arising out of the capital gain treatment that General Eisenhower was able to secure with respect to payments for his war memoirs. The favorable tax treatment for Eisenhower's earnings from writing did not go unnoticed by Hemingway. Writing to Edmund Wilson on 8 November 1952, Hemingway cracked that "When Eisenhower received his tax free money from the Democrats for his book he became a Republican" (*SL* 793).

In any event, professionals who were "in the business of writing," and therefore unable to have their literary property meet the definition of a "capital asset," attempted to get around that by "splitting" their copyright interest in literary works. Royalties—payments to an author for the right to publish his or her work—were taxed as ordinary income. But the right to use the same literary property as the basis for a television program or a motion picture might legitimately be viewed as a *separate* right arising out of their copyrighted published materials. If so, an author could claim that because he or she was not "in the business" of supplying stories to the television or motion picture industry, the sale of that separate right was eligible for capital gains tax treatment.[7]

It is unclear to what extent Hemingway pursued or was successful in securing capital gains treatment for the sale of motion picture rights arising out of his literary works. However, the subject of how best to structure payments from television and motion picture studios was given careful consideration by the author and his advisors, including Rice and Hotchner.[8]

Deductions From Income

> I hope you will point out to the Internal Revenue people that it is necessary to spend money to make money.
>
> —Ernest Hemingway (*SL* 832)

In the event that funds received for writing were not excluded from income, and were therefore taxed either as ordinary income or capital gain, the amount of tax could be reduced by expenditures incurred in connection with the production of the income.

In general, "ordinary and necessary" expenses incurred in a trade or business are deductible from income and, therefore, can reduce the bottom-line tax that is owed. For capital assets, expenditures relating to the property may increase the property owner's "basis" (in other words, the amount invested) in that property. This is important because only amounts received in excess of basis are taxed when the property is sold. From the government's standpoint, the key question is whether deductions claimed by a taxpayer were actually business-related, or whether they were non-deductible personal expenses.

Establishing that expenses are ordinary and necessary can be difficult for a writer. The cost of paper is clearly a deductible expense. But could the same be said for expenses incurred on an African safari which later formed the basis of a popular short story or best-selling novel? The answer to that question, like many things in the tax law, is not "black and white" and will depend on the facts and circumstances of each case.

In a 12 July 1954 letter to Alfred Rice, Hemingway argued persuasively that deductions attributable to his 1953–54 African safari, as well as his field work for the movie version of *The Old Man and the Sea*, were absolutely legitimate, ordinary, and necessary expenses incurred in connection with the production of income. Even so, Hemingway recognized that his inability to obtain receipts in small Cuban coastal villages or in the heart of Africa could pose a problem when it came time to substantiate those expenses: "You can't go along the Cuban coast writing checks and checks don't get you very far in Africa where people will not even take paper money" (*SL* 833).

Even much earlier in his career, Hemingway was clearly aware of the importance of deductions, as well as the difficulties that could be encountered when trying to claim them. In a 12 August 1930 letter to Maxwell Perkins, for example, Hemingway made the tongue-in-cheek remark that he had "6 more cases of beer good for 6 more chapters," adding that "[i]f I put in an expense account on this bull fight book it would be something for the accounting Dept to study" (*SL* 327). On a more serious note, Hemingway once complained to Alfred Rice that "This time I have really wonderful stuff to write but now when I should be writing I am chasing receipts and writing letters like this" (*SL* 832).

As he grew older, Hemingway lamented the fact that writers, due to the nature of their profession, were limited in their ability to claim deductions for the full range of expenses they incurred. As Hemingway saw it, he had literally worn himself out—in car accidents, airplane crashes, and other events—in an effort to further his work as a writer. Yet he was afforded little or no tax relief for this, unlike other taxpayers who could reduce their income with deductions for depreciation as they tapped into and wore out *their* diminishing resources. It seemed unfair to Hemingway, who wrote Alfred Rice that he figured to "make more money for the Government than any Texas oilman that get's his depreciation" (*SL* 833).

Successfully Navigating, and Complying with, the Internal Revenue Code

> Since I am not familiar with the new Revenue laws Mary has listed things and left it up to you to decide whether they are deductible (833).
>
> —Ernest Hemingway

To one degree or another, the tax law has always been confusing. Even the courts, which regularly analyze and interpret the law, have recognized this. One judge, prefacing his written analysis of a tax issue, put it this way: "We shall now embark on a voyage through the various sections of the Income Tax Regulations which are enough to boggle the mind of an English-speaking U.S. citizen" (qtd. in Katz 623).

No matter how well-versed one is in tax law, there are some tax issues and concepts which are difficult even for attorneys and judges. In Hemingway's estimation, his own attorney, Alfred Rice, had not always gotten things right and, on at least one occasion, had committed some troubling "tax mistakes" (qtd. in DeFazio 273).[9]

The Internal Revenue Service (which was known as the Bureau of Internal Revenue until 1952) conducts "audits" to ensure that the tax laws are being correctly interpreted and applied by taxpayers. In an audit, the key question is whether the taxpayer has reported and paid the correct amount of tax. More often than not, the examining agent will propose adjustments at the end of the audit, resulting in an increased tax liability and penalties.

While both the IRS and the courts recognize that arranging one's tax affairs to minimize tax is permissible tax avoidance, legitimate tax avoidance can sometimes evolve into tax evasion, a criminal violation under United States law. The difference between avoidance and evasion hinges on a taxpayer's intent, which can be difficult to ascertain due to the complicated nature of the tax laws. Indeed, intent is so important in criminal tax cases that the law imposes a burden on the government to "negat[e] a defendant's claim of ignorance of the law or a claim that because of a misunderstanding of the law, he had a good-faith belief that he was not violating any of the provisions of the tax laws" (Chase).

Accordingly, one of the keys to successfully navigating the tax laws, at least in terms of avoiding the most severe types of tax penalties, rests with good-faith efforts to comply with the law. The flipside to a good-faith intent to comply with the tax law is *mens rea* or the "guilty mind."

Tax Crimes

> And he lay now, with no kindly blurring, denied all that chemical courage that
> had soothed his mind and warmed his heart for so many years, and wondered
> what the department had, what they had found and what they would twist, what
> they would accept as normal and what they would insist was evasion . . .
>
> —Ernest Hemingway (*THHN* 234)

In the passage quoted above, Hemingway describes the plight of an executive anguishing over the state of his tax affairs as he spends the night on a yacht lying at a finger pier in the Key West marina: "On one of the largest yachts, a handsome, black, barkentine rigged three-master, a sixty-year-old grain broker lay awake worrying about the report he had received from his office of the activities of the investigators from the Internal Revenue Bureau" (*THHN* 233).

The grain broker is unable to dull the pain of those worries with Scotch high balls, having been forbidden such comforts by his doctor, who has informed him that drinking as usual will kill him. This makes the situation insufferable and, as his mind races through the night, he reflects on his life and on the tax problems at hand: "His remorse was to think if only he had not been quite so smart five years ago. He could have paid the taxes then without any juggling, and if he had only done so he would be all right now" (*THHN* 236).

Over the course of several pages, Hemingway describes the inner workings of the grain broker's mind. It is precisely these types of thoughts that a good prosecutor will endeavor to present to a jury in order to prove the existence of *mens rea* needed to obtain a conviction.

Hemingway's "To Whom It May Concern" Memorandum

> My wife Mary at no time believed or considered that I had ever committed any illegal act of any kind. She had no guilty knowledge of any of my finances nor relations with anyone. . . . She knew nothing of any misdeeds nor illegal acts and had only the sketchiest outline of my finances and only helped me in preparing my [tax] returns on material I furnished her.
>
> —Ernest Hemingway (*SL* 909. Bracketed insert by Baker)

As noted throughout this article, Hemingway repeatedly dealt with substantive tax questions during his career, for years on end. He had Speiser and then Rice available to assist him with such matters and, from his correspondence, it appears that he had a good grasp of basic tax concepts and that his tax affairs were in good order. That being the case, his 4 December 1960 "to whom it may concern" memorandum, quoted above, is not only puzzling, but seems oddly out of place and out of character. What prompted that sort of an unsolicited pronouncement?

Hemingway's poor health offers the most likely explanation. By the time he turned sixty in July 1959, Hemingway's physical health and emotional condition were plainly deteriorating, as described in detail by Michael Reynolds in *Hemingway: The Final Years* (321–322, 329–330). James Michener, in his introduction to *The Dangerous Summer*, summed it up this way: "In 1959 Hemingway went back to Spain and during that long, lovely summer . . . he was already beginning to suffer the ravages which would in the end destroy him—monomania about being spied upon, suspicion of his most trusted friends, doubt about his capacity to survive . . ." (12).[10]

In a very real sense, however, many of Hemingway's physical and psychological problems had begun to manifest themselves long before he turned sixty in the summer of 1959. Hemingway had, for example, previously experienced a variety of serious physical ailments with lingering effects, such as the concussions he sustained from an automobile accident in 1944 and two airplane crashes in 1957. In addition, Hemingway had been prone to periodic "cycles" of depression (or "black ass"), at least as far back as 1919 and especially pronounced during the 1943–1944 period. Such depressions were usually linked to the completion of novels, and often exacerbated by other factors, such as tax or financial matters (Reynolds 91, 235–36, 306). Finally, according to Hemingway's biographer Michael Reynolds, the writer had exhibited signs of paranoia and an "irrational fear of the law" as early as his mid-teens (Reynolds 116).[11]

But unlike prior bouts with depressed or other ailments, when Hemingway would eventually re-emerge as his old self after a period of "re-balancing," it was clear by the end of 1960 (if not earlier) that there would be no such recovery this time around. Thus, while at least some of Hemingway's tax problems in 1959 and 1960 were similar to those he had experienced in the past, the true nature and extent of those problems (to the extent there even was a problem) had been magnified many times over in his mind.

Carlos Baker believed that the "to whom it may concern memorandum" was "an unsolicited memorandum designed to free Mary from accusations of complicity in supposed illegal acts in the event that the FBI or the IRS should ever decide to prosecute, as of course they never did, having no cause" (SL 909, fn. 1). While there probably was no rational reason to fear IRS or FBI inquiries, the concern was real enough in Hemingway's mind, and remained that way for the remaining months of his life.

Continuing Fears About Taxes in 1961

In the midst of erratic mood swings, paranoia, and worsening depression, Hemingway purchased *The Operators,* a nonfiction book by Frank Gibney describing the prevalence of "white collar" crime and including a lengthy discussion of criminal tax offenses (1–7, 174–224). Hemingway's purchase of Gibney's book, published in 1960, is confirmed by a January 1961 receipt from Scribner's Book Store, as well as by the book's presence in his Ketchum home at the time of his death (Brasch 30–31, 160). While there is probably no way to know for certain whether Hemingway actually read *The Operators,* it seems likely that he did read it and found its contents unsettling.

Hemingway was admitted to the Mayo Clinic in Rochester, Minnesota on 30 November 1960. On 22 January 1961, he was discharged and returned to his home in Ketchum, Idaho, where he convalesced with his wife, Mary. In the early part of 1961 in Ketchum, Hemingway and his wife engaged in a routine of long morning walks and, in the evenings, "they read from the more than thirty new volumes ordered from the Scribner Book Store . . ." (Reynolds 352). One of those books was *The Operators,* which began with a scenario about a hypothetical executive's workday, demonstrating how seemingly ordinary business decisions, which might be viewed as unremarkable in and of themselves, could actually constitute multiple criminal violations of United States tax laws. The very first criminal violation included in Gibney's scenario is an executive's failure to pay Social Security taxes on the wages paid to his family's maid (1). The possible consequences of such a failure are listed just two pages later, as follows: "Penalty for willful nonpayment of employer's Social Security contributions: $10,000 fine and/or five years in jail" (Gibney 3).

Within a few months after returning to Ketchum, Hemingway, who had seemed somewhat better at first, began to exhibit "more disturbing symptoms of his returning depression" and, "[a]round the solstice, March 21, what began as a simple question—had Mary paid Social Security tax on their maid, Mary Williams—evolved into a full-scale emotional explosion" (Reynolds 353). In short order, the explosion escalated into a "three-day war" (Reynolds 354).

While it could be coincidence (which seems unlikely), the example of the maid in *The Operators* may well have sparked the bitter argument that erupted between Hemingway and his wife over the question of whether Social Security taxes had been paid with respect to *their* maid. During the course of that three-day battle, Mary Hemingway attempted in vain to assuage his fear that if the FBI came to investigate the issue, they would surely look at her checkbook to see whether the taxes had been paid (Reynolds 353–354).

The concerns about the payment of the maid's payroll taxes were not the only examples of tax-based fears expressed by Hemingway in 1961. By April of that year, after being readmitted to the Mayo Clinic in Rochester for a second time, Hemingway continued to articulate deep worries about his federal income tax liability for 1960. He was concerned about whether the funds in his special bank account (which he used to escrow for taxes) would be sufficient to cover both his obligations to the IRS and possible problems with *state* income taxes. And he was also worried about whether FBI agents were monitoring his activities (Reynolds 356–358).

More than forty years after Hemingway's death, it is difficult (if not impossible) to specifically pinpoint the genesis of, or the specific reason for, each one of the tax concerns that manifested themselves with such intensity in 1960 and 1961. However, this much is clear: when it came to tax issues, the *reality* of the situation for Hemingway was that along with financial success as a writer came increased federal income tax obligations which were with him year-in and year-out, a constant source of stress, making demands on his time and energy right up to the end of his life.

The "True Gen" on Hemingway and Taxes

In the late 1940s, Hemingway was audited by the Bureau of Internal Revenue (*SL* 657), not surprising considering the level of success and income that he attained in the prime of his career. Large incomes tend to generate heightened scrutiny. But given all of the time, effort, and money that Hemingway spent on the analysis, preparation, filing, and payment of his taxes during his life, how well or poorly did he actually do when it came to the handling of his own tax affairs?

The short answer is that only Hemingway would know. Carlos Baker, for one, believed that "As a man [Hemingway] loved, and ordinarily did his best to follow, the attributes of fortitude, courage, honor, and thoroughgoing honesty in the conduct of his affairs, including the financial" (*SL* xviii). The present writer agrees.

While Hemingway frequently complained about taxes and was never pleased by paying exorbitant amounts,[12] the overall attitude he expressed about his role and responsibility as a United States taxpayer was exemplary, and right in line with IRS views about how a system based on "voluntary compliance" should function. Consider, for example, the following instructions that Hemingway gave to his attorney, Alfred Rice, in a letter dated 15 December 1948, regarding his 1944 income tax return:

> I do not want you ever to initiate any action for any refunds of taxes without first consulting me and presenting the matter fully to me so that I may judge whether it is an honorable and ethical action to take, not simply legally, but according to my own personal standards. I have been crippled, financially, by taxes but I am as proud of haveing helped my Government in that way as of any aid I was able to give in the field. I do not wish to squawk about being hit financially any more than I would squawk about being hit physically. I need money, badly, but not badly enough to do one dishonorable, shady, borderline, or "fast" thing to get it. I hope this is quite clear. (*SL* 655. Footnote by Baker omitted.)

In tax law, as in any other field, perfection is rare and, in many instances, is simply unobtainable. Even the federal courts have observed that "the law does not require the filing of a perfect tax return" (St. Clair). While it would be a safe bet to conclude that Hemingway's tax affairs were not always perfect, an outlook like the one found in the 1948 letter to Rice can go a long way in the tax world and, for that matter, may be about as perfect as it gets.

NOTES

The author wishes to thank the University of South Carolina for the use of its libraries, and his colleagues at Richardson, Plowden, Carpenter & Robinson, P.A., particularly Vonja Huff (his paralegal), for supporting his efforts to prepare and publish this article.

1. The most conspicuous example of a tax issue appearing in Hemingway's novels is the multi-page discussion of tax problems experienced by the grain broker in *To Have and Have Not* (233–238), mentioned in the text of this article. Taxes are also discussed in *For Whom the Bell Tolls,* when Robert Jordan "explained how the income tax and inheritance tax worked" (207), and there are at least two references to European tax evaders in *Across the River and into the Trees,* including "a particularly notorious multi-millionaire non-taxpaying profiteer of Milan ..." (38, 57). Hemingway's work also contains numerous references to financial matters not directly related to taxes, particularly to the lack of income, such as the early days in Paris when "we were young and nothing was simple there, not even poverty, nor sudden money ..." (*MF* 58).

2. In 1953, the exclusion provision, which had previously allowed an unlimited amount of foreign-earned income to escape United States taxation, was amended to cap the exclusion, so that it applied only to the first $20,000 of foreign-earned income.

3. With respect to payments as an "actor," Hotchner wrote to Hemingway that "Al [Rice] was counting on your pay as 'actor' to up your take because it is tax-free, since it is performed in Cuba" (qtd. in DeFazio 121. Bracketed insert by DeFazio).

4. There are several clear examples of timing issues found in *Selected Letters,* such as the following passage from Hemingway's 21 October 1941 letter to Charles Scriber: "I'll let you know how we want to handle the money business once the picture situation is cleared up. May get quite a good piece of money from there and if that comes this year will want to let all other money go over until next year" (*SL* 519). Other examples of attempts to "time" the receipt of income are quoted in the text of this article.

5. A notable example of 1950s-era tax planning involved William Holden and his contract to perform in *The Bridge on the River Kwai.* His contract reportedly ensured that he would receive 10% of the gross profits of the film, to be paid out in annual installments not exceeding $50,000 per year. Based on the film's

expected earnings as of 1958 (when Holden was about forty years old), the $50,000 per year payments were projected to continue until long after his eightieth birthday, causing some commentators to wonder whether a lump-sum payment, though subject to heavy tax, would have been preferable from an economic standpoint (Gibney 222).

6. The definition of a "capital asset" is set forth in the Internal Revenue Code of 1954, at Section 1221.

7. Despite opposition from the IRS, which rejected the separate asset argument (on the grounds that copyrights were indivisible), the United States Court of Claims issued a ruling in 1952 holding that the exclusive grant of motion picture rights to the copyrighted novel *Forever Amber* (by Kathleen Winsor) was a sale of a capital asset. That court decision was based on facts which predated the Revenue Act of 1950, however, which added a provision specifically defining a copyright as a non-capital asset.

8. There are several good examples of discussions about potential sales of rights for television and movie productions in Albert J. DeFazio's edition of the Hemingway-Hotchner correspondence. *Dear Papa, Dear Hotch* (96–98, 111–13,119–22).

9. Hemingway viewed one of Rice's "tax mistakes," neglecting to report $45,000 on Hemingway's 1957 tax return, as particularly troublesome, so much so that he described it as a *bajonazo* when writing to Hotchner on 7 December 1957 (qtd. in DeFazio 229). A *bajonazo* is a bullfighting term defined in *Death in the Afternoon* as "a deliberate sword thrust into the neck . . ." (*DIA*, "An Explanatory Glossary"). Further details on this particular "tax mistake" are found at pages 328–329 of Michael Reynolds' *Hemingway: The Final Years*.

10. Michener's assessment of Hemingway's state of mind in 1959 is consistent with firsthand accounts from others, including Valerie Hemingway. In *Running with the Bulls*, she observes that, to Hemingway, "[t]axes were always a hidden enemy, waiting to attack" (132). She also describes a plan he devised to disguise her earnings in Cuba, paying her from a fund so it "would not show up anywhere in his own finances," due to concerns about her visa (144).

11. Hemingway's "irrational fear of the law" may have begun in 1915, after he was pursued by a game warden in Michigan for illegally shooting a blue heron.

Hemingway was sixteen at the time and, according to Reynolds, the experience "continued to haunt Hemingway, becoming in his imagination more serious than it was, more threatening" and also represented "the first of several encounters with law enforcement that always produced in Hemingway a visceral response more intense than the event might warrant" (255).

12. One of Hemingway's most frequently cited quips about the payment of taxes is found in a 19 July 1941 letter to his ex-wife, Pauline: "If anyone asks the children what their father did in Mr. Rooseveldts war they can say 'He paid for it.' Practically everything of all that work on the book has gone or will have to go for taxes" (*SL* 525).

WORKS CITED

Brasch, James D., and Joseph Sigman. "Hemingway's Library: A Composite Record" (pdf). Originally published New York and London: Garland, 1981. *Ernest Hemingway On-Line Resources.* 2000. John F. Kennedy Presidential Library and Museum. 18 March 2007. <http://www.jfklibrary.org/Historical+Resources/ Hemingway+Archive/Online+Resources/>.

Chase, David. "Tax Problems Peculiar to an Author." *N.Y.U. Institute of Federal Taxation* 7 (1949): Cheek v. United States. No. 89–658. Supreme Ct. of the U.S. 8 January 1991.

DeFazio, Albert J. III, ed. *Dear Papa, Dear Hotch: The Correspondence of Ernest Hemingway and A.E. Hotchner.* Columbia: U of Missouri P, 2005.

Gibney, Frank. *The Operators.* New York: Harper Brothers, 1960.

Hemingway, Ernest. *Across the River and into the Trees.* New York: Scribner's, 1950.

———. *Death in the Afternoon.* New York: Scribner's, 1932.

———. *Ernest Hemingway: Selected Letters, 1917–1961.* Ed. Carlos Baker. New York: Scribner's, 1981.

———. *For Whom the Bell Tolls.* New York: Scribner's, 1940.

———. "The Great Blue River." In By-Line: Ernest Hemingway, Selected Articles and Dispatches of Four Decades. Ed. William White. New York: Scribner's, 1967. 403–416.

———. *To Have and Have Not.* New York: Scribner's, 1937.

————. *A Moveable Feast*. New York: Scribner's, 1964.

Hemingway, Valerie. *Running with the Bulls, My Years with the Hemingways*. New York: Ballantine-Random House, 2004.

Internal Revenue Code of 1939. Pub. L. 76–1, 10 Feb. 1939. 53 Stat.

Internal Revenue Code of 1954. Pub. L. 83–591. 16 Aug. 1954. 68A Stat.

Katz, Farley P. "The 'Infernal' Revenue Code." *Tax Lawyers* 50 (1997): 617–24.

Kragen, Adrian and John K. McNulty. *Federal Income Taxation, Individuals, Corporations, Partnerships*. 4th ed. St. Paul: West Publishing Co., 1985.

Michener, James. Introduction. *The Dangerous Summer*. By Ernest Hemingway. New York: Scribner's, 1985. 3–40.

Reynolds, Michael. *Hemingway: The Final Years*. New York: W.W. Norton, 1999.

St. Clair v. United States. No. 5–91-CV-138. United States District Court for the District of Minnesota. 3 May 1993.

Scott, Patrick. "An Overview of the Collection." *The Speiser and Easterling-Hallman Foundation Collection of Ernest Hemingway*. 16 July 2002. University of South Carolina. 18 May 2007. <http://www.sc.edu/library/spcoll/amlit/hemingway/hem1.html>

Speiser, Maurice, and G. Campbell Becket. "Memorandum with Regard to Requested Clarification of Section 107 of the Internal Revenue Code." Rpt. in *A Guide and Analytical Index to the Internal Revenue Acts of the United States, 1909–1950: Legislative Histories, Laws and Administrative Documents*. Ed. Bernard D. Reams, Jr. Vol. 35. Buffalo, NY: W.S. Hein, 1979. 3401–3402.

Hemingway and Cultural Geography

The Landscape of Logging in "The End of Something"

Laura Gruber Godfrey

I visited Ernest Hemingway's house outside Ketchum, Idaho in the fall of 2004. The late September weather was golden, crisp, perfect—the skies an intense western blue, long ribbons of quaking aspen and cottonwood trees lining the graceful curves of the Big Wood River. On that late afternoon visit, I watched as a herd of elk grazed quietly in a meadow below Hemingway's yard, next to the river, and to the north the Boulder/White Cloud mountains glowed brown and violet in the sun. The house itself, now under the care of the Nature Conservancy, has undergone few changes, and so when I peeked through the kitchen window I knew that the faded, worn curtains I could see were probably chosen by Mary, Hemingway's fourth wife, and

Reprinted with permission from *The Hemingway Review* 26.1 (Fall 2006). Copyright © 2006 The Ernest Hemingway Foundation. Published by the University of Idaho, Moscow, Idaho.

that the kitchen table was one at which he had often sat. There is a picture, in Kenneth Lynn's massive biography, of Hemingway in the Ketchum house in the winter of 1959, eating dinner with his cat at the kitchen counter; I glimpsed that same counter through the window. And there was the large green door on the south side of the house that marks the entrance to the foyer, where Hemingway used his double-barreled 12-gauge shotgun to take his own life on 2 July 1961.

It struck me that afternoon that every detail of the place, although Hemingway and his wife had long been absent, sang with the history of his life. To the ~ outside observer the house might appear as an increasingly-shabby structure on a spectacular piece of property—the slightly sagging deck with its chipped green paint, the forlorn white bench sitting outside the basement door, and the splintered, peeling wood on the windowsills make an odd juxtaposition with the stunningly beautiful landscape (and the land itself is surrounded by houses that are, needless to say, more reflective of Ketchum, Idaho property values). But to anyone familiar with Hemingway's life story, each tiny detail of the property carries enormous weight and significance. I found myself taking a ridiculous number of pictures of any image I could catch—a worn patch of grass, a refrigerator visible through a window, a cloud shadow on the Boulder Mountains—bringing these images like prizes back to my baffled yet amused American Literature students, who had just begun reading *In Our Time*.

Geography and place lie at the heart of Hemingway's art, as they did in his life: perhaps this fact explains the powerful urge Hemingway scholars and fans have to *see* the places where he situated and composed that art. Critical discussion of Hemingway's sense of place is no new enterprise, and what we may call "place-centered" criticism of his work continues to be an active field of discussion. As an author Hemingway presents again and again his disciplined and exacting aesthetic for landscapes (inspired by landscape painters like Cézanne); Susan Beegel reads Hemingway's Nick Adams stories and their "ecological comprehension" of the surrounding landscapes (102), and Terry Tempest Williams calls Hemingway "a powerful mentor, in terms of what it means to create a landscape impressionistically on the page, to make it come alive, pulse, breathe" (11).

As these authors point out, many of Hemingway's geographies do more for his narratives than simply elevate or give depth to the stories; these landscapes are also invested with both aesthetic and cultural meaning. Perhaps one passage that best demonstrates this awareness of the *cultural* geographies of places comes in the middle of Hemingway's *Green Hills of Africa,* where he describes the train of thoughts that come to him while fishing in the Gulf Stream:

> . . . when, on the sea, you are alone with it and know that this Gulf Stream you are living with, knowing, learning about, and loving, has moved, as it moves, since before man, and that it has gone by the shoreline of that long, beautiful, unhappy island since before Columbus sighted it and that the things you find out about it, and those that have always lived in it are permanent and of value because that stream will flow, as it has flowed, after the Indians, after the Spaniards, after the British, after the Americans and after all the Cubans and all the systems of governments, the richness, the poverty, the martyrdom, the sacrifice and the venality and the cruelty are all gone. . . . (149)

While the sentiments expressed in the passage might be called a kind of homage to the permanence of nature, or a sort of deep-ecological awareness of the timelessness of the natural world, also striking is Hemingway's interweaving of geography with cycles of both human *and* natural change. Place here is created from, influenced, and shaped by both natural (the flowing stream, the ancient shoreline) and human (politics, poverty, martyrdom, cruelty) forces. This kind of awareness of place is a cornerstone of cultural geography.

To impact the natural, historical, and cultural meanings of his settings, Hemingway investigates and presents these places on multiple planes, often documenting the changes that have played out there on human and natural levels; his sensitivity to topography and to the nuances of geography and landscape show him, then, to be a cultural geographer in the contemporary sense of the term. Hemingway himself once remarked that when it comes to art in general, "'[u]nless you have geography, background, you have nothing'" (qtd. in McComas 46). *In Our Time* was originally published by Charles Scribner's Sons in 1925, some fifty years prior to the humanist renaissance in the field of geography. In connecting Hemingway's short fiction to this more recent field, however, I want to show that his early short fiction engenders its own geographies.

This essay documents the ways that one of Hemingway's early short stories from *In Our Time*, "The End of Something," demonstrates his acute spatial awareness in the form of cultural geography. I am not so much interested, here, in Hemingway's "nature" as in his interweaving of "nature" with "culture." Cultural geographers are not simply naturalists studying the ecological nuances of a landscape or ecosystem; nor are they merely geologists, painting pictures of how the landscape was formed or of the science behind its topography; nor are they political or social scientists, studying only the histories and lives of human movements on a given landscape.[1] To be a literary artist in the vein of a cultural geographer means that the writer must encompass some mixture of these elements all at once. It invokes a kinetic, dynamic presentation of place. Rather than presenting landscape, geography, or topography as fixed or static, then, Hemingway in "The End of Something" writes of a place that has shifted, is shifting, and will continue to be in flux due to a variety of forces. Everything about his northern lake setting in this piece is in a state of transition, and the spaces he depicts here have a tangible physicality of their own. Hemingway achieves this sense of force in the narrative by detailing—again, always suggestively—the long standing cycles of history and change that have taken place on the landscape and within this particular Michigan geography.

"The End of Something" and the Landscape of Logging

In a number of the stories within the *In Our Time* collection, logging serves as a driving force behind Hemingway's fluctuating, potent, and multi-layered landscapes and behind the emotional dramas of the characters. In "The Doctor and the Doctor's Wife," for example, Hemingway describes a moral struggle about whether to take abandoned logs left by the local mill, and in "Big Two-Hearted River" Nick Adams travels through a burnt-out landscape, passing through the town of Seney which has also burned to the ground—the charred landscape a reminder of the "devastating fires that spread repeatedly through the [northern lakes] region" in the early 20th century—fires ignited from "the great piles of slash waste left on the forest floor after the cut-out-and-get-out" method of lumber industries there (M. Williams 158). But in "The End of Something," Hemingway evokes a particularly rich and detailed sense of the connection between the dynamic geographies surrounding his characters and the characters' own emotional geographies.

Alfred Kazin once wrote that "[n]o nature writer in all America literature save Thoreau has had Hemingway's sensitiveness to color, to climate, to the knowledge of the physical energy under heat or cold, that knowledge of the body thinking and moving through a landscape that Edmund Wilson, in another connection, has called Hemingway's 'barometric accuracy'" (334). Yet this "barometric accuracy" applies not only to Hemingway's documentation of human progression through and existence in landscape, but also to the cycles of change and flux (not simply natural, organic change) that exists in any landscape, in any geography. "The End of Something" presents just such a multi-layered awareness of geography, and so when Kazin writes further that "the landscape of *In Our Time* had meaning only as the youth [Nick Adams] learned from it" (328), or when Constance Cappel Montgomery remarks that Hemingway's settings in this story are used as "background[s] [...] important only in that they give the reader a sense of time and place," I must disagree (129). In the reading that follows, I want to show that the "background" of Hemingway's "The End of Something" is really no "background" at all—the geographies of its northern Michigan setting are instead presented as dense with their own histories and changes.

"The End of Something" is a break-up story, where the characters Nick Adams and Marjorie find their relationship coming to a quiet, anticlimactic conclusion. Hemingway begins this brief story with a description of Hortons Bay and its abandoned atmosphere. Hemingway often begins his fiction, both short stories and novels, with intricate yet deceptively simple descriptions of place—five of the *In Our Time* stories (not to mention the interchapter vignettes) and seven of the later *Men Without Women* stories begin with some form of detailed description of topography, place, or geography. Of the opening descriptions in "The End of Something," H. R. Stoneback writes that while some critics find such details "lumbering" and "ponderous," he "rather like[s] Hemingway's landscape-opening. At one level, put most simply, 'The End of Something' is an elegy for a *place* [. . . .]" (66).

Place, rather than character, frames the narrative. More specifically, Hemingway opens "The End of Something" not only with a description of place, but of place as it relates to history, to economics, to local industry; he focuses on the economic, or human, forces that shaped the town's identity. Hortons Bay saw its prime long ago, and Hemingway anchors us in the present scene by giving us a glimpse of the past. "In the old days," he begins, "Hortons Bay was a lumbering town" (*CSS* 79). Each of these ten words has meaning and purpose. Far more complex than a beginning depiction of "place," here is an entire local economy, landscape, history, and folklore distilled into its most compact form. The description continues:

> Then one year there were no more logs to make lumber. The lumber schooners came into the bay and were loaded with the cut of the mill that stood stacked in the yard. All the piles of lumber were carried away. The big mill building had all its machinery that was removable taken out and hoisted on board one of the schooners by the men who had worked in the mill. (*CSS* 79)

With such evocatively simple images, Hemingway gives readers the clear sense that more than one "ending" is being documented in the narrative. Before we learn that Nick and Marjorie's relationship is ending, we are given a dismal picture of the gradual dismantling of the lumber mill—a mill that was once the lifeblood for this entire town. This parallel of setting to human drama gives depth to the story, for the setting not only serves as a dramatic backdrop for the love conflicts between Nick and Marjorie, but also—in its dismantled, "ruined" state—parallels the human drama itself. The lumber mill was built and remained active while there were still resources to harvest; Hortons Bay was built up around the lumber mill the way towns are always born around industry, resources, and capital. Once the center is removed from the town, though, it falls apart. The same is true for Nick and Marjorie: our sense is that some "center" that held them together has dwindled and then died.

This parallel between the setting of "The End of Something" and its characters is often noted in critical discussions of Hemingway's early fiction and in discussions of this story in particular. The presence of the ruined, abandoned lumber mill has been understood for years as symbolic representation of the decayed, dying status of the relationship between Nick Adams and Marjorie. However, the story's setting—that embodied presence of this community's historical past—deserves closer inquiry. From this opening narrative frame, the reader comes to understand that Nick and Marjorie are only two members of a broader community that has its own stories, its own folklore, its own important histories; this we know from Hemingway's opening sentence, written as if he is embarking on the retelling of some myth, or legend: "In the old days, Hortons Bay was a lumbering town." The language of this brief opening frame evokes a sense of cultural geography in its mimicry of the intonations of oral histories.[2] The repetitive, soothing incantations of the words themselves bear resemblance to some of the oldest patterns within oral traditions, stories passed down from generation to generation that served as the very fabric of local cultures and communities.

"The End of Something," then, maintains its emphasis on the importance of cultural geography not only in content, but in sound and form. Hemingway begins his story "[I]n the old days," in a time almost outside of time. He describes the common condition of the people who populated this long-ago place, noting that "no one who lived in [the town] was out of sound of the big saws in the mill by the lake." He then shifts, again in keeping with that oral-storytelling style, explaining simply that "[t]hen one year there were no more logs to make lumber" (CSS 79). The architecture of Hemingway's sentences and the rhythm of their movement support his emphasis on geography, on place, on local history. While it was once the lumber mill that held this community together, the fabric of the space is, arguably, kept intact now by memories and stories.

The language in "The End of Something," then, suggests longstanding knowledge of and involvement with place and history. Hemingway considered such knowledge of place, history, and geography as one of the most important—indeed, essential—kinds of critical thinking and responsible cultural awareness. He once took Yale instructor Charles Fenton (who was crafting a dissertation on Hemingway's writing at Oak Park High School as well as on his journalism at the Kansas City *Star*) to task precisely for his ignorance of cultural geography, or local history. Hemingway's written reprimand to Fenton bears repeating in its entirety:

> . . . Did anyone in the old days have any right to work on a man's past and publish findings while the man was alive unless he was running for public office or was a criminal?. . . . I don't know whether you went to Oak Park or just wrote out there. But I do know that the impression you would get from it is quite false.
>
> It used to have a North Prairie and a South Prairie. The North Prairie ran from a block beyond your (our) house as far out as the Des Plaines River which then had plenty of pickerel in it up to Wallace Evan's game farm where we used to poach. Where you see an apartment building now there was usually a big old house with a lawn. Where you see subdivisions and row after row of identical houses there used to be gypsy camps in the fall with their wagons and horses.
>
> Oak Park had its own artesian water supply and some of us kids used to bring pickerel from the Des Plaines River and put them in the reservoir at night and we watched them grow big for years and never told anybody. We caught goldfish out of the creek and breeding ponds in the game farm and brought them back in minnow buckets and stocked the reservoir to make feed for the pickerel. In the deep water the goldfish all turned silver or silver and black mottled. . . .
>
> Any picture you would get of Oak Park now would be false. . . . The point I am trying to make by talking all around it is that when you come into something thirty-five years late, you do not get the true gen. You get Survivors' gen. You can get statistics and badly remembered memories and much slanted stuff. But

it is a long way from true gen and I do not see what makes it scholarship . . ." (qtd. in M. W. Hemingway 299)

Deeply offended and upset by publicized (or to-be-publicized) interpreta- tions of the geographies of his own life, Hemingway attempts to correct Fenton's misunderstanding of Oak Park as place. He does so by creating for Fenton a miniature cultural geography that cites the varying forces that made Oak Park, Illinois what it once was—the social forces, the natural forces, the economic development. To make this place more "real" for Fenton, Hemingway populates Oak Park with specific names, explanations for now-altered landscapes, localized traditions, childhood rituals, and memories. But here he also emphasizes the way Fenton's mind and eye would be fooled into great misunderstandings by looking at Oak Park as it would have appeared to him, an outsider to this cultural geography, an observer who would be entirely ignorant of any personal or local history or meaning. The point to take away from this letter is that, for Hemingway, *memory* or place—its history, its cycles of growth, expansion, development, change—has as much to do with a landscape's meaning as do the landscape's actual physical features.

Hemingway's exacting aesthetic for writing place moves beyond a faith- ful mimesis of what the eye can see, attempting in addition to capture the aesthetics of memory. Memory as key component to a full knowledge of place plays an important role in "The End of Something," and the memories of the local landscape are kept alive through stories and retellings. Turning from a broad commercial picture of this landscape's decline, Hemingway moves into a dramatic enactment of the economic forces that drove the lumber mill out of business, and desolated the local geography. In a sense, he "remembers" this history aloud for his readers, recalling the time when the local lumber mill fell apart, and its lumber and machinery were taken away:

The lumber schooners came into the bay and were loaded with the cut of the mill that stood stacked in the yard. All the piles of lumber were carried away. The big mill building had all its machinery that was removable taken out and hoisted on board one of the schooners by the men who had worked in the mill. The schooner moved out of the bay toward the open lake carrying the two great saws, the traveling carriage that hurled the logs against the revolving, circular saws and all the rollers, wheels, belts and iron piled on a hull-deep load of lumber. Its open hold covered with canvas and lashed tight, the sails of the schooner filled and it moved out into the open lake, carrying with it everything that had made the mill a mill and Hortons Bay a town. (*CSS* 79)

While this mill and its machinery once were the driving force behind the economy, landscape, and livelihoods of the area, its pieces are now "covered with canvas and lashed tight," rendered powerless. It is not clear where the schooner is headed—it is simply moving "out into the open lake." Hemingway thus emphasizes the human (economic) forces that have shaped the geography of Hortons Bay, stressing the mill's influence not only on the local natural landscape, but also its impact on the entire town structure.

But there can be no complete remembrance of this local history without including people from the past or the places they once inhabited. Hemingway seems to recognize this need as he shifts gradually into describing another "layer" of the cultural geography of this place: the town itself. "The one-story bunk houses," he writes "the eating-house, the company store, the mill offices, and the big mill itself stood deserted in the acres of sawdust that covered the swampy meadow by the shore of the bay" (*CSS* 79). Again, the local landscape has been undeniably altered by the human economic forces exerted upon it—as is true for many of the topographies described in Hemingway's fiction. Here is a veritable ghost town, resting on a bed of sawdust, the sawdust itself a remnant of the trees that once blanketed the area and which were subsequently processed by the mill. We gain a clear image of the cycles of change that have taken place in Hortons Bay, almost as if watching time-lapse photography: the geography morphed from a landscape blanketed with deep forest, to a thriving, booming town and lumber mill, to a deserted ghost town where most of the first-generation timber has been removed and the people are either merely scraping by or have moved away. The visuals of the human and the economic forces shift again at the close of this brief passage, focusing instead on the purely "natural" elements of landscape: the "swampy meadow" and the "shore of the bay." In this brief, seemingly simple opening to the story, Hemingway has managed to present a distilled version of the long history of this one small cross-section of landscape—a cultural, economic, and natural history all in one. The landscape of this story as presented by Hemingway is alive with history and with stories from the past.

Like the humanist geographers of the later 20th century, Hemingway also shows his readers in "The End of Something" that culture and geography are interrelated constructions rather than separate or discreet entities. Understanding the history of the timber industry in the Northern Lakes region of the United States illuminates the ways that Hemingway's fiction accurately depicts the artificiality, or constructedness, of the landscape left behind by the logging culture there. Hemingway's landscape in "The End of Something" is a geography made by logging; here is not a depiction of "nature," but rather of what happens when "nature" and "culture" collide. Such "collisions" between nature and culture—between forest and logger, between the landscape and its human inhabitants—make up the very fabric of the local histories of this area. Logging was an industry that created its own landscape, never more so than with the rise of commercial, industrial-scale logging in the United States during the 19th century:

> The new scale and form of logging was a response to the increasing demand for lumber from a growing population and an increasingly industrialized economy and society. From a mere 0.5 billion board feet cut in 1801, the amount of lumber cut rose to 1.6 billion board feet in 1839, and the rate of cutting quickened at each successive decade to form a new and upward sloping curve which reached 8 billion board feet in 1859, 20 billion in 1880 and a peak of 46 billion board feet in 1904, an amount never reached since. (M. Williams 152)

Hard as it is for us to conceive, then, portions of the northern lake geography of Michigan Hemingway documents in his 1925 collection of fiction would have seemed to him, growing up as a boy there each summer, in some ways like a geography abandoned—by the early 20th century, much of the forest there had been harvested, cleared, and hauled away. As Frederic Svoboda notes, "the young Hemingway hunted and fished in Michigan, but he really did not know a Michigan wilderness. That was long gone by the time he came there" (16). One of the only ways for Hemingway to keep the memories and stories of the area alive would be to accurately record those histories in his fiction.

For Hemingway, an accurate and honest depiction of these geographical spaces is one that includes stories suggesting the great changes wrought by the local logging industry. Logging—as a livelihood, as a culture, and as an industry—wove itself into the cultural context of this landscape, altering the lives, the vocations, and the natural environments of the locals. As an industry it could do so swiftly and relentlessly. Michael Williams further describes the quick ruthlessness of this boom-and-bust, resource-based economy when he notes that:

> The landscape of commercial logging reached its characteristic form and epitome in the Lake States where the assiduous application of new inventions, with the addition of steam skidders, ice roads, and logging railroads, enabled exploitation to proceed efficiently and ruthlessly. The logging landscape had two faces: there was the landscape of the processes of exploitation and the landscape of depletion. (156)

The methods employed by the burgeoning lumber industry in this region were particularly harsh; by the time timber companies established themselves in the Pacific Northwest in the later decades of the 20th century, a somewhat more careful harvesting process was in place, and Williams points out that while "cutting had been careless" in the northern Lakes region, "on the whole, there was far less cutover land in the Northwest than in any other region" (158, 161). Still, it is safe to assume that Hemingway himself would have been very familiar with the appearance of "cutover" land. Susan Beegel notes that these "cutovers," or clearcuts, amounted to a "wasteful assault on the Michigan forests," and goes on to explain that memories of these ecological "wounds" exist throughout much of Hemingway's Nick Adams stories:

Those wounds are everywhere [. . .] in the burned-over terrain of "Big Two-Hearted River" [. . .] in the abandoned mill town of Hortons Bay in "The End of Something," and in the clearcuts of Hemingway's final, posthumously published Nick Adams story, the aborted novel "The Last Good Country" [. . .] "Fathers and Sons," and the reduction of its hemlock forest to "open, hot, shadeless, weed-grown slashing," are [also] a vital part of this lineage. (85)

Although his family's vacation home, Windemere at Walloon Lake, was itself the embodiment of a pastoral escape, much of the geographical subtext in "The End of Something" hints that some of the nearby landscapes are in the process of recovering from the impact of logging. "There was nothing," Hemingway writes, "of the mill left except the broken white limestone of its foundations showing through the swampy second growth as Nick and Marjorie rowed along the shore" (CSS 79). And while the second-growth timber—forming a dense, dark border along the lake shore—serves as partial reminder of this altered landscape, we can assume that other areas:

... [would have been] strewn with debris and massive stumps, often cut many feet above the ground. . . . [often] the cutovers were (and still are in places) dotted with unpainted and sagging farmhouse structures. . . . In the deserted fields occasionally one still sees a lilac bush or a heaped-up pile of stones where a chimney once stood, both markers of an abandoned homestead, the whole scene a mute and melancholy testimony to abandoned hopes. (M. Williams 158–9)

Hemingway's deep cultural awareness of this local geography is present in the following dialogue between Marjorie and Nick:

"There's our old ruin, Nick," Marjorie said.
   Nick, rowing, looked at the white stone in the green trees.
   "There it is," he said.
   "Can you remember when it was a mill?" Marjorie asked.
   "I can just remember," Nick said.
   "It seems more like a castle," Marjorie said. (CSS 79)

The force and speed with which the logging industry cleared and then abandoned these landscapes gives that industry's former presence an almost mythical quality. For Nick and Marjorie, "the old days" seem more legend than reality, a legend of a time when the local landscape thrived with activity and prosperity and trees seemed in boundless supply. There are layers of cultural meaning attached to this geography as humans, their lives, and their economies interact with it; in this sense the natural world, for Hemingway, is never simply "nature" untouched and pristine. The "natural world" and its geographies are, instead, spaces either altered or being altered, filled with reminders of cultural history. In Hemingway's fictional world, the categories "nature" and "culture" are equally influenced by one another, and this mutual alteration is communicated through the weight of geographical detail. Elaine Scarry discusses a similar "weight" of aesthetic detail in Thomas Hardy's novels when she notes that:

> [t]hus [the human body] is . . . forever rubbing up against and leaving traces of itself . . . on the world, as the world is forever rubbing up against and leaving traces of itself . . . on the human creature. . . . Fleeting gestures become materials with shape, weight, and color. . . . A patch of paint or blood is a patch of history. (50–51)

In "The End of Something," Hemingway's geographical portraits suggest that same sense of "mutual alteration" between nature and cultural forces. As Marjorie and Nick sit by the fire on the shore of the lake, Hemingway reasserts that "[i]n back of them was the close second-growth timber of the point and in front was the bay with the mouth of Hortons Creek" (CSS 81). The existence of the second-growth timber, here, evokes that history full of "shape, weight, and color." The ruins of the mill and the recovering forest both are "patches of history." Hemingway constructs a changing, altered geography in the narrative, a careful combination of the cultural and natural elements of topography, and a suggestive depiction of the long cycles of change, history, and industry that have taken place here.

The abandoned mill's presence in Hemingway's fictional landscape, then, is more than the presence of a ruin. From their brief exchange of dialogue, Nick and Marjorie show their longstanding awareness of the evolution of this community's geography: Nick can just remember the time when the mill was part of the local economy, and each time he glimpses it he can feel for himself the many layers of history, culture, and change that have occurred within this community. He is reminded of the decline of the smaller logging operations in northern Michigan, of the fact that a once-bustling and prominent town is no longer so bustling, and in the forests that surround him he sees the remaining impact of the logging in the form of the second-growth timber. This understanding of the place gives him a deeper sense of what it means to live here as well as a deeper understanding of his own relationships. Beyond chronicling the observations of a naturalist or escapist adventures in the woods "The End of Something" demonstrates the careful interweaving of human characters with their communities and their landscapes, and serves as evocative portrayal of how the local logging industry influenced the history and emotion of one American geography.

In the discussion of cultural geography, too little attention has been paid to literary artists—artists who were entirely separate from the fields of geography or cultural geography, but who played important roles in the developing emphasis on the "constructedness" of space and place. In terms of critical discourse on Hemingway's fictional geographies, my hope is that emphasizing his awareness of geography as multi-layered, kinetic, and constructed will broaden the discussions of his spaces and places beyond the old critical binaries of "nature to be conquered" or "nature as escape," whether that escape be from war or women. In "An Old Newsman Writes," an article written for *Esquire* in 1934, Hemingway commented that "All good books are alike in that they are truer than if they had really happened and after you are finished reading one you will feel that it all happened to you and afterwards it all belongs to you; the good and the bad, the ecstasy, the remorse and sorrow, the people and the places and how the weather was" (*BL* 146). Hemingway attempted, in his writing, to create pictures of landscape reminiscent of the beauty and simplicity of Cézanne, but his writing was also an attempt to pass along the histories, memories, and emotional fabrics of the varying communities he observed and of which he was part.

NOTES

1. As a field, cultural geography "concentrates upon the ways in which space, place, and the environment participate in an unfolding dialogue of meaning" (Shurmer-Smith 3). The humanist geographers of the 1970s began this dialogue, reacting against more positivist mid-century geographers like Carl Sauer for whom culture—and by relation, "place"—was a monolithic concept—treated as an entity that individuals merely "participate in" or "flesh out" (Jackson 18). Such reification "severely limits the questions that may be asked" about culture as construction, and indeed removes the agency almost entirely from the human (Jackson 18). Rather than viewing "culture," "geography" and "place" as separate, autonomous absolutes, the humanist geographers of the 1970s believed that "these concepts were entities *created* by different societies. These geographers, perhaps most famously Yi Fu Tuan in his 1977 work *Space and Place,* reacted against purely scientific and economic readings of geography and space, creating theories that often articulated space and place according to more emotional and personal characteristics. For humanist geographers like Tuan, space becomes place only by our interaction with and understanding of it: place (like culture) becomes a construct of perspective, rather than an independent factual entity.

   Gillian Rose, in her 1993 work, *Feminism and Geography,* argues against defining place as bounded or safe, or as an environment for total belonging or as an enclosed or separate space—arguing instead for a more chaotic, kinetic, honest depiction of place. Similarly, Doreen Massey also theorizes place as ever-changing, always in flux, as unfixed as the social and economic and gender relations that exist within it. Thus, there is always—and has always been—a fluid quality to the identity of places, simply because the people *in* places are always changing and moving. Both Rose and Massey consistently highlight the constructedness of space and landscape, arguing that "'space itself—and landscape and place likewise—far from being firm foundations for disciplinary expertise and power, *are insecure, precarious and fluctuating*'" (qtd. in Ekinsmyth 64, my emphasis).

2. Stories rooted in an oral tradition contain characteristics, or "markers" of their own, both in terms of form and content. Formal characteristics include repetitions and word patterns at openings of sentences, as evident in this creation story recorded in the early 20th century from the Pima tribe of the American Southwest:

> And the moon he made in the same way and tried in the same places. . . .
>
> But when he made the stars he took the water in his mouth. . . .
>
> And now for a time the people increased till they filled the earth . . . But Juhwertamahkai [the Pima culture's original human in their creation story] did not like the way his people acted. . . . (Thin Leather 23)

Formal parallels between orally-rooted creation stories such as this and "The End of Something" include the cadences as well as the openings to the sentences. Listening to Hemingway's words read aloud evokes a similar sense of oral patterns and tones, and underscores the parallel content: "In the old days," "No one who lived in it," "Then one year," "Ten years later . . ." are all opening "markers" eliciting the sense that Hemingway is embarking on a story rooted in his community's own unique oral tradition, about to tell a story that binds that community together with a common history.

WORKS CITED

Baker, Carlos. *Ernest Hemingway: A Life Story.* New York: Avon Books, 1968.

Beegel, Susan F. "Second Growth: The Ecology of Loss in 'Fathers and Sons.'" In *New Essays on Hemingway's Short Fiction.* Ed. Paul Smith, 75–110. Cambridge: Cambridge UP, 1998.

Ekinsmyth, Carol. "Feminist Cultural Geography." In *Doing Cultural Geography.* Ed. Pamela Shurmer-Smith, 53–65. London: Sage, 2002.

Hemingway, Ernest. "The End of Something." In *The Complete Short Stories of Ernest Hemingway: The Finca Vigía Edition,* 79–82. New York: Simon and Schuster, 1998.

————. *Green Hills of Africa.* New York: Scribner's, 1935.

————. "An Old Newsman Writes: A Letter from Cuba." 1934. In *By-Line: Ernest Hemingway.* Ed. William H. White, 179–185. New York: Scribner's, 1967.

Hemingway, Mary Welsh. *How It Was.* New York: Knopf, 1976.

Jackson, Peter. *Maps of Meaning: An Introduction to Cultural Geography.* London: Unwin, 1989.

Kazin, Alfred. *On Native Grounds: An Interpretation of Modern American Prose Literature.* New York: Harcourt, Brace, 1942.

Massey, Doreen. *Space, Place, and Gender.* Minneapolis: U of Minnesota P, 1994.

McComas, Dix. "The Geography of Ernest Hemingway's 'Out of Season.'" *The Hemingway Review* 3.2 (Spring 1984): 46–49.

Montgomery, Constance Cappel. *Hemingway in Michigan.* New York: Fleet, 1966.

Scarry, Elaine. *Resisting Representation.* New York: Oxford UP, 1994.

Shurmer-Smith, Pamela, ed. *Doing Cultural Geography.* London: Sage, 2002.

————. "Reading Texts." In *Doing Cultural Geography.* Ed. Pamela Shurmer-Smith, 123–136. London: Sage, 2002.

———— and Carol Ekinsmyth. "Humanistic and Behavioural Geography." In *Doing Cultural Geography.* Ed. Pamela Shurmer-Smith, 19–27. London: Sage, 2002.

Stoneback, H. R. "'Nothing Was Ever Lost': Another Look at 'That Marge Business.'" In *Hemingway: Up in Michigan Perspectives.* Eds. Frederic J. Svoboda and Joseph J. Waldmeir, 59–76. East Lansing: Michigan State UP, 1995.

Svoboda, Frederic J. "False Wilderness: Northern Michigan as Created in the Nick Adams Stories." In *Hemingway: Up in Michigan Perspectives.* Eds. Frederic J. Svoboda and Joseph J. Waldmeir, 15–22. East Lansing: Michigan State UP, 1995.

———— and Joseph J. Waldmeir, eds. *Hemingway: Up in Michigan Perspectives.* East Lansing: Michigan State UP, 1995.

Thin Leather. "The Story of the Creation." Recorded by J.W. Lloyd. In *The Norton Anthology of American Literature, Shorter Sixth Edition.* Ed. Nina Baym, 21–24. New York: Norton, 2003.

Tuan, Yi-Fu. *Space and Place: The Perspective of Experience.* Minneapolis: U of Minnesota P, 1977.

Williams, Michael. "The Clearing of the Forests." In *The Making of the American Landscape*. Ed. Michael P. Conzen, 146–168. New York: Routledge, 1990.

Williams, Terry Tempest. "Hemingway and the Natural World: Keynote Address, Seventh International Hemingway Conference." In *Hemingway and the Natural World*. Ed. Robert Fleming, 7–17. Moscow, ID: University of Idaho Press, 1999.

Pilgrimage Variations

Hemingway's Sacred Landscapes

H. R. Stoneback

> I want to make the small pilgrimage to see you . . . I prayed for you sincerely
> and straight in Chartres, Burgos, Segovia and two minor places . . . Sorry not
> to have made the home office of Santiago de Compostella / sic / . . .
>
> Hemingway to Bernard Berenson (8/11/53, 2/2/54), *SL*

Pilgrimage, the notion and motion of spiritualized travel, is at the
center of Hemingway's religious vision and his work from his earliest stories
to the final, unfinished and posthumously published novels and memoirs.
Pilgrimage variations in his work range from individualized quests to places
that are sacralized by the achieved journey, to traditional pilgrimages long
held sacred by centuries of pilgrims. Most notable in the latter category of
pilgrimage is Hemingway's longstanding devotion to the specifically Catholic
Pilgrimage of Santiago de Compostela.

Although my primary concerns here are not biographical, it may be
useful, as prelude, to outline Hemingway's personal religious profile. Indeed

Reprinted with permission from *Religion and Literature* 35.2–35.3 (Summer–Autumn 2003). Copyright
© Notre Dame University. Published by Notre Dame University Press.

■ 457

given the vast countervailing weight of the pervasive popular culture Myth of
Papa Hemingway as well as most Hemingway biographies, which lead readers
to notions such as Hemingway-the-Nihilist, Hemingway-the-Non-believer,
Hemingway-the-amoral Existentialist, etc. ad infinitum, it is essential to clarify
the biographical facts: (1) Hemingway was baptized, confirmed and raised
in the Congregational Church. As a boy, as a teenager, he sang in the church
choir, he spoke at youth fellowship meetings. His adult conversion to Roman
Catholicism must be understood against the background of his boyhood
experience of mainstream social-gospel Protestantism. (2) Beginning with
his wounding and near-death experience on an Italian battlefield in 1918,
and continuing with increasing intensity through the early and mid-1920s,
Hemingway's personal religious pilgrimage takes him through a rejection of
Puritanism, and far beyond the social-gospel brand of Protestantism, into
an ever-deepening discovery of Catholicism. This personal faith-journey is
manifest, in his life and his work, by profound engagement with the aesthetic
and historical and spiritual sensibility centered in ritual and ceremony (e.g.,
most obviously, as in the world of *Toreo*, or the bullfight; and, less obviously, in the vision of life-as-pilgrimage). Hemingway's rootedness in the
sacramental sense of experience, in the incarnational paradigms of Catholic
Christianity, grows ever deeper. Before his twenty-eighth birthday (in 1927),
he has accepted the tradition, the authority, and the discipline of Rome and
formalized his conversion. Far from being a "nominal" or "bogus" Catholic
as some biographers would have it, Hemingway is a devout practicing
Catholic for much of his life. He believed that "the only way he could run
his life decently was to accept the discipline of the Church," and he could
not imagine taking any other religion seriously (Baker 1969, 333). I have
documented these biographical matters in considerable detail elsewhere,
and students of Hemingway's *life* are urged to consult the complete printed
record (see e.g. Stoneback 1991).

What matters for students of Hemingway's *writing*, and what matters most
for me, is that his fiction from *The Sun Also Rises* (and arguably even before,
from the earliest short stories) through *Men Without Women, A Farewell to
Arms, Winner Take Nothing, For Whom the Bell Tolls, Across the River and*

into the Trees, The Old Man and the Sea and on through all the posthumously published work to *True at First Light* is rooted in his religious sensibility, and the work is most deeply accessible through an understanding of his Catholic vision. Prose, Hemingway famously said, is architecture, not interior decoration. The spirituality, or if the reader prefers, the faith, the religion, the Catholicism of Hemingway's prose is architecture not mere interior decoration. And the foundational mode of that architecture is pilgrimage.

The ever-recurring center of Hemingway's work, then, is the notion of pilgrimage. Pilgrimage, in its many avatars, serves his fiction as deep structure, as externalized mysticism, as road map to the sacred landscapes of his fiction, as cartography of both the individualized and elusive *Deus Loci,* as well as the communal and binding historicity of actual landscapes rendered numinous by the millennial motions of millions of pilgrims who have traveled that way before.

The word—pilgrimage—has been subject to so much loose and leveling usage in popular culture that we must clarify at the outset how the term will be deployed here. (For example, I happened to overhear quite accidentally, while preparing this essay, two minor celebrities chattering on some television talk show about their seasonal "pilgrimages" to buy clothes at certain boutiques. This leveled eviscerated usage will not be in play here; if every motion is construed as pilgrimage, if every landscape—including a shopping mall—is considered sacred, the very possibility of authentic pilgrimage is rendered impossible.) Dictionary hierarchies of definition point to three categories of pilgrimage: (1) the journey of religious devotees to a specific shrine or numinous place, e.g., the Pilgrimage to Rome, or to Santiago de Compostela; (2) the more generalized notion of personal quest for some end individually construed as exalted, as morally or spiritually significant, e.g., the veteran's pilgrimage to a war memorial, or the desert aficionado's journey to Death Valley; (3) the trivialized notion of pilgrimage as any journey of any traveler for any reason. As indicated above, this latter false or attenuated sense of pilgrimage is here rejected. The first sense, the specific communal religious pilgrimage, and to some extent the second sense, the generalized notion of the individual quest, both involve to varying degrees the deeply felt necessity to seek out the numinous place (the spiritually elevated location), to travel through (or to) a *paysage moralisé* or symbolic landscape and approach the *Deus Loci*, or Spirit of Place, in the deliberate composed mood of expiation, or vow-fulfillment, seeking renewal or redemption.

To be sure, within the sacred space of authentic pilgrimages, there may be found both true pilgrims and false pilgrims. T. S. Eliot provides a useful touchstone for distinguishing the two types in his *Four Quartets* where he addresses the true pilgrim who must "put off / Sense and notion. You are not here to verify, / Instruct yourself, or inform curiosity / Or carry report. You are here to kneel / Where prayer has been valid" (Eliot 139). Thus, when Hemingway as devout Catholic makes the Pilgrimage of Santiago de Compostela, he cannot be a mere curious tourist, nor even the well-informed traveler and writer intent on carrying "report" or verifying anything—he is there "to kneel / Where prayer has been valid." The same holds for Jake Barnes, Hemingway's narrator in *The Sun Also Rises;* e.g., when Jake prays in the Cathedral of Pamplona (a major way-station on the great Pilgrimage Road of Santiago) he knows where he is and why he is there—"to kneel / Where prayer has been valid." And when he tells us he's "a rotten Catholic" but it is a "grand religion" he confirms his authentic pilgrim-identity (*SAR* 97). He may be accompanied by false pilgrims, friends and acquaintances who are in Pamplona only for the carnivalesque aspects of fiesta and pilgrimage, or worse, mere tourists curious about the local color of the bullfights. But Jake lives the true pilgrim's code, dwells in the sacred landscape, and quests renewal and redemption.

The Sun Also Rises, far from being the chronicle of an aimless "lost generation" that it is often taken for, is Hemingway's first great meditation on the theme of pilgrimage. Rather than rehash the details and arguments of my numerous essays on this matter, published over the last three decades, it must suffice here to recapitulate briefly the essential information: 1) from 1925 (the time of Hemingway's composition of *The Sun Also Rises*) and throughout his career, the Pilgrimage of Santiago de Compostela remains a benchmark in Hemingway's life, a touchstone in his writing; 2) the deep structure of *The Sun Also Rises* is determined by this pilgrimage; and Jake

Barnes, who designs the scrupulously precise movement of the novel on the Road of Santiago–from Paris to Bayonne to Roncevaux to Pamplona—is the conscious authentic pilgrim. Moreover, Jake (and Hemingway) know the moral and spiritual anguish and joy of the true pilgrim, the specifically Catholic pilgrim on the exact and exacting pilgrimage route, and they are very much in touch with the history, the ritual, the moral and aesthetic and salvific legacy of the great medieval—and modern—Pilgrimage of Santiago de Compostela.

II.

This seems to be getting very solemn for the hour which is 0930 but then I have heard Mass at that hour in Santiago de Campostella / sic / . . . I stayed there three summers trying to learn when I was working on my education.

—Hemingway to Bernard Berenson (10/24/55), SL

Hemingway's Compostelan pilgrimage variations reverberate throughout his works; and twenty-six years after *The Sun Also Rises,* in the last major fiction published during his lifetime, *The Old Man and the Sea,* the sacred landscape—or seascape—of pilgrimage is once again a major motif. For many years I have routinely remarked in passing, in hundreds of lectures and addresses dealing with the subject of Hemingway and Pilgrimage, that an important key to *The Old Man and the Sea* is provided if we understand that the novella's protagonist, Santiago, represents the culmination of Hemingway's lifelong preoccupation with the Pilgrimage of Santiago de Compostela. And I once wrote, in an essay published nearly two decades ago, that although Jake Barnes is clearly a Compostelan Pilgrim, he does not complete the pilgrimage, whereas Hemingway's Santiago does complete the pilgrimage "in a figurative or incarnational sense" (Stoneback 1986, 5). My concern here is to clarify and expand these passing remarks.

In 1954 Hemingway wrote to Father Robert Brown: "You know about Santiago and you know the name is no accident" (Hemingway-Father Brown

Correspondence). This was at the beginning of an important correspondence (unpublished) of several years' duration, which had been initiated by Brown's general inquiries regarding Hemingway's Catholicism and specific questions about *The Old Man and the Sea*. Let us consider here that one telling sentence; Hemingway writes *you* know, i.e., *you*, Father Brown, a priest with a sense of history and a knowledge of pilgrimage, *you* know even if all my other readers do not know about Santiago-Saint James-Saint Jacques and the Pilgrimage of Compostela; and, *you* know—even if other readers are blind to the fact—that it is "no accident," that I have named my old Cuban fisherman after Saint James, and more particularly, after the avatars of Saint James associated with Compostela. So Father Brown knew about Santiago, and Hemingway knew, and as informed readers aware of the depth of Hemingway's writerly iceberg, we must know.

There are, of course, biblical resonances that link Hemingway's old fisherman, Santiago, to James the fisherman and the calling of St. James to apostleship. These biblical resonances may be passed over here for they are not, strictly speaking, the matter of Santiago with which Hemingway is most deeply concerned; his matrix of signification is primarily generated by St. James of Compostela, by matter, that is to say, which is extra-biblical, which is specifically Catholic and medieval, the stuff of pilgrimage legend, lore, and tradition.

Tradition holds that after St. James-Santiago was beheaded in Jerusalem, thus becoming the first martyred apostle, his body was transported by arduous sea voyage in a small open boat to the northwestern coast of Spain, near the site of what would become the city and shrine of Santiago de Compostela. By the twelfth century, Santiago had achieved his full complex identity, through the two principal configurations: 1) the Pilgrim Saint for all of Europe and 2) Santiago Matamoros (or "moor-slayer"), champion of the Spanish armies in the reconquest of Spain for Christendom. In his manifestation as Santiago Matamoros, one of the "Seven Champions of Christendom," he appears rather directly in *The Old Man and the Sea* as, in Hemingway's words, "Santiago El Champeón." For a long time after his epic struggle with and final conquest of the "negro from Cienfuegos," everyone calls him "The Champion" (*OMATS*

69–70). And yet, for the most part, Hemingway de-emphasizes Santiago Matamoros in order to emphasize the avatar of Santiago who is the opposite of the knightly warrior-champion, who evokes the feeling and vision, the humility and gentleness, the poverty and resolution and endurance of St. James the Pilgrim.

Consider Hemingway's repeated references to the stars, how the old man on the first night at sea knows his location and direction "from watching the stars," how he repeatedly checks his course by looking "at the stars" (47). On the second night at sea, he watches the "first stars" appear and he knows that "soon they would all be out and he would have all his distant friends." He knows he must kill the great fish but he is glad, he says aloud, "we do not have to try to kill the stars." He assures himself that he is "clear enough" in the head: "I am as clear as the stars that are my brothers" (74–77). These and other references to the stars function as a primary allusion to Santiago de Compostela, which has manifold associations with the stars. The popular derivation of Compostela is from *campus stellae*, the "field of the star," and the pilgrimage road to Compostela was known as the *via lactea*, the Milky Way which pointed pilgrims the way to the shrine of St. James.

In Hemingway's terms, then, Santiago the pilgrim-fisherman knows where he is and who he is ("brother" of the stars) because of the field of the star, the Compostela, or *campus stellae*. But Hemingway also knows, as all students of Compostela know, that the more likely derivation of Compostela is from the Latin *compostum*, suggesting not only the "little graveyard" of St. James, but death and the grave in general, and—perhaps for Hemingway's ear—the compost heap of dying, dead, and decaying matter which is the always-imminent destination of all nature, great fish and humble fisherman alike. The true pilgrim knows this well, and that is why the pilgrimage is made.

The great strangeness that is at the heart of *The Old Man and the Sea* is anchored in a profoundly intensified consciousness of participation in the mysteries of nature; and the quintessential mystery of nature, I would add, has to do with the triumph of the human spirit. Hemingway and Santiago said it better: "A man can be destroyed but not defeated" (103). Above all others, pilgrims know this truth of the spirit, pilgrims who suffer and endure much in their lonely journey through and struggle with nature, pilgrims who participate profoundly in nature's mysteries, pilgrims who seek expiation and redemption, pilgrims who chant the litany of brotherhood, who practice humility and charity and compassion even as they fight off the sharks on their long journey through the sacred seascape toward the field of the star *and* the compost heap of all things living and dying. This great strangeness of the "strange old man" (a phrase used by Hemingway to characterize both Santiago and himself) and his journey is finally only approachable as mystery, through the discipline of mysticism, that mysticism which is a form of internalized pilgrimage, as pilgrimage is externalized mysticism.

Since there is not sufficient space here to consider all of the allusions, resonances, and patterns in Hemingway's skillful narrative deployment of the Pilgrim-Saint of Compostela, we must settle for a few more key details. Readers will recall that Hemingway's Santiago promises "to make a pilgrimage to the Virgin of Cobre" if he catches the great fish (*OMATS* 65). (The Christological associations of the great fish are obvious, and need not be belabored here.) We note that just as *Nuestra Señora del Pilar,* the Virgin patroness of Spain, is associated with Santiago de Compostela, so is the Virgin of Cobre, Cuba's Virgin patroness, associated first with the sacred place of Santiago de Cuba where she was enshrined in the Cathedral of Santiago, and second with Hemingway's Santiago who has made the *interior* pilgrimage to the Virgin of Charity and promises the physical pilgrimage. The most intricate aspect of Hemingway's overall narrative strategy is that at the same time that he constructs a pattern of allusions to the universal matter of the Pilgrimage to Santiago, and to the local Cuban matter of Pilgrimage to the Virgin of Cobre, he presents the transcription of Santiago's actual pilgrimage at sea.

This pilgrimage motif was rounded off and underlined, extratextually, when Hemingway gave his Nobel Prize Medal to the shrine of the Virgin of Cobre. At a fiesta in his honor in Hemingway's hometown in Cuba, with 400 villagers present including 45 fishermen, Hemingway presented his medal, symbol of his life's work, his long personal and creative pilgrimage, to the major pilgrimage site of Cuba. Or to be more precise, Hemingway gave his medal not to the Cuban state, not to the Cuban people (as is often said in Cuba), not to any museum, but to the Virgin: "*Quiero dar esta medalla,*" he said, "*al Nuestra Señora la Virgen de Cobre.*" In that speech to his neighbors and fisherman-friends, more revealing than his formal Nobel Prize Address, Hemingway bore witness to his long pilgrimage, his engagement with Santiago de Compostela that began decades before in *The Sun Also Rises.*

The Old Man and the Sea, then, is a complex study of pilgrimage, not only in the way that it connects with the history and legend of a particular saint, but in its deconstruction (for want of a better word) of Santiago de Compostela, not for purposes of debunking or dismissal, but in order to reconstruct a version of the original, historical saint—anchored in time, immersed in nature, rooted in the bright particularity and dailiness of lived saintliness. That is to say, the old fisherman Santiago is Hemingway's version of St. James the Fisherman grown old not as an Apostle, but as a fisherman-pilgrim; and he is Hemingway's version of Santiago de Compostela, stripped of legend and lore, presented in his fundamental human identity as pilgrim. With his reconfiguration of Santiago's namesake and pilgrim-brother, Santiago of Compostela, Hemingway reconstructs the paradigm of pilgrimage, relocates the "field of the star" to the Caribbean, and creates in the Gulf Stream off Cuba one of the most compelling sacred landscapes in world literature.

III.

> dépaysement . . . change of scene, disorientation.
>
> —*Larousse Dictionnaire*

The Old Man and the Sea, while it was the last fiction published in Hemingway's lifetime that dealt with pilgrimage and sacred landscape, is not the final pilgrimage variation in the Hemingway canon. Posthumously published works such as *The Garden of Eden* and *True at First Light* remain centrally concerned with pilgrimage, the hermeneutics of mobility, and sacred landscape. *The Garden of Eden,* for example, involves another specifically Catholic and traditional pilgrimage: the ancient and venerable Provençal and pan-European "Gypsy Pilgrimage" of the Holy Marys of the Sea, with its annual celebrations and processions in les Saintes-Maries-de-la-Mer, France, on the Camargue coast of Provence. It was this pilgrimage that the Catholic newlyweds Ernest and Pauline Hemingway participated in during their honeymoon in 1927. It was this pilgrimage, with its links to the Pilgrimage of Santiago, that would figure importantly in Hemingway's ambitious but unfinished *The Garden of Eden.* The pilgrimage motif is clearly present in the manuscript, if less so in the unfortunate much-edited posthumously published version (Stoneback 1999). And *True at First Light,* Hemingway's most recently published (1999) unfinished work, is essentially the story of his African Pilgrimage, which will be considered in some detail below. Another late, unfinished and posthumously published work that may be considered a pilgrimage variation is the long "short story," or more precisely, the unfinished novel "The Last Good Country." This work is the narrative of Nick Adam's flight into the wilderness of northern Michigan, after he commits a violation of hunting laws and believes he must go on the run from the game wardens who are after him. As a tale of flight, an escape story, it may seem to fall under a questionable rubric of pilgrimage-under-duress, until we remember that the medieval sentence for some crimes was indeed a required pilgrimage. Moreover, even if it is a pilgrimage that is set in motion by the fear of pursuit, the real focus is on the individualized quest to a place that is sacralized by the journey, the difficult travel through and to a symbolic landscape. The adolescent Nick is accompanied in this quest for the sacred landscape at the heart of the wilderness by his little sister. They must fight their way through the "long bad slashings," nearly impenetrable thickets of downed timber, must traverse a "real swamp," a "bad swamp," to get to the "secret place beyond all this slashing" (*CSS* 515). When they reach the "virgin timber," Nick tells his little sister: "This is the way forests were in the olden days. This is about the last good country there is left. Nobody gets in here ever." She replies: "I love the olden days. But I wouldn't want it all this solemn" (*CSS* 516).

The solemnity of the virgin forest makes them both "feel very strange."
As is usual in Hemingway's fiction, the inscription of the great strangeness at
the "secret" heart of nature ("the last good country" where almost "nobody
gets . . . ever") leads directly into the spiritualization of the landscape, and
the specifically religious aspects of the journey. Nick is not "afraid" in this
secret place but, as he reiterates: "I always feel strange. Like the way I ought
to feel in church." His sister agrees: "this kind of woods make me feel awfully
religious." Then, there in the Michigan wilderness, they have this remarkable
exchange:

> "That's why they build cathedrals to be like this."
>
> "You've never seen a cathedral, have you?"
>
> "No. But I've read about them and I can imagine them. This is the best
> one we have around here."
>
> "Do you think we can go to Europe some time and see cathedrals?"
>
> "Sure we will. But first I have to get out of this trouble and learn how to
> make some money" (CSS 517).

Thus, in the midst of their individualized quest of the "secret place" in
the woods where they will be safe from the game wardens of northern
Michigan, they entertain a traditional religious pilgrimage to the cathedrals
of Europe. While the story remains unfinished and inconclusive regarding
the escape-journey, there is sufficient evidence that the deep structure of
this Edenic pilgrimage variation has more to do with patterns of innocence-
fall-banishment-redemption than with mere flight. Hemingway writes that
Mr. John, one of the key characters in the community from which Nick has
fled, "liked Nick Adams because he said he had original sin. Nick did not
understand this but he was proud." And Mr. John tells Nick that "one of the
best things there is" is to have things to repent: "You're going to have things
to repent, boy" (CSS 523). "The Last Good Country" is fundamentally a
pilgrimage of penance and expiation to the "cathedral" of the deep secret
forest. We cannot know how Hemingway would have completed this
unfinished story, but we can discern the patterns. We can see how Nick,

the experienced pilgrim, instructs his younger sister in the mysteries of the secret woods, in fishing and hunting and drinking from sacred springs, and how, after a difficult journey, these two young brother-sister pilgrims are redeemed by pristine spiritual love in the virgin woods, far from the law of the game wardens.

This unfinished pilgrimage variation from late in Hemingway's career, "The Last Good Country," connects in a very direct fashion with his earliest pilgrimage tale, the journey into the deep, secret, and redemptive Michigan northwoods in "Big Two-Hearted River." Dating from the early 1920s, Hemingway's first masterpiece is sometimes read as one of the "greatest fishing stories," but it is much more than that; indeed it should not be construed even as a story since it is, strictly speaking, the concluding chapter of the Nick Adams *Bildungsroman, In Our Time.* As "Big Two-Hearted River" begins, we find Nick Adams, a wounded war veteran, returning to the Michigan northwoods where he fished in his pre-war youth. At first the entire country seems like a wasteland; the town of Seney is burned to the ground; the foundation stones of the buildings are "chipped and split by the fire"; nothing else is left of the town—"even the surface had been burned off the ground" (CSS 163). Nick's pilgrimage from the wasteland of war-torn Europe seems to have brought him to another wasteland. But the river is there, and it is full of trout. And that is why Nick has come to the Two-Hearted River. As he does with many of his pilgrimage narratives, Hemingway centers this one simultaneously on the fishing (or hunting) quest and the search for peace, for inner spiritual harmony and serenity.

Nick's heart tightens and he feels "all the old feeling" as he watches the trout move in the river (CSS 164). Then he sets off hiking through the countryside beyond the burned-out town; at first the country is all "burned over and changed"—even the grasshoppers have "turned black from living in the burned-over land." But Nick keeps hiking, "sweating in the sun," knowing the country "could not all be burned" (CSS 164–65). Finally he gets beyond the fire line, into the good country, the ankle-high sweet ferns, the island of tall pines and the meadow by the river where he will make his camp. Very carefully, he prepares his campsite, pitches his tent. Every action is charged with precision, as he makes order out of chaos. He crawls into his tent, thinking:

> Already there was something mysterious and homelike. Nick was happy as he crawled inside the tent. He had not been unhappy all day. This was different though. Now things were done. There had been this to do. Now it was done. It had been a hard trip. He was very tired. That was done. He had made his camp. He was settled. Nothing could touch him. It was a good place to camp. He was there, in the good place. He was in his home where he had made it. (*CSS* 167)

This passage might well serve as the Pilgrim's Credo, the essence of the individualized quest with no traditional pilgrimage associations—there are no shrines in these Michigan woods except the one the pilgrim constructs. The pilgrim-protagonist makes a difficult journey through the wasteland, arrives at a numinous place, made numinous in part by his creative discipline and order-making activities. The landscape is sacralized by the pilgrim's ordering of it, the home he *makes* "in the good place." This is not to say that "Big Two-Hearted River" is allusion-free; certainly the deep structure of the tale echoes T. S. Eliot's *The Waste Land,* with Nick Adams playing the role of the Fisher King, questing redemption in the "good place" beyond the ruined Wasteland. Nick's fishing activities throughout the rest of the narrative, like those of Santiago in *The Old Man and the Sea,* resonate with Christological associations.

Such pilgrimage variations abound in Hemingway's work from his early fiction to his last works. Indeed a year-long course of study could be built around the pilgrimage variations in Hemingway's work that we often miss, because we approach the narratives with a circumscribed predisposition—e.g., *A Farewell to Arms,* a novel almost always viewed exclusively through the lens of "love and war." Yet this is a novel suffused with pilgrimage designs, difficult journeys through hard country, the flight from the Italian army, the flight to Switzerland from Stresa; all of these actions are conditioned by a pilgrimage paradigm. Moreover, Frederic Henry is imaged as a Fisher King figure in the Stresa fishing scenes, just before the midnight flight to

Switzerland. That flight is both escape and pilgrimage, made in the name of love, renewal, and redemption from the wasteland of war. Then there is the Abruzzi motif in *A Farewell to Arms,* which may be seen as an instance of the road not taken, the pilgrimage that should have been made. The Abruzzi is not a traditional Catholic Pilgrimage site, but it acquires that significance in Hemingway's text: the high clean place of honor and dignity and good manners, where, as the Priest tells Frederic Henry, "it is understood that a man may love God. It is not a dirty joke" (*AFTA* 71). The Abruzzi functions as the symbolic matrix of the novel, Hemingway's anagogical place-referent, the emblem of his sacral geography and the desired journey to the numinous place in flight from a desacralized world.

Then there are the so-called "hunting stories" in the Hemingway oeuvre that, like the fishing stories, are almost always designed as quest and pilgrimage narratives. Consider "The Snows of Kilimanjaro," where the protagonist has undertaken a pilgrimage-safari to Africa with the hope that he can find personal and creative renewal and redemption there, with the hope "that in some way he could work the fat off his soul" (*CSS* 44). What he finds on this African pilgrimage is redemption and death and the flight of his soul to Kilimanjaro (which, as Hemingway reminds us, means the "House of God")—"as wide as all the world, great, high, and unbelievably white in the sun. And then he knew that there was where he was going" (*CSS* 56).

Africa, and the sacred landscape around Kilimanjaro, are once again at the center of Hemingway's last major pilgrimage narrative—*True at First Light.* Yet another unfinished and posthumously published work (1999), it provides all the evidence necessary to declare that pilgrimage remains Hemingway's most enduring theme. Ostensibly a hunting tale, it is more importantly a straightforward pilgrimage narrative that subsumes all of the pilgrimage variations found throughout Hemingway's work, incorporating elements of the traditional pilgrimage and the individualized quest in a new and quite specifically religious synthesis.

True at First Light is a fictionalized memoir of Hemingway's 1953 African safari. It is also a pilgrimage variation that stresses, more than Hemingway's other pilgrimage narratives, the desire to become a part of the place to which the pilgrimage is made. It is rooted, as most pilgrimage narratives are, in a sense of *dépaysement,* in the desire for a "change of scene" and the simultaneous "disorientation" that accompanies the change, the motion of the pilgrim. If the pilgrimage is to be judged efficacious, the "disorientation" leads through catharsis to a profound reorientation that leaves the pilgrim feeling a part of the place to which the pilgrimage has been made, feeling authentic connection with, rootedness in, the sacred landscape. Most discussions of *True at First Light* stress the primary theme of the "Africanization" of Hemingway, who is, in *propria persona,* the narrator and major actor. At the beginning, Hemingway states his love for Africa, and then he narrows the range of that love to a specific part of Africa, Kenya, and then to the particular tribal part of Kenya that he loves—ultimately the sacred country in the shadow of Kilmanjaro (or the "House of God"), which is the goal of his pilgrimage. He is there not as a tourist, not as just another rich and fashionable hunter and maker of safaris, but "to learn and to know about everything" (*TAFL* 73) and to do this not to serve some anthropo-missionary goal but in order to become increasingly a part of local tribal life. He stresses an intense localism of identity throughout. The primary mode of identity in this Hemingway work, as in most, is tribal and local, the pilgrim outsider become insider. Nearly every chapter has some indication of Hemingway's identification with, then his participation in, and finally his membership in the Kamba tribe.

Near the end of the book his wife Mary says that she wants "to go and really see something of Africa. You don't have any ambition. You'd just as soon stay in one place." To which Ernest replies: "Have you ever been in a better place?" And against, more firmly: "I'd rather live in a place and have an actual part in the life of it than just see new strange things" (*TAFL* 301–02). Of course, contrary to the popular view and the usual biocritical view, this was always the fundamental Hemingway mode of being: in France, or Spain, or Cuba, or Africa. He is never a tourist, always a pilgrim in the process of being localized, a purposeful traveler longing to be a member of a select community, or *creating* a new tribe or community rooted in the best traditions of the best places. It is a version of pilgrimage in which the pilgrim who goes to Rome or Santiago, stays in Rome or Santiago, or longs to stay forever.

At the very heart of Hemingway's African pilgrimage is the question of religion. Religious motifs and images are so pervasive that they can only be sketched here. When I talked to Hemingway's son Patrick as he was editing the book (omitting a great deal of the manuscript), he stressed one thing: "It's full of talk about the Baby Jesus and all this stuff foreshadowing the coming of Christmas, but Christmas never comes." When I received my pre-publication copy, the first thing I did after reading it through was to begin a count of the key passages and allusions dealing with religion; I stopped counting after marking 85 such passages. Likewise, with the references to the marijuana-effect Christmas Tree that Mary quests so assiduously for, I stopped counting after 35 references. And there are many references to the "Birthday of the Baby Jesus" and other formulations, some serious, some hilarious, involving the words "Baby Jesus"—e.g., when they go to dip up the magic Christmas Tree, Hemingway says they are "working for the Forestry Department of Our Lord, the Baby Jesus" (*TAFL* 296). Also I noted immediately the dozens of citations of the Mountain-God Kilimanjaro. When portions of this manuscript were first published, decades ago, in *Sports Illustrated,* it was presented as a hunting narrative; but the editor noted that religion was important, and though often used for humorous purposes, religion was not a laughing matter for Hemingway. Not enough time has passed since this published version of *True at First Light* came into print four years ago for there to be any established critical contextualizations, but the majority of Hemingway students and scholars tend to adopt a dismissive stance toward the book's religious concerns, viewing the matter as comic relief. But religion is never comic relief for Hemingway. Pilgrims don't make pilgrimages just for laughs.

It seems a safe bet that there are already dissertations and books in progress dealing with Hemingway's "New Religion" in *True at First Light.* It seems an equally safe bet that many such studies will view the "new religion" as Hemingway's Pagan Pilgrimage, his rejection of Christianity, or his farewell to Catholicism (and thus miss the point of Hemingway's Catholicism yet once more). Others will be sophisticated enough, it is to be hoped, to recognize that Hemingway's lifelong preoccupation with pilgrimage led him to a vision of Catholicism in relation to his African tribal religion that is subsumptive; that beneath all the comic play with religion, there is a syncretic religious thesis at work, a syncretistic drive to reconcile, to localize and thus truly universalize his fundamental Catholic beliefs. Under the rubric of syncretism *True at First Light* might seem to some students of Church history to be an adumbration of post–Vatican Two trends, and Hemingway might be seen as a kind of forerunner, a prophet of ecumenical inclusiveness and new modalities of worship. Here, for example, is Papa describing what Mary calls "Papa's religion": "We retain the best of various other sects and tribal laws and customs. But we weld them into a whole that all can believe" (*TAFL* 79). At times, it sounds like Papa's Postmodern Pilgrimage for Everyman. All on one page "Papa's religion" is described as a "new religion," as a "frightfully old religion," as a religion that Papa makes "more complicated every day," as a "revealed" religion rooted in Papa's "early visions" (*TAFL* 79). Whatever is serious, whatever is joking, one theme remains constant: the world-pilgrim's syncretistic drive to reconcile the local and the universal.

There is much more in the religious design—throw in Gitchy Manitou, the great Spirit, the Happy Hunting Grounds, add sacred trees and mountains and African religious ceremonies, animistic, Hindu, and Muslim references, meditations on the soul, pilgrimage allusions involving Rome, Mecca, and Santiago de Compostela, and you have some notion of how rich the mix is. The reader who has not studied the omitted portions of the manuscript should tread cautiously before drawing conclusions about this seriocomic mélange, and should remember also that Hemingway is always serious about religion and pilgrimage, which is precisely why he jokes about it. Never preachy, *True at First Light* rides on the syntax of spirituality, moves in religious rhythms that alternate between mystical meditation and epiphanic moments, and the self-deprecatory mockery of Papa, the pilgrim-leader of the "new religion."

One striking example may be seen in the sequence of movements that begins with the death of Mary's lion, the object of her achieved quest. First, there is ceremonial drinking; then Hemingway writes: "I drank and then lay down by the lion and begged his pardon for us having killed him and while I lay beside him I felt for the wounds. I drew a fish in front of him with my forefinger in the dirt" (*TAFL* 169). This Ichthus-ceremony (calling to mind the countless Christological associations of Hemingway's fishing pilgrimages) then flows directly into a meditation on the dark night of the soul and leads eventually to a quasi-Eucharistic meal: "it was wonderful to be eating the lion and have him in such close and final company and tasting so good" (*TAFL* 200). These incarnational moments of epiphanic communion with and in and through the body and blood of the lion are followed almost immediately by a sequence of self-mockery and mocking of religious clichés. Papa, paraphrasing the eighteenth-century Protestant hymn-writer Isaac Watts, tells his friend G. C. (which stands for Gin Crazed): "Satan will find work for idle hands to do." He asks—in inflated preacherly mode—if G. C. "will carry these principles into Life." Drinking a ceremonial beer (and beer drinking functions throughout the work as a ritual act of communion), G. C. says, "Drink your beer, Billy Graham" (*TAFL* 203–04). If we read Hemingway accurately and well, such joking does not undercut but underlines the seriousness of religious matters. Beyond all irony, Hemingway's work is about carrying principles into action, and he is a king of pilgrim-evangelist always inculcating ethical and moral and spiritual codes of conduct and communion.

Readers of *True at First Light* should be reluctant to make sweeping judgments regarding Hemingway and pilgrimage, Hemingway and religion, based on this published version, which might seem to suggest, for example, that Hemingway's African Pilgrimage had led him to go truly native, to become an actual pagan worshiper of the Mountain-God Kilimanjaro. Before reaching such a conclusion, consider carefully such omitted manuscript passages as this one: "We all worshiped the mountain with our borrowed and insecure religion but she belonged to another people and we loved her but we knew that we were strangers and we looked at her as a boundary and a delight and a source of coolness and something to be enjoyed and loved. But she was another people's God" (Hemingway Collection). The true pilgrim, that is to say, salutes all sacred landscapes, but holds fast to his own God. It may also be useful to remember that while Hemingway was writing his African pilgrimage variations, he was still praying at the Cathedrals of San Marco and Chartes and Burgos and Segovia, and still remaking segments of his old beloved Catholic Pilgrimages of Santiago de Compostela and les Saintes-Maries-de-la-Mer.

. . . . .

A few years ago, I had a conversation with a road-weary pilgrim in a café in the pilgrimage town of les Saintes-Maries-de-la-Mer, where I was living, after having made the pilgrimage several times, after having been chosen through some providential intervention to be the first American in history to carry the Saints into the sea at the pilgrimage. Thus, in that place, pilgrimage is always very much on my mind. The pilgrim, who was also a poet and a professor, was on his way back from Santiago de Compostela. "If the true pilgrim is always the quintessential anti-tourist, how would you define the pilgrim's hermeneutics of mobility?" I asked him. (He was, after all, a French poet and professor so it seemed safe to use the word hermeneutics after sundown.) "First," he said, "*dépaysement,* a hunger for change, of place and self. Then, a new Composition of Place rooted in cathartic vision—and, with luck, visions—of sacred landscape. Landscapes where you leave part of yourself, your remorse, where change, expiatory transformation, sweeps away the old self. Sacred landscapes that live within you forever." "That sounds a lot like Hemingway," I said, "like the pilgrimages he created in his work." "Oh," he said, "was Hemingway a pilgrim?" "Yes," I said, "and you are walking in his footsteps, abiding in his sacred landscapes."

WORKS CITED

Baker, Carlos. *Ernest Hemingway: A Life Story.* New York: Scribner, 1969.

———, ed. *Ernest Hemingway: Selected Letters 1917–1961.* New York: Scribner, 1981.

Eliot, T. S. *The Complete Poems and Plays.* New York: Harcourt, 1952.

Hemingway Collection. Manuscript. John F. Kennedy Lib. Boston, Massachusetts.

Hemingway, Ernest. *The Complete Short Stories of Ernest Hemingway.* New York: Scribner, 1987.

———. *A Farewell to Arms.* New York: Scribner, 1929.

———. *The Garden of Eden.* New York: Scribner, 1986.

———. Hemingway-Father Brown Correspondence. Hemingway Collection. U of Texas Lib. Austin, Texas.

———. *The Old Man and the Sea.* New York: Scribner, 1952.

———. *The Sun Also Rises.* New York: Scribner, 1926.

———. *True at First Light.* New York: Scribner, 1999.

Stoneback, H. R. "From the rue Saint-Jacques to the Pass of Roland to the 'Unfinished Church on the Edge of the Cliff.'" *Hemingway Review* 6 (Fall 1986): 2–29.

———. "In the Nominal Country of the Bogus: Hemingway's Catholicism and the Biographies." *Hemingway: Essays of Reassessment.* Ed. Frank Scafella, 105–40. New York: Oxford UP, 1991.

———. "Hemingway and the Camargue: Van Gogh's Bedroom, the 'Gypsy' Pilgrimage, Saint-Louis, the Holy Marys, Mireio, Mistral, Mithra, and Montherlant." *North Dakota Quarterly* 66.2 (1999): 164–95.

PART 5

Endings

Suzanne del Gizzo
Susan Beegel
William E. Cain

Going Home

Hemingway, Primitivism, and Identity

Suzanne del Gizzo

For a long time I had identified myself with the Wakamba and now had passed over the last important barrier so that the identification was complete.

—Hemingway, *True at First Light*

This was the beginning of the end of the day in my life which offered the most chances of happiness.

—Hemingway, *True at First Light*

"I'm going to be Kamba," Ernest Hemingway announces through his alter ego "Ernie" in *True at First Light,* a posthumously published account of his 1953–54 East African safari (242). Although this proclamation may seem surprising to those familiar with Hemingway, the great *American* writer, his initiation into the Kamba tribe was, for him, the culmination of a lifelong fascination with African culture. During his first safari in 1934–35, Hemingway had developed a profound connection to Africa; he explains in *Green Hills of Africa:* "I felt at home and where a man feels at home outside of where he's born, is where he is meant to go" (284). Even before the trip was over, Hemingway lamented his departure, claiming that he would lie awake

Reprinted with permission from *Modern Fiction Studies* 49.3 (Fall 2003). Copyright © the Purdue Research Foundation by the Johns Hopkins University Press.

at night listening to the sounds of Africa, "homesick" for it already. Writing nearly twenty years later, he returned to this theme of Africa as home, when he explains: "I had been a fool not to have stayed on in Africa and instead [I] had gone back to America where I had killed my homesickness for Africa in different ways" (*TAFL* 161). Certainly Hemingway's reference to Africa as "home" is tainted by an unmistakable note of imperialism, but it nonetheless reveals how deeply he wished to connect to Africa and African culture and to convey its personal significance for him.[1] A keen student of different cultures, Hemingway traveled frequently and adopted local customs easily and enthusiastically. For this reason, his insistence on Africa as "home" is all the more meaningful and compelling. Thus, when Hemingway finally returned to Africa for the 1953–54 safari, he took the opportunity to intensify his connection to the land and the people by becoming a member of the Kamba tribe.[2] Although the details of his "initiation" remain sketchy, *True at First Light* gives readers a glimpse into the experience as the narrator, "Ernie," "goes primitive"—ritualistically shaving his head, dyeing his clothes the pink ochre of the Masai tribe, and hunting naked at night with only a spear in hand.[3]

Although this encounter with the primitive is certainly the most explicit and colorful in his oeuvre, it would be a mistake to think of it as a departure from the themes and concerns of his overall work. In fact, the primitive—in many different forms and manifestations—exerts itself as a powerful force and defining factor at nearly every major intersection of Hemingway's life and career. During his childhood in suburban Chicago, the young Hemingway was exposed to the primitivist rhetoric of the "back to nature" and "recreation" movements, which celebrated the moral and physical healing properties of a "return to nature." This general cultural rhetoric was reinforced by his personal experiences with his father, an avid nature lover, and with the Native American cultures of Northern Michigan during his summer vacations. Later, as an aspiring writer in postwar Paris, Hemingway was again influenced by what had become the all-encompassing cultural phenomenon of Primitivism, which extended into areas of art, literature, language, and science as well as into popular culture and fashion, influencing the work of

Pablo Picasso, Gertrude Stein, and Ezra Pound, among others. But even after the vogue of Primitivism as a major cultural force had passed, Hemingway continued to return to its themes and ideas, working through them almost obsessively in his final and unfinished works, in particular *The Garden of Eden* and *True at First Light*.

As is evident from just this brief sketch, the word "primitive" in Western culture is a broad and slippery term that can denote many things from native peoples and cultures to folkways and natural environments. In addition, it can connote a wide range of sentiments, including "gentleness" and "innocence" as well as "fierceness" and "violence" (Torgovnick 1990, 7), not to mention the fact that it can be and has been deployed in the service of disparate political and cultural agendas. For this reason, discussions of the primitive often tend to be emotional and confused. More importantly, however, the very existence of the category of "the primitive" introduces the complications of cross-cultural interaction. Whatever else the primitive may come to mean, it is usually invoked in comparison to the West's level of progress and/or standards for civilization, culture, and civilized behavior. As the "other" of the West, the primitive becomes an empty holding place that reflects Western desires and anxieties about its own culture and identity—the primitive acts like an inverted mirror, showing the West aspects of itself that help define it by what it believes it is not, or more compellingly, by what it believes it has missed or lost. As Marianna Torgovnick argues, "the real secret of the primitive in [the twentieth] century has often been the same secret as always: the primitive can be whatever Euro-Americans want it to be" (Torgovnick 1990, 9). The primitive, then, reflects a fascination with not only a specific "primitive" culture and the "other," but ultimately with Western culture and the self as well. Although this account of primitivism as a hazy construction that overlaps with and informs a variety of Western cultural formations may be accurate, it is important to recognize that such an understanding limits the ability to imagine the capacity of primitivism for critique because it presents primitivism as always already incorporated into Western culture. While the primitive is always and only primitive in comparison to the West, there are different levels and kinds of Western engagement with the primitive. When invoked in relation to pristine natural environments or quaint folkways, the primitive is qualitatively different from the experience of direct involvement with or immersion in a culture considered to be primitive. It is useful and necessary to make a distinction between Western cultural discourse about primitivism and the actual experience of cross-cultural interaction. Cultural exchange, especially when it occurs on the turf of the "other" with a Westerner attempting to accept and live by that society's rules and customs, reveals the ways in which primitivism is capable of offering a meaningful critique of Western cultural norms and concepts. As we will see, for my purposes here, this critique is made possible not because of an explicit criticism on the part of the members of a "primitive" culture, but because the experience of belonging to two different cultures at once creates an awareness of hybridity on the part of the Western subject.

Although Hemingway initially exploited assumptions about the primitive, specifically its resonance in Anglo-American culture with physicality and authenticity, to cultivate and fuel his public persona in the early years of his career, ultimately it was his engagement and identification with primitive cultures that allowed him to distance himself from that persona and articulate a profound self-critique. His self-conscious attempt to become a member of the Kamba tribe through a ritualistic initiation and his decision to assume or perform a new identity as Kamba (however imperfectly), created a space of critique from which he reconsidered not only his public image, but also arguably Western notions of essential, unified selfhood as well. Hemingway's relationship to the primitive, then, reveals not only an unexpected side of the writer and artist engaged in a questioning of his persona, but also provides insight into the critical dialogue between primitivism and Western notions of identity.

. . . . .

The "primal scene" for Hemingway's interest in the primitive can be found in his childhood. His father, Clarence "Ed" Hemingway, shared his love of nature with his children and exposed them to his personal admiration for Native American culture. Ed Hemingway had been a student of Indian life since his own childhood; he was a meticulous collector of Indian artifacts and took particular pride in a nickname, Ne-teck-ta-la (Eagle Eye), that Indian friends had given him celebrating his skill as a marksman (Mellow 28). These early encounters with Native Americans and their culture through his father arguably gave Hemingway an understanding of the conditions of modern Indian life. They also introduced him to the idea of the primitive as a socially sanctioned alternative to the mainstream values and priorities emphasized by his suburban upbringing. According to Peter Hays, for the young Hemingway, as for many boys and girls of his generation, the Native American past came to represent a primitive ideal (48)—a time when man lived more intimately and harmoniously with nature—that implicitly, but productively, questioned the valorization of rapid, unthinking industrialization and urbanization. During his adolescence, however, Hemingway's interest in primitivism took a somewhat bizarre turn when his admiration of Native Americans developed into an assertion that he was, in fact, part Indian himself, claiming that he had Indian blood from the Edmonds side of his father's family (Mellow 29). While this identification may not be totally surprising in an impressionable young boy—biographer James Mellow speculates that it was merely a form of "[teenage] rebellion against his family and Oak Park values" (30)—what is surprising is its persistence. At various times over the course of his life and well past the years of "teenage rebellion," Hemingway alleged that he was part Indian—sometimes Ojibwa, sometimes Cheyenne, sometimes unspecified. Although later in life many of his references to Native American culture appear superficial and playful—like his use of an affectionate "Choctaw lingo" among his friends (whom he referred to collectively as a "fine tribe")—he continued to insist with some seriousness that he was at least "⅛ Indian" (SL 659).

The persistence of Hemingway's claim to Indian blood can be found in another curious act of identification—Hemingway's initiation into the Kamba tribe at the age of fifty-four. Interestingly enough, his claim to Native American ancestry re-intensified during and after this second visit to Africa. He said of his initiation experience specifically: "I was the first and only white man or 1/8 Indian who was ever Kamba, and it is not like President

Coolidge being given a war bonnet by tame Blackfoote [*sic*] or Shoshone"
(qtd. in Lewis 480). Hemingway uses the declaration of an ancestral primitive
bloodline (imagined though it may be) to justify or heighten his connection
to the Kamba and to separate himself from other white men interested in
the primitive. This gesture lends an air of authenticity to his experience,
which he insists was certainly more meaningful than President Coolidge's
fraudulent war bonnet.

Although many critics have taken up the issue of primitivism in Hemingway's work, particulary with regard to Native Americans, they often discuss
it in generic terms and in theoretical contexts.[4] In the process, they miss what
is perhaps most striking and most puzzling about Hemingway's fascination
with the primitive—his *identification* with primitive peoples and cultures.
He did not simply observe or study them, appropriating select aspects of the
culture; he sought in many instances, through some rite of initiation or feat of
analogy, to become one of them. Moreover, it is significant that Hemingway's
interest in the primitive was generated not merely by ideas, theories, and
reading, but also and principally by physical contact and interpersonal
relationships. By reifying Hemingway's encounters with the primitive into a
vague set of non-specific values, qualities, and practices, previous critics have
circumvented the political and social complexities of a white, American man
in physical contact with primitive peoples and cultures. In addition, such an
approach diminishes the significance of Hemingway's desire to reconfigure
his ethnic and/or racial make-up and to fabricate identities that distanced
him from whiteness, Americanness, and masculinity.

Hemingway's interest in the primitive also resonates with what Susan
Gubar calls "racechanges" to the extent that his fascination hinges on a desire
for cross-cultural or cross-racial identification, a longing to occupy or perform
the identity of the "other." For Gubar, "racechange" is a term that describes the
phenomenon of white people imitating "characteristic" behaviors, gestures,
or speech patterns of people, usually African Americans for her purposes,
considered racially "other." Throughout his life, Hemingway participated in
behavior consistent with Gubar's notion of racechange. For example, he was
fond of recounting a story about the time (true or not) when he had been

mistaken for a Cheyenne boy by an old Indian while visiting the Wind River Reservation (Mellow 29), spoke in what he called his "Choctaw" lingo, and was almost obsessive about tanning and darkening his skin. What is interesting and unusual, however, about Hemingway's racechanges is his desire to establish a connection to Native Americans specifically (and by extension to all primitive peoples) via bloodlines and ancestry. This claim reveals a sense of urgency and a desire to move his identification beyond the realm of superficial physical alterations or behaviors. Such a proud, albeit fabricated claim to mixed blood fed directly into cultural taboos about miscegenation and blood mixing, exacerbating early-twentieth-century anxieties about racial authenticity and purity. But Hemingway asserted that he was racially mixed in order to position himself to claim a greater authenticity—a direct connection through his ancestors to the primitive. In this way, Hemingway's fictional Native American identity, somewhat daring in its implication of miscegenation, remains thoroughly rooted in the mythology of the primitive by accepting the primacy of blood and the connection between blood and race. At the same time, while this fictive identity is still clearly a performance (in the way that racechange is a performance), Hemingway's blood claim flirts directly with the rhetoric of authenticity and, more profoundly, the relationship between performance, authenticity, and identity.

Robert Lewis alone hints at the significance of Hemingway's preoccupation with Native Americans and its connection to his sense of identity. Lewis speculates that "references and allusion to Indians run throughout [Hemingway's] public fiction and nonfiction and the private letters, not as a major element, but perhaps as a *trace element essential to psychic health*" (211; emphasis added). Although I would broaden this statement to read "references and allusions to the *primitive*," Lewis's observation does clarify the link between primitivism, identity, and recreation in the early twentieth century. During his childhood, Hemingway pieced together his ideas of the primitive through his contact with Native Americans during his summer vacations, which indelibly linked the primitive to recreation in his mind, as well as through his readings of novels by Rudyard Kipling and accounts of former President Roosevelt's 1909–10 East African safari. Hemingway caught his first direct glimpse of Africa as a boy in the Chicago Field Museum, when his father took him to see the artifacts and mammals that Carl Akeley had sent back from his famous "brightest Africa" expeditions. As an adult, sports, such as bullfighting and big game fishing and hunting, became the locations where he was most likely to encounter primitive cultures and/or behavior. It was not by chance that Hemingway's interactions with primitive cultures most often occurred in the context of some recreational activity. His personal experience of the interconnectedness of primitivism and recreation reflects a more general tendency. Recreation, primitivism, and health came together to form a kind of recuperative matrix in the early twentieth century: a space of rebirth and reassessment that defined itself in reaction to what were believed to be the debilitating effects of mainstream culture and civilization.

Primitivism and recreation were connected insofar as they were portrayed as liminal spaces on the fringe of mainstream society that enabled one to objectify the society's values and gain perspective on them. Spaces that are socially and spatially liminal, however, have long been regarded as culturally central by critics such as Victor Turner. This observation is literally true with regard to the rise of recreational spaces at the turn of the century when pristine natural spaces were quickly becoming regulated national parkland in the name of healthful recreation. At this time, the concept of specifically primitive or natural recreation as an antidote to cultural malaise was a sentiment that was very much at the center of social concerns. Recreation and the primitive were united by their capacity to provide a break or an escape from the dominant culture and encourage a radical exploration of self unfettered (at least theoretically) from society, even if this gesture itself were interpolated into the dominant cultural logic. Such an exploration of self, it was allowed, would often involve deviating from expected norms—literally letting "one*self* go." As such, recreation and primitivism tended to be associated not only with liberation and freedom, but also with transgression—breaking the rules or behaving out of character, a practice that often involved some version of racechange or imitating behaviors considered to be representative of a primitive "other." Recall, for example, Mellow's contention that Hemingway first claimed to be Native American as a form of "rebellion" against his family and their turn-of-the-century suburban values. It is perhaps in this spirit that Lewis suggests that an identification with Native American culture (and primitivism) contributed to Hemingway's "psychic health"—it provided a socially sanctioned outlet or escape from a culture that he found oppressive and limiting. But Lewis's insistence on the ultimate "healthful" results of this rebellion further reveals the way in which primitivism was largely used in the service of producing and maintaining Western notions of an essential, whole, unified self and by extension, individuals who could function productively in mainstream culture. While this association between primitivism and recreation, then, does contain the concept of critique, it is ultimately more of a "pressure release valve" designed to maintain social norms.

· · · · ·

As a young artist in Paris, Hemingway discovered that his childhood connection between primitivism and rebellion came to be a more self-consciously deployed tactic on the part of modernists, who were searching for a position from which to critique mainstream culture and society.[5] Although there are elements of sincere critique in modernist interest in the primitive, for example its celebration of the instinctual and sexual, it was quickly popularized and commercialized, becoming more of a fashionable bourgeois stance than a profound cultural reassessment. Modernist interest in the primitive, however, does contain the seeds of a more radical critique insofar as it puts primitivism explicitly in dialogue with issues of identity. Hemingway was part of a generation defined by a feeling of alienation from the dominant society in the wake of World War I, a generation that had lost its sense of rootedness and for whom expatriation and exile became defining motifs. Georg Lukàcs's theory of "transcendental homelessness" captures the nature of this modern experience. It is, as Marianna Torgovnick explains, a "form of alienation . . . from the self [and] from society" (Torgovnick 1990, 227), a feeling of disconnection from the mechanisms that help individuals create a sense of themselves in the world. Transcendental homelessness is related to the belief that individuals are cast adrift and left to their own devices to forge their identities and create their personae. Identity is up for grabs. If one is no longer defined by one's origins, if one is homeless, then the burden of forming the self is entirely one's own; it is not pre-determined by factors such as nation, class, and, more radically, race or gender affiliation. The result is an intense focus on the self and the process of self-creation.

Within this open field of self-creation in modern culture, primitivism, as depicted in artistic modernism, promised something occult, mysterious, and ancient, all the lure and the hope of an historical and/or psychic origin—a home, in its most basic sense. Freud explains the connection between this desire for origins and the primitive in *Civilization and its Discontents*. He argues that his longing for the "oceanic" (15), a comforting feeling of "eternity" (11), is merely a residual, primitive stage of mental development that is "commonly preserved alongside" our more advanced, adult minds (16). The primitive, then, was imagined as offering the hope of connection, union, and intimacy both with others and the surrounding environment. Torgovnick connects these two major themes of the modern period when she links transcendental homelessness to primitivism. She suggests that the condition of exile or cultural estrangement contained in the concept of "transcendental homelessness" is marked by a longing to "go home" and that this desire to "go home" "turn[s] up as the grounding condition for interest in the primitive in a surprising number of important writers" (1990, 187). Torgovnick observes that "going home," like "going primitive," is a metaphor for a return to origins (1990, 185).

At the same time, however, the search for identity and the need to create the self invites existential uncertainties about the possibilities of accessing truth and authenticity. While transcendental homelessness produces a longing for home, its focus on self-creation and self-determination calls into question the entire concept of a genuine "at-homeness" itself (North 1994, 32). In the process of searching for origins, one becomes aware that this exercise compromises the idea of origins in the first place, since origins and at-homeness rely on static categories of social and cultural identity that individuals feel comfortable with and, therefore, take for granted. Thus, this process often entails an attendant realization that all identities are in some sense performed, a realization that in turn gives rise to anxieties about "falseness" and "authenticity."

As one of the principal figures of "la generation perdu" and as an expatriate, it is perhaps not surprising that Hemingway became fixated, however ambivalently, on the idea of "home." But like many of his generation, his search for home was compromised by his awareness that traditional identity markers were not only unreliable and misleading but were also potentially limiting. Hemingway's search for home was further complicated by his fascination with authenticity and honesty. In both his writing and his life, he seemed dedicated to capturing authentic action and emotion—the "true gen," as he called it—and was very wary of any false emotion. This pronounced preoccupation with authenticity has filtered into critical perceptions of Hemingway and his work as well. Hugh Kenner called Hemingway a "recorder of authenticities" (145), and Malcolm Cowley believed that Hemingway's interest in the primitive was motivated by a search for the authentic (Lewis 207). But Hemingway's desire for authenticity comes into direct conflict with the concept of performance inherent in his notions of identity. In recent years, critics such as Debra Moddelmog and Leonard Leff have suggested that Hemingway's conscious construction of a public persona, which was so clearly a performance in some respects (not to mention his attempts to identify himself as Native American and Kamba), complicates his stated insistence on authenticity. At this point, it is not news that Hemingway was actively involved in the creation of a public persona, but the full ramifications of this realization and what it reveals about Hemingway's concept of self, especially its relationship to issues of primitivism and authenticity in Hemingway's life and work, still need to be teased out. To begin this exploration, I will look at the narratives of Hemingway's two trips to Africa, in particular his second trip in 1953–54, where issues of identity, authenticity, and primitivism collide.

. . . . .

Hemingway's interest in Africa spanned nearly sixty years and coincided with the decline of colonialism on that continent. As a result, his attitudes about and relationship to Africa and its peoples were informed by these sociopolitical developments. It must immediately be noted that Hemingway's loudly professed love and appreciation for Africa was rooted firmly in a self-centered sense of it as a space of recreation that could help him discover or recover aspects of himself. As Moddelmog points out, in Hemingway's work, as "in so much of American and British literature written by white men, Africa ... [remains] the stage of the white male's individuation in which black African natives serve as stage hands without histories or scripts of their own" (109). Nonetheless, although Hemingway never fully stepped outside of a traditional dynamic of the modern Westerner selfishly encountering the primitive, it is possible to detect significant changes in his attitude toward Africa and African peoples as well as toward himself by studying the writing and fiction that emerged from his two visits.

I will not examine the narratives that resulted from the first safari (1934–35), which include "The Snows of Kilimanjaro," "The Short Happy Life of Francis Macomber," and *Green Hills of Africa,* in any detail since I am interested in this trip principally to establish a comparison with the later safari.[6] Suffice it to say that the 1934–35 safari was an expensive, white-hunter-led expedition that participated in an imperialistic and disrespectful relationship to the African land and peoples. Despite Hemingway's attempts to portray the conditions as rustic and to emphasize the austerity of camp life in stories like "The Snows of Kilimanjaro," the safari was relatively luxurious (according to Leff, it cost nearly 25,000 1934 dollars). The majority of the trip was dedicated to trophy hunting or the killing of game for sport. It is curious that while Hemingway appears to be attracted to Africa because of its pristine hunting conditions, he does not fully recognize the way in which his presence and the presence of others like him compromises this situation. Moreover, he expresses his enthusiasm for Africa using imperialistic language that compares America and Africa: "Our people went to America because it was the place to go then. It had been a good country and we had made a bloody mess of it and I would go, now, somewhere else as we had always had the right to go somewhere else and as we had always gone" (*GHOA* 285). Throughout *Green Hills of Africa,* Hemingway creates and maintains a firm distinction between "our people" and the native Africans.

The writings he produced based on this safari portrayed the African natives who accompanied him on it as members of what Toni Morrison refers to as Hemingway's "array of enabling black nursemen" (82). The "black nursemen," who Morrison compares to Tonto of the Lone Ranger tales (a comparison, which, incidentally, reinforces the link I have been tracing between Native Americans and Africans in Hemingway's work) are faithful attendants who "do everything possible to serve . . . without disturbing [the] indulgent delusion that [the white hero] is alone" (Morrison 82). Africa as portrayed on this safari merely serves as a backdrop or "stage" for personal exploration and redemption. When Hemingway is not concerned with affirming his masculinity and prowess through the trophy hunt, he obsesses over the demands of his life as a professional writer. The fusing of these concerns is so complete that in an infamous review of *Green Hills of Africa* in *The New York Times,* John Chamberlain claimed that Hemingway "went all the way to Africa to hunt, and then when he thought he had found a rhinoceros, it turned out to be Gertrude Stein" (19). Thus, while Hemingway was physically there and anxious to enjoy Africa, his cultural and personal concerns put a barrier between him and any significant experience of it. As a result, Hemingway indirectly supports imperialist policies by his refusal to engage in the issues of the foreign occupation of Africa, the devastating environmental impact of the safari industry, and by his inability, or perhaps his unwillingness, to recognize the situation of the politically disenfranchised natives, who, despite the fact that they were experiencing horrible famine during his visit, he persists in envisioning as living harmoniously with the land (*GHOA* 284). In this way, Hemingway participates in a "state of mind that is produced by and in turn helps to produce imperialistic attitudes toward another nation and thus subjects its people to dependency and domination" (Moddelmog 110).[7]

Nonetheless, Hemingway enjoyed this trip to Africa and, almost as a foreboding, was preoccupied by the fear that he might never be able to return. It would, in fact, take nearly twenty years and a World War before Hemingway was able to go back to Africa. When he finally stepped onto East African soil again in 1953, he did so in an entirely different ideological, social, and political context. Whereas East Africa had been very much a set of British colonies in the 1930s, the post-World War II East Africa of the 1950s was already experiencing the stirrings of political independence. Hemingway was not oblivious to these changes; he sums up the difference succinctly in *True at First Light*: "Things were not too simple in this safari because things had changed very much in East Africa" (13).

I should perhaps pause here to say a few words about the challenges involved in working with *True at First Light*.[8] As a posthumously published work, edited by Hemingway's son, Patrick, it presents some critical complications worthy of mention. One issue that inevitably arises is the extent to which my readings may or may not be affected by Patrick's editorial choices. I have studied both the published version and the manuscript, known to Hemingway scholars as the *African Journal*, and have used only passages that appear in both. Although Patrick did expunge parts of the manuscript, I do not feel that any of the passages left out of the published text enhanced my readings here or altered my overall perception of the book. Another, slightly more vexing issue revolves around the nettling question of accuracy and the extent to which the book or the manuscript can be read as a non-fictional account of the safari.[9] Although many of the events in the journal are corroborated by other sources such as letters and diaries, I prefer to respond to this concern using another approach. I would suggest that *True at First Light* and its manuscript are best treated as narratives that, like all narratives, exist in an imperfect relationship to fact. I choose to read *True at First Light* as a fictional memoir that regardless of where the lines between truth and fiction are drawn sheds light on Hemingway's personal attempts at identity construction.

Nevertheless, *True at First Light* marks a significant change in Hemingway's attitudes and approach to Africa and Africans. Whereas in *Green Hills of Africa* Hemingway believes he had the "right" to hunt in any pristine country he could find—"I would go, now, somewhere else as we had always had the *right* to go somewhere else and as we had always gone" (282; emphasis added)—in *True at First Light*, he adopts a much more reticent and self-aware posture. Although *True at First Light* uses the language of "rights" as well, their valence has changed significantly, as Hemingway circumspectly confesses that he "want[ed] to know more about [Africa] than [he] had any *right* to know" (39; emphasis added). The native African safari workers, though not fully developed characters, are more individualized and are treated with more respect than in *Green Hills of Africa.* Hemingway notes how his interaction with the natives has changed: "Twenty years ago I had called them boys too and neither they nor I had any thought that I had no *right* to" (*TAFL* 16; emphasis added). Moreover, one of the subplots of *True at First Light* concerns the Mau Mau rebellion, an intense, if scattered uprising against British authority. Over the years, then, Hemingway witnessed profound changes in the relationship between Westerners, native Africans, and the land they both occupied.

For critical purposes, the 1953–54 safari can be divided into two parts—the portion of the trip, only about a month or so, when Hemingway and his wife, Mary, were accompanied by a photographer, Earl Theisen, for *Look* magazine, which ran a photo article on the trip, and the three months after Theisen left. This distinction is useful because there are two significantly different versions of this second safari: the *Look* story (made up predominantly of Theisen's photographs) and *True at First Light,* which begins after Theisen leaves. Moreover, Hemingway was in some sense "on duty" as the "famous author" as long as Theisen was in the safari party, but he was able to let his guard down once Theisen was gone.

With or without Theisen there, however, Hemingway does not at any point present the trip as a pure recreational escape. Rather, he goes through some trouble in both the *Look* article and *True at First Light* to portray the safari as a full-scale alternative life. Hemingway explains in *True at First Light* that this safari was not one of those expensive "White-Hunter-chaperoned" ordeals (perhaps an allusion to his first safari). He has accepted a "job" working as a Game Warden for the Kenyan Game Department and lives in a (relatively) simple camp that sends its "warriors" out to kill animals for the food it needs to survive, while providing a service to the surrounding native communities by protecting them from dangerous animals. The camp is portrayed as a working safari in every respect. Hemingway enthusiastically embraces this new world, immersing himself in its details, protocol, and responsibilities. Although the mood changes depending on whether one is reading the *Look* article or *True at First Light,* in both cases the second safari is an attempt to create a different, more intimate connection that reflects an interest in being involved in Africa and not simply being in Africa. Hemingway does retain many unthinking primitivist propositions, particularly with regard to the link between primitivism, physicality, and, specifically, sexuality, but he is engaged in an attempt to gather as much information as possible and to live according to tribal rules.[10] As such, the 1953–54 safari presents an encounter with the primitive rooted less in vague cultural fantasies linked to Anglo-American ideas of recreation and more in disciplined, ascetic immersion into the other culture that involved learning rituals, languages, and customs. Although Hemingway remains interested in Africa principally for its ability to offer a personally transformative experience, this safari is more invested in engagement and contact, opening up the borders of the self rather than protecting them. This approach is made possible by not only the change in the political climate, which encouraged more equal relationships between Westerners and natives, but also arguably by Hemingway's increasing sense of frustration with and alienation from his public persona.

· · · · ·

The two known and readily accessible versions of the 1953–54 safari reveal very different sides of Hemingway and his interaction with Africa and African peoples. Unlike the 1934–35 safari, where the primitive space of Africa was used principally as a background for a public rant that only served to confirm Hemingway's public persona, this later trip, which is distinguished by his embrace of the primitive in many respects, compelled in him a deep study of self and a re-imagination of identity. The differences between the *Look* article, titled "Safari," and *True at First Light* demonstrate how this safari, in particular, challenged Hemingway's notions of self and highlighted issues of identity and authenticity that are central, but sometimes unexamined, in his earlier work. The *Look* article portrays Hemingway as a civilized and knowledgeable white man protecting and teaching his African friends by bringing aspects of Western culture with him on safari, while *True at First Light* reveals a Hemingway on the verge of dissociating himself from Western culture and "going native." Although both narratives rehearse established patterns of the white man's experience in Africa—going native is as familiar a gesture as acting to maintain Western ideals in the face of the primitive—the juxtaposition and simultaneity of these two narratives make them interesting. They suggest not only that Hemingway consciously negotiated the images of his visit to Africa for the public, but also that, as one man playing both roles—the civilized Westerner and the Westerner gone primitive—he struggled both with issues of his identity and with those of mastery of and/or immersion in another culture.

The cover of the January 26, 1954, issue of *Look* magazine features Hemingway's familiar patriarchal face with a white beard, his watchful eyes looking alertly out into the distance. An African man in the background follows his gaze. This photograph captures the essence of the specific Hemingway persona in Africa portrayed by the *Look* article—a calm, wise, quintessentially American man and adventurer who advises and directs Africans and who is admired by them. Across the bottom of the cover, a banner proclaims: "Hemingway Writes on Africa." The irony of this phrase, of course, lies in its double meaning. In addition to its intended meaning that Hemingway will write *about* Africa for readers of *Look,* it also suggests that Hemingway, like other Westerners before him, will write his own story *over* Africa, at the expense of Africa itself, by bringing his American ideals and standards with him. The banner continues to read: "America's great author takes you on safari." The use of the singular—"great author"—confirms Hemingway's expertise and cultural clout not only as a Westerner in Africa, but in America as well. In fact, the article works consistently through this double logic—it portrays Hemingway as both the Western man advising backward Africans in a number of scenarios, but it also makes it clear that he is advising "us"/Americans/Westerners about travel to an exotic and primitive locale.

The finished article is sixteen pages long, fifteen of which are filled with photographs. Hemingway wrote only one full page of text and captions for the article, but in that small space of writing, he works to do two things: to familiarize American readers with Africa and to convince them that it is a safe vacation destination. The article exploits Hemingway's reputation as an experienced reporter and seasoned war correspondent. These qualifications, the article continually implies, make him capable of assessing the safety of foreign cultures, and the entire article works to confirm this image of Hemingway as expert.

In order to familiarize *Look* readers with Africa, Hemingway compares the foreign landscape to America. At one point, he is reminded of "Wyoming west of Cheyenne," and at another of "Tombstone, Arizona" ("Safari" 20). The fact that Hemingway is reminded of places in the American West tacitly equates Africa to the American frontier. This gesture not only domesticates the primitive landscape, it also suggests that Africa holds the promise of an experience now lost in America forever, since by the 1950s the American frontier was only a memory. Invoking the frontier plays to the American nostalgia that Hemingway keenly felt for a lost pristine space that was metaphorically as well as literally open and full of opportunity. At the same time, the wildness of the West is diminished due to its pastness, making it an emotionally effective but benign comparison. The familiarization process continues by making references to institutions such as Woolworth and Barclay's Bank and by deploying a tone familiar in the magazine world, that of an expert advising readers on social etiquette. These efforts are part of Hemingway's attempt to counter reports of the violence of the Mau Mau rebellion. Again, to drive his point home, he compares the Kenyan capital to various American cities. Here is the extended, almost comical quotation: "Nairobi for a foreigner with no one with a grudge against him is safer than New York, five times safer than parts of Memphis, West Memphis or Jacksonville, infinitely safer than parts of Chicago and most certainly safer than Brooklyn, the Bronx, Central Park at night or Cook City Montana, on the date of the celebration of the Old Timers Fish Fry" ("Safari" 20).

If this emphasis on safety seems odd for Hemingway, a man who tended to gravitate to wars and extreme experiences, it may be better understood by explaining that the 1953–54 safari was, in part, a carefully engineered publicity event and business deal. Hemingway agreed to write a brief article for *Look* and to allow Earl Theisen to photograph the beginning of the safari because the money he made on the deal paid for the entire trip. Furthermore, a young ranger with the Kenyan Game Department, Denis Zaphiro, welcomed Hemingway and *Look,* in the hope that coverage of the author's visit would boost interest in safari tours, which had been lagging due to the Mau Mau rebellion (Burwell 136)—a glimpse into the odd partnerships forged by globalization! But, of course, it is implied that Hemingway engages Africa on a level the average tourist will not. He strives to present himself as a traveler in a world of tourists, a man with a qualitatively different relationship to Africa than the average person could ever have. After all, he is employed by the Kenyan Game Department to protect natives from marauding animals—so Africa remains dangerous for him even as he tells readers it is safe for them.

Most of the photographs that compose the article rehearse a number of cultural performances that reinforce the message of safety and familiarity in Hemingway's text; they meet expectations of the white man's role in an increasingly post-colonial Africa. Hemingway is portrayed less as an adventurer and more as an ethnographer and/or cultural emissary, making Africa safer by making it more Western. Among the roles that Hemingway assumes in the picture story are protector, teacher, advisor, and doctor. The attitude toward hunting portrayed in the *Look* article, where Hemingway is pictured only once with a hunting trophy (a leopard that, incidentally, he did not shoot), is entirely different from that of the 1934–35 safari, which focused on trophy hunting and killing animals for sport. Hemingway repeatedly claims that animals are only killed for food or to protect natives. There are two instances of Hemingway as protector in the article, where he is asked to kill a troublesome and dangerous animal that is threatening the native population. In the first instance, he kills a lioness that had attacked a Masai camp. Despite the presence of seventeen Masai warriors, Hemingway shoots the lioness single-handedly, testifying to the superiority of Western techniques and tools. In another instance, a game ranger enlists his help to kill a wounded and therefore very dangerous rhino. Hemingway's expertise and bravery as a hunter are dramatized in the caption where he tells us: "I let the [rhino] come much further than it was good for either of us in order to be truly sure" ("Safari" 27). In a photograph titled, "Clinic," Hemingway is pictured demonstrating another skill, as he diagnoses and treats natives using the wonder of modern Western medicine—antibiotics. And in another picture, this time of Hemingway sparring with "Tony," a native scout, Hemingway's expertise is again emphasized as he knowingly assesses Tony's technique and informs us that he will "never make a good heavyweight" ("Safari" 30).

Hemingway's fourth wife, Mary, appears in relatively few photographs, but when she does appear, it is usually to emphasize the domestic effect her presence as a woman had on the safari. Despite the fact that Mary also hunted animals and participated in the rigors of camp life, as we know from *True at First Light,* she is pictured with a gun only once in the *Look* article and even then, it is pointed down while she stops to admire the scenery. In the most extensive set of pictures featuring her, Mary takes in and cares for "Baa," a Grant gazelle that has been abandoned by his mother. The Baa photographs confirm Mary's innate femininity by presenting the gazelle as a surrogate baby—the baby Mary and Ernest could not have. Mary is pictured fawning over Baa, feeding him from a bottle, and allowing him to kiss her face. Femininity and domesticity are deployed to further familiarize Africa and make camp life look like suburbia.

The *Look* article seeks not only to present a reassuring narrative of a Westerner's visit to East Africa, but also to reaffirm our picture of a patriarchal, knowledgeable Papa and his loving wife living peaceably with nature and the natives—an image that is profoundly altered in *True at First Light.* But the seamlessness of the article's narrative is disturbed in an unsettling and problematic closing gesture: the article ends with a photograph of a hawk attacking a guinea fowl. The caption describe the hawk's brutal attack in graphic detail and explains that the "hawk started to eat the guinea alive and the guinea protested vocally" ("Safari" 34). Hemingway explicitly contemplates the politics of intercultural interaction in the caption that concludes: "They were obviously different tribes. Watching this action I was not wholly sure of white man's role in Africa" (34). In the final words of the article, Hemingway casts vivid doubt on the role of the Westerner in Africa and goes so far as to invert typical cultural associations by casting the white man as similar to the hawk, a bird that eats other birds, or in other words, something akin to a cannibal.

True at First Light picks up where the *Look* article leaves off both in terms of chronology—the photographer, Earl Theisen, has already departed as the narrative opens—and in terms of theme. While there is still an element of Papa as protector and expert in *True at First Light*, these roles are less secure and much more ambiguous than in the *Look* article, as is the Westernized domesticity of camp life. In *True at First Light*, Africa becomes less a place to find safety and reaffirm social roles than a space in which to take risks and invert traditional relations. Hemingway is no longer a master intent on sharing Western culture with Africans; he is a student immersed in the ways of different tribal customs. While the *Look* article focuses on Hemingway "at work" within a recreational field, cameras capturing "America's great author" on safari, the events in *True at First Light* occur once the cameras are gone and the "vacation" proper begins, albeit a vacation whose general atmosphere is one of discipline and work. In this somewhat different context, away from the cameras and public expectations, Hemingway is more inclined to explore the transgressive elements of his encounter with the primitive.

True at First Light reveals Hemingway's personal attraction to African life and his attempts to explore his own identity by identifying with African culture as opposed to Western culture. Hemingway captures both the discomfort and fascination with African peoples that marks Western relations to those they consider primitive. He seems at once to mock their rituals, culture, and spirituality, while also striving to be a part of them. The narrative is divided into two major sections. The first follows Ernie (the character) as he helps Mary (the character) hunt a lion. The image of "Miss Mary" (as she is called throughout the book) actively hunting diverges from the image of her implied by the *Look* article. In addition, throughout the book, Hemingway and Mary share a more equal relationship with each other and with the natives than was suggested by the article. The second section of the book begins with Mary's departure to do Christmas shopping in Nairobi and ends when she returns. In this section, the tone of the narrative changes dramatically as Hemingway "goes native," exploring the tribal traditions of the Kamba and the Masai.

I will concentrate on the second section of *True at First Light*, since it is here that the image of Hemingway in the *Look* magazine article is most clearly complicated. Although Hemingway expresses a desire to "know more about [Africa] than [he] had any right to know" throughout the book, it is not until Mary leaves for Nairobi that he feels free to act out his deepest desires. As a white woman and his wife, Mary signifies those elements that most police Hemingway's conscience, regardless of their personal experimentation and transgressions, which I will discuss later. Once Mary is gone, Hemingway begins to embrace the "other" cultures of the Kamba and the Masai by engaging in their rituals. He has been having a relationship with a Kamba woman named Debba, an affair that he problematically associates with his desire to "know" Africa, but he has limited the time he has spent with her to minimize tensions with Mary. Shortly after Mary leaves, Hemingway shaves his head in a fashion Mary later describes as like a girl of the Masai tribe, kills a leopard, drinks to excess, breaks a safari cot with his Kamba fiancée (as Debba is called), dyes his clothes the pink ochre of the Masai, and goes hunting naked with only a spear in the middle of the night. In these activities, Hemingway's position as expert, so central to the logic of the *Look* article, is inverted; he is now a novice, an outsider, trying to learn, however haphazardly, the ways of another tribe. As a result, his relationship to the other men at the camp is altered. They begin to advise him on the necessary form and procedures for the rituals he attempts to undertake. For example, because Keiti, a camp elder, does not condone Hemingway's familiarity with Debba at meal time, he prevents Hemingway from eating at the table with her, an intervention that would not have been tolerated in the past. In fact, Keiti and Mwindi, another tribesman, frequently steer Hemingway through the nuances of tribal ritual and behavior.

Although Hemingway's version of initiation into the Kamba tribe seems to mix actual tribal customs with his own romantic notions of primitivism, such as drinking to excess, engaging in unusual sexual practices, and hunting a leopard, his desire to perform a racechange and to live as a Kamba and according to tribal law (at least for the most part) reveals a complex repudiation of identity. At one point, "Ernie" puts a piece of wounded leopard's shoulder blade into his mouth; it cuts the inside of his cheek and his blood mixes with the leopard's blood (*TAFL* 239). Although portrayed in the section where he is going primitive, this mixing of animal and human blood is not part of the initiation ritual. The episode reveals how Hemingway's desire to integrate into the tribe sublimates his own anxieties and fantasies about racial and cultural authenticity. Throughout the book, Hemingway flirts with racechange, claiming that he and Mary are "not white," but once he "goes native," he makes every attempt to disassociate himself from his identity as a "White Man," physically as well as socially and politically; he explains: "it seemed to me stupid to be white in Africa and . . . I was burned dark enough to pass as half-caste" (*TAFL* 201). Later, while tracking a wounded leopard with a Kamba friend, Ngui, Hemingway recounts his dissociation from the more abstract political and social roles of the "White Man" in Africa: "We were both very serious now and there was no White Man to speak softly and knowingly from his great knowledge, nor any White Man to give violent orders astonished at the stupidity of his 'boys' and cursing them on like reluctant hounds" (*TAFL* 239). Here, through his capitalization of the term, "White Man," and his rearticulation and revalencing of the expected power relations, Hemingway emphasizes that he does not feel nor does he want to claim the power dynamic and privilege that "White Men" are supposed to feel and claim in relation to Africans. Rather, he wants to be Kamba and prefers to identify himself on equal-footing with other members of the tribe. At the same time, however, even though he is a new member of the tribe, Hemingway immediately attempts to claim the seniority of age as well as the status of a warrior within his new culture. He explains: "I was a Mzee which means elder as well as still having the status of a warrior" (*TAFL* 264). Regardless of his position within the tribe, these episodes make it clear that Hemingway longs to embrace a different identity, and through this longing he presents a critique of his identity as a "White Man."

But it is Hemingway's behavior in his private life, after the safari was over, that best expresses how deeply he was affected by his experiences on this second phase of the safari. While working on the manuscript of *True at First Light,* he became obsessed with the idea of carrying some "markers" of his membership in the Kamba tribe into his daily life. One example of his persistence can be seen in what Mary termed the "earring crisis." Mary explains that Hemingway "developed a fever for some outward sign of kinship with the Kamba" (426). His fever apparently grew so intense that Mary wrote him a note on October 4, 1955, detailing the reasons why he should not pierce his ears. She writes:

> Everything you do sooner or later gets into print, and I feel truly that your wearing earrings or having your ears pierced with have a deleterious effect on your reputation both as a writer and a man. If you were a chorus boy, it wouldn't make any difference. But you are an important man with a reputation for seeing reality and the truth more clearly than any other writer of your time. The fiction that having your ears pierced will make you a Kamba is an evasion of the reality, which is that you are not and never can be anything but an honorary Kamba, and it is out of harmony with your best character which is that of a wise, thoughtful, realistic adult white American male.
>
> I know you are impassioned about Africa and the Africans, writing about them, and allured by the mystery and excitement of becoming one of them. And you know I love the fun of make-believe as much as you do. But the attempt to convert fantasy into actuality can only result, I think, in distortion and failure. (qtd. in Eby 178–79)

Mary's argument, then, is that because Hemingway is a "realistic adult white American male" (notice the lack of commas, as if it were one concept) and because he is famous, he should not/could not go through with his desire to pierce his ears and express his identification with the Kamba. Mary's letter puts into direct conflict and tension Hemingway's public identity and his personal wishes. She insists that mainstream expectations of him and his conformity to them should override his personal desires. Moreover, she suggests that these desires belong to and should remain firmly rooted in the land of "make-believe." Although the reasons for Mary's prohibition are clear, Hemingway's desire, and more importantly, the significance with which he regarded this desire, remains enigmatic. As Torgovnick observes, when Westerners re-enact rituals they consider to be primitive, there is usually a gap in meaning between their performance of the ritual and the performance of the ritual in its original context. What motivates Hemingway, a fifty-four year old, white, American writer, to want to become Kamba? There are several possible answers, all of which are related to the themes of Mary's letter.

The first explanation for Hemingway's desire to "go native" concerns his wish to distance himself from Western culture and by extension from guilt over the destruction of Africa by Euro-American imperial culture. Several times in *True at First Light,* Hemingway corrects Africans who refer to him as a European; at one point, even identifying transnationally with an East Indian store owner, he says, "One thing must always be clear. I am not a European. Mr. Singh and I are brothers" (178). This sentiment, along with Hemingway's frequent insistence throughout the book that he and Mary are "not white," picks up on his desire for the universal "brotherhood" among like individuals despite nationality, race, and even gender. By seeking to identify with the Kamba, by going native, Hemingway attempts to minimize his connection to Westerners who have had a hand in abolishing the local customs and practices, and, in the process of identification, to recover elements of his own personality repressed by that same domineering culture. This motivation for identifying with the "other" in order to distance himself from Western culture participates in what Gubar calls in her discussions of racechange "white remorse about racial inequality," which she claims "turns out to be a more significant motive in twentieth-century aesthetic productions than many critics have realized" (xix).

Another explanation is that Hemingway's interest in going primitive satisfies a particular quality of his own psychosexual make-up, one which Carl Eby thoroughly explores in his book *Hemingway's Fetishism.* With the posthumous publication of *True at First Light* and, earlier, in *The Garden of Eden* (1986), critics have glimpsed a part of the author's personality that was generally kept private during his lifetime—a Hemingway interested in abdicating authority and transgressing boundaries. In *The Garden of Eden,* Hemingway overtly explores sexual role reversal through the characters of David and Catherine Bourne, who not only experiment with swapping gender roles in bed, but who also begin to alter their appearance (particularly their hairstyles and skin color) as a physical indication of this private exploration. Hemingway and his wife, Mary, appear to have engaged in similar practices, often referring to each other in inverted sexual terms—more than once Mary refers to herself as Hemingway's "brother"—and in a letter from the safari, Mary describes Hemingway's shaved hairstyle as similar to the fashion popular among Masai girls. Moreover, Mary's safari diary, *How It Was,* contains several entries in Hemingway's hand that playfully refer to sexual role reversal and experimentation. One such entry reads:

> Reporter: Mr. Hemingway, is it true that your wife is a lesbian?
> Papa: Of course not. Mrs. Hemingway is a boy.
> Reporter: What are you favorite sports, sir?
> Papa: Shooting, fishing, reading and sodomy.
> Reporter: Does Mrs. Hemingway participate in these sports?
> Papa: She participates in all of them. (369)

Other diary entries continue this theme of gender inversion by playing with cross-gendered name combinations (Eby 179), which also occurs in *The Garden of Eden,* such as when Catherine insists on being called "Peter," while calling David "Catherine."

As Eby demonstrates, this sexual experimentation was in Hemingway's mind intricately related to ideas of primitivism and racial difference. In *The Garden of Eden,* a book whose very name invites us to consider the notion of the primitive, David writes stories about his childhood in Africa as he honeymoons with his wife on the French Riviera. Catherine and David "tan" themselves excessively, and Catherine goes so far as to express a desire to be the "darkest white girl in the world." Furthermore, in an expunged part of the edited published text, the couple plans a trip to Africa because they believe it will heighten the intensity of their sexual relationship (Eby 159). Toni Morrison notes that Catherine's desire to become David's "African girl" and to travel with him to Africa reveals "the associations constantly made between darkness and desire, darkness and irrationality, darkness and the thrill of evil" (87). In this way, Hemingway rehearses a prevalent association of race and by extension primitivism with a desire to explore sexuality in a way forbidden by Western culture. In fact, Hemingway explicitly links the practice of sexual inversion to primitivism, despite acknowledging the fact that it is not a legitimate association, when he writes to Mary that what they do in the night is "outside all tribal law" (qtd. in Eby 176). Even the *Look* article hints at the "inside joke" between Hemingway and Mary when she claims that the dusty landscape reminds her of the "Bible in the part where Lot's wife looked back and they turned her into a pillar of salt" (20). What is unsaid here, of courses, is that Lot's wife was looking back on the destruction of the forbidden cities of Sodom and Gomorrah. In other words, for Hemingway, Africa and the primitive, despite his personal experience of Kamba culture and its laws and restrictions, remain associated with a desire for liberation from the sexual restrictions of Western culture—a space in which gender can be transcended and forbidden practices explored.

A final explanation for Hemingway's interest in becoming Kamba is that, as he mentions several times in *True at First Light,* the Kamba tribe had no writers. Hemingway's achievement and identity as a writer was of no consequence within these cultures. For years, Hemingway had felt trapped by fame and the pressure it put on him to produce, a sentiment first expressed in *Green Hills of Africa.* In 1954, bitter for having been passed over the year before for the Nobel Prize,[11] Hemingway may have been seeking to become a member of a culture without writers—a place where he would have the opportunity to explore himself and re-define his identity on other terms. Hemingway had become famous so early in life that his sense of identity was intricately linked to his persona. As Michael North has noted when discussing the fame of Charlie Chaplin, people with that level of visibility are "foreign to no one" and yet perversely become "foreign to [themselves]";

in other words, the fame that makes (in this case) Hemingway "at home everywhere depends on a more fundamental alienation of the reproducible image from its unique source that makes him feel uncomfortably dissociated even at home" (North 1999,17). Oddly enough, it is precisely on these grounds—his fame as an author with a reputation—that Mary objects to his desire to pierce his ears as an outward show of kinship with the Kamba; she is afraid it will damage his reputation "as a writer and a man." It is not possible to her way of thinking to be both a Kamba and a preeminent American author at once. Hemingway's longing to be a member of society where his public role or profession does not even exist is an expression of his desire to abdicate authorship and by extension authority. At the same time, significantly, this desire does not eradicate his identity as a writer; rather, it coexists with it.

Hemingway's experience with the Kamba, then, points to a critique of self made possible by his immersion into a primitive culture and his attempt at racechange, but it is certainly not a critique of primitivism itself. Thus, although Hemingway continues to rely on Western cultural assumptions about the primitive, he nonetheless becomes, through cross-cultural interaction and cross-racial identification, a hybridized subject—not just the self or the other, but rather some combination of the two based partly on fact and communication and partly on fiction and misunderstanding. Still, his status as hybrid reveals the capacity of primitivism to critique Western culture. All three of his motivations for going native—and I think there is truth to each of them—point to a similar phenomenon—the desire for self-effacement. Part of the lure of the primitive for the Westerner is the opportunity to suspend "the normative conditions of the Western self" and to dissolve the boundaries that Western notions of self are predicated upon (Torgovnick 1997, 8). *True at First Light* reveals Hemingway's attempts to renounce the identity traits that he is best known for—he renounces his identity as a Westerner by actively identifying with a non-Western culture and practicing its rituals, as a man through transgender sexual experimentation and identification, and as a writer by joining a culture where there are no writers. In this way, he uses the primitive recreational space of Africa as a space of transgression as well as of self-exploration and in the process emerges with a critique not only of the cultural norms and restrictions of his society (such as the prohibition against men wearing earrings), but also with a profound critique of self through which he begins to imagine a life apart from the public persona that he created. Most importantly, in this case, the primitive is not used to secure a healthful reconfirmation of unified selfhood, but rather leads to the realization that the self can consist of contradictory desires. The fact that Hemingway was engaged in his activity as a writer when he experienced the "earring crisis" reveals that he wanted to be both writer and Kamba at once and that he realized, on some level, that the self does not have to be unified or coherent.

In addition, Hemingway's performance of rituals and practices of another culture highlights the performative nature of the more familiar Western roles he plays in the *Look* article. In other words, there is no reason to believe that one of these narratives is more true than the other. There is fiction in the article and truth in *True at First Light*. Malcolm Cowley claimed that Hemingway's interest in the primitive was motivated by a search for the "authentic," but I believe Hemingway's interest in the primitive was ultimately motivated by what I would call strategic performances of authenticity. In other words, with the Indians in childhood, and Africans later on, Hemingway recognized the capacity of the primitive as a space in which he could re-imagine and rejuvenate himself, literally re-write himself and his origins—so that as a teenager, he became "part Indian" and as an old man, he became "Wakamba." Neither of these claims is "authentic" and yet they are true to the way Hemingway preferred to see himself in his act of self-creation. Hemingway is generally understood to be a modernist author who adamantly believed in truth, but in reality, he was well aware of how elusive, if not unattainable, Truth was. Hemingway's struggle, then, was to make sense of himself in a world where identity is created through a complex interaction of culture, history, society, and personal experience, where representations of the self are always incomplete and flawed and where a thing that appears "true at first light" will appear "a lie by noon" (*TAFL* 189), or even more problematically where multiple, contradictory things can be true at the same time. Our realization of Hemingway's struggle invites us to see him not as Hugh Kenner once did as a "recorder of authenticities" but rather as their creator.

NOTES

1. Despite his interest in Africa and his attempts, particularly in his later writing, to be ethnographically exact, Hemingway often does not make clear distinctions between African geography and African cultures, which are linked for him by the idea of "primitivism." In this way, he perpetuates an elision between land and people that is highly problematic in discussions of Africa. Still, as we will see over the course of the argument, Hemingway attempts to arrive at ever more specific understandings of different African tribes.

2. Although Hemingway generally refers to the tribe as the "Wakamba" in *True at First Light,* "Wakamba" is a Swahili word. "Kamba" is the name of the tribe in Akamba (the language of the tribe), so I have chosen to use this word throughout. I am indebted to Carl Eby and Jeremiah Kitunda for setting me straight on this issue.

3. The authenticity of Hemingway's initiation is questionable. Hemingway's initiation appears to have combined elements of actual tribal customs (although mixing the customs of different tribes, specifically the Kamba and the Masai) with other rituals or practices that Hemingway found personally meaningful. Although this issue will be discussed in more detail later, it, nonetheless, remains difficult to ascertain whether the initiation was recognized as legitimate by members of the Kamba tribe.

4. Here I have in mind critics like Paul Civello, Peter Hays, and Jeffrey Meyers. Hays and Civello, in particular, offer readings of Hemingway's interest in primitivism as based on abstract ideas of ritual. Civello, for example, reads primitivism in "Big Two-Hearted" through the work of Mircea Eliade and cyclic theory in his article "Hemingway's Primitivism: Archetypal Patterns in 'Big Two-Hearted River.'"

5. Many modern artists used African-inspired or primitive voices within their work, including Gertrude Stein in "Melanctha," Marcel Janco and Richard Huelsenbeck

in "African" masks, and Ezra Pound and T. S. Eliot in their dialect experiments. According to Michael North in *The Dialect of Modernism,* these identifications with primitive voice (he focuses specifically on the use of African-American dialect by American modernists) are a kind of verbal masking that enabled modern artists to create a sense of distance from established cultural norms.

6. For an excellent reading of the short stories, in particular their relation to issues of imperialism, see Debra Moddelmog's *Reading Desire: In Pursuit of Ernest Hemingway.*

7. That said, it is important to realize that this posture toward Africa—its use as a backdrop for his explorations of self—is more a product of Hemingway's ego and personality than a conscious acceptance of imperial policy. During his lifetime, he traveled extensively and frequently attempted to adopt, however superficially, the local customs, costumes, and even linguistic phrasing (for example, the bullfight culture in Spain, intellectual culture in France, sea culture in Cuba), while relegating the indigenous population to the background. Those countries and his relationship to them are not viewed through the same lens, that of imperialism, which necessarily comes into play with regard to Africa. In other words, Hemingway's attitude toward Africa probably has less to do with Africa and Africans that with his own demeanor for encountering foreign cultures. All the same, this fact does not erase the importance of imperialism as an issue and factor that must be addressed.

8. Hemingway worked on the original manuscript from July 1954 until August 1956, but the document remained unpublished during his lifetime (Burwell xxv). It was edited and published as *True at First Light* by Patrick Hemingway in 1999.

9. The exact level of accuracy of *True at First Light* is impossible to ascertain. I call it a "fictional memoir" in an effort to suggest that the material is largely based on fact but may have been lightly fictionalized at points. The working title of the manuscript—*The African Journal*—however, suggests that the piece was principally non-fictional in nature. In addition, Hemingway chooses to maintain the names of the principal players—Ernie (himself) and Mary (his wife). Moreover, certain members of the safari party, or their parents, accompanied Hemingway on his earlier 1934–35 safari. This continuity suggests that

in many ways *True at First Light* is a sequel of sorts to *Green Hills of Africa*, his "absolutely true book." Many of the events in the book are also corroborated by information in letters; for example, Hemingway's relationship to Debba is mentioned in letters to friends as well as within the book. But as we have seen, Hemingway was prone to telling fictions in real life as well—so it is difficult to be sure.

10. An important issue that I won't discuss explicitly in this article, however, is the degree to which Hemingway's attempt to assimilate into Kamba culture is sincere. As I have mentioned above, the initiation ritual appears to have consisted of a combination of actual tribal customs and his personal ideas about what primitive initiation should entail. Throughout *True at First Light*, Hemingway knows that he will leave Africa, that it is ultimately a "vacation" that will end, despite his attempt to create a sense of timelessness. From this perspective, his willingness to engage in significant tribal customs with legal ramifications within the tribe and to take a Kamba fiancée is stunningly problematic and raises questions about his sincerity, not to mention his morality.

11. Hemingway's desire to win the Nobel Prize had been increasing with age, although most of his references to the prize are defensive in nature. Biographer James Mellow explains: "For years, Hemingway had coveted the Nobel Prize but always denied wanting it. He made a point of ridiculing the prize itself and, generally, those who received it" (588). For example, he wrote to Charles Scribner in 1941, after winning the Limited Editions Club gold medal for *For Whom the Bell Tolls*, that "[c]hances are there aren't going to be any Nobel prizes any more and anyhow this is what I wanted instead" (*SL* 532); in 1952, he wrote to Lillian Ross: "I cannot help out very much with the true dope on God, as I have never played footy-footy with him . . . nor won the Nobel Prize" (*SL* 807).

WORKS CITED

Burwell, Rose Marie. *Hemingway: The Postwars Years and the Posthumous Novels.* New York: Cambridge UP, 1996.

Chamberlain, John. Rev. of *Green Hills of Africa,* by Ernest Hemingway. *New York Times* 25 Oct. 1935.

Civello, Paul. "Hemingway's Primitivism: Archetypal Patterns in 'Big Two-Hearted River.'" *Hemingway Review* 13.1 (1993): 1–16.

Eby, Carl. *Hemingway's Fetishism: Psychoanalysis and the Mirror of Manhood.* Albany: State U of New York P, 1999.

Freud, Sigmund. *Civilization and Its Discontents.* Ed. and trans. James Strachey. New York: Norton, 1961.

Gubar, Susan. *Racechanges: White Skin, Black Face in American Culture.* New York: Oxford UP, 1997.

Hays, Peter L. "Hunting Ritual in *The Sun Also Rises.*" *Hemingway Review* 8.2 (1989): 46–48.

Hemingway, Ernest. *Ernest Hemingway: Selected Letters 1917–1961.* Ed. Carlos Baker. London: Panther, 1985. 532–33, 658–61, 807–08.

———. *The Garden of Eden.* Ed. Tom Jenks. New York: Macmillan, 1986.

———. *Green Hills of Africa.* 1935. New York: Macmillan, 1987.

———. "Safari." *Look Magazine* 26 Jan. 1954: 20–34.

———. *True at First Light.* Ed. Patrick Hemingway. New York: Scribner, 1999.

Hemingway, Mary. *How It Was.* New York: Random, 1976.

Kenner, Hugh. *A Homemade World: The American Modernist Writers.* New York: Morrow, 1975.

Leff, Leonard J. *Hemingway and His Conspirators: Hollywood, Scribners, and the Making of American Celebrity Culture.* New York: Rowan, 1998.

Lewis, Robert W. "'Long Time Ago Good, Now No Good': Hemingway's Indian Stories." In *New Critical Approaches to the Short Stories of Ernest Hemingway.* Ed. Jackson J. Benson. Durham: Duke UP, 1990. 200–12.

Lukàcs, Georg. *Theory of the Novel.* Trans. Anna Bostock. Cambridge: MIT P, 1971.

Mellow, James R. *Hemingway: A Life Without Consequences.* New York: Houghton, 1992.

Meyers, Jeffrey. *Life into Art.* New York: Cooper, 2000.

Moddelmog, Debra A. *Reading Desire: In Pursuit of Ernest Hemingway.* Ithaca: Cornell UP, 1999.

Morrison, Toni. *Playing in the Dark: Whiteness and the Literary Imagination.* New York: Vintage, 1993.

North, Michael. *The Dialect of Modernism: Race, Language and Twentieth-Century Literature.* New York: Oxford UP, 1994.

———. *Reading 1922: A Return to the Scene of the Modern.* New York: Oxford UP, 1999.

Torgovnick, Marianna. *Gone Primitive: Savage Intellects, Modern Lives.* Chicago: U of Chicago P, 1990.

———. *Primitive Passions.* New York: Knopf, 1997.

Thor Heyerdahl's *Kon-Tiki* and Hemingway's Return to Primitivism in *The Old Man and the Sea*

Susan Beegel

A now-crumbling dust jacket tells the story. *The Chicago Tribune* called the book "the fiction of a Conrad or a Melville brought to reality . . . a superb record of the triumph of the human spirit." *The Saturday Review of Literature* glowed: "Superbly written . . . certainly one of the greatest narratives of the sea of our day. It has almost every quality that can raise the spirit of all of us who . . . are enthralled by the daring and the hardihood of man." "Undoubtedly one of the great epics of the sea," said the *San Francisco Chronicle,* "It will keep almost any reader utterly fascinated from beginning to end." The *New York Herald Tribune* added, "It is the deep connection with nature and a tremendous simplicity that makes this book great as few books of our time are great." London newspapers agreed. The *Daily Mail* described it as "a book to restore one's faith in twentieth century mankind," while the *Sunday Times* asserted that it was "certain to be one of the classics of the sea" (Jacoby 267).

These could easily be quotations from early reviews of Ernest Hemingway's *The Old Man and the Sea.* But instead they describe explorer Thor Heyerdahl's narrative, *Kon-Tiki: Across the Pacific by Raft,* first published in Norway in 1948 and translated into English in 1950, two years before Hemingway's own triumph. Together with five companions, sailing in the Humboldt Current, Heyerdahl had successfully crossed 4,300 nautical miles of the Pacific Ocean—a distance equal to that from Moscow to Chicago—on a primitive balsa log raft named *Kon-Tiki* for the high priest and sun-king of an ancient Peruvian race. An amateur archeologist who believed that the Polynesian islands were peopled in about 500 A.D. by light-skinned Amer-Indians from South America, Heyerdahl navigated his Stone Age craft from the coast of Peru to an unnamed islet in the Tahitian group in order to demonstrate that prehistoric peoples were "capable of undertaking immense voyages over the open ocean" (1950, 297).

Kon-Tiki, the narrative of Heyerdahl's remarkable voyage, was both a Book-of-the-Month Club selection and a runaway bestseller, topping the *New York Times* nonfiction lists for over a year (Lear 204). The book's immense popularity was augmented by Heyerdahl's film of the voyage, reaching some thirty million viewers in theaters after being cut, spliced, enlarged, sharpened, and generally massaged by RKO Studios into an Academy Award winning documentary (Jacoby 272–273, 278). "Kon-Tiki Fever" swept the world—Kon-Tiki hotels and Kon-Tiki restaurants with exotic dishes and cocktails sprang up overnight. There was a Kon-Tiki fashion craze, including Kon-Tiki ties, shorts, dresses, scarves, and of course, Kon-Tiki bathing suits. The name "Kon-Tiki" appeared, without Heyerdahl's consent, on products including drinks, candy, perfume, paints, cookies, butter, sardines, leather goods, porcelain, silverware, toys, souvenirs, matches, and even insecticides. The world's first manned satellite, from Russia, was launched with Kon-Tiki chocolate bars on board. Beautiful young women rode a California Rose Bowl parade float made of flowers in the shape of the Kon-Tiki raft. Little boys and grown men built rafts of every possible material from ping-pong balls to gasoline cans and launched themselves on bodies of water ranging in size from ponds to oceans. The Kon-Tiki raft itself was enshrined in an Oslo museum, while scientific controversy about the validity of Heyerdahl's theories raged not only in academic congresses, but in tabloid newspapers blaring headlines such as "Kon-Tiki Voyage Humbug" and "Is the Kon-Tiki Voyage a Publicity Stunt?" And Heyerdahl underwent America's inevitable ordeal for celebrities—a spurious lawsuit—this one mounted by a hula-dancing Tahitian princess wanting $150,000 in damages for her appearance in the Kon-Tiki film (Jacoby 274–280, 294).

Hemingway, who purchased a copy of *Kon-Tiki* for his library at the Finca Vigía (Brasch 174), must have watched the frenzy over Heyerdahl's book with something akin to bitter envy. His own 1950 offering to the American reading public, the novel *Across the River and into the Trees,* was a shattering critical failure, the most devastating of the author's career. Hemingway had published nothing since the acclaimed bestseller *For Whom the Bell Tolls* in 1940, and expectations for his new novel were especially high. Critics greeted *Across the River,* the story of the dying Colonel Cantwell's May-December romance with a teenage Venetian aristocrat, with a dismay proportionate to the length of time they had been kept waiting. For Morton Dauwen Zabel, writing in *The Nation,* the novel was "an occasion for little but exasperated depression" (377). Alfred Kazin, on behalf of *The New Yorker,* felt "pity, embarrassment that so fine and honest a writer can make such a travesty of himself" (378). "The fact is," Isaac Rosenfeld wrote for *The Kenyon Review,* "a good deal of it is trash" (385). Evelyn Waugh was more sympathetic in *The Tablet,* but nevertheless noted that "[A]ll the leading critics. . . . have been smug, condescending, derisive, some with unconcealed glee, some with an affectation of pity; all are agreed that there is a great failure to celebrate. It is the culmination of a whispering campaign of some years' duration, that 'Hemingway is finished'" (382). Particularly unnerving was Zabel's intimation that *Across the River and into the Trees* might be sufficiently awful to efface Hemingway's earlier achievements "in at least two novels and a score of brilliant tales," and to subject his entire life's work to "some severely revised judgments in the coming years" (377).

To salvage his career from the disaster of *Across the River and into the Trees,* Hemingway needed an overwhelming popular success. Since 1945, he had been struggling with a large manuscript he sometimes called "the Sea Book," posthumously published as *Islands in the Stream* (Burwell 51). Thor Heyerdahl's *Kon-Tiki* and its effulgent reviews may have demonstrated to Hemingway the type of alchemy needed to transform his own experience of the sea into literary gold. *The Old Man and the Sea* took shape rapidly in the wake of *Kon-Tiki,* embracing—as the soon-to-be-abandoned *Islands in the Stream* did not—many of the elements responsible for Heyerdahl's success, and particularly the subject matter and philosophy of primitivism.

Kon-Tiki is, to be sure, a well-told narrative of an exciting, twentieth-century "voyage of discovery." But its unprecedented popularity suggests, as Heyerdahl's biographer Arnold Jacoby has observed, that there was "something peculiar to the age that made a success of these dimensions possible. People were living in a postwar period of lost ideals and broken illusions, struggling to satisfy material demands and uncertain of what the future might have in store. If they took refuge in the world of books for an hour or two, there was little comfort to be found in the mass of war literature and profound psychological novels" (281). A philosopher cited in Jacoby's work, Dr. Robert Jungk of Vienna, felt that the story of the *Kon-Tiki* voyage fulfilled—particularly for Americans—an emotional need that went beyond mere escapism: "'Material satisfaction is not enough. Man is not content with his limitations on the spiritual level; and he grows bored. Man has proved himself unable to master the technical development of modern civilization by spiritual means. We no longer know for what we are striving. . . . In America people are trying to escape from these problems. The popularity of the *Kon-Tiki* voyage is a consequence of this'" (Jacoby 281).

Just five years after the conclusion of World War II, Americans in 1950 were at war again, this time in a frightening Atomic Age that they themselves had created. North Korean troops swept through South Korea unhindered, and President Truman ordered U.S. armed forces into battle. France appealed to the United States for aid in containing communism in Vietnam, and Truman sent military advisors. As the Soviet Union tested nuclear weapons, shot down a U.S. bomber over Latvia, and signed a mutual defense treaty with China, Truman ordered work on a hydrogen bomb designed to be 1,000 times more powerful than the atomic bombs that had destroyed Hiroshima and Nagasaki, despite the warnings of some scientists that such potent nuclear weapons had the capacity to destroy all life on the planet. Americans read pamphlets on how to defend against atomic attack, and began building fallout shelters in their yards and basements. Anti-communist hysteria swept the country when Senator Joseph McCarthy claimed that communist sympathizers had infiltrated the federal government. Congress passed the "anti-American acts" over a presidential veto. When U.S. troops under General Douglas MacArthur reached the Yalu River, China's border with North Korea, The People's Republic entered the war on North Korea's side and pressed U.S. forces all the way back to Korea's 38th parallel. Truman declared a "state of emergency" and imposed wage and price controls on American industries to boost defense production. While the threat of atomic warfare rocked the nation, other new technologies also revealed their dark side. What was then the worst disaster in aviation history took place when a chartered airliner crashed in Wales, killing 80 people. More tragic crashes followed, in Wisconsin, Florida, and France. A study showed for the first time what we now take for granted—that in 1950 American children spent as many hours watching television as they did in school, and more time watching "Six Gun Playhouse," the "Ed Sullivan Show," and professional wrestling than doing their homework (Daniel 674–691; Urdang 353–354).

In one of the bleakest and most terrifying years of the new Atomic Age, then, the *Kon-Tiki* expedition offered a return to a time when the human spirit dominated technology, rather than the other way around. Since boyhood, Heyerdahl had been swept up by the early twentieth century's "back to nature" movement—passionate in the study of natural history, creating his own museum of specimens, hiking, camping, mountain-climbing, and yearning to be an explorer. In 1936, then aged 21, Heyerdahl and his new bride Liv Coucheron Torp lived for a year on the island of Fatu-Hiva in the Marquesas, the paradise of Melville, building a bamboo hut and fishing and gathering fruit to sustain themselves. The subject of Heyerdahl's first book, *Pa Jakt efter Paradiset* (1938), recast as *Fatu-Hiva: Back to Nature* in 1974, and of his late memoir *Green was the Earth on the Seventh Day* (1996), the Fatu-Hiva experiment took for its goals "To try and cut off all ties with civilization and walk into a tropical wilderness empty-handed and barefoot, as a man at one with nature. . . . To attempt a farewell to life in a civilized community. . . . To study our own civilization from the outside" (Heyerdahl 1996, 21, 22).

Civilization suffered in the comparison. By the time the *Kon-Tiki* set sail in 1947, Heyerdahl, with the experience of World War II behind him, believed more firmly than ever that there could be "no progress from Paradise" as God created it, and that the study of "people and cultures living in intimate harmony with nature" might hold some important lessons for the modern world (1996, 20, 27). These beliefs form the ideological basis of the *Kon-Tiki* narrative, and underlie passages such as Heyerdahl's ironic description of his primitive raft's construction at an "ultramodern" naval dockyard in Lima:

> Down in the naval dockyard lay the big balsa logs from the Quevedo forest. It was really a pathetic sight. Fresh-cut round logs, yellow bamboos, reeds, and green banana leaves lay in a heap, our building materials, in between rows of threatening gray submarines and destroyers. . . . In these coastal waters, where Inca legends affirm that their ancestors first learned to sail such rafts from Kon-Tiki's vanished clan, modern Indians were forbidden to build such rafts by men of our own race. Sailing on an open raft can cost human lives. . . . Bamboo and balsa belong to the primitive past; here, too, life is marching on—to armor and steel. (1950, 82–83)

Later, after the raft is finished, Heyerdahl notes:

> When the raft began to take shape and lay there among the warships, golden and fresh with ripe bamboos and green leaves, the minister of marine himself came to inspect us. We were immensely proud of our vessel as she lay there, a brave little reminder of Inca times among the threatening big warships. But the minister of marine was horrified. I was summoned to the naval office to sign a

paper freeing the navy of all responsibility for what we had built in its harbor
... [and] a paper saying that if I left the harbor with men and cargo on board,
it was entirely on my own responsibility and at my own risk. (86)

Here Heyerdahl unmasks the arrogance of modern civilization in assuming
that its evolution from bamboo and balsa to armor and steel is "progress,"
and points out the absurdity of a society that has created weapons of mass
destruction questioning the safety of a log raft.

In January and February 1951, as the capital of South Korea fell to Chinese
and North Korean forces after violent hand-to-hand fighting, radioactive
fallout from nuclear weapons testing sifted down on American cities and
killed livestock in the West, and the United States geared up to try Julius
and Ethel Rosenberg for the theft of atomic secrets (Baker 490–91, Daniel
692–696), Hemingway began drafting a novel about a voyage nearly as
anachronistic as the *Kon-Tiki* expedition. Santiago's boat is almost as timeless
in its construction as Heyerdahl's balsa raft; the old subsistence fisherman,
like generations of his ancestors before him, goes to sea in a wooden skiff
far smaller than the eighteen-foot marlin he eventually catches (*OMATS* 97,
122), a vessel powered by his own strength with oars and thole pins, or by
the wind with a mast and a sail patched with flour sacks that he can carry
over one shoulder. Santiago's fishing "technology" consists of "the wooden
box with the coiled, hard-braided brown lines, the gaff and the harpoon
with its shaft. The box with the baits . . . . under the stern along with the
club that was used to subdue the big fish" (15). Heyerdahl's balsa raft is a
"pathetic sight" to the naval officers of the "ultramodern dockyard" (1950,
82–83); Santiago's skiff is a pathetic sight to the young fishermen of his
village, who make fun of the old man (*OMATS* 11). They have "advanced"
to 18- and 24-foot motorboats, bought with profits from the war years,
and to free-floating fishing rigs of baited hooks hung at various depths,
rather than lines worked off their boats or in their hands (*OMATS* 29–30;
Farrington 27–30).

In the *Kon-Tiki* narrative, the business of escaping from the ties of
civilization to "peace and freedom" on the sea is fraught with peril (127). A

motorboat arrives to tow the raft out of the harbor to the tug *Guardian Rios,* despite Heyerdahl's desperate plaints that some of the members of his crew are not yet on board. Cast off from its moorings, the raft is nearly smashed against the wooden piles of the quay by a long swell. Once the raft has been towed to the *Guardian Rios,* the tugboat takes over and attempts to move the *Kon-Tiki* out to the Humboldt Current, free of the coastal shipping lanes. But the tow rope breaks, and in retrieving the rope, Heyerdahl's men are badly stung by poisonous jellyfish. When the *Guardian Rios* is ready for another attempt, the *Kon-Tiki* is swept under the tug's overhanging stern, and the raft narrowly escapes being crushed by the motor vessel. The towing takes all night and threatens "to shake the raft to bits." Finally, the "last coast light disappears astern," and the men of the *Kon-Tiki* board the *Guardian Rios* to have their position shown to them on their chart and to take a "ceremonious farewell of all on board." Then the towrope is cast off, and the raft is "alone again." Not until "the black column of smoke" from the tug has "dissolved and vanished over the horizon" do the men of the *Kon-Tiki* "shake their heads and look at one another" (96–100).

For Santiago, too, the escape from the bonds of the human community on land comes as a relief. Ashore, he is surrounded by reminders of his eighty-four days without a fish and of his slow spiral down into a humiliating and dependent old age. Mocked by the young fishermen, pitied by the old fishermen, living on the charity of his village, the old man is caught in a poverty trap—too poor to buy food, he has lost his apprentice Manolin, and sold the cast net he uses to catch bait for the fishing that is his livelihood. "'First you borrow, then you beg,'" Santiago tells Manolin, predicting his own future (18). But when the boy offers to bring Santiago fresh bait, the old man feels "his hope and his confidence. . . . freshening as when the breeze rises" (13), as does the reader when, in the lovely paragraphs of the novel's dawn scene—a kind of fisherman's *aubade*—Santiago leaves "the smell of the land behind"—a smell that includes the stench of the local shark factory, of the industrial exploitation of nature—and rows out "into the clean early morning smell of the ocean" (11–12, 28). The passage offers an objective correlative for Heyerdahl's telling sentiment: "It was as though the fresh salt tang in the air, and all the blue purity that surrounded us, had washed and cleansed both body and soul" (1950, 127).

Once at sea, both the men on the *Kon-Tiki* and Santiago in his skiff attain, rather unexpectedly, a satisfying solitude free from surveillance by the most distinctive technology of the recent World War—the airplane. A few days after Heyerdahl's departure, the American ambassador flies out from Lima "to bid us a last good-by [*sic*] and to see what we looked like at sea" (109). Despite the fact that the men give their position as exactly as they can and send direction-finding radio signals, the ARMY-119 aircraft circles round and near and never spots the raft. "It was not easy to find the low raft down in the trough of the seas," Heyerdahl writes. "At last the plane had to give it up and returned to the coast" (110). When Santiago does not return from his fishing voyage by the following morning, his community searches for him—unsuccessfully—"with coast guard and with planes." "The ocean is very big and a skiff is small and hard to see," the old man tells the boy (124).

Thor Heyerdahl, loathing "push buttons and turning knobs," and wishing to keep the *Kon-Tiki* voyage as authentic as possible, fought engineer Herman Watzinger's insistence that the expedition carry a short-wave radio. "'Radio!' I said, horrified. What the hell do we want with that? It's out of place on a prehistoric raft'" (1950, 43). Safety considerations carry the argument, but Heyerdahl's anti-technology stance expresses itself as the radio becomes something of a malevolent presence on the raft—dishing out electric shocks to unsuspecting crew members who wander too close, causing gastric distress to a pet parrot who eats part of the antenna and excretes metal bits for several days, forcing the men to spend a frantic day drying and reassembling water-logged parts to call off a rescue that isn't needed, and blaring out canned hula music from the United States as the men attempt to enjoy an authentic Polynesian paradise. Heyerdahl consoles himself: "Even though the ghost words carried through the air by short wave were an unheard of luxury in Kon-Tiki's early days, the long ocean waves beneath us were the same as of old and they carried the balsa raft steadily westward as they did then, fifteen hundred years ago" (1950, 196).

No radio compromises the primitivism of Santiago's voyage. In his world, only "the rich have radios to talk to them in their boats" (*OMATS* 39). When Santiago thinks of radios at all, he never considers their value as safety equipment, as a means of calling for help or of receiving weather reports. Rather, on the two occasions in the novel when the old man does wish for a radio, he considers the technology as a means of easing his loneliness and boredom at sea by bringing him "the baseball" (39). "I wonder how the baseball came out in the grand leagues today, he thought. It would be wonderful to do this with a radio" (48). Yet each time Santiago thinks about having a radio in his boat, he rejects the technology as an intrusion distracting his attention from his relationship with the sea and the practice of his craft: "Then he thought, think of it always. Think of what you are doing" (48). Hemingway's own anti-technology stance shows forth in a passage exemplifying the type of minute observation of nature short-circuited by baseball games on the radio:

> Now is no time to think of baseball, he thought. Now is the time to think of only one thing. That which I was born for. There might be a big one around that school, he thought. I picked up only a straggler from the albacore that were feeding. But they are working far out and fast. Everything that shows on the surface today travels very fast and to the north-east. Can it be the time of day? Or is it some sign of the weather that I do not know? (*OMATS* 40)

One of the startling and enchanting aspects of the *Kon-Tiki* narrative is the profound sense of safety that pervades every page and surely helps account for the book's popularity in the anxious year 1950. In *Green Was the Earth on the Seventh Day*, Heyerdahl recalled: "If any of us on board the *Kon-Tiki* had been prepared for disaster by the unanimous warnings from sailors and scientists before we left, we all began to relax after the first week in the choppy sea of the Humboldt Current. The behavior of the raft, which always rode on top of the waves and never became water-logged, gave us a feeling of complete security and merry excitement" (1996, 261). Even a major storm at sea, the subject at first of "strained anticipation and anxiety," becomes instead "an exciting form of sport" once the men recognize that the raft can handle 25-foot waves, and that the tons of water coming aboard simply flow away over the stern, or out between the logs (1950, 202–203). The young Scandinavians "delight in the fury round about us which the balsa raft mastered so adroitly," and think of it as a form of skiing: "[W]hen the raft glided up and down over the smoking waste of sea we always thought of racing downhill amid snowdrifts and rock faces" (202).

A sense of safety also pervades *The Old Man and the Sea*. As with the *Kon-Tiki* raft, the primitive qualities of Santiago's skiff are her virtues: "Her lightness . . . is my safety," the old man thinks (76), and she rides "gently with the small sea" that rises with the easterly wind (66–67). Heyerdahl's observations about the *Kon-Tiki* apply as well to Santiago's skiff:

> [T]he elements seemed to ignore the little raft. Or perhaps they accepted it as a natural object, which did not break the harmony of the sea but adapted itself to current and sea like bird and fish. Instead of being a fearsome enemy, flinging itself at us, the elements had become a reliable friend which steadily and surely helped us onward. While wind and waves pushed and propelled, the ocean current lay under us and pulled, straight toward our goal. (Heyerdahl 1950, 127)

Rowing out to fish in the morning, Santiago "let[s] the current do a third of the work." Fishing, he "drift[s] with the current" (*OMATS* 30). Sailing home at night, he lets the evening onshore breeze carry him home against the Gulf Stream: "The wind is our friend anyway" (120).

Like Santiago, the men of the *Kon-Tiki* know that the wind is not always the mariner's friend. Their safety at sea depends on their intimate knowledge of their environment. Lacking modern equipment for weather forecasting, they observe the sky for signs of changes in the weather, and make their preparations accordingly: "[O]ur first storm . . . started by the trade wind dying away completely, and the feathery, white trade wind clouds, which were drifting over our heads up in the topmost blue, being suddenly invaded by a thick black cloud bank which rolled up over the horizon from southward" (Heyerdahl 1950, 201). Santiago too can do without a radio for weather forecasts because he understands his region's weather patterns and can read the sky:

> He thought of how some men feared being out of sight of land in a small boat and knew they were right in the months of sudden bad weather. But now they were in the hurricane months and, when there are no hurricanes, the weather of hurricane months is the best weather of all. If there is a hurricane you always see the signs of it in the sky for days ahead, if you are at sea. They do not see it ashore because they do not know what to look for. (*OMATS* 61)

White cumulus clouds like "friendly piles of ice cream" tell him the weather will be good for a time (*OMATS* 61).

To conserve the authenticity of their voyage, Heyerdahl and his crew navigate by the stars: "The night watch could sit quietly in the cabin door and look at the stars. If the constellations changed their position in the sky, it was time for him to go out and see whether it was the steering oar or the wind that had shifted" (Heyerdahl 1950, 197). Santiago too, like Heyerdahl's ancient Polynesians, uses "the starry sky . . . [as] a great glittering compass revolving from east to west" (Heyerdahl 1950, 198). Hemingway writes: "Once he stood up and urinated over the side of the skiff and looked at the stars and checked his course" (*OMATS* 47). Lacking even such basic navigation equipment as a sextant, chart, or compass, Santiago thinks of the stars as "all his distant friends" (75). While critic Robert Weeks finds such "cosmic camaraderie" in *The Old Man and the Sea* "forced" (40), comparison of Hemingway's novel to Heyerdahl's narrative suggests that the affection of mariners without navigation technology for the guiding stars "marching across the vault of the sky" is quite genuine (Heyerdahl 1950, 197).

The physical wilderness of the ocean—the world of wind, waves, and stars—is also one of surpassing biological wealth and beauty. The *Kon-Tiki* narrative makes explicit what *The Old Man and the Sea* implies, that the "ancient mariner" whose raft or skiff moves in harmony with the elements, and without the dissociating clamor of technology, is uniquely positioned to observe the ocean's inhabitants:

> The sea contains many surprises for him who . . . drifts along slowly and noiselessly. A sportsman who breaks his way through the woods may come back and say there is no wild life to be seen. Another may sit down on a stump and wait, and often rustlings and cracklings will begin and curious eyes peer out. So it is on the sea, too. We usually plow across it with roaring engines and piston strokes, with the water foaming around our bow. Then we come back and say there is nothing to see far out on the ocean. (117)

Far from finding "nothing to see," both Heyerdahl and Hemingway enrich their texts with detailed observations that serve not only to describe marine creatures, but to express the intimacy of their primitive voyagers with the natural world.

The Norwegian's workmanlike prose (as translated by F. H. Lyon) contrasts sharply with Hemingway's lyricism, but the content is the same. To give just two examples, the *Kon-Tiki* narrative reads:

> [O]ne day we came into a school of porpoises which seemed quite endless. The black backs tumbled about, packed close together, right in to the side of the raft, and sprang up here and there all over the sea as far as we could see from the masthead. (113)

And *The Old Man and the Sea*:

> He did not dream of the lions but instead of a vast school of porpoises that stretched for eight or ten miles and it was in the time of their mating and they would leap high into the air and return into the same hole they had made in the water when they leaped. (81)

Heyerdahl writes:

The dolphin (dorado) . . . is a brilliantly colored tropical fish. . . . We jerked
on board one which was four feet eight inches long with a head thirteen and
a half inches high. The dolphin had a magnificent color. In the water it shone
blue and green like a bluebottle with a glitter of golden-yellow fins. But if we
hauled one on board, we sometimes saw a strange sight. As the fish died, it
gradually changed color and became silver gray with black spots and, finally,
a quite uniform silvery white. (144)

And Hemingway:

Just before it was dark, as they passed a great island of Sargasso weed that
heaved and swung in the light sea as though the ocean were making love with
something under a yellow blanket, his small line was taken by a dolphin. He saw
it first when it jumped in the air, true gold in the last of the sun and bending
and flapping wildly in the air. . . . When the fish was at the stern, plunging and
cutting from side to side in desperation, the old man leaned over the stern
and lifted the burnished gold fish with its purple spots over the stern. . . . [H]e
clubbed it across the shining gold head until it shivered and was still. (73)

Later, "the dolphin was cold and a leprous gray-white now in the starlight"
(78).

In the marine wilderness, both physical and biological, the men of the
Kon-Tiki crew create a "home" on their balsa log raft (171). The crew's sense
of comfort in the palm-thatched bamboo hut that comprises their "cabin"
augments the narrative's portrayal of men living in domestic harmony with
nature, unhindered by the material luxuries of civilization. In a vignette
titled "At Sea in a Bamboo Hut," Heyerdahl writes:

Inside the bamboo cabin we found shade and the scent of bamboos and withered
palm leaves. The sunny blue purity outside was now served to us in a suitably
large dose through the cabin wall. . . . It was remarkable what a psychological
effect the shaky bamboo cabin had on our minds. . . . [T]his primitive lair gave us
a greater feeling of security than white-painted bulkheads and closed portholes

would have given in the same circumstances. . . . The longer the voyage lasted, the safer we felt in our cozy lair, and we looked at the white-crested waves that danced past outside our doorway as if they . . . convey[ed] no menace to us at all. (172)

The passage almost seems to echo Hemingway's 1925 short story, "Big Two-Hearted River," where a tent has a similarly soothing effect on returned veteran Nick Adams:

Inside the tent the light came through the brown canvas. It smelled pleasantly of canvas. Already there was something mysterious and homelike. Nick was happy as he crawled inside the tent. . . . Nothing could touch him. He had made his camp. . . . . He was there, in the good place. He was in his home where he had made it. . . . It was quite dark outside. It was lighter in the tent. (*CSS* 215)

Santiago lives in equivalent simplicity. Ashore, he dwells in a traditional "shack made of the tough budshields of the royal palm which are called *guano* and in it there was a bed, a table, one chair, and a place on the dirt floor to cook with charcoal" (15). "On the brown walls of the flattened, overlapping leaves of the sturdy fibered *guano*" he has two colored religious pictures, and a shelf for his clean shirt (15–16). Like the *Kon-Tiki* hut, Santiago's palm frond shack is penetrated by the elements—the smell of the land breeze wakens him each morning (25). In *A Naturalist in Cuba,* Thomas Barbour, a contemporary of Hemingway's, writes: "I suspect that [this] method of house building [was] in use before the arrival of the first Spanish conquistadors" (10).

At sea, Santiago's physical ordeal with the fish prohibits his finding the degree of comfort experienced by Heyerdhal's crew in their dwelling, but still the old man is eminently "at home" in his skiff. Easing his straw hat on his head, drinking from the water bottle under the bow, resting on the un-stepped mast and sail, warming and shielding himself with a sack he has dried in the sun atop the bait box, Santiago thinks of himself as "almost comfortable" in conditions that, as Hemingway pointedly reminds readers, a civilized man would find "intolerable" (46).

In their descriptions of huts and shacks, as well as of home-like "comforts" at sea or onshore, both the *Kon-Tiki* narrative and *The Old Man and the Sea* reject technology and its accompanying materialism for a Thoreauvian philosophy of "shelter":

> The very simplicity and nakedness of man's life in the primitive ages imply this advantage at least, that they left him still but a sojourner in nature. When he was refreshed with food and sleep, he contemplated his journey again. He dwelt, as it were, in a tent in this world, and was either threading the valleys, or crossing the plains, or climbing the mountaintops. But lo! Men have become the tools of their tools (Thoreau 25).

A raft or a skiff on the ocean carries out this philosophy more thoroughly than a cabin at Walden Pond, for at sea man's dwelling is a "sojourner in nature" along with him. Viewing their raft from a rubber dinghy, the *Kon-Tiki* crew marvels at how "the low cabin with the wide doorway and the bristly roof of leaves . . . bobbed up from among the seas" (170). Santiago too lives always in contemplation of the journey. No landed asceticism can be so complete—the primitive mariner removes himself from civilization to make a home where all the world seems "empty and blue" (171).

The sea proves a bountiful larder for those at home there. "To starve to death was impossible," Heyerdahl writes of the *Kon-Tiki*'s voyage in the rich waters of the Humboldt Current. Using handlines, the men pluck tuna and dolphin fish from the sea with the ease of Marquesan islanders collecting fruit from the trees: "As a rule, it was enough to warn the cook twenty minutes in advance if we wanted fish for dinner" (146). The men strain plankton from the ocean and find that "if it was mostly deep-sea fish ova, it tasted like caviar and now and then like oysters" (140). Yet even the modest labor of fishing is not always necessary in the narrative's maritime Eden. The *Kon-Tiki* crew nibbles on the "fresh and delicate" barnacles that grow beneath the raft and on the tiny pelagic crabs that wash across her deck (144). They eat "seaweed as a salad" (144). Young squid, tasting "like a mixture of lobster and India rubber," land on the cabin roof in the night

(155). Even "large bonitos, delicious eating," swim aboard with the waves washing over the raft (132). Torstein awakens one morning to find a sardine on his pillow (114). Best of all are the flying fish:

> [W]e were in a maritime land of enchantment where delicious fish dishes came hurling through the air. . . . The cook's first duty, when he got up in the morning, was to go out on deck and collect all the flying fish that had landed on board during the night. There were usually half a dozen or more, and once we found twenty-six fat flying fish on the raft. Knut was much upset one morning because, when he was standing operating with the frying-pan, a flying fish struck him on the hand instead of landing right in the cooking fat. (114)

The self-reliant Santiago, fishing in the rich waters of the Gulf Stream, is in no danger of starvation either. Although not subject to the veritable rain of seafood we see in the *Kon-Tiki* narrative, the old man easily catches all he needs to maintain his strength during the ordeal with the marlin. As the novel begins, he effortlessly pulls a ten-pound tuna from the sea (38–39). Santiago intends the fish for bait, but after he has begun his struggle with the marlin, the tuna with its "strong full-blooded" and "not unpleasant" meat nourishes the fisherman (38–39, 58–59). Later in his voyage, needing sustenance again, Santiago knows that he is in a part of the current where he can get a dolphin fish (65–66), and he shortly thereafter not only hooks one but, despite the dolphin's "acrobatics," lands it with his left hand while working the marlin with his right (71–72). He collects "very tiny" shrimp from a floating mat of Sargasso weed, and chews them shells and all—"they were nourishing and they tasted good" (98). Like the men of the *Kon-Tiki*, the old man enjoys eating flying fish, and knows that he could attract them on board if only he had a light: "I wish a flying fish would come on board tonight. But I have no light to attract them. A flying fish is excellent to eat raw and I would not have to cut him up" (66).

Fresh water is the critical survival problem for men at sea in open boats, as Coleridge's "Ancient Mariner" ironically observed: "Water, water, every where, / Nor any drop to drink" (20). Sea water, because of its high salt content, only exacerbates thirst and accelerates dehydration, making the ability to obtain and ration fresh water one of the most important tests of making a "home" on the ocean. The *Kon-Tiki* crew carries fresh water for their voyage in primitive containers—thick canes of giant bamboo stopped "with a plug or with pitch or resin" (131). When after two months their fresh water begins to "grow stale and have a bad taste," they capture rain water in various containers (131). But Heyerdahl also recognizes another method for obtaining desperately needed moisture at sea:

> The old natives knew well the device which many shipwrecked men hit upon during the war—chewing thirst-quenching moisture out of raw fish. . . . . It does not taste good if one has anything better to drink, but the percentage of salt is so low one's thirst is quenched. (132)

Santiago uses the same method to conserve the limited supply of fresh water he carries in a bottle throughout his three-day ordeal. When he eats the raw tuna, he adjures himself to "chew it well . . . and get all the juices" (58). Later in the novel, his decision to rebait a line and catch a dolphin fish is prompted not only by his hunger, but by the fact that his water is "low in the bottle" (65).

"The closer we came into contact with the sea and what had its home there," Heyerdahl writes, "the less strange it became and the more at home we ourselves felt" (159). The men of the *Kon-Tiki* live in "neighborly intimacy" with the marine creatures of the Pacific (114). A school of dolphin fish travels under the raft, finding a "magical attraction in being able to swim in the shade with a moving roof above them" and food "in our kitchen garden of seaweed and barnacles that hung like garlands from all the logs" (143). Small black-and-white striped pilot fish also accompany the *Kon-Tiki* "with such a childlike confidence that we . . . had a fatherly protective feeling toward them" (150). When the men wash their dishes alongside, "It was as if we had emptied a whole cigar case of pilot fish among the scraps" (150). A pelagic crab takes up residence on board, and becomes a "marine pet" (151). Named Johannes, the crab learns to take scraps of biscuit or fish out of Heyerdahl's fingers with his claws (137). The men even develop a fondness for the sharks that sometimes follow the raft, "jumping up like a begging dog" for food (186). The men feed and tease the sharks with leftovers, and think of them as "half fierce, half good-natured and friendly dog[s]" (186). Their deepest affection, however, is reserved for marine mammals, the whales and porpoises that sometimes surface near the raft to breathe: "It was so unusual to hear real breathing out at sea, where all living creatures wriggle silently about without lungs and quiver their gills, that we really had a warm family feeling for our old distant cousin[s]" (141–142).

Santiago too has a "neighborly feeling" towards the marine creatures of the Gulf Stream. Flying fish are his "principal friends on the ocean" (29). He "love[s] green turtles and hawk-bills with their great elegance and speed" (36). A man-of-war bird, following schooling fish from the air, is "a great help" to Santiago (38). The old man befriends and talks to an exhausted migrating warbler that perches on his skiff, and like Heyerdahl with the pilot fish, seems to experience a "fatherly protective feeling" engendered by the bird's "childlike confidence"—"'How old are you?. . . . Is this your first trip?. . . . Stay at my house if you like, bird. . . . I am sorry I cannot hoist the sail and take you in with the small breeze that is rising'" (55). The great marlin is Santiago's "friend" and "brother" (55, 92). The old man even admires the mako shark—"He is beautiful and noble and knows no fear of anything" (106)—and picks up Heyerdahl's domestic dog simile to describe the *galanos*—"the sharks hit the carcass as someone might pick up scraps from the table" (119). Once again like the men of the *Kon-Tiki*, Santiago possesses a "warm family feeling" for marine mammals, the porpoises who roll and blow around his skiff in the night: "'They are good. . . . They play and make jokes and love one another. They are our brothers like the flying fish'" (48).

For the men of the *Kon-Tiki* expedition, many of them veterans of World War II and of Nazi Germany's occupation of Norway, the voyage across the Pacific Ocean on a balsa log raft is a marine version of Hemingway's "Big Two-Hearted River." As Hemingway wrote to Charles Poore on 23 January 1953, that masterful short story, composed in the wake of World War I, was "about a boy who has come back from the war. The war is never mentioned though. . . . This may be one of the things that helps it" (*SL* 798). In all of the three hundred pages of *Kon-Tiki,* Heyerdahl barely mentions the war, sketching his own experience in just two sentences: "Right face, left face, about face. Washing barracks stairs, polishing boots, radio school, parachute—and at last a Murmansk convoy to Finnmark, where the war-god of technique reigned in the sun-god's absence all the dark winter through" (25–26). Later, he briefly mentions that crew member Knut Haugland had been decorated for taking part "in the parachute action that held up German efforts to get the atomic bomb" and had shot his way out of a building surrounded by Gestapo (43–44). Torstein Raaby had followed the movements of the German battleship *Tirpitz* in and out of occupied Norway's harbors, radioing her position to the British, providing information that eventually guided bombers to destroy her (44). Knut and Torstein, Heyerdahl surmises, "would be glad to go for a little trip on a wooden raft" (45). For them, as for Nick at the Big Two-Hearted River, the natural world—"where the sea curved away under us as blue upon blue as the sky above"—becomes a place of refuge and recovery (Heyerdahl 1950, 171).

Hemingway's own experience of World War II was as grim as Heyerdahl's. Heyerdahl knew the now legendary terrors of the Murmansk convoy—ships torpedoed by German submarines, frozen corpses floating in the sea, and Arctic storms sweeping men and munitions from destroyer decks—and he witnessed the burned villages and mined snowfields of Finnmark, Norway's northernmost province (Jacoby 190–203). Hemingway, working as a war correspondent, attended the taking of Fox Green Beach in the D-Day invasion of France, and experienced the battle of Hürtgen Forest with a regiment of 3,000 men that took 2,678 casualties (Meredith 63). But while Hemingway wrote about these things in his journalism, and sketched the Hürtgen Forest debacle as part of Colonel Cantwell's past in *Across the River,* he never depicted them at any length in his published fiction. In the manuscript of *Islands in the Stream,* Hemingway does make Thomas Hudson's Caribbean submarine hunt central, yet he set that unfinished work aside for *The Old Man and the Sea,* a book that mentions the war obliquely only once, as the source of profits for the young fisherman's motorboats and new fishing technology "bought when the shark livers had brought much money" (30)—in other words, when war in the North Atlantic closed the Grand Banks cod fishery and with it the world supply of Vitamin A from cod liver (Ellis 39). War, in the last novel Hemingway published during his lifetime, is the stench from the shark factory that hangs over Santiago's village like a pall (*OMATS* 11–12).

For Americans still in recovery from World War II and already involved in another war, such hastily sketched experiences had great resonance. They too would be glad to go "for a little trip on a wooden raft"—or in a wooden skiff. But more is at stake in the *Kon-Tiki* narrative and *The Old Man and the Sea* than mere escapism. If these texts did nothing more than treat nature as a place of peace and freedom, of refuge from civilization and of neighborly feeling and brotherhood with other creatures, then both might be accused, as Suzanne Clark notes Hemingway is often accused, of using "modernist primitivism" solely in the service of a "reactionary nostalgia" (63). In fact, "Big Two-Hearted River" is by far the more reactionary text, as Nick literally feels "a reaction" against "going on into the swamp," where creatures "almost level with the ground" slither beneath the "low-growing branches" (*CSS* 231). In the swamp, in the primordial ooze Nick associates with evolution, fishing will be "a tragic adventure," and Nick does not want it (231). But both *Kon-Tiki* and *The Old Man and the Sea* embrace fishing as a tragic adventure, and, like *Moby-Dick* before them, as a means to explore whether man has "progressed" far enough away from animals to govern his own sharkishness, to abandon nature's essential violence. In a world where, as Hemingway had observed in *For Whom the Bell Tolls*, the shadows of Heinkel bombers move "over the land as the shadows of sharks pass over a sandy floor of the ocean" (76), the question was one of utmost importance.

Both the *Kon-Tiki* narrative and *The Old Man and the Sea* address the primal violence of the marine food chain in the Humboldt Current and the Gulf Stream, where dolphins pursue flying fish, bonito and tuna pursue dolphins, and larger fish, including porpoises, marlin, and sharks, pursue bonito and tuna. In a *Kon-Tiki* vignette titled "Blood Bath in the Sea, Blood

Bath on Board" Heyerdahl uses the language of war to describe a feeding frenzy that takes place after a great storm:

> When the weather moderated, it was as though the big fish around us had become completely infuriated. The water round the raft was full of sharks, tunnies, dolphins, and a few dazed bonitos, all wriggling about close under the timber of the raft and in the waves closest to it. It was a ceaseless life-and-death struggle; the backs of big fishes arched themselves over the water and *shot off like rockets,* one chasing another in pairs, while the water around the raft was tinged with thick blood. The *combatants* were mainly tunnies and dolphins. . . . The tunnies were the *assailants;* often a fish of 150 to 200 pounds would leap high into the air holding a dolphin's bloody head in its mouth. . . . Now and again the sharks, too, seemed to become blind with rage, and we saw them catch and fight with the big tunnies, which met in the shark a *superior enemy.* (204; my emphasis)

To "bring order to the sanguinary chaos" that surrounds them, the crew of the *Kon-Tiki* decides to fish for sharks (205). Throughout the narrative, they have methodically killed the sharks following the raft to give themselves a safety zone for washing, swimming, and bathing. Now the crew battles with the sharks for five exhausting hours, hauling them aboard the raft with heavy handlines until "wherever we walked on deck, there were big sharks lying in the way" and "we became completely befuddled as to which sharks were quite dead, which were still snapping convulsively if we went near them, and which were quite alive and were lying in ambush for us with their green cat's eyes" (206).

Far from bringing order to nature's sanguinary chaos, the violent participation of the men only intensifies it. The next day, there are fewer dolphins and tunnies around the raft, but "just as many sharks" (206). The men begin again to kill sharks, until they realize that "all the fresh shark blood that ran off the raft only attracted still more sharks" (206). Peace is finally restored when they halt their own killing, throw the dead sharks overboard, wash the deck clean of blood, and replace the bloodied and torn bamboo deck mats with new, golden-yellow ones. Yet the memory of the "blood bath" haunts them—"[W]hen we turned in on those evenings in our mind's eye we saw greedy, open shark jaws and blood. And the smell of shark meat stuck in our nostrils" (206). For the first time, a member of the expedition expresses a desire to "stretch . . . out comfortably on the green grass on a palm island . . . to see something other than cold fish and rough sea" (206–207).

The Old Man and the Sea also erupts in "sanguinary chaos" when Santiago harpoons his marlin in the heart, and the resulting flow of blood summons a great mako shark "from deep down in the water as the dark cloud of blood had settled and dispersed in the mile deep sea" (100). Knowing that "the shark was not an accident" (100)—that its appearance is part of the order of nature—and having no hope that his intervention can prevent "the bad time" that is coming, Santiago nevertheless kills the mako (101–103). More sharks come—galanos with shovel-shaped heads, brown dorsal fins, and "yellow cat-like eyes" (108)—following the scent of blood, "a trail for all sharks as wide as a highway through the sea" (111). Santiago thinks of them not as friends or brothers, but as enemies—"hateful sharks, bad smelling, scavengers as well as killers" (107–108). Blood calls to blood in an orgy of violence that mounts geometrically, as Santiago hacks, clubs, and stabs at the repeated waves of sharks arriving for a feeding frenzy.

The Kon-Tiki narrative seems to suggest that man, by remembering his humanity, might learn to temper his own sharkishness and "progress" away from violence. In contrast, Santiago is invested in protecting the marlin—his independence for the winter—from the sharks, and the desperate killing in The Old Man and the Sea ends only when there is "nothing more" for the sharks to eat (119). The old man reminds us that natural violence has redemptive qualities; it is an essential ingredient of competition to survive and the wellspring of vitality for both the individual and the race. Yet, like Heyerdahl's narrative, Hemingway's novel is critical of man's conscious participation in nature's primal violence. Harpooning the mako prompts the old man's meditation on sin, as he questions the pleasure he took in killing the shark. Santiago understands that man, with his knowledge of good and evil, cannot be an innocent killer, and he acknowledges his kinship with the mako: "He lives on the live fish as you do" (105). The old man's self-absolution for killing sharks is more Darwinian than Christian: "I killed him in self-defense. . . . And I killed him well. . . . Besides . . . everything kills everything else in some way" (106). Santiago's moral thinking advances beyond this concern—and beyond the *Kon-Tiki* narrative—when he wonders whether it is also a sin to kill the marlin, despite his love and respect for the great fish, and despite hunting him in the mindful and sacral way of the primitive who celebrates his brotherhood with the life that nourishes his own (105).

The old fisherman believes that man's position on the food chain and the concomitant violence of our nature is an unchanging law—man "*has to . . .* live on the sea and kill [his] true brothers" (75; my emphasis). Thus Santiago illuminates the "tragic adventure" of fishing that young Nick avoids. In his sorrow for the marlin, Santiago hints at his resentment of the law; he "does not understand" why God has laid the necessity for killing on man (75). Therefore the old man experiences the final loss of the meat he is defending and the end of his need to kill as a release—"He only noticed how lightly and how well the skiff sailed now there was no great weight beside her" (119). Like the men of the *Kon-Tiki,* when the shark massacre ends Santiago feels his first longing to return to land and to a human community which can supply something other than "cold fish and a rough sea"—"[H]e sailed the skiff to make his home port as well and as intelligently as he could. . . . He knew where he was now and it was nothing to get home" (119–120). He does not yearn to "stretch out comfortably on the green grass," but he does yearn for his bed: "Bed is my friend. Just bed, he thought. Bed will be a great thing" (120).

The *Kon-Tiki* narrative begins to draw to a close, and to extend its primitivist thinking, as the expedition makes real and metaphoric landfall at a "seductive, green palm island" in Polynesia's Tuamotu group, where "all was Paradise and joy" (227). From the raft, as it rises on the waves, the men can see "the peace over the bright, green palm forest that stood and beckoned to us, the peace over the white birds that sailed around the palm tops, the peace over the glassy lagoon and the soft sand beach" (227). This Eden, however, is girdled not by Cherubims and a flaming sword "to keep the way of the tree of life" (Gen. 3.24), but by a naked coral reef with pounding surf, "the rust-red sword which defended the gates of heaven" (Heyerdahl 1950, 227). Heyerdahl describes this supremely dangerous natural barrier not only with Biblical imagery, but with images connected to war and to sharks. The reef resembles "a torn-up barricade of rusty iron ore"; the surf is "a frothing moat" that sounds like "cannonading and [the] roll of drums" (226–227). Circle the island as they may, the men of the *Kon-Tiki* cannot find safe passage through the compact reef, which lies "gnashing its blood-red teeth ominously in the foam" (226).

Both the *Kon-Tiki* narrative and *The Old Man and the Sea* celebrate endurance. Heyerdahl investigates several islands in search of a safe landing, but because all are coral atolls, ringed by reefs, he finds that each island "like a bulging basket of flowers," each "little bit of concentrated paradise" is surrounded by "a half-submerged fortress wall" (253). Eventually, the men find themselves "drifting helplessly toward the Raroia reef" (245), and the true ordeal of the *Kon-Tiki* voyage begins as the raft is sucked into the crushing surf and jagged coral blocks. The men cling to the raft for their lives, all of them pounded by the massive weight of 15- to 20-foot waves, some bruised by the falling masts and collapsing cabin as the raft begins to break up. With each repeated wave, not knowing whether they will reach the inside of the reef and safety before the *Kon-Tiki* is destroyed altogether, the young men hold out against this battery and in the process discover what Hemingway's old man already knows: "[W]e had all one single thought—hold on, hold on, hold, hold, hold! . . . [I]t demanded more endurance than we usually have in our bodies. There is greater strength in the human mechanism than that of muscles alone. I determined that, if I was to die, I would die in this position, like a knot on the stay" (Heyerdahl 1950, 248).

Santiago has no reef to cross to land his marlin and reach the longed-for bed where he may sleep. Instead, the ravening packs of sharks constitute the barrier of "gnashing . . . blood-red teeth" that stands between him and his own island. The old man fights the sharks for an afternoon and through the night into the small hours of the next morning, adjuring himself, like the men of the *Kon-Tiki* battling waves on the reef, to "think of nothing and wait for the next ones" and "'Fight them. . . . I'll fight them until I die'" (111, 115). Santiago is "beaten now finally and without remedy" (119); the sharks strip the marlin of its flesh until nothing is left but "the white naked line of his backbone and the dark mass of the head with the projecting bill and all the nakedness in between" (121). Yet the old man remains unconquered in spirit—his last act in the battle with the sharks is to spit blood into the ocean and declare "'Eat that, *galanos*. And make a dream you've killed a man'" (119).

The "winner take nothing" theme first appears in the Hemingway canon in an early short story, "The Undefeated" (1924). But the foregrounding of the same theme in the *Kon-Tiki* narrative may have prompted Hemingway's return to this successful message. The battering taken by the raft on the reef effectively destroys the *Kon-Tiki* in the moment of her triumph—landfall in Polynesia after three long months on the Pacific Ocean and a successful passage from South America. Heyerdahl writes:

> The *Kon-Tiki* was wholly changed, as by the stroke of a magic wand. The vessel we knew from weeks and months at sea was no more; in a few seconds our pleasant world had become a shattered wreck. . . . The hardwood mast on the starboard side was broken like a match, and the upper stump, in its fall, had smashed right through the cabin roof, so that the mast and all its gear slanted at a low angle over the reef on the starboard side. Astern the steering block was twisted round lengthways and the crossbeam broken, while the steering oar was smashed to splinters. The splashboards at the bow were broken like cigar boxes, and the whole deck was torn up and pasted like wet paper against the forward wall of the cabin, along with boxes, cans, canvas, and other cargo. Bamboo sticks and rope ends stuck up everywhere, and the general effect was of complete chaos. (249)

Like the skeleton of Santiago's marlin, the *Kon-Tiki* is "a wreck, but an honorable wreck" (253–254).

With the *Kon-Tiki* stranded on the reef, the men are eventually able to swim and wade through the interior lagoon to reach an uninhabited island.

Happily likening themselves to Robinson Crusoe, they build a fire, dine on crab meat and fresh coconut milk, and sleep on "beds of fresh palm leaves" amidst "the insinuating scent of blossoms" from "wild flowering bushes" (261). Yet this is no Eden; the violence of fallen nature remains unchanged. There are serpents in this paradise: the seemingly tranquil lagoon is full of the nastiest creatures encountered on the *Kon-Tiki* voyage—"frightful eel[s] with long poisonous teeth that could easily tear off a man's leg" (266)—and another battle reminiscent of the shark massacre occurs. Fishing in the lagoon,

> [The men] were suddenly attacked by no fewer than eight large eels.... The slimy brutes were thick as a man's calf and speckled green and black like poisonous snakes, with small heads, malignant snake eyes, and teeth an inch long and as sharp as an awl. The men hacked with their machete knives at the little swaying heads which came writhing towards them; they cut the head off one and another was injured. The blood in the sea attracted a whole flock of young blue sharks which attacked the dead and injured eels. (266–267)

Rescued by natives, the *Kon-Tiki* crew is taken to Raroia, a nearby inhabited island that also seems a Paradise at first glance, despite its human population. The village welcomes them with crowns and necklaces of flowers, with titles (Heyerdahl is anointed "Varoa Tikaroa"—spirit of the island's first king, an Adamic figure), with a banquet of "roast suckling pigs, chickens, roast ducks, fresh lobsters, Polynesian fish dishes, breadfruit, papaya, and coconut milk," and with "hula dancing on a grand scale" (281). Yet nearby a child lies dying of an abscess, with a temperature of 106 degrees, and when the *Kon-Tiki* voyagers successfully cure him with penicillin, they discover that "there was no end to the maladies which cropped up in the village. Toothache and gastric troubles were everywhere, and both young and old had boils in one place or another" (287). Although he does not discuss it in *Kon-Tiki*, Heyerdahl, who during his sojourn on Fatu-Hiva had witnessed fatal epidemics caused by European diseases, and who knew that the toothaches and gastric troubles were caused by Western diet and the boils by mosquitoes introduced by white men, equated medicine with civilization. For him, as for Hemingway years before in "Indian Camp," Western medicine was not always a blessing, but a technological panacea for imbalances in nature (Heyerdahl 1996, 99–100). The recovered child, in a vignette predicting the island's future, wants "to look at pictures from the white man's strange world where there were motorcars and cows and houses with several floors" (287).

No extravagant Polynesian ceremony of welcome awaits Santiago on his return to his Cuban village. When he sails "into the little harbour the lights of the Terrace were out and . . . everyone was in bed" (*OMATS* 120). Stiff, sore, and deeply exhausted by his ordeal, he must drag his skiff up on the shingled beach, and carry the heavy mast to his shack. His lonely bed covered with newspapers, and eventually a can of coffee—"hot and with plenty of milk and sugar in it"—brought by the boy Manolin constitute his welcome (123). Yet the company of the boy, his recognition of Santiago's achievement in bringing the giant marlin to gaff, and Manolin's loving promise to bring Santiago all the newspapers from the time he was away, a clean shirt, something to eat, and salve for his damaged hands, fulfill all the old man's emotional and physical needs on his return from the sea.

Despite the warmth of Santiago's relationship with Manolin, his island is no more a paradise than is Heyerdahl's. The old man remains subject to the curse God laid upon Adam at the expulsion from Eden—"In the sweat of thy face shalt thou eat bread, till thou return to the ground" (Gen. 3.19)—Santiago's only "hope" for the future is a return, with the boy as his apprentice, to the existential ordeal of fishing, to labor until he dies. Given, as Bickford Sylvester was among the first to suggest (91), that Santiago is probably dying ("'In the night I spat something strange and felt something in my chest was broken'" (*OMATS* 125), his projected return to the sea is a dignity-conserving "fiction" between him and the boy, like the non-existent cast net and the pot of yellow rice he pretends to have at the novel's beginning (16). But whether fictional or not, the old man's return to fishing presupposes a return to killing his true brothers, the marlin, and a renewed battle with the sharks. He requires new and improved weaponry to replace his broken knife: "'We must get a new killing lance and keep it always on board. You can make the blade from a spring leaf from an old Ford. We can grind it in Guanabacoa. It should be sharp and not tempered so it will break'" (125).

For Santiago, Paradise is not an actual island surrounded by a dangerous reef, but a primitivistic dream reaching back to an Edenic past, and forward to a millennial restoration of Eden. The old man dreams of "Africa when he was a boy and the long golden beaches and the white beaches, so white they hurt your eyes, and the high capes and the great brown mountains. He lived along that coast now every night and in his dreams he heard the surf roar and saw the native boats come riding through it" (24–25). It is a *Kon-Tiki*-like dream of "the white peaks of the Islands rising from the sea" (*OMATS* 25). It is a dream from the age of sail, from a time when ships moved with, rather than against the elements—"He smelled the tar and oakum of the deck as he slept" (25). But most of all, it is a vision of peace in nature, exemplified by the "lions on the beach" that play "like young cats in the dusk," the lions that the old man loves as he loves the boy (25). These are not the militant "young lions" of Psalm 104, who "roar after their prey and seek their meat from God" (21).[1] They belong instead to the millennial paradise of Isaiah, where natural law is overturned: "The wolf also shall dwell with the lamb, and the leopard shall lie down with the kid; and the calf and the young lion and the fatling together; and a little child shall lead them. . . . They shall not hurt nor destroy in all my holy mountain: for the earth shall be full of the knowledge of the Lord, as the waters cover the sea" (11.6, 11.9).

"One can't buy a ticket to Paradise," Heyerdahl ruefully concluded at the end of his Fatu-Hiva experiment (1974, 269), and the same is true of the *Kon-Tiki* expedition. The *Kon-Tiki* narrative ends when the 4,000 ton Norwegian steamer, *Thor I,* is diverted from Samoa to Tahiti to pick up the explorers and the remains of their raft, now just nine balsa logs hauled off the Raroia reef and towed to Papeete harbor. *Thor I* swings out "a huge iron arm and lift[s] her small kinsman up onto the deck" while "loud blasts of the ship's siren echo over the palm-clad island" (Heyerdahl 1950, 295). Engines roar, propellers whip the water, and the return to civilization begins: "Waves were breaking out on the blue sea. We could no longer reach down to them.

White trade-wind clouds drifted across the blue sky. We were no longer traveling their way. We were defying Nature now. We were going back to the twentieth century which lay so far, far away" (296).

Chief Teriieroo has told the men that if they wish to return to Tahiti, they must throw their flower wreaths into the lagoon as the steamer goes, the classic parting gesture of tourists vacationing in the islands. And so the narrative ends as "in the lagoon at Tahiti six white wreaths lay alone, washing in and out, in and out, with the wavelets on the beach"—emblems of man's desire to return to a paradise that no longer exists on earth (296).

Like the steamer *Thor I*, returning the *Kon-Tiki* and her crew to civilization, the conclusion of *The Old Man and the Sea* returns the reader, if not Santiago, to the twentieth century that has lain "so far, far away" throughout most of the text. A party of tourists lunching at the Terrace looks down and sees Santiago's marlin, "now just garbage waiting to go out with the tide" (126). "'What's that?'" a woman tourist asks a waiter. "'Tiburon,' the waiter said. 'Eshark.' He was meaning to explain what had happened. 'I didn't know sharks had such handsome, beautifully formed tails,'" the woman responds. "'I didn't either,' her male companion said" (127). The tourists are emblematic of many things—not only a new coastal economy that will overtake and destroy Santiago's way of life, as all the "civilized" world attempts to buy a "ticket to Paradise," but also twentieth century man's alienation from, and continuing nostalgia for the world of nature. Heyerdahl might have been glossing this passage when he wrote in *Green Was the Earth on the Seventh Day*, "[tourists] sit all day at a desk . . . eleven months out of twelve to earn money for cars and big houses. Then, with the money they've saved, they rush away . . . for a few weeks' vacation. . . . To look for a place in the sun. To hunt, to fish, to pick berries, to stroll in the woods, climb the hills or swim. Primitive man's work has become modern man's leisure" (1996, 225).

Readers of *The Old Man and the Sea* have more in common with the tourists at the Terrace than with Santiago, yet our voyage through the novel has given us what they lack, a greater understanding of the richness of his world, and the impoverishment of our own. The final sentence of the novel—"The old man was dreaming about the lions"—functions in part like

Heyerdahl's flower necklaces in the surf, a reminder of our own longing for a lost communion with nature, and our hope for a return.

The Old Man and the Sea won the overwhelming critical success Hemingway required after the debacle of *Across the River and into the Trees.* The reviews, albeit with a literary cast, echoed those of *Kon-Tiki.* Mark Schorer, writing in *The New Republic,* spoke of Santiago's "Conradian victory, which means destruction and triumph" (412). Malcolm Cowley, in the *New York Herald Tribune Book Review,* was among the many who compared the book favorably with Herman Melville's *Moby-Dick* (106–107). Harold Gardiner, reviewing the novel for *America,* lauded its deep connection with nature: "There is the extraordinary feel for the cleanness of the sea winds, the mysterious life under the waves, the lone majesty of the sunset" (Hanneman 442). Carlos Baker, in *Saturday Review,* noted Hemingway's celebration of the daring and hardihood of man—"What Santiago has at the close of his story is what all the heroes of Hemingway have had—the proud, quiet knowledge of having fought the fight, of having lasted it out, of having done a great thing to the bitter end of human strength" (Hanneman 440). No less a reader than William Faulkner, writing for *Shenandoah,* saw the novel as a restoration of faith: "This time, [Hemingway] discovered God, a Creator" (414–415). Like the *Kon-Tiki* narrative, *The Old Man and the Sea* was hailed as a classic from the moment of publication: "Everywhere the book is being called a classic," wrote Schorer (410); "[D]estined to become a classic of its kind," asserted Baker (Hanneman 440); "The writing has the quality of being familiar yet perpetually new that is the essence of classical prose," opined Cowley (107). "[N]o page of this beautiful masterwork could have been done better or differently" wrote Cyril Connolly in the London *Sunday Times* (Hanneman 441). The novel swiftly captured the Pulitzer Prize, and most affirming of all was the Nobel Prize Committee's belief that *The Old Man and the Sea* was the "work of ideal tendencies" required to anoint Hemingway as the 1954 recipient of the Nobel Prize for Literature (Baker 510, 528).

While not quite the equal of "*Kon-Tiki* fever," public enthusiasm for *The Old Man and the Sea* ran high. Published in *Life* magazine, the novel reached 5,318,650 readers almost instantaneously. It was the largest print run in the magazine's history, and sold out in 48 hours (Reynolds 258; Baker 504). Like *Kon-Tiki, The Old Man and the Sea* was a Book-of-the-Month Club selection, with 153,000 copies distributed to members (Reynolds 258). Yet despite this seeming saturation of the market, regular book sales too were brisk. Scribner's first edition of 50,000 copies sold out in ten days, and the novel remained on the *New York Times* best-seller list for 26 weeks (Reynolds 258). Hemingway was deluged with letters and telephone calls from hysterical fans; people burst into tears at the sight of him, challenged him to fist fights, and named their dogs Santiago. Rabbis and ministers preached sermons on the text (Baker 505). Almost immediately, Hollywood came calling with a proposal to turn *The Old Man and the Sea* into a film starring Spencer Tracy and a mechanical rubber fish, and Hemingway received a "Medal of Honor" from a Cuban Tourist Institute unconscious of irony (Hanneman 444). "[T]his five million readers at a time is spooky," Hemingway wrote to Wallace Meyer on 26 September 1952 (*SL* 783). He and his wife Mary fled on *Pilar* to the uninhabited islet they called Paraíso Key, there to fish and swim naked in a lagoon protected by a barrier reef (Reynolds 262).

The same cultural conditions that helped contribute to *Kon-Tiki*'s success still obtained when *The Old Man and the Sea* was published. Kenneth Lynn has observed that "larger historical circumstances . . . figured in the response the novel aroused" and that "it expressed a collective mood of disillusionment no less surely than had *The Sun Also Rises*" (566). In 1952, Allies staged the largest air strike of the Korean War, pummeling the ancient city of Suan from dawn to dusk with bombs, machine gun bullets, and napalm, while six thousand American troops with flamethrowers and tanks smashed a communist prison on Korea's Koje Island. General Dwight D. Eisenhower and running mate Richard Nixon won the presidency in a landslide, vowing to end the Korean War with honor. Meanwhile, the war in Vietnam widened, as French soldiers pressed north of Hanoi. The British sent troops to Kenya to suppress the Mau Mau rebellion. The United States dedicated the world's first atomic submarine, and Britain a long-range bomber capable of crossing the Atlantic in eight hours. Congress deplored the proliferation of violent crime shows and advertisements for alcohol on television, and General

Fulgencio Batista seized the government of Cuba in a lightning coup d'état. The first flashing "Don't Walk" signs were installed in New York City, and Peter During, a 41-year-old steel worker from Bethlehem, Pennsylvania, became the first man to receive a mechanical heart (Daniel 713–724).

Only two critics have written about *The Old Man and the Sea* in its historic context. Gerry Brenner elaborates on that context only to dismiss its importance: "the story *ignores* events contemporaneous with its composition, publication, or reception." The novel's "long-standing appeal lies in its remoteness from our world" and the "timeless quality of *The Old Man and the Sea* . . . contributes to the work's stature as a masterpiece" (3, 7; my emphasis). Kenneth Lynn, by contrast, felt that "whether by deliberate design or by unconscious groping, the Korean War and all its implications" are reflected in the novel. He likens the story both to the dismissal by President Truman of war hero General Douglas MacArthur for his attempts to carry the Korean War to China, and to the immensely popular 1952 Western movie *High Noon,* about a retired marshal who, despite a pacifist bride and a cowardly populace that does not want a fight, returns to duty to face four outlaws in the dusty streets (567–569). For Lynn, *The Old Man and the Sea* too was a story of "a conscientious return ending in alienation and departure, a victory with a taste as sour as defeat" (569). Whereas Brenner reads the novel as apolitical—perhaps even socially irresponsible—in its deliberate refusal to engage current events, Lynn sees it as reactionary in politics, reading *Old Man* as a Cold War drama of "beset manhood" (Clark 91), playing out MacArthur's "Old soldiers never die, they just fade away," or Sheriff Kane's "A man's gotta do what a man's gotta do."

Both readings have validity, but both avoid the novel's setting on the sea entirely, as if nature played no part in the story's politics. And it is in *The Old Man and the Sea*'s primitivism, as Suzanne Clark reminds us, in its rejection of the artifice and corruptions of the modern world for a life of freedom, innocence, and simplicity lived on the sea, that we may locate the novel's "progressive politics" and advocacy of "more communal forms of living" (63). Such has been one important role of primitivism in American thought and literature since the first Europeans encountered the pristine nature of the new continent, early identified, as M. H. Abrams notes, with both "the golden age of the past and the new millennium to come" (137). If, by the 1950s, the fresh green breast of the new world had long since been despoiled, the physical sea had remained, at least for Hemingway, the same as it was "since before Columbus" (*GHOA* 149). For Heyerdahl as well, the sea was "the absolute common measure of history—endless unbroken darkness under a swarm of stars" (1950, 173).

Hemingway was no stranger to primitivism, either in his life or his art. Born fifteen years before Heyerdahl, he too had been steeped in the "back-to-nature" movement—studying natural history with the Agassiz Club, preparing animals for its museum taxidermy collections, hunting, fishing, hiking, camping, and hoping one day "'to do pioneering or exploring work in the last 3 great frontiers Africa southern central South America or the country around and north of Hudson Bay'" (Beegel 2000, 77–78). For Hemingway, as for Heyerdahl, the sea would gradually displace the rivers, lakes, forests, and mountains of his boyhood as "the last wild country there is left" ("OTBW" 237). Although he never deserted civilization and its discontents as completely as Heyerdahl in the Fatu-Hiva experiment, Hemingway's adult removal to the tropical islands of Key West and Cuba certainly constituted a similar rejection of the workaday urban and suburban worlds of most Americans.

And like Heyerdahl in *Kon-Tiki*, Hemingway in *The Old Man and the Sea* could approach the natural world with a veteran's perspective that included not only such horrors of World War II as the D-Day landings in Normandy and the mechanized slaughter of Hürtgen Forest, but equivalent grim memories of the Spanish Civil War, the Greco-Turkish War, and World War I, as well. Hemingway in his most successful fiction—the Nick Adams stories and the novels *The Sun Also Rises, A Farewell to Arms,* and *For Whom the Bell Tolls*—had used to great effect the ironic juxtaposition of nature, a place of refreshment and healing, with scenes of war and postwar despondency. Perhaps the most obvious progenitor of *The Old Man and the Sea* is Hemingway's Spanish Civil War short story "Old Man at the Bridge," which juxtaposes the ruined life of an old man almost reminiscent of St.

Francis of Assisi, a 76-year-old refugee "without politics," a peasant who was "only looking after animals," with the Fascist advance on the Ebro (*SS* 79–80). The old man's life and impending death, like Santiago's, constitute a devastating critique of modern warfare—and the fact that *The Old Man and the Sea*, like "Big Two-Hearted River" before it, does not mention the war, does not make the story less political—or less effective—than "Old Man at the Bridge." Although Delmore Schwartz felt that with *The Old Man and the Sea* Hemingway had moved away from the "hysterical fury against modern warfare" that had marred *Across the River and into the Trees* (416), F. W. Dupee was shrewd enough to recognize that "If his feeling for nature receives in [*The Old Man and the Sea*] an uncommonly ideal expression, that does not mean that the anger is any the less. It may mean that the anger has now reached the stage of the ineffable" (420–421).

Hemingway's best work, as Leo Marx observed long ago, "invoke[s] the image of a green landscape—a terrain either wild or, if cultivated, rural—as a symbolic repository of meaning and value" while at the same time acknowledging "the power of a counter-force, a machine or some other symbol of the forces which have stripped the old ideal of its meaning." This "complex pastoralism," Marx continues, "acknowledges the reality of history" (362–363). Why Hemingway chose to abandon a primitivistic stance for the almost undiluted materialism of *Across the River and into the Trees*—a novel whose own spiritual malaise derives from its obsessive concern with the best hotels and restaurants, jewels, coiffures, and brand-name products including Sollingen cutlery, Rolex watches, Buick Roadmasters, and Burberry raincoats, as well as Boss and Purdey shotguns—must remain conjectural. But if there was little Thor Heyerdahl could teach Hemingway about either writing or the literary uses of primitivism, both the story of the *Kon-Tiki* voyage and the wild popular acclaim that greeted it had a great deal to teach Hemingway about value of a return to nature—and to his roots as a writer.

NOTE

1. Consciously or unconsciously, Hemingway may have wanted to invoke a comparison with Irwin Shaw's *The Young Lions* (1948), a critically acclaimed, best-selling war novel well-known to the contemporary audience of *The Old Man and the Sea*. He had special reason to feel competitive with the younger Shaw, who had not only beaten the old lion Hemingway to a classic, bestselling novel of World War II, but had also beaten him to his fourth and final wife Mary, who had an affair with Shaw before her marriage to Hemingway.

WORKS CITED

Abrams, M. H. *A Glossary of Literary Terms*. 3rd ed. New York: Holt, Rinehart and Winston, 1971.

Baker, Carlos. *Ernest Hemingway: A Life Story*. New York: Charles Scribner's Sons, 1969.

Barbour, Thomas. *A Naturalist in Cuba*. Boston: Little, Brown, 1945.

Beegel, Susan F. "Eye and Heart: Hemingway's Education as a Naturalist." In *A Historical Guide to Ernest Hemingway*. Ed. Linda Wagner-Martin, 53–92. New York: Oxford UP, 2000.

———. "A Guide to the Marine Life in *The Old Man and the Sea*." *Resources for American Literary Study* 30 (2006): 236–315.

———. "Santiago and the Eternal Feminine: Gendering *La Mar* in The Old Man and the Sea." In *Hemingway and Women: Female Critics and the Female Voice*. Eds. Lawrence R. Broer and Gloria Holland, 131–156, 305–307. Tuscaloosa: University of Alabama Press, 2002.

Brasch, James D., and Joseph Sigman. *Hemingway's Library: A Composite Record*. New York: Garland, 1981.

Brenner, Gerry. *The Old Man and the Sea: Story of a Common Man*. New York: Twayne Publishers, 1991.

Burwell, Rose Marie. *Hemingway: The Postwar Years and the Posthumous Novels*. New York: Cambridge UP, 1996.

Clark, Suzanne. *Cold Warriors: Manliness on Trial in the Rhetoric of the West*. Carbondale: Southern Illinois UP, 2000.

Coleridge, Samuel Taylor. *The Rime of the Ancient Mariner*. 1834; New York: Dover, 1970.

Cowley, Malcolm. "Hemingway's Novel Has the Rich Simplicity of a Classic." In *Twentieth Century Interpretations of The Old Man and the Sea*. Ed. Katharine T. Jobes, 106–108. Englewood Cliffs, NJ: Prentice-Hall, 1968.

Daniel, Clifton, ed. *Chronicle of the Twentieth Century*. Mount Kisco, NY: Chronicle Publications, 1987.

Dupee, F. W. "Rev. of *The Old Man and the Sea*." In *Hemingway: The Critical Heritage*. Ed. Jeffrey Meyers, 417–421. Boston: Routledge and Kegan Paul, 1982.

Ellis, Richard. *The Book of Sharks*. New York: Alfred A. Knopf, 1996.

Farrington, S. Kip. *Fishing with Hemingway and Glassell*. New York: David McKay Company, 1971.

Faulkner, William. "Rev. of *The Old Man and the Sea*." In *Hemingway: The Critical Heritage*. Ed. Jeffrey Meyers, 414–415. Boston: Routledge and Kegan Paul, 1982.

Hanneman, Audre. *Ernest Hemingway: A Comprehensive Bibliography*. Princeton, NJ: Princeton UP, 1967.

Hemingway, Ernest. *Across the River and into the Trees*. New York: Charles Scribner's Sons, 1950.

———. *Ernest Hemingway: Selected Letters, 1917–1961*. Ed. Carlos Baker. New York: Charles Scribner's Sons, 1981.

———. *For Whom the Bell Tolls*. New York: Charles Scribner's Sons, 1940.

———. *Green Hills of Africa*. New York: Charles Scribner's Sons, 1935.

———. *The Old Man and the Sea*. New York: Charles Scribner's Sons, 1952.

———. "On the Blue Water: A Gulf Stream Letter." *Esquire*. April 1936. In *By-Line: Ernest Hemingway*. Ed. William White. New York: Charles Scribner's Sons, 1967. 236–244.

———. *The Short Stories of Ernest Hemingway*. New York: Charles Scribner's Sons, 1938.

Heyerdahl, Thor. *Fatu-Hiva: Back to Nature*. New York: Doubleday, 1974.

———. *Green Was the Earth on the Seventh Day*. New York: Random House, 1996.

———. *Kon-Tiki: Across the Pacific by Raft*. Trans. F. H. Lyon. Chicago: Rand McNally, 1950.

———. *Pa Jakt efter Paradiset*. Oslo: Gyldendal, 1938. Jacoby, Arnold. *Señor Kon-Tiki: The Biography of Thor Heyerdahl*. Chicago: Rand McNally, 1967.

Jobes, Katharine T., ed. *Twentieth Century Interpretations of* The Old Man and the

Sea. Englewood Cliffs, NJ: Prentice-Hall, 1968.

Kazin, Alfred. "Rev. of *Across the River and into the Trees*." In *Hemingway: The Critical Heritage*. Ed. Jeffrey Meyers, 378–381. Boston: Routledge and Kegan Paul, 1982.

Lear, Linda. *Rachel Carson: Witness for Nature*. New York: Henry Holt, 1997.

Lynn, Kenneth. *Hemingway*. New York: Simon and Schuster, 1987.

Marx, Leo. *The Machine in the Garden: Technology and the Pastoral Ideal in America*. New York: Oxford University Press, 1964.

Meredith, James H. "The Rapido River and Hürtgen Forest in *Across the River and into the Trees*." *The Hemingway Review* 14.1 (Fall 1994): 60–66.

Meyers, Jeffrey, ed. *Hemingway: The Critical Heritage*. Boston: Routledge and Kegan Paul, 1982.

Reynolds, Michael. *Hemingway: The Final Years*. New York: W.W. Norton, 1999.

Rosenfeld, Isaac. "Rev. of *Across the River and into the Trees*." In *Hemingway: The Critical Heritage*. Ed. Jeffrey Meyers, 385–393. Boston: Routledge and Kegan Paul, 1982.

Schorer, Mark. "Rev. of *The Old Man and the Sea*." In *Hemingway: The Critical Heritage*. Ed. Jeffrey Meyers, 408–413. Boston: Routledge and Kegan Paul, 1982.

Schwartz, Delmore. "Rev. of *The Old Man and the Sea*." In *Hemingway: The Critical Heritage*. Ed. Jeffrey Meyers, 415–416. Boston: Routledge and Kegan Paul, 1982.

Shaw, Irwin. *The Young Lions*. New York: Random House, 1948.

Sylvester, Bickford. "Hemingway's Extended Vision in *The Old Man and the Sea*." In *Twentieth Century Interpretations of* The Old Man and the Sea. Ed. Katharine T. Jobes, 81–96. Englewood Cliffs, NJ: Prentice-Hall, 1968.

Thoreau, Henry David. *Walden and Civil Disobedience*. Ed. Owen Thomas. New York: W.W. Norton, 1966.

Urdang, Laurence, ed. *The Timetables of American History*. New York: Simon and Schuster, 1981.

Waugh, Evelyn. "Rev. of *Across the River and into the Trees*." In *Hemingway: The Critical Heritage*. Ed. Jeffrey Meyers, 382–385. Boston: Routledge and Kegan Paul, 1982.

Weeks, Robert P. "Fakery in *The Old Man and the Sea*." In *Twentieth Century*

Interpretations of The Old Man and the Sea. Ed. Katharine T. Jobes, 34–40. Englewood Cliffs, NJ: Prentice-Hall, 1968.

Zabel, Morton Dauwen. "Rev. of *Across the River and Into the Trees.*" In *Hemingway: The Critical Heritage.* Ed. Jeffrey Meyers, 375–377. Boston: Routledge and Kegan Paul, 1982.

Death Sentences

Rereading *The Old Man and the Sea*

William E. Cain

Perhaps the familiarity of *The Old Man and the Sea* has prevented us from perceiving its terrible power. Hemingway's novel has become so taken for granted that we have not appreciated how disturbing it is: for all of its intrepid dignity on the surface, it is deeply disquieting in its themes. The best known of Hemingway's books, *The Old Man and the Sea,* is also the most misunderstood.

Life magazine published the entire text of *The Old Man and the Sea* in its September 1, 1952 issue and 5.3 million copies were sold in the first forty-eight hours. Scribner's first printing of 50,000 became available the next week and the book soon reached the best-seller list, where it remained

Reprinted with permission from *The Sewanee Review,* 114.1 (Winter 2006). Copyright © 2006 by William E. Cain. Published by The University of the South by Johns Hopkins University Press.

for six months. The Book-of-the-Month Club chose it as a main selection with a first printing of 153,000 copies, and it was translated into nine foreign languages within the year. Soon *The Old Man and the Sea* was being taught in middle schools and high schools, and it became a favorite outside the classroom as well.

Not all of Hemingway's biographers and critics admire *The Old Man and the Sea,* and some have spoken about it harshly. Jeffrey Meyers, for example, emphasizes its "radical" weaknesses, including sentimentality, self-pity, and "forced and obtrusive" Christian symbolism. "In the highly acclaimed *Old Man and the Sea,*" he states, "Hemingway either deceived himself about the profundity of his art or expressed his contempt for *Life,* Scribner's, the reading public, the critics, and religion by writing an ironic and mock-serious fable that gave them exactly what they wanted and expected." Kenneth Lynn reaches the same conclusion: "Today, there is only one question worth asking about *The Old Man.* How could a book that lapses repeatedly into lachrymose sentimentality and is relentlessly pseudo-Biblical, that mixes cute talk about baseball . . . with crucifixion symbolism of the most appalling crudity . . . have evoked such a storm of applause from highbrows and middlebrows alike—and in such overwhelming numbers?"

These are minority reports, however. Hemingway scholars usually refer to *The Old Man and the Sea* in respectful terms, describing it as Hemingway's "recovery" from the disaster of *Across the River and into the Trees,* published two years earlier, and as a noble evocation of the Hemingway code. But at present *The Old Man and the Sea* has only a marginal place in Hemingway studies. It says little about sexuality and gender—for decades these have been the dominant topics for Hemingway scholars—and hence it is briefly praised and bypassed. For most Hemingway scholars, what counts are the ambitious projects he pursued during the 1940s and 1950s, none of which he finished but which, in heavily edited and cut forms, have been published attached to his name: *A Moveable Feast* (1964), *Islands in the Stream* (1970), *The Dangerous Summer* (1985), *The Garden of Eden* (1986), and *True at First Light* (1999).

As revealing as these edited books are about Hemingway's personal and sexual preoccupations, in my view they do not possess the authority of the works he completed and saw through to publication in his lifetime. The climax of Hemingway's career is *The Old Man and the Sea:* this is the point at which his journey as a published writer ended. The novel lacks the range and scale of his best books of the 1920s, but it is, I believe, the work of a master, and in retrospect it strikes me as the only possible ending for his career.

I am simply proposing that we give *The Old Man and the Sea* another look and in the process allow it to display its strange brilliance. From first to last Hemingway's sentences in *The Old Man and the Sea* take surprising turns, as when he concludes the opening paragraph with a sentence about Santiago's skiff: "The sail was patched with flour sacks, and, furled, it looked like the flag of permanent defeat." "Permanent" accents the point, making it unmistakable, and thus the sentence that comes a few lines later seems a contradiction: "Everything about him was old except his eyes and they were the same color as the sea and were cheerful and undefeated." This adjustment in our response is part of Hemingway's narrative strategy: the later sentence corrects the earlier one—or, rather, it corrects our interpretation of the earlier one. The flag does not signify defeat, though to some it might be misread in that way. Hemingway is prompting us to see the difference between how something appears (and what it might mislead us to believe about a person) and who someone is.

It is frequently said that in his final books Hemingway lost contact with the shape and sound of his prose and was no longer seeing and hearing the interaction of the sentences he set down on the page. You might conclude from the novel's opening that the references first to "permanent defeat" and then to "undefeated" bear witness to the supposition that in his sentences Hemingway is not in control. But the contradiction is deliberate and dramatizes that we are inclined to make superficial judgments: we know less than we think we do. In miniature it teaches us that the reality of an experience or the essence of a person cannot be judged from surfaces. The lesson pertains to our experience and our understanding of *The Old Man and the Sea* as a whole.

This claim about Hemingway's craft can be taken further. In *The Old Man and the Sea* Hemingway is oriented critically toward his style: he reflects on its strengths and limitations and even exposes its absurdity—the arbitrariness, and yet the necessity, of choosing this word rather than that one for a sentence, and indeed the larger issue of being a writer at all. *The Old Man and the Sea* is not a recovery for Hemingway; it should not be characterized as a return to his style of the 1920s. Instead it is an advance, an effort to do something new. Hemingway seeks in this fiction to make the tragic and comic coincide, coalescing the heroic and the laughable in his sentences. Santiago is brave and ridiculous, self-aware and out of his mind. He endures; he shows grace under pressure. He is absurd, committed to a mission and a task that matter not against the dissolution performed by time.

The storyline and plain prose of *The Old Man and the Sea* invite a rapid reading for pleasure, but the risk then is not taking the novel seriously—by which I mean with full seriousness. Hemingway's ideal audience consists of readers who pause over sentences and savor the spaces in between—the perfectly modulated sequences of notes and silences that Hemingway deploys as breathtakingly as the jazz geniuses Louis Armstrong and Miles Davis. "None of these scars were fresh," he writes of Santiago, "They were as old as erosions in a fishless desert." Hemingway gives the sense of wearing away in the sound of "old as erosions," and he implies that the scars are impossibly old, reaching backward to a desert that was once a sea. He reminds us of the span of time—that the sea in which the old man fishes will also eventually become a desert, boundless and bare.

Later, as evening falls and as the great fish that Santiago has caught continues to pull his boat, Hemingway writes:

It was dark now as it becomes dark quickly after the sun sets in September. He lay against the worn wood of the bow and rested all that he could. The first stars were out. He did not know the name of Rigel but he saw it and knew soon they would all be out and he would have his distant friends.

"The fish is my friend too," he said aloud. "I have never seen or heard of such a fish. But I must kill him. I am glad we do not have to try to kill the stars."

Killing the stars may sound far-fetched—some of Hemingway's critics have mocked this phrase. But there is no lapse here: such language is not far-fetched for an old fisherman tired from battle with his huge catch. This is how Santiago's mind drifts and fixes on an object of attention. The double "dark" in the first line connects Hemingway to his character—Hemingway has experienced the conditions that Santiago contends against. The vowels in "the worn wood of the bow"—the assonance of the phrase—evoke the feel of the wood's smoothness; what Santiago feels Hemingway has felt, and that is why this writer can strike the phrase that instills in us the same feeling. "The first stars were out" changes the rhythm, which is followed by Hemingway's break in point of view as he cites knowledge of a detail not known to his character and then lays down the passage of dialogue, quiet and meditative but edged with craziness.

People do talk to themselves, especially fisherman; Santiago knows he does, and Hemingway mentions this point in essays about fishing he wrote in the 1930s (e.g., "On the Blue Water," *Esquire,* April 1936). But there is more to it than that. No one else is with Santiago; he is alone at sea, occupying a jot of space amid immensity. There are no witnesses except for the reader to whom Hemingway tells the story. Those on shore, described in the final pages, see only the bare bones of the marlin; they do not know the facts and sensations of the struggle, and there is no indication that Santiago will talk about them.

Manolin, the person closest to Santiago, was not there for the contest with the marlin and the fight against the sharks either. Whatever he does hear from Santiago will be a diminished rendering of what took place. Moreover the sense of exhaustion Hemingway expresses in his character after Santiago returns to shore suggests to me that he will die very soon. Every life story ends in death, and no one knows what another person has gone through on his or her way there: the best we can achieve are approximations.

Santiago is detached from all others: nearly everyone else is a name in the newspaper or a dim recollection or a presence encountered on trips back and forth to his boat. Santiago says he loves Manolin, but it not clear what his love amounts to. This old man would take to sea whether Manolin existed or not. His photograph of his wife is underneath his shirt on the shelf in the corner, it made him lonely to see it, so he removed it from the wall. He does not dream about her, nor does she come to his mind when he is at sea.

Does Santiago, this figure of stark isolation, possess the grandeur that critics have attributed to him? In some measure he does, yet in truth he is just a fisherman, an old man alone, like Robert Frost's old man who can't keep a house. For many days Santiago catches no fish; he then catches a great fish only to lose it. On bad days and good days he returns to his shack, and, as Manolin is aware at the outset, this old man may not realize that some of the things he says are untrue.

There are determination and resilience in Santiago, in his devotion to his work at hand, akin to that of Hemingway rising with the sun to write and count that day's allotment of prose. This is a form of grandeur. But no exertion prevents death—the black oblivion (the other side of the white page of an author's book) into which all subsides. Day after day this knowledge pressed on Hemingway, and he is working through it in his depiction of Santiago. No writer was more severely driven by the imperative to work, nor was any writer more cut to the quick by the hopelessness of work shadowed by extinction.

In *The Old Man and the Sea* Hemingway recounts Santiago's story to express the majesty and the pointlessness of human effort. It is not that he is using Santiago as an analogy for himself as a writer. He is saying he and Santiago are the same. It is simple: one fishes, one writes, both die. This is not sentimental or self-pitying: it is the truth for Hemingway about what it means to be alive—that each of us is dying. When we are young we believe otherwise, as does Nick Adams in trailing his hand in the warm water on a sharp chilly morning at the close of "Indian Camp," the first story of *In Our Time* (1925): "In the early morning on the lake sitting in the stern of the boat with his father rowing, he felt quite sure that he would never die." The questions Hemingway confronted were these: Since finally we know that everyone dies, how should we live? Why should we live?

For Hemingway these questions do not depend upon God. Not for him is the promise of the New Testament: "the last enemy that shall be destroyed is death" (1 Corinthians 15:26). Hemingway wrote against death; he professed that his best sentences could embody a feeling forever even as he knew that his forever could never be forever. A great book is a postponement of the inevitable: there is no defense against Time's scythe. If you think that something will last forever, you are not looking far enough ahead. It is punitive to think in such terms, which is why Hemingway often claimed that his work might win an eternal life after all. It was pretty to think so.

Facing eternity, or the lack of it, each day, Hemingway wrote until he could write no longer, and then, in July 1961, he killed himself. He kept going after *The Old Man and the Sea,* but the thousands of pages of sentences and half-sentences he produced would not cohere as books and that was because he had nothing left to say. Santiago was inherent in the Nick Adams of "Indian Camp," in the frailty of the overinsistent "quite sure" that he would never die. In *The Old Man and the Sea,* Hemingway gave life to the character that was always waiting for him, the person whom in a sense he always was, even when he was a handsome young man in his twenties, full of promise in Paris. A friend of his first wife, Hadley Richardson, remembered him: "You wouldn't believe what a beautiful youth Ernest was. . . . He laughed aloud a lot from quick humor and from sheer joy in being alive." It is miraculous that this writer lasted as long as he did. He wrote with a gun to his head every day.

. . . . .

I have not yet done justice to *The Old Man and the Sea.* This novel is more extreme than I have suggested—than I even want to suggest. It has an unyielding power in its scenes and in its vision that expose dimensions of experience that are almost impossible to face and that bring home with intensity the feelings that Hemingway explored. When the sentences of *The Old Man and the Sea* are lingered over, the experience of the novel becomes unforgettable and unforgiving: it wounds the reader's consciousness. This novel's extremity is evident early in the action, as Santiago prepares for a new day of fishing: "The successful fishermen of that day were already in and had butchered their marlin out and carried them laid full length across two planks, with two men staggering at the end of each plank, to the fish house where they waited for the ice truck to carry them to the market in Havana. Those who had caught sharks had taken them to the shark factory on the other side of the cove where they were hoisted on a block and tackle, their livers removed, their fins cut off and their hides skinned out and their flesh cut into strips for salting."

The verb *butchered* describes the activity of preparing the marlin for sale but carries with it the connotation of unflinching slaughter, which Hemingway amplifies in the final sentence, with its hoisting, removing, cutting, and skinning. The impact is visceral and is meant to elide differences between marlins and sharks and human beings. Hemingway makes us remember that we are as permeable as are these creatures; our flesh is vulnerable to the knife—we can be cut into pieces—and our bodies will be degraded too. The humiliations of lifelessness are contained in us.

Hemingway was a fisherman, hunter, ambulance driver, war reporter, soldier; he was wounded and injured countless times and knew what a knife could do. The rending of bodies appears throughout his nonfiction reportage on wars and battles (journalism is one-third of his total output) and in his fiction from the woman in "Indian Camp" whom Nick's father sews up after the Caesarean and her husband who cuts his throat from ear to ear to the mutilated Jake Barnes, the bloodied Frederic Henry and the hemorrhaging Catherine Barkley, and the wounded, broken down, dying, or dead figures of Harry Morgan, Robert Jordan, Colonel Cantwell, and Thomas Hudson.

"Gee I was sorry when I heard that you were to go under the knife," Hemingway wrote to his sister Marcelline, May 20, 1921, after she had told him about an operation ahead. "There's nothing bothers me like having a dear old friend or relative go under the knife," he says again in this letter, and he repeats the phrase "under the knife" eight more times before he is done. Hemingway truly was his father Dr. Clarence E. Hemingway's son: cutting was in his blood.

The blood flows in *The Old Man and the Sea,* as when Manolin recalls his first boat trip with Santiago: "I can remember the tail slapping and banging and the thwart breaking and the noise of the clubbing. I can remember you throwing me into the bow where the wet coiled lines were and feeling the whole boat shiver and the noise of you clubbing him like chopping a tree down and the sweet blood smell all over me."

To my ear the phrase "the wet coiled lines" does not fall within the range of Manolin's voice. Neither does "feeling the whole boat shiver." The rhythm is right for Hemingway himself, whereas for Manolin it is instead the phrase "the noise of you clubbing him" that expresses how he would speak. Hemingway wants it this way: his voice resonates within the voice of the character he is presenting; his voice is in the midst of his character's words. We will miss the power of the scene if we fail to see how subtle and intimate it is. It affirms companionship that partakes of repulsion and joy, bloody and sweet.

A later sequence of sentences, describing Santiago's baits, extends and toughens this pointed piteous effect: "Each bait hung head down with the shank of the hook inside the bait fish, tied and sewed solid and all the projecting part of the hook, the curve and the point, was covered with fresh sardines. Each sardine was hooked through both eyes so that they made a half-garland on the projecting steel. There was no part of the hook that a great fish could feel which was not sweet smelling and good tasting."

Feel the hook passing through your eyes. The helplessness of each fish, the mutilation inflicted upon it, show us what we are capable of and do all the time: this is what we do to fish, and what throughout history human beings have done to one another. Santiago enjoys his occupation; he is an expert. The fish he hopes to catch is "great" literally and figuratively, and its meat and blood are sweet. The play of light, the salt smell in the breeze, the endurance of this aged fisherman—the scene is seductive yet horrific, calling to mind Oedipus gouging his eyes in Sophocles' play and the tormentors in *King Lear* who bind the corky arms of Gloucester and grind his eyes to sightlessness.

The Old Man and the Sea is a theater of cruelty with a flesh-piercing array of images and terms that complicate the novel's renderings of nature's wonder and humankind's courage. One could characterize *The Old Man and the Sea,* as some have done, as an existentialist novel, but while the writings of existential philosophers such as Jean-Paul Sartre and Albert Camus offer contrast and comparison, they are not directly relevant to the inquiry that Hemingway undertook: he came to questions of life and death on his own and was brooding over them when he was in his teens. He forged his style by studying Sherwood Anderson, Gertrude Stein, and James Joyce, among others, even as he developed his conceptions of identity and nature within the contexts of his family, his hometown of Oak Park, Illinois, with its schools and churches, his summers in Michigan, and his experiences in love and war.

Here is Santiago thinking about the "big sea turtles": "Most people are heartless about turtles because a turtle's heart will beat for hours after he has been cut up and butchered. But the old man thought, I have such a heart too and my feet and hands are like theirs." The first sentence records a fact that at first makes no sense: one might have expected the sight of the turtle's heart continuing to beat after it is slaughtered to lead us to the opposite of "heartless." It is a grotesque image; if you read the sentence, it will stay with you. We are heartless when we see this sight because we have no hearts ourselves. But Santiago says that he does and that his hands and feet are turtlelike; he is one of them. If at this moment he is different from us, it is because at this moment he is not human.

If he is human, it is because he is a killer. As the marlin eats the bait, Santiago says: "Eat it so that the point of the hook goes into your heart and kills you, he thought. Come up easy and let me put the harpoon into you. All right. Are you ready? Have you been long enough at table?" His tone is beguiling and ruthless; he loves his prey heartlessly. The domesticity of the marlin "at table" makes the scene more dreadful: Santiago's love for the marlin coincides with his intention to kill it. He kills the creature he loves, and he loves it because he can and will kill it.

Once the marline is hooked, Santiago cuts away one line and connects it to "the two reserve coils": "It was difficult in the dark and once the fish made a surge that pulled him down on his face and made a cut below his eye. The blood ran down his cheek a little way." The "him" refers to Santiago, but for a second we interpret it as the fish because this is the noun that has come just before. The pronoun *him* is the fish and is Santiago too, who has cut the fish but who now is bloodied himself, like the sardines hooked through the eyes, and like the fish clubbed until its sweet blood covers Manolin.

To give himself strength, Santiago eats pieces of tuna: "Holding the line with his left shoulder again, and bracing on his left hand and arm, he took the tuna off the gaff hook and put the gaff back in place. He put one knee on the fish and cut strips of dark red meat longitudinally from the back of the head to the tail. They were wedge-shaped strips and he cut them from next to the back bone down to the edge of the belly. . . . I wish I could feed the fish, he thought. He is my brother. But I must kill him and keep strong to do it. Slowly and conscientiously he ate all of the wedge-shaped strips of fish."

"Brother" implies one level of relationship, but this bond evolves toward a deeper one that declares Santiago's identity with his prey, an identity to which Hemingway testifies in sentences as the novel moves toward its climax and conclusion: "But I must get him close, close, close, he thought. I mustn't try for the head. I must get the heart." "The shaft of the harpoon was projecting at an angle from the fish's shoulder and the sea was discolouring with the red of the blood from his heart. . . . I think I felt his heart," he thought. "He did not want to look at the fish. He knew that half of him had been destroyed. . . . He liked to think of the fish and what he could do to a shark if he were swimming free." The killing of the marlin is savage and heartbreaking, brutal and erotic. By killing the fish he loves, Santiago becomes one with it as the ambiguous "half of him had been destroyed" suggests. It is not just that he has taken life, but also that he has experienced what it is like to die.

In Hemingway's work it is unclear whether it is more painful to die or more painful to live. The wrenching pain of life is signified in *The Old Man and the Sea* when Santiago sees two sharks approaching the boat: "'*Ay*,' he said aloud. There is no translation for this word and perhaps it is just a noise such as a man might make, involuntarily, feeling the nail go through his hands and into the wood." There is no translation for this word because the feeling knows no bounds: no language, not Spanish or English or any other, can name it. It may not even be a word but, rather, a "noise," an expression of utterly helpless incoherence.

Nowhere in the accounts of the crucifixion in the Gospel narratives is mention made of nails going through Jesus' hands and into the wood of the cross. Nailing, however, rather than binding with rope, was a common practice, and the story of Thomas's doubt of Jesus' resurrection (John 20:24–31) is keyed to his desire to see and feel "the print of the nails." For Hemingway, the nails are crucial, so much so that I am almost tempted to say we should not dwell upon the crucifixion of Jesus itself when we read Hemingway's lines, but, instead, imagine as acutely as we can the word we would cry out or the noise we would make if it were our hands through which nails were driven. "My wounds were now hurting," Hemingway said in a letter to his parents (August 18, 1918) after he had been wounded, "like 227 little devils were driving nails into the raw."

We know that Hemingway was captivated by representations of Jesus on the cross and pondered them often. The image figures, for example, in many paintings by the Old Masters he revered and examined in the Louvre, the Prado, and other museums. "Lots of nail holes," says Frederic Henry about Andrea Mantegna in *A Farewell to Arms*, alluding to Mantegna's "The Lamentation over the Dead Christ" (c. 1490), a painting in the Brera National Art Gallery in Milan, where in the summer and fall of 1918 the nineteen-year-old Hemingway recovered from the wounds he described in his letter to his parents. He was haunted by bodies pierced, lacerated, and cut, in anguish like the body of the crucified Jesus.

In Madrid in mid-May 1926, Hemingway wrote a short story entitled "Today is Friday," which presents the conversation of three Roman soldiers late in the evening of the day of the crucifixion. The second soldier wants to know why Jesus did not come down from the cross, and the first soldier replies that Jesus did not want to—"that's not his play." The second soldier insists that everyone wants to come down from the cross: "Show me one that doesn't want to get down off the cross when the time comes." "What I mean is," he continues, "when the time comes. When they first start nailing him, there isn't none of them wouldn't stop it if they could." The third soldier then says, "The part I don't like is the nailing them on. You know, that must get to you pretty bad." Hemingway uses his pronouns keenly: Is "you" the person being nailed, or the person watching the nailing, or the person watching who feels as if he is being nailed himself? Or is the "you" intended above all to wound the reader, impelling each of us to imagine how we would feel if we were nailed to a cross?

Later Santiago shoulders the mast as he walks ashore, and soon he rests on his bed with "his arms out straight and the palms of his hands up." Santiago is the crucified Jesus, by which I mean that the pain he has gone through has taken him as close to the divine as any man can be. But the identification that matters is less with Jesus himself than, more specifically, with Jesus' pain—the weight of a cross cutting into the shoulder, the nails pounded through hands and feet, and above all this cry: "And about the ninth hour Jesus cried with a loud voice, saying, 'Eli, Eli, lama sabachthani?' that is to say, 'My God, My God, why hast thou forsaken me?'" (Matthew 27:46). Echoing the first line of Psalm 22, this is for me the most searing passage in the Gospels. It brings before us the voice of absolute abandonment, a pain no language or translation is adequate to, a question cast into a void. This is life at its most essential, as Hemingway understands it: forsaken man crucified, alone, emits an appeal to which there is no reply.

For Hemingway, Jesus was not the Redeemer but the peerless embodiment of a life of pain. Jesus accepted a mission: he knew he was dead the moment he was born. He embraced it freely because he knew that through his death was eternal life for all humankind. This is a promise of salvation in which Hemingway did not believe. For him there was no life after death, and his abiding concern increasingly came to be why and how a dying person—we are always dying—makes art. Santiago toward the end in fact wonders whether he might be "already dead," but then he realizes he "was not dead," and he knows he is not because he feels "pain." Pain confirms for the old man he is alive, and as long as he is alive, he works.

. . . . .

Hemingway's son John said after his father's death: "I keep thinking what a wonderful old man he would have made if he'd learned how. I don't think he had faced up to becoming old." Yet the pain cut deeper, as another of his sons, Gregory, suggested when he said his father lived "with the knowledge of what the edge of nothingness is like." It was not only what Hemingway could not face but also what he did face. Returning to the harbor, Santiago reflects: "And what beat you, he thought. 'Nothing,' he said aloud. 'I went out too far.'" He pulls in the boat by himself because "there was no one to help him." Far out, Hemingway saw nothing and that was the vision that gives such desperation to the disciplined books he wrote. As he said two years later in his Nobel Prize acceptance speech, he had made a commitment to be a writer "driven far out past where he can go, to where no one can help him."

Hemingway realized he wanted from his sentences more than sentences in books, however great, could give. For this reason I think he did not care much about his books once they were done. What Hemingway cherished was the act of writing them, the experience of making them—of moving his pencil across the page, of making, revising, and honing sentences. In the introduction he wrote in 1948 for a new edition of *A Farewell to Arms*, he explained what it felt like to write this novel:

I remember living in the book and making up what happened in it every day. Making the country and the people and the things that happened I was happier than I had ever been. Each day I read the book through from the beginning to the point where I went on writing and each day I stopped when I was still going good and when I knew what would happen next. The fact that the book was a tragic one did not make me unhappy since I believed that life was a tragedy and knew it could only have one end. But finding you were able to make something up; to create truly enough so that it made you happy to read it; and to do this every day you worked was something that gave a greater pleasure than any I had ever known. Beside it nothing else mattered.

Inside the world of the book while it was being written, it was possible for Hemingway to feel nothing else mattered, including the reality of death. This for him was the thrill of creation—a form of happiness oblivious to its own impermanence. In the midst of his sentences as he wrote them, Hemingway could experience the feeling of immortality: I am not immortal but, at this moment, I feel as if I were. But when the final sentence was written and the book was done, where was he? What next?

He would have to attempt to do it again, writing himself into a place where nothing mattered. He knew all the time that his story could only have one end.

Index